Intuitions of Justice and the Utility of Desert

Intuitions of Justice and the Utility of Desert

Paul H. Robinson

OXFORD
UNIVERSITY PRESS

OXFORD
UNIVERSITY PRESS

Oxford University Press is a department of the University of Oxford. It furthers the University's objective of excellence in research, scholarship, and education by publishing worldwide.

Oxford New York
Auckland Cape Town Dar es Salaam Hong Kong Karachi Kuala Lumpur Madrid
Melbourne Mexico City Nairobi New Delhi Shanghai Taipei Toronto

With offices in
Argentina Austria Brazil Chile Czech Republic France Greece Guatemala Hungary
Italy Japan Poland Portugal Singapore South Korea Switzerland Thailand
Turkey Ukraine Vietnam

Published in the United States of America by
Oxford University Press
198 Madison Avenue, New York, NY 10016

Library of Congress Cataloging-in-Publication Data

Robinson, Paul H.
Intuitions of justice and the utility of desert/Paul H. Robinson.
p. cm.
Includes bibliographical references and index.
ISBN 978-0-19-991772-3 ((hardback): alk. paper)
1. Criminal justice, Administration of—Philosophy. 2. Criminal justice, Administration of—Public opinion. 3. Criminal justice, Administration of—Moral and ethical aspects. 4. Criminal law—Philosophy. 5. Criminal law—Public opinion. 6. Criminal law—Moral and ethical aspects. I. Title.
K5001.R64 2013
364.01—dc23

2012033073

9 8 7 6 5 4 3 2 1

Printed in the United States of America on acid-free paper

Note to Readers
This publication is designed to provide accurate and authoritative information in regard to the subject matter covered. It is based upon sources believed to be accurate and reliable and is intended to be current as of the time it was written. It is sold with the understanding that the publisher is not engaged in rendering legal, accounting, or other professional services. If legal advice or other expert assistance is required, the services of a competent professional person should be sought. Also, to confirm that the information has not been affected or changed by recent developments, traditional legal research techniques should be used, including checking primary sources where appropriate.

(Based on the Declaration of Principles jointly adopted by a Committee of the American Bar Association and a Committee of Publishers and Associations.)

This book is dedicated to
John M. Darley
Warren Professor of Psychology at Princeton
in thanks for his ideas and inspiration

TABLE OF CONTENTS

Preface and Acknowledgments xvii
Selected Robinson Bibliography xix
List of Tables and Figures xxi

PART I } **The Nature of Judgments about Justice**

1. **Judgments about Justice as Intuitional and Nuanced** 5
2. **Judgments about Justice as a Human Universal: Agreements on a Core of Wrongdoing** 18
3. **The Origins of Shared Intuitions of Justice** 35
4. **Disagreements about Justice** 63
5. **Changing People's Judgments of Justice** 70

PART II } **Should the Criminal Law Care What the Lay Person Thinks Is Just?**

6. **Current Law's Deference to Lay Judgments of Justice** 96
7. **Current Law's Conflicts with Lay Judgments of Justice** 110
8. **Normative Crime Control: The Utility of Desert** 141
9. **Building Moral Credibility and the Disutility of Injustice** 176
10. **Deviations from Empirical Desert** 189
11. **Implications for Criminal Justice and Other Reform** 208

PART III } **The Content of Lay Judgments of Justice**

12. **Rules of Conduct: Doctrines of Criminalization** 239
13. **Rules of Conduct: Doctrines of Justification** 277
14. **Principles of Adjudication: Doctrines of Culpability** 301
15. **Principles of Adjudication: Doctrines of Excuse** 336

16. **Principles of Adjudication: Doctrines of Grading** 362

17. **Law-Community Agreement and Conflict, and Its Implications** 401

PART IV } **Empirical Studies of Lay Judgments of Justice as a Law and Policy Tool**

18. **Explaining History: Shifting Views of Criminality** 415

19. **Testing Competing Theories: Blackmail** 439

20. **Testing Competing Theories: Justification Defenses** 472

21. **Guiding Judicial Discretion: Extralegal Punishment Factors** 493

22. **Intuitions of Justice & the Utility of Desert** 533

Table of Cases 537
Table of MPC 541
Index 545

DETAILED TABLE OF CONTENTS

Preface and Acknowledgments xvii
Selected Robinson Bibliography xix
List of Tables and Figures xxi

PART I } **The Nature of Judgments about Justice**

1. Judgments about Justice as Intuitional and Nuanced 5
A. Judgments about Justice as Intuitional 5
B. The Common Wisdom: Judgments about Justice as Vague or at Best Unspecific 8
C. The Reality: Nuanced Judgments 12
1. Making Many Distinctions among Cases 12
2. Small Factual Differences among Cases Can Produce Significant Liability Differences 13
D. Conclusion 16

2. Judgments about Justice as a Human Universal: Agreements on a Core of Wrongdoing 18
A. The Intuition That Serious Wrongdoing Should Be Punished 19
1. Questionnaire Studies 19
2. Behavioral Economics Studies 20
3. Cross-Cultural Studies 21
4. Are There Exceptions? 22
B. Intuitions on the Relative Seriousness of Wrongdoing 23
1. Previous Domestic Studies 23
2. Cross-Cultural Studies 26
C. Testing the Limits of Agreement 28
1. Study 1: In-Person Testing 29
2. Study 2: Internet Testing 32
D. Conclusion 34

3. The Origins of Shared Intuitions of Justice 35
A. An Evolutionary Explanation for Intuitions of Justice 36
B. Empirical Support for an Evolutionary Explanation 41
1. Animal Studies Evidence 41
2. Brain Science Evidence 44
3. Child Development Evidence 48
4. Summary of Evidence 54

C. Alternative Explanations: General Social Learning and Efficient Norms 56

1. Spontaneous Social Learning 56

2. Accumulated Social Learning 58

D. Conclusion 62

4. Disagreements about Justice 63

A. Apparent Disagreements among Intuitions of Justice 63

B. True Disagreements among Intuitions of Justice: Studies 3 and 4 65

1. Method: Studies 3 and 4 65

2. Study 3 Results 66

3. Study 4 Results 67

C. Conclusion 68

5. Changing People's Judgments of Justice 70

A. Proposals to Change Intuitions of Wrongdoing and Blameworthiness 70

B. Difficulties in Changing Intuitions 71

C. Which Intuitions of Justice Can Be Changed and Which Cannot? 74

D. How Can Judgments of Justice Be Changed? 77

1. Public Education to Manipulate the Analogy to Core Wrongs 77

2. Internalization of Group Beliefs 79

E. Criticisms of Claims Regarding Agreement and Its Implications 82

1. What Is Included in the "Core"? 82

2. Possible Points of Disagreement with BKH 87

3. Conclusion 93

PART II } **Should the Criminal Law Care What the Lay Person Thinks Is Just?**

6. Current Law's Deference to Lay Judgments of Justice 97

A. Rules 97

1. Recognizing Excuse Defenses 98

2. Failing to Take Account of Factors Relevant to Coercive Crime-Control Principles 100

3. Creating a False Impression That Resulting Harm Is Significant by Including Result Elements in Offense Definitions 101

B. Standards 103

1. Explicit Reliance upon Lay Judgments of Justice 104

2. Vague Standards 104

3. Rules Requiring Jury Speculation 106

C. Explanations for Deference to Lay Judgments of Justice 108

7. Current Law's Conflicts with Lay Judgments of Justice 110

A. Common and Recurring Minor Conflicts 110

B. Modern Coercive Crime-Control Rules in Conflict with Desert 111

1. Three Strikes and Other Habitual Offender Statutes 112
2. Drug Offense Penalties 113
3. Adult Prosecution of Juveniles 114
4. Abolition or Narrowing of the Insanity Defense 115
5. Strict Liability 117
6. Felony Murder 119
7. Criminalization of Regulatory Violations 119
C. Testing the Perceived Justice of Modern Crime-Control Doctrines 120
1. "Milestone" and "Crime-Control" Scenarios 121
2. Study Design and Methodology 123
3. Study Results and Discussion 124
D. How Can a Democratic Process Produce Liability Rules That the Community Sees as Unjust? 128
1. Media Omission of Facts Vital to Understanding Sentences 130
2. Media Coverage of General Crime Issues; Government as Information Source 131
3. Assuming Headline Crimes to Be Paradigmatic 134
4. Public Fear 136
5. Next-Election Vulnerability 138
E. Conclusion 139

8. Normative Crime Control: The Utility of Desert 141
A. Limitations on the Traditional Coercive Crime-Control Principles: Deterrence, Incapacitation, and Rehabilitation 142
1. Deterrence 144
2. Rehabilitation 148
3. Incapacitation of the Dangerous 149
B. Normative Crime Control: Why People Obey the Law 152
1. Harnessing the Power and Efficiency of Normative Social Influence through Stigmatization 154
2. Avoiding Vigilantism 155
3. Avoiding the Resistance and Subversion Produced by a System That Is Seen as Doing Injustice or Failing to Do Justice 156
4. Having a Role in Shaping Societal Norms: The Persuasive Power of the Law 161
5. Gaining Compliance an Borderline Cases 162
C. Deontological Desert and Empirical Desert 163
1. Two Conceptions of Desert 164
2. Where the Two Conceptions Agree 165
3. Where the Two Conceptions Disagree 166
D. Criticisms of Empirical Desert as a Distributive Principle 167
1. Notions of Desert as Hopelessly Vague 167
2. Hopeless Disagreement as to Notions of Desert 168

3. *People Intuitively Assess Punishment According to Deterrence or Incapacitation 169*
4. *Empirical Desert as Inevitably Draconian 171*
5. *Empirical Desert as Potentially Immoral 172*

E. Conclusion 174

9. Building Moral Credibility and the Disutility of Injustice 176

A. Recent Empirical Studies on the Disutility of Injustice 177
1. *Study A Design and Methodology 177*
2. *Study A Results and Discussion 179*
3. *Study B Design and Methodology 181*
4. *Study B Results and Discussion 182*

B. Previous Studies 184

C. Conclusion 188

10. Deviations from Empirical Desert 189

A. Inevitable Deviations: The Problem of Moral Divisions within the Community 190

B. Right-Spirited Deviations: Promoting Justice in a Complex World 191

C. Justifying Deviations from Empirical Desert 193
1. *Deviations to More Effectively Control Crime 194*
2. *Deviations to Advance Interests Other Than Crime Control 196*

D. Deviations to Change Social Norms: Altering Empirical Desert 196
1. *The Importance of Moral Credibility to Social Reformers 197*
2. *Limitations on and Techniques for Changing Norms 199*
3. *Managing Benefits versus Risks of Reform Programs: Persuasion versus Contempt 200*

E. Deviation to Promote Legitimacy 202
1. *Points of Tension 203*
2. *Resolving the Conflict 205*

11. Implications for Criminal Justice and Other Reform 208

A. A Central Concern for Doing Justice 208

B. Abolition of Punishment and "Restorative Justice" 209

C. Reforms to Existing Deviations from Empirical Desert 215
1. *Criminal Justice Reforms 215*
2. *Employing Civil Rather Than Criminal Processes 216*

D. Sharpening the Criminal-Civil Distinction 218
1. *Why Have Two Legal Systems?: The Layperson View of the Criminal-Civil Distinction 218*
2. *The Detrimental Effect of Blurring the Criminal-Civil Distinction 219*

E. Expanding the Reach of Blamelessness: Exercising Mercy 222

1. The Nature of Mercy 222
2. Lay Intuitions on XPFs and the Problem of Undermining the Law's Moral Credibility 223
3. Disagreements about XPFs and the Problem of Disparity in Application 224
F. Breaking New Ground: Are We Responsible for Who We Are? 226
1. Traditional Excuse Theory and the Inadequacy of a "But For" Cause as an Excuse: Judge Bazelon in Brawner and Alexander 227
2. Coercive Indoctrination under Normative Crime Control: The Case of POW Richard Tenneson 230
3. Testing the Limits of a Coercive Indoctrination or a "Rotten Social Background" Excuse: The Case of Alex Cabarga 231
4. "Rotten Social Background" and Empirical Desert 234

PART III } **The Content of Lay Judgments of Justice**

12. Rules of Conduct: Doctrines of Criminalization 239
A. Research Methodology in Testing Lay Judgments of Justice 240
B. An Illustration: Testing the Objective Requirements for Attempt Liability 247
C. Desistance, Renunciation, and Undoing in Attempt 253
D. Creating a Criminal Risk 257
E. Objective Requirements of Complicity 261
F. Omission Liability 268
G. Secondary Prohibitions: A Summary 275

13. Rules of Conduct: Doctrines of Justification 277
A. Use of Deadly Force in Self-Defense 278
B. Use of Force in Defense of Property 287
C. Citizens' Law Enforcement Authority 293
D. Justification Defenses: A Summary 299

14. Principles of Adjudication: Doctrines of Culpability 301
A. Offense Culpability Requirements and Mistake/Accident Defenses 302
B. Culpability Requirements for Complicity 310
C. Voluntary Intoxication 318
D. Individualization of the Objective Standard of Negligence 327
E. Summary 334

15. Principles of Adjudication: Doctrines of Excuse 336
A. Insanity 336
B. Immaturity and Involuntary Intoxication 346
C. Duress and Entrapment Defenses 353
D. Summary 360

16. Principles of Adjudication: Doctrines of Grading 362
A. Grading Distinctions among and within Offenses 362
B. The Seriousness of the Offense: Sexual Offenses 369
C. The Culpability of the Person: Felony Murder 377
D. The Strength of the Person's Connection with the Prohibited Result: Causation Requirements 385
E. Punishment for Multiple Offenses 393
F. Summary 399

17. Law-Community Agreement and Conflict, and Its Implications 401
A. Law and Community Commonly Agree 402
B. Law and Community Also Commonly Disagree 402
C. Binary versus Category Judgments: Legality and Normative Power in Code Drafting 406
D. Criminal Liability without Punishment 408
E. The Jury as a Resolver of Law-Community Conflicts 410

PART IV } **Empirical Studies of Lay Judgments of Justice as a Law and Policy Tool**

18. Explaining History: Shifting Views of Criminality 415
A. Theories for a Pattern of Criminalization Difference between Common Law and Modern Codes 416
1. A Doctrinal Shift in Views of Criminality from Common Law to Modern Codes? 416
2. Objectivist vs. Subjectivist (Traditionalist vs. Modernist) Views of Criminality 419
3. Testable Empirical Issues 421
B. Identifying Objectivist versus Subjectivist Views of Criminality 421
C. The Results 423
1. Issues of Offense Grading 423
2. Issues of Offense Minimum Requirements 425
3. An Analysis of Response Patterns of Individual Subjects 428
D. Implications 429
E. Conclusion 434
1. Limitations of the Study 434
2. Implications for Existing Criminal Law 435

19. Testing Competing Theories: Blackmail 439
A. Competing Theories of Blackmail 440
1. Theories of Blackmail as a Crime against the Threat Recipient 441
2. Theories of Blackmail as a Crime against Third Parties 443

3. *Theories of Blackmail as a Societal Harm 447*
4. *Theories of Blackmail as Non-crime: The Abolitionist Position 449*

B. Statutory Approaches 450

C. Testing Community Views 453
1. *Design and Methodology 453*
2. *Theory Predictions 455*
3. *Statutory Liability Patterns 462*
4. *Results and Discussion 464*

D. Conclusion 470

20. Testing Competing Theories: Justification Defenses 472

A. Competing Theories of Justification 473
1. *Unknowingly Justified Actor 474*
2. *Mistake as to a Justification 475*

B. Liability Predictions 477
1. *Contrast Cases 478*
2. *Test Cases 480*

C. Liability Results 484
1. *Contrast Cases 484*
2. *Cases for Which the Theories of Justification Have Different Predictions 486*

D. Implications for Criminal Law Reform 487
1. *Formulation and Grading Offenses 487*
2. *Formulation of Defenses 488*
3. *Reform of Acquittal Verdict Forms 490*

E. Conclusions 492

21. Guiding Judicial Discretion: Extralegal Punishment Factors 493

A. Extralegal Punishment Factors 494
1. *Offender Reaction to the Offense: Remorse, Apology, and Acknowledgment of Guilt 495*
2. *Victim or Public Reaction to the Offense (Unrelated to Desert): Victim Forgiveness; Demand for More Punishment, or for Less; Public Outrage 498*
3. *Offender Status or Characteristics (Unrelated to Commission of the Offense): Past Good, or Bad, Character or Deeds; Rehabilitation; Special Talents 501*
4. *Suffering Apart from Official Punishment: Special Hardship from Offense or from Punishment, for Offender or Family or Others; Payment of Civil Compensation 506*

B. A Study of Lay Intuitions of Extralegal Punishment Factors 512
1. *Methodology 513*
2. *Methodological Note: A Shift from Implicit to Explicit Ranking 517*

3. *Support for Adjusting Punishment in Light of Extralegal Punishment Factors* 518
4. *Effect of Baseline Offense on XPF Adjustments to Punishments* 521
5. *Relative Relation among XPFs by Popularity* 522
6. *Demographic Differences* 525
7. *Summary of Study Conclusions* 528

C. Implications for Criminal Justice Rules and Practices 529
1. *Disagreements about XPFs and the Problem of Disparity in Application* 529
2. *Strong Support for, or Opposition to, an XPF and the Problem of Undermining the Law's Moral Credibility* 531

D. Conclusion 532

22. Intuitions of Justice & The Utility of Desert 533

Table of Cases 537
Table of MPC 541
Index 545

PREFACE AND ACKNOWLEDGMENTS

As with several earlier volumes—most notably *Structure and Function in Criminal Law* (Oxford 1997) and *Distributive Principles of Criminal Law* (Oxford 2008)—this book is less the presentation of new ideas—although there are some here—and more the bringing together into an integrated coherent whole of the ideas contained in several dozen articles. See the bibliography below.

As the bibliography shows, I have been writing about these issues since 1994. The work began with a series of studies of lay judgments of justice in 1993 that culminated in the publication with John Darley of *Justice, Liability & Blame: Community Views and the Criminal Law* (1995). (That volume has been out of print for many years, unfortunately, but its most important points are included here within part III.)

In the several decades since, I have had the good fortune to work with many excellent coauthors, including Sean Jackowitz, Daniel Bartels, Michael Reisig, and Josh Bowers. My greatest intellectual debts are to coauthors Rob Kurzban, Geoff Goodwin, Michael Cahill, and Owen Jones. Above all, it was John Darley who contributed to and inspired my work in this area, and to him I dedicate this volume.

To all my coauthors, I thank them for their contributions and for their permissions to include our work here. (The source from which a chapter or section is drawn is noted at its start.) My thanks also go to research assistant Melissa Krain for an exceptional job in helping me to pull these materials together and to Rebecca Blake for her careful work during proofing and review.

Finally, I express my usual unending debt to Sarah McAlpine Robinson, who, in so many different ways, made this work possible.

—Paul H. Robinson
Bryn Mawr, Pennsylvania
May 1, 2012

SELECTED ROBINSON BIBLIOGRAPHY

Selected works by Paul H. Robinson and coauthors related to the subject matter of this volume are listed below. A complete bibliography of Robinson's articles, together with their download links, is available at http://ssrn.com/author=47441.

Extralegal Punishment Factors: A Study of Forgiveness, Hardship, Good-Deeds, Apology, Remorse, and Other Such Discretionary Factors in Assessing Criminal Punishment, 65 *Vanderbilt Law Review* 737–829 (2012) (with Sean Jackowitz and Daniel M. Bartels)

The Disutility of Injustice, 85 *New York University Law Review* 1940–2033 (2010) (with Geoff Goodwin and Michael Reisig)

Perceptions of Fairness & Justice: The Shared Aims & Occasional Conflicts of Legitimacy and Moral Credibility, ?? *Wake Forest Law Review* ??-?? (2012) (with Josh Bowers)

Are We Responsible for Who We Are? The Challenge for Criminal Law Theory in the Defenses of Coercive Indoctrination and "Rotten Social Background," 2 *Alabama Civil Rights & Civil Liberties Law Review* 53–77 (2012)

Mercy, Crime Control & Empirical Desert, in Austin Sarat (ed.), Merciful Judgments 99–122 (Cambridge University Press 2011)

Realism, Punishment & Reform, 77 *University of Chicago Law Review* 1611–1632 (2010) (with Robert Kurzban and Owen Jones)

Competing Theories of Blackmail: An Empirical Research Critique of Criminal Law Theory, 89 *Texas Law Review* 291–352 (2010) (with Michael Cahill and Dan Bartels)

Criminalization Tensions: Empirical Desert, Changing Norms & Rape Reform, in Antony Duff, Lindsey Farmer, Sandra Marshall, Massimo Renzo, Victor Tadros, eds., *The Structure of Criminal Law* 186–202 (Oxford 2011)

The Ongoing Revolution in Punishment Theory: Doing Justice as Controlling Crime (First Annual Shoen Lecture), 42 *Arizona State Law Review* 1089–1111 (2010)

Empirical Desert, in Robinson, Garvey & Ferzan, eds., *Criminal Law Conversations* 29–39, 61–66 (2009)

Competing Conceptions of Modern Desert: Vengeful, Deontological, and Empirical, 67 *Cambridge Law Journal* 145–175 (2008)

Intuitions of Justice: Implications for Criminal Law and Justice Policy, 81 *Southern California Law Review* 1–67 (2007) (with John Darley)

The Origins of Shared Intuitions of Justice, 60 *Vanderbilt Law Review* 1633–1688 (2007) (with Robert Kurzban and Owen Jones)

Concordance & Conflict in Intuitions of Justice, 91 *Minnesota Law Review* 1829–1893 (2007) (with Robert Kurzban)

How Psychology Has Changed the Punishment Theory Debate, in B. Brooks-Gordon & M. Freeman, *Current Legal Issues 2006: Law & Psychology* 94–104 (Oxford 2006)

Testing Lay Intuitions of Justice: How and Why, in Symposium: Is Justice Just Us? A Symposium on the Use of Social Science to Inform the Substantive Criminal Law 28 *Hofstra Law Review* 611–634 (2000)

Why Does the Criminal Law Care What the Lay Person Thinks is Just? Coercive vs. Normative Crime Control, 86 *Virginia Law Review* 1839–1869 (2000)

Objectivist vs. Subjectivist Views of Criminality: A Study in the Role of Social Science in Criminal Law Theory, 18 *Oxford Journal of Legal Studies* 409–447 (1998) (with John Darley)

Testing Competing Theories of Justification, 76 *North Carolina Law Review* 1095–1143 (1998) (with John Darley)

The Utility of Desert, 91 *Northwestern University Law Review* 453–499 (1997) (with John Darley)

Competing Theories of Justification: Deeds vs. Reasons, in A.T.H. Smith & A. Simester, eds., *Harm and Culpability* 45–70 (Clarendon, Oxford 1996)

The Criminal–Civil Distinction and the Utility of Desert, in Symposium on the Intersection of Crime and Tort, 76 *Boston University Law Review* 201–214 (1996)

Popular Press

Crime, Punishment, and Prevention, 142 *The Public Interest* 61–71 (Winter 2001)

Moral Credibility and Crime, *The Atlantic Monthly* 72–78 (March 1995)

A Failure of Moral Conviction? in Symposium on "The Black Crime Gap," 117 *The Public Interest* 40–48 (Fall 1994)

Social Psychology Literature

Why Do We Punish? Deterrence and Just Deserts as Motives for Punishment, 83 *Journal of Personality and Social Psychology* 284–299 (2002) (as coauthor after Kevin Carlsmith and John Darley)

The Ex Ante Function of the Criminal Law, 35 *Law and Society Review* 165–189 (2001) (as coauthor after John Darley and Kevin Carlsmith)

Incapacitation and Just Deserts as Motives for Punishment, 24 *Law and Human Behavior* 659–683 (2000) (as coauthor after John Darley and Kevin Carlsmith)

Community Standards of Criminal Liability and the Insanity Defense, 19 *Law and Human Behavior* 425–446 (1995) (as coauthor after Daniel Bails, John Darley, and Tracy Waxman)

The Severity of Intermediate Penal Sanctions: A Psychophysical Scaling Approach for Obtaining Community Perceptions, 11 *Journal of Quantitative Criminology* 71–95 (1995) (as coauthor after Robert E. Harlow and John M. Darley)

LIST OF TABLES AND FIGURES

No.	Title
1	Process and Content in Two Cognitive Systems 7
2	Results from Study 1 30
3	Six Face Drawings 31
4	Results from Study 2 33
5	Results from Study 3 67
6	Results from Study 4 68
7	Lay Person versus Law's Liability Assessment for Complicity 111
8	Control Scenarios—"Milestone Markers" 122
9	"Crime-Control" Scenarios 123
10	Subjects' Mean Rankings of Scenarios 125
11	Subjects' Mean Sentences for Scenarios Compared to Actual Sentences 126
12	Comparison of Subjects' and Law's Sentences for "Crime-Control" Cases 127
13	Distributive Principles 143
14	Strengths & Weaknesses of Deterrents 148
15	Strengths & Weaknesses of Rehabilitation and Incapacitation 152
16	Summary of Distributive Principles and Their Strengths and Weaknesses 174
17	Questions on the Effect of Moral Credibility on the Criminal Justice System 178
18	Study A Pre-and Post-Stimulation Averages 180
19	Study A Baseline and Study B Results 182
20	Tenneson Liability Survey 230
21	Sentencing Survey for Alex Cabarga 234
22	Punishment Scale 242
23	Attempt Scenarios 244
24	Liability for Various Degrees of conduct toward a Completed Theft Offense 250
25	Liability for Various Degrees of Conduct toward Theft 251
26	Percentage of Subjects Assigning No Liability or Liability But No Punishment 251
27	Effect of Renunciation in Reducing Liability 255
28	Liability for Creation of Risk 259
29	Liability as a Function of Risk and Injury 260
30	Liability as Related to Object Requirements of Complicity 263
31	Liability Assigned to the Accomplices as a Function of His Involvement 266
32	Effects of Success or Failure of Killing on Liability for the Accomplice 266
33	Liability for Commission and Omission 271
34	Respondents' Perceptions of Commission and Omission Cases 272
35	Liability as a Function of the Degree of Sacrifice Necessary to Rescue 273
36	Self-Defense Liability 280
37	Liability Assigned for Defensive and Nondefensive Killing Scenarios 281

38 Liability as a Function of Maximum Force Allowed 283
39 Subjects' Perceptions of Self-Defense Cases 284
40 Liability for the Use of Force in Protection of Property 288
41 Subjects' Perceptions of the Use of Force in Protection of Property 289
42 Liability for Exercise of Citizens' Law Enforcement Authority 295
43 Effect of Use of Deadly and Non-Deadly Force on Liability for Exercise of Citizens' Law Enforcement Authority 297
44 Subjects' Perceptions of the Exercise of Citizens' Law Enforcement Authority 298
45 Liability for Mistake/Accident 305
46 Liability as a Function of Culpability Level 306
47 Liability as Related to Culpability Requirements for Complicity 313
48 Subjects' Perceptions as to Culpability Requirements for Complicity 314
49 Liability as a Function of Accomplice's Culpability as to Resulting Death 315
50 Liability for Voluntary Intoxication 321
51 Liability as a Function of Pre-Intoxication Culpability as to Killing 323
52 Liability as a Function of Pre-Intoxication Culpability as to Becoming Intoxicated 323
53 Liability and Culpability in Core Cases 331
54 Factors in Individualization of Negligence Standard 332
55 Respondents' Perceptions of Cognitive and Control Dysfunctions 340
56 Liability as Related to Insanity 341
57 Questions for Common and Legal Language Formulations 344
58 Respondents' Perceptions of Cognitive and Control Dysfunction: Agreement with Common and Legal Language Formulations 345
59 Liability as Related to Immaturity and Involuntary Intoxication 348
60 Subjects' Perceptions of Immaturity and Involuntary Intoxication Cases 349
61 Liability and Subjects' Perceptions as Related to Duress and Entrapment 356
62 Average Seriousness Rating Given to 140 Offenses in Baltimore Survey 363
63 Liability for Sexual Offenses 370
64 Subjects' Perception of Sexual Offenses 371
65 Liability for Felony Murder 380
66 Liability as a Function of Role and State of Mind as to Killing 381
67 Liability as Related to Causation 387
68 Subjects' Perception of Causation 389
69 Liability for Perpetrator and Lookout in Causation Scenarios 389
70 Liability as Related to Causation 391
71 Liability for Multiple Offenses 395
72 Total Liability as a Function of Number of Offenses (no time delay) 396
73 Total Liability as a Function of the Interval between Two Offenses 397
74 Identifying Objectivist and Subjectivist Responses 422
75 Liability Results and Their Objectivist -Subjectivist Implications 423
76 A Discounting Model of Grading 431
77 Estimate of Discount Size 432
78 Discounting Models for Murder Cases 433
79 Text of Scenarios 454
80 Manipulation-Check Questions for Criteria of Each Theory 455
81 Manipulation-Check "Correct Answers" 456

82 Criminalization Predictions for Each Theory 456
83 Legal Criminalization Criteria 462
84 Legal Liability Analysis 463
85 Manipulation-check Results 464
86 Criminalization Results (and Comparisons) 466
87 Subject Evaluations of Extent of Demand Disclosure & Secrets 469
88 Interrelation of Contact Cases 1 through 4 479
89 Summary of Liability of Predictions 483
90 Liability Means 484
91 Baseline Scenarios 513
92 Scale Used by Subjects to Assign Punishment to Hypothetical Offenders 514
93 ESN Scale 514
94 Extralegal Punishment Factor Variations 515
95 Average Punishment for Each Baseline Scenario 518
96 XPF Popularity and Magnitude, Ordered by Overall Popularity 519
97 Frequency of XPF Adjustment Amounts 521
98 Effects of Baseline Crime Scenarios on XPF Magnitude 523
99 Rank by Popularity of XPFs for Each Scenario 524

PART } I

The Nature of Judgments about Justice

Let me briefly sketch the main themes of the five chapters in part I. The common wisdom was that there was nothing on which people agreed or ever could agree regarding what was just punishment in specific cases. This would seem to follow from the fact that such judgments seem so subjective, so complex, and so value dependent. Yet the studies in chapter 2 show the common wisdom to be false. There are indeed points of agreement, indeed agreement that exists across demographics and at a high level. It is not agreement on the absolute amount of punishment that a particular offender deserves, but rather agreement on the relative blameworthiness among different cases. And it is not agreement on cases involving all offenses and all factors, but only some—what one might call the "core" of wrongdoing—because they represent the point of high agreement. As the studies reported in chapter 4 show, as one moves away from this "core" of agreement by adding other factors or offenses, the extent of agreement among people breaks down. The chapter 2 agreement studies find high agreement only in offenses of theft and violence; the chapter 4 disagreement studies show disagreement on a wide variety of offenses like drunk driving, drug offenses, date rape, prostitution, alcohol use, abortion, and bestiality. The larger point here is that there is not a sea of disagreement on everything, as was thought, but rather a continuum from high agreement to high disagreement, from a core of issues on which there is almost near unanimity to increasing disagreement as one moves out to the periphery.

The single most interesting, indeed perplexing, finding of this research is that a core of agreement exists at all. How could this be so? How could people's views about relative blameworthiness—which seem so highly subjective and complex—*ever* produce such high agreement *on any liability and punishment issues in any context*? Chapter 3 explores this puzzling development.

How do humans come to their judgments about relative blameworthiness? Are those judgments in some part the product of a specialized learning system, or just the product of the standard general learning mechanism? Chapter 3 concludes that, while there are reasons to prefer the former, there is still insufficient evidence to settle the issue. For the larger project regarding the relevance of intuitions of justice to the law, however, it is irrelevant which of these two mechanisms produce the shared intuitions of justice. As noted in chapter 3 and reemphasized in chapter 5, both of these alternative mechanisms lead to the same conclusion on the point that is relevant to criminal law: Whatever the source of people's shared intuitions of justice, those shared intuitions are something to which system designers and social reformers would be wise to give special attention.

Reformers ought not to assume that they can simply educate people out of a core intuition of justice the way they would persuade people to change their views on purely reasoned matters. This is true if core judgments about justice are the result of a specialized learning mechanism, but is also true if they are formed through general social learning. The key factor is not the source of the agreement but rather the high agreement across demographics, for this suggests that whatever the source of the judgments of justice, they are deeply embedded and not easily modified.

Imagine the variety of factors that can influence human judgments about relative blameworthiness. Different demographics—income, education, race, political orientation, marital status, religion, gender—can create profound differences in life experience. The fact that any core of high agreement exists suggests that such judgments are held in a manner that insulates them from the standard influences of everyday life. If that is true, how are social reformers to significantly change those views? This is the subject of chapter 5.

Intuitions at the "core" are perceived by people as facts, not reasoned conclusions—and what seem to them to be quite obvious facts. People generally have little access to why they feel the way they do about these matters. While it is certainly possible for rational argument to override even a deeply felt core intuition of justice, we suspect that liberal democracies are not likely to feel comfortable with the kind of coercive intrusion into the lives and thinking of citizens that might be required to change these shared core intuitions—intuitions that have already shown themselves to be immune from even the powerful influence of demographic differences.

As explained in chapters 5 and 11 in part II, this reduced malleability of the high agreement issues at the "core" has implications for social reformers. Reformers should understand that some views will be easier to change than others; they should be wise in the battles they choose to fight and how they fight them. For example, they ought to think carefully before they invest time and energy in a program to persuade the community not to punish serious wrongdoing, as some reformers would do;[1] or to persuade the community that serious resulting harm, such as causing death, ought to be insignificant in assessing punishment, as others would do.[2] Chapter 5 also attempts to give reformers insights on how best to change people's judgments about justice. The greater the level of existing disagreement, the greater the likelihood that peoples' views on relative blameworthiness can be successfully modified. That same chapter has a how-to section for reformers, showing them how they can use high agreement on the "core" issues to help shift people's views on issues out from the "core."

---

[1] See chapter 11, section A.

[2] *See, e.g.*, Stephen J. Schulhofer, *Harm and Punishment*, 122 U. Pa. L. Rev. 1497, 1498–1503 (1974); Larry Alexander, Kimberly Kessler Ferzan, and Stephen Morse, Crime and Culpability (2009). The Model Penal Code drafters generally seek to minimize the significance of resulting harm by grading attempts (other than murder) the same as the completed offense. Model Penal Code §5.05(1). However, most states, even those following the Model Code, reject this approach and grade completed offenses higher than attempt. See authorities collected at Paul H. Robinson, *The Role of Harm and Evil in Criminal Law*, J. Contemp. Leg. Issues 299, 305, n. 18 (1994).

1 }

Judgments about Justice as Intuitional and Nuanced

Until recently, the common wisdom has been that people's judgments about justice are at best vague, which is expected given that they involve such complex analyses of so many different factors that must be weighed. Yet the empirical evidence paints a quite different picture, not only about the judgments themselves but also about how they are reached.

This chapter is drawn primarily from portions of my articles with Robert Kurzban, *Concordance and Conflict in Intuitions of Justice*; and with John Darley, *Intuitions of Justice: Implications for Criminal Law and Justice Policy*.[3]

A. Judgments about Justice as Intuitional

It is common to believe that our judgments about criminal liability and punishment are the result of a well-reasoned analytical process. It is generally assumed that one makes such judgments in the same way that one makes any other complex judgment, through reasoning based upon experience and education—Should I go to the grocery store now or later? For whom should I vote for president? Should I invest money in that stock fund?[4]

Yet social science research paints a different picture. It suggests that many judgments about justice are commonly intuitional rather than reasoned. Their intuitional nature means that these judgments are derived quickly and with strong confidence, but that their basis is essentially inaccessible to the people who make them. This section explores the intuitional nature of our judgments about justice and what that nature means in practice.

The primary claim here is that humans have an internal system that produces intuitive judgments that is importantly different from the system that produces the

[3] Paul H. Robinson and Robert Kurzban, *Concordance and Conflict in Intuitions of Justice*, 91 MINN. L. REV. 1829, 1832–1846 (2007); Paul H. Robinson and John M. Darley, *Intuitions of Justice: Implications for Criminal Law and Justice Policy*, 81 S. CAL. L. REV. 1, 4–6, 31–43 (2007).

[4] This section is drawn primarily from Robinson and Darley, *Intuitions of Justice*, *supra* note 3, at 4–6.

deliberate operations of reasoned judgments. Since the 1970s, a group of judgment and decision-making psychologists have documented the fact that people frequently produce decisions via heuristic processes, in contrast to the conscious, deliberative processes that we think of as reasoning processes.

One of the earlier demonstrations of intuitive judgments was made by Amos Tversky and Daniel Kahneman.[5] They showed that people, even if well trained in statistical reasoning, often gave quickly expressed intuitive solutions to statistical problems, and that these solutions differed from the calculated solutions to these problems, calculations that these experts knew thoroughly and often spent considerable time teaching to students. Further, these intuitive judgments were frequently wrong, in the sense that they importantly deviated from the demonstrably correct calculated results. Moreover, the statisticians often relied on the results of these flawed intuitions not only when they were making quick, off-the-cuff judgments, but when they were making consequential decisions about the conduct of research.

Three decades of research on "heuristics and biases" have demonstrated that people frequently use intuitive, shortcut methods to come to decisions and then go on to act on those decisions. Robin Hogarth, in 2001, gave a thorough review of the domains of these intuitive decisions,[6] which led Tversky and Kahneman to suggest that these "intuitive judgements occupy a position—perhaps corresponding to evolutionary history—between the automatic operations of perception and the deliberate operations of reasoning."[7] The intuitive system involves processes that parallel those of the perceptions system, in that "they are typically fast, automatic, effortless, associative, implicit (not available to introspection), and often emotionally charged; they are also governed by habit and are therefore difficult to control or modify. The operations of . . . the reasoning system are slower, serial, effortful and more likely to be consciously monitored and deliberately controlled; they are also relatively flexible and potentially rule governed."[8]

The relation of these alternative systems is summarized in Figure 1.[9] As it shows, the intuitive processes are identical to those of the perception system—a fact that suggests why intuitions, like perceptions, are often taken by "the intuitor" as just as unproblematically correct as all of us take our perceptions to be. Thus, there are a set of intuition-produced decisions, choices, and problem solutions that are experienced as summaries of the ways "the world is," because the person having the intuition is unaware of the complex, potentially incorrect, cognitive processes that produced them.

---

[5] Amos Tversky and Daniel Kahneman, *Belief in the Law of Small Numbers*, 76 Psychol. Bull. 105–110 (1971).

[6] Robin M. Hogarth, Educating Intuition (2001).

[7] Daniel Kahneman, *A Perspective on Judgement and Choice: Mapping Bounded Rationality*, 56 Am. Psychol. 697, 697 (2003) [hereinafter Kahneman, *Judgement and Choice*].

[8] *Id.* at 698.

[9] *Id.* at 698.

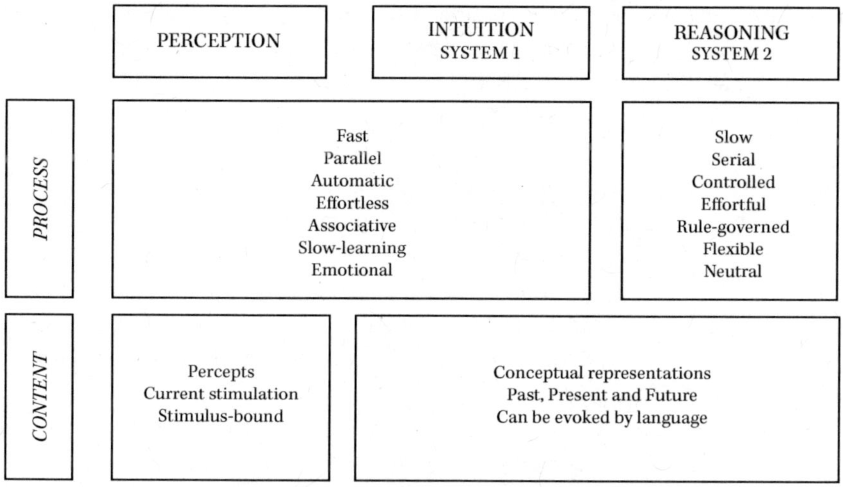

FIGURE 1. Process and Content in Two Cognitive Systems

As Kahneman explains, the perceptual system and the intuitive system "generate impressions of the attributes of objects of perception and thought. These impressions are neither voluntary nor verbally explicit."[10] He then goes on to suggest that the assignment of degrees of "badness" to various stimulus situations is an intuitive system assessment, a suggestion quite relevant to the conceptualization of the intuitive judgments of blameworthiness of wrongdoers. "Some attributes, which Tversky and Kahneman called natural assessments, are routinely and automatically registered by the perceptual system or by (the intuitive system) without intention or effort.... The evaluation of stimuli as good or bad is a particularly natural assessment. The evidence, both behavioral and neurophysiological, is consistent with the idea that the assessment of whether objects are good (and should be approached) or bad (and should be avoided) is carried out quickly and efficiently by specialized neural circuitry."[11]

In Jonathan Haidt's work on "moral dumbfounding," people report strong intuitions about things that are morally wrong, such as consensual, nonreproductive incest, but are unable to provide a principled explanation for their judgments.[12] Similarly, Hauser, Young, and Cushman looked at judgments of morally permissible actions using the "trolley problem,"[13] in which some number of people can be saved from being killed by a runaway trolley if some action is taken (or not taken), resulting in the death of a smaller number of people—often a single individual.[14]

---

10 *Id.* at 699.

11 Kahneman, *Judgement and Choice*, *supra* note 7, at 701.

12 *See* Jon Haidt, *The Emotional Dog and Its Rational Tail: A Social Intuitionist Approach to Moral Judgement*, 108 PSYCH. REV. 814, 814 (2003) [hereinafter Haidt, *Emotional Dog*].

13 Philippa Foot, *The Problem of Abortion and the Doctrine of Double Effect*, 5 OXFORD REV. 5 (1967).

14 Marc Hauser et al., *Reviving Rawls' Linguistic Analogy*, in MORAL PSYCHOLOGY AND BIOLOGY [20–21] (W. Sinnott-Armstrong ed., 2008).

People are asked what choice should be made in these difficult situations and to explain their reasoning. While subjects commonly have strong and clear views on the proper result, they also commonly are unable to offer an explanation for their conclusions. For example, in one variation of the trolley problem, the subject can avoid the death of five people on the track by (a) pushing a bystander on the track whose body and backpack will jam the trolley's wheels, stopping it, but killing that person; or by (b) throwing a switch to divert the trolley to a side track where it will kill one person. Despite the fact that the results of the two actions are identical, 89 percent of the subjects considered the latter action moral, but only 11 percent judged the former to be moral. More interesting for present purposes, 70 percent of the subjects could give no plausible explanation for their judgment. This mirrors Haidt's results concerning incest.

Based on his review of the existing social science literature, Haidt concludes that "moral judgments" derive from "quick automatic evaluations (intuitions)."[15] Similarly, Hauser concludes that "much of our knowledge of morality is... intuitive, based on unconscious and inaccessible principles...."[16] In other words, there is at least some degree of consensus that many moral judgments are made by a deeply intuitive system. If such judgments were the product of a set of principles of morality learned from others, it would seem to be a straightforward matter to derive the "wrongness" of acts from these principles, just as mathematical inferences can be made from a set of axioms and subsequently explained with reference to them. But "moral dumbfounding" and related effects in the psychological literature suggest that this is not how these judgments are made.

To summarize, the belief that serious wrongdoing should be punished and judgments of the relative blameworthiness of different acts of wrongdoing are commonly intuitive rather than reasoned judgments. This being so, these judgments come quickly to mind and are accompanied with strong feelings of certainty. The fact that these judgments are the product of interpretative habits is obscured from the person, because the processes that produce them are automatic and rapid and leave no "mental traces."

B. The Common Wisdom: Judgments about Justice as Vague or at Best Unspecific

Many writers, including many sympathetic to the importance of doing justice, see desert as a vague concept. Some writers have a related but slightly different objection: It is not that the concept of desert is too vague to have any meaning, but rather that the notion of desert has discernible content that only provides guidance as to

[15] Haidt, *Emotional Dog*, *supra* note 12, at 814.

[16] Marc Hauser, Moral Minds: How Nature Designed Our Universal Sense of Right and Wrong 125 (2006).

the outer limits of appropriate punishment. It can identify injustice and failures of justice—outer boundaries that should not be crossed—but cannot specify a punishment that *should* be imposed.

Such claims of vagueness are matters subject to empirical testing. Do lay persons have specific intuitions of justice, specific enough to reliably distinguish among a variety of cases? Or, do people's intuitions of justice have hopelessly vague content—or do they specify only outer limits of proper punishment—such that they could not be the basis for constructing a workable criminal justice system?

This section seeks to answer such questions by an examination of existing research in this and other countries. The picture that emerges is quite striking: Intuitions of justice among lay persons exist on a wide variety of liability and punishment issues. They are quite nuanced, no matter a person's level of education. They produce specific conclusions regarding deserved punishment, not simply broad generalities or outer limits.

To start, consider the common wisdom that existed until recently. Writers commonly criticized what they saw as the "vagueness of desert"[17]:

> Everyone may agree that five years in prison is unjustly harsh desert for shoplifting, or that a five dollar fine is unjustly lenient desert for rape, but beyond such clear cases our intuitions seem to fail us. Is two years, five years, or ten years the proper sanction for a rape?...Our sense of just deserts here seems to desert us.[18]

Further, it is argued, even if theoretically there is a meaningful concept of desert, it simply is impossible to operationalize it with sufficient specificity:

> Insofar as we seek a morally sensitive scale in which to weigh subjective guilt, to classify the individual criminal on the long continuum from unblemished virtue to unmitigated evil...[t]he criminal law is unfitted for such issues. It faces an adequacy of difficulties without addressing such ethical nuances. It is necessarily generalized rather than related to the moral quality of the specific act....
>
> ...Questions of guilt will thus be weighed on the imprecise scales of the criminal law which can allow for only a few subjective qualifications to the objective gravity of the crime.[19]

Some writers may be willing to concede that desert has some meaning but argue that it cannot specify a particular amount of punishment that is deserved; it can only identify what is a seriously disproportionate punishment. Indeed, this seems to be the underlying assumption of the American Law Institute's 2007

[17] *See, e.g.,* JOHN BRAITHWAITE AND PHILIP PETIT, NOT JUST DESERTS: A REPUBLICAN THEORY OF CRIMINAL JUSTICE 180 (1990) ("The vagueness of desert...masks mistakes.").

[18] Leo Katz, *Criminal Law*, *in* A COMPANION TO THE PHILOSOPHY OF LAW AND LEGAL THEORY 80–81 (Dennis Patterson ed., 1996).

[19] Norval Morris, THE FUTURE OF IMPRISONMENT 74 (1974).

adoption of a revised Model Penal Code Section 1.02(2)(a), setting out the purposes of the sentencing provisions and the principles governing their interpretation and application:[20]

> Subsection (2)(a) embraces Morris's observation that moral intuitions about doing justice in specific cases are almost always rough and approximate—and that most people experience them as such. Even if a decisionmaker is well acquainted with all the circumstances of a particular crime, and has a rich understanding of the offender, it is seldom possible (except in an extreme case) for the decisionmaker to say that the deserved penalty is *precisely x*. In Morris's phrase, the "moral calipers" possessed by human beings are not sufficiently fine-tuned to reach exact judgments. He postulated instead that most people's moral sensibilities, for most crimes, will orient them toward a range of permissible sanctions that are "not undeserved." At the perimeters of the range, some punishments will appear clearly excessive to do justice, and some will appear clearly too lenient—but there will nearly always be a gray area between the two extremes.
>
> Subsection 1.02(2)(a)(i) codifies Morris's idea of an approximate retributive ballpark when it speaks of a "*range* of severity" of proportionate punishments.[21]

Part of the confusion here is a mistaken notion by some that desert associates an absolute amount of punishment with a particular act of wrongdoing. Modern desert theorists make no such claim and have no need to do so. What they argue is that desert requires that punishment be proportional to an offender's personal blameworthiness.[22] In other words, modern notions of desert are ordinal rather than cardinal. If the continuum of punishment is altered—for example, some societies permit the death penalty and others do not, some societies provide

---

[20] The text provides:

§1.02(2). Purposes; Principles of Construction.

(2) The general purposes of the provisions governing sentencing, applicable to all official actors in the sentencing system, are:

(a) in decisions affecting the sentencing of individual offenders:

(i) to render sentences in all cases within a range of severity proportionate to the gravity of offenses, the harms done to crime victims, and the blameworthiness of offenders;

(ii) when reasonably feasible, to achieve offender rehabilitation, general deterrence, incapacitation of dangerous offenders, restoration of crime victims and communities, and reintegration of offenders into the law-abiding community, provided that these goals are pursued within the boundaries of sentence severity permitted in subsection (a)(i); and

(iii) to render sentences no more severe than necessary to achieve the applicable purposes from subsections (a)(i) and (ii);...

American Law Institute, Model Penal Code Amendment (Adopted May 16, 2007), section 1.02(2).

[21] Model Penal Code §1.02(2)(a)(i) (as adopted May 16, 2007).

[22] John Kleinig, Punishment and Desert 114 (1973) ("What follows from [attempts to exactly define desert] is not the absurdity of specific desert claims but only the absurdity of expecting them to function like statements of empirical quantity.").

long prison terms while others do not—then desert would distribute punishment differently.[23]

Desert requires a specific amount of punishment not because there is some magical connection between the offense and that amount of punishment, but rather because that amount of punishment is the amount needed to set the offender in his appropriate relative position in relation to other offenders and acts of wrongdoing on the continuum of deserved punishment. Given the large number of distinctions that lay persons make among cases and the limited number of distinguishable units on the punishment continuum, each case ends up on a specific point, not a range.

The punishment continuum theoretically has an infinite number of different points—one could break terms of imprisonment, for example, down to not only a specific number of months, but also days, hours, or minutes. But in practice the punishment continuum is limited because people do not see meaningful differences between sentences that are only minutes or hours apart. In fact, as one moves up the punishment continuum, the increase in punishment required to be seen as meaningfully different becomes larger. A day's difference might matter if the sentences are 4 days versus 5 days, but not if they are 4 month versus 4 months and a day. When one sentence is 10 years, a meaningfully different sentence may have to be months, not just days, more. This dynamic reduces the punishment continuum to one of limited units. Given the ease with which lay persons can distinguish two cases on blameworthiness grounds, the number of distinguishable cases probably meets (or exceeds) the number of distinguishable punishment units on the punishment continuum, thus forcing every case to a specific point on the continuum in order to distinguish it from cases of different perceived blameworthiness.

It may still be argued that even this blameworthiness ranking of offenses is beyond the ability of people's intuitions of justice—that those intuitions are simply too vague to do more than to roughly distinguish between "serious" cases and "less serious" cases and cannot provide the kind of nuance needed to construct a workable criminal justice system. As Justice Breyer explains in his opposition to basing the United States Sentencing Commission sentencing guidelines on desert:

> The "just deserts" approach would require that the Commission list criminal behaviors in rank order of severity and then apply similarly ranked punishments proportionately. For example, if theft is considered a more serious or harmful crime than pollution, then the thief should be punished more severely than the polluter....

---

[23] Desert demands only that each person's offense be punished according to the person's relative degree of personal blameworthiness. There is nothing central in desert theory that demands a particular higher or lower endpoint on the continuum of punishment. On the other hand, while desert primarily concerns itself with the relative blameworthiness, it may have some useful things to say in a debate about the continuum endpoint. *See* chapter 8, section C.

> ...[T]he Commission soon realized that only a crude ranking of behavior in terms of just deserts, based on objective and practical criteria, could be developed....
>
> ...[T]hose who advocated "just deserts"...could not produce a convincing, objective way to rank criminal behavior in detail ."[24]

C. The Reality: Nuanced Judgments

The average state criminal code distinguishes a dozen grades of offenses. Modern sentencing guidelines make even more distinctions.[25] Are lay intuitions of justice nuanced enough to distinguish among cases with this level of specificity or more? Or, do they suggest only broad categories?

1. MAKING MANY DISTINCTIONS AMONG CASES

A common measure of whether a person makes nuanced judgments is the number of distinctions she makes in her judgments. In studies in which subjects are given categories into which to sort offenses, they in fact use most or all of the categories. Sellin and Wolfgang, for example, asked raters to evaluate the seriousness of violations using a scale ranging from 1 (least serious) to 11 (most serious), with instructions that "[e]ach of the eleven categories is an equal step on the scale."[26] Walker surveyed 650 individual residents of Sheffield and 40 first-year sociology students, asking subjects to rank the seriousness of 11 offenses scenarios—"He steals 1 pound of the money and alters the books"—on a scale ranging from 1 to 11.[27] Gottfredson, Young, and Laufer similarly used 11 categories of "seriousness" in their survey of 159 subjects.[28] In all three studies, subjects used the full range or nearly the full range of the scale values that were available to them.

The more nuanced people's intuitions of justice are, the easier it should be for people to see two cases as distinguishable. A variety of studies ask participants to

---

[24] Stephen Breyer, *The Federal Sentencing Guidelines and the Key Compromises upon Which They Rest*, 17 HOFSTRA L. REV. 1, 15–17 (1988) (footnotes omitted).

[25] The United States Sentencing Guidelines represent the far end of this spectrum, with 43 offense levels. U.S. Sentencing Guidelines Manual §5A (Nov. 2010) *available at* http://www.ussc.gov/Guidelines/2010_guidelines/Manual_PDF/Chapter_5.pdf.

[26] THORSTEN SELLIN AND MARVIN E. WOLFGANG, THE MEASUREMENT OF DELINQUENCY 131, 140 (1967).

[27] Monica A. Walker, *Measuring the Seriousness of Crimes*, 18 BRIT. J. CRIMINOLOGY 348, 348–349 (1978) (comparing relative rankings of crimes across social status and gender using category and ratio scales; showing that very serious and very trivial offenses were excluded because other studies had already shown substantial agreement between people with regard to these crimes; also presenting evidence that the entire scale was used, even when the ranges of offenses were restricted—giving further evidence of nuanced intuitions).

[28] Stephen D. Gottfredson, Kathy L. Young, and William S. Laufer, *Interaction and Additivity in Offense Seriousness Scales*, 17 J. RES. CRIME & DELINQ. 26, 29 (1980).

compare two or more cases or to rank cases against one another. In no instance in which subjects were presented with such a task were they unable to complete it. Similarly, Walker, noted above, used the "paired comparison" method, in which subjects were asked to judge which in each pair of offenses is more serious. There is no evidence that participants had any difficulty with this task.[29]

Another testing methodology—magnitude estimation—suggests the same conclusion. In Sellin and Wolfgang's survey of 575 individuals across Pennsylvania, subjects were asked to rate the seriousness of 51 offenses and to rate the seriousness of each offense relative to a bicycle theft, which was given an arbitrary value of "10."[30] Thus, if an offense was judged twice as serious as a bicycle theft, that offense would be given a value of "20." Subjects' responses covered an extremely broad range of values covering nearly three orders of magnitude.[31]

In the 1977 National Crime Survey, which surveyed 60,000 persons across the United States, subjects were read vignettes of 25 specific criminal events and asked to rate how serious the crime was relative to a baseline offense (the same bicycle theft used by Sellin and Wolfgang). Not all subjects rated all items; a total of 204 offenses were evaluated. Judgments of the severity of the crimes covered an extremely broad range: two and a half orders of magnitude.[32] Such vast ranges in estimates of the seriousness of different offenses are not consistent with the claims that intuitions regarding crime seriousness are simplistic or only generalized.

Even clearer evidence of enormous nuance is shown in the study reported in chapter 2, in which subjects had little difficulty rank ordering 24 crime scenarios (and showed astounding agreement among themselves in doing so).

2. SMALL FACTUAL DIFFERENCES AMONG CASES CAN PRODUCE SIGNIFICANT LIABILITY DIFFERENCES

The fact that small factual differences among scenarios produce significant differences is another indication of the level of nuance in intuitions of justice about the amount of punishment that subjects think is deserved. The studies described in part III nicely and repeatedly illustrate the point. In each of 18 studies, participants were given a series of scenarios that follow the same basic story but vary the facts in a variety of ways. Participants were then asked to give deserved liability and punishment judgments for each scenario. Changes in responses among the scenarios could

---

[29] *See* Walker, *supra* note 27, at 361.

[30] Each subject rated the same 21 offenses and an additional 30 offenses drawn from a pool of 120 additional offenses. *Id.*

[31] Each order of magnitude refers to an offense being 10 times more serious than another. Two orders of magnitude would mean that the most serious offense was considered 100 times as serious as the least serious offense, and so on. *See* SELLIN AND WOLFGANG, *supra* note 26, at appendix E-2, 389–390.

[32] Alfred Blumestein and Jacqueline Cohen, *Sentencing of Convicted Offenders: An Analysis of the Public's View*, 14 L. & SOC. REV. 223, 223 (1980) (concluding that there was "considerable agreement across various demographic groups on the relative severity of the sentences to be imposed for different offenses, but disagreement over the absolute magnitude of these sentences.").

then be attributed to the varied facts. The results dramatically and repeatedly illustrate how small changes in facts can produce large differences in the punishment judged to be deserved on a wide array of criminal law issues.

For example, in a study concerning the objective requirements for attempt liability, participants dramatically altered the liability and punishment they would impose according to just how far the actor had gone toward committing a coin store robbery. When the person visits the store to plan the robbery carrying a special tool that he will need, and tells friends of his plan, but is caught before he goes to the store to rob it, his average punishment is just under two weeks. However, if he takes the additional step of going to the store and starting work on the safe, his liability jumps to 1.7 years.[33] If he voluntarily renounces his attempt before being caught, 85 percent or more of participants would impose no punishment, but if he voluntarily renounces after committing the offense, few would give him a defense.[34]

In a study that examines the use of deadly force in self-defense, most people impose no punishment if such force was unavoidable for defense, but impose an average punishment of 9.6 months if the person could have safely retreated,[35] unless the person is in his own house, in which case there is no punishment even if the person could have safely retreated.[36] And, in comparison to the 9.6 months that he gets if he can safely retreat in a public place, if he mistakenly believes that he cannot retreat, then he gets no punishment.[37] But if his mistake is not about whether he can safely retreat but about the legality of using deadly force in the situation, then his average punishment is 5.8 years.[38] (Interestingly, most of the distinctions that participants make here track criminal law doctrine, even though participants generally do not know the criminal law rules.)

Similarly, if a person has consensual intercourse with a partner that he knows is under the legal age, then his average punishment is 1.6 years, but if he believes she is over the legal age but is aware of a possibility that she might not be, then his punishment is six months.[39] If her being underage never occurs to him but would have occurred to the reasonable person, then his punishment is six days.[40] If the reasonable person would not have thought she was underage, then he has no punishment.[41]

Another study examined the effect of mistake in various contexts. Where a person burns a house that he thinks he just bought, his punishment is 1.6 years if he disregards a risk that the house has not yet been legally conveyed to him (which turns out to be the case), but his punishment is only 4.4 months if the risk never occurs to him

---

33 *See* chapter 12, section B (compare scenario 3 to 5).
34 *Id.*, compare scenarios 3a and 5a to 6a and 6b.
35 *See* chapter 13, section A (compare scenario 2 to 4).
36 *Id.*, scenario 5.
37 *Id.*, compare scenario 4 to 7.
38 *Id.*, scenario 9.
39 *Id.*, compare scenario 6a to 6b.
40 *Id.*, scenario 6c.
41 *Id.*, scenario 6d.

but would have occurred to the reasonable person.[42] But if he disregards the risk that ownership has not yet been conveyed to unimproved property, rather than to a house, then his punishment is nine months rather than 1.6 years.[43] But if the risk—that the unimproved property is not legally his—never occurred to him but would have occurred to the reasonable person, then his liability is 2.4 months rather than nine.[44]

In a study concerning objective requirements for complicity liability, participants dramatically altered the liability and punishment they would impose according to how much assistance the accomplice provides. The man who helps a woman in planning the killing of her husband by directing her to a gun store is given an average liability of five years, while the man who helps her by giving her his gun so she does not have to go to the store gets an average of life imprisonment.[45] But if he offers her his gun but she says she does not need it (because she already has one), then 85 percent say no punishment.[46]

Another study examined the effect on liability and punishment of different causal chains between a stabbing and a resulting death. Where the death is immediate, the average penalty is life imprisonment; but if death results because a careless nurse at the hospital injects the wrong medication during treatment, the attacker's punishment is only 19.5 years; and if death results because the victim flees the attack and happens to be running under a construction crane when its cable breaks, then the attacker's punishment is 10.2 years[47] (about the same as it would be for an attempted murder under similar circumstances[48]). If the victim's death results from a rare allergic reaction to a common drug during treatment at the hospital, then the attacker's punishment is about 26 years, rather than life (for the immediate death);[49] but if death results later from an auto accident on the way to the hospital for post-operative treatment, then the attacker's punishment is only 15 years.[50]

Another study tested the effect of various conditions on punishment for an omission to act that results in a death. The person who fails to throw a stranger a life preserver gets punishment of 7.5 weeks, but if the person is a security guard for the pier, his liability jumps to 3.8 years.[51] Forty-six percent of the participants would assign no punishment for the person who fails to throw the life preserver. If the person is required to swim to save the stranger (assuming the person is a strong swimmer), 62 percent would assign no punishment. However, if the person knows that sharks inhabit that body of water, 86 percent would say no punishment.[52]

---

[42] *See* chapter 14, section A (compare scenario 3b to 3c).

[43] *Id.*, compare scenario 4b to 3b.

[44] *Id.*, scenario 4c.

[45] *See* chapter 12, section E (compare scenario 4 to 5).

[46] *Id.*, scenario 2.

[47] *See* chapter 16, section D (compare scenario 5 to 7).

[48] *Id.*, scenario 2.

[49] *Id.*, compare scenario 1 to 4.

[50] *Id.*, scenario 6.

[51] *See* chapter 12, section F (compare scenario 1 to 3).

[52] *Id.*, scenario 5.

In a study concerning coercion and entrapment, a truck driver gets two years for voluntarily delivering drugs, but only 4.8 months where he is coerced to make the delivery by his employer's threat to fire him if he does not.[53] But where he makes the delivery because his family was threatened, his punishment is only about four weeks.[54]

One study concerns accomplice liability for a perpetrator's killing another for a killing during a store robbery. Where the accomplice agrees beforehand to the shooting, his punishment is 30 years to life when the principal shoots the store owner, but if the accomplice thought the principal's gun would be unloaded, his liability is only 6.6 years for the owner's death.[55] And if the principal shoots a cofelon rather than the store owner, then the surviving cofelon's punishment is only 12 months.[56]

Jacoby and Cullen's study also found substantial variation in preferred punishment depending on specific factors (e.g., harm caused, dollar loss, etc.), again supporting the view that punishment preferences are nuanced. Further, their results show that a factor that mediates seriousness for one crime does not necessarily do so for another. For example, the dollar amount stolen changes seriousness judgments for theft but not for theft in the context of rape.[57] That the effect of mediating factors depends on the type of crime again indicates quite nuanced intuitions.

Changes in the characteristics of the offender also influence judgments. In a study concerning immaturity and other excuses, an 18-year-old intentionally sets another boy on fire to kill him while he sleeps, getting an average punishment of 25.5 years. A 14-year-old who does the same thing gets 6.2 years; and a 10-year-old gets 11 months.[58] (The adult gets on average a split between life imprisonment and the death penalty.[59]) Rossi, Simpson, and Miller similarly found that punishments varied according to not only on the consequences of the crime, but also features of the victims and offenders.[60]

D. Conclusion

In short, the evidence from multiple testing methods supports the view that intuitions of justice are finely nuanced. Durham summarizes the surveys this way: "Virtually

---

[53] *See* chapter 15, section C (compare scenario 1 to 3).

[54] *Id.*, scenario 2.

[55] *See* chapter 16, section C (compare scenario 4 to 6).

[56] *Id.*, scenario 9.

[57] S. D. Gottfredson, K. L. Young, and W. S. Laufer, *Additivity and Interactions in Offense Seriousness Scales*, 17 J. Res. Crime and Delinquency 26, 39 (1980) ("The studies described above suggest that we consider not only the type of offense and the amount of loss incurred (measured in dollars) when judging the seriousness of criminal or delinquent acts, but also the interaction between the two.").

[58] *See* chapter 16, section B, scenarios 7, 8, and 9.

[59] *Id.* at scenario 1.

[60] *See* Peter H. Rossi, Jon E. Simpson, and Joanne Miller, *Beyond Crime Seriousness: Fitting the Punishment to the Crime*, 1 J. Quantitative Criminology 59, 60–61 (1985).

without exception, citizens seem able to assign highly specific sentences for highly specific events."[61] The conclusion suggested by the empirical evidence is that people take account of a wide variety of factors and often give them quite different effect in different situations. That is, people's intuitions of justice are not vague or simplistic, as claimed, but rather sophisticated and complex.

[61] Alexis M. Durham III, *Public Opinion Regarding Sentences for Crime: Does It Exist?*, 21 J. CRIM. JUSTICE 1, 2 (1993).

2}

Judgments about Justice as a Human Universal: Agreements on a Core of Wrongdoing

While people may have quite nuanced and specific notions regarding criminal liability and punishment, as chapter 1 suggests, these views might be quite different across various groups and individuals. This has certainly been the common wisdom for some time.

> [E]ven assuming retribution in distribution is appropriate, there is a classic epistemological problem. How do we know how much censure, or "deserved punishment," a particular wrongdoer absolutely deserves? God may know, but as countless sentencing exercises have shown, peoples' intuitions about individual cases vary widely.[1]
>
> There is... reason to doubt that anything like a consensus exists on the seriousness of criminal conduct. While there may be some agreement on relative levels of harm, there appears to be great variation in perceptions of the absolute magnitude of harm represented by various criminal acts, and in either the relative or absolute level of culpability represented by various criminal actors.[2]

This view, together with the view that only crude rankings of offenses by seriousness could be made, has been used to justify important policy decisions, including the drafting of the United States Sentencing Commission sentencing guidelines:

> [S]ome students of the criminal justice system strenuously urged the Commission to follow what they call a "just deserts" approach to punishment....The difficulty that arises in applying this approach is that different Commissioners have different views about the correct rank order of the seriousness of different crimes....Considering the inherent subjectivity of such a trade-off process, the

---

[1] Michael Tonry, *Obsolescence and Immanence in Penal Theory and Policy*, 105 COLUM. L. REV. 1233, 1263 (2005).

[2] John Monahan, *The Case for Prediction in the Modified Desert Model of Criminal Sentencing*, 5 INT'L J. L. & PSYCHIATRY 103, 105 (1982). *See also* David Dolinko, *Three Mistakes of Retributivism*, 39 UCLA L. REV. 1623, 1638–39 (1992); Ernest van den Haag, *Punishment: Desert and Crime Control*, 85 MICH. L. REV. 1250, 1254 (1987).

> Commission soon realized that only a crude ranking of behavior in terms of just deserts...could be developed.[3]

Again, however, the empirical evidence paints a very different picture than this common wisdom, concluding that across demographics there can be an astounding level of agreement on a wide variety of liability and punishment issues.

Section A reviews a variety of studies that show a nearly universal intuition that serious wrongdoing should be punished. Section B investigates views on the relative seriousness of different wrongdoings and finds a similar degree of consensus. This is not to say that individuals agree on the specific sentence for each case, but rather, that people agree upon the relative blameworthiness among a set of cases. However, given a punishment continuum with a limited number of meaningfully different units and a high number of distinguishable cases, each case must end up associated with a specific sentence. Finally, section C describes two recent studies designed to test the outer limits of agreement. The level of agreements in rank ordering scenarios is so high that the studies failed to find the limits of shared intuitions of justice on core wrongdoing, although clearly there are limits.

This chapter is drawn primarily from portions of my article with Robert Kurzban, *Concordance and Conflict in Intuitions of Justice*.[4]

A. The Intuition That Serious Wrongdoing Should Be Punished

Using a range of techniques, previous empirical studies confirm a nearly universal human intuition that serious wrongdoing deserves punishment.

1. QUESTIONNAIRE STUDIES

In much of the existing research, subjects have been given an option to assign no punishment. Yet, people overwhelmingly chose to assign punishment even though they could have assigned none. For example, a study by Boydell and Grindstaff gave participants the opportunity to indicate the penalty they believed should be applied to an offense, as well as the minimum and maximum penalty applicable to that offense.[5] For the least serious offense they investigated, a mere 4 percent of people indicated that the minimum penalty they would apply was "no punishment."[6] For all other crimes, "no punishment" was chosen as the appropriate penalty by less

---

[3] Stephen Breyer, *The Federal Sentencing Guidelines and the Key Compromises Upon Which They Rest*, 17 HOFSTRA L. REV. 1, 15–17 (1988).

[4] Robinson & Kurzban, *Concordance and Conflict*, *supra* note 3, at 1846–80.

[5] Craig L. Boydell and Carl F. Grindstaff, *Public Opinion Toward Sanctions for Crimes of Violence*, 65 J. CRIM. L. 113, 116 (1974).

[6] *See id.* at 114. (Note: The penultimate column, labeled "education," is mislabeled and should read "execution" (see p. 115 for a confirmation of this error) and should therefore not be interpreted as a preference for "no punishment.")

than four percent of the respondents. Indeed, in the majority of cases, "no punishment" was selected by no participants, even as the minimum punishment for the offense.[7]

Similarly, a study by Wolfgang et al. allowed people to indicate zero in their magnitude estimation task when questioned about the appropriate punishment for certain offenses.[8] The frequency of zeros is not reported, but the average value assigned for even the offense judged least serious ("a person under 16 years old plays hooky from school") was statistically different from zero.[9] On average across all regions investigated, even the least serious offense was judged to deserve some punishment.

In studies in which "no liability" was not an option, it is clear that the experimenter assumed that all subjects would believe that all acts described in the study deserved some punishment. This itself is noteworthy. Researchers from multiple disciplines over the course of decades have routinely assumed that no significant fraction of subjects would believe that the offenses in question deserved no punishment. In short, even the experts in these fields discount the possibility that subjects would not want to punish. If all of these researchers are wrong, there likely would be evidence in the studies of subjects refusing to assign punishment, such as subjects responding with only the minimum possible amount of punishment in each case or by responding randomly. Yet these types of results did not occur, vindicating the researchers' views.

Taken together, these facts suggest that every study conducted supports the view that people share the intuition that serious wrongdoing should be punished.

2. BEHAVIORAL ECONOMICS STUDIES

In questionnaire studies, people are asked about how much punishment is "right" or "justified" or "deserved." They are not, however, required to pay any cost to inflict punishment. In some experiments, however, people must actually bear a cost to punish. These experiments typically investigate breaches of perceived norms, such as fairness, rather than criminal offenses. That is, the wrongdoing being punished here typically is dramatically less serious than the kind of wrongdoing involved in criminal violations. Thus, to the extent that persons are demonstrated as willing to bear the cost of punishment for violation of a civil norm, it seems reasonable to assume that they would similarly be willing to bear the cost of punishment—or pay much more to punish—in cases of criminal wrongdoing.

One game used in such studies that tests the willingness to bear the costs to punish perceived unfairness is the so-called Ultimatum Game. In the typical version,

---

[7] *Id.*

[8] MARVIN E. WOLFGANG ET AL., THE NATIONAL SURVEY OF CRIME SEVERITY, app. A at 137 (1985) (the instructions read: "If YOU think something should not be a crime, give it a zero.") (emphasis in original).

[9] *See id.* at 158–61.

experimental subjects are brought into the laboratory and randomly assigned to one of two experimental "roles," either that of the Proposer or the Responder. The Proposer is provisionally allocated a sum of money, called an "Endowment," often 10 dollars. The Proposer suggests a split of the Endowment with the Responder, for example, 6 dollars for the Proposer, 4 dollars for the Responder. The Responder is then given the option of accepting the option, in which case the money is split as designated by the Proposer, or he can reject the proposal, in which case the 10 dollars is not given to the subjects.

Proposers generally offer between 40 and 50 percent of the Endowment to Responders,[10] but our interest is in situations in which a very unequal split is proposed. Under these conditions, Responders will often reject the proposals, costing them the amount offered by the Proposer, and thus depriving the Proposer of his portion of the money. Such rejections are interpreted by researchers as cases in which Responders are punishing Proposers for making unfair offers. This happens even when the subjects do not physically interact with one another, do not know one another's identities, and when even the experimenter does not know the Responder's decision. In short, people punish perceived unfairness at a cost to themselves even when there are no instrumental consequences or experimenter expectations that might be at work. Even more strikingly, there is evidence that people will pay to punish another person even when they are not directly involved in the transaction if they perceive that the person has behaved intentionally unfairly.[11]

3. CROSS-CULTURAL STUDIES

If notions of wrongdoing and punishment were absent from a culture, study respondents presumably would have difficulty understanding the task put to them or would be expected to randomly answer questions about these topics. There is no report that any researcher who has attempted to gather data on judgments about wrongdoing or punishment has had difficulty in conveying the relevant questions and in obtaining coherent responses.[12] In fact, cross-cultural data suggest that questionnaire studies yield similar results in all of the cultures that have been studied. While one cannot deny that there are important cultural differences, the intuition that those who commit wrongs should be punished seems to be universal. There is no documented case of a culture in which the intuition to punish serious wrongdoing does not exist.

Experts commenting on this element of human culture show broad agreement. Cultural psychologist Paul Rozin and his colleagues conclude that "Moral judgment and the condemnation of others, including fictional others and others who have not

---

[10] This varies considerably depending on the details of the experimental procedure. *See* COLIN CAMERER, BEHAVIORAL GAME THEORY: EXPERIMENTS IN STRATEGIC INTERACTION 50–52 (2003).

[11] Daniel Kahneman et al., *Fairness and the Assumptions of Economics* (Part 2), 59 J. BUS. S285, S285–S300 (1986).

[12] *See* John R. Snarey, *Cross-Cultural Universality of Social-Moral Development: A Critical Review of Kohlbergian Research*, 97 PSYCHOL. BULL. 202, 213 (1985).

harmed the self, is a universal and essential feature of human social life."[13] Similar sentiments have been expressed by developmental psychologist Jerome Kagan, who includes this intuition as one of "a limited number of universal moral categories that transcend time and locality."[14] Philosopher Ray Jackendoff concludes: "Thus in our culture, the legal system punishes not only physical aggression like assault, but also economic aggression like stealing. Similar institutions are found in some form in every culture, even in the absence of written legal codes."[15] Anthropologist Donald Brown, in his exhaustive review of the cross-cultural data, includes intuitions surrounding justice and punishing transgressors as a "Human Universal."[16] In short, experts from multiple disciplines have been unambiguous in their assertion that, despite cultural differences, the intuition to punish is a key aspect of what it means to be a member of the human species.

4. ARE THERE EXCEPTIONS?

The previous discussion is not meant to imply that no human could conceive of a social structure in which people were not punished for their transgressions. For example, some religious writings might be taken to urge such a view, such as the biblical injunction to "turn the other cheek." However, the significant point here is that this injunction is given precisely because it is understood to run counter to strong intuitions to punish serious wrongdoing. More importantly, it is hardly evidence contradicting the existence of shared intuitions of justice that some people have called for the abolition of punishment if the call is rarely, if ever, answered.

Of course, one might argue that there are, in fact, historical figures who have believed that people should not be punished for their wrongdoing. For example, some might argue that Jesus Christ or Mahatma Gandhi were persons who would in fact "turn the other cheek," disproving the claim of a universal human intuition to punish serious wrongdoing. There is reason to believe that even such icons of love and forgiveness in fact believed in punishment of wrongdoing. Biblical passages of Christ's teachings are full of references calling for punishment.[17] And one might observe that Mahatma Gandhi advocated strikes and sit-ins meant to punish the British. But the important point here is not the conduct of these persons and others

---

[13] Paul Rozin, Laura Lowery, Sumio Imada, & Jonathan Haidt, *The CAD Triad Hypothesis: A Mapping Between Three Moral Emotions (Contempt, Anger, Disgust) and Three Moral Codes (Community, Autonomy, Divinity)*, 76 J. PERSONALITY & SOC. PSYCHOL. 574, 574 (1999).

[14] JEROME KAGAN, THE NATURE OF THE CHILD 118 (1984).

[15] RAY JACKENDOFF, LANGUAGE, CULTURE, CONSCIOUSNESS: ESSAYS ON MENTAL STRUCTURE 185–86 (2007).

[16] DONALD E. BROWN, HUMAN UNIVERSALS 138 (1991).

[17] "These will go away into eternal punishment." *Matthew*, 25:46. There are other biblical references to punishment. *See, e.g., Thessalonians* 1:5–10, especially 9: "...they will be punished with everlasting destruction, forever separated from the Lord and from his glorious power..." Note that Paul does not seem to shy away from punishment in the present. He indicates that an individual in power "does not bear the sword in vain; for he is the servant of God to execute His wrath on the wrongdoer" (*Romans* 13:4).

like them, but rather the fact that they have become historic figures precisely because they seemed to advocate a position so difficult for ordinary persons to achieve and so counter to human nature. Their historic status only serves to illustrate and confirm the strength of the human intuition to punish serious wrongdoing.

B. Intuitions on the Relative Seriousness of Wrongdoing

As is apparent from the quotations at the start of this chapter, some writers might concede the existence of a shared intuition that serious wrongdoing should be punished but might dispute nonetheless that there is agreement on how punishment ought to be distributed across cases of wrongdoing. However, a substantial body of research has accumulated that indicates a broad consensus regarding the relative seriousness of different wrongdoings and the relative amount of punishment appropriate.

It is not that everyone agrees on a specific sentence for each case. On the contrary, some people would generally give more harsh punishment and others generally less harsh punishment. But whether they prefer harsh or lenient punishments, people tend to agree on the relative degree of blameworthiness among a set of cases. That is, while they may disagree as to the endpoint of the punishment continuum, they agree on the relative placement of cases along that continuum. As noted previously, once a society determines the end point of the punishment continuum, shared intuitions of justice will set each case on a specific point on the continuum in order to put it in its appropriate place relative to other cases. The specific amount of punishment due in each case is fixed not because there is some magical connection between that amount of punishment and that particular offense, but rather because that is the amount of punishment needed to distinguish that case from cases of noticeably greater and lesser blameworthiness on the limited punishment continuum.[18]

The existing studies reveal an extraordinary extent of agreement in this regard across a variety of issues and demographics. While a variety of testing techniques and subjects have been used, the conclusions are all essentially the same, confirming the existence of shared intuitions as to relative blameworthiness of different variations on wrongdoing.

1. PREVIOUS DOMESTIC STUDIES

The most well-known study is that of Sellin and Wolfgang, who in 1964 surveyed 575 individuals across Pennsylvania.[19] As noted previously, subjects were asked about the seriousness of 51 offenses—such as, "An offender forces a female to

---

[18] See text at chapter 1, section B.

[19] *See* THORSTEN SELLIN & MARVIN E. WOLFGANG, THE MEASUREMENT OF DELINQUENCY 268 (1964).

submit to sexual intercourse. No other physical injury is inflicted." The researchers used two test methods. One asked subjects to place offenses on a scale ranging from 1 to 11. Another asked subjects to assign the offense a number to indicate its seriousness relative to bicycle theft, which was assigned a value of 10, a "magnitude estimation task." The results show broad agreement. The researchers conclude that "[t]he most strongly supported conclusion... is that all the raters... tended to assign estimations [so] that the seriousness of the crimes is evaluated in a similar way, without significant differences, by all the groups" and, further, that a "pervasive social agreement about what is serious and what is not appears to emerge."[20] This study has been replicated, with results that support its original conclusions.[21]

Since Sellin and Wolfgang, there have been many other studies using a variety of methods that all reach similar conclusions. Here is a sampling of five that are representative. Jacoby and Cullen surveyed a national sample of 1,920 adults who, during 30-minute telephone interviews, were read 8 crime vignettes.[22] "Respondents agreed, on average, on the ordering of the twenty-four crimes in seriousness and deserved sentence length."[23] The researchers reported that the "amounts of variation in sentencing accounted for by the individual characteristics studied was quite small, less than 10 percent."[24]

Blumstein and Cohen surveyed 603 residents of Allegheny County, Pennsylvania. Subjects were asked to assign the length of a prison sentence[25] that "best fits the seriousness of the offense" for 23 offenses that were presented in the form of brief crime scenarios.[26] The researchers found no strong effects of demographics including gender, race, religious affiliation, and level of education on the ordering of sentences in terms of how much punishment was warranted. That is, different groups tended to agree on which crimes should be punished more than other crimes. They concluded that there was "considerable agreement across various demographic groups on the relative severity of the sentences to be imposed for different offenses."[27]

Rossi et al. interviewed 125 whites and 75 blacks in Baltimore, with a roughly equal number of males and females, asking people to categorize each of 80 offenses

---

[20] *Id.* at 268.

[21] *See* Jeffrey A. Roth, *Prosecutor Perceptions of Crime Seriousness*, 69 J. CRIM. L. & CRIMINOLOGY 232 (1978).

[22] *See* Joseph E. Jacoby & Francis T. Cullen, *The Structure of Punishment Norms: Applying the Rossi-Berk Model*, 89 J. CRIM. L. & CRIMINOLOGY 245, 263 (1998).

[23] *Id.* at 285. The researchers also noted that "[The subjects] did not agree on the appropriate value for seriousness or sentence length." *Id.*

[24] *Id.* at 205.

[25] *See* Alfred Blumestein & Jacqueline Cohen, *Sentencing of Convicted Offenders: An Analysis of the Public's View*, 14 L. & SOC. REV. 223, 229 (1980).

[26] A sample scenario: first-degree murder: "The offender is convicted of first degree murder after he intentionally killed a person who witnessed a crime he had committed." The offenses represented a significant contribution to present prison populations in the United States (i.e., first-degree murder, narcotics sales, etc.). *Id.* at 228.

[27] *Id.* at 223. They also noted, however, that there was "disagreement over the absolute magnitude of these sentences."

into 9 categories according to how serious the offense was perceived to be.[28] The correlations between ratings of blacks and whites, males and females, and more and less educated groups were 0.89, 0.94, and 0.89, respectively, indicating a substantial amount of agreement. The researchers concluded that "the amount of consensus among subgroups is impressive"[29] and that "[t]he norms defining how serious various criminal acts are considered to be are quite widely distributed among blacks and white, males and females, high and low socioeconomic levels, and amount levels of educational attainment."[30]

Hamilton and Rytina conducted face-to-face interviews with 391 subjects in the Boston area in which subjects were asked to rank each of 17 offenses using a "magnitude estimation task" similar to the one described above.[31] A comparison of the individuals' judgments of seriousness and desired punishments with the sample's average judgments gave high correlations, ranging from .71 to .78, suggesting "a high level of consensus."[32] An analysis of the demographic differences among the subjects—age, race, income, and sex—showed no strong effects.[33]

Thomas, Cage, and Foster surveyed 3,334 households, asking subjects what they felt would be a "fair sentence" for each of 17 offenses.[34] They reported finding "evidence of a remarkable level of consensus, even after separating the sample on the basis of their sex, race, age, income, occupational prestige, and educational attainment."[35] They concluded that the findings, "regardless of the type or category of offense examined, are not supportive of any prediction that suggests variations between different categories of the population in either perceptions of relative seriousness of these offenses, or the level of sanctions that are viewed as appropriate."[36]

The above studies asked subjects about crime seriousness, preferred sentences, or both. These two kinds of inquiries are related but not identical. The second includes a broader range of factors, beyond the seriousness of the criminal act itself, such as the consequences of the act; features of the perpetrator, such as prior history; and features of the victim. Nonetheless, testing of both offense seriousness and deserved punishment consistently show substantial consensus.

Indeed, there is reason to think that these studies *understate* the extent of agreement. When two people are given a skeletal description of an offense, as most of

---

[28] Peter H. Rossi et al., *The Seriousness of Crimes: Normative Structure and Individual Differences*, 39 AM. SOC. REV. 224, 226 (1974). Sample offenses ranged from the "planned killing of a police officer" to "being drunk in public places."

[29] *Id.* at 231.

[30] *Id.* at 205.

[31] V. Lee Hamilton & Steve Rytina, *Social Consensus on Norms of Justice: Should the Punishment Fit the Crime?*, 85 AM. J. SOC. 1117, 1124 (1980).

[32] *Id.* at 1132.

[33] *Id.* at 1134.

[34] Charles Thomas, Robin Cage & Samuel Foster, *Public Opinion on Criminal Law and Legal Sanctions: An Examination of Two Conceptual Models*, 67 J. CRIM. L. & CRIMINOLOGY 110, 112 (1976).

[35] *Id.* at 116.

[36] *Id.*

these studies provide, each of the persons is likely to visualize a "story" of the offense, and different people may well "fill in" different details to complete the picture. Demographic differences could prompt different details to be filled in, reflecting the different life experiences from which the details are drawn. If subjects visualize slightly different stories, one would expect them to give slightly different assessments of relative seriousness even if they in fact agreed in their intuitive judgments. This potential for these studies to understate the extent of agreement becomes greater as the crime descriptions become more skeletal, and is at its worst when researchers use crime labels rather than factual descriptions, as in some of the studies reported above, because different people are quite likely to visualize different stories when given just the bare offense label. Despite this serious potential to underestimate the extent of agreement, the studies consistently show a significant level of agreement on intuitions of justice, even across demographics.

Rossi and Berk, in their review of the literature through 1997, suggest that the studies converge on the view that people share intuitions about the relative seriousness of wrongdoing.[37] There is a "[f]airly strong consensus on the seriousness ordering of crimes, with those involving actual or threatened physical harm to victims generally considered to be the most serious."[38] In fact, their summary of previous studies suggest that "there is very little, if any evidence that there exist subgroups within the American population with radically different views about sentencing norms"[39] and that "[t]here is no evidence for a normative order that is an alternative to what the overwhelming majority of the American population believe."[40]

2. CROSS-CULTURAL STUDIES

The cross-cultural evidence appears to support the view that people everywhere share some intuitions of justice about the relative blameworthiness of serious wrongdoing. Of the large body of literature, here are four studies that are representative.

O'Connell and Whelan surveyed 623 individuals in the greater Dublin area, asking subjects to rate 10 offense descriptions on a 1 to 11 scale of seriousness.[41] Clear ordering of offenses emerged, suggesting textured intuitions regarding seriousness and deserved punishment. A comparison of the Irish data with a British sample from a decade earlier found that, "Irish perceptions of crime... have much in common with those in other jurisdictions," especially with regard to more serious crimes.[42]

---

[37] *See, e.g.*, Peter H. Rossi & Richard A. Berk, A National Sample Survey: Public Opinion on Sentencing Federal Crimes 193 (1995)

[38] Peter H. Rossi & Richard A. Berk, Just Punishments: Federal Guidelines and Public Views Compared 12 (1997).

[39] Rossi & Berk, *supra* note 98 at Appendix C.

[40] *Id.* at 209.

[41] Michael O'Connell & Anthony Whelan, *Taking Wrongs Seriously: Public Perceptions of Crime Seriousness*, 36 Brit. J. Criminology 299, 302–04 (1996).

[42] *Id.* at 316.

Following in the tradition of Sellin and Wolfgang, Hsu administered a survey to 600 Chinese persons in Taiwan including students, policemen, and judges.[43] Subjects were asked for seriousness judgments of 14 offenses, which were the 14 index offenses of Sellin and Wolfgang translated into Chinese, on an 11-point scale. Hsu found broad agreement across the three Taiwanese samples (students, police, and judges), with correlation coefficients all above .90, and similar ordinal judgments in the relative ranking of the 14 offenses between the Chinese and American samples, with a coefficient of .84 (.95 among male subjects).[44] The Sellin and Wolfgang study has been replicated in many other studies in other countries, reaching similar conclusions about shared intuitions of justice.

Newman sampled 2,360 individuals from a number of different cultures—India (512), Indonesia (500), Iran (479), Italy (200), United States (169), Yugoslavia (500)—chosen for their supposed important cultural differences.[45] Subjects were asked to rate serious offenses, described very briefly, with a minimum of surrounding circumstances, on a 12-point scale.[46] Newman reports that, "If one were to order the acts according to the proportions of each country sample criminalizing them, one would find a general consensus across all countries as to the extent that all acts should be tolerated."[47] Newman also reports that "At the general level of analysis, it is apparent that there was considerable agreement as to the amount of punishment appropriate to each act" and that looking at relative rankings indicates "general agreement in ranks across all countries."[48]

Cross-cultural agreement exists on issues beyond just ranking of harm seriousness. Bersoff and Miller presented 180 adults and children aged 8 to 10 years old in the United States and India with vignettes in which an offender harmed another person or committed a violation of property rights, such as theft; and where the circumstances of the offense varied, being either accidental or intentional.[49] The accidental offenses were distinguished from the intentional offenses and were exculpated across cultures and age ranges: 91 and 100 percent of the time across samples.[50] This indicates intent, as a mediating factor, has broad cross-cultural support. Other studies reach similar conclusions.

These studies represent only a fraction of the evidence regarding cross-cultural similarities. In their review of the cross-cultural evidence, when discussing the variability in what cultures consider immoral, Haidt, Koller, and Dias suggested,

---

[43] Marlene Hsu, *Cultural and Sexual Differences on the Judgement of Criminal Offenses: A Replication Study of the Measurement of Delinquency*, 64 J. CRIM. L. & CRIMINOLOGY 348, 350 (1973).

[44] *Id.* at 350.

[45] GRAEME NEWMAN, COMPARATIVE DEVIANCES: PERCEPTION AND LAW IN SIX CULTURES 140 (1976).

[46] *Id.* at 116 tbl.4.

[47] *Id.* at 115.

[48] *Id.* at 140–41. (*See* tbl.12, pp. 142–43).

[49] David M. Bersoff & Joan G. Miller, *Culture, Context, and the Development of Moral Accountability Judgments*, 29 DEVELOPMENTAL PSYCHOL. 664, 666 (1993).

[50] Emotional duress or immaturity of the agent showed some developmental and substantial cross-cultural variability. *Id.*

"Harm, broadly construed to include psychological harm, injustice, and violation of rights, may be important in the morality of all cultures."[51]

C. Testing the Limits of Agreement

While earlier studies establish the existence of agreement on intuitions of justice, one may wonder at what point the agreement breaks down. Just how nuanced could the shared intuitions be? Just how far and with how wide a range of factors could one push lay persons in making distinctions among cases and still retain general agreement? The study described here attempted to answer these questions.

The tests sought to find the outer limits to the nuance and variety of scenarios on which subjects would express consensus. Could subjects distinguish two dozen scenarios on a single continuum of punishment—making quite subtle differences between each adjacent pair—yet still reach a high level of agreement in their rank ordering? Could subjects make fine distinctions, and agree in their judgments when they were judging not just cases that differed in tangible harms, like physical injury, but also differed in intangible harms, such as the extent of intrusion of privacy, or differed in mitigating and excusing conditions, or differed in the vulnerability of the victim?

The first task was to design a method that minimized testing factors that obscure the extent of agreement. For example, it was speculated that both the use of factual descriptions rather than abstract offense labels and the use of full rather than skeletal fact patterns would reduce the problem of inadvertently creating cases that would be perceived differently by different subjects. The study used a card sorting procedure with scenario headings that might allow an increase in the number and complexity of the distinctions that subjects were asked to make.

The same test instrument was used in two different sets of studies. In the first set, reported here as Studies 1 and 3, the test instrument was administered in person to subjects who rank ordered 24 cards on a large table. In the second set of studies, identified here as Studies 2 and 4, subjects performed the task over the Internet, using a software program in which they "dragged" each scenario to its appropriate place among the other scenarios. (Studies 1 and 2 are discussed in this chapter; Studies 3 and 4 are discussed in chapter 5.) The use of the Internet introduced certain complications in assuring that subjects understood and were motivated to undertake the relatively demanding tasks, but it also allowed for the collection of data from a greater number of subjects with a wider range of demographic characteristics.

To signal the results, the testing found that despite the dramatically greater difficulty of the task over those of previous studies, the levels of agreement in rank ordering were astonishingly high. In other words, the tests failed to find the limits of shared intuitions of justice for the core wrongdoing.

---

[51] Jonathan Haidt, Silvia Helena Koller, & Maria G. Dias, *Affect, Culture, and Morality, or Is It Wrong to Eat Your Dog?*, 65 J. Personality & Soc. Psych. 613, 613 (1993).

1. STUDY 1: IN-PERSON TESTING

a. Method. Participants were given 24 short scenarios, each on a separate card describing an event during which "John" engages in conduct that may be a criminal offense. Participants were asked to rank order the cards on a table to reflect the amount of punishment, if any, that John deserves. The scenarios included such offenses as theft by taking; theft by fraud; property destruction; assault; burglary; robbery; kidnapping; rape; negligent homicide; manslaughter; murder; and torture, in a variety of situations, including self-defense, provocation, duress, mistake, and mental illness. (The kinds of offenses in the scenarios represent 94.9 percent of the offenses committed in the United States.[52]) When the participant completed the rank ordering, he or she was asked to reconsider each pair of scenarios to confirm that each pair was ordered as wished. This task typically took participants between 30 and 40 minutes. Each participant also filled out a form that collected demographic information.

b. Results. Table 2 orders the scenarios in the modal order produced by the subject pool as a group. The first four scenarios were most commonly rated as deserving no liability or punishment. Scenario 5 was a borderline case. About a quarter of the subjects thought there should be no punishment, while the remainder thought there should be, but most subjects agreed that it should be ranked as more aggravated than the four no punishment scenarios and less aggravated than the other 19 scenarios. Mean ranks in ordinal data obviously have limited usefulness but are provided here simply to give a heuristic sense of the distribution for each scenario.

The task asked of the subjects was quite complex. Ranking each scenario required a comparison of each scenario to each of the other scenarios. It was expected that an unavoidable amount of "noise" in the data would reflect the fact that many subjects would have difficulty sustaining the required level of concentration for the length of time required for the task, which was longer than most research tasks require. Thus, it was quite surprising that the results, nonetheless, were rather clear and dramatic.

For the first four scenarios, there was overwhelming consensus that "no punishment" was appropriate. Ninety-two percent of the time subjects agreed that no punishment was deserved. (The 64 subjects each judged these four scenarios—a total of 256 judgments—and in 235 instances concluded that no punishment was deserved.)

Each of the 64 subjects could have deviated from the group modal ranking as to each of the 190 pair-wise judgments, for a total number of 12,160 possible deviations from modal pair-wise ranking. Note that if a subject ranks a scenario different from the modal ranking it may produce many pair-wise "deviations." For example, a subject who agreed with the modal ranking in every respect, except that he ranked S11 much higher—say, as more serious than S19—would by his ranking

[52] *See* Bureau of Justice Statistics, National Crime Victimization Survey 2003, Table 1, Number, percent distribution, and rate of victimizations, by type of crime.

TABLE 2. } Results from Study 1

Scenario	Mode Rank	% Assigning "No Liability"	Mean Rank
S1 (defending)	no punish	91	**
S2 (coercion)	no punish	92	**
S3 (umbrella)	no punish	92	**
S4 (hallucination)	no punish	92	**
S5 (pies)	5	27	3.9
S6 (T shirt)	6	8	6.3
S7 (short change)	7	9	6.8
S8 (radio)	8	5	7.6
S9 (drill)	9	3	8.8
S10 (microwave)	10	2	9.9
S11 (TV)	11	2	10.4
S12 (slap)	12	0	12.1
S13 (headbutt)	13	2	13
S14 (stitches)	14	0	14.1
S15 (necklace)	15	0	14.8
S16 (robbery)	16	0	15.6
S17 (clubbing)	17	0	16.8
S18 (pit bulls)	18	0	18.2
S19 (infant)	19	3	18.6
S20 (stabbing)	20	0	19.7
S21 (ambush)	21	0	20.9
S22 (abduction)	22	0	21.7
S23 (burning)	23	0	23
S24 (ransom)	24	0	23.9

N = 64

** The means for these four scenarios are 0.6, 0.3, 1.4, 0.3, respectively, when a response of "no punishment" is given a value of 0.

of that one scenario produce 8 deviations. That is, he would have deviated from the judgments the other subjects in 8 different pair-wise judgments, S11 versus S12, S11 versus S13, etc.

The subjects had a total of 480 deviations, meaning that the subjects reversed the modal pair-wise ranking only 4 percent of the time. This means that subjects agreed with the modal pair-wise ranking 96 percent of the time, as compared to the approximately 50 percent agreement rate that a random ranking of pairs would give.

More sophisticated statistical methods of analysis are available, most important Kendall's coefficient of concordance, which measures agreement (concordance) among different sets of rank orderings of the same set. (This measures the concordance shown in the entire ranking, not just in set pairwise comparisons.) A coefficient of 1.0 indicates perfect agreement, a 0.0 indicates no agreement.

For the 24 scenarios in the study, the Kendall's W is .95 (with $p < .001$). This is an astounding level of agreement.

c. Discussion. Preliminarily, note that the present study confirms the rather basic conclusion of section A, above, that people do indeed share an intuition that serious wrongdoing should be punished. Each subject in the study could have judged "no liability" for any or all of the 24 scenarios presented. Instead, subjects typically chose "no liability" only for the first 4 scenarios, which were designed to elicit a judgment of full exculpation.[53] For every other scenario, subjects typically expressed an intuition that at least some punishment was deserved.

As to shared intuitions regarding the relative seriousness of wrongdoing, discussed in section B, above, the amount of agreement shown in the study—96 percent of all pair-wise judgements, and a Kendall's W of .95—represents an extraordinary result. To appreciate its significance, consider some points of comparison. For example, American men who ranked the attractiveness of women with different WHRs (waist-to-hip ratios), generally agreed in their rankings, showing a Kendall's W of .54.[54] On the other hand, when economists were asked to rank the top 20 economic journals according to quality, the Kendall's W was .095.[55]

Very high Kendall's W scores typically are found only in tasks that seem quite obvious, as when subjects are asked to rank order images according to their brightness, yielding a Kendall's W of .95[56] or, to take another example, when subjects are asked to rank the following six drawings of faces according to how much pain they show, giving a Kendall's W of .97.[57]

One may wonder how this amount of agreement could exist when judging such a complex matter as relative blameworthiness. It would seem to call for a matter of complex and subjective judgment—like judging the relative talent of 20 movie actors or athletes, the beauty of 20 flower arrangements or paintings, the awkwardness of 20 embarrassing situations, or the humorousness of 20 comedians or clowns.

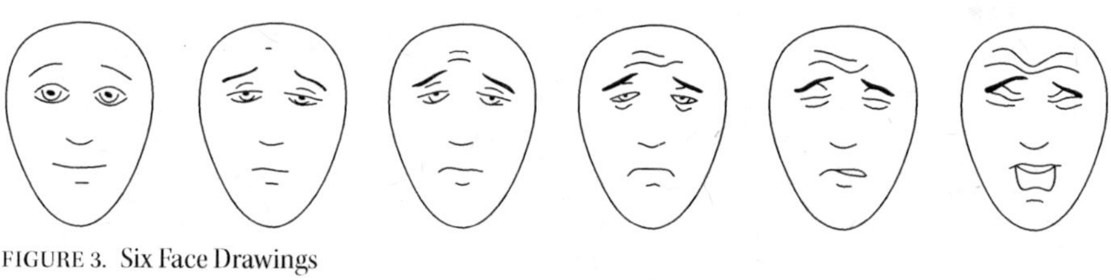

FIGURE 3. Six Face Drawings

[53] *See* tbl. 1, column 3. In these four scenarios, the act that caused harm was either unintentional (a mistake or a hallucination), coerced, or self-defense.

[54] Frank Marlowe & Adam Wetsman, *Preferred Waist-to-Hip Ratio and Ecology*, PERSONALITY AND INDIVIDUAL DIFFERENCES 30, 481–489 (2001).

[55] Kostas Axarloglou & Vasilis Theoharakis, *Diversity in Economics: An Analysis of Journal Quality Perceptions*, 1 J. EUROPEAN ECON. ASSOC. 1402, 1421–22 (2003).

[56] C. M. M. DE WEERT & N. A. W. H. VAN KRUYSBERGEN, ASSIMILATION: CENTRAL AND PERIPHERAL EFFECTS, PERCEPTION, 26, 1217–1224 (1997). The images are made up of black and white splotches. The more white splotches, the brighter the image appears.

[57] K. A. Herr, P. R. Mobily, F. J. Kohout, & D. Wagenaar, *Evaluation of the Faces Pain Scale for Use with the Elderly*, 14 CLINICAL J. PAIN 29, 29 (1998).

How is it that people can agree so much with one another when asked to judge the relative punishment deserved in 24 crime scenarios, a task that would seem to involve equally complex matters of judgment? The existence of this level of agreement presents an intriguing puzzle in itself, which is discussed further in chapter 3.

2. STUDY 2: INTERNET TESTING

In a follow-up study, 246 subjects rank ordered the same 24 scenarios using a computer-based program over the Internet. Despite the potential for a large increase in the amount of "noise," the results were essentially the same.

a. Method. In the computer-based test, each Internet participant would "drag" each scenario to the location in a "stack" of scenarios that reflected the proper rank of the scenario with regard to the amount of punishment deserved. As in the paper-based administration, subjects were free to identify any or all scenarios as deserving of no punishment.

Study 2 was conducted through the National Science Foundation's TESS program (Time-Sharing Experiments for the Social Sciences), which resulted in some important differences with respect to the first study. First, subjects were recruited using a random sampling procedure that draws broadly from across the United States. Subjects came from a variety of socioeconomic, religious, and racial backgrounds. Participants were presented with a web-based interface that asked them to perform the same task as described above. Of course, because no experimenter was present at the time the task was performed, there is substantially increased potential for "noise" as there is no way to directly observe whether subjects were attending to the task. The motivation of subjects sitting in front of a computer terminal may be considerably less than that when they have face-to-face contact with a human researcher. For a task that demands as much time and concentration as the rank ordering of 24 scenarios, the lack of personal motivation, as well as the lack of quality control that comes from personal observation, meant that the resulting data could be quite "noisy."

b. Results. Table 4 presents the scenarios in the modal order of the participants as a group. As in paper-based Study 1, the first four scenarios were typically ranked as not deserving punishment. Scenario 5 was seen as a borderline case for which subjects disagreed about whether punishment was deserved but agreed that it should be ranked as more aggravated than the 4 "no punishment" scenarios but less aggravated than the other 19 scenarios. As with Table 2, mean ranks in ordinal data obviously have limited usefulness but are provided here simply to give a heuristic sense of the distribution for each scenario.

As in the previous study, the first four scenarios were judged to merit "no punishment" by an overwhelming proportion of subjects: 82 percent, 75 percent, 87 percent, and 71 percent for the four scenarios respectively.

TABLE 4. Results from Study 2

Scenario	Modal Rank	% Assigning "No Liability"	Mean Rank
S1 (defending)	no punish	82	**
S2 (coercion)	no punish	75	**
S3 (umbrella)	no punish	87	**
S4 (hallucination)	no punish	71	**
S5 (pies)	5	8	5.4
S7 (short change)	6	6	7.1
S6 (T shirt)	7	1	7.4
S8 (radio)	8	0	8.4
S9 (drill)	9	0	9.2
S10 (microwave)	10	0	10.2
S11 (TV)	11	0	10.6
S12 (slap)	12	0	11.6
S13 (head-butt)	13	2	12.2
S14 (stitches)	14	0	13.7
S15 (necklace)	15	0	13.6
S16 (robbery)	16	0	15.3
S17 (clubbing)	17	1	16.7
S18 (pit bulls)	18	0	17.8
S19 (infant)	19	1	19
S20 (stabbing)	20	0	20.1
S21 (ambush)	21	0	20.9
S22 (abduction)	22	0	21.4
S23 (burning)	23	0	22.2
S24 (ransom)	24	0	23.5

N = 246

** The means for these four scenarios are 1.2, 2.3, 0.3, 1.7, respectively, when a response of "no punishment" is given a value 0.

Each of the 246 subjects could have deviated from the group modal ranking as to each of the 190 pair-wise judgments for a total number of 46,740 possible deviations from modal pair-wise ranking. Recall that if a subject ranks a single scenario different from the modal ranking, it may produce many pair-wise "deviations." The subjects had a total of 4,317 deviations, meaning that the subjects reversed the modal pair-wise ranking only 9.2 percent of the time. That is, they agreed with the pair-wise modal rank 91.8 percent of the time, as compared to the roughly 50 percent agreement rate that a random ranking of pairs would give.

The most common deviation, as one might guess, was for a subject to "flip" the ranking of two scenarios that were adjacent in the group's modal ranking—for example, a subject rank ordering the scenarios as S6, S8, S7, S9, "flipping" scenarios S7 and S8. There were 1,447 such "adjacent flip" deviations, or about a third of all deviations. If these simple "flips" of adjacent scenarios are excluded, the percentage of pair-wise rankings that deviate from the mode is only 6.1 percent.

As in paper-based Study 1, a Kendall's coefficient of concordance for the subjects' rankings was calculated. Recall that a coefficient of 1.0 indicates perfect agreement, a 0.0 indicates no agreement. For the 246 subjects rank ordering the 24 scenarios, the Kendall's W is 0.88 (with $p < .001$), again, a surprisingly high level of agreement.

c. Discussion. The results of computer-based Study 2 reinforce the conclusions of paper-based Study 1. Both studies show an exceptionally high level of agreement among the participants. The result in Study 2 is all the more surprising given the great potential for "noise" in a study where researchers cannot supervise or even observe the participants as they perform the task. The subjects agreed with the modal pair-wise ranking 92 percent of the time and, if the "flips" of adjacent scenarios are excluded, they agreed with the modal pair-wise ranking 94 percent of the time. The Kendall's W coefficient of concordance was 0.88. This confirms the astounding level of agreement shown by Study 1's Kendall's W of 0.95, in performing what appears to be a rather complex and subjective judgment task.

Chapter 4 reports Studies 3 and 4 of this same project, which focus on showing where lay persons' intuitions of justice do disagree.

D. Conclusion

As the previous sections have demonstrated, contrary to the common wisdom, available evidence suggests that human intuitions of justice about "core" wrongdoing—both the sense that serious wrongdoing should be punished and the sense of the relative seriousness of wrongdoing—are widely shared. While chapter 4 will show that there are disagreements about the relative blameworthiness of wrongdoing out from the "core," the "core" wrongs themselves—physical aggression, takings without consent, and deception in exchanges—are often the subject of nuanced and specific intuitions on which there is high agreement across demographics.

The existence of such shared intuitions of justice can have important implications for criminal justice debates, as later sections will show, including the abolition of punishment (chapter 11, section B), the distribution of punishment according to principles that conflict with the community's shared intuitions of justice (chapter 8), and programs to change people's views on what constitutes serious wrongdoing (chapter 5).

3 }

The Origins of Shared Intuitions of Justice

The somewhat astounding level of agreement among intuitions of justice, even across demographics described in chapter 2, presents an intriguing puzzle: How can it be that people with such varied situations and backgrounds agree on judgments that are so complex and subjective?

Section A offers an evolutionary explanation: Human success as a species came in large part from their sociability—their ability to work together in a group. This success was possible only with group cohesion and cooperation. Conduct undermining the same had to be prohibited, but the available mechanisms of enforcement during most of human history typically required engaging in prohibited conduct (physical aggression, taking of property). Thus, if enforcement of the essential norms was not to trigger further violations, setting off a downward spiral into chaos, humans had to share some common understating of what kind of punishment was appropriate for what kind of violations and to mark these out as not themselves a violation of the norms but rather as vindication and reinforcement of them. In other words, there was an enormous evolutionary advantage, indeed a necessity for survival, to humans sharing a view that punishing serious wrongdoing was necessary and not itself a new violation, and also a general sense of the relative seriousness of different wrongs to guide the amount of appropriate punishment.

While one cannot know, on present information, if the evolutionary hypothesis is correct, one can test it by examining existing data on related issues. Section B examines findings from animal studies, brain science research, and child development research. While none of the evidence can offer definitive proof, it supports the evolutionary explanation, and no evidence exists that conflicts with it.

Section C considers the best alternative explanation: social learning—the claim that shared intuitions of justice are learned through interaction with one's surroundings. Several versions of the theory are possible. In one version, shared intuitions of justice are spontaneously learned by each individual and match those of others because of the similarity among the interactions that all humans experience. In another version, shared intuitions of justice are developed over multiple generations and passed to each individual through a shared predisposition to adopt the notions of justice of others in one's group. While some of these theories work better than others, all have problems, and none are as consistent with available evidence as an evolutionary explanation.

This chapter is drawn primarily from my article with Robert Kurzban and Owen Jones, "The Origins of Shared Intuitions of Justice."[1]

A. An Evolutionary Explanation for Intuitions of Justice

This section describes how evolutionary processes, most notably natural selection, operate to preserve both anatomical and behavioral traits that helped to solve challenges regularly encountered by ancestors over evolutionary time. It explains how the process of solving these challenges can lead to common psychological preferences in humans, including some general moral preferences. More specifically, it suggests how evolutionary processes can result in shared intuitions of justice relating to punishment for wrongdoing.

Given the influence of genes, environments, and evolutionary processes on human problem solving through evolved behavioral predispositions, including moral ones, it is a small but significant logical step to suggest that shared intuitions of justice, specific to punishments for transgressions of varying seriousness, also reflect the common human evolutionary history. It is argued here that human sociality has laid the foundation for an evolved predisposition to acquire shared intuitions of justice and that such intuitions benefit the individuals that bear them. Further, it is argued that there is reason to believe that evolution has in particular contributed to intuitions that physical harm, taking of property, and cheating in exchanges are matters for particular attention and condemnation.[2]

1. Human Sociality and the Predisposition to Acquire Shared Intuitions of Justice. The predisposition to acquire human intuitions of justice likely arose from the deeply and irretrievably social nature of the human species. Humans have been described as "ultrasocial" by anthropologists because of the many ways in which they interact with one another, particularly in the context of cooperation between individuals and within groups.[3] Group cooperation is relatively uncommon in the biological world—though there are exceptions such as certain group-living insects—and captures the attention of biologists because evolution, broadly, tends to favor genes that lead to selfish behavior. Humans, however, behave altruistically in many contexts: family relations, friendships, and within-group cooperation. How does such extensive cooperation come to pass? The evolution of cooperation in humans and other species is relevant to the argument here.

---

[1] Paul H. Robinson, Robert Kurzban, & Owen D. Jones, *The Origins of Shared Intuitions of Justice*, 60 VAND. L. REV. 1633, 1639–87 (2007).

[2] *See also* Marc D. Hauser, MORAL MINDS: HOW NATURE DESIGNED OUR UNIVERSAL SENSE OF RIGHT AND WRONG 108–109 (2006).

[3] Peter J. Richerson & Robert Boyd, *The Evolution of Human Ultra-Sociality*, in INDOCTRINABILITY, IDEOLOGY, AND WARFARE: EVOLUTIONARY PERSPECTIVES 71, 71 (Irenaus Eibl-Eibisfeldt & Frank Salter eds., 1998).

It has been shown both theoretically and empirically that cooperation can evolve through several independent but overlapping processes. The one most relevant for the immediate purpose concerns the mutually beneficial effects of reciprocity: if you share with me today in exchange for my sharing with you yesterday, we are both better off than if neither of us share. In social animals, reciprocity can involve such things as alerting other group members when food has been discovered, sharing food over time, and supporting a comrade in action against others.

But underlying this rosy picture is a darker shadow. While it is evident that reciprocators can outperform loners, a cheater could theoretically outperform both if he were able to regularly take benefits without repaying them. Consequently, an evolutionary arms race ensues in social animals between various predispositions toward cooperation and exploitation. In the end, the most successful cooperators are not those who always cooperate, but rather those who cooperate *selectively* with other cooperators, thus discriminating (passively or aggressively) against those who are not reliable partners in cooperative endeavors.[4] Put another way, effective cooperation requires rewarding good behavior and punishing bad behavior.

For this to work, one must be able to evaluate the individual costs and benefits of various kinds of things (such as different objects, acts, and information) and similarly evaluate others' valuation of those objects. One must, in turn, be able to discern unfairness, such as an inequitable distribution of resources or a violation of reciprocity. One must also be able to recognize individuals and remember recent interactions with them, so as to discriminate in future in favor of some and against others. These are precisely the features one tends to observe in the most highly social animals.

Those features are also precisely the features that likely underlie the functional advantage of the specific learning capacity in humans for acquiring shared intuitions of justice. Humans have a universal and uniquely nuanced propensity for engaging in social exchange. Indeed, gains from social exchange form the basis of the modern economy and infiltrate nearly every aspect of life, both in formal markets and in personal relationships. The psychology that underpins exchange requires deep intuitions and complex computational capacities to operate.

In particular, one critical capacity for successful social exchange is the intuition that one should punish individuals who injure others or cheat in an exchange. If one is engaged in transactions with the same person over time, then allowing another individual to injure or to cheat without punishment is an invitation to exploitation without end. Therefore, to be most successful in social exchange, one must have the capacity not only to detect but also to punish such persons.

This implies that there might have been selection in humans for the cognitive mechanisms designed to detect inequities and, similarly, for the cognitive mechanisms that yield intuitions that motivate the punishment of people who violate the most ancient and fundamentally necessary principles of social exchange. In other words, the evolutionary history of social exchange has likely led to the development

---

[4] *See, e.g.*, Robert Axelrod, EVOLUTION AND THE THEORY OF GAMES (1984).

of a reliable psychological system that is able to compute when someone has injured or cheated, as well as to a motivation to punish them.

2. Intuitions of Justice as Generating Benefits for Individuals. The argument sketched so far may explain why people have intuitions that lead them to believe that people who have harmed or cheated *them* ought to be punished. However, this does not explain why people have intuitions that punishment should be imposed on wrongdoers in transactions in which they have no part. This question—why people care about third party transactions at all—is an important mystery. Most nonhuman organisms attend very little to transactions that occur between unrelated others (though there are some important exceptions). Why do humans care so much about these interactions? The analysis follows along these lines: Once individuals possess intuitions about being wronged, detecting when others have been wronged is possible using the same set of intuitions. This does not itself explain why individuals should care that someone else has been wronged; it merely explains the origin of the ability to detect wrongful acts toward others.

What may explain the interest in wrongdoing to others is that individuals themselves need to make decisions about the people with whom they interact; engage in social exchange; form groups and coalitions and more generally, socialize. One observing a third party committing a wrong against another person has important information about the perpetrator of the wrong, which may make the observer less likely to choose that person for social interactions.

Another puzzle exists: Why do people have the intuition that wrongs to others should be punished? The evolutionary advantage of this intuition can be debated, but this chapter advances some ideas that help explain the preference. The logic begins with the uncontroversial premise that humans evolved in relatively small groups that consisted of people with whom they had a large number of transactions over a sustained period of time.[5] Consider two kinds of groups: first, one in which individuals whose acts of unprovoked violence, theft, or cheating in exchanges is left unpunished; and second, one in which these acts are punished. In the second group, the individuals in the group benefit because they are less likely to be subject to violence, theft, or cheating. Thus, each person has an incentive to take it upon himself to inflict punishment on those who commit such offenses to gain that benefit. Such punishment is potentially costly, so the long-term benefits of punishing must outweigh the long-term costs if it is to be selected.[6] And very recent experimental evidence in humans suggests that under such circumstances, given a choice, even prior transgressors choose to be in a group that punishes over one that is punishment free.[7]

---

[5] *See generally* Christopher Boehm, Hierarchy in the Forest: The Evolution of Egalitarian Behavior (1999).

[6] *See* Richerson & Boyd, *supra* note 121.

[7] Ozgur Gurek et al., *The Competitive Advantage of Sanctioning Institutions*, 312 Science 108 (Apr. 2006).

However, personally punishing wrongdoers need not be the only way to increase the chances of being in a group in which undesirable acts are punished. One need not inflict punishment oneself. One can decrease the cost of inflicting punishment on wrongdoers by supporting or defending those who do inflict the punishment. A third party punisher has a smaller risk of retaliation if group members endorse the punishment meted out by the third party. So, an individual benefits by having intuitions that support the punishment—by some individual—of those who transgress.

If it is true that (1) individuals prefer that wrongdoers be punished, and (2) individuals may not want to bear the costs of inflicting punishment, it is not surprising that means have been developed to satisfy these two preferences, though the means may differ across the centuries and cultures. For example, in some cultures,[8] one person has special responsibilities and duties in the context of such punishment. In the West, punishment is put into the hands of a system of criminal justice, including legislatures, police, judges, and so on. In the small groups in which humans evolved, the marginal benefit of having each individual support punishment for wrongdoings might have had an impact on making the group one in which transgressions were reduced, and thus protect an individual's health, property, and ability to make contracts.

In short, shared intuitions of justice contribute to the ability of an individual or group to be able to punish, which in turn provides evolutionary advantage to all. In other words, there is an evolutionary advantage to an understanding of victimhood and to the concurrent condoning of the punishment of one who has engaged in wrongful conduct. This is important because the imposition of punishment—the imposition of costs against the wrongdoer—is itself something that normally would be seen as a wrongful act. To produce conditions that avoid a never-ending spiral of wrongful acts, intuitions of justice must specify that wrongful acts can be punished without eliciting the further intuition that the punishers should themselves be punished.

To be able to distinguish deserved punishment, which is permitted, from undeserved punishment, which is not, the group obviously must share some sense of what constitutes wrongful conduct and the amount of punishment appropriate in any one case relative to that in other cases. If everyone in a group agrees on this, stability and cooperation, and its consequent benefits to members of the group, can be achieved.[9]

Contributing to the institutional arrangement for punishment may not be the only reason that intuitions of justice evolved. Because social exchange is mutually beneficial, participation in exchange is desirable. When there are many people in a social group, there is competition to be selected as a partner in exchange. It should

[8] *See* Bruce G. Trigger, THE CHILDREN OF AATAENTSIC: A HISTORY OF THE HURON PEOPLE TO 1660, 59, 60 (1976).

[9] *See* Robert Boyd & Peter Richerson, *Solving the Puzzle of Human Cooperation*, in EVOLUTION AND CULTURE 105 (Stephen C. Levinson & Pierre Jaison eds. 2005).

therefore be expected that natural selection would favor predispositions that signal to others that one is a good candidate for participation in such exchanges. If one shares others' moral intuitions—that cheating in an exchange is condemnable, for example—then one can expect selection to favor those who signal having such an intuition. Krebs and Denton recently made this argument explicitly: "Persuading others that you are a fair, honest, generous, responsible and moral person who will make an attractive exchange partner may induce them to bestow benefits on you."[10]

The emergence of intuitions of justice has a self-sustaining character. Once the intuitions exist in a group, actions that violate others' intuitions invite censure and punishment. Once the intuitions of justice exist, it is disadvantageous to publicly reject the principles of that system or to behave in ways that conflict with others' intuitions. Thus, persons who do not reliably behave in a manner consistent with those intuitions or do not signal their agreement in such shared intuitions will be disadvantaged as opposed to those who do.

To illustrate that core intuitions of justice should reliably develop in all humans, consider the fate of a mutation that causes individuals not to develop such intuitions. Such individuals would be punished by those who they injured, stole from, or cheated, and would not be desired as social exchange partners or as members of groups. For a social creature, such a fate would have been a reproductive disaster.[11] The individual costs associated with having diverging intuitions from those shared by others are a powerful force for homogenizing the intuitions of justice.[12] Thus, once such intuitions of justice are in place, there would be strong pressure favoring any variant in humans that acquires those intuitions, stabilizing them, and making them essentially universal in the species.

One might wonder why some details of human intuitions of justice are widely shared, while others are not. Intuitions of justice that were advantageous no matter what the context should be relatively consistent across individuals, and should develop reliably regardless of one's local environment.[13] These core intuitions probably include the notions that unjustified physical aggression, taking of another's property, and cheating in exchanges are all wrong and should be punished.[14] In contrast, the less that conduct directly prevents beneficial social interaction or the more it is dependent upon social, economic, or other contexts, the less likely it is to be included in the "core" intuitions that have reliably developed today in all

---

[10] Dennis Krebs & Kathy Denton, *Toward a More Pragmatic Approach to Morality: A Critical Evaluation of Kohlberg's Model*, 112 Psychol. Rev. 629, 642 (2005).

[11] Robert Kurzban & Mark R. Leary, *Evolutionary Origins of Stigmatization: Social Exclusion*, 127 Psychol. Bull. 187, 192 (2001).

[12] *See, e.g.,* Joseph Henrich & Robert Boyd, *The Evolution of Conformist Transmission and the Emergence of Between-Group Differences,* 19 Evol. & Hum. Behav. 215 (1998).

[13] *See* Jerome Kagan, The Nature Of The Child 123, 189 (1984). *See also* Richard A. Shweder & Jonathan Haidt, *The Future of Moral Psychology: Truth, Intuition and the Pluralist Way*, 4 Psychol. Sci. 360, 363 (1993).

[14] *See* Owen D. Jones, *Proprioception, Non-Law, and Biolegal History,* 53 Fl. L. Rev. 831, 847–67 & Fig. 9 (2001).

environments. This is reflected in the cross-cultural and even intra-group divergence on such things as drug use or prostitution, in which the core intuitions regarding harm, theft, and deception are not violated.

B. Empirical Support for an Evolutionary Explanation

Section A provides an evolutionary explanation for the little-acknowledged but stunningly consistent and widely shared intuitions of justice. On present evidence, one cannot know whether this specific evolutionary explanation is correct. Unlike bones, behavior does not fossilize, and one can only test the accuracy of evolutionary accounts of behavior by triangulating from presently available sources of information. That requires combining theories, offered in section A, with the observations and experiments discussed in this section.

There is a good deal of empirical work that needs to be done, but in the meantime, it is useful to look to three existing areas that shed some light on the hypothesis. First, this section considers animal studies that suggest evolved, rudimentary notions of fairness and blaming. Second, it considers brain science studies that reveal identifiable physiological processes at work when humans make moral judgments. Finally, it examines the field of developmental psychology, which shows a common path in the development of moral reasoning in the human child across demographics and cultures. One may conclude that all three of these provide evidence consistent with the evolutionary hypothesis above. In contrast, there is no known data in direct conflict with it.

1. ANIMAL STUDIES EVIDENCE

If the evolutionary explanation for shared intuitions of justice is correct, one might expect to find in other animals rudimentary forms of humans' core intuitions about what constitutes wrongdoing and the intuition that it should be punished, especially among primates. In fact, a number of socially cooperative species appear in some circumstances to exhibit these characteristics of "punishing" aggressors and cheaters. And a number of researchers now suggest that such behaviors may reflect a rudimentary moral sense or intuition of justice. Individuals that deviate from various group norms and expectations are sometimes avoided or aggressed against by the victims, the victim's relatives, or others. These phenomena are not limited to primates or even to mammals.

Here are a few of many examples. Within the highly social naked-mole rat communities, queens appear to focus attacks on lazy workers.[15] In one social species of wren, "helpers" assist by providing food when the young are being raised. Helpers

---

[15] Hudson K. Reeve, *Queen Activation of Lazy Workers in Colonies of the Eusocial Naked Mole-Rat*, 358 NATURE 147 (1992).

experimentally removed from the group during that period are usually attacked and harassed upon their return, while helpers absent at other times of the year are never attacked.[16] Wolves apparently refuse to play with those who violate the social rule against injurious play-fighting, and the latter both leave the group and die at higher rates than average.[17]

Researchers studying animal punishment patterns have found that behavior akin to theft is one particular target for retribution.[18] For example, elephant seal pups caught trying to nurse from a female who is not their mother are not just shooed away; they are often bitten severely and sometimes killed.[19] Young male deer attempting to sneak copulations with females being guarded by adult males are regularly attacked.

With respect to an animal sense of fair treatment, a leading researcher has concluded that a wide variety of animals are capable of discerning when a situation is not equitable.[20] For example, in a recent and widely reported experiment with capuchin monkeys, different combinations of two adjacent monkeys regularly alternated returning granite tokens for slices of cucumber. Once the experimenter began to provide one monkey in a dyad with a grape (a more highly valued food) in exchange for the same token that continued to yield mere cucumbers for the other monkey, the other monkey often manifested considerable distress. It sometimes jumped up and down, throwing the token or the cucumber at the researcher, refusing to eat the cucumber, and the like.[21] This led the authors of the study to conclude that capuchins are capable of comparing their own reward to the reward others receive, and accepting or rejecting rewards according to their relative, not absolute, value.[22] Similarly, chimpanzees reportedly will often refuse to participate in an exchange once another chimpanzee is receiving a more valued reward for the same amount of effort.[23] Thus, both capuchins and chimpanzees behave in ways suggesting both that they can perceive unfairness and that it often agitates them.

Behavior suggesting an ability to perceive inequities appears to underlie a great deal of social behavior in primates, in whom transgressive acts are most systematically punished. By way of background, many primates regularly exhibit sophisticated cooperation, which ranges from simple reciprocal grooming and food sharing to complex tool-using and coalitional behavior. For example, in olive baboons there is a

---

[16] Raoul A. Mulder & Naomi E. Langmore, *Dominant Males Punish Helpers for Temporary Defection in Superb Fairy-wrens*, 45 ANIM. BEHAV. 830 (1993).

[17] Marc Bekoff, *Wild Justice, Cooperation, and Fair Play*, *in* THE ORIGINS AND NATURE OF SOCIALITY 53 (Robert W. Sussman & Audrey R. Chapman eds., 2004).

[18] Tom H. Clutton-Brock & Geoff A. Parker, *Punishment in Animal Societies*, 373 NATURE 209, 211 (1995).

[19] *Id.* at 212 (citing Joanne Reiter, et al., *Northern Elephant Seal Development: The Transition from Weaning to Nutritional Independence*, 3 BEHAV. ECOL & SOCIOBIO. 337 (1978).

[20] Sarah Brosnan, *Nonhuman Species' Reactions to Inequity and their Implications for Fairness*, 19 JOURNAL OF SOCIAL JUSTICE 153 (2006).

[21] Sarah Brosnan & Frans de Waal, *Monkeys Reject Unequal Pay*, 425 NATURE 297 (2003); Sarah Bosnan & Frans de Waal, *Reply*, 428 NATURE 140 (2004).

[22] *Id.* at 140.

[23] Brosnan, *supra* note 138.

strong correlation between A's prior support for a fellow baboon B, in a conflict, and A's successful recruitment of B to a new conflict in which A is later involved.[24] In both vervet monkeys[25] and macaques,[26] individuals have been observed to support unrelated others, who have in the past supported them, by intervening in conflicts on their behalf.[27] Vervet monkeys tend to preferentially groom individuals who have groomed them in the past.[28] In chimpanzees, when one chimpanzee grooms another earlier in the day, the latter is more likely to share food with him later.[29] And chimpanzees experimentally engaging in tasks requiring collaboration with another chimpanzee quickly determine which among different potential collaborators is most effective and recruit that individual preferentially for subsequent collaborative tasks.[30]

On the other hand, failure to cooperate regularly yields sharp consequences. Negative acts are the flip side of the cooperation coin. Authors of a leading paper on the subject conclude that the intensity of punishments often increases with the increasing harm caused by transgressors.[31] The worse the harm, the more severe the punishment. In rhesus macaques, for example, those who discover food and are caught having failed to alert the group to its discovery often become targets of significant aggression.[32] In chimpanzee societies, those reluctant to share when they have food are more likely to encounter aggressive responses when they later approach those who have food.[33] Chimpanzees will attack former allies who failed to assist them in conflicts with third parties.[34] And many primates, including chimpanzees, tend to intervene most often against those others who have most often intervened against them.[35] These patterns have prompted leading researchers to refer to such negative reciprocities as a "revenge system."[36]

---

[24] Craig Packer, *Reciprocal Altruism in Papio anubis*, 265 NATURE 441 (1977).

[25] Julia A. Horrocks & Wayne Hunte, *Maternal Rank and Offspring Rank in Vervet Monkeys*, 31 ANIM. BEHAV. 772 (1983).

[26] Frans de Waal & Lesleigh M. Luttrell, *The Similarity Principle Underlying Social Bonding Among Female Rhesus Monkeys*, 46 FOLIA PRIMATOLIGICA 215 (1986).

[27] Jessica C. Flack & Frans de Waal, *"Any Animal Whatever": Darwinian Building Blocks of Morality in Monkeys and Apes*, *in* EVOLUTIONARY ORIGINS OF MORALITY (Leonard D. Katz ed., 2000).

[28] Robert M. Seyfarth & Dorothy L. Cheney, *Grooming, Alliances and Reciprocal Altruism in Vervet Monkeys*, 308 NATURE 541 (1984).

[29] Frans B.M. de Waal, *Food Sharing and Reciprocal Obligations among Chimpanzees*, 18 J. HUMAN EVO. 433 (1989).

[30] Alicia P. Melis et al., *Chimpanzees Recruit the Best Collaborators,* 311 SCI. 1297 (2006).

[31] Clutton-Brock & Parker, *supra* note 136, at 211.

[32] Marc D. Hauser, *Costs of Deception: Cheaters Are Punished in Rhesus Monkeys*, 89 PROC. NATL. ACAD. SCI. 12137, 12137 (1992).

[33] Frans B. M. de Waal, *Food Sharing and Reciprocal Obligations among Chimpanzees*, 18 J. HUMAN EVO. 433 (1989).

[34] FRANS DE WAAL, CHIMPANZEE POLITICS 207 (1989).

[35] Joan B. Silk, *The Patterning of Intervention Among Male Bonnet Macaques: Reciprocity, Revenge, and Loyalty*, 33 CURRENT ANTHRO 318 (1992).

[36] *See, e.g.,* Frans de Waal & Lesleigh M. Luttrell, *Mechanisms of Social Reciprocity in Three Primate Species: Symmetrical Relationship Characteristics or Cognition*, 9 ETHOL. & SOCIOBIO. 101 (1998); Fillipo Aureli et al., *Kin-oriented Redirection Among Japanese Macaques: An Expression Of a Revenge System?,* 44 ANIMAL BEHAV. 283 (1992).

Indeed, among chimpanzees (which, along with bonobos, are the closest relatives of humans), retribution is sufficiently common that researchers consider retaliation "an integral part of [a] system of reciprocity."[37] Because sharing and other cooperative behavior exists in a "multi-faceted matrix of relationships, social pressures, delayed rewards, and mutual obligations,"[38] the most successful individuals are those who can distinguish good colleagues from bad, and deal with each accordingly. A leading chimpanzee scientist consequently describes their community as "a 'market' of reward and punishment,"[39] with "balance sheets" on social interactions,[40] and reciprocity rules consisting of "'one good turn deserves another' and 'an eye for an eye, a tooth for a tooth.'"[41] "Not only are beneficial actions rewarded," he concludes, "there seems to be a tendency to teach a lesson to those who act negatively."[42] Reward good deeds and punish bad deeds.

The data available, of which the foregoing is only a sample, do not alone prove that some core aspects of human intuitions of justice are evolved adaptations. Nor, even if they are adaptations, did they necessarily arise from the same roots as related intuitions in other species. However, tolerance of wrongdoing in highly cooperative species is evolutionarily unstable. Punishment of wrongdoing is likely a logically necessary companion of cooperation in ultrasocial species such as ours. And the intersecting vectors of available animal evidence point toward that conclusion. Moreover, the close relationship of humans, chimpanzees, and other primates suggests that it is best not to assume that there are different causes in humans for the same behaviors in other animals.[43] It is not surprising, then, that the leading animal researchers believe that evolution has supplied the "building blocks" of human morality,[44] and that the question is not whether, but rather to what degree, biology has influenced the development of human moral systems.[45] "Evolution" they believe, "has produced the requisites for morality: a tendency to develop social norms and enforce them."[46]

2. BRAIN SCIENCE EVIDENCE

Some people may balk at the notion that intuitions of justice could be the product of evolution even in an indirect way because views of justice are obviously matters of complex judgment making. The design of one's visual system might be the

---

[37] Frans B. M. de Waal, Good Natured: The Origins of Right and Wrong in Humans and Other Animals, 157–58 (1996).

[38] *Food Sharing and Reciprocal Obligations*, *supra* note 147, at 452.

[39] *Id.*

[40] Good Natured, *supra* note 155, at 157–59.

[41] Frans de Waal, Chimpanzee Politics 207 (1989).

[42] Good Natured, *supra* note 155, at 159.

[43] *Id.* at 64.

[44] Flack & de Waal, *Any Animal, supra* note 145.

[45] *Id.* at 3.

[46] Good Natured, *supra* note 155, at 39.

product of evolution, but how could evolution affect a person's judgment concerning what punishment is deserved?

Of course, specialized brain structures and brain processes determine all decision making, no matter how complex. Neuroscience has begun to provide details on what does what. As demonstrated below, it is now known that specific brain regions perform certain kinds of judgment tasks, and moral judgment making, in particular, has been shown to involve specific brain regions and, indeed, those regions interact differently depending upon the exact nature of the moral decision being presented.

Contrary to prior assumptions, it is known today that the brain is anatomically and functionally specialized. Different parts of the brain acting in varying combinations perform different information-processing tasks that, in turn, influence a person's behavior. Scientists have investigated what part of the human brain does what by observing what happens when different brain locations are experimentally stimulated, different regions of the brain are removed or damaged, or a person within a brain scanning device is experimentally engaged in decision making.

A wealth of experimental evidence has shown that artificial stimulation of different areas of the brain affect perception, cognition, and behavior in different ways. With invasive electrical stimulation, for example (most studies of which have, for obvious reasons, involved nonhuman primates), researchers have manipulated the activity of small groups of neurons, ultimately establishing causal links between the activities of those cells and specific aspects of perception or cognition.[47] And with noninvasive stimulation studies on humans (such as transcranial magnetic stimulation), researchers have discovered predictable interference with different cognitive tasks when the activity of a specific portion of the brain is artificially disrupted.[48]

With respect to discoveries arising from cases of brain damage, consider the well-studied case of Phineas Gage, a reliable and personable railroad worker of normal social disposition, who had a metal tamping rod pass cleanly through his skull and brain, after a spark ignited the dynamite he was tamping into its hole. After the rod removed Gage's medial prefrontal cortex, he retained all his mental faculties but became bizarrely antisocial.[49] Similarly and more recently, a variety of studies have identified ways in which relatively localized and discrete brain damage and lesions in particular brain areas can result in severe impingement on the acquisition of social knowledge, social behavior, and moral reasoning.[50] For example,

---

[47] Marlene R. Cohen & William T. Newsome, *What Electrical Microstimulation has Revealed about the Neural Basis of Cognition*, 14 Current Op. In Neurobio. 169 (2004) (providing overview of studies).

[48] Alvaro Pascual-Leone et al., *Transcranial Magnetic Stimulation in Cognitive Neuroscience—Virtual Lesion, Chronometry, and Functional Connectivity*, 10 Current Op. In Neurobio. 232 (2000).

[49] *See* Antonio R. Damasio, Descartes' Error: Emotion, Reason, and the Human Brain (1994); Hanna Damasio et al., *The Return of Phineas Gage: Clues About the Brain from the Skull of a Famous Patient*, 264 Sci. 1102 (1994).

[50] Joshua Greene, *Cognitive Neuroscience and the Structure of the Moral Mind* (forthcoming ?? in 1 Innateness and the Structure of the Mind 6 (Peter Carruthers et al., eds.) [hereinafter *Cognitive Neuroscience*].

damage to the ventromedial prefrontal cortex, particularly of a young child, renders that person essentially morally incompetent.[51] A condition known as "acquired sociopathy" often results from damage to the orbitomedial or polar frontal cortex, the anterior temporal lobe, or the superomedial frontal lobe.[52]

Even more significant are the results of brain imaging studies. Functional magnetic resonance imaging (*f*MRI), which tracks both locations and amplitudes of activity in the brain, has shown that specific parts of the brain—the orbital and medial sectors of the prefrontal cortex, as well as the superior temporal sulcus, among others—are involved in moral reasoning,[53] and also has shown how the subareas work together in predictable ways during the process of making a moral decision.[54]

Not only does this work reveal the underappreciated extent to which processes of evolution and development have yielded highly specialized brain operations, evolutionary premises explicitly underlie the hypotheses of some of the most significant studies of moral decision making. For example, Joshua Green and colleagues started from the premise that elements of basic emotions (such as fear, jealousy, and anger) are evolved shortcuts to behaviors that were adaptive for their bearers, on average, in deep ancestral environments. That is, compared to more cumbersome analysis and deliberation, emotions are generally "reliable, quick, and efficient" ways of dealing with commonly encountered circumstances.[55]

These researchers therefore predicted that the more closely a moral scenario aligns with regular features of ancestral environments, the more likely it is to invoke evolved emotional reactions, rather than dispassionately cognitive and deliberative ones. And the results were consistent with those predictions. Specifically, more physically personal dilemmas, such as whether to *push* one person into harm's way, thereby deflecting that harm from several people, yields greater activity in the brain areas associated with emotions, while a less personal but analogous dilemma, such as whether to *throw a switch* that would deflect an oncoming harm onto one person instead of several, yields greater activity in a different brain area, associated with less passionate analysis and calculation.[56]

Of course, such evidence does not suggest that there is a single, evolved, discretely bounded "morality module" in the brain.[57] The situation is more complex.

---

[51] DESCARTES' ERROR, *supra* note 167 at 79.

[52] Jorge Moll et al., *Morals and the Human Brain: A Working Model*, 14 NEUROREPORT 299, 300 (2003) (collecting citations).

[53] *See, e.g.,* Jorge Moll et al., *The Neural Correlates of Moral Sensitivity: A Functional Magnetic Resonance Imaging Investigation of Basic and Moral Emotions,* 22 J. OF NEUROSCI. 2730 (2002); *An fMRI Investigation*, *infra* note 178; *The Neural Basis*, *infra* note 172 (citing studies).

[54] *See generally* Greene, *Cognitive Neuroscience*, *supra* note 168; Qian Luo et al., *The Neural Basis of Implicit Moral Attitude—An IAT Study Using Event-Related fMRI*, 30 NEUROIMAGE 1449 (2005) [hereinafter, *The Neural Basis*] (providing useful bibliography); Jorge Moll et al., *Morals and the Human Brain: A Working Model*, 14 NEUROREPORT 299 (2003).

[55] Joshua Greene, *The Secret Joke of Kant's Soul*, in THE NEUROSCIENCE OF MORALITY: EMOTION, DISEASE, AND DEVELOPMENT 33 (Walter Sinnott-Armstrong ed. 2007).

[56] Greene, *Cognitive Neuroscience, supra* note 168.

[57] *See id.* at 6.

Some of the regions associated with moral decision making are also associated with other brain activities. But what is clear is that identifiable subsets of the brain's regions, despite anatomical dissociability, are regularly and intimately networked in assessing moral dilemmas. And the interaction of these regions changes predictably as the nature of the moral dilemma changes.[58]

In another study, researchers found that people make faster decisions, and with less activity in the deliberating temporal poles, when moral scenarios involve bodily harm than when they do not.[59] Another study showed significantly greater activity in the right amygdala, left medial orbitofrontal cortex, and medial frontal gyrus when subjects are shown interpersonal violence than when shown vandalism or violence to objects.[60] Compared to scenarios with unintentional harm, scenarios involving intentional harm yield greater activity in areas associated with emotion (such as the orbitofrontal cortex and the temporal pole), with correspondingly less activity in areas associated with deliberative cognition (such as the angular gyrus and superior frontal gyrus).[61] Moral scenarios in which action and inaction result in the same amount of harm yield greater activity in areas associated with deliberative cognition (such as the dorsolateral prefrontal cortex) and correspondingly less activity in areas associated with emotion (including the orbitofrontal cortex and temporal pole), than do analogous nonmoral scenarios. This suggests that "[i] ndividuals will utilize varying combinations of cognitive and emotive facilities to address moral challenges, but, overall, certain types of moral scenarios are likely to be processed in characteristic areas."[62] And removing emotive components of decision making does not render people hyper-ethical, it instead renders them "unable to feel the rightness and wrongness of simple decisions and judgments."[63]

This area of research is relatively new. But the foregoing, in conjunction with other studies, has led a variety of researchers to conclude that moral intuitions are built on evolved and widely shared building blocks.[64] Marc Hauser, for example, concludes that the evidence points to "all humans [being] endowed with a moral faculty."[65] Joshua Greene argues that the evidence suggests that "the form of human moral thought is importantly shaped by the innate structure of the human

---

58 *See* sources cited *supra* note 172.

59 Hauke R. Heekeren et al., *Influence of Bodily Harm on Neural Correlates of Semantic and Moral Decision-Making*, 24 NEUROIMAGE 887 (2005).

60 Jana Schaich Borg et al., *Consequences, Action, and Intention as Factors in Moral Judgments: An fMRI Investigation*, 18 J. COG. NEUROSCI. 803 (2006).

61 *Id.* at 803.

62 *Id.* at 815–16.

63 Jonathan Haidt & Fredrik Bjorklund, *Social Intuitionists Answer Six Questions about Moral Psychology*, *in* THE COGNITIVE SCIENCE OF MORALITY: INTUITION AND DIVERSITY 17 (Walter Sinnott-Armstrong ed., 2007).

64 *See, e.g.*, Greene, *Cognitive Neuroscience*, *supra* note 168, at 11.

65 Marc Hauser et al., *Reviving Rawls' Linguistic Analogy: Operative Principles and the Causal Structure of Moral Actions*, *in* THE EVOLUTION OF MORALITY: INTUITION AND DIVERSITY 1 (Walter Sinnott-Armstrong ed., 2007). While some of Marc Hauser's work has been controversial, the material cited throughout this book has held up as a valuable contribution to how we think about morality.

mind and that some basic, pro-social tendencies probably provide human morality with innate content."[66] And both argue that, while moral decision making is networked, rather than unitary, it is networked in a way distinctly analogous to the brain's innate grammar (which is the basic grammar design one is born with, and which underlies all human languages despite regional cultural variation).[67] That is to say, these authors and others conclude that the basic moral sentiments humans share are products of evolutionary processes.

3. CHILD DEVELOPMENT EVIDENCE

The child development literature provides much collateral support for the evolutionary theory offered in section A. First, there is evidence that children across cultures go through a consistent set of stages of development of their intuitions of justice. In the same way that baby teeth grow from gums and adult teeth replace baby teeth, intuitions about morality and justice seem to come online according to a relatively predictable sequence. Second, the cognitive skills that underpin these intuitions are precocious, with children able to make important conceptual distinctions relevant to morality and justice at young ages. Finally, the content of the intuitions of justice track the core intuitions discussed above, with intuitions about injury, theft, and fairness being among the first principles of justice understood by young children. The following studies are far from a comprehensive collection, but rather simply a few illustrations.

a. Predictable Stages of Development. There is a great deal of data about the development of moral reasoning in children. The classic—if somewhat dated—body of research in the area is Kohlberg's work,[68] recently described as "the most widely researched description of moral development available."[69] Kohlberg's view is that people go through a predictable sequence of phases of moral thinking.[70] As Kagan suggests, this is as one would expect if the capacity for learning moral reasoning were like the capacity for learning language.[71] That is, reliable, consistent, cross-situational development is a hallmark of the existence of a specific set of psychological mechanisms designed for this particular function by natural selection.

For the present purposes, it is not important whether Kohlberg's scheme is the best way of describing the various stages of development. What is significant is the

---

[66] Greene, *Cognitive Neuroscience, supra* note 168, at 19.

[67] *Id.*; Hauser, *supra* note 183, at 1.

[68] *See, e.g.*, Lawrence Kohlberg, *The Psychology of Moral Development*, 2 ESSAYS IN MORAL DEVELOPMENT (1984); Lawrence Kohlberg, *From Is to Ought: How to Commit the Naturalistic Fallacy and Get Away With It*, in COGNITIVE DEVELOPMENT AND EPISTEMOLOGY (Theodore Mischel, ed., 1971). *See also* THE MEASUREMENT OF MORAL JUDGMENT, vols. 1–2 (Anne Colby & Lawrence Kohlberg eds., 1987).

[69] LARRY P. NUCCI, EDUCATION IN THE MORAL DOMAIN 81 (2001).

[70] *See generally* Lawrence Kohlberg, *The Philosophy of Moral Development*, in 1 ESSAYS ON MORAL DEV. (1981) (linking cognitive and moral development).

[71] Jerome Kagan, *Introduction*, in THE EMERGENCE OF MORALITY IN YOUNG CHILDREN x (Jerome Kagan & Sharon Lamb eds., 1987).

evidence, particularly from recent research (see below), of a predictable developmental path for all humans, however that path might be conceptualized and described. To the extent that children everywhere go through similar stages of moral reasoning about justice, at roughly the same ages, the evolutionary explanation for the origins of intuitions of justice receives collateral support. As suggested by Kagan, "temporal concordance implies a biologically based preparedness to judge acts as right or wrong, where preparedness is used with the same sense intended by linguists who claim that two-year-old children are prepared to speak their language."[72]

Imagine the reverse case. If there were no specific developmental system for the acquisition of moral intuitions—if intuitions of justice were simply a matter of general social learning—then the developmental route of the acquisition of intuitions of justice would depend on the environment in which the child developed. This would include acts the child witnessed, ideas communicated through language, pedagogy from various sources, and so forth. Because all of these elements are likely to differ widely across cultures and even across family and peer groups within cultures, such a general learning system would yield very different paths and timing in the acquisition of intuitions of justice for different individuals.

b. Making Subtle and Complex Judgments at an Early Age. Early research in this area seems to have vastly underestimated the sophistication of children. More recent research has shown that children are able to make much more sophisticated judgments and much finer distinctions than those predicted by Kohlberg's proposed sequence. Indeed, although evidence now suggests that moral reasoning develops relatively early, it is likely that research still does not yet fully reveal the precociousness of moral reasoning.[73] Darley and Schultz, in their broad review, suggest that "children are capable of making moral judgments at a much earlier age than previously thought. According to the recent literature, "moral capacity is well developed, although by no means completely developed, in the third year of life."[74] These precocious abilities of young children support the evolutionary argument in section A. To the extent that intuition, knowledge, and conceptual distinctions are made by very young children, especially universally, the probability that each child acquires these by general learning processes becomes less likely, and a more innate developmental sequence becomes more likely.

i. Distinguishing Moral, Conventional, and Prudential Rules. In one early and crucial experiment, Smetana tested very young children's beliefs about justice to determine if they make distinctions between violations of moral rules—acts that are wrong and deserve punishment (for example, one child hitting another)—and violations of conventional rules—acts that deviate from a convention (for example,

---

72 *Id.* at x.

73 *See* Lawrence Kohlberg, *A Current Statement on Some Theoretical Issues*, in LAWRENCE KOHLBERG: CONSENSUS AND CONTROVERSY 485, 491 (Sohan Modgil & Celia Modgil eds., 1986). *See also* John M. Darley & Thomas R. Shultz, *Moral Rules: Their Content and Acquisition*, 41 ANN. REV. PSYCHOL. 525, 537 (1990).

74 Darley & Shultz, *Moral Rules, supra* note 191, at 552.

failing to say grace before a snack).[75] Smetana used pictures indicating the acts in order to demonstrate violations. To elicit responses, a pictorial scale (different size frowns) was used to gauge seriousness. Smetana also used a verbal assessment of how harshly the offender should be punished: not at all, a little, or a lot. One group of subjects consisted of children between two-and-a-half to roughly three-and-a-half years old. The other group consisted of children between roughly three-and-a-half and almost five years old. Moral offenses included both physical harm (hitting) and theft (taking someone else's apple). Both groups indicated that the moral transgressions were more serious and deserved more punishment than the conventional transgressions. The children indicated that the moral offenses, compared with the violations of convention, would be wrong even if "there was no rule about it."[76]

These results suggest that children even at this very young age distinguish moral wrongs from violations of convention and apply a different logic to them. Moreover, children seem to consider moral offenses serious; the majority of subjects in both groups rated the moral offenses a four on the four-point scale. When tested two to three weeks later, subjects' responses were similar to their earlier responses, suggesting a consistency in judgments.

The importance of these results should not be underestimated. The fact that such young children believe immoral acts are wrong even in the absence of rules, indicates a precocious, universalist view of morality.[77] In sharp contrast, children believe that conventions apply to a particular group at a particular time and can be changed. Dunn has concluded that the evidence suggests that "by three and four years old, children respond differently to different kinds of rule breaking or transgression" and that "[a]lthough the data do not show unambiguously a clear distinction between transgressions of social convention and of moral standards, they demonstrate that three-year-olds are sensitive to different kinds of cultural breach."[78]

Somewhat older children similarly distinguish between moral rules and "prudential rules"—rules that are in place to protect people from harm (for example, climbing on the back of a sofa). Tisak and Turiel gave children (in groups of roughly age 7, 9, and 11) stories about acts that violated either moral rules (regarding theft, hitting) or prudential rules (regarding running and falling).[79] Subjects reported that

---

[75] *See* Judith Smetana, *Preschool Children's Conceptions of Moral and Social Rules*, 52 Child Dev. 1333, 1333–34 (1981).

[76] Judith G. Smetana, *Toddlers' Social Interactions Regarding Moral and Conventional Transgressions*, 55 Child Dev. 1767 (1984).

[77] *See* Judith G. Smetana et al., *Preschool Children's Judgments About Hypothetical and Actual Transgressions*, 64 Child Development 202 (1993).

[78] Judith Dunn, *The Beginnings of Moral Understanding: Development in the Second Year*, in The Emergence of Morality in Young Children 91, 93 (Jerome Kagan & Sharon Lamb eds., 1987). Other scholars take an even stronger view, *see, e.g.,* Charles C. Helwig et al., *Morality: Its Structure, Functions and Vagaries*, in The Emergence of Morality in Young Children 155, 170 (Jerome Kagan & Sharon Lamb eds., 1987).

[79] Marie Tisak & Elliot Turiel, *Children's Conceptions of Moral and Prudential Rules*, 55 Child Dev. 1030 (1984).

the violation of the moral rule was more wrong and that it would be more wrong to change moral rules (that is, it's more acceptable for the prudential rule to be modified). The comparison between moral rules and prudential rules indicates judgments that go beyond consideration of consequences of rule-violating actions. Again, the results of Tisak and Turiel suggest the development of nuanced views at early ages.

ii. Judging the Relative Seriousness of Wrongful Conduct. Studies suggest that even young children intuitively appreciate the relative seriousness of different kinds of wrongful conduct, and that the sophistication of the distinctions they make increases with age. One of the first principles of morality acquired by children is the idea that it is wrong to hurt others.[80] By age three, this principle is understood;[81] and by age four, the foreseeability of harm is taken into account.[82]

Findings also indicate that "children consider moral transgression resulting in physical harm to be more wrong than moral transgressions resulting in property violations."[83] This suggests that children have complex intuitions across different domains. Additional evidence comes from studies in which children are asked to give examples of moral transgressions. Children give physical acts of harm as the most common examples. Acts of physical aggression are "prototypical" moral violations to children.

Children are, of course, not always able to articulate the reason why it is wrong to hit, and might even use superficially self-serving language to express themselves. (The inability to justify oneself is common among adults as well.[84]) Research shows that by age seven, ideas about injury are fairly well elaborated, and these ideas include a calculation as to the *intention* of the person doing the injury when making judgments about blame and punishment.[85]

This conclusion—that the first moral concept to appear in children is the concept that physical aggression is wrong—is relevant to the evolutionary argument. It seems likely to be more than mere coincidence that this is also the first step in the offered account of the evolutionary origins of intuitive justice.

In contrast, very young children might *not* seem to have a firm grasp on notions of fairness in exchange or social contracts. It has been argued that it is not until later in the development of a child, perhaps around nine years of age, that adult-like conceptions of fairness emerge.[86] Young children are frequently heard announcing that

---

[80] Nucci, Education in the Moral Domain, *supra* note 187.

[81] Phillip David Zelazo et al., *Intention, Act, and Outcome in Behavioral Prediction and Moral Judgment*, 67 Child Dev. 2478 (1996).

[82] Sharon A. Nelson-LeGall, *Motive-Outcome Matching and Outcome Foreseeability: Effects on Attribution of Intentionality and Moral Judgments*, 21 Dev. Psychol. 332 (1985).

[83] Marie Tisak et al., *Preschool Children's Social Interactions Involving Moral and Prudential Transgressions: An Observational Study*, 7 Early Education & Dev. 137, 139 (1996).

[84] *See* Richard E. Nisbett & Timothy D. Wilson, *Telling More Than We Can Know: Verbal Reports on Mental Processes*, 84 Psychol. Rev. 231 (1977).

[85] *See* Dale T. Miller & C. Douglas McCann, *Children's Reactions to the Perpetrators and Victims of Injustices*, 50 Child Dev. 861, 866 (1979).

[86] Larry P. Nucci, *Because It Is the Right Thing to Do*, 45 Human Dev. 125 (2002).

some outcome is "unfair." However, this often means that the outcome is unfavorable to the speaker, rather than violating a social contract or norm.[87] Nonetheless, Damon has suggested that young children can show "consistent, patterned reasoning about [fair distribution of property, ownership, and the like]."[88]

The integration of multiple factors relevant to estimation of seriousness also begins early, perhaps around age seven. In a study performed by Elkind and Dabek, children were divided into groups based upon age (average age of the groups was roughly five-and-a-half, seven-and-a-half, and nine).[89] The children listened to stories about different crimes. The offenses described in the stories varied in terms of whether an offense was intentional or not and whether the damage was to a person or to property. The children then assessed blame and were asked about punishment. On average, the children viewed damage to a person to be more serious, and they judged intentional damage to be more serious than nonintentional damage (though this varied by age). Children of all ages viewed intentional personal injury to be more serious than unintentional property damage. Interestingly, the youngest group of children (average age roughly five) thought that unintentional personal injury was more serious than intentional property damage, suggesting the importance of personal injury. This pattern was not found in the older children. These results are mirrored in later work that suggests that while very young children focus on either intention *or* harm, older children (four and five) use both harm *and* intention when making decisions about punishment.[90] Such conclusions strongly imply that children have sophisticated views on desert, and possess the ability to weigh multiple factors by age seven.[91]

iii. Judging Blameworthiness with Factors Beyond Offense Seriousness. Children's intuitions of justice are sophisticated enough to include more than just an assessment of the seriousness of the wrongful conduct. They will, for example, take account of a person's culpable state of mind—whether the violation was intentional or accidental—as noted above. Further, children as young as seven years old take into account various exculpating or mitigating circumstances.[92]

---

[87] NUCCI, EDUCATION IN THE MORAL DOMAIN, *supra* note 187.

[88] William Damon, *Early Conceptions of Positive Justice as Related to the Development of Logical Operations*, 46 CHILD DEV. 301, 302 (1975).

[89] David Elkind & Ruth F. Dabek, *Personal Injury and Property Damage in the Moral Judgments of Children*, 48 CHILD DEV. 518 (1977).

[90] Zelazo et al., *supra* note 199, at 2478–92.

[91] *See also* Charles C. Helwig & Urszula Jasiobedzka, *The Relation Between Law and Morality: Children's Reasoning About Socially Beneficial and Unjust Laws*, 72 CHILD DEV. 1382 (2001) (concluding that children apply moral concepts of harm, rights, and justice to evaluate laws" and these findings imply that children develop textured views of legal issues by around age six).

[92] *See* Adrian F. Furnham & Steven H. Jones, *Children's Views Regarding Possessions and Their Theft*, 16 J. MORAL EDUCATION 16, 18–30 (1987). *See also* Darley & Shultz, *Moral Rules, supra* note 191, at 535 (suggesting that their results "indicated a fairly sophisticated use of a variety of the moral concepts by children from 5 years of age.... They also used information on intention and negligence to assign moral responsibility and information on restitution to assign punishment.").

The sense of justice held by young children also incorporates a feature present in adult intuitions of justice: the effect of a mistaken belief of an offender. When they make judgments regarding blame, children aged five and seven (but not three[93]) take into account the fact that others might have incorrect beliefs.[94] Their judgments are quite nuanced: if a person's beliefs that differ from the child's relate to matters of fact—that is, beliefs concerning what is true (as opposed to what is morally right)—a mitigation often is permitted. However, if the belief that differs from the child's concerns what is right and wrong (for example, a teacher who thinks it is acceptable to discriminate against one depending on gender), the person's mistake does not exculpate.[95] This implies that children have a sophisticated understanding of others' beliefs and the role they play in the commission of moral offenses. Further research has shown similar results in older children.[96]

Summing up this research, Smetana et al. suggest that "by 4 years of age, middle-class, primarily European American children, as well as African American preschoolers from lower socioeconomic backgrounds, reliably evaluate moral transgressions pertaining to physical or psychological harm and fairness as very serious, deserving of punishment, generalizably wrong, and wrong regardless of whether a rule or a teacher prohibits the act."[97] In short, even young children seem to have textured and specific views regarding deserved punishment, and these views are not derived simply from the dictates of authority.

c. Cross-Cultural Developmental Studies. Substantial research demonstrates that the developmental sequence for moral reasoning is not unique to the Western world. In a recent review of the evidence, Yau and Smetana conclude that despite cultural differences, "Children as young as 3½ to 4 years of age have been found to treat moral transgressions as very serious, generalizably wrong, and wrong independent of rules and authority sanctions. In contrast, they treat conventional transgressions as less serious, contextually relative, and contingent on rules and authorities."[98]

This last point, that children believe moral rules to be universally applicable, bears expansion. As discussed above, children distinguish between fundamental issues of justice—such as the belief that wrongdoing should be punished, property should not be forcibly taken, and so on—and issues of convention or collateral societal

---

[93] *See generally* Simon Baron-Cohen, MINDBLINDNESS: AN ESSAY ON AUTISM AND THEORY OF MIND (1995); Alan M. Leslie, *Pretense and Representation: The Origins of Theory of Mind*, 94 PSYCHOL. REV. 412 (1987); Alan M. Leslie, *Pretending and Believing: Issues in the Theory of ToMM*, 50 COGNITION 211 (1994).

[94] *See* Cecilia Wainryb & Sherrie Ford, *Young Children's Evaluations of Acts Based on Beliefs Different from Their Own*, 44 MERRILL-PALMER Q. 484 (1998).

[95] *Id.*

[96] *See, e.g.*, Larry P. Nucci & Elsa K. Weber, *Social Interactions in the Home and the Development of Young Children's Concepts of the Personal*, 66 CHILD DEV. 1438, 1445 (1995).

[97] Judith G. Smetana et al., *Children's Moral and Affective Judgments Regarding Provocation and Retaliation*, 49 MERRILL-PALMER Q. 209, 210 (2003).

[98] Jenny Yau & Judith G. Smetana, *Conceptions of Moral, Social-Conventional, and Personal Events Among Chinese Preschoolers in Hong Kong*, 74 CHILD DEV. 647, 647 (2003).

issues—such as the objects over which individuals can be said to have a property right and the conventions that a society established for which clothing can be worn by which type of people. Children acknowledge that the latter—conventions—could be other than as they are, and that if another group of people had a different convention, it would not be "wrong."[99]

The capacity of children to make this distinction is relevant to the frequently cited argument that cultures differ in their morality, found in Schweder et al.'s cross-cultural investigation of the relative rankings of wrongful acts as judged by Hindu Brahman children.[100] Of the 39 acts listed, the children judged the most serious wrong on the list to be this: "[t]he day after his father's death, the eldest son had a haircut and ate chicken."[101] They judged as one of the least serious transgressions—ranked 35th of the 39—the case of a husband who beats a wife because she repeatedly goes alone to the movies.

These results might seem to conflict with the notion of shared intuitions of justice; Western children would make no such ranking. However, the rankings must be understood in the context of the underlying beliefs held by the raters. Because the father's soul is put in jeopardy by the son's act, the son's act is judged as a most serious harm. Similarly, the raters' understanding that the wife's act is a serious breach of a clear contractual and social obligation helps explain why the husband's beating of her is not ranked as being more wrongful. In short, while underlying intuitions regarding principles of justice may be similar, different social conventions create different perceptions about the wrongfulness of specific conduct. As Wainryb put it, "what appears to be moral variation may be due not to diversity in ethical concepts but rather to differences in informational assumptions."[102] This is an important point in judging the locus of genuine variability in beliefs surrounding intuitions of justice.

4. SUMMARY OF EVIDENCE.

The hypothesis that shared intuitions of justice derive in large measure from the relentless effects of evolutionary processes on human brains and consequent sentiments and behavioral predispositions, connects at a deep level with modern developments in biology and psychology. The hypothesis also appears to explain why these intuitions appear to be so stunningly consistent across demographics and cultures yet so subtle in their complexities. This chapter has not attempted a definitive

---

[99] *Cf.* Leigh Shaw & Cecilia Wainryb, *The Outsider's Perspective: Young Adults' Judgments of Social Practices of Other Cultures*, 17 Brit. J. Dev. Psychol. 451 (1999) (reaching similar conclusions with a Chinese sample).

[100] Richard A. Schweder et al., *Culture and Moral Development, in* The Emergence of Morality in Young Children 1–83 (Jerome Kagan & Sharon Lamb eds., 1987).

[101] *Id.* at 40.

[102] Cecelia Wainryb, *Understanding Differences in Moral Judgments: The Role of Informational Assumptions*, 62 Child Dev. 840, 849 (1991).

proof of the evolutionary hypothesis. However, it also has explored in overview three different areas in which the data are consistent with the hypothesis.

The animals studies suggest that humans are not alone in punishing violations of norms of cooperation, reciprocity, and fairness. That so many social species exhibit these behaviors, and in such very specific ways, suggests that there is an evolutionary and adaptive root to these behavioral predispositions. And this in turn suggests that similar human behavior may stem from the same root. The data are consistent with the idea that tolerance of wrongdoing is an evolutionarily unstable and unsuccessful trait. Some form of punishment appears to exist as a prerequisite for certain kinds of cooperation such as social exchange. This requires an ability to perceive wrongful behavior, to remember transgressors, and to treat them differently than non-transgressors. And this is not only seen in other social animals, but also specifically in contexts of inflictions of physical harm, the taking of resources, and the violations of norms of reciprocity.

From the rapidly expanding field of brain science, it may observed how evolutionary processes and development have yielded very anatomically and functionally specialized human brains—again that tend to function very similarly in individuals across the species. Damage to specific regions can result in dramatic social and moral behavioral aberrations (suggesting that those areas of the brain are sufficiently specialized to be necessary for social and moral activity). Imaging studies reveal widely shared patterns in neural activity, consistent with evolutionary hypotheses, when subjects are confronted with various moral scenarios. More personal and evolutionarily salient scenarios invoke evolved neural shortcuts to a greater extent than alternative scenarios. And far from responding with generic neural activity, human brains are intriguingly similar and differentially focused when considering such things as bodily injury, violations of cooperation norms, and the like. This all suggests that human brains typically process certain kinds of transgressions in characteristic ways, which in turn raises the possibility that they have evolved that specific capacity to do so.

In the child development literature, the experimental evidence demonstrates an understanding at a very early age that some acts are wrong and deserve punishment. Indeed, the intuition appears to exist at the point at which children are first able to communicate these types of ideas. The notion of physical injury as a wrong seems to be one of the first elements to emerge in children, followed soon after by notions of fairness and reciprocity. These intuitions become increasingly textured as children grow older and change from simplistic notions of strict equality to more sophisticated notions such as equity, which take into account a person's capacities, contributions, and needs. Most strikingly, there is growing evidence that the development of these rather sophisticated intuitions follow similar patterns cross-culturally, though there remains debate about the extent of cross-cultural developmental similarities.[103]

---

[103] *See* Richard A. Schweder et al., *Culture and Moral Development,* in The Emergence of Morality in Young Children 1–83 (Jerome Kagan & Sharon Lamb eds., 1987).

While no single study or field of research conclusively proves the evolutionary hypothesis for the origins of shared intuitions of justice, the triangulation of the theoretical foundations from biology and psychology generally, alongside behavioral data in humans and other species, recent studies of human brain operations, and broad research into characteristically human development of moral psychology, present a strong case.

C. Alternative Explanations: General Social Learning and Efficient Norms

Evolutionary explanations inevitably evoke the riposte that perhaps the phenomenon in question is simply due to "learning" or "culture." Could the consensus documented in chapter 3 be the result of social learning rather than evolution? Perhaps the norms adopted simply reflect human propensity to copy others' norms, hence the observed consensus without the need for an evolutionary explanation. Or perhaps, groups adopt the same norms because the norms are efficient for all groups.

In one sense, the social learning claim—that shared intuitions of justice are the product of social learning from the surrounding culture—is not really in conflict with the evolutionary theory in section A, for it is argued there that intuitions of justice are indeed "learned" in a sense. Babies do not come into the world with intuitions of justice intact; rather, they acquire them over time in a predictable and largely sequential way through interaction with their environment. In this sense, the evolutionary explanation envisions some involvement of the surrounding culture, just as the special human mechanism for acquiring language involves the surrounding culture.

However, non-evolutionary explanations go a step further. Their claim is that intuitions of justice result *entirely* from general social learning with no reliance upon an evolutionarily developed mechanism for acquiring intuitions of justice. In other words, the non-evolutionary explanations claim that people acquire views of justice in the same way that they learn most other knowledge or come to most other opinions—that views of justice are learned, reasoned out, or chosen through rational decision making.

1. SPONTANEOUS SOCIAL LEARNING

One non-evolutionary explanation, which might be called "spontaneous social learning," could go something like this: the views of justice upon which there is so much agreement are those views that are most efficient for a group to hold, perhaps because they permit productive social cooperation, much like the advantages discussed in the evolutionary account given in section A. This explanation, as you may notice, relies on no special mechanism for the acquisition of intuitions of justice. But this explanation for the shared views of justice faces several difficulties.

a. Preferring Group Interests Over Individual Interests. First, for this explanation to work, it depends upon the individual choosing to adopt views of justice that are efficient *for the group*. But there is little reason to believe that people are predisposed toward preferring norms that are efficient for the group, rather than norms that are efficient for their own self-interest. To make this explanation plausible, one would have to show that people would prefer what is good for the group over what is good for themselves, a preference that the available data do not support.[104] Instead, evidence from both the laboratory and the real world support the view that when group interests are pitted against self-interest, what has been referred to as "social dilemmas," it more likely that self-interest will prevail.[105] Acts of littering, pollution, overfishing, and limitless other examples are all cases in which people choose to accommodate their own interests rather than to do what is good for the group.[106]

In the lab, the question of self-interest versus group interest has been addressed by using "public goods" games or "commons dilemma" games. In these games, people are put into groups and given an allotment of money. Subjects can keep some or all of the money, or put some or all of it in a group pot. Money in the group pot is multiplied by the experimenter at some rate and subsequently divided among all the members of the group. Because money in the pot is multiplied and subsequently split among the group members, everyone in the group is made best off if everyone contributes all their money to the group pot, in effect making the "pie" everyone shares larger. However, each person is individually better off by keeping all their own allotment of money for themselves. With a few exceptions, when people play these games in the same group over time, people keep greater and greater amounts of their endowment, reaching nearly purely selfish behavior over time.[107] In short, when individual selfishness is pitted against group interest in the lab, selfishness eventually wins.

b. Complexity of Determining Efficient Norms as Beyond Individual Capacity. Even if people preferred a norm that is efficient for the group as a whole, though not necessarily good for them personally, another difficulty for the spontaneous social learning explanation arises from the fact that determining what is an efficient norm is an exceedingly complex matter, probably well beyond the capacity of an individual. Studies of human cognitive skills confirm their limitations. Substantial experimental evidence suggests that when people are presented with tasks that require the use of a general ability to reason using the rules of formal logic, they typically do not perform well.[108] Even in experiments in which the financial

---

[104] Richard Dawkins, THE SELFISH GENE (1976).

[105] Robyn Dawes, *Social Dilemmas,* 31 ANN'L REV. OF PSYCH. 169 (1980).

[106] Samuel S. Komorita & Craig D. Parks, SOCIAL DILEMMAS (1996).

[107] John Ledyard, *Public Goods: A Survey of Experimental Research*, in HANDBOOK OF EXPERIMENTAL ECONOMICS 111–94 (J. Kagel & A. Roth eds., 1995).

[108] Leda Cosmides & John Tooby, *Cognitive Adaptations for Social Exchange*, *in* THE ADAPTED MIND: EVOLUTIONARY PSYCHOLOGY AND THE GENERATION OF CULTURE 183 (Jerome H. Barkow et al., eds., 1992).

stakes are very high, in which one might assume that people would have an incentive to reason as logically and carefully as possible, behavior deviates substantially from wealth-maximizing rationality. As Nobel Laureate Herb Simon put it, "[A]ctual human rationality-striving can at best be an extremely crude and simplified approximation to the kind of global rationality that is implied... by game theoretical models."[109]

These limitations are vividly illustrated in Jared Diamond's recent account of the failure of civilizations.[110] In the cases presented, the human inability to foresee the consequences of the way that societies organize themselves and to regulate the use of resources, played crucial roles in their eventual downfall. Among the Mayans and the Rapanui of Easter Island, for example, the mismanagement of resources, due to the inability to foresee how cultural practices would affect long-term growth and stability, played central roles in the collapse of those civilizations. This differs little from modern times, in which economists and others reach little consensus on policies that will improve economic growth, because of the complexity of the system in question and the limitation of human cognitive abilities to understand and predict complex social systems. Diamond's analysis in many ways continues analyses by economists such as Smith and as Hayek,[111] that neither the aggregate decisions of a democratic society nor the guiding hand of a dictator (for example, among the Mayans) is sufficient.[112]

In short, the spontaneous social learning explanation for the agreement on views of justice is inconsistent with what is known about the limits of human calculation, including the sharp limits on the human cognitive capacity for deduction, the common human tendency to rely on simplifying heuristics, and other limitations on cognition. In contrast, the evolutionary explanation for intuitions of justice offered in section A involves a process that "tests" alternative intuitional systems (or any other features of an organism) through the sieve of natural selection. The feedback loop on genes allows only a narrow range of developmental programs to be selected. The spontaneous social learning explanation has no such power.

2. ACCUMULATED SOCIAL LEARNING

One might try to save a social learning explanation from this last flaw—that it is beyond the cognitive ability of a single individual, or a single group—by altering the explanation in one respect: one might argue that such efficient norms are not learned spontaneously by each person or each group but rather are the product of accumulated social learning across several generations. That is, groups may move

---

[109] Herbert Simon, *A Behavioral Model of Rational Choice,* 69 Q. J. Econ. 99, 101 (1955).

[110] Jared Diamond, Collapse: How Societies Choose to Fail or Succeed (2005).

[111] Adam Smith, An Inquiry into the Nature and Causes of the Wealth of Nations (1776); F. A. Hayek, The Fatal Conceit: The Errors of Socialism (1989).

[112] Collapse, *supra* note 228, at 177.

toward efficient norms over many generations and may perpetuate those norms because they are efficient and lead to success.

In a sense, this argument borrows the refinement mechanism of evolutionary theory and makes it available to the general social learning explanation. In other words, the claim is that groups with efficient norms grow, do better, and spread their norms; and thus over time there comes to be a great deal of agreement because of the diffusion of the efficient norms.[113] The explanation is "evolutionary" in a sense in that it involves change over time, with less successful norms losing out to more successful ones. However, it differs from the evolutionary explanation in section A, because here the selection occurs strictly through the operation of social learning, rather than through gene selection. But this revised social learning explanation, which might be called "accumulated social learning," still faces a number of serious difficulties.

a. Absence of Variation in Intuitions of Justice Among Groups Despite Large Differences in Situation and Culture. There exist vast differences in ecology, history, demographics, social structure, and many other variables from one group and culture to another. These differences are so striking and of such a nature that it seems odd that all groups would find the same norms to be the most efficient and, further, that each group is equally effective in teaching these norms to each successive generation. It would seem surprising that dramatic differences in social structure and social resources would have no effect on how, when, and what a generation would learn about justice from each previous generation. One would expect some groups to be better than others at approximating the efficient norm and some groups to be better than others at teaching that approximation to the succeeding generation.

Yet, as documented in chapter 2, there is a consensus on the core intuitions of justice even across demographics and cultures. How could one explain this consensus if those views simply reflect the efficient norm for each group? This seems a difficult task. It would require finding a set of conditions that are universal to all human groups, no matter their circumstances and culture, and showing that it is these universal conditions alone that set the efficient norms for the group's views of justice. If any other factor, other than these universal conditions, had influence in shaping the core views of justice, then one would find differences between groups according to the differences of these nonuniversal factors. Perhaps others will take up this challenge—finding these universal conditions and showing how these alone determine core views of justice—but until such can be found, or even imagined, it would seem to make the spontaneous social learning explanation implausible. In contrast, the evolutionary explanation suffers no such problem. Evolutionary

---

[113] *See, e.g.*, Emile Durkheim, DIVISION OF LABOR IN SOCIETY (1893); ALFRED REGINALD RADCLIFFE-BROWN, STRUCTURE AND FUNCTION IN PRIMITIVE SOCIETY (1952).In the more modern anthropological literature, this is referred to as "cultural group selection." *See, e.g.*, Joseph Soltis et al., *Can Group-functional Behaviors Evolve by Cultural Group Selection? An Empirical Test*, 63 CURRENT ANTHRO. 473, 474 (1995). For a recent, comprehensive treatment of this and related issues, see Peter J. Richerson & Robert Boyd, NOT BY GENES ALONE: HOW CULTURE TRANSFORMED HUMAN EVOLUTION (2004).

explanations, dependent as they are upon evolutionarily evolved mechanisms that all humans share, fit naturally with human universals.

b. Inconsistency with Developmental Data. Even more problematic for the accumulated social learning explanation is the fact that it simply does not fit the developmental data summarized above in section B.3. For example, children's views of morality emerge early and are nuanced from a young age. Recall that even very young children—around three years of age—are precocious universal moralists, believing that certain offenses are wrong even if there were no rule about the act, and they distinguish moral rules from rules of convention. In particular, children believe that unprovoked physical harm is wrong and, further, very young children distinguish among offenses (harm versus theft) and take intent and extenuating circumstances into account in evaluating blameworthiness for violations, suggesting nuanced views of justice.

If views of justice were the result of social learning, one would expect that young children would have to be taught distinctions such as those between precautionary rules and moral rules. But it seems implausible that these abstractions could be taught to such young children, who seem to come to these important distinctions precociously. The development of these intuitions seem to parallel more closely, say, the growth of teeth—they simply develop according to a pre-programmed timetable for all children, as opposed to, say, chess, which must be taught systematically and over a period of time with explicit instruction. Indeed, chess has a small number of rules, as compared to the intricacies of moral judgment, and yet the learning of morality, somewhat paradoxically, seems to come much more easily and naturally to children than chess.

While it is not impossible that the ideas that children have about wrongs and punishment are transmitted to them by parents and peers while they are young, the fact that these intuitions come online across children in a reliably developing sequence at roughly the same time throughout the world, without differences reflecting the different practical, social, and cultural conditions, makes these intuitions look as though they are part of a specific, developed learning mechanism, rather than the result of general social learning that is necessarily dependent upon the child's environment, which will differ substantially from place to place.

c. Intuitional Knowledge Having Distinct Characteristics from Learned Knowledge. Even if the social learning explanation was not inconsistent with the developmental data, it nonetheless would appear problematic because it is inconsistent with current knowledge about the nature of views of justice: their intuitional nature. If views of justice were learned from others, one would expect such views to have the character of other learned knowledge. That is, a social learning explanation assumes that individual judgments about justice are like many other judgments that are made in each person's daily lives, such as the following: How fast should I drive on this stretch of road, or how long should I cook this sandwich in the microwave, or how carefully should I take notes of this lecture? These judgments are the product of reasoning, promoted by life experience and education.

However, social science evidence suggests that judgments about justice, especially for violations that might be called the core of criminal wrongdoing, are more the product of intuition than reasoning. As discussed in chapter 1, their intuitional nature means, among other things, that they are judgments quickly arrived at, even by people with little education or life experience, that they frequently are held with strong feelings of certainty, and that the reasons they hold such judgments are generally not consciously accessible.

Recall Jon Haidt's work on "moral dumbfounding," for example, in which people report strong intuitions about things that are morally wrong, such as consensual, nonreproductive incest, but are unable to provide a principled explanation for their judgments;[114] and Hauser, Young, and Cushman look at the "trolley problem,"[115] in which some number of people can be saved from being killed by a runaway trolley if some action is taken (or not taken), resulting in the death of a smaller number of people, often a single individual. People are asked what choice should be made in these difficult situations, and also asked to explain their reasoning. While subjects commonly have strong and clear views on the proper result, they also commonly are unable to offer an explanation for their conclusions.

In sum, there is at least some degree of consensus that many moral judgments are made by a deeply intuitive system. If such judgments were the product of a set of principles of morality learned from others, it would seem to be a straightforward matter to derive the "wrongness" of acts from these principles, just as mathematical inferences can be made from a set of axioms and subsequently explained with reference to them. "Moral dumbfounding" and related effects in the psychological literature suggest that this is not how these judgments are made.

d. Difficulties in Teaching Inarticulate Lessons. Further undermining the social learning explanation for shared views of justice is the fact that, to the extent that people are unable to articulate the principles that underlie their intuitions of justice, it would seem difficult to transmit those principles verbally to others. In other words, the intuitional nature of judgments about justice undermines the argument that they are socially learned from others through language. Of course, learning through nonlinguistic means is possible, but the social transmission of information is vastly more difficult without natural language. The psychological literature is replete with examples of this general principle,[116] but the general idea is well illustrated by two relevant phenomena.

First, consider that social transmission is rare in nonhumans, restricted to narrow domains such as song learning in birds. Without language, nonhuman animals are confined to very modest social learning, so much so that each case of social learning

---

[114] *See* Jonathan Haidt, *The Emotional Dog and Its Rational Tail: A Social Intuitionist Approach to Moral Judgment*, 108 Psychol. Rev. 814 (2001).

[115] Philippa Foot, *The Problem of Abortion and the Doctrine of Double Effect*, 5 Oxford Review 5 (1967).

[116] For a recent example, *see* Bjørn Sætrevik et al., *The Utility of Implicit Learning in the Teaching of Rules*, 16 Learning & Instruction 363 (2006).

is considered an extraordinary case.[117] Second, consider some vivid examples from everyday life. The game of "charades" (or, more recently, "Pictionary") is fun precisely because, deprived of natural language, conveying simple ideas, even individual words, is difficult. Similar examples can be seen in the difficulty in understanding what prelinguistic infants are trying to communicate, and familiar to anyone who has tried to ask even rudimentary questions of someone with whom one does not share a common language. Social learning without language is not impossible, but is certainly difficult. If individual words and simple questions already pose a challenge, consider how much more difficult abstract complex notions of deontic principles would be to convey nonlinguistically. If people themselves do not have explicit access to these principles, it is unlikely that they are being socially transmitted.

In addition to these failings of the accumulated social learning explanation, recall that it also suffers the objection raised with regard to the original "spontaneous social learning" explanation: that such an explanation depends upon individuals putting group interests above their own individual interests. As noted above, the available evidence suggests that such altruism has serious limits. Until it can be shown that there are special circumstances and reasons that prompt such altruistic behavior, the accumulated social learning explanation is on this ground as implausible as the spontaneous social learning explanation.

D. Conclusion

On present evidence, the explanation for the "puzzle" of the existence of shared intuitions of justice is more likely a specific evolved human mechanism for acquiring these core intuitions than general social learning derived from some set of conditions and life experiences universal to all humans and all human groups. The latter cannot be ruled out on present evidence but seems implausible, while the former is consistent with the available data.

Ultimately, whatever conclusion one comes to on this question, it does not alter the existence of important implications that follow. Whatever is the source of shared intuitions of justice, it is a source that is not easily altered. Even if the source is general social learning, it must be social learning arising *only* from an aspect of human life experience that is so fundamental as to be essentially universal to all persons without regard to circumstances or culture. In other words, it is not a source that is open to easy change or manipulation. If it were not so fixed, if it were easily manipulatable, then the natural variations in circumstance and culture would have altered it and produced variations in intuitions of justice, and there would not be the agreement that does exist.

---

[117] *See* Michael Tomasello, *Culture and Cognitive Development*, 9 Current Directions in Cog. Sci. 37, 37 (2000).

4}

Disagreements about Justice

While there is wide agreement on a core of wrongdoing, as chapter 2 has shown, disagreements on intuitions of justice do exist. However, many apparent disagreements are not true disagreements. Such false positives occur for a variety of reasons. Testing methods may exaggerate levels of disagreement. The use of ambiguous crime scenarios will produce disagreement, but only disagreement about the case facts and not about its relative blameworthiness. Also, the fact that some people prefer more harsh punishment generally, while others prefer more lenient punishment generally, tends to obscure the agreement between the two groups on the relative blameworthiness of different offenders. These and related issues are discussed in section A.

Not all appearances of disagreement are false positives, however. Section B reports two studies that demonstrate true disagreements. The studies suggest that the high level of agreement seen for a "core" of wrongdoing breaks down as the case facts moves out from the "core" to include more culturally dependent factors. And while much of lay judgments about justice are intuitive, not all are. Especially as a case moves out from the core, reasoned judgments, engaging life experiences, and personal values come into play; and these, of course, can differ among people.

This chapter is drawn primarily from portions of my article with Robert Kurzban, *Concordance and Conflict in Intuitions of Justice*.[1]

A. Apparent Disagreements among Intuitions of Justice

People obviously do disagree about many things relating to crime and punishment, as the endless public debates make clear. What can be said about the issues on which there is agreement and the issues on which there is not?

Some apparent sources of disagreement are simply misleading. For example, poor testing methods will predictably underestimate the extent of agreement. When a test scenario is written ambiguously so that different test participants perceive it

[1] Paul H. Robinson & Robert Kurzban, *Concordance and Conflict in Intuitions of Justice*, 91 Minn. L. Rev. 1829, 1846–80 (2007).

differently, the existence of shared intuitions of justice will itself predict different judgments among the participants. So too, when a case with social or political implications is reported in the headlines, it is common that its relevant facts will be perceived differently by different people. What one makes of the police testimony in the O. J. Simpson case or the Rodney King case may depend upon one's experiences and one's peers' experiences with police officers in daily life. If people draw different conclusions from the testimony, they may have different views of the relevant facts of the case, which would predict different views on the liability and punishment deserved.

A related effect that exaggerates the extent of disagreement is the abstraction and politicization process. When people are asked whether they support or oppose the death penalty, for example, their answers may be different from when the question is put in terms of a specific set of facts with a specific offender and victim.[2] The larger point is that when a criminal punishment issue or case takes on a broader public profile, it often carries baggage that can distort what a person otherwise would judge as deserved punishment. This phenomenon has analogs in other areas. When persons in need are specific identified individuals, for which specific and concrete information is provided, people are more likely to help them than when such information is not provided.[3] Stereotypes are more commonly applied to groups (for example, black males) than to specific individuals in the category.[4] In both of these instances, as with the death penalty, the difference between the abstract and the specific can change the responses.

Another source of apparent disagreement arises from the fact that some people may generally prefer harsher punishments while others prefer more lenient ones. That is, some people may tend to set the most severe end of the punishment continuum noticeably higher than others, which would predict different sentences for individual cases, even if the people agreed on the relative blameworthiness of different offenders.

There is evidence that attitudes toward the general severity of punishment tend to vary with some demographics, such as race and socioeconomic status. For example, whites have been found to support the death penalty more than blacks.[5] Similarly, whites are more supportive of "three strikes" laws that produce long prison terms.[6] Religious variables have also been found to have effects on issues such as the

---

[2] *See* Craig Haney, DEATH BY DESIGN: CAPITAL PUNISHMENT AS A SOCIAL-PSYCHOLOGICAL SYSTEM 76 (2005).

[3] Tehila Kogut & Ilana Ritov, *The "Identified Victim" Effect: An Identified Group, or Just a Single Individual?*, 18 J. BEHAV. DECISION MAKING 157, 163 (2005).

[4] *See* Michael J. Gill, *Biased Against "Them" More Than "Him": Stereotype use in Group-Directed and Individual-Directed Judgments*, 21 SOC. COGNITION 321, 321 (2003).

[5] Robert L Young, Race, *Conceptions of Crime and Justice, and Support for the Death Penalty*, 54 SOC. PSYCHOL. Q. 67, 67 (1991).

[6] L. Peña Yesilernis, Christopher Federico, & Jim Sidanius, "Race and Support for the Criminal Justice System: A Matter of Asymmetry," *available at* http://www.russellsage.org/sites/all/files/u4/Pena,%20Federico,%20%26%20Sidanius_Race%20%26%20Support%20for%20the%20Criminal%20Justice%20System.pdf, 29 Table 1 (2002) (unpublished manuscript).

death penalty, though their effects are not straightforward.[7] Generally, women have been found to be less punitive than men.[8] Data from Canada and elsewhere indicate that those of lower education and incomes tend to be more punitive in the sense that they report that sentences are "not severe enough,"[9] though the role of education on policies relating to punitiveness is somewhat complex.[10]

Differences are also seen cross-culturally. Average prison sentences vary widely from nation to nation. American offenders were required to serve an average of 29 months after conviction in 1999.[11] In contrast, the average offender in the Netherlands was released after 5 months,[12] while Colombian offenders were not released until a mean of 140 months.[13] Moreover, even within a culture, community attitudes toward punishment severity can vary over time.[14] One effect of these different views on punishment severity generally is to obscure existing agreement on the relative blameworthiness of specific cases.

B. True Disagreements among Intuitions of Justice: Studies 3 and 4

Notwithstanding the many phenomena and influences that obscure the existing agreement on the relative blameworthiness of core wrongdoing, it nonetheless is true that there are relative blameworthiness issues on which people do disagree. Two additional studies we conducted, using the same participant pools as Studies 1 and 2 described in chapter 2, illustrate the potential for disagreement and may hint at its source.

1. METHOD: STUDIES 3 AND 4

After completing the paper-based rank ordering of the 24 scenarios of Study 1, participants being tested in person were given an additional 12 scenarios. The methodology was the same as used in Study 1: each scenario was printed on a separate card, which the participants were asked to rank order on a large table according to

---

[7] Robert L. Young, *Religious Orientation, Race and Support for the Death Penalty*, 31 J. Sci. Study of Religion, 76, 82 (1992).

[8] Felicia Pratto, Lisa M Stallworth, & Jim Sidanius, *The Gender Gap: Differences in Political Attitudes and Social Dominance Orientation*, 36 British J. Soc. Psychol. 49, 49 (1997).

[9] Carla Cesaroni & Anthony N. Doob, *The Decline in Support for Penal Welfarism: Evidence of Support Among the Elite for Punitive Segregation*, 43 British J. Crim. 434, 438 (2003).

[10] Michael J Leiber, Kimberly Schwarze, Kristin Y Mack, & Margaret Farnworth, *The Effects of Occupation and Education on Punitive Orientations Among Juvenile Justice Personnel*, 30 J. Crim. Justice 303, 303 (2002).

[11] United Nations Survey of Crime Trends and Operations of Criminal Justice Systems, at 480.

[12] *Id.* at 308.

[13] *Id.* at 66.

[14] *See*, e.g., Michael Tonry, Sentencing Matters 137 (1996) (noting that the average prison sentence for violent offenses in the United States tripled between 1975 and 1989).

the amount of punishment deserved, if any. In addition, they were asked to show the punishment deserved in these 12 scenarios, compared to that of the first set of 24 scenarios, by laying the 12 new cards out on the table next to the original 24 cards, using the placement of the card to indicate the proper punishment in relation to the previously ranked scenarios. (Participants could place the 12 new scenarios either next to or between the previously ranked 24 scenarios.)

The 12 scenarios of this second group included offenses of drunk driving, prostitution, marijuana purchase, purchase of alcohol for use by teenagers, bestiality, late-term abortion, cocaine purchase, date rape, third felony offense (jewelry grab), large-scale cocaine selling, and very large-scale cocaine importation and distribution. While a majority of these offenses are committed with much lower frequency than the offenses in Study 1, they are each in their own turn an offense on which there has been public debate.

In the final study, Study 4, the same Internet participants who had ranked the first 24 scenarios using the procedures in Study 2, now ranked the same additional 12 scenarios used in paper-based Study 3, just described. In the Internet version, however, participants simply ranked the 12 scenarios among themselves, without indicating how they compared to the 24 scenarios they had previously ranked in Study 3. This was largely a concession to logistic limitations of the web-based interface.

2. STUDY 3 RESULTS

Table 5 lists the scenarios in the order in which the subjects as a group ranked them, according to mean rank. Recall that the subjects are using their ranking of the first set of 24 scenarios as their "rank calibration," as it were, in ranking this second set of 12 scenarios. Thus, the point of reference for understanding the ranks in Table 5 below are the ranks established in Study 1. (The lettering of the scenarios indicates the order of seriousness as reflected in the statutory penalties commonly associated with each offense.[15] Scenario A typically carries the lowest statutory penalty, scenario L the highest.)

Note the low number of responses that created the modal response for each scenario, suggesting that the responses were quite scattered.

Each of the 64 subjects could have deviated from the group modal ranking as to each of the 66 pair-wise judgments, for a total number of 4,224 possible deviations from modal pair-wise ranking. Recall that if a subject ranks a single scenario different from the group's overall ranking, it may produce many pair-wise deviations. The subjects had a total of 561 deviations, meaning that the subjects reversed the overall group's pair-wise ranking 13.3 percent of the time, as compared to the roughly 50 percent disagreement rate one would see for a random ranking of pairs. This suggests more than three times the 4 percent disagreement rate among the same subjects when they ranked the first set of 24 scenarios, in Study 1. A similar implication

[15] *See* Robinson & Kurzban, *supra* note 236, at appendix D.

TABLE 5. } Results from Study 3

Scenario	Mean Rank*	Mode Rank (frequency)**	% Assigning "No Liability"
E (bestiality)	5.1	no punish (27)	42.2
B (prostitution)	7.3	no punish (15)	23.4
C (marijuana)	7.4	no punish (14)	21.9
G (cocaine)	10.2	11–12 (9)	9.4
A (drunk crash)	12	11–12 (9)	3.1
D (teen alcohol)	12.2	17–18 (10)	4.7
I (3rd theft)	13.6	11–12 (12)	0
F (late abortion)	14	no punish, 17–18 (8)	12.5
H (unwanted sex)	15.5	17–18 (17)	1.6
K (cocaine dealer)	16.5	17–18 (21)	3.1
L (cocaine importer)	17.4	17–18 (24)	0
J (rape)	18.6	17–18 (18)	0

N = 64

* Recall that subjects' ranks in this Study relied upon the rankings they had given in the first set of scenarios, in Study 1. Thus, the 18.6 mean rank for scenario J suggests that subjects most closely associated this scenario with the seriousness of scenarios 18 and 19 of Study 1.

** A mode of 11–12 on the table indicates that the most common subject response was to rank the scenario as being between the scenarios in the first set that she had ranked as 11th and 12th. The number in parentheses indicates the number of subjects who gave that modal response.

might be drawn from the fact that the standard deviations of the rank means in the second set of 12 scenarios are higher than those for the first set of 24 scenarios, even though they should be lower by virtue of the smaller number of scenarios.[16]

Again, this analysis of pair-wise comparisons, rank mode frequencies, and standard deviations of mean ranks is designed only to give the reader some general commonsense view of the data. The more reliable and sophisticated analysis is the use of Kendall's W coefficient of concordance, which measures agreement among sets of rank orderings. (Recall that a W of 1.0 indicates perfect agreement, 0.0 indicates no agreement.) For the 12 scenarios in Study 3, the Kendall's W is .55 ($p < .001$), as compared to the Kendall's W of .95 for the same participants ranking the 24 Study 1 scenarios.

3. STUDY 4 RESULTS

Table 6 shows the mean rankings of the same 12 scenarios as ranked by the 246 subjects who did Internet-based rankings for Study 4. (Remember that in this study, as opposed to paper-based Study 3, the subjects ranked the 12 scenarios among themselves, and not in relation to the 24 scenarios they had previously ranked for Study 2. Thus, the mean rankings in Table 6 can be compared to an ideal set of mean rankings of from 1 to 12.)

[16] *See id.*, at 1886, Table 7.

TABLE 6. } Results from Study 4

Scenario	Mean Rank	Modal Rank	% Assigning "No Liability"
C (marijuana)	2.2	**	33
B (prostitution)	2.4	**	30
G (cocaine)	4	**	19
E (bestiality)	4.2	**	16
D (teen alcohol)	4.8	5	6
A (drunk crash)	6.2	6	0
I (3rd theft)	7.1	7	0
F (late abortion)	7.5	12	11
K (cocaine dealer)	7.9	9	6
H (unwanted sex)	8.7	11	1
L (cocaine importer)	8.9	10	6
J (rape)	11.1	12	0

N = 246

** These scenarios had a modal rank of "no punishment."

Each of the 246 subjects could have deviated from the group modal ranking as to each of the 66 pair-wise judgments, for a total number of 16,236 possible deviations from modal pair-wise ranking. The subjects had a total of 3,362 deviations, meaning that the subjects reversed the overall group's pair-wise ranking 20.7 percent of the time, as compared to the roughly 50 percent disagreement rate one would see for a random ranking of pairs. This is noticeably higher than the 9.2 percent rate of disagreement among the same subjects when they ranked the first set of 24 scenarios, in Study 2.

Again, this analysis of pair-wise comparisons and mean ranks is designed only to give the reader some general commonsense view of the data. The more reliable and sophisticated analysis is the use of Kendall's W coefficient of concordance, which measures agreement among sets of rank orderings. (Remember, a W of 1.0 indicates perfect agreement, 0.0 indicates no agreement.) For the 12 scenarios in Study 4, the Kendall's W is .51 ($p < .001$).

C. Conclusion

As compared to the extremely high Kendall's W of .95 and .88 for the 24 scenarios in Studies 1 and 2, respectively, the Kendall's W for the 12 scenarios in these two studies, of .55 and .51, respectively, show that both paper-based and Internet-based subjects have considerably less agreement on the second set of scenarios than on the first set. Why should there be more disagreement among subjects over the proper ranking of the Study 3 and 4 scenarios than over the Study 1 and 2 scenarios?

Each of the second set of offenses has its own story as to the reasons for its controversial nature.[17] But there may be systematic differences between the kind of scenarios of the first set and those of the second set that invite further exploration. Note, for example, that the second set of scenarios is different from the first in that they concern conduct outside the core of wrongdoing (physical injury, taking without consent, and deception and exchanges). This conclusion is consistent with the explanations for agreement offered in chapter 3. Some wrongs are so central to effective group cooperation that one might speculate that they must exist in any group in any culture and would be included in any evolutionary pressure to create a human predisposition for such learning. Other wrongs are less essential to group cooperation.

One might speculate that views about punishment of conduct out from the core may not be the product of intuition at all, but rather the product of social learning and reasoning. The more this is true, the more the situational context and the demographic characteristic of the subject may shape the punishment judgment. The results here might suggest generally that the closer conduct is to the core—of physical injury of persons or property, takings without consent, and deception in exchanges—the greater will be agreement about its relative blameworthiness. The more conduct is tied to these fundamental wrongdoings only by analogy; the greater will be the disagreement over its seriousness, to an extent analogous to the extent of disagreement over the strength of the analogy.

---

[17] For example, one arguing for enhanced drunk driving penalties may point to the number of serious automobile accidents caused by intoxicated drivers, while others may suggest that the existing punishments for impaired drivers are disproportionate to the sanctions for similarly reckless conduct, such as driving grossly over the speed limit in a residential area.

5 }

Changing People's Judgments of Justice

Whatever one concludes from the analysis of chapter 3—whether the striking existence of widely shared intuitions of justice is the result of evolutionary pressures or is the result of universal social learning—it is clear that such intuitions about the core of wrongdoing are immune from the powerful forces of life experience and demographics. If this were not the case, one would not find the high degree of agreement across demographics demonstrated in chapter 2.

This reality has important implications for social reformers. Can people's intuitions of justice be changed? If so, how? Section A reviews some recent reform campaigns that touch such matters of community judgments about wrongdoing. Section B considers the difficulties with changing shared intuitions of justice, followed by section C examining what can and cannot be realistically changed. Drawing on this analysis, section D then offers advice to reformers about how best to accomplish their goals. The subject of reforming a community's intuitions of justice is taken up again in chapters 10 and 11, after the analysis has been further developed by the intervening chapters' demonstration of the value of following community views of justice and the costs to criminal law of conflicting with them.[1] A final section in this chapter considers a set of criticisms that has been offered against the points presented in this part.

Sections A through D of this chapter are drawn primarily from portions of my article with John M. Darley, *Intuitions of Justice: Implications for Criminal Law and Justice Policy*.[2] Section E of this chapter is taken mainly from my article with Owen Jones and Robert Kurzban, *Realism, Punishment, and Reform*.[3]

A. Proposals to Change Intuitions of Wrongdoing and Blameworthiness

A standard form of political and social activity, and "norms theory" debate, is the wish to change people's views and ultimately their conduct to that which the

[1] See in particular chapter 10, section D (Deviations to Change Social Norms: Altering Empirical Desert) as well as chapter 11 generally (Implications for Reform).

[2] Paul H. Robinson & John M. Darley, *Intuitions of Justice: Implications for Criminal Law and Justice Policy*, 81 S. Cal. L. Rev. 1, 13–18 & 51–66 (2007).

[3] Paul H. Robinson, Owen Jones, & Robert Kurzban, *Realism, Punishment, and Reform*, 77 U. Chi. L. Rev., 1611 (2010).

reformer sees as preferable. With advent of recognition of an "expressive function" of criminal law and punishment, it also is common to have criminal law play a central role in this social engineering process. The typical plan is, with the help of criminal law manipulation, to get people to view conduct disapproved by the social engineers as condemnable or more condemnable (or, alternatively, to dissolve the condemnation with which people currently view the conduct sought to be promoted). In other words, the reform programs are in the business of trying to alter people's judgments of justice.

The list of recent reform programs is substantial. Reformers concerned about date rape have attempted to eradicate the notion that women often pretend to withhold consent to intercourse to appear more alluring or simply to avoid appearing "promiscuous," rather than as a genuine indication of not wanting to engage in sexual activity.[4] Antismoking activists have sought to stigmatize smoking in the presence of nonsmokers who did not consent to inhaling secondhand smoke.[5] The campaign against domestic violence sought to raise the general level of societal condemnation of the abuser.[6] A coalition of governmental and nongovernmental organizations hoped to alter people's views on drug use in order to reduce usage.[7] The nonprofit group Mothers Against Drinking and Driving sought to change public perceptions about the harms inherent in drunk driving.[8] Reformers pressed changes in public views on the acceptability of sexual harassment in the work place.[9] Finally, proponents of same-sex marriage have sought to build public acceptance of both same-sex intercourse and the legal recognition of same-sex unions.[10]

B. Difficulties in Changing Intuitions

As noted above, given the universal and intuitional nature of core judgments about justice, it seems likely these judgments cannot easily be changed to the extent they are based on intuitions rather than reasoning. However, intuitions sometimes can be overridden by the reasoning system. One of the functions of the reasoning

---

[4] *See* Steven J. Schulhofer, UNWANTED SEX: THE CULTURE OF INTIMIDATION AND THE FAILURE OF LAW at Chapter 2 (1998). *See also* Daniel Kahan, *Gentle Nudges vs. Hard Shoves: Solving the Sticky Norms Problem*, 67 UNIV. CHI. L. REV. 607, 608 (2000) [hereinafter Kahan, *Gentle Nudges*]

[5] *See infra* section E.1

[6] For a review of antidomestic violence norm-changing techniques, *see* Kahan, *Gentle Nudges*, *supra* note 256, at 629–31.

[7] *See* Above the Influence Website, *Drug Facts* http://www.abovetheinfluence.com/facts/drugfacts (last visited July 22, 2011).

[8] *See* MADD Website, *MADD Online: Victims*, http://www.madd.org/victims (last visited July 22, 2011).

[9] *See* Kahan, *Gentle Nudges*, *supra* note 256, at 634–40.

[10] *See* Human Rights Campaign Website, *Marriage & Relationship Recognition*, http://www.hrc.org/issues/marriage.asp (last visited July 22, 2011).

system is to monitor the quality of the mental products of the intuitive system. But apparently this monitoring is quite intermittent, perhaps because of the feelings of certainty produced by the automaticity of the intuitive system. Reviewing many studies, Daniel Kahneman and Shane Frederick conclude "that [the reasoning system's] monitoring of the products of the intuitive system is normally quite lax and allows many intuitive judgments to be expressed, including some that are erroneous."[11] It is also the case, however, that the products of intuitive thinking can be quite accurate. Malcolm Gladwell's thesis in his book *Blink* is that intuitive judgments are often startlingly accurate, sometimes more accurate that reasoned judgments.[12] Because it is likely that people only infrequently conclude that their intuitions of justice are in error; their reasoning system does not habitually scan their intuitive judgments of justice.

What is it that might trigger the reasoning system into a long-lasting override of shared moral intuitions? Certainly frequent discoveries of disagreements with other citizens will not do this. As demonstrated in chapter 2, there is a remarkable degree of consensus among citizens about the relative severity of punishments due wrongdoers for various transgressions. If one became convinced that, for instance, a Benthamite version of deterrence theory was the appropriate guide to sentencing either as a matter of principal or as a conclusion of the best way to reduce the rate of criminal acts, one might then conclude that judgments of the appropriate punishment for any crime should be guided by deterrence calculations, even if they conflicted with shared intuitions of justice. But this seems like both a rare event, perhaps limited primarily to academics or policy wonks, and a point of view that would be difficult to sustain. As discussed in chapter 3, the two contending explanations for a citizen's intuitions of justice are cultural socialization and evolutionary readiness, and both produce intuitions that are quite deep seated.

Evidence suggests that it takes a dramatic, concerted effort to fundamentally alter a person's intuitive notions of justice. Such changes in core judgments have been notably observed in cases of coercive indoctrination, often referred to as "brainwashing." While there remains scholarly dispute over the precise definition and nature of brainwashing, the mechanisms to produce effective changes in an individual's views have been persuasively demonstrated, for example, in their effective application by the Chinese military on American soldiers captured during the Korean War. Effective coercive indoctrination manifested itself in the acceptance of the Chinese Communist ideology by POWs, some of whom, at least temporarily, had their personal ideologies seriously altered.[13]

---

[11] Daniel Kahneman & Shane Frederick, *Representativeness Revisited: Attribute Substitution in Intuitive Judgment*, in HEURISTICS AND BIASES 49–81 (2002).

[12] Malcolm Gladwell, BLINK: THE POWER OF THINKING WITHOUT THINKING (2005).

[13] *See generally* Edgar H. Schein with Inge Schneier & Curtis H. Barker, COERCIVE PERSUASION; A SOCIO-PSYCHOLOGICAL ANALYSIS OF THE "BRAINWASHING" OF AMERICAN CIVILIAN PRISONERS BY THE CHINESE COMMUNISTS (1961)

Coercive indoctrination commonly can be achieved through three stages:[14] isolation; destruction of the preexisting self; and construction of a new, indoctrinated self. Isolation is used to exert complete control over the subject's access to information, physical condition, and environment. Destruction of self is then achieved through the psychological and physical degradation of the subject. The subject is destabilized through a combination of physiological stressors (starvation, insufficient sleep, poor sanitation, physical abuse) and psychological pressures (ritual confession, peer pressure, renunciation of values). Finally, the subject's identity is reconstructed into a new self, adopting as his own the beliefs and values of the indoctrinator.

However, even such highly controlled and intrusive coercive indoctrination procedures have success only within limits. As applied by the Chinese, one of the more successful and systematic employments of the technique of brainwashing was found to work only on a small number of soldiers. Out of 4,428 Korean War POW survivors, only 192, about four percent, were deemed chargeable of a serious misconduct offense for siding with the enemy.[15] Thus, brainwashing would hardly seem effective if the goal is to change the views of large populations. Further, even on the persons who succumb to brainwashing, the effects often fail to hold without continued reinforcement, leading to a reversion in beliefs. After the war, without constant reinforcement, most indoctrinated POWs lost their devotion to the communist cause and, when repatriated to the United States, abandoned their attitudes concerning the superiority of communism.[16]

Thus, even using a method as extreme as coercive indoctrination, one can fail to permanently separate a person from his preexisting beliefs and values. To effectively change such views would require intensive and intrusive coercion to bring about the initial change and a continuous reinforcement of the newly adopted views. As a practical matter, this appears impossible to replicate broadly, and as a moral and political matter the coercion involved would not be tolerated in a modern liberal democracy.

What might be seen as a weaker form of coercive indoctrination is the well-documented "Stockholm Syndrome."[17] In this, victims of hostage situations come to positively associate themselves with their captors, often adopting a sympathetic view of the captor's ideals or even, as in the heavily publicized case of Patty Hearst, to join the captors.[18] In many respects, Stockholm Syndrome is induced and functions similarly to the more extreme version of coercive indoctrination described above. The hostage, faced with constant anxiety and/or physical abuse (or threat thereof) begins to deconstruct himself and seek the protection of the

---

[14] *Ibid.*

[15] Donald Manes, *Barbed Wire Command*, 10 MIL. L. REV. 1, 2 (1960).

[16] *Id.*

[17] *See generally* Thomas Strentz, *The Stockholm Syndrome: Law Enforcement Policy and Hostage Behavior*, in VICTIMS OF TERRORISM, 149–61 (Frank Ochberg & David Soskis eds., 1982).

[18] *See* Paul H. Robinson, CRIMINAL LAW: CASE STUDIES & CONTROVERSIES 725–33 (2005).

captor, who controls the situation. In the process, the captive adopts the perspective of the captor, creating both emotional and ideological bonds.

Thus, in Stockholm Syndrome the degradation and reconstruction process are vital to changing basic intuitions and beliefs. Isolation and anxiety alone, while capable of producing elevated levels of personal sympathy, are likely not sufficient to effect dramatic changes in a person's belief structure. This demonstrates the resilience of intuitive views. While captives may identify on a personal level with captors from isolation alone (Stockholm Syndrome can develop in a relatively brief amount of time so long as there is sufficient contact between the captor and the captive), it takes extreme interventions in order to relegate a captive to the condition necessary to be able to fully internalize a new set of values.

This again points to the difficulty in effecting societal-wide changes in intuitive notions. While it may be possible to find isolated nations where leaders manipulate the anxiety of their citizens to induce feelings of loyalty as Stockholm Syndrome writ large, even this weak form of coercive indoctrination would be incompatible with the functioning of a modern liberal democracy and, in any case, is likely to produce little other than affection for the person of the leader.

The best-known case in which the legal authorities of the United States sought to produce change in thought and action patterns of the populace was the "noble experiment" of Prohibition.[19] In 1920, the 18th amendment to the Constitution came into effect, followed soon by the National Prohibition Act (the Volstead Act) by which the sale and consumption of alcoholic drinks was banned. The consumption of alcohol was a rather poor candidate for criminalization in the minds of the citizens. Alcohol consumption does not fit the paradigm of an act that deliberately inflicts harm on others. Within many of the sub-cultures of citizens of the United States, alcohol consumption was perceived as a harmless activity, embedded in treasured subcultural practices. Realizing this, some of the advocates of Prohibition raised the specter of impoverished wives and children abused by drunken fathers, to make salient the prototype of the act of alcohol consumption inflicting harms on others. But this was not persuasive, or at least not persuasive enough to maintain support for Prohibition.[20]

C. Which Intuitions of Justice Can Be Changed and Which Cannot?

The picture is not entirely bleak for social engineers. Some intuitions of justice can be changed in some respects using certain methods. The means by which intuitions of justice can be changed is a function of their intuitive nature. Acknowledging and learning from that nature will in the end be more effective than ignoring or denying it.

---

[19] *See supra* chapter 8, section B.3.

[20] *See generally* Edward Behr, PROHIBITION: THIRTEEN YEARS THAT CHANGED AMERICA (1996).

The more intuitive the justice judgment, the more likely it is to be resistant to change. One indication of the highly intuitive nature of a view is high agreement on it across demographics and cultures. That there is agreement across demographics and cultures illustrates just how immune these intuitions are to the influence of normal human experience that varies so greatly across demographics and cultures.

The studies showing high levels of agreement suggest that the core intuitions include at least three kinds of violations: physical aggression against others, the unconsented-to taking of property, and dishonesty or deception in exchanges,[21] which also happen to be those prohibitions that a society would need to promote the cooperation that allows it to exist. Other kinds of studies support similar conclusions. The intuitive core of wrongdoing seems to start with direct personal action such as hitting or stabbing another individual.[22] Greene's neuroscience studies support a core of such direct aggression or pushing another in a way that places him in the path of harm.[23]

The practice by older law books of calling actions that are "wrong in and of themselves" offenses that are *malum in se* captures this idea. Although this is a phrase that has gone out of common usage in modern criminal law theory,[24] it somewhat accurately describes ordinary citizens' responses when they are asked, for instance, why it is wrong to murder another. Their answer, often, is that it is just wrong. It is an answer often given with some emotion, and brain imaging work suggests that emotional areas of the brain are involved in responding to these sorts of core wrongs.[25]

As this perspective suggests, it would be very difficult to bring persons to intuit acts that do direct harm to others as acts that are not morally wrong. And the nearer other acts are to doing direct harm to others, the more the difficulty there will be in getting them perceived as not wrong. The wrongness of taking "candy from a baby"—more generally, taking sustenance from a weaker person—seems an intuition that is easily connected to a "do not do harm to others" prototype.

The other prohibitions that appear difficult to change, such as the one on breach of agreement or deception in exchanges, may have this status for one of two

---

[21] Note, for example, that nearly all of the scenarios used in the recent Robinson-Kurzban study, which showed such a high level of agreement on scenario ranking, involved these "core" wrongs. This study is described at length throughout chapters 1.C, 2, and 4.

[22] As military trainers know, it is extremely difficult to get a military recruit to shoot to kill an enemy. David Grossman, who has extensively studied the problem, suggests that "there is a powerful,, innate human resistance toward killing one's own species." David Grossman, ON KILLING: THE PSYCHOLOGICAL COST OF LEARNING TO KILL IN WAR AND SOCIETY, xxix (1996).

[23] *See* Joshua D. Greene, Leigh E. Nystrom, Andrew D. Engell, John M. Darley, & Jonathan D. Cohen, "The Neural Bases of Cognitive Conflict and Control in Moral Judgment," 44 NEURON 389, 389–400 (2004).

[24] See, *e.g.*, WAYNE R. LAFAVE, PRINCIPLES OF CRIMINAL LAW §1.6(B) (2003) (reviewing difficulties in giving workable meaning to distinction between malum in se and malum prohibitum).

[25] *See* Greene et al., *supra* note 275.

reasons. First, they may be intuitively wrong because of their analogical closeness to inflicting direct personal harm on another. As suggested above, unjust takings of another's foodstuffs could have this character. More generally, "crimes against property" may be perceived as wrong because it is intuitively easy to make the connection between physically taking property and physically harming another as related forms of aggression. In the case of intuitions such as prohibitions against failure in keeping one's commitments, an independent underlying prototype may have been evolutionarily prepared for. At this moment, research on prototypes of wrongdoing actions is not far enough advanced to enable knowledge of how many prototypes there are of wrongdoing actions.

It is also the case that the development of a generalized desire to punish those who transgress these core prohibitions is an extremely useful mechanism for a society to develop. Two sets of studies have examined the underpinnings of "the urge to punish" those who transgress these rules. Experimental gaming studies have demonstrated that participants have a propensity to punish defectors in prisoners' dilemma and other games that allow a person to make a "defecting" choice. These defecting choices are generally interpreted by those that suffer from them as a breach of contract, or at least of fairness, which generates considerable anger at the defector. The important finding here is that a player will expend resources to punish a defector. This is true even when steps are taken to ensure that the player has no rational reason to inflict the punishment. One would rationally expend resources to punish a person who has defected if that would establish a reputation of being a person who "does not tolerate double-crossers." Thus, those constructing the games make clear that the player will never play against that defector again, and make clear to the player that he will never encounter the defector outside the game context again. Therefore, there is no self-interested reason for the player's costly infliction of punishment to establish a reputation of being willing to retaliate against defections. Still, the experiments demonstrate, the player will expend resources to punish the soon-to-disappear defector.[26]

The second set of relevant studies is brain imaging studies. They illuminate what could motivate this punishment response. These studies have demonstrated that when a person who has been defected against witnesses a third party punishing the defector, brain areas associated with rewards are activated. In other words, they take satisfaction in seeing the defector punished, even if the punishment is administered by others.[27]

---

[26] Joseph Henrich, Richard McElreath, Abigail Barr, Jean Ensminger, Clark Barrett, Alexander Bolyanatz, Juan Camilo Cardenas, Michael Gurven, Edwins Gwako, Natalie Henrich, Carolyn Lesorogol, Frank Marlowe, David Tracer, & John Ziker, *Costly Punishment Across Human Societies*, 23 SCI. 1767, 1767–70 (2006).

[27] Dominique J.-F. de Quervain, Urs Fischbacher, Valerie Treyer, Melanie Schellhammer, Ulrich Schnyder, Alfred Buck, & Ernst Fehr, *The Neural Basis of Altruistic Punishment*, 27 SCI. 1254, 1254–58 (2004).

D. How Can Judgments of Justice Be Changed?

If a judgment of justice is of a sort that can be meaningfully altered, the previous discussions on the origin and changeability of such judgments hints at how change might most effectively be brought about. There are two potentially effective methods: public education campaigns to manipulate the strength of analogies to core wrongs and the internalization of group beliefs. These are not mutually exclusive; a reform program might combine aspects of each approach.

1. PUBLIC EDUCATION TO MANIPULATE THE ANALOGY TO CORE WRONGS

First, it is possible through public education both to inform people about negative effects of conduct that had not previously been fully appreciated and to analogize the conduct sought to be condemned with conduct that already is seen as condemnable. This approach changes judgments of what constitutes wrongdoing not by fighting the existing intuition but by harnessing it, by demonstrating that the conduct at issue really does have the condemnable character or effect that people's intuitions abhor.

Two examples illustrate how intuitions may be changed by such a public education campaign. For both drunk driving and cigarette smoking in banned areas, which has been either criminalized or given more severe penalties in recent years, criminalization was "successful" in that the community came to think of the actions as appropriately condemnable and properly criminalized.

For drunk driving, the path to criminalization involved changing the identity of the "victim" of drunk driving from the driver himself to the innocent bystander injured by the driver's actions. Groups such as Mothers Against Drunk Driving (MADD), formed of mothers who had children killed or injured by drunk drivers, who were tragically motivated to make drunk driving criminal, educated the public as to why it was that these actions fit the "moral wrong" prototype. Previously, the stereotype of drunk driving was one of a "foolish fellow," likely to crash into large objects, injuring only himself if anyone. The MADD parents, holding up childhood or graduation pictures of their dead children, or photographs of the horrible results of car accidents caused by drunk drivers, provided a persuasive message that drunk driving was indeed conduct highly dangerous to others.

Cigarette smoking was a bit of a more complicated case, but similar in that it worked by building an analogy to condemnable physical aggression. Rather than being able to use the direct linkages to obvious victims that were effective in anti-drunk driving campaigns, the process of changing intuitive notions concerning cigarette smoking required incrementally expanding the understanding of who suffered from the smoking.

Initially, as evidence began to accumulate that cigarettes had remarkably harmful effects on smokers and that they were for, at least some people, highly addictive, cigarette sales were prohibited to minors. This was justified on the basis that minors are as a group unable to reason rationally about risks. However, this did not warrant prohibiting the sale of cigarettes to adults or restricting where smokers could smoke. Smoking was seen as creating risks for the smoker, but conventional wisdom coded these as risks that adult persons could not be stopped from *choosing* to take, since they were risks only to themselves.[28]

The next expansion of cigarette prohibitions followed the release of research showing that "secondhand smoke"—smoke inhaled by (innocent) bystanders who were in rooms filled with smoke—produced similar although reduced health risks to the nonsmokers. As a result, many jurisdictions turned to banning cigarette smoking in private spaces such as offices and meeting places as well as public spaces in which smokers and nonsmokers congregated. As the public became educated on the potential harm caused by secondhand smoke, people came to see that smokers inflicted real harm on other, nonconsenting people. Therefore, laws were passed to prohibit the infliction of these harms. However, regulations did not extend to certain public establishments such as restaurants and bars, where other options such as "smoke-free" sections or the ability of patrons to simply stay home were seen as appropriate reasons to continue to allow indoors, public smoking.

To shift the public's judgments on the appropriateness of smoking in restaurants and bars, public education was used to change the focus from the effects on other patrons to the effects on the employees. Unlike other patrons, the waitresses, waiters, and bartenders who were exposed to secondhand smoke were portrayed as struggling young workers, often the sons and daughters of people like us, who had not voluntarily consented to contracting cancer; they were innocent victims working in needlessly dangerous areas, driven by need for their wages. This resulted in a growing number of cities deciding to ban smoking in these last bastions of cigarette smoking. The rate at which the "immoralization" of smoking has spread through society is remarkable—fueled by the ability of antismoking advocates to demonstrate the harmful effects of smoking on discreet categories of nonsmokers.

The ability to replicate the results of these two public education campaigns in order to change judgments on other actions relies on the ability to analogize a given action to a clearly condemnable harm suffered by another person or group of people. The current effort to change judgments concerning "insider trading" is an example of both the possibilities of and the limitations on changing intuitions. Insider trading, buying and selling stocks or bonds based on information that a person has that is not yet known to the public, has been criminalized. However,

[28] The film, *Thank you For Smoking* (Fox Searchlight Pictures 2006) reproduces the contention of the cigarette companies that smoking is an entirely voluntary act, an argument that exists in uneasy relationship with the fact that smoking is addictive, and that many who are trying to stop smoking are in the grip of an addiction that the wish they never had started.

despite high profile prosecutions for violations, public judgments of the criminality of insider trading remain somewhat complex.[29]

As predicted by this subsection's argument, when the action of insider trading results in the selling of a stock shortly prior to the price of the stock falling, it is easier for the public to view this as intuitively criminal. This occurs because a "victim" can be established in the subsequent purchasers who suffer personal or institutional economic harm. Hence, in the case of the collapse of Enron, a great deal of attention was paid to the fact that many employees had their retirement savings invested in the company.

In the opposite situation, buying stock on insider information prior to it gaining value, it is more difficult to identify a victim class and thus more difficult to change judgments on the condemnability of such action. In this case, insider trading is an action that is some distance away from what is generally considered a core prohibition, in which one person harms another. The action harms all other, later, buyers of the stock, because the buying actions of those who bought on insider information slightly raised the price of the stock at which the later buyers bought in. These later buyers constitute a large and non-personified class of actors who are harmed in some fairly abstract ways. Given this, it could be predicted that criminalizing this version of insider trading would be met with some skepticism from the general public.

2. INTERNALIZATION OF GROUP BELIEFS

Another mechanism for changing judgments operates in a more indirect way. Once a substantial group comes to see the conduct differently, their views can be used to help change the views of others. This might be predictable given the evolutionary and social group utility of a person adopting the judgments of justice of others in his group.[30]

There is a considerable social psychological literature on conformity that demonstrates that an individual who is surrounded by a group of people who voice a uniform and unanimous opinion comes to express the same opinion.[31] And there are specific conformity studies that demonstrate that people do conform on judgments of a moral sort, when they face uniform disagreement from others. When an action is "tagged" by the group that surrounds the person, as the sort of act that should not be done, it may become persistently and perhaps permanently perceived as morally wrong.

During the childhood period in which the child is socialized into, among other things, the moral thinking of the culture, the child often accepts the norms presented in an initially uncritical way. It is often the task of the child to articulate for herself the

---

[29] *See* Joan MacLeod Heminway, *Save Martha Stewart? Observations about Equal Justice in U.S. Insider Trading Regulation*, 12 TEX. J. WOMEN & L. 247, 250–53 (2003) (examining the public indifference to insider trading and the Justice Department's actions in high-profile cases).

[30] *See* chapter 3, sections A & B.

[31] Solomon Asch, SOCIAL PSYCHOLOGY (1955).

underlying reasons for the moral norm in question.[32] The child, cued by the expressions of disgust on the faces of adults, for example, comes to understand that spreading her baby food into her hair or the living room rug is a transgression.

Alternately, it is possible that the person's group-induced conclusion about the act will fade over time. In psychological terms, this is the question of whether the intuition produced by the group has been "internalized" by the individual and made part of his own individual thinking, or is only the result of an identification with the group that is temporary in nature, and the intuition will revert to some previously held content as the memories of the group opinion fades. A broad generalization from the research literature is that opinions or intuitions voiced while in the orbit of groups tend to revert to prior states.[33]

However, there may be reason to doubt that moral opinions initially expressed because of conformity pressures from others will always revert. Groups provide a particularly powerful source of persuasive cues for moral judgments. If many others like him think that some novel complex action is a wrong action, this is a good cue to a person that he too would think that action is wrong if he reflected on it. He then may be motivated to search for reasons why the others think the action is wrong. The search is likely to be biased to find confirmation. If the processes are initiated while the individual is under the influence of the group consensus, then the change in the judgment can become more far reaching or "internalized" by the individual, to use the current vocabulary.

An example of this process comes from social scientists studying the developmental steps in the radicalization of those who protest against abortion. For a considerable group of Americans, the story, in brief, is this. Many who opposed abortion did so initially because they thought abortion was an act in opposition to their religious beliefs. They then began to involve themselves in protests, at which point they were surrounded by others who opposed abortion. The sharing of their antiabortion attitudes shifted the group norms against abortion in a more extreme direction.

Apparently many antiabortion sympathizers became much more extreme in their beliefs when they witnessed a film of a sonogram of an abortion of a fetus, looking childlike, and horribly, apparently struggling to avoid the abortionist's needle. They saw, "with their own eyes, that abortion was murder of a child."[34] Witnessing this event with others who already thought that abortion was a wrong, amplified the processes by which everyone's belief became more extreme. It was from people with this set of experiences that many of the "rescuers" came. "Rescuers" were

---

[32] Richard A. Shewder & Nancy C. Much, *Determinations of Meaning: Discourse and Moral Socialization*, in William M. Kurtines & Jacob L. Gerwitz, MORAL DEVELOPMENT THROUGH SOCIAL INTERACTIONS 197–244 (1987).

[33] Richard E. Petty & John T. Cacioppo, ATTITUDES AND PERSUASION: CLASSIC AND CONTEMPORARY APPROACHES 259 (1981).

[34] *The Silent Scream*, film by Dr. Bernard Nathason, 1984 (depicting the abortion procedure via ultrasound where the fetus appears to react in pain).

those who became willing to inflict violence on those who performed abortions, and several did so.[35]

As this suggests, it is often the case that the group will actively provide the reasons that an action should be considered morally wrong, generally by analogizing it to a paradigm of one person doing physical harm to another. This predisposition to take account of others' expressed views on wrongdoing and blameworthiness can create a potential for change, in concert with the processes of recruiting beliefs that support that change. In modern society, one's relevant "group" may be a social, political, ethnic, religious group, or whatever it is with which the person identifies.

These processes may work in the service of either "immoralizing" behavior previously thought allowable or de-"moralizing" behavior previously thought wrong. As an example of the latter, consider the rookie on the high school football team. He begins with the usual taboos about harming others. But he discovers that all the older team members, the people he looks up to and from whom he desperately wishes acceptance, express that certain aggressive rule-breaking behavior on the sports fields is the right way to play. He may then begin to provide reasons, which will be justifications, for that view from his own mind. It would occur to him that enemy players are well padded by the protective gear they wear and will not really be hurt. He might be reminded of other times he has learned that the real rules that govern behavior are not always the ones in the rulebooks. And so on. In other words, the person is conducting a search for information about the moral rightness of an action, but the search is a biased one, seeking to find the reasons that the group might think it right.[36]

Another example may make this clearer and an unpleasant but realistic one comes to mind. In some so-called male "affinity groups," young men engage in partially organized, partially spontaneous, aggressive sexual assaults on women. Investigations often discover that the ideology of the group, into which they socialize new members, centers around what social scientists call "rape myth beliefs." These beliefs contest whether nonconsensual sexual intercourse, inflicted on a woman, is "harm." An example of this is the view that "girls often say no when they really mean yes."[37] Those holding these beliefs consider sexual relations to be based on getting what one wants from the other, and that coercive force is an appropriate way to get it.

Thus, the mechanism of conformity that is used to change intuitions can motivate individuals to internalize either enhanced or diminished views of the criminality of certain behaviors. The difficult challenge for this approach to change is not the initial changing of the view under group influence but rather is causing the view to be internalized such that it will survive a diminishing influence of the group.

---

[35] James Risen & Judy L. Thomas, WRATH OF ANGELS: THE AMERICAN ABORTION WAR (1998).

[36] Robert J. Lifton, THE NAZI DOCTORS: MEDICAL KILLING AND THE PSYCHOLOGY GENOCIDE 102–44 (1986).

[37] Martha Burt, *Cultural Myths and Supports for Rape,* 38 J. PERSONALITY & SOC. PSYCH. 217, 217–30.

For a further discussion of changing people's judgments of justice, with special focus on rape reform, see chapter 10, section D (discussing having criminal law deviate from existing community views in order to help change those views).

E. Criticisms of Claims Regarding Agreement and Its Implications

In their article *Some Realism about Punishment Naturalism*,[38] Professors Braman, Kahan, and Hoffman [hereinafter BKH] offer criticisms of many of the points contained in the previous chapters, many of which originally appeared in the articles *Concordance and Conflict in Intuitions of Justice* [hereinafter *C&C*],[39] *The Origins of Shared Intuitions of Justice* [hereinafter *Origins*],[40] and *Intuitions of Justice: Implications for Criminal Law and Justice Policy* [hereinafter *Implications*].[41] My coauthors Owen Jones and Robert Kurzban and I responded to these criticisms in our article *Realism, Punishment, and Reform*.[42] This section is drawn from that article.

We think that some of the BKH criticisms are actually false disagreements; others are not. Section 1 below examines claims that BKH attribute to us that are not our views. Section 2 considers what we believe to be possible points of real disagreement with BKH.

1. WHAT IS INCLUDED IN THE "CORE"?

Professors Braman, Kahan, and Hoffman represent the studies on punishment agreement and disagreement that are reported in chapters 2 and 4 as claiming that

(1) the vast majority of wrongful acts are part of the core of agreement,[43]
(2) people agree as to all aspects of all offenses that are part of the core,[44] and

---

[38] Donald Braman, Dan M. Kahan, & David A. Hoffman, *Some Realism about Punishment Naturalism*, 77 U. CHI. L. REV. 1531 (2010).

[39] Robinson & Kurzban, *Concordance and Conflict in Intuitions of Justice*, 91 MINN. L. REV. 1829–1907 (2007). This article is the major source for chapter 1.C, 2, and 4.

[40] Paul H. Robinson, Robert Kurzban, & Owen D. Jones, *The Origins of Shares Intuitions of Justice*, 60 VAND. L. REV. 1633 (2007). This article is the major source of chapter 3.

[41] Paul H. Robinson & John M. Darley, *Intuitions of Justice: Implications for Criminal Law and Justice Policy*, 81 S. CAL. L. REV. 1 (2007).

[42] *See* Robinson, Jones, & Kurzban, *supra* note 255.

[43] BKH represent us as claiming that people have broadly share intuitions about "most forms of crime and punishment" 77 U. CHI L. REV. at 1532–33 and "the vast majority of wrongful acts." *Id.* at 1600. As support for their characterization of our view, BKH cite *C&C, supra* note 291, text at note 172, the methodology discussion of the study, not the analysis or implications section. That passage simply points out that we picked common offenses for the study. The passage makes no claim that there is high agreement as to all offenses, as BKH represents. It also makes no hint that people agree on *all aspects or instances* of these offenses, as BKH also represents.

[44] BKH explains, as if it were in contradiction of our view, that there are "significant controversies within the three categories of core offenses" and "there is substantial disagreement about what constitutes wrongdoing" as related to the core offenses. 77 U. CHI. L. REV. at 1566.

(3) people also agree as to what conduct should be criminal,[45] and what conduct is justified.[46]

Unfortunately, or fortunately, these are not claims that we make. In fact, we do not know any respectable scholar who makes such claims.

Regarding (1) & (2). What is the "core"? BKH suggest that its contours are quite vague and difficult to identify,[47] but what constitutes the "core" is not a matter of speculation or theory, or even of interpretation. It is a matter of empirics. The "core" is, *by definition*, that on which there is high agreement across demographics, like that demonstrated in the *C&C* agreement study.[48]

What cases are included in the core? Those cases on which there is high agreement across demographics. What kinds of cases are those? The *C&C* agreement study showed that one could find this level of agreement in cases involving offenses of violence and theft. Could there be other offenses where one might find cases of such high agreement? Possibly. That will require further research. As we explain in the methodology section to the *C&C* agreement study, we focused on the most common offenses that actually occur in practice.[49] If there are other offenses, they are not likely to be common ones.

What aspects of these offenses are included in the core? BKH seem to assume that we claim that all aspects, all cases, involving any of these offenses are part of the core,[50] but this could hardly be the situation. Our research scenarios intentionally used factors upon which we judged there was high agreement. To the extent that one substitutes a factor on which there is disagreement, obviously the level of agreement on the relative seriousness of the case would have to decline. If, instead

[45] BKH says, for example,"Another reason to be skeptical of the suggestion that we share intuitions about most classes of wrongful acts is that the classes of acts listed also exclude acts that a substantial number of Americans believe should be crimes, but which are not. . . ." *Id.* at 1554. "[N]aturalists hold that while individuals may disagree about how much to punish bad acts, they agree on what *constitutes* a bad act. As such, on the whole, the population should agree that, in each case, the defendant is either guilty or innocent." *Id.* at 1590.

[46] For example, BKH begins their Article with a justification case on which they note there is disagreement, *id.* at 1532, as if this were in contradiction to our view. BKH also has many discussions of the justification of self-defense. *See id.* at 1578–88.

[47] BKH says, for example, "We doubt that naturalists will discover some independent way to distinguish the core of harms from the periphery. . . ." *id.* at 1556 and "One reason to be unsatisfied with the core/periphery distinction is that it fails to tell us what, exactly, distinguishes the important core from the unimportant periphery of crimes." *Id.* at 1557.

[48] In *Origins*, *supra* note 292, we certainly give reasons why we think there is high agreement on the cases at the core, but these theories are not the *definition* of the core but rather are offered as possible *explanations* of the core.

[49] *C&C*, *supra* note 291, at note 172.

[50] BKH says, "If individuals have an intuitive sense of how wrongful acts are relative to each other, then we would expect a person with [different] cultural profiles like Ron and Linda to agree—perhaps not on precisely how much punishment a person deserves, but at the very least on the relative culpability of the two defendants. For naturalism, dissensus in the core of wrongdoing remains a puzzle." 77 U. Chi. L. Rev. at 1592.

of stealing a clock radio from the car, as appears in one scenario, the offender steals the ashes of the car owner's father, obviously the prior high agreement on the relative blameworthiness of the offender will diminish with the extent of the disagreement on the relative value of a father's ashes, which might vary widely across cultures and even across individuals within a culture.

What cases beyond those in the *C&C* agreement study are included in the "core"? We would feel quite comfortable extrapolating well beyond the specific scenarios used in the study. Most objects have an agreed upon value, like the clock radio; most do not have the disputed value of a father's ashes. But until the research is done, of course, we cannot know for sure what level of agreement attaches to what facts.[51]

In *C&C* (Appendix B), we show the reader just how we were able to construct the 24 scenarios on which our subjects had such high agreement: by relying upon, and only upon, principles that we suspected were deeply embedded intuitions of near unanimity. Specifically, there exist a number of general principles of liability and punishment that are widely accepted, for example, damage to person is more blameworthy than damage to property; purposely causing a harm is more blameworthy than doing so recklessly, which in turn is more blameworthy than doing so negligently; the greater the extent of a personal injury, the greater the blameworthiness; the greater the extent of an expectation of privacy, the greater the blameworthiness of an intrusion; etc. Our suspicion was that the high agreement on these general principles had practical consequences for the level of agreement in individual cases as well, suggesting that one *could* create high agreement in judging the relative blameworthiness of individual cases, in contradiction of the common wisdom. The *C&C* agreement study confirmed that the high agreement on the general principles does translate into high agreement on individual cases.

As you can imagine, we found the BKH article quite difficult to understand, given its false assumptions about our claims. For example, it has an entire section showing disagreements in cases of deception in exchanges. Whether somebody is deceived in an exchange obviously is a function of one's expectations about the terms of the exchange, and those expectations could be highly culturally dependent or, even within a culture, highly dependent on context. The case we used in the study was one of a store clerk shortchanging a customer. We used it precisely because it seemed to us that such shortchanging offered an example of a violation of a nearly universal expectation of this most common form of exchange, a purchase. People who agree to make an exchange typically believe that they have a shared understanding of the terms of the exchange. Thus, within any culture, there is likely to be shared expectations when an exchange takes place but, obviously, not always.

---

[51] We aren't entirely ignorant about such matters. There is existing research that gives some hits on a wide range of criminal law issues. *See generally* PAUL H. ROBINSON & JOHN DARLEY, JUSTICE, LIABILITY, AND BLAME (Westview 1995), excerpted in part III.

Even more puzzling is BKH having a section showing disagreements about sexual offenses,[52] as if this were in contradiction of our claim.[53] Recall that the *C&C* disagreement study itself demonstrates that there is *high dis*agreement with respect to many kinds of sexual offenses.[54] It is hard to know why BKH would want to lecture us on disagreement on sexual offenses when our study may be the best available empirical evidence in support of that disagreement.

Generally, BKH have our claim reversed. The point of the *C&C* agreement study is not to show that people agree on everything, or even a lot, but rather to expose as false the common wisdom of the day that, at least in terms of individual cases, people agree on nothing. It is difficult for us to see the value in BKH presenting an exaggerated view of our claims, then criticizing them for being exaggerated.

The important point here is that, simply because one can find or create disagreement by introducing facts on matters in dispute, it does not take away from the fact that there does exist a core of high agreement. And, as discussed further in section 2 below, that high agreement has implications for the malleability of people's intuitions of justice.

Regarding (3). We see the same pattern of misunderstanding when BKH represent us as claiming that there exists high agreement as to what is criminal. A primary theme of the *C&C* disagreement study is to show just the opposite—it shows not just disagreements about relative blameworthiness, but also about whether the conduct should even be criminal. In two of the scenarios, more than 20 percent of the subjects assign no liability. In another, more than 40 percent find no liability.[55] (This is so, even though all three scenarios are criminal under current law.)

Indeed, even in our *C&C* agreement study, we specifically demonstrate that people can agree on the relative blameworthiness of different offense cases yet disagree as to where on the continuum of blameworthiness should be drawn the line marking off the minimum point for criminal liability and punishment. We designed one of our scenarios as an intentionally borderline case (taking food away from an all-you-can-eat buffet in violation of the buffet rules). It was no surprise that people disagreed about whether the case should trigger criminal liability. The important point to us was to show that, despite this, there was still near consensus on where the case ranked on the continuum of relative blameworthiness. The larger point here is that it is judgments about relative blameworthiness on which people can have high agreement, not necessarily judgments about exactly where the line is to be drawn for minimum blameworthiness for criminal liability.

---

[52] 77 U. Chi. L. Rev. at 1573–77. BKH also discusses disagreement over the criminality of the sexual offenses of prostitution, bestiality and unwanted sex. *Id.* at 1555–56.

[53] "But there most manifestly is not consensus in American society on how rape should be defined, and in particular whether a man who engages in sex with a woman who says repeatedly tells him "no" before and during intercourse has committed "rape" or merely succeeded in achieving "unwanted sex," or over how severely, if at all, to punish such a man." [pg. 54, para. 3, line 5.]

[54] *See C&C, supra* note 291, at 1884, 1885, Tables 6 and 7.

[55] *See id.* at 1885, Table 6.

BKH similarly misunderstand our view as claiming that people agree not only on all aspects of what is criminal but also on what is justified.[56] That is, they go beyond what criminal law theorists call "prohibitory norms"—what should be prohibited as wrongful—to include "justificatory norms"—what admittedly wrongful conduct might be tolerated under special justifying circumstances. (Indeed, BKH give no indication that they are aware of this distinction or that they have crossed from one to the other.) They begin their article with a hypothetical about a person deciding whether to steal a bus ticket in order to make an important appearance at a wedding. They point out that Americans might think it was wrong to take the ticket in this situation but that Indians might not, suggesting that we would claim that everyone would agree about this case.

Contrary to the way in which they present it, the hypothetical is not a simple case about whether people disagree on whether theft is wrongful. Presumably the person in the hypothetical believes stealing is wrong. The issue presented is a different one: whether the conduct (theft of the ticket), *which all agree is wrongful*, may nonetheless be justified in this instance because of a special competing interest of sufficient importance (the need to get to the wedding) that might justify the otherwise wrongful conduct. The case is not a test of whether people think theft is wrongful, but rather a test of the comparative value of the competing justification interests.

As above, if one compares interests on which people agree (or that are so disparate that people's minor disagreements are irrelevant), then one will get agreement. On the other hand, if one compares interests, one (or both) of which people disagree about—like the value of a father's ashes or the importance of getting to a wedding—then people will disagree on the comparison. In this instance, the value one places on the importance of one's wedding responsibilities is culturally dependent. BKH suggest that Indians give it greater value than Americans, and we do not know enough about it to disagree.

Consider, however, what else the hypothetical might illustrate. We suspect that there is high agreement on the general principle that special justifying circumstances can outweigh the prohibition of conduct that is itself wrongful. And, as we have shown in the *C&C* agreement study, that high agreement on a general principle can translate into high agreement in individual cases, if those cases involve only factors on which there is agreement. Introducing into a case a factor on which there is disagreement, obviously will reduce the previous level of agreement.

BKH might ask themselves why it is that both Americans and Indians, and every other group on the planet that recognizes property rights, agree that taking another person's property of value is wrongful *and thus would require some justification*. No doubt there is considerable cultural diversity about what counts as "another's property," as well as considerable diversity on the value that different cultures put on different kinds of property. But how is it that diverse cultures all seem to agree with the basic rule: taking another person's property of value without consent

[56] *See supra* note 298.

is wrongdoing. Indeed, there is probably further agreement: that, the greater the value, the greater the wrongdoing. Do the Punishment Realists believe that they can find societies, or could create societies, in which people would believe that there was nothing wrong with taking another's property without consent; or that, if people see such taking as wrongful, that they could be made to believe that the greater the value of the property taken, the lesser the wrongdoing?

2. POSSIBLE POINTS OF DISAGREEMENT WITH BKH

As one might imagine, we have found it difficult to engage with much of the BKH article, based as it is on a representation of our views that we often do not recognize. The experience has left us with little confidence that we understand BKH's position, and thus we are hesitant to make claims about their views. On the points below, we suspect there may be real disagreement, but we think it prudent to simply identify possible points of disagreement and leave it to BKH to confirm or deny that these are their views.

There is No Core of Agreement. It might be that BKH's view is that: there are no aspects of any offenses on which there is high agreement as to an offender's relative blameworthiness. This, of course, was the common wisdom prior to the *C&C* study. It is hard to see how this could continue to be a plausible claim, yet BKH seem to act as if this were the case, by continuing to deny that there is a difference between core and noncore cases.

There Is a Core of Agreement But It Is Meaningless. It may be more likely that the BKH position is slightly different. They may concede that we have shown a core of high agreement, but may believe that this is in some sense a false appearance of agreement or at least an appearance of agreement that has no real significance.[57] If that is their view, then presumably BKH are claiming that the kinds of cases in our agreement study, which we identify as part of the "core" of high agreement, are no different in terms of their potential for agreement or disagreement than the kinds of noncore cases in our disagreement study.[58] That is, they may be arguing that there is nothing meaningful about the apparent core of agreement that we show, because people's agreement or disagreement about relative blameworthiness is something that can be created and dissolved and re-created and re-dissolved at will. No set of issues relating to blameworthiness is any different from any other set of issues in this respect; all are subject to the same potential for agreement or disagreement.

---

[57] BKH says, for example: "None of [the categories that comprise 'the core of wrongdoing'] is composed of acts free from dissensus, and the nature of *the systematic dissensus that pervades each of these categories is at least as interesting and informative as any agreement that can be found.*" 77 U. Chi. L. Rev. at 1568–69 (emphasis added).

[58] For BKH's view that no meaningful distinction exists between the core and the noncore cases, *see supra* note 299. BKH also argues that there is disagreement both among the core cases and among the noncore cases, so the distinction is not meaningful with regard to disagreement. 77 U. Chi. L. Rev. at 1566. *See supra* note 290 at 1566.

The results in our *C&C* agreement study (and presumably our disagreement study as well), they may argue, are just one of an infinite variety of patterns of agreement and disagreement that a researcher or reformer could create or dissolve at will by manipulating the facts or by giving reasons.

We think that BKH are simply wrong on the empirics. We offer them this challenge: using the noncore cases in the *C&C* disagreement study, create the same level of agreement across demographics that we did using core cases in the *C&C* agreement study. If core and noncore cases have no meaningful difference, as BKH seem to believe, then they should be able to create the same level of high agreement using the noncore cases that we claim is unique to the core cases. We do not believe it can be done.[59] Contrary to BKH's claim, core and noncore cases are importantly different.

Even If There Is a Core of Agreement, It Has No Effect on the Malleability of People's Judgments about Justice. We think the core of high agreement has practical significance because these intuitions will be harder to modify than judgments on other cases and issues. That the high agreement on the core cases can be reduced if one adds factors about which there is disagreement, does not make people's intuitions concerning the core cases any more malleable. The issues at the core remain as difficult to modify whether they appear with or without factors on which there is disagreement.

BKH seem to think that all judgments about justice are malleable.[60] They seem to think that social reformers should see all judgments about justice as equally fair game for modification. Again, we believe that BKH are simply wrong on the empirics. As we note above, the existence of a high degree of agreement across demographics shows that the view is sufficiently deeply embedded as to be insulated from the powerful forces of social influence inherent in the wide variety of demographic factors at work in the world. If these core intuitions are immune from the influence of these forces, why would one expect that they nevertheless would be susceptible to easy modification by reformers?

---

[59] Nor do we believe that BKH can construct a set of scenarios on which there is low disagreement as to their proper ranking, then modify the scenarios *by adding information* and thereby create high agreement. If BKH is correct that there is no such thing as a core of agreement, surrounded by factors and offenses of increasing disagreement out from that core, then BKH should be able to create, dissolve, and re-create agreement simply by their manipulation of the facts. We do not believe that it can be done. Once the high agreement of the core is destroyed by adding facts on which there is disagreement, there is no getting it back by adding more facts. The only way to get it back is to drop the disagreement-inspiring facts that were added. There is a core of agreement that is different from other blameworthiness issues and cases.

[60] BKH says, for example: "[P]unishment realism is based on the premise that while individuals do hold deep and abiding intuitions regarding wrongdoing and responses to it, these intuitions depend on social constructs that are demonstrably plastic." 77 U. Chi. L. Rev. at 1533. "The diversity of positions political communities have adopted on them—over place and over time—make us conscious of the plasticity of social norms. . . ." *Id.* at 1535. "Where we see mutability in norms, and hence the inescapability of collective responsibility for their content, the Naturalist apprehend their stability, and warn of the futility and even perversity of using criminal law as an instrument of norm reform." *Id.* at 1536. BKH wants to "learn how our moral intuitions are shaped and to develop means of fostering conceptions of justices that are both satisfying to us and compatible with our collective welfare." *Id.* at 1532.

The most obvious data point here is the shared intuition that serious wrongdoing should be punished.[61] There is an active abolitionist movement, which we discuss and document in *Implications*. However, given the strength and near unanimity of the intuition that serious wrongdoing should be punished, it strikes us as unrealistic that this movement will ever gain much support, let alone be implemented by any society. If, as BKH claim, this intuition can be modified; and if, as the abolitionist arguments make clear, there are good reasons to think that punishing wrongdoing might not be the best course for a society, why have no societies of which we are aware ever rejected having a punishment system? Given the diversity of societies in the world, and across time, BKH owes us at least an explanation as to why this particular intuition of justice has apparently never been overridden.

Indeed, one can read BKH as essentially conceding our point that there are some intuitions of justice so deeply embedded as to make it unrealistic to think that they can be changed. BKH suggest that reformers need not worry about widely shared intuitions about justice because they do not "address a *live* policy debate."[62] Presumably, they mean that the current debate about the abolition of punishment, for example, is a "dead" debate—which is simply another way of saying that it is unrealistic to expect that the abolitionists could ever prevail. But if BKH think that all intuitions of justice are malleable, without regard to the degree of agreement on an intuition, why should not the debate be a "live" one? How can BKH see the abolitionist debate as not "live," without conceding that there are important and predictable differences in malleability that attach to core intuitions?

In fact, BKH also are wrong in claiming that intuitions of justice that are hard to change are at the heart of "live" debates. As we discuss in *Implications*, the abolitionist debate has taken on a more modern form in the guise of "restorative justice." There can be little doubt that the founder of that movement, John Braithwaite, has as his principal motivation an anti-punishment agenda.[63] There are many different forms of restorative processes, some more inclined to defeat deserved punishment than others. The debates over which processes to prefer are in large part debates over the extent to which just punishment can and should be frustrated. Consistent with our prediction, restorative processes are currently typically limited in their application to cases involving juveniles or minor offenses, precisely because broader application, to more serious offenses, would conflict with people's shared intuitions that serious wrongdoing should be punished. I have argued in print that there could be great value in using restorative processes in cases of serious offenses, and that reformers would be better advised to drop their anti-punishment agenda in order to promote such broader use.[64]

---

[61] As we have said above, where to draw the line of demarcation between criminal and noncriminal conduct can be a matter of dispute. However, for those cases that are seen as serious wrongdoing, there is little dispute that punishment should be imposed. *Implications*, *supra* note 293, at 9.

[62] 77 U. Chi. L. Rev. at 1597 (emphasis added).

[63] See Paul H. Robinson, *The Virtues of Restorative Processes, the Vices of Restorative Justice*, 2003 Utah L. Rev. 375, 377–78, 380.

[64] *Id.* at 387.

To go beyond the broad intuition that serious wrongdoing should be punished, consider an example of a specific criminal liability rule. People overwhelmingly have a strong intuition that resulting harm matters—for example, that murder should be punished more than attempted murder and that manslaughter should be punished more than reckless endangerment, even if whether a death results is to some extent a matter of bad luck. The strength of this widely held intuition has been repeatedly documented across demographics and cultures.[65]

It is easy enough to see the rational argument against giving punishment significance to resulting harm, as every criminal law professor has used to regale his or her class. Why should an offender's liability and punishment vary because of a factor over which he has no control—the intended target happens to bend down to tie his shoe at the moment the shot is fired; the pedestrian who would have been killed by the reckless driver is running a bit late that day and gets to the crosswalk just after the reckless driver has passed.

No doubt some professors are able to persuade some members of their criminal law class that rational analysis supports ignoring resulting death. But there is a difference between persuading a student of the irrationality of the rule and getting the students to feel that justice requires that resulting death be ignored. And even if one could persuade a student on the justice point—and some minority of the particularly rational students are indeed persuaded each year—it does not follow that this victory of intellectualization over intuition could be repeated for shoe salesmen and mold-press operators, and certainly not at the rate that would change a shared societal view. Anyone who thinks this kind of reform of a core intuition is possible has not spent enough time talking with ordinary people.

If BKH were to begin a broad-based campaign to change people's intuitions about the significance of resulting death, it is likely that the vast majority of people would not take them seriously. Remember, people tend to see such intuitions as analogous to observable facts; there is no need for discussion, the fact is clear and obvious. If it is near impossible to persuade more than a minority of one's highly rational criminal law students on the justice point, it seems hard to imagine what it would take to create a consensus, or even strong support among a broad community. It should give BKH some pause that, no matter how irrational it may seem to give significance to resulting death, we are aware of no societies on earth in which people support a conception of blameworthiness that ignores it.

We think BKH are not only wrong to dismiss the difference between core and noncore issues as relevant to malleability, but also to ignore the difference between intuitional and reasoned judgments. (We suspect that most aspects of the core are intuitional judgments, but matters out from the core also may be intuitional in part.) As we discuss in *Implications*, intuitions about justice have quite different qualities than reasoned judgments about justice. The former are perceived as facts, held with great confidence, and give the holder little access to why they hold that view.

---

[65] *See* chapterh 12.A.

It would seem obvious that the distinction between intuitive and reasoned judgments about justice would be important to reformers. As to the latter, the reformer can change the judgment simply by presenting a better reasoned argument. Changing the former, the intuitive judgment, however, requires something more. To start, the reformer must get the person to think that their strongly held intuition is worth reexamining. And, even if that hurdle is cleared, it does not follow that the intuition can be changed simply by presenting a reasoned argument. Lay people are not going to disavow the significance of resulting harm simply because a law professor can demonstrate its irrationality. When BKH ignore the difference between intuitions of justice, like those at the core of agreement, and reasoned judgments about justice, like those out from the core, they do social reformers a disservice. To be effective, a reform program aimed at changing intuitions would likely be quite different than one aimed at changing reasoned judgments.

There Is No Value In Having Criminal Liability and Punishment Rules Track the Intuitions of Justice of Those Governed by the Rules. BKH appear to reject the notion that there is a cost to criminal law relying upon rules that conflict with people's judgments of justice.[66] (Note that this argument does not depend upon the existence of global agreement on any justice judgments. It simply urges that a criminal code reformer adopt rules that will maximize the code's moral credibility *with the community that it governs*. That is, it provides a workable guide for law reformers even if their community has different notions of justice than those of other communities with other criminal codes.[67])

BKH certainly had good company in their view a decade or two ago; modern crime-control doctrines have been quite indifferent about producing results that conflict with the community views of justice.[68] However, we think scholars' views are changing in light of common sense, anecdotal evidence, and empirical studies. On purely anecdotal grounds, most people would probably concede that a criminal justice system perceived as unjust will have little or no normative influence and will instead prompt resistance and subversion rather than acquiescence and assistance. The Soviet criminal justice system, for example, lacked moral credibility and probably few were surprised that it seemed unable to gain much deference in the absence of direct coercive force. This is simply common sense: Why would people defer to a system as a moral authority when it has shown itself to be so regularly indifferent to injustice?

Empirical studies have more clearly shown the connection between a criminal justice system's moral credibility and people's willingness to assist and defer to it. Studies reported in *Implications*,[69] as well as additional studies since,[70] have shown

---

[66] To our claim that criminal law's intentional conflicts with community views can undermine the law's moral credibility, producing detrimental practical consequences, BKH refers sarcastically as "these admittedly terrifying prospects." 77 U. Chi. L. Rev. at 1594.

[67] *Implications*, *supra* note 293, at 37–38.

[68] *See* chapter 7, sections A and B.

[69] *Implications*, *supra* note 293, at 26.

[70] *See* chapter 7, section C.

that by manipulating the former, one can produce a change in the latter. If BKH disagree with this view, what studies showing contrary results have they presented?

Our Reform Realism Means We Must Be Conservative Anti-Reformers. BKH claim that our views make us conservative anti-reformers.[71] We found this claim particularly bizarre. BKH have it backwards. Our program is designed to give reformers tools for more effective reform. BKH's "Punishment Realism," in contrast, offers damaging advice that can hurt reform efforts and provides excuses for keeping the status quo in the face of glaringly unjust punishment rules that reformers have long wanted to change.

The analysis set out in *Implications* suggests two recommendations to social reformers. First, it may often be unwise to invest limited reform resources on trying to change intuitions of justice that will be difficult to change, or at least not changeable within the resources and authority that the reformers have available to them. In other words, be smart and pick one's fights carefully.

Second, when developing a program to change people's intuitions of justice, it will often be a better investment to harness people's core intuitions of justice rather than fight them; such core intuitions are a power that reformers can use for their own purposes. If one wants people to take domestic violence more seriously, emphasize the violence part and de-emphasize claims that it is somehow exempt because it is domestic. If one wants people to see downloading music as more condemnable, build up the analogy to physical taking that we know to be part of the core of agreement.

It is not just these two recommendations that can help reformers, but a more sophisticated understanding of the complexities of making strategic choices, including an appreciation for the need of reformers to build and harness the moral credibility of the criminal law in order to use it to help them change norms, as we discuss in *Implications*. As an illustration, see the discussion of effective rape reform in chapter 10, section D.[72]

BKH, in contrast, stand as the protectors of the status quo. Our program challenges the dominant theory of crime control in the United States for the past several decades, one based upon intentionally and regularly doing injustice in the name of general deterrence and incapacitation, by its reliance upon doctrines like three strikes, high penalties for drug offenses, adult prosecution of juveniles, abolition or narrowing of the insanity defense, the felony-murder rule, and the use of strict liability as is discussed at length in chapter 7. We show that, in judgments of relative blameworthiness, these criminal law doctrines dramatically conflict with the community's

---

[71] BKH says: "We do feel deep concern . . . over what we take to be the politically conservative resonances with which the Punishment Naturalist has been needlessly infused. It is, simply put, extremely difficult to take in the corpus of work that the Punishment Naturalists have amassed without sensing a deep commitment on their part to the status quo—to popular retributive sensibilities as they are (or are depicted with a high degree of uniformity to be) and to laws that conform (or are depicted as conforming) to them." 77 U. Chi. L. Rev. at 1602.

[72] Paul H. Robinson, *Criminalization Tensions: Empirical Desert, Changing Norms & Rape Reform*, in Duff, Farmer, Marshall, Renzo & Tadros eds., The Structure of the Criminal Law 186–202 (2012).

intuitions of justice, and we argue that even the good utilitarian ought to reject these crime-control doctrines because of injustice they produce.

BKH's "Punishment Realism" offers a quite different reaction to these injustices. By discounting the significance of perceived injustice and by offering instead the false lure of widespread malleability about justice judgments, BKH protect the status quo of injustice. They suggest, and some scholars in fact have argued,[73] that we ought not worry about these injustices. People's blameworthiness rankings are all malleable. The lesson BKH teach is that we can keep the injustices and simply change people's views about what constitutes injustice. We should train people to think that justice is really whatever most effectively deters or whatever is necessary to incapacitate dangerous offenders, as if such changes were a realistic possibility. Distributing criminal liability so as to optimize deterrence or incapacitation might be legitimate goals, but, disconnected as they are from moral blameworthiness, they are different from doing justice. More importantly, it is not reasonable to think that one could persuade a community that such programs, rather than moral blameworthiness, are the criteria for doing justice. Yet it is these kinds of injustice-assuring programs that BKH's approach protects, by offering the false hope of malleability of community intuitions of justice.

3. CONCLUSION

Our program is to make reformers smart and effective. How BKH has transformed this into a conservative anti-reformer program is unclear. We think that reformers ought to invest their limited time and energies with due regard for the comparative difficulties and potential effectiveness of alternative strategies. Wasteful or ineffective reform programs are not to be preferred.

By contrast, what is the positive contribution that BKH's "Punishment Realism" provides to enhance the program of social reform? Is the BKH contribution the insight that the world is full of disagreements about what is justice? Who would dispute this? In fact, there is no danger anyone would think otherwise given that not long ago the common wisdom was that there existed *only* disagreements about judgments of justice. Or is the BKH contribution the insight that people's views about justice are commonly influenced by socially dependent factors?[74] That point too seems to be well known and long understood. How could it be otherwise? Or is the BKH contribution the insight that reformers should try to understand the

---

[73] *See, e.g.,* Alice Ristroph, *The New Desert*, in Robinson, Garvey & Ferzan, eds., CRIMINAL LAW CONVERSATIONS 46 (2009) ("Desert requires external values to give it content. If those values change and produce revised sentencing policies—if we decide to emphasize incapacitation over rehabilitation, for example—the assessment of how much punishment is deserved is likely to change as well.").

[74] BKH says: "Realists just want to know what those extra-legal influences are and how they manifest themselves so that they can better predict legal outcomes and manipulate policy to enhance whatever social welfare, fairness, or expressive concern they favor." 77 U. CHI. L. REV. at 1566–67.

socially dependent factors?[75] We suspect that anyone in the social reform business figured this out long ago. On the other hand, there is no harm in repeating it. The same cannot be said, however, about the other BKH advice.

Is it a positive contribution of the "Punishment Realists" to advise reformers that there is no difference between core and noncore issues, so reformers ought to give no attention to the existence of high agreement on some issues when they design their reform programs? Is it good advice that reformers should go ahead and invest in eliminating people's demand that serious wrongdoing should be punished, and invest in convincing people that resulting death should be ignored? Encouraging reformers to invest limited resources in programs likely to be ineffective does not seem like a positive contribution.

Is the positive contribution of "Punishment Realism" to advise reformers that a proposed law's potential for injustice can be ignored, and that such injustice will have no effect on the long-term success of the reform program? Common sense, history, and now empirical studies show this also to be bad advice. Reformers act at their peril when they promote liability rules that will be perceived as unjust by those governed by them.

Ultimately, it is likely that the primary contribution of BKH's "Punishment Realism" is to debunk a notion of "Punishment Naturalism" to which none of us subscribe. But now that that straw man is on the ground, one may wonder whether "Punishment Realism" has any continuing value.

[75] This seem to be the main point of Punishment Realism: that justice judgments commonly are influenced by social factors. "For the most part these extra-legal influences will move legal actors to agree, but sometimes they will move them to disagree." *Id.* at 1566.

PART } II

Should the Criminal Law Care What the Lay Person Thinks Is Just?

One may ask whether there is any reason why the criminal law should care about people's judgments of justice, or about changing them. Certainly the history of modern crime control, with its focus on general deterrence and incapacitation—what I will call "coercive crime control"—shows considerable indifference to whether the distribution of punishment provided by those programs conflicts with people's shared intuitions of justice. However, in this part, I will argue that it may be costly for the criminal law to adopt principles for assessing criminal liability and punishment that conflict with the shared judgments of justice of the community it governs. Gaining a reputation for "getting it wrong"—for regularly and intentionally relying upon rules that do injustice—can promote subversion and resistance to the system, can undermine the effective yet inexpensive normative influence of stigmatization, can reduce people's willingness to defer to the law in cases of normative ambiguity, and can subvert the criminal law's ability to shape community norms and to induce people to internalize the norms expressed in the criminal law.

Part I reviewed empirical research suggesting that lay intuitions of justice are often nuanced, specific, and universal. Is this striking picture relevant to criminal law? Should lay intuitions help shape criminal law? Do they?

Chapter 6 shows that current criminal law does indeed commonly defer to lay intuitions. For example, even though the American Law Institute's Model Penal Code was drafted in accordance with the traditional instrumentalist principles of deterrence, incapacitation, and rehabilitation, its deference to lay intuitions of justice is both explicit and implicit in its liability and punishment rules. However, as chapter 7 makes clear, modern codes still regularly adopt doctrines that seriously conflict with lay judgments of justice. Most of these are modern crime-control programs, which are well-known and highly popular with today's politicians.

Chapters 8 and 9 are a pivotal part of the book. They explain why such striking conflicts with community views of justice are so problematic. They make the case for the importance of tracking community views and show the cost—typically ignored in the past—of deviating from those views. Chapters 10 and 11 end part II with a discussion of the implications that flow from the conclusions of the previous chapters. They suggest the kinds of reforms that the criminal justice system ought to consider if it seeks to track community views, but they also discuss how reformers might change those views if necessary.

6 }

Current Law's Deference to Lay Judgments of Justice

Nothing in the criminal law theory of the past half century suggests that lay judgments of justice should be relevant to criminal law drafters. Retributivists care about desert, but only desert of the deontological sort—desert as reasoned out by moral philosophers. Crime-control utilitarians traditionally have not cared about desert, so why would they care about lay conceptions of it? Yet, as this chapter shows, current American criminal law, even that of the explicitly utilitarian Model Penal Code, often quietly defers to lay judgments of justice.[1]

Examples of such deference appear in the adoption of rules that explicitly call for decision makers to look to their own judgments of justice, as well as in rules for which the drafters must have known, and perhaps intended, that in practice the decision makers could hardly do anything other than look to their own judgments of justice. Particularly interesting here are attempts by the drafters to hide those aspects of the code that most conflict with people's shared intuitions. Why should the drafters bother hiding what the code does if they believe there are good instrumentalist reasons for the provisions? One explanation might be that the drafters implicitly understood, even if not expressed in their writings, that effective crime control required a criminal code that did not too obviously conflict with the community's shared judgments of justice. The next chapter gives a fuller account of why this should be so.

A. Rules

Consider three sorts of rules common in modern criminal codes that reflect a deference to lay judgments of justice.

---

[1] This chapter is drawn primarily from Paul H. Robinson, *Why Does the Criminal Law Care What the Layperson Thinks Is Just? Coercive Versus Normative Crime Control*, 86 Va. L. Rev. 1839, 1841–61 (2000).

1. RECOGNIZING EXCUSE DEFENSES

Every state's criminal law recognizes a variety of excuse defenses[2]—defenses given in situations where a violation of the rules of conduct may be admitted but where the defendant claims exculpation because some abnormal characteristic, circumstance, or condition excuses his violation. Social science research makes clear that such excuse defenses are part of lay persons' intuitions of justice. Legal defenses such as insanity, involuntary intoxication, immaturity, and duress have all been tested and found to be supported in some form by lay intuitions.[3]

But why should an instrumentalist code recognize excuse defenses? Any recognition of an excuse defense or mitigation undercuts the criminal law's general deterrent threat. It creates the possibility that an offender may escape liability even though he has committed the offense. Even if they do not legitimately qualify for a defense, some potential offenders will calculate that they can manipulate the system to get one nonetheless. This is true even if the defense is, in fact, difficult to abuse. It is a potential offender's perception of whether he or she can manipulate the system, not the reality, that matters. This is a significant point, especially given the evidence that people tend to exaggerate the ease of obtaining an excuse defense. The most famous example may be the persistent public overestimate of the rate at which insanity defenses are successful.[4] Thus, even if an excuse is rarely given, its recognition—the possibility that it might be given—incrementally undermines the strength of the deterrent threat.

Indeed, a general deterrence strategy might suggest just the opposite rule for excuse cases. Instead of giving a defense, the system could treat these cases as a special opportunity to demonstrate the seriousness of the deterrent threat. By punishing an insane offender, for example, the law can say, "Look! This shows how seriously we take the criminal law's prohibitions! If even the insane offender will be punished, you can be sure that you will be too."

The recognition of excuse defenses might be consistent with a strategy of special deterrence—deterring the offender at hand (rather than general deterrence which focuses on deterring others). If the nature of the excusing dysfunction prevents the potential offender from appreciating or responding to the deterrent threat, punishment would be a wasteful expenditure. Punishment will not deter one who cannot make the logical connection between criminal conduct and punishment, or deter one who cannot resist the impulse to commit the criminal conduct no matter how clear the resulting liability or how unpleasant the consequences.

---

[2] For a list of excuse defense authorities for each state, *see* Paul H. Robinson, CRIMINAL LAW DEFENSES § 171 n.1, § 173 nn.1–5, § 174 nn.1–3, § 175 nn.1–2, § 176 nn.1–3, § 177 n.1, § 82 nn.1–2, § 183 n.1, § 184 n.1, § 185 n.1, § 191 nn.1–3, § 194 nn.15–20 (1984 & Supp. 2000).

[3] *See* ch. 15; Paul H. Robinson & John M. Darley, JUSTICE, LIABILITY AND BLAME 127–55 (1995).

[4] *See* Richard Pasewerk et. al., *Opinions About the Insanity Plea*, 8 J. FORENSIC PSYCHOL. 63, 64–66 (1981); Valerie P. Hans & Dan Stater, *"Plain Crazy:" Lay Definitions of Legal Insanity*, 7 INT'L J.L. & PSYCHOL. 105, 105 (1984).

But few, if any, excuses or mitigations are justified by lawmakers on grounds of special deterrence. It is general deterrence that drives much of modern criminal law theory. Special deterrence arguments tend to be more of an afterthought. More importantly, excuse defenses generally are not formulated according to the demands of special deterrence—whether the offender is able to make the logical connection between crime and sanction. Excuse defenses typically look at the extent of the cognitive or control dysfunction that caused the person to commit this offense—a focus on blameworthiness. A duress defense is given under the Model Penal Code, for example, when "a person of reasonable firmness in [the actor's] situation would have been unable to resist" the coercion.[5] It does not look to whether the dysfunction is such as to prevent a future deterrent effect.

The recognition of excuses and mitigations is all the more puzzling from a deterrent perspective because these defenses weaken the deterrent threat at just the moment when it needs to be strengthened: when other forces are leading the offender toward the offense. Consider the first-time offender who struggles, but fails, to resist coercion to commit an offense. If acquitted based on a duress defense, the lesson the defendant learns from such an acquittal may reduce his or her motivation to resist if the situation were to reoccur. That is, the availability of the excuse defense undermines the disincentive to commit a crime in just those situations in which a determined special deterrence strategy would increase it.

From the view of incapacitation and rehabilitation strategies, the recognition of excuse defenses is even more inexplicable. Excuse defenses are allowed in cases where it has been conclusively demonstrated that some special condition, circumstance, or characteristic has caused the offender to commit an offense. That puts the offender in a group that the criminal justice system should have a great interest in detaining for treatment or incapacitation. At the very least, legal custody would give an opportunity to investigate fully the likelihood of recurrence of the offense, or of a similar offense, and would provide the legal jurisdiction for a probationary period and supervised release. Especially when the condition causing the offense continues to exist—as is common with insanity and immaturity, for example—it seems odd indeed for an instrumentalist code to release such an offender.

Civil commitment mechanisms have been created to recapture some of these offenders acquitted under one of these excuses—insanity. But if the criminal justice system is in the business of coercive crime control, why should it have to resort to civil commitment to protect the public from those who have already committed a criminal offense?

The recognition of excuse defenses is odd for another reason. Incapacitation and rehabilitation crime-control strategies are commonly plagued with behavioral science's limited ability to predict future conduct. Law enforcement is hesitant to

[5] Model Penal Code § 2.09(1) (duress).

incapacitate when so many predictions of future criminality are wrong. But excuse cases are a select group for which this weakness is of less concern. By definition, these are cases where the excusing circumstance, condition, or characteristic has already led to criminal conduct, providing a ground to justify governmental intrusion on liberty at least sufficient to test for continuing dangerousness.

2. FAILING TO TAKE ACCOUNT OF FACTORS RELEVANT TO COERCIVE CRIME-CONTROL PRINCIPLES

Not only does current law take account of factors that a purely coercive crime-control system should ignore, such as an offender's perceived blamelessness, it also fails to take account of factors that a purely coercive system should treat as central. Consider, for example, the difficulty that law enforcement officials face in capturing an offender. The effect of a deterrent threat is a product of both the severity of the threatened punishment and the likelihood of its imposition after a violation. In other words, the likelihood of detection and capture is an important variable in the deterrence formula. This means that offenses for which arrest rates are low—for example, burglary and motor vehicle theft—ought to be graded more severely than they would be otherwise to compensate for their low detection rates. Perhaps offenses for which the difficulty in detection ranges widely from case to case ought to have a grading factor in the code that adjusts the punishment in each case accordingly. Thus, the offender who works hard at and creates a significant possibility of avoiding detection ought to suffer greater punishment when captured.

Yet, likelihood of capture appears to play essentially no part in current criminal law. Difficulty of detection is rarely if ever used as a grading factor for offenses. Nor is difficulty of detection commonly taken into account by criminal code drafters in initially setting the grade of an offense. Why not?

The same kind of omission is seen in relation to the crime-control mechanisms of incapacitation and rehabilitation. There is strong social science evidence to support the importance of such things as prior employment, age, and family situation, for example, in predicting future criminality. Yet, there is no indication that such factors are used either as a grading factor or in initially setting the grade of an offense.[6] Why does criminal law not include these and other predictors of future criminality as explicit factors in defining and grading offenses?

Such factors might be quietly taken into account by some sentencing judges in highly discretionary sentencing systems, but these factors have not made the

---

[6] The Model Penal Code never uses employment history as a factor in the grading of an offense, although it is used as a factor in determining appropriate sentencing. *See, e.g.,* Model Penal Code § 7.07(3). Nor is age a factor when grading an offense, although it is a factor at the sentencing stage. *See, e.g., id.* at § 7.03(1) (prohibiting sentencing someone under the age of 21 as a "persistent offender whose commitment for an extended term is necessary for protection of the public"). *See also id.* § 210.6(1)(d) (excluding a death sentence for those under 18 years of age).

transition to the articulated sentencing guideline systems.[7] Indeed, the legislation governing the United States Sentencing Commission guidelines expressly prohibits the use of those factors, as well as others that have obvious relevance to coercive crime-control mechanisms.[8] If such factors are highly relevant in predicting future criminality, why are they not included in the guideline calculations?

The answer, of course, is the same as the answer to the question of why difficulty in detection is not taken into account despite its centrality to effective deterrence: The factors relevant to future criminality are ignored because lay persons do not see them as relevant to justice. Some reliance upon them may exist in a purely discretionary system, where such reliance is not easily or clearly discernible. In an articulated sentencing guideline system, however, there is too much danger that use of such factors would become known and would damage the system's reputation for doing justice among lay persons.

3. CREATING A FALSE IMPRESSION THAT RESULTING HARM IS SIGNIFICANT BY INCLUDING RESULT ELEMENTS IN OFFENSE DEFINITIONS

To illustrate more fully attempts by code drafters to use but hide their reliance on coercive crime-control factors that are inconsistent with lay judgments of justice, consider one last example. When a person engages in conduct that intends or risks causing a prohibited result, it is of limited relevance for coercive crime-control purposes whether the result comes about as hoped or risked or whether it luckily does not. A person who shoots at another in an attempt to kill is no less dangerous because the intended victim bends down to tie a shoe and is spared. Nor is the need to deter such conduct any less pressing. Similarly, a person who dumps toxic chemicals near a school yard is no less dangerous nor the conduct any less in need of deterrence if the dumping is discovered before any child is poisoned. Because the coercive crime-control mechanisms are forward looking—attempting to avoid future crime—the fortuitous results in the case at hand are of little importance; only the offender's conduct and state of mind matter. Why does current law include result elements in offense definitions? Why not just criminalize specific conduct committed with a specified state of mind—conduct by which one intends to cause a prohibited harm or risk?

Again, the answer is that lay persons feel strongly that resulting harm is important in assessing just punishment.[9] Social science research confirms that lay persons

---

[7] Indeed, when it established the United States Sentencing Commission, Congress explicitly stated its opinion that sentencing guidelines should not take such factors into account: "[t]he Commission shall assure that the guidelines and policy statements, in recommending a term of imprisonment or length of a term of imprisonment, reflect the general inappropriateness of considering the education, vocational skills, employment record, family ties and responsibilities, and community ties of the defendant." 28 U.S.C. § 994(e) (1999).

[8] *See id.*

[9] *See, e.g.*, chapter 16, section D.

have a strong intuition that an unsuccessful killing should be punished at a lower level than a successful killing—as only attempted murder.[10] Toxic dumping ought to be punished at a lower level when no harm occurs than when children are actually injured or killed—as only endangerment or as risking catastrophe.[11] Resulting harm is highly significant to lay persons, who think it ought to aggravate liability and punishment.

Thus, the Model Penal Code drafters faced a difficult situation: a strongly held lay intuition in direct conflict with effective coercive crime control. People would never tolerate a criminal code that defined the substantive offense of rape or arson or theft as simply doing an act with the intention to commit rape, arson, or theft. People would insist that their criminal code distinguish the "real" offense—an actual rape, arson, or theft—from a mere attempt. To ignore whether a forced intercourse did occur, whether a person's house was burned, or whether a person's property was taken, might be seen as trivializing the victim's suffering.

In response to this, the drafters came up with a rather clever solution. They defined full substantive offenses and appropriately distinguished them from inchoate offenses. By including resulting harm in the definitions of substantive offenses, the Model Code could look like the code people expected, with the offenses of rape, arson, theft, and a host of others requiring proof of the prohibited harm. However, in a separate provision governing the grading of inchoate offenses, the drafters provided that, with few exceptions, the completed offense and the inchoate offense were to have the same punishment grade.[12]

Thus, while rape and attempted rape are distinct offenses in name, they are the same offense in effect. The Code's definition of rape requires intercourse,[13] just as its definition of arson requires a building be set on fire or exploded,[14] and its definition of theft requires an unconsented-to taking.[15] In fact, these resulting harm requirements are irrelevant to liability. If any are missing, the offender is liable "only" for attempt, but that attempt carries a grade of liability identical to the full offense. The drafters achieved their coercive crime-control distribution principle, but preserved the appearance of a code that seems to track shared lay intuitions.

Of course, there is always the danger that the illusion will be dispelled. If the deception is discovered, there is the added danger that the public may become cynical, wondering what other deceptions are as yet unrevealed. Once such cynicism sets in, a criminal law may have difficulty gaining moral credibility even if it does in fact track lay intuitions of justice. Perhaps because of these dangers to a code's

---

[10] *See id.* at 14–28, 181–89.

[11] *See id.*

[12] See Model Penal Code § 5.05(1). The one exception maintained the traditional distinction between inchoate and completed offenses for first degree felonies, essentially murder and aggravated kidnapping. *See id.*

[13] *See id.* § 213.1(1).

[14] *See id.* § 220.1(1).

[15] *See id.* § 223.2.

moral credibility, or perhaps because not all state code drafters share the Model Penal Code drafters' commitment to coercive crime-control strategies in place of doing justice, the Model Penal Code's attempt grading scheme has been frequently (but not always[16]) rejected, even by state codes that otherwise are heavily influenced by the Model Code.[17]

The conclusion to be drawn from each of these three kinds of examples is the same: even highly instrumentalist criminal code drafters are careful to construct a criminal law that at least appears to be not too inconsistent with lay judgments of justice. The next section's examination of the standards used in doctrinal formulations reinforces this conclusion.

B. Standards

Precision and specificity would seem to be obvious virtues in a criminal code designed to deter future crime. Vagueness in the definition of conduct rules (the rules defining what conduct is prohibited, or permitted or required) reduces the possibility of compliance. Potential offenders may not understand what conduct is prohibited and may engage in conduct that they otherwise would avoid if the prohibition were clear.

Similarly, vagueness in adjudication rules (rules that determine what rule violations by what kind of offenders will be given what kind of liability) creates the possibility, and therefore creates the hope among potential offenders, that violators will escape liability. A vague defense provision creates the possibility of a defense beyond that intended by the drafters. A vague liability provision, such as that governing complicity or causation, creates the possibility of more narrow liability than that intended by the drafters.

Therefore, one would think that vagueness should be avoided in an instrumentalist criminal code. Vagueness seems all the more problematic when it arises from a doctrinal formulation that defers to reliance upon lay intuitions of justice. This is not just random vagueness, the instrumentalist might worry, but intractable vagueness. It is a vagueness that cannot be remedied by artful judicial construction but must be left vague.

---

[16] The following jurisdictions have adopted the Model Penal Code's formulation of attempt grading: Connecticut, Delaware, Indiana, Mississippi, New Jersey, New Hampshire, North Dakota, and Pennsylvania. An additional five jurisdictions have gone beyond the code's formulation by not exempting first degree felonies: Delaware, Hawaii, Maryland, Montana, and Wyoming. *See* Paul H. Robinson, *The Role of Harm and Evil in Criminal Law: A Study of Legislative Deception?*, 5 J. CONTEMP. LEGAL ISSUES 299, 320 n.67 (1994).

[17] The following jurisdictions have codes heavily influenced by the Model Penal Code but have refused to adopt the Code's inchoate grading provision: Alabama, Alaska, Arizona, Arkansas, California, Colorado, Florida, Georgia, Idaho, Illinois, Kansas, Kentucky, Louisiana, Maine, Michigan, Minnesota, Missouri, Nebraska, Nevada, New Mexico, New York, Ohio, Oklahoma, Oregon, Puerto Rico, South Dakota, Tennessee, Texas, Utah, Washington, and Wisconsin. *See id.* at 321 n.69.

Formulating criminal law rules in a way that defers to lay intuitions also is problematic for coercive crime control because available social science data suggests that lay intuitions in assigning criminal liability and punishment do not look to the factors that are central to deterrence, incapacitation, and rehabilitation—but look instead to desert, as is discussed in chapter 8, section D.3.

Thus, a criminal code designed to advance the mechanisms of coercive crime control would have every reason to actively avoid the use of vague or imprecise standards that have the decision maker defer to lay intuitions of justice. But consider the following provisions common in American criminal codes, even the highly instrumentalist and tightly drafted Model Penal Code.

1. EXPLICIT RELIANCE UPON LAY JUDGMENTS OF JUSTICE

It is not uncommon for a code to incorporate explicitly within its liability assessment doctrines a call for the jury to look to their own intuitive notions of justice. The Model Penal Code defines an adequate causal connection, for example, as one that "is not too remote or accidental in its occurrence *to have a [just] bearing on the actor's liability or on the gravity of his offense*."[18] Thus, the juror is explicitly left to look to her own sense of what should have a "[just] bearing on the actor's liability." Similarly, a violation of the rules of conduct is to be exempt from liability if it is "too trivial *to warrant the condemnation of conviction*."[19] To apply this standard, the juror must look to her own sense of what warrants the condemnation of criminal conviction. There is no source of guidance in applying these provisions other than one's own judgment of justice or what deserves condemnation.

2. VAGUE STANDARDS

Other provisions use standards so open that they inevitably invite a juror to look to her own intuitions of justice. For example, it is an offense if one "fails to take reasonable measures" to control or report a fire,[20] to return lost property,[21] or to prevent a catastrophe.[22] The juror must divine what are "reasonable measures," and therefore noncriminal; and what are not, and therefore criminal. It is an offense to make "unreasonable noise"[23] or to treat a corpse in such a way that "outrages ordinary family sensibilities."[24] A reckless homicide is murder, and an assault is aggravated assault if it "manifest[s] extreme indifference to the value of human life."[25] The juror must decide how much indifference is "extreme" and what will

[18] Model Penal Code § 2.03(2)(b), (3)(b) (alteration in original) (emphasis added).

[19] *Id.* at § 2.12(2) (emphasis added).

[20] *See id.* at § 220.1(3).

[21] *See id.* at § 223.5.

[22] *See id.* at § 220.2(3).

[23] *Id.* at § 250.2(1)(b).

[24] *Id.* at § 250.10.

[25] *Id.* at §§ 210.2, 211.1(2)(a).

manifest such. Similarly, what would otherwise be murder is only manslaughter if "there is a reasonable explanation or excuse" for a defendant's "extreme emotional disturbance."[26]

Indeed, every offense that requires recklessness—the default culpability level in the code[27]—or requires negligence or uses the term "reasonable" (which is defined as nonreckless and nonnegligent[28]) employs such a vague standard. Both recklessness and negligence are defined to require a finding that the actor disregarded, or should have been aware of, respectively, "a substantial and unjustifiable risk" that the offense elements exist or will result.[29] The disregard or unawareness must be "a gross deviation from the standard of [conduct/care] that a [law-abiding/reasonable] person would observe."[30] It is the juror who must decide whether the risk was "substantial" or "justifiable" and whether the defendant's disregard/unawareness of the risk was "a gross deviation" from what the law-abiding/reasonable person would have done. Ultimately, this is not far from asking the juror to apply her own intuitions of justice in assessing liability.

Such an invitation also commonly appears in the Code's general liability provisions. For example, conduct constitutes an attempt when it has gone so far as to take "a *substantial step*" toward commission of the offense.[31] The juror must decide in each case when mere (noncriminal) preparation has become a criminal attempt. Similarly, a violation is to be exempted if it is "within a customary license or tolerance"[32] or if there exist "such . . . extenuations that it cannot reasonably be regarded as envisaged by the legislature in forbidding the offense."[33] It is for the decision maker to decide what must have been "reasonably envisaged" and what violations are generally tolerated.

Open-ended provisions are even more common in code provisions assessing whether a violation is to be exculpated. For example, an offense is to be exculpated if "the harm or evil sought to be avoided by such conduct is greater than that sought to be prevented" by the offense.[34] The juror must determine the interests in conflict, give value to each, and then determine their relative value. A duress defense is given if "a person of reasonable firmness in [the actor's] situation would have been unable to resist [the coercion]."[35] The juror must decide whether the amount of coercion the defendant was subjected to would have coerced a person of "reasonable firmness." Another provision of the Model Code excuses otherwise criminal behavior if it results from "*reasonable* reliance upon an official statement of the law."[36] The juror

---

26 *Id.* at § 210.3(1)(b) (emphasis added).

27 *See id.* at § 2.02(3).

28 *See id.* at § 1.13(16).

29 *Id.* at § 2.02(2)(c), (d) (emphasis added).

30 *Id.* at § 2.02(2)(c), (d).

31 *Id.* at § 5.01(1)(c) (emphasis added).

32 *Id.* at § 2.12(1).

33 *Id.* at § 2.12(3).

34 *Id.* at § 3.02(1)(a).

35 *Id.* at § 2.09(1).

36 *Id.* at § 2.04(3)(b) (emphasis added).

must intuit what reliance exculpates and what does not. An accomplice can escape liability if he "makes *proper effort* to prevent the commission of the offense."[37] The bounds of the withdrawal defense are then for the juror to determine, with reference to her own assessment of what would be "proper" in the situation.

Another well-known example is found in the formulations of the insanity defense. Research suggests that it does not matter which of the common insanity formulations is used: the ALI's "lacks substantial capacity"[38] or M'Naghten's "defect[s] of reason" or "insane impulse controlling their will or judgment."[39] The liability result in any given case will be the same under all formulations. These results make sense if one concludes that the formulations are all so open ended that they simply invite the juror or study participant to rely upon her own intuitions of justice; that is, her own intuitions of whether a person with that dysfunction in that situation could reasonably have been expected to have avoided committing that offense.

Such a liability assessment scheme may be exactly what one would hope for if one were in the business of expressing community notions of justice. But, for a criminal law that seeks to engage the mechanisms of deterrence, incapacitation, and rehabilitation, such deference to lay intuitions of justice is odd indeed.

3. RULES REQUIRING JURY SPECULATION

Another way in which even the Model Penal Code incorporates lay intuitions of justice is through reliance on factual issues that cannot be resolved other than through jury speculation. Such speculation inevitably invites the juror to take account of his or her own intuitions of justice for how the case should be resolved. When a juror is required to speculate about a fact, and the juror believes the criminal justice system to be in the business of doing justice, logic suggests that the juror is more likely to reach a factual conclusion legally consistent with the perceived "proper" result in the case.

Most common among the issues upon which a jury must speculate are those regarding a defendant's state of mind at the time of the offense. Did he "believe or hope" that a result would occur?[40] Or, was he just "practically certain that" the result would occur?[41] Did he believe that such force was "immediately necessary for the purpose of protecting himself"?[42]

Frequently the juror is asked to determine a purely hypothetical state. Would the actor "have been aware of the risk had he been sober"?[43] At other times, the juror is asked to speculate about the state of mind of persons other than the defendant.

---

[37] *Id.* at § 2.06(6)(c)(ii) (emphasis added).

[38] *Id.* at § 4.01(1).

[39] Parsons v. State, 2 So. 854, 857, 863 (Ala. 1887).

[40] Model Penal Code § 2.02(2)(a)(ii).

[41] *Id.* at § 2.02(2)(b)(ii).

[42] *Id.* at § 3.04(1).

[43] *Id.* at § 2.08(2).

Would "a person of reasonable firmness"[44] have been coerced to commit the offense? Would a person "other than [one] who [is] ready to commit [the offense]"[45] have been induced by the police conduct? Sometimes the jury is asked to speculate about what the defendant thought about what another person thought. Did the defendant think the other person was acting under "a false impression"[46] about the nature of the property?

The jury is even asked to guess what the defendant thought about what another person would have thought in a hypothetical situation. Did he "believ[e] that the owner, if present, would have consented"[47] to the taking if he had been asked? Did the defendant believe the owner "would have licensed him"[48] to enter had he been asked before the trespass?

It seems highly likely that a juror will draw upon his or her own life experience in determining what the defendant or the other person would have thought or what the defendant thought about what the other person thought when given such speculative tasks. The juror's conclusion will also be shaped in some significant part by the juror's overall sense of how the case should come out. From the same objective facts, a juror may see more charitable interpretations of a defendant's beliefs and motivations if the juror is inclined against liability. Whether a defendant actually believed that "the force used was immediately necessary for the purpose of protecting [herself]"[49] may end up being a function of whether the juror thinks the defendant ultimately should be criminally liable for what she did. Why should an instrumentalist coercive crime-control code use rules that call for such factual speculation?

The invited speculation is all the more an invitation to an open-ended "justice" judgment because in most instances the issue put to the jury is not simply whether the defendant "believed" a certain fact—whether the owner would have, for example, given consent had she been asked—but whether the defendant "reasonably believed" a certain fact.[50] A belief is "reasonable" if it is "not reckless or negligent,"[51] that is, if it does not satisfy the definition of negligence.[52] In the process of determining, as that definition requires, whether a defendant "should [have been] aware of a substantial and unjustifiable risk" of the offense elements, and whether the risk was "of such a nature and degree that the actor's failure to perceive it, considering the nature and purpose of his conduct and the circumstances known to him, involves a gross deviation from the standard of care," using as the standard "the standard of

---

44 *Id.* at § 2.09(1) (duress).

45 *Id.* at § 2.13(1)(b) (entrapment).

46 *Id.* at §§ 223.3(1), (3).

47 *Id.* at § 223.1(3)(c).

48 *Id.* at § 221.2(3)(c).

49 *Id.* at § 3.04(1).

50 *See id.* at §§ 223.3(1), (3); *see also id.* at § 221.2(3)(c).

51 *Id.* at § 1.13(16).

52 *Id.* at § 2.02(2)(d).

care that a reasonable person would observe in the actor's situation," the jury can hardly do anything but consult their own lay intuitions of justice.

The point here is not to criticize these statutory formulations. On the contrary, a criminal law that seeks to track society's complex notions of justice must ask the jury to engage in such speculations on points where those intuitions are complex. The point here is to see that such inquiries are in fact explainable only by the apparent quest for justice as the community sees it, for they would be counterproductive if offered as a determined system of coercive crime control.

C. Explanations for Deference to Lay Judgments of Justice

One might argue that reliance upon lay judgments of justice is not inconsistent with the mechanisms of deterrence, incapacitation, and rehabilitation because people's intuitions naturally track the demands of these mechanisms. That is, lay persons naturally understand the demands of these crime-control mechanisms and naturally think of the imposition of criminal liability as the means for advancing these mechanisms. Certainly this is true of many economists and law professors; perhaps it is true of lay persons as well. If this were true, it might undercut the claim that doctrinal standards inviting the use of lay judgments are inconsistent with the coercive strategies. Such reliance upon lay judgments, it could be argued, is not deference to lay intuitions of justice, but rather to lay intuitions that naturally take account of deterrence, incapacitation, and rehabilitation.

The available evidence does not support this claim. Lay persons do not intuitively apply principles of deterrence, incapacitation, and rehabilitation when they assess criminal liability and punishment. To the contrary, the studies show that lay assessments of criminal liability and punishment conflict with, rather than track, coercive crime-control strategies. Chapter 8, section D.3 reviews the studies on this point, but some evidence of this has already been noted above. Lay intuitions assign liability and punishment in ways that systematically conflict with the rules of liability and punishment that coercive crime-control strategies would follow. For example, lay intuitions support the recognition of excuse defenses[53] and take account of resulting harm[54] but do not support taking into account the difficulty in detection.[55]

Another example from above is the Model Code drafters' treatment of attempt grading, where they work to obscure their use of coercive strategies that conflict with strong lay intuitions that resulting harm is significant. If the lay audience took the coercive crime-control view, which would make resulting harm insignificant, there would be no need to obscure the coercive strategy. Criminal codes could

---

[53] *See, e.g.*, ch. 15.

[54] *See* ch. 16.C.

[55] *See, e.g.*, Kevin M. Carlsmith, John M. Darby, & Paul H. Robinson, *Why Do We Punish? Deterrence and Just Deserts as Motives for Punishment*, 83 J. PERS. & SOC. PSYCH. 284 (2002).

openly declare the insignificance of resulting harm, by defining offenses solely in terms of conduct with a particular state of mind, without reference to resulting harm. Yet no criminal code takes this approach.

A more plausible explanation for the deference to lay intuitions of justice is that the drafters understood, although they did not make it explicit, that a criminal code could not openly conflict with the community's shared intuitions of justice without losing moral credibility with the community it governs, and that such a loss of credibility would undermine the criminal law's crime-control power. This will be discussed further in chapter 8.

7}

Current Law's Conflicts with Lay Judgments of Justice

While the Model Penal Code drafters were careful not to advertise their move toward coercive crime-control doctrines that did not track lay notions of justice, as the previous chapter shows, the intervening 50 years have seen a more public shift to criminal law doctrines openly violating community notions of justice in pursuit of modern crime control. This chapter catalogues many of these doctrines, showing with empirical studies just how seriously they conflict with community notions, a conflict that can have serious repercussions, as the next chapter explains.[1]

Section A considers the many ways in which current law systematically deviates from community views in a host of small ways. (Part III of the book gives dozens of other examples of such deviations found within a wide variety of specific doctrines.) Section B examines seven popular crime-control doctrines, most of which have been introduced or expanded since the Model Penal Code-based codifications of the 1960s and '70s. A recent study reviewed in section C shows just how seriously these popular doctrines conflict with community views. Section D will address how such conflicts were able to arise in a democratic society.

A. Common and Recurring Minor Conflicts

Current criminal law systematically conflicts with community notions of justice in many subtle ways. To give one example of a subtle difference, consider the law's rules governing the liability of an accomplice to crime, as compared to the community's views.

As you see in the graphic, the extent of the accomplice's assistance increases along the horizontal axis; the extent of criminal liability increases along the vertical axis. The legal rules provide full liability for the object offense as soon as the extent of assistance meets the minimum legal requirements—see the vertical line in the middle of the graphic and the horizontal line at the top. Lay persons' views,

[1] Sections B through D of this chapter are drawn primarily from Paul H. Robinson, Geoffrey P. Goodwin, & Michael D. Reisig, *The Disutility of Injustice*, 85 N.Y.U. L. Rev. 1940, 1949–1995 (2010).

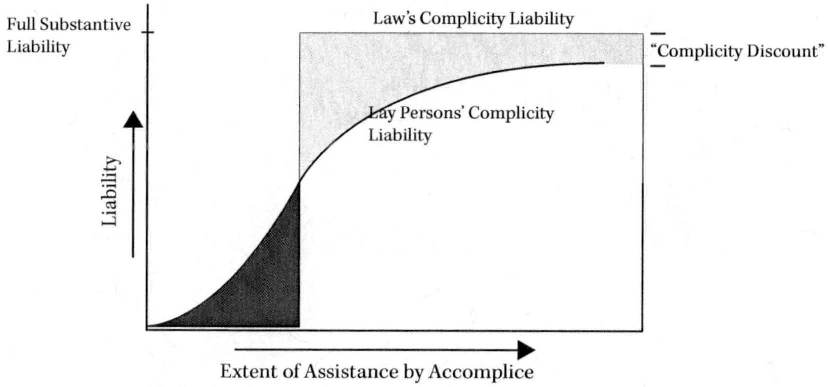

FIGURE 7. Lay Person versus Law's Liability Assessment for Complicity

in contrast, gradually increase the degree of liability according to the extent of assistance provided—see the curved line. Note that this curved line never reaches the level of full liability but tops out at some amount less than this—what might be called the "complicity discount." Lay persons' intuitions of justice would punish the actual perpetrator more than the accomplice; in contrast, the formal legal rules provide the same degree of liability.

An analogous situation exists for setting the liability for inchoate offenses, such as attempt. The law in some states punishes the attempt the same as the object offense, and applies this full liability as soon as the offender has met the minimum requirements for attempt liability. People, in contrast, increase the amount of punishment for attempt gradually as the offender comes closer to completing the offense, but attempt liability never reaches the full level of liability for the offense. A more in-depth look at the conflict between community views and criminal law doctrine is presented in part III of this book.

Happily for the criminal law, minor subtle discrepancies between the legal rule and the community's views are not likely to have a serious effect in undermining the law's moral credibility. The law is seen as providing a rough approximation of what people see as just, and that may well be tolerated as adequate. However, there are other criminal law rules that more seriously conflict with the community's judgments of justice, in ways that can seriously undermine the criminal justice system's moral credibility with the community when the pattern of conflicts become known.

B. Modern Coercive Crime-Control Rules in Conflict with Desert

Described below are seven of the most common and politically popular criminal justice doctrines. They are expressly based upon instrumentalist coercive crime-control strategies—usually those of general deterrence and incapacitation. The case examples given to illustrate each doctrine are not necessarily the statistically most common application of each doctrine, but neither are they an aberrant application by a rogue judge. Each instance is a sound application that was expected and intended by the terms of the doctrine, and many, if not most, have been reviewed and approved on appeal—some by the United States Supreme Court. These are the legal doctrines for which people's judgments of justice are tested in the study reported in part C.

1. THREE STRIKES AND OTHER HABITUAL OFFENDER STATUTES

The case of William James Rummel is not unusual. In 1964, the 21-year-old Texan used his employer's credit card to pay $80 for four new tires without permission. He later pled guilty to felony fraud. In 1969, Rummel forged a check for $28.36 to pay rent at a hotel, another felony. Over a course of years, Rummel was convicted of similar frauds over four more times. On a hot August day in 1972, Rummel entered a bar in San Antonio and noticed that the air conditioner was broken. He told the bar's owner that the unit needed a new compressor and offered to fix it for free if the owner would pay for the necessary part. The owner gave him $120.75 for the compressor, but Rummel never returned to the bar. After the owner decided to press charges, Rummel was arrested.[2] Rummel was guilty of a felony theft,[3] which typically would receive a sentence of 2 to 10 years.[4] However, because this was Rummel's third felony conviction, he was charged under a Texas recidivism statute and received a sentence of life imprisonment.[5] His sentence was affirmed by the United States Court of Appeals and by the U.S. Supreme Court.[6]

In another case, 59-year-old Charles Almond became frustrated by the constant arguing of his two adult sons (who still lived at home) over which television program to watch. He picked up a .22 caliber revolver that his oldest son had left on the table and shot out the television's screen. Thirty years earlier, Almond had twice been convicted of burglarizing an unoccupied building, and 25 years earlier, he was convicted of throwing "a missile" (a rock) at an automobile driven by his father-in-law. On another occasion, he was convicted for stealing electricity. Because of Almond's decades-old felony convictions, a sentence of 15 years was imposed in the television-shooting case, for "possession of a firearm as a felon" combined with a "career offender" statute.[7]

---

[2] Paul H. Robinson, Criminal Law Case Studies 28 (4th ed. 2010).

[3] Paul H. Robinson, Would You Convict? Seventeen Cases that Challenged the Law 32 (New York University Press 1999) [hereafter Robinson, Would You Convict].

[4] *Id.* at 29.

[5] *Id.* at 32. Under the controlling Texas law, Rummel would have been eligible for parole after serving 12 years of his sentence with good behavior. Tex. Code Crim. Pro. Ann. art. 42.12 §15(a) (Vernon 1974) (amended 2009).

[6] Rummel v. Estelle, 445 U.S. 263, 285 (1980); Rummel v. Estelle, 587 F.2d 651, 654 (5th Cir. 1978). For more details on the *Rummel* case, *see* Robinson, Would You Convict, *supra* note 386, at 22.

[7] Paul H. Robinson & Michael T. Cahill, Law Without Justice: Why Criminal Law Doesn't Give People What They Deserve 132–33 (Oxford 2005) [hereafter Robinson & Cahill, Law Without Justice].

Such "three strikes" and other habitual offender legislation commonly impose long prison terms on offenders who have committed previous crimes. The underlying rationale for these statutes is typically incapacitation.[8] Advocates of such statutes reason that the offender's past recidivism shows that he cannot be deterred from future crime, and that incapacitation may be the most effective means of preventing future offenses.[9]

Similar habitual offender statutes, which became common in the 1990s,[10] typically set high mandatory sentences for felonies committed after the offender has been convicted of two prior felonies. The most common form taken by such statutes (used in 15 jurisdictions) requires the two previous felonies to be of a violent nature.[11] Another 10 jurisdictions allow certain other felonies to be included, such as drug trafficking violations.[12] Other jurisdictions have habitual offender statutes other than the famous "three strikes" formulation.[13]

2. DRUG OFFENSE PENALTIES

In another not-unusual case, Anthony Papa was asked by a bowling partner to deliver an envelope containing cocaine to another nearby town in exchange for $500. The courier who gave him the envelope is an undercover drug enforcement officer, and Papa was arrested when he delivered the envelope, which contained 4.5 ounces of cocaine. Under the controlling statute, the court imposed the required sentence of 15 years to life.[14]

Similarly, in the case of *Harmelin v. Michigan*, the subject was driving through Detroit in the early morning when he made an illegal U-turn through a red light. After Harmelin was pulled over and arrested for marijuana possession, a police search uncovered 672 grams of cocaine in the car's trunk—an amount approximately

---

[8] *See* authorities and examples collected at Paul H. Robinson, *Punishing Dangerousness: Cloaking Preventative Detention as Criminal Justice*, 114 HARV. L. REV. 1429, n.2 (2001). Might be easier to just list them here. Or at least some representative examples.

[9] *Id.* at 1429 n.7.

[10] *See* Nat'l Conference of State Legislators, "Three Strikes" Sentencing Laws 24 (1999) (noting that between 1993 and 1999, 24 states and the federal government enacted "three strikes" laws and that nearly all states have some type of sentence enhancement applicable to habitual offenders).

[11] Arkansas, Colorado, Connecticut, Florida, Kansas, Maryland (requires 4 strikes), Montana, New Jersey, New Mexico, North Carolina, Pennsylvania, Tennessee, Vermont, Virginia, Wisconsin. *See* John Clark, James Austin & D. Alan Henry, NATIONAL INSTITUTE OF JUSTICE, "THREE STRIKES AND YOU'RE OUT": A REVIEW OF STATE LEGISLATION 7–13 (1997), *available at* http://www.ncjrs.gov/pdffiles/165369.pdf.

[12] California, Georgia (2 strikes for violent felonies, 4 strikes for others), Indiana, Louisiana, Nevada, North Dakota (2 strikes), South Carolina (2 strikes), United States (only 1 prior conviction can be drug related, other must be violent), Utah, Washington. *See* 18 U.S.C. §3559(c) (2006); *Id.* at 7–13.

[13] Alabama, Alaska, Arizona, Delaware, District of Columbia, Hawaii, Idaho, Illinois, Iowa, Kentucky, Maine, Massachusetts, Michigan, Minnesota, Mississippi, Missouri, Nebraska, New Hampshire, New York, Ohio, Oklahoma, Oregon, Rhode Island, South Dakota, Texas, West Virginia, Wyoming. *See* Clark et al., *supra* note 394, at 7–13.

[14] *See* Rebecca Tuhus-Dubrow, *Talking With Anthony Papa*, THE NATION, Dec. 9, 2004, *available at* http://www.thenation.com/doc/20041227/tuhusdubrow. Papa serves 12 years of his sentence before being granted clemency.

equal in size to one and a half soda cans. Harmelin, who had no prior police record, was convicted under a Michigan drug statute and was sentenced to a mandatory term of life in prison without the possibility of parole—a sentence that the U.S. Supreme Court upheld as constitutional and not in violation of the Eighth Amendment prohibition of cruel and unusual punishments.[15]

In *United States v. Prince*, Leroy Prince rented a room from Sydney Griffith, owner of a nearby furniture store. Prince frequently helped move furniture from the house to Griffith's business. In exchange, Griffith agreed to provide furniture when Prince moved out of his rented room into an apartment. On one occasion, at Griffith's request, Prince helped unload boxes at the house where Prince rented a room. He smelled marijuana during the unloading and confirmed its presence by partially opening a box. He continued to help with the unloading but insisted that the marijuana boxes be stored in a place other than the house where he lives. He helped move the boxes to the basement of a nearby grocery store. Customs inspectors later seized 47 boxes, containing a total of 1,169 kilograms of marijuana. After being given downward adjustments under the U.S. Sentencing Guidelines due to his minor role in the offense, his lack of knowledge of the drug's presence beforehand, and his guilty plea, he was sentenced to five years imprisonment without the possibility of early release.[16]

Though they had traditionally been governed only by state law, the past several decades have seen increasing federal jurisdiction over drug-related crimes.[17] In an attempt to increase deterrent effects, federal sentencing for drug crimes has become quite harsh. The average federal sentence for drug-related crimes in 2005 was 85.7 months. If marijuana-related crimes are removed, that average rises to 98.9 months. As a point of comparison, the average federal sentence for all violent crimes is 95.2 months. Homicide has an average sentence of 118.3 months—less than 20 percent higher than for non-marijuana drug offenses.[18] Harsher federal penalties mean that an ever-increasing number of cases that could be brought in state courts are being prosecuted in federal court.[19]

3. ADULT PROSECUTION OF JUVENILES

It is no longer unusual for prosecutors to try to punish juveniles as adults, even with long prison terms.[20] Nathaniel Brazill, 13 years old, was upset about being suspended from school for 10 days, just before summer vacation, for throwing water balloons. He returned to the middle school to say goodbye to friends. When told

---

[15] Harmelin v. Michigan, 501 U.S. 957, 995–96 (1991).

[16] U.S. v. Prince, 110 F.3d 921, 926 (2d Cir. 1997).

[17] *See, e.g.*, Edward L. Glaeser et al., *What Do Prosecutors Maximize? An Analysis of the Federalization of Drug Crimes*, 2 Am. L. & Econ. Rev. 259 (2000).

[18] All sentencing statistics are taken from U.S. Department of Justice, Bureau of Justice Statistics, Sourcebook of Criminal Justice Statistics tbl. 5.25.2005 (2005), *available at* http://www.albany.edu/sourcebook/pdf/t5252005.pdf.

[19] *See* Glaeser et al., *supra* note 400, at 260.

[20] *See infra* notes [26–30].

by a seventh grade teacher (with whom he had a good relationship) that he had to leave, he pulled out a pistol and pointed it at him. The gun discharged, hitting the teacher in the head and killing him. After being tried and convicted as an adult, he was sentenced to 28 years in prison without the possibility of parole.[21]

In another case, Zachary Eggers, a 16-year-old, was given two natural life terms for killing his parents.[22] Witnesses testified that Eggers was upset at his parents because he considered them to be too strict.[23] His attorney suggested that Eggers was intoxicated at the time of the killings.[24]

All jurisdictions in the United States allow, in at least some cases, juveniles to be transferred to criminal court and tried as adults.[25] Transfers can be by discretionary, presumptive, or mandatory waiver of juvenile court jurisdiction, as well as by specific statutory criteria, and can be limited to specific offenses.

The lowest age for which transfer is allowed differs from jurisdiction to jurisdiction. Three jurisdictions do not list any minimum age for transfer.[26] Seven jurisdictions allow transfer at ages 10 to 12.[27] Thirty-two other jurisdictions allow transfer at ages 13 or 14.[28] Ten jurisdictions retain a somewhat higher age for transfer, such as 15 or 16.[29]

4. ABOLITION OR NARROWING OF THE INSANITY DEFENSE

Eric Clark was a typical teenager until mental illness took over his life. He was diagnosed with paranoid schizophrenia, a subtype of schizophrenia characterized by delusions and hallucinations. He would not drink tap water, because he was fearful of lead poisoning. He believed that alien life forms from another planet were after him. Clark set up a fishing line with beads and wind chimes throughout his home as an alarm system for alien invasions. He also started to keep a bird in his car to warn him of any airborne poison. He sometimes circled the neighborhood, blaring loud music in an attempt to keep the aliens away. Clark thought that the aliens were commonly disguised as government agents.

---

[21] *See* Kate Randall, *Another Florida Teenager Receives Harsh Adult Prison Sentence*, World Socialist Web Site, Aug. 3, 2001, http://www.wsws.org/articles/2001/aug2001/flor-a03.shtml.

[22] Kim Smith, *Teen gets life for killings of his parents*, Ariz. Daily Star, Sept. 23, 2005, at B4.

[23] Mitch Tobin, *Teen guilty in 2 killings*, Ariz. Daily Star, Aug. 25, 2005, at B1.

[24] *Id.* When detectives searched his house, they found marijuana in his room. Appellee's Answering Brief at 3, State v. Eggers, No. 2 CA-CR 05-0320, 2005 WL 5829847 (Ariz. Ct. App. 2005).

[25] *See* Patrick Griffin et al., U.S. Department of Justice, Trying Juveniles as Adults in Criminal Court: An Analysis of State Transfer Provisions 1 (1998).

[26] Maine, South Dakota, West Virginia. *Id.* at 14–15.

[27] Colorado, Indiana (only Murder), Kansas, Missouri, Montana, Vermont, Wisconsin (only Murder). *Id.*

[28] Alabama, Arkansas, California, Connecticut, Delaware, Florida, Georgia, Hawaii, Idaho, Illinois, Iowa, Kentucky, Louisiana, Massachusetts, Michigan, Minnesota, Mississippi, Nevada, New Hampshire, New Jersey, New York, North Carolina, North Dakota, Ohio, Oklahoma, Pennsylvania, South Carolina, Texas, United States (18 U.S.C. §5032), Utah, Virginia, Wyoming. *Id.*

[29] Alaska, Arizona, District of Columbia, Maryland, Nebraska, New Mexico, Oregon, Rhode Island, Tennessee, Washington. *Id.*

After neighbors called the police to report the excessive noise he was making, Clark was pulled over by a police officer. Believing the policeman to be an alien, and not wanting to be abducted or killed, Clark shot and killed the officer. Clearly, Clark was dangerous in his current state and needed to be civilly committed for as long as he remained so. Yet it seems difficult to assess his blameworthiness without taking account of his serious mental illness. However, the Arizona statutes have so narrowed the availability of defenses and mitigations related to mental illness that his disease was essentially legally irrelevant to his court case. He was convicted of first degree murder and sentenced to life imprisonment. The Supreme Court upheld as constitutional the Arizona supreme court's *Mott* rule, which precludes the use of evidence of diminished capacity caused by mental illness to negate the mens rea elements of a crime.[30]

Consider, similarly, the case of Andrea Yates. She, her husband, and their four young boys lived in a renovated bus. They were deeply religious, often prayed together, and wanted as large a family as possible. Unfortunately, Andrea increasingly manifested signs of mental illness. On one occasion, she attempted to commit suicide by swallowing pills. Though given prescriptions for multiple medications, including antipsychotics, Andrea did not often take them. She often shook, failed to feed her children, mutilated herself, and claimed that there were cameras in the ceilings. Her husband Rusty stopped a second, nearly successful, suicide attempt but did not report the incident to her physicians. The Yateses were warned against having more children because of Andrea's precarious mental state, but they soon had a fifth child, a baby girl. The family moved from the bus into a house, and Andrea's condition initially improved—but the improvement was short lived. Andrea was soon cutting herself again and refusing to feed her children. She worried that her mental illness rendered her a bad mother and that, as their minister preached, her children would then be doomed to eternal torment in hell. One morning, after Rusty left for work, Andrea filled the bathtub with water, then drowned each of her children. Her son Noah tried to run, but Andrea grabbed him and held him under the water as he struggled to escape. She believed that by killing her children she was saving them from a horrifying existence of eternal torment.

Again, one would think that her serious mental illness would significantly reduce or eliminate her blameworthiness. Yet she was convicted of capital murder and sentenced to life imprisonment (though the conviction was later overturned because of questionable testimony by a state witness).[31] Yates did not qualify for an insanity defense in Texas because the state limits it to individuals who, owing to mental illness, do not know that their conduct is criminal.[32] Presumably, Yates did know that

---

[30] *See* Clark v. Arizona, 548 U.S. 735, 779 (2006). Arizona law does not allow evidence of mental illness to be introduced to negate specific intent elements for any crime. State v. Mott, 931 P.2d 1046, 1051 (Ariz. 1997). The State does allow a general insanity defense, but only one that is narrow in scope and that puts the burden on the defendant to prove "by clear and convincing evidence" that he was insane. ARIZ. REV. STAT. §13-502(A) (LexisNexis 2008).

[31] Yates v. State, 171 S.W.3d 215, 216–22 (2005).

[32] The Texas Penal Code provides: "It is an affirmative defense to prosecution that, at the time of the conduct charged, the actor, as a result of severe mental disease or defect, did not know that his conduct was wrong." TEX. PENAL CODE ANN. §8.01(a) (Vernon 2003). "Wrong" in this sense is interpreted under Texas law to mean "illegal." Ruffin v. State, 270 S.W.3d 586, 592 (Tex. Crim. App. 2008)

her conduct was in violation of the state's rules, even though she thought she was doing the right thing in order to save her children.

Today, two jurisdictions do not allow an insanity defense, although they do allow evidence of mental illness to be used more narrowly to negate offense mens rea requirements.[33] Another 31 allow an insanity defense based only upon a cognitive dysfunction; no defense is allowed for a control dysfunction no matter how severe the impairment.[34] The remaining 19 allow an insanity defense for either a cognitive or control impairment.[35]

5. STRICT LIABILITY

It is now not uncommon for even a serious offense, such as statutory rape, to become one of strict liability. Under such a regime, a culpable state of mind need not be proven with respect to a sexual partner's age. Consider the case of Raymond Garnett, a 20-year-old mentally retarded man with an IQ of 52. He was introduced to Erica, who said that she was 16—a fact confirmed by her friends. Garnett and Erica talk on the phone on and off—he enjoyed talking to someone who did not make fun of him. One night, around 9 p.m., he was stranded without a ride home, but noticed Erica's house nearby. As he approached the house, Erica opened her upstairs bedroom window and invited him in, directing him to use a nearby ladder.

---

[33] Montana, Mont. Code Ann. §46-14-201 (2007); Utah, Utah Code Ann. §76-2-305 (2008).

[34] *See* United States, 18 U.S.C. §17 (2006); Alabama, Ala. Code §15-16-2 (LexisNexis 2008); Alaska, Alaska Stat. §12.47.010 (2008); Arizona, Ariz. Rev. Stat. Ann. §§13-502(A)-(B) (2008); Arkansas, Ark. Code Ann. §5-2-312 (2008); California, People v. Drew, 583 P.2d 1318 (Cal. 1978); Colorado, Colo. Rev. Stat. §§16-8-101(1), -104, -105(2) (2007); Delaware, Del. Code Ann. tit. 11, §§304a, 401 (2007); Florida, Fla. R. Crim. P. §3.217; Illinois, 720 Ill. Comp. Stat. Ann. 5/6-2 (LexisNexis 2008); Indiana, Ind. Code Ann. §§35-41-3-6, -4-1(b) (West 2004); Kansas, State v. Roadenbaugh, 673 P.2d 1166 (Kan. 1982) and State v. Grauerholz, 654 P.2d 395 (Kan. 1982); Louisiana, La. Rev. Stat. Ann. §14:14 (2007); Maine, Me. Rev. Stat. Ann. tit. 17-A, §39 (2006); Minnesota, Minn. Stat. Ann. §611.026 (West 2009); Mississippi, Herron v. State, 287 So. 2d 759 (Miss. 1974); Missouri, Mo. Ann. Stat. §552.030 (West 2009); Nebraska, Neb. Rev. Stat. §29-2203 (2009); Nevada, Poole v. State, 625 P.2d 1163 (Nev. 1981); New Hampshire, State v. Plummer, 374 A.2d 431 (N.H. 1977); New Jersey, N.J. Stat. Ann. §2C:4-2 (West 2005); New York, N.Y. Penal Law §40.15 (Consol. 2008); North Carolina, State v. Vickers, 291 S.E.2d 599 (N.C. 1982); Oklahoma, Munn v. State, 658 P.2d 482 (Okla. 1983); Pennsylvania, 18 Pa. Cons. Stat. Ann. §315 (West 1998); South Carolina, S.C. Code Ann. §17-24-10 (2007); South Dakota, State v. Kost, 290 N.W.2d 482 (S.D. 1980); Tennessee, State v. Clayton, 656 S.W.2d 344 (Tenn. 1983); Texas, Tex. Penal Code Ann. §§2.04, 8.01 (West 2003); Washington, Wash. Rev. Code Ann. §10.77.030(2) (West 2002).

[35] *See* Connecticut, Conn. Gen. Stat. §53a-13(a) (2007); District of Columbia, Bethea v. United States, 365 A.2d 64 (D.C. 1976); Georgia, Ga. Code Ann. §16-3-3 (2007); Hawaii, Haw. Rev. Stat. §704-400 (2009); Idaho, State v. White, 456 P.2d 797 (Idaho 1969); Iowa, Iowa Code Ann. §701.4 (West 2003); Kentucky, Ky. Rev. Stat. Ann. §504.020 (West 2008); Maryland, MD. CODE ANN., CRIM. PROC. §3-109 (LexisNexis 2008); Massachusetts, Commonwealth v. McHoul, 226 N.E.2d 556 (Mass. 1967); Michigan, Mich. Comp. Laws Ann. §768.21(a) (West 2008); New Mexico, N.M. STAT. ANN. §31-9-3 (LexisNexis 2009); Ohio, State v. Anders, 277 N.E.2d 554 (Ohio 1972); Oregon, Or. Rev. Stat. §161.295 (2009); Rhode Island, State v. Johnson, 399 A.2d 469 (R.I. 1979); Vermont, Vt. Stat. Ann. tit. 13, §4801 (2009); Virginia, Godley v. Commonwealth, 343 S.E.2d 368 (Va. Ct. App. 1986); West Virginia, State v. Lockhart, 490 S.E.2d 298 (W. Va. 1997); Wisconsin, Wis. Stat. Ann. §971.15 (West 2007); Wyoming, Wyo. Stat. Ann. §7-11-304 (2009).

They talked for a long time, had consensual intercourse, and Garnett left at about 4:30 a.m. When Erica gave birth eight and a half months later, her parents contacted police, who arrested Garnett for statutory rape. Erica was 13 years old at the time of their intercourse. Garnett was charged with second degree rape. Because the offense was one of strict liability, he was not allowed to introduce evidence at trial showing that his mistake as to her age was a reasonable one for him to make.[36]

In another case, 19-year-old Ras Haas let two runaway girls stay at his apartment. They told him they were 18 years old, and at different times had consensual intercourse with him. He was later arrested and charged with two counts of sexual assault of a child because the girls, in fact, were 14 and 15 years old. At trial he was not allowed to present evidence that he reasonably believed the girls were over the age of 16, which was the age of consent required by state law. Because the offense was one of strict liability, such reasonableness was irrelevant. He was sentenced to 20 to 30 years imprisonment for each count, with the terms to be served consecutively.[37]

Roswold Adkins had consensual intercourse with a 14-year-old girl who intentionally misrepresented her age. During deliberations, the jury, apparently concerned about the issue, asked the judge about taking the intentional misrepresentation into account in assessing liability, and was told that it was irrelevant to liability because even a reasonable mistake is no defense. Adkins was convicted of two counts of criminal sexual conduct and sentenced to two concurrent terms of 6.5 to 22 years.[38]

Thirty-three jurisdictions reject a defense even for a mistake as to age that a reasonable person would have made.[39] While other serious offenses, such as driving

---

[36] Garnett v. Maryland, 632 A.2d 797 (Md. 1993). Garnett's prison sentence is suspended and he is put on probation. ROBINSON & CAHILL, LAW WITHOUT JUSTICE, *supra* note 390, at 63–65.

[37] State v. Haas, No. A-05-804, 2006 WL 996535, at *5 (Neb. Ct. App. 2006).

[38] People v. Adkins, No. 257845, 2006 WL 142120, at *1 (Mich. Ct. App. 2006).

[39] *See* United States, 18 U.S.C. §1111(a) (2006); Alabama, ALA. CODE §13A-6-2(a)(3) (2009); Alaska, ALASKA STAT. §11.41.110(a)(3) (2008); Arizona, ARIZ. REV. STAT. ANN. §13-1105(A)(2) (2010); California, CAL. PENAL CODE §1-8-1-189 (West 2008); Colorado, COLO. REV. STAT. ANN. §18-3-102(1)(b) (West 2009); Connecticut, CONN. GEN. STAT. ANN. §53(a)-54(c) (West 2007); District of Columbia, D.C. CODE §22-2101 (LexisNexis 2010); Florida, FLA. STAT. ANN. §782.04 (West 2007); Idaho, IDAHO CODE ANN. §18-4003(d) (2004); Illinois, 720 ILL. COMP. STAT. ANN. 5/9-1(a)(3) (West 2002); Indiana, IND. CODE ANN. §35-42-1-2, -3 (West 2004); Iowa, IOWA CODE §707.2.2-.3 (2007); Kansas, KAN. STAT. ANN. §21-3401(b) (2007); Louisiana, LA. REV. STAT. ANN. §14:30(A)(1) (2007); Maine, ME. REV. STAT. ANN. tit. 17-A, §202(1) (2006); Maryland, MD. CODE ANN., CRIM. LAW §2-201(a)(4) (LexisNexis 2002); Massachusetts, MASS. ANN. LAWS ch. 265, §1 (LexisNexis 2008); Michigan, MICH. COMP. LAWS ANN. §750.316(1)(b) (West 2004); Minnesota, MINN. STAT. ANN. §609.185(a)(2)-(3) (West 2009); Mississippi, MISS. CODE ANN. §97-3-19(1)(c) (2005); Montana, MONT. CODE ANN. §45-5-102(1)(b) (2009); Nebraska, NEB. REV. STAT. §28-303(2) (2009); Nevada, NEV. REV. STAT. §200.030(1)(b) (2009); New Jersey, N.J. STAT. ANN. §2C:11-3.a(3) (West 2005); New York, N.Y. PENAL LAW §125.25(3) (Consol. 1998); North Carolina, N.C. GEN. STAT. ANN. §14-17 (West 2000); North Dakota, N.D. CENT. CODE §12.1-16-01(1)(c) (1997); Ohio, OHIO REV. CODE ANN. §2903.01(B) (West 2006); Oregon, OR. REV. STAT. §163.115(1)(b) (2009); Rhode Island, R.I. GEN. LAWS §11-23-1 (2002); South Carolina, S.C. CODE ANN. §16-3-20(c)(a)(1) (2003); South Dakota, S.D. CODIFIED LAWS §22-16-4(1) (2006); Tennessee, TENN. CODE ANN. §39-13-202(a)(2)-(3) (2006); Utah, UTAH CODE ANN. §76-5-203(2)(d) (LexisNexis 2008); Vermont, VT. STAT. ANN. tit. 13, §2301 (2009); Virginia, VA. CODE ANN. §18.2-32 (2009); West Virginia, W. VA. CODE ANN. §61-2-1 (2005); Wisconsin, WIS. STAT. ANN. §940.03 (West 2005); Wyoming, WYO. STAT. ANN. §6–2-101(a) (2009).

under the influence, can be ones of strict liability,[40] the bulk of strict liability offenses are more minor, such as "public welfare offenses,"[41] speeding and other vehicular offenses, as well as liquor, narcotics, and food regulation infractions.[42] A few state courts have invalidated the use of strict liability for offenses that impose significant prison sentences or create an unreasonable expectation of knowledge in the offender.[43] The Model Penal Code attempts to restrict the use of strict liability to "violations" rather than crimes,[44] although it too imposes strict liability for the serious felony of aggravated statutory rape.[45]

6. FELONY MURDER

The felony murder doctrine punishes as murder all deaths caused in the course of a felony no matter how accidental the killing, and applies such murder liability not just to the person causing the death but to all accomplices in the underlying felony.[46] The case of Jerry Moore is not unusual. Moore agreed to help Montejo (an acquaintance) burglarize a house while the house's owner was away. Neither man was armed. When the resident returned unexpectedly, Moore was surprised to see Montejo shoot and kill the owner with a gun he apparently found in a nightstand. Moore was convicted of murder for Montejo's shooting and was sentenced to life imprisonment at hard labor without the possibility of parole.[47]

The most popular version of the rule, used by 40 jurisdictions, allows only inherently dangerous felonies (such as arson or drug trafficking) to trigger the rule's use.[48] Ten jurisdictions allow the commission of any felony to be used.[49] Two jurisdictions have abolished the felony murder rule.[50]

7. CRIMINALIZATION OF REGULATORY VIOLATIONS

Tom Lindsey, 26, took his brother and six friends on a rafting and camping trip in the popular Hell's Canyon National Recreation Area, a park created and regulated

---

[40] *See* Leocal v. Ashcroft, 543 U.S. 1, 8 n.5 (2004) (listing states where driving under the influence is treated as a strict liability offense).

[41] *See, e.g.,* Morissette v. U.S., 342 U.S. 246, 255 (1952); Francis Bowes Sayre, *Public Welfare Offenses*, 33 COLUM. L. REV. 55, 84-88.

[42] Wayne R. LaFave, CRIMINAL LAW 272 n.1 (4th ed. 2003).

[43] *Id.* at 279.

[44] MODEL PENAL CODE §2.05(1)(a) (Proposed Official Draft 1962).

[45] *Id.* at §213.6(1).

[46] *See* LaFave, *supra* note 425, at 744–65.

[47] Louisiana v. Moore, 2006-KA-1979, p. 2 (La. App. 1 Cir. 3/28/07); 2007 WL 914637, at *1.

[48] *See supra* note 422.

[49] *See* Arkansas, ARK. CODE ANN. §5-10-102(a)(1) (2006); Delaware, DEL. CODE ANN. tit. 11, §636(a)(2) (2007); Georgia, GA. CODE ANN. §16-5-1 (2007); Missouri, MO. REV. STAT. §565.021.1(2) (1999); New Hampshire, N.H. REV. STAT. ANN. §630:1-b (2007); New Mexico, N.M. STAT. ANN. §30-2-1-A(2) (2004); Oklahoma, OKLA. STAT. ANN. tit. 21, §701.7(B) (West 2002); Pennsylvania, 18 PA. CONS. STAT. §2502(b) (1998); Texas, TEX. PENAL CODE ANN. §19.02(b)(3) (West 2003); Washington, WASH. REV. CODE ANN. §9A.32.030(1)(c),-050(1)(b) (2009).

[50] *See* HAW. REV. STAT. §707-701 (LexisNexis 2008); KY. REV. STAT. ANN. §507.020 (LexisNexis 2008).

by federal law.[51] Lindsey acquired the necessary permits to both raft and camp in the area, but did not strictly follow the relevant regulations. In order to fish in the mornings, Lindsey and his friends launched their raft at 7:00 a.m., instead of waiting until 9:00 a.m., as the regulations required. Additionally, they camped below the high water mark of the river, which was technically state and not federal land, in order to evade a federal regulation forbidding campfires during the summer. Forest Service agents arrested Lindsey and his brother. They later sent Lindsey a letter informing him that his permits had been revoked. Lindsey and his brother were indicted on felony charges of camping without a permit and building a campfire without a permit.[52]

The federal criminal code, in particular, has seen "unprecedented expansion" in recent years.[53] Between 1980 and 2004, there was a 30 percent increase in federal offenses that have criminal penalties.[54] Many of these new laws criminalize behavior typically handled through civil regulatory actions, including such things as the expansion of criminal liability for copyright infringement,[55] environmental offenses,[56] and fiduciary irresponsibility.[57]

The phenomenon is not limited to federal law, although the continuing expansion of state criminal codes has taken place in a much longer time frame than has the federal code expansion. The Illinois Criminal Code is a particularly striking example. In 1856, the Code contained 131 crime definitions; by 1951 this number had ballooned to 460.[58] Perhaps more telling is the expansion of Illinois's modern code: though when written in 1961, the code was 72 pages long, it had expanded to 1,200 pages by the year 2000.[59] Such rapid expansion is not unique to Illinois, and in most cases is the result of a number of factors including the continuous adoption of "designer offenses" covering actions already made illegal by more general statutes, the passage of laws covering "crimes *du jour*" that garner heavy news coverage and public outrage, and other forms of ad hoc code amendments tending to expand the range of criminal statutes.[60]

C. Testing the Perceived Justice of Modern Crime-Control Doctrines

The crime-control doctrines described in section B were used as the basis for a study testing the extent to which the law's treatment of those cases matched community

---

[51] *See* ROBINSON & CAHILL, LAW WITHOUT JUSTICE, *supra* note 390, at 187.

[52] *Id.* at 187-89.

[53] Sara Sun Beale, *The Many Faces of Overcriminalization: From Morals and Mattress Tags to Overfederalization*, 54 AM. U. L. REV. 747, 755 (2005).

[54] *Id.* at 754.

[55] *See, e.g.,* 17 U.S.C. §101 (2004); 17 U.S.C. §1204 (2004).

[56] *See, e.g.,* 33 U.S.C. §1319(c) (2004) (enacted August 18, 1990).

[57] *See, e.g.,* 7 U.S.C. §2009. *See also* U.S. v. Ntshona, 156 F.3d 318 (2d Cir. 1998); U.S. v. Goldstein, 883 F.2d 1362 (7th Cir. 1989).

[58] *See* William J. Stuntz, *The Pathological Politics of Criminal Law*, 100 MICH. L. REV. 505, 513.

[59] George H. Ryan, *Executive Order to Rewrite and Reform the Illinois Criminal Code (Exec. Order No. 9)* (May 4, 2000).

[60] Michael T. Cahill & Paul H. Robinson, *Can a Model Penal Code Second Save the States from Themselves?*, 1 OHIO ST. J. CRIM. L. 169, 170-73 (2003).

views. Subjects were asked to rank and then assign a specific punishment to each of a dozen of the cases noted above, and these rankings and assigned punishments were then compared to the rankings and punishments that the law gave the cases. This study is drawn from my article with Geoffrey Goodwin and Michael Reisig, *The Disutility of Injustice*.[61]

1. "MILESTONE" AND "CRIME-CONTROL" SCENARIOS

Subjects were first asked to rank order, and then to assign specific punishments to a collection of 12 common sorts of cases that ranged along the full length of punishment continuum. These 12 cases then provided "milestones," as it were, for the subject's punishment continuum, against which the 12 "crime-control" test cases embodying the coercive crime-control doctrines could be compared. If all we knew from a subject was a punishment amount, say five years in prison, we could not tell what that punishment alone indicated about the relative seriousness of the case being tested. Depending upon the subject's view about the general severity of punishment, that five-year sentence might mean the subject saw the test case as something similar in seriousness to a minor assault, or perhaps to an aggravated robbery, or perhaps to an intentional homicide. By having the subject put common offenses on the punishment continuum as "milestones," we could then better understand what they thought about the relative seriousness of a case in their sentencing of the crime-control test cases.

The "milestone" scenarios were taken from the studies presented in chapters 2 and 4 of the book.[62] Recall that in those studies, subjects rank ordered 24 crime scenarios according to the amount of punishment deserved by the described offender. The studies found that the subjects had little difficulty performing the task. The two studies' results showed a level of concurrence of a Kendall's W of .95 and .88, which is an astounding level of agreement across demographics in the ordinal ranking of the scenarios.[63]

In the present study, only 12 of the original 24 scenarios were used to make up the given "milestone markers."[64] Table 8 shows the control cases that were used as "milestone markers." As is apparent, this collection of cases represents the full punishment continuum, from cases where subjects impose no liability (scenarios 1 and 2), to cases of common minor offenses, such as petty theft, to cases of common serious offenses, such as first degree murder. As it happens, each of the scenarios represents a different legal offense from the others, named in the second

---

[61] Paul H. Robinson, Geoffrey P. Goodwin, & Michael D. Reisig, *The Disutility of Injustice*, 85 N.Y.U. L. Rev. 1942, 1961–1978 (2010).

[62] They are originally from Paul H. Robinson & Robert Kurzban, *Concordance and Conflict in Intuitions of Justice*, 91 Minn L. Rev. 1829, 1867 (2007).

[63] See chapter 2, section C for an explanation of Kendall's W.

[64] The text of each of these 12 "milestone" scenarios may be found in Robinson, Goodwin & Reisig, *supra* note 444, at 2027–08.

TABLE 8. } Control Scenarios—"Milestone Markers"

Scenario	Offense	Model Penal Code Grade*	Avg. State System Term**	USSC Guideline Sentence***
12. Ambush shooting	First Degree Murder	felony—death eligible (§210.2(1)(a), §210.6(3)(h))	10.5 years	life §2A1.1
11. Stabbing	Second Degree Murder	felony 1st degree (§210.2(1)(a))	10.5 years	19.5–24.5 years §2A1.2
10. Accidental mauling by pit bulls	Manslaughter	felony 2d degree (§210.3(1)(a))	4.7–8.4 years	2.25–2.75 years §2A1.4(a)(2)(A)
9. Clubbing during robbery	Aggravated Robbery	felony 2d degree (§222.1(1)(b))	4.3 years	6.5–8 years §2B3.1(b)(2)(D) & (3)(B)
8. Attempted robbery at gas station	Attempted Robbery	felony 2d degree (§222.1(1)(b))	(<4.3 years)	4.25–5.25 years §2B3.1(b)(3)(B)
7. Stitches after soccer game	Aggravated Assault	felony 2d degree (§211.1(2))	2.6 years	3.75–4.75 years §2A2.2(b)(2)(B) & (3)(B)
6. Slap and bruising at record store	Assault	misdemeanor (§211.1(1)(a))	(<2.6 years)	4–10 months §2A2.3(b)(1)(A)
5. Microwave from house	Burglary	felony 3d degree (§221.1(1))	2.4 years	2–2.5 years §2B2.1(a)(1)
4. Clock radio from car	Theft	misdemeanor (§223.1(2)(b))	1.5 years	0–6 months §2B1.1(a)(2)
3. Whole pies from buffet	Petty Theft	petty offense (§223.1(2)(b))	–	–
2. Wolf hallucination	Assault – insanity defense	no liability (§4.01(1))	–	–
1. Umbrella mistake	Theft – culpability defense	no liability (§2.02(1))	–	–

* MODEL PENAL CODE (Official Draft 1962).
** BUREAU OF JUSTICE STATISTICS, *First Releases from State Prison: Sentence Length, Time Served, and Percent of Sentence Served, By Offense*, in National Corrections Reporting Program, NCJ 219082 (2003), *available at* http://www.ojp.usdoj.gov/bjs/dtdata.htm#ncrp.
*** U.S. SENTENCING GUIDELINES MANUAL (2008).

column. The differences in seriousness perceived by the subjects in the earlier study generally match the differences in offense grade assigned by typical American criminal codes (based, as they are, upon the Model Penal Code), as is noted in the third column. The ranking of those subjects also matches, in a general way, the average sentences given to state offenders, listed in the fourth column; and the sentencing of federal offenders provided by the federal sentencing guidelines, listed in the last column.

After considering the 12 "milestone" scenarios, subjects were provided with 12 additional "crime-control" test scenarios and asked to include them in their ranking exercise. Each of these scenarios summarizes the basic facts of one of the specific real-world cases used to illustrate the operation of the seven crime-control doctrines discussed in part B. Table 9 shows the real-world case upon which each scenario is

TABLE 9. } "Crime-Control" Scenarios

Scenario	Case Name	Offense	Crime-Control Doctrine	Actual Court Sentence
L. Accidental teacher shooting	*Brazill*	Murder	Adult Prosecution of Juveniles	28 years w/o parole
K. Drowning children to save them from hell	*Yates*	Murder	Narrowing Insanity Defense	life
J. Accomplice killing during burglary	*Moore*	Felony murder, burglary	Felony Murder	life at hard labor w/o parole
I. Killing officer believed to be alien	*Clark*	Murder	Narrowing Insanity Defense	life
H. Cocaine overdose	*Heacock*	Felony murder, unlawful distribution of controlled substance	Felony Murder	40 years
G. Cocaine in trunk	*Harmelin*	Complicity in unlawful distribution of controlled substance	Drug Offense Penalties	life w/o parole
F. Air conditioner fraud	*Rummel*	Petty fraud	Three Strikes	life w/o parole
E. Sex with female reasonably believed overage	*Haas*	Statutory rape	Strict Liability	40 to 60 years
D. Underage sex by mentally retarded man	*Garnett*	Statutory rape	Strict Liability	5 years
C. Marijuana unloading	*Papa*	Unlawful possession of controlled substance	Drug Offense Penalties	8 years
B. Shooting of TV	*Almond*	Unlawfully discharging firearm	Three Strikes	15 years w/o parole
A. Incorrect lobster container	*Blandford*	Violation of importation regulations	Criminalizing Regulatory Violations	15 years to life

based, the crime-control doctrine that it illustrates, and the actual sentence imposed under that doctrine.

2. STUDY DESIGN AND METHODOLOGY

The study was administered and funded by the National Science Foundation's Time Sharing Experiments in the Social Sciences (TESS). The 317 subjects were recruited broadly from across the United States and were demographically heterogeneous, representing a wide range of socioeconomic, racial, and religious backgrounds.[65] The task was computerized and was run over the Internet using a sample of subjects

[65] For more on TESS and the demographics of this study, see Robinson, Goodwin & Reisig, *supra* note 444, at n.101.

that were recruited by TESS. In the first part of the task, subjects were presented with a vertical array on the left side of the screen, which was labeled "Most serious case (person most blameworthy)" at the top; and "Least serious case (person least blameworthy)" at the bottom. A description of each new case was presented on the right side of the screen. Subjects read the description of each case and then dragged the case with a mouse cursor to a point on the vertical array corresponding to its relative rank order of blameworthiness. Once subjects had ranked all 24 cases, they were prompted to review and finalize the order they had constructed.

Subjects then assigned exact punishment amounts to the 24 cases they had previously rank ordered. Each case was displayed on the right side of the screen in the rank order that the subject had previously decided upon. The subjects' task was to drag each case to a punishment amount that they felt was appropriate given the blameworthiness of the offender. The sentence table contained slots corresponding to no punishment, including a "liability but no punishment" option, as well as a "no liability" option.

3. STUDY RESULTS AND DISCUSSION

Table 10 below sets out the subjects' mean ranking for each scenario. The "milestone" scenarios are in bold, and the test cases are in italics. The rank order among the milestone scenarios matches that of the previous study from which they were taken, as was described in chapter 2. Together they present a continuum of blameworthiness along which the modern "crime-control" scenarios, in italics, can be placed. Consistent with previous research, subjects tended to agree very strongly on the rank ordering of the milestone cases (Kendall's W = .86, $p < .001$). (There was also moderate agreement on the rank ordering of the "crime-control" cases; Kendall's W = .52, $p < .001$.) The table lists the scenarios in the order in which they were ranked by the subjects on average.

Perhaps the most striking feature of Table 10 is the locations of the modern "crime-control" scenarios. Recall from Table 9's last column that most of these cases were given very high sentences: the top eight (E–L) were given sentences comparable to that of murder—life imprisonment or its equivalent. If the subjects' rankings had followed the law's treatment of these cases, they would have been ranked at the top of the list, above or between the milestone murder scenarios of 11 and 12. Instead, the top three crime-control cases are ranked as being less serious than the milestone manslaughter case involving an accidental killing by dogs. The next two crime-control cases are ranked as being even less serious—between the "stitches after soccer game" and "attempted robbery at a gas station" scenarios. The next two crime-control cases (both of which the law treats as comparable to murder), are ranked by subjects between the "stealing a microwave from a house" and the "slap and bruising at the record store" scenarios. The last case treated by the law as similar to murder is ranked somewhere between "stealing a radio from a car" and "stealing a microwave from a house." The same dramatic disparity is also

TABLE 10. } Subjects' Mean Rankings of Scenarios

Scenario	Legal Analysis	Mean Rank
12 Ambush shooting	**First Degree Murder**	**23.3**
11 Stabbing	**Second Degree Murder**	**22**
10 Accidental mauling by pit bulls	**Manslaughter**	**19**
L Accidental teacher shooting	*Murder—by juvenile*	*18.8*
K Drowning children to save them from hell	*Murder—mental illness*	*18.4*
J Accomplice killing during burglary	*Felony murder, burglary*	*17.9*
9 Clubbing during robbery	**Aggravated Robbery**	**17.3**
8 Attempted robbery at gas station	**Attempted Robbery**	**16**
I Killing officer believed to be alien	*Murder—mental illness*	*15.6*
H Cocaine overdose	*Felony murder, unlawful distribution of controlled substance*	*14.7*
7 Stitches after soccer game	**Aggravated Assault**	**13.9**
6 Slap and bruising at record store	**Assault**	**11.8**
G Cocaine in trunk	*Complicity in unlawful distribution of controlled substance*	*11.5*
F Air conditioner fraud	*Petty fraud—prior record*	*10.6*
5 Microwave from house	**Burglary**	**10.1**
E Sex with female reasonably believed overage	*Statutory rape—lack of culpability*	*9*
4 Clock radio from car	**Theft**	**8.7**
D Underage sex by mentally retarded man	*Statutory rape—lack of culpability*	*7.8*
C Marijuana unloading	*Unlawful possession of controlled substance*	*7.2*
B Shooting of TV	*Unlawfully discharging firearm—prior record*	*6.4*
3 Whole pies from buffet	**Petty Theft**	**6.2**
A Incorrect lobster container	*Violation of importation regulations*	*5.8*
2 Wolf hallucination	**Insanity defense**	**5.6**
1 Umbrella mistake	**Culpability defense**	**2.2**

seen in the remaining four crime-control cases, for which the modern crime-control doctrines give sentences of 5 to 15 years or more. The subjects, in contrast, treat the cases as almost trivial violations—more like "taking pies from an all-you-can-eat buffet," but less serious than "taking a radio from a car." It seems indisputable that the modern crime-control doctrines are treating cases in ways that dramatically conflict with lay people's judgments of justice.

The same serious disparity is evident when comparing the sentences that the subjects gave the scenarios to the actual sentences that courts gave the crime-control cases, as set out in Table 11 below.[66] As before, the scenarios are listed in the order in which they were ranked by the subjects.

TABLE 11. Subjects' Mean Sentences for Scenarios Compared to Actual Sentences

Scenario	Subjects' Mean Sentence	Actual Court Sentence
12 Ambush shooting	**between life and death**	
11 Stabbing	**essentially life**	
10 Accidental mauling by pit bulls	**20.6 years**	
L Accidental teacher shooting (juvenile)	*19.2 years*	*28 years w/o parole*
K Drowning children to save them from hell (insanity)	*26.3 years*	*life*
J Accomplice killing during burglary (felony murder)	*17.7 years*	*life at hard labor w/o parole*
9 Clubbing during robbery	**12.0 years**	
8 Attempted robbery at gas station	**9.1 years**	
I Killing officer believed to be alien (insanity)	*16.5 years*	*life*
H Cocaine overdose (felony murder)	*10.7 years*	*40 years*
7 Stitches after soccer game	**5.0 years**	
6 Slap and bruising at record store	**3.9 years**	
G Cocaine in trunk (drugs)	*4.2 years*	*life w/o parole*
F Air conditioner fraud (3 strikes)	*3.1 years*	*life w/o parole*
5 Microwave from house	**2.3 years**	
E Sex with female reasonably believed overage (strict liability)	*2.9 years*	*40 to 60 years*
4 Clock radio from car	**1.9 years**	
D Underage sex by mentally retarded man (strict liability)	*2.3 years*	*5 years*
C Marijuana unloading (drugs)	*1.9 years*	*8 years*
B Shooting of TV (3 strikes)	*1.1 years*	*15 years w/o parole*
3 Whole pies from buffet	**8.3 months**	
A Incorrect lobster container (regulatory)	*9.7 months*	*15 years to life*
2 Wolf hallucination	**1.1 years**	
1 Umbrella mistake	**1.8 months**	

The data is graphically presented in Figure 12 below. The solid lines show the subjects' punishment decisions—dark for the milestone cases and lighter for the crime-control cases. The dotted lines show the law's actual sentences.

The difference in the slope of the solid line versus dotted line for the same case shows the extent of the disparity between the subjects and the law for the test cases. Note that the punishment scale is exponential rather than linear (to reflect the way

[66] Subject responses of "death" were coded as 50 years and of "life" were coded as 40 years. Using these values, the mean sentences for Scenarios 12 and 11 were 44.5 and 38.9 years, respectively.

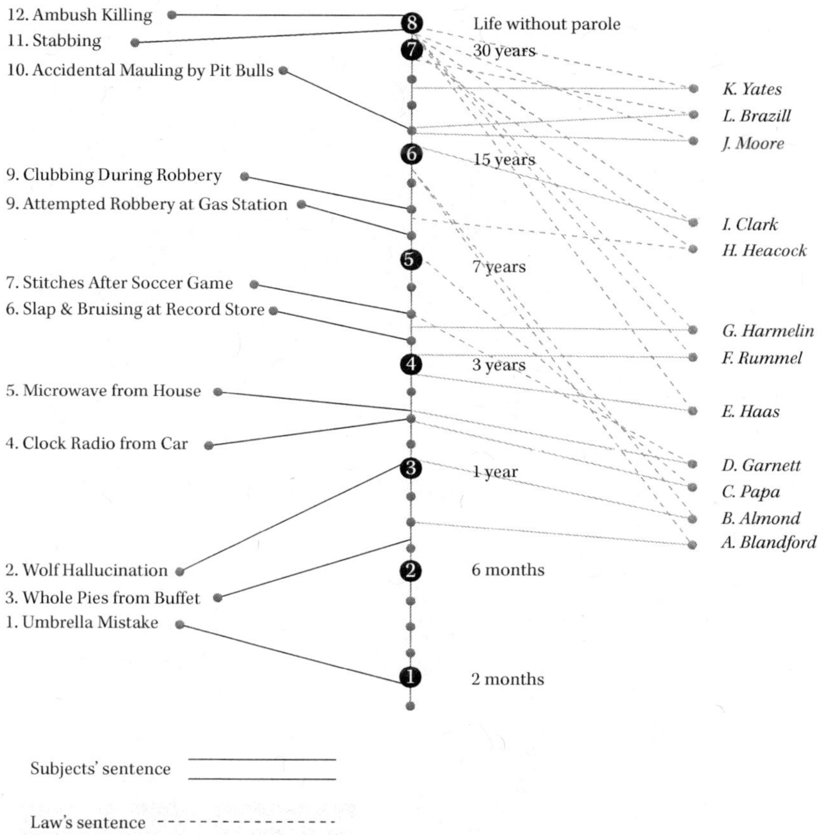

FIGURE 12. Comparison of Subjects' and Law's Sentences for "Crime-Control" Cases

American criminal codes define offense grades and the way lay people think about punishment differences[67]); moving up the scale from one large dot to the next may reflect a doubling or tripling of the punishment. Thus, the differences in slope that the graphic shows represent enormous disparities.[68]

Among this sampling, the crime-control doctrines most divergent from community views include drug offense penalties, three strikes (habitual offender) doctrines, strict liability offenses, and felony murder. The differences between community intuitions and legal treatment are sometimes astonishing: 40–60 years instead of 2.9 years (*E*–strict liability), life without parole instead of 3.1 years (*F*–three strikes),

---

[67] For a more detailed explanation of the scale, *see* chapter 12, section A; PAUL H. ROBINSON & JOHN DARLEY, JUSTICE, LIABILITY, & BLAME: COMMUNITY VIEWS AND THE CRIMINAL LAW 8 (Westview 1995)

[68] Subjects' sentences were less severe than the law's for each test case considered on its own, all *ps* < .001. And the subjects' sentences for the test cases were, on average, 20 years less severe than the sentence actually handed down in the case, a difference that is highly significant (t (307) = 78.81, $p < .001$).

40 years instead of 10.7 (*H*–felony murder), and life without parole instead of 4.2 years (*G*–drug offense).[69]

These differences appear even though our TESS Internet sample of subjects seems quite punitive. Indeed, they are considerably more punitive than the criminal courts typically are when dealing with cases such as those represented by the milestone scenarios. The sentences that the subjects imposed in these cases (see Table 11, column 2, bold entries) are often double or triple the punishment imposed in real-world practice (compare Table 8, column 4, also column 5).[70] Thus, in the subjects' view, the law in the milestone cases is doing no injustice to offenders whatever. (Indeed, if the subjects have a complaint, it is that the law is not punishing the offenders enough.) Yet, the modern crime-control doctrines produced sentences that dramatically exceeded those of the subjects.

D. How Can a Democratic Process Produce Liability Rules That the Community Sees as Unjust?

By this point, one central question must have struck the reader: How can freely elected and presumably accountable legislators enact criminal justice provisions that are responsive to public sentiment regarding crime, but yet in conflict with the community's shared judgments of justice? The concept itself seems to be a contradiction in terms: how can a law be responsive to public sentiment, but at the same time be contrary to community intuitions? Indeed, politicians often cite public demand as the prime motivation behind enactments of strict criminal law provisions, indicating that they at least publicly believe themselves to be fulfilling their democratic function.[71]

There is no short answer to be found here, except that the seeming conflict here is real, and can be at least partially explained by a number of factors that shape society, community perceptions, and the mechanisms of state and national legislation. Though no one factor is responsible on its own for the enactment of popularly

[69] The two insanity cases, *I* and *K*, were given two of the highest rankings and sentences among the "crime-control" cases (although not nearly as high as the courts gave). Those mean rankings and sentences are the result of a bimodal distribution (the only two cases of the 24 to have such) and both stood out as having the highest standard deviations (6.1 and 6.3, respectively, for rankings, and 16.7 and 19.0, respectively, for sentences) of the 24 cases. As earlier studies have suggested, lay intuitions are quite sympathetic to mitigations and excuses for seriously mentally ill offenders, even though the law is increasingly hostile. *See* Robinson & Darley, *supra* note 450, at 132 tbl. 5.2.

[70] Compare the law's sentences for the milestone cases as shown by the average state sentences on Table 8, column 4, to the subjects' sentences shown on Table 11, column 2, in bold. Only in "milestone" case 5 (microwave from house) does the law's average sentence exceed the subjects' average sentence (2.4 years versus 2.3 years, respectively). On average the milestone cases did not produce nearly as much deviation from the law as did the test cases, (t (307) = 87.08, $p < .001$).

[71] John Darley contributed much to the development of the ideas and the research contained in this section.

supported policies that conflict with community views of justice ("empirical desert"), a number of complex processes play a role in leading legislatures to criminalize actions that the citizens do not feel are criminal, or to assign excessively lengthy sentences to crimes.

A good deal of scholarship on the topic suggests that voter views are a major force behind increases in criminal sentence lengths. Social scientists reviewing public opinion studies on criminal justice matters comment that "The influence of the public on policy in the area of sentencing and parole should not be under-estimated. Many sentencing commissions and judges are to some degree affected by public pressure to make sentences harsher."[72] Sentencing Commission recommendations must commonly be enacted or approved by legislatures, and legislators voting on these enactment bills will be aware of voter opinions.

Interestingly, however, another line of thinking regarding popular concern for crime issues argues that while there may be some latent crime-control concern present in the public consciousness, it would be erroneous to conclude that public pressures often lead to harsher criminal law enactments. Rather, it may be such that the reverse is true: expressed concern over and attention paid to crime issues by politicians seems to spur public interest in the issue, thereby making it seem as if voter demand has caused certain legislative enactments—when in fact, the public may have been merely "riding the wave" of concern actuated by a politician's previous comments.[73]

Notwithstanding *how* they arrived at their desires, it seems clear at first glance that voters *do*, in fact, desire higher sentences. Polling studies frequently ask citizens some variation on the question of whether they think sentences for crimes are too lenient, too harsh, or about right. Consistently, those polled think that current sentences are too lenient and wish them to be harsher. Furthermore, citizens report that a politician's position on sentencing affects their vote: about 80 percent of voters surveyed report that if a candidate advocates tougher sentencing policies, they are more likely to vote for that candidate.[74]

The results of these polls are widely reported; thus it would be easy to conclude that politicians feel that they are fulfilling the will of the people when they vote for longer sentences for various crimes. It is also the case that by doing so, they are avoiding being charged by election year opponents as "being soft on crime." Still, this is not a complete picture of the factors that shape public opinion regarding criminal law, all of which combine to cause enactments that seem to have popular support but for a number of reasons do not reflect the actual preferences of the

---

[72] Julian V. Roberts & Loretta J. Stalans, PUBLIC OPINION, CRIME, AND CRIMINAL JUSTICE 197 (Westview Press 2000).

[73] KATHERINE BECKETT, MAKING CRIME PAY: LAW AND ORDER IN CONTEMPORARY AMERICAN POLITICS 78 (Oxford 1997) [hereafter BECKETT, MAKING CRIME PAY].

[74] Michael J. Hindelang, *Public Opinion Regarding Crime, Criminal Justice, and Related Topics*, 11 J. RES. IN CRIM. & DELINQUENCY 101, 108 (1974).

community. A selection of these factors will be discussed in order to shed light on this conflict.

1. MEDIA OMISSION OF FACTS VITAL TO UNDERSTANDING SENTENCES

Current research suggests that there is a complex story behind "what voters want." It is often the case that voters are only informed about the duration of sentences assigned in specific cases through media reports: whether in print, on television, or via the Internet. In one study, researchers asked Canadian and U.S. citizens to read sentencing stories printed in newspapers, then asked the study subjects to judge the sentence given in each case.[75] Large majorities of readers reported that the sentences assigned in the cases were too lenient and were quite confident in their ratings. The researchers note that most of the crime stories in newspapers are relatively brief and commonly report the sentence given, but generally omit or gloss over the reasoning that lies behind the assigned sentences. The study found that "the modal reaction to these stories was to regard the criminal sentences reported in them as too lenient,"[76] finding such a result in 13 of the 16 stories. Furthermore, in spite of the fact that in the stories, "little information was conveyed on which to base a reasoned evaluation of the appropriateness of the sentence," the respondents reported a high degree of confidence in their view that the sentences were too lenient.[77]

These findings are consistent with other studies. It appears likely that media accounts of crimes are the source that voters generally use to form their judgments on courtroom sentencing. By reading the newspaper or watching television news accounts—which cover a disproportionately high number of violent, as opposed to routine crimes, and which generally do not highlight extenuating circumstances or the judge's reasoning—readers and viewers quickly come to the conclusion that the sentences assigned are too lenient. Reading further news reports strengthens this conclusion. In fact, over 90 percent of respondents to one study reported that the media was their most important source of information regarding the crime problem in America today.[78]

This should make it clear that the media holds the central role in shaping the public's perceptions that sentencing is too lenient. Realizing this, Roberts and Doob examined how the public would perceive sentences if they had a different source

---

[75] Julian Roberts & Anthony Doob, *News Media Influences on Public Views of Sentencing*, 14 LAW & HUM. BEHAV. 451 (1990).

[76] *Id.* at 456. Generally speaking, "the sentences reported by the newspapers... confirmed the a priori view held by most respondents that sentences are generally too lenient." *Id.*

[77] *Id.* at 457. "[I]n 58 percent of the ratings, subjects indicated that they were "very confident" of their evaluations. In an additional 35 percent, subjects indicated they were "somewhat" confident. In only 7 percent were subjects "not at all confident." *Id.*

[78] RAY SURETTE, MEDIA, CRIME, AND CRIMINAL JUSTICE: IMAGES AND REALITIES 197 (2d ed. 1998).

of accounts of the cases.[79] These researchers derived an account of the newspaper case from the official courtroom records, creating a summary from actual quotes from the proceedings, or paraphrasing actual documents. Importantly, the summary included much information that is generally not found in news reports—the offender's previous convictions, a brief description of the offense, the defense's and prosecution's arguments regarding sentencing for the offender, a summary of the presentence reports, and the final comments offered by the judge.

The study proceeded by separating the subjects into two groups: one received a copy of the "court documents" account including all relevant information, and a second matched sample of the subjects received a newspaper account of the same crime. The two groups' reactions to the material were vastly different. Whereas 63 percent of the newspaper group thought that the sentence was too lenient, only 19 percent of the "court documents" group thought the sentence too lenient—while 52 percent thought it too harsh. Perhaps unsurprisingly, those who read the "court documents" account evaluated the offense as less serious, and the offender as a better person than did subjects who had read the newspaper story.[80]

The takeaway point from these studies is that at least part of the reason why the public at large reports a desire for stricter criminal law is because they are, in fact, underinformed about the actual nature of most crimes and offenders. The nature of news reporting is in some ways antithetical to disclosure of the whole fact pattern that leads to any particular criminal sentence. After all, what is newsworthy is the sentencing itself, not the actual cause therefor. With limited space in which to print or report (coupled with a not-insignificant desire to simplify the news for cross-demographic comprehension), news outlets end up leaving gaps in the "whole story" behind any particular sentencing decision. These gaps often cause people to assume that the sentence imposed was simply too light, which, if it happens in enough cases, can entice society at large to believe that harsher set of sentencing guidelines (or any other proposed legislation *du jour*) is necessary in order to rectify the "problem" in criminal law.

2. MEDIA COVERAGE OF GENERAL CRIME ISSUES; GOVERNMENT AS INFORMATION SOURCE

As mentioned previously, the news media is the primary source of information that people rely on when judging the operation of the criminal law. This would not be problematic if the news media were able to provide a truly neutral and inclusive picture of the criminal law. Unfortunately, this is not the case. As shown in the previous subsection, the news media commonly skews perceptions of sentences in individual criminal cases by not providing all of the relevant information. Perhaps more significant, however, is the news media's coverage of more general criminal issues—

[79] Roberts & Doob, *supra* note 459, at 461.

[80] *Id.* at 463.

illustrated by specials highlighting the "war on drugs," or by breaking news reports delivered whenever a study reports an uptick in the crime rate. This coverage (and the innumerable examples of similar reports on other issues) is not by itself problematic; it is the function of the news to report on what is important and relevant to society. Rather, the larger issue in terms of the media's role in shaping public perceptions of the criminal law is traceable to the sources delivering the news to the media in the first place. Though it is often assumed that the democratic process follows a pattern beginning with news reports, which then shape public opinion, which itself then shapes governmental action, studies have shown that this is often not the case.

In fact, governmental actions are often the prime motivation behind change in public opinion, spurred by popular news reports. "[The ability of governmental sources] to supply frequent and conveniently formatted 'news' meant that the use of state sources also satisfied the organizational needs of news workers," concludes Beckett. Her study of news "packages" promoted to news agencies by official sources found that, during four time periods in which all crime-related stories printed in the *New York Times*, *Los Angeles Times*, and the *Washington Post* were analyzed for content, 65 percent of all "packages" (that is, defined issues presented in certain ways) reflected state sponsorship—meaning reliance on a governmental agent as the source of the news contained therein. An additional study analyzing the sources behind drug-related television news reports in the 1980s came to an even more striking conclusion: 76 percent of all news stories containing identified "packages" of information about drugs and related criminality were attributable to state sources.[81]

These studies, however, only tell half of the story. That the state is a source of news is not shocking; it is perhaps not even surprising that more than half of all crime-related news coverage is in some way attributable to the government. Such involvement in newsmaking is only relevant to a discussion of popular opinions regarding criminal sentencing and policy if it can be shown that the news does not, in fact, reflect preexisting concerns held by society as a whole. It is assumed that legislators are responsive to the desires of society; there are a number of reasons, external to the scope of this discussion, why this is so in a democracy. One cannot assume, however, that those desires are organic. It is known that people on the whole are influenced by and shape their opinions according to what is presented by the media. However, if the picture painted by the media is itself a creation of the very legislators who work to enact stricter criminal law, then they themselves are the force behind those laws, not the demanding public. In other words, governmental influence on the media contributes to the enactment of legislation that deviates from desert if it is shown that public interest in the crime-related problems reported by the media (using government sources of information) lags behind the news reports—thus showing that they have a hand in causing said interest—rather than preceding them.

---

[81] Beckett, Making Crime Pay, *supra* note 457, at 76.

In many instances, this is in fact the case. While one cannot conclude that a media report can cause any particular change in the opinions of the public, "it is undoubtedly a crucial component of the context in which political opinions are formed. It is quite likely that the media's reproduction of the official view of crime and drugs played an important role in generating support for crime and drug policies" that were advocated by politicians in power at the time of the study.[82] Between 1964 and 1974, political initiatives and media coverage were strongly correlated with public concern about crime—and the concern only arose *after* the political moves were initiated.[83] In contrast, the actual crime rate was not correlated with public concern.[84] In the next analyzed time frame (1985–1992), the study found that political initiatives regarding drug laws were strongly correlated with public concern over the drug problem—but that the actual rate of drug use was not.

It is important not to make too much of these studies. Politicians and the media are not the only factors influencing public opinion, and it is certainly not the case that politicians always lead the public by the nose—public opinion and the actions of politicians are more likely mutually reinforcing,[85] and the demands of elections will generally make political actors at least try to do what the public demands. Still, the evidence is striking: in June of 1993, only 7 percent of respondents to a national poll identified crime as the nation's most important problem; by August of 1994, this number had increased to 52 percent.[86] Amazingly, this increase contradicted the crime trends at the time; victimization studies indicated that most types of crime decreased in prevalence over that time frame. However, then-President Clinton's January 1994 State of the Union address spent significant time addressing the crime problem in the country,[87] and—most important—one of the country's most significant crime-control bills, the Violent Crime Control and Law Enforcement Act of 1994, was debated in Congress and passed that year. There is no doubt that these political events contributed significantly to the rise in public concern over crime policy that occurred between 1993 and 1994.

In sum, it is clear that the media is a prime motivator of public opinion. While it is often assumed that the media is reporting objective fact and unbiased information, this may not always be the case. It is problematic, then, to assume that politicians are strictly responsive to the will of the people. Though this may seem to demand stricter crime-control laws, it may simply be that public opinion has been shaped by the very politicians claiming to only follow public opinion. The previous section noted that public opinion regarding individual instances of sentencing would be significantly different if the public were able to consider the entire facts behind

---

[82] *Id.* at 78.

[83] *Id.* at 21.

[84] *Id.*

[85] *Id.* at 23.

[86] Beckett, Making Crime Pay, *supra* note 457, at 25.

[87] President William J. Clinton, Address Before a Joint Session of the Congress on the State of the Union (January 25, 1994), *available at* http://www.gpoaccess.gov/sou/index.html.

the decision. It is not too large a leap to conclude that public demands regarding stricter criminal law would be different if the public were given similarly inclusive and unbiased accounts of the more general criminal statutes and proposals in force at any given time. Finally, while politicians claim to be responsive to public demands by enacting harsher criminal penalties, this may be less than true. Evidence exists to show that public interest in crime policy follows rather than causes legislative activity. To unequivocally state that harsher criminal enactments are simply a response to public demand therefore is to mischaracterize the situation.

3. ASSUMING HEADLINE CRIMES TO BE PARADIGMATIC

As mentioned previously, the media is the chief source upon which the public bases its opinions regarding criminal law. Another related cause of the general finding that citizens think that criminal sentences are too lenient involves the ways citizens imagine the crime when they answer the opinion poll asking "whether penalties for crimes are too lenient, too severe, or about right." Recall that the majority of citizens choose the "too lenient" answer to this question. Evidence suggests that when asked this question, people bring to mind violent crimes and this is disproportionately done by those who give the "too lenient" answer.[88] One cause for this distortion is the reality that only the most heinous or most significant crimes receive significant news coverage.

When a citizen thinks about the appropriate sentence for a crime, he calls to mind a prototype or exemplar of the crime. The citizen does not do what the legislative system must do, which is to consider the necessary and sufficient conditions for having committed that crime. That is, the law must specify what counts as, for instance, murder or rape. If the citizen is judging whether "life" is an appropriate prison sentence for "murder," she will imagine her prototype of murder, and report that indeed, life is the appropriate sentence. Yet, that does not mean that she thinks that life in prison is the just sentence for a person who brings to an end the life of her terminally ill husband who is in terrible pain, for example. In fact, the citizen would be shocked at the severity of the sentence in that instance, despite it being an example of "murder."

There is a systematic distortion here, because the prototype of the crime that the citizen brings to mind is the clear, unqualified case of deliberate murder, and not the cases of murder that would require qualifying descriptions about how they occurred. In other words, when thinking of murder cases, the citizen does not consider mercy killings or killings done under provocation. Such distortions of the content of specific offenses occur for other crimes besides murder, as well. The dynamic is exacerbated by the fact that news coverage present a somewhat misleading perspective of the crime occurring. In one analysis, 25 percent of media crime stories were about murder, yet murder is involved in less than 1 percent of crimes.[89]

---

[88] Roberts and Doob, *supra* note 459, at 464–65.

[89] *Id.* at 452–453.

Additionally, this "over-broadening of the category" can be brought about when a certain sort of law is passed. The most salient example is found in the expansion of sex offender laws. Many states find that when a terrible incident occurs, such as a child being kidnapped, sexually molested, and perhaps eventually killed, the legislators feel that public opinion demands a hardening of the criminal penalties that can be mobilized if similar incidents occur in the future. Often when a category such as "sexual offender" is created, the sentence for "sexual offending" is also legislatively specified, and quite long sentences are often mandated for the crime. Further, some continuation of confinement for "mentally ill offenders" is often mandated after sexual offenders have completed their prison terms—and it is often the case that most offenders are found by the reviewing panels to be "mentally ill." Finally, laws may be enacted to prohibit the freed offender from living within various distances of spots where children may congregate.[90]

The prototype of the sexual offense—the kidnapping and rape of a child—that comes to mind when people think of the sexual offender may justly warrant the sentence just described. However, the sexual offender laws, as they are currently written, often criminalize a number of actions that are morally quite distant from the prototype. For example, in New Jersey, a teenage person who has sexual intercourse with another teenage person who is just under the legal age of consent has committed a sexual offense. In this instance the offense is "criminal sexual contact," because the victim is a minor.[91] Despite the striking dissimilarity between this crime and the paradigmatic sex offense, both will be referred to as such under the law.

However, the news media reporting of the legislature's movement toward passing sexual offender laws, not surprisingly, continues to invoke the actual case that triggered the legislature into action. The reports pay much less attention to other, less offensive cases that would also fall under the scope of the law. Therefore, the public does not focus on whether the scope of the proposed laws will be overly broad and inflict too severe of sentences on persons who commit these less morally repugnant crimes. The unjust consequences of these new laws are downplayed, and thereby hidden from public view.

What emerges is an account of crime sentencing policies that is much more complicated than the standard account. The standard account holds that the legislatures are doing "the will of the people" when they pass "harsh measures" against crimes. Instead, social and political scientists suggest that when citizens are asked relatively simple questions about crimes, they respond in terms of their momentary interpretations on the question. In order to answer the questions, they think of the crimes

---

[90] Consider this description of the relevant Georgia state law: "The law, described when it was adopted in 2006 as the nation's toughest restriction on sex offenders, prohibited them from living within 1,000 feet of schools, churches or any other place that children might congregate, including more than 150,000 school bus stops in the state. The ban applied even when a school, a church or the like opened in an area where an offender was already living." Brenda Goodman, *Georgia Justices Overturn a Curb on Sex Offenders*, N.Y. TIMES, November 22, 2007, at A26.

[91] N.J. STAT. ANN. § 2C:14–3 (West 2005).

that the media has shown them, which are usually violent ones presented in dramatic and one-sided terms. They use their answers about sentence duration to make the point that crime is bad and deserves sanction. However, when the question set gives the citizens the chance to give a more tempered and nuanced view of what to do about crimes, they take that chance.[92] A more nuanced presentation of the crime at hand inevitably leads to a more nuanced liability judgment by the person asked.

To summarize, a third dynamic arises from citizens' tendencies to think about crimes using the prototypes of crimes that are quickly and automatically recalled when a crime category is discussed. Here, the prototype is generally a "perfect" version of the category—a murder, for example, is a highly deliberate killing of an innocent victim, and not the more complex mix of intention, provocation, and human error that is the case with many non-paradigmatic murders. By conceptualizing the question about penalty severity as an inquiry into the appropriate severity of penalties that should be assigned to the prototype versions of the crime, the citizen tends to signal a desire for more severe penalties in general. This masks the fact that that citizen is really only expressing a desire for relatively severe penalties being assigned to the "perfect" (and thus most severe) instances of these crimes. Yet, the resulting sentencing practices enacted by legislation allow for those harsher sentences to be assigned for much lesser forms of the offense, and the public remains unaware.

4. PUBLIC FEAR

People's opinions about the sentences required for proper criminal punishment fluctuate as a function of their current perceptions of the threat of crimes, and more generally, their state of fear. If, as the news media brings about, people feel that the threat of crimes is high, they will report that criminals need to be locked away to reduce that threat. Long sentences are a way to reduce the threat of crime. People are expressing a desire for crime to be controlled when they answer that sentences are too lenient, and at the moment they answer, they perceive increasing the duration of sentences as one way of achieving that end.

The point here is that people take different perspectives in answering the questions they are asked in surveys depending on their perceptions of crime rates—whether or not their perceptions are actually correct. Perhaps more importantly, people tend to generalize their feelings toward crime overall when answering specific questions. If they are asked these questions when they are primarily concerned with conveying the message that they want more attention paid to crime prevention, then they will answer *all* questions about their favorability toward actions that they perceive as having a crime prevention component in a strongly supportive direction. Thus, they may report they support "harsher prison sentences," but would think, if they were to stop and reflect, that some of the specific examples of harsh sentences are

---

[92] Dena M. Gromet & John M. Darley, *Restoration and Retribution: How Including Retributive Components Affects the Acceptability of Restorative Justice Procedures*, 19 Soc. Just. Res. 395, 421 (2006).

actually unduly harsh and thus unjust. However, this is not the question they perceive themselves as answering. Instead, they see themselves as expressing approval of policies that incapacitate criminals by incarcerating them, or policies that seek to deter criminal conduct among the general population.

Further, studies have demonstrated that people report support for deterrence and incapacitation as crime-control practices.[93] Here, the argument is importantly different from that of other subsections. In the previous subsections, the general suggestion was that the public was in some sense being misled, often by mass media reports, into supporting sentences that would be unjust. Now, the suggestion is that the public sometimes construes questions concerning sentencing practices as questions about their favorability toward achieving crime control overall, without factoring in their own judgments about appropriate crime sentence durations or their sense of the injustice in draconian sentence durations. Put simply, if any person has a general desire for more "crime control," they will tend to consistently answer that crimes should have stricter punishments, without stopping to consider that perhaps some current punishments are already strict enough—or too strict.

Another related effect of high levels of public fear or concern is the passage of "designer laws" designed to address very specific events that have been widely reported or that enter the popular consciousness. Imagine, for example, a brutal attack on a mother and child, committed by polo-clad youths pretending to practice their golf swings in a public park. Media coverage is unrelenting, saturating the airwaves with updates on the case, and with other reports of intimidation by 9-iron. Though the vast majority of teenagers merely want to work on their short game, concerned citizens demand legal action to counter the heavily publicized threat. Out of concern for the sensibilities of the public (and wanting to look "tough on crime"), legislators "view these incidents with alarm" and criminalize possession of a golf club or other "weaponized sporting equipment" inside of certain "safety zones," such as within a half mile of any school or public park. The penalty for possession, of course, is severe—in fact, many demand that all instances of "criminal possession of a golf club" be punished as severely as was the assault that triggered the public's outrage in the first place. Sadly, this scenario is less farfetched than it seems. Legislatures have passed numerous harsh criminal statutes as direct responses to fear based on coverage of a crime that captures the public consciousness[94]—often disregarding prior

---

[93] Kevin M. Carlsmith, *On Justifying Punishment: The Discrepancy between Words and Actions*, 21 Soc. Just. Res. 119, 133 (2008).

[94] "Many of the laws passed in the 1990s—Megan's law, Three Strikes, sexual predator statutes, the reintroduction of children's prisons, pedophile registers, and mandatory sentences…are designed to be expressive, cathartic actions, undertaken to denounce the crime and reassure the public….Typically these measures are passed amidst great public outrage in the wake of sensational crimes of violence, often involving a disturbingly archetypal confrontation between a poorly controlled dangerous criminal and an innocent, defenseless middle-class victim." David Garland, The Culture of Control: Crime and Social Order in Contemporary Society 133 (University of Chicago Press 2002).

legislative enactments that already criminalize the covered activity. The consequences of such new, fear- or panic-driven legislation are often disastrous.[95]

5. NEXT-ELECTION VULNERABILITY

During the 1970s and '80s, a quite powerful specific version of the law and economics perspective emerged and quickly gained adherents. It is called the "public choice perspective," and it helps illuminate why legislators in general will sometimes vote for measures that they know are bad ones from a public policy standpoint, and specifically, will vote for draconian sentencing legislation. The basic assumption of the public choice perspective, applied to legislators, is that legislators, like other political actors, will rationally maximize their own self-interest. In other words, when a legislator is elected, the electorate has not created a saint who will consistently work for the public good; instead, a personally ambitious person has been placed into a seat in the legislature from which he or she will keep a keen eye on his or her own personal interests.

One such interest pointed out by public choice theorists is in getting reelected.[96] The legislator faces the need to raise money for increasingly expensive reelection campaigns and to take legislative stands that will attract voter support in later elections. The fact that campaigns are expensive can be useful for the incumbent legislator, since it provides a high barrier to entry for candidates running against him. Therefore, one task of the incumbent is to cast votes that do the bidding of various "interest groups." The interest group's task is to "pay off" the legislator for the favorable vote. The payoffs can be campaign contributions, votes that the interest group can mobilize for the candidate, or implicit promises of future campaign contributions (and sometimes—a current favorite—a promise of a lobbying position in the interest group organization or in lobbying firms the interest group controls after the politician leaves office).

Commonly, a legislator's primary goal is to remain in office. Even when considering a post-legislature career, the legislator will be more valuable to an interest group if he has served several terms in the legislature. So, not surprisingly, the successful legislator is alert to occasions or actions that might derail his ability to accumulate campaign funds or attract votes in coming elections. Votes on criminal codes and sentence durations have the possibility of causing such derailing.

---

[95] Many of these sorts of ad hoc additions to criminal laws, generated in haste in response to a perceived public demand, often criminalize actions that already are criminalized in the general sections of the criminal code, do so in ways that are inconsistent with the penalties set for the acts in the general codes, and often generate considerable legal complexities. *See* Paul H. Robinson & Michael T. Cahill, *The Accelerating Degradation of American Criminal Codes*, 56 HASTINGS L.J. 633, 637–38 (2005). *See also id.* at 103–39.

[96] To get a sense of the public choice position, *see* Brian Tamanaha, LAW AS A MEANS TO AN END: THREAT TO THE RULE OF LAW 193–95 (Cambridge University Press 2006). As Tamanaha remarks, "Public choice theory... has a startlingly cynical cast." *Id.* at 193.

One way of stating the problem has already been mentioned: allowing an opponent to cast one's voting record as "soft on crime." The dynamic that links citizens' apparent support of harsh sentencing, detailed above, to legislative increases in prison sentences is the concern of legislators in being perceived as "soft on crime," and thus vulnerable to attack by opponents during election cycles. Negative campaigning involving distortions of the meaning of voting patterns by incumbents is a well-known political phenomenon, and it would make sense for a politician to go to considerable lengths to avoid leaving any voting record that could make him or her vulnerable to such charges—after all, no politician wants to be seen as supporting the "crime lobby."[97] The commonly cited example of this kind of campaign is the "Willie Horton" ads that associated Governor Dukakis (who, at the time, was running for president against eventual winner George H. W. Bush) with the prison furloughing of a criminal who committed a murder while on release.[98] How often these negative attacks happen in practice is not clear, but the knowledge of their possibility may be enough for many politicians to be leery of association with crime legislation that does anything else but treat crime harshly. This fear of being seen as "soft on crime" is a self-perpetuating cycle—if no party is willing to risk such a label, sentencing standards will only spiral upward, whether or not that outcome is in accord with community views.

E. Conclusion

The reader should by now realize that public opinion is subject to the influence of many factors, none of which can be definitively identified as primary but all of which have some effect. Unfortunately, as a result, the true feelings of the population are not always reflected in legislative activity or even in public opinion polls. The influence of the media in shaping public opinion often causes people to profess opinions that they would not hold if given all of the information in any particular case. People's generalization of crime opinions, and their construction of crime archetypes upon which they base their sentencing judgments, often simplify their thinking to the point that because only the worst crimes are reported and come to mind, they, when polled, often want to impose only the worst punishments. As such, any particular legislator can look to this flawed public opinion and conclude that the majority support harsher crime laws, when in fact they do not.

Another reason for the passage of legislation that can conflict with desert is the nature of the democratic process on the whole. The media's crime reporting is often based on information provided by the government—and it has been shown

---

[97] *See, e.g.,* Douglas Husak, Overcriminalization: The Limits of the Criminal Law 16 (Oxford 2008).

[98] *See generally* Steve Takesian, Willie Horton: True Crime and Its Influence on a Presidential Election (2002).

that public concern about crime often *follows* legislative consideration of crime issues, rather than being the cause of said action. Additionally, the legislators' self-preservation interest dictates that they not put themselves in a position that could be vulnerable to attack by a rival—a situation that is often brought about by advocating sentencing reduction or opposing harsher penalties, even if such reforms would be in accord with lay judgments of justice.

The takeaway point here is this: while one cannot pinpoint a single reason why the democratic legislative process produces crime laws that conflict with the intuitions of justice of the community, it is possible to identify a number of factors that work together to cause such results. It is incontrovertible that these outcomes do happen. Laws passed are often not in accord with the community's sense of justice, as the study reported in section C makes clear. Knowing some of the reasons why this happens, however, may help to avoid such deviant enactments in the future. Doing so would harness more of the benefits of keeping the law in accord with shared community perceptions of justice, and would reduce the harmful consequences of deviations from desert, the topic of the next chapter.

8 }

Normative Crime Control: The Utility of Desert

Should the criminal law care what the lay person thinks is just? This chapter, and part II generally, tries to show that it should care very much. The incorporation of community judgments of justice into law's liability and punishment rules is essential to law's crime-control effectiveness because it is only by earning moral credibility with the community it governs that the criminal law can, among other things, harness the powerful forces of social influence and internalized norms. This chapter examines the arguments in support of this theory of "normative crime control" and the role that criminal law can play in harnessing normative forces.[1]

Section A considers the traditional "coercive crime-control" programs that use deterrence, incapacitation of the dangerous, and rehabilitation as distributive principles for criminal liability and punishment. At first glance, these principles seem like alternatives to desert that might more effectively avoid future crimes, a goal which every society ought to strive for. Upon closer inspection, however, each suffers serious limitations. While they might (or might not) provide a marginal increase in deterrence, incapacitation, or rehabilitation over that already inherent in a desert-based system of distribution, any such marginal increase in crime control is likely outweighed by the costs of a criminal law system viewed by the community as being unjust.

Section B makes the case for the crime-control benefits of a distributive principle that maximizes criminal law's moral credibility with the community, primarily by having its liability and punishment rules track the community's judgments of justice. This "empirical desert," as it is called, has some considerable overlap with the "deontological desert" that moral philosophers reason out, but the two also have differences, as section C discusses. While there are good reasons to find empirical desert an attractive distributive principle, it also has problems. Section D offers a critique of empirical desert's strengths and weaknesses.

---

[1] Section A is drawn primarily from Paul H. Robinson, *The Ongoing Revolution in Punishment Theory: Doing Justice as Controlling Crime*, 42 ARIZ. ST. L.J. 1089, 1090–1104 (2010); sections B and D from Paul H. Robinson & John M. Darley, *Intuitions of Justice: Implications for Criminal Law and Justice Policy*, 81 S. CAL. L. REV. 1, 18–31 (2007); and section C from Paul H. Robinson, *Competing Conceptions of Modern Desert: Vengeful, Deontological, and Empirical*, 67 CAMBRIDGE L.J. 145, 148–55 (2008).

A. Limitations on the Traditional Coercive Crime-Control Principles: Deterrence, Incapacitation, and Rehabilitation

Empirical desert ends up being an attractive distributive principle for criminal liability and punishment in part because of the limitations and costs of its alternatives. Before considering each of those alternatives, a few preliminary comments on "distributive principles" in general may be useful.

How is one to determine who is to be punished within the criminal justice system, and how much? This is a central question, perhaps the central question, in criminal law and theory. It is not a mere scholarly inquiry but one of enormous practical significance. If a code drafter or judge must decide whether to adopt a given formulation of a rule or adopt a particular code interpretation or impose a particular sentence, what kind of rational guidance can he be given? It is common to have them look to what have been called the alternative "purposes" of punishment and to adopt the formulation, interpretation, or sentence that those purposes suggest. In this usage, however, the "purposes" of criminal law are being used as principles for determining how to distributive criminal liability and punishment; hence, the reference here to them as "distributive principles."

As shown below, the difficulty with just directing the decision maker to consult the various alterative principles is that different principles suggest different answers. Thus, the central question in criminal law theory and practice becomes which of the alternative principles (or what defined combination of principles) should criminal law rely upon?[2]

For terminological purposes, let me list what I mean by each of the alternative principles to be discussed.

Each of the alternative distributive principles looks to a different criterion and therefore would distribute different amounts of liability and punishment to different people in different situations. Consider, for example, the case of the elderly man who was once a Nazi torturer. If one is focusing purely on *deserved* punishment, this would be an easy case for imposing liability because what the person has done is so horrible. Similarly, if your focus is general deterrence—using this case as an opportunity to dissuade others by the threat of liability and punishment for engaging in such conduct in the future—then again, there is good reason to punish. On the other hand, if one's focus is incapacitation or rehabilitation, punishment in such a case might be a waste of resources. The offender may no longer be a danger or in need of rehabilitation.[3]

Or consider the question of whether the criminal law ought to recognize an excuse defense for people who are seriously mentally ill and have, because of that

---

[2] For a detailed answer to this fundamental question, *see* PAUL H. ROBINSON, DISTRIBUTIVE PRINCIPLES OF CRIMINAL LAW: WHO SHOULD BE PUNISHED HOW MUCH? (Oxford University Press 2008).

[3] Or, if the focus is special deterrence—imposing punishment in order to deter future offenses by the offender at hand—punishment again may be a waste of resources if this offender will never have the opportunity to engage in such horrors or any other sort of serious wrongdoing.

TABLE 13. } Distributive Principles

Distributive Principle	Distributive Criterion	Examples of Factors Relied upon to Determine Amount of Punishment to be Imposed
Desert—deontological and empirical	Offender's blameworthiness	Nature and extent of harm, culpability level, justifying circumstances, personal capacities
Incapacitation	Offender's dangerousness	Period during which the offender remains sufficiently dangerous to need restraint
Rehabilitation	Offender's susceptibility to rehabilitation	Period required to rehabilitate the offender
Deterrence—special	What will deter crime by this offender	Proportional to seriousness of offense; more than that imposed for previous offense; perhaps low punishment for first offense
Deterrence—general	What will deter crime by others	Proportional to seriousness of offense; increase as publicity level increases; increase as capture rate decreases

illness, committed an offense without realizing its wrongfulness. If the focus is desert, there is no blameworthiness and therefore no reason to punish. Similarly, if the focus is special deterrence, such people may well be sufficiently dysfunctional that they simply do not understand, or cannot respond in a rational way to, the deterrent threat. On the other hand, as discussed previously,[4] there may be a very good reason to deny an excuse defense and impose liability on the seriously mentally ill offender if one's distributive principle is incapacitation or rehabilitation. The person has already demonstrated that his mental illness makes him dangerous. Finally, if the distributive principle is general deterrence, liability in such cases could be an effective way of signaling to all non-insane potential offenders that the criminal law is quite serious about punishing this kind of conduct, and that they ought not to hold out some hope that they can commit the offense but find an insanity loophole. Indeed, denying an insanity defense can present a useful opportunity to reinforce the seriousness of the deterrent threat.

Notice, most interestingly, that not only do different distributive principles answer the insanity defense question differently, but that the alignment of principles on each side of the question is different for the issue of the insanity defense than it was for the previous issue of what to do with the elderly Nazi torturer. Other questions will similarly generate altogether different alignments. Consider, for example, the question before a criminal code commission that must decide whether to have attempts punished the same as the completed offense or punished less. A distributive principle of incapacitation or rehabilitation would suggest that they be punished the same, at least in the common case in which the attempter and the

[4] *See* chapter 6, section A.1.

successful offender are equally dangerous. Yet general and special deterrence and at least some forms of desert would suggest that the attempter be punished less.

In other words, the distributive principle adopted for the criminal justice system really does make a difference. To give a hint at where the chapter is headed, it turns out that none of the alternative distributive principles are perfect. All have flaws. However, some may be clearly better than others.

1. DETERRENCE

The most obvious strength of general deterrence is its enormous potential efficiency. By punishing a few people, there is the potential for influencing the conduct of thousands or hundreds of thousands of other potential offenders. And there can be little dispute that having a criminal justice system that is known by all to impose punishment for violations has a general deterrent effect. What is less clear is whether manipulating of criminal law's liability and punishment rules—in other words, using general deterrence as a *distributive principle for criminal liability and punishment*—can provide a deterrent effect greater than, say, that already inherent in a principle that imposes deserved punishment.

There can be no deterrent effect unless certain basic prerequisites are satisfied. First, the target must know the rule by which the law seeks to influence the person's conduct. Second, the target must be able and willing to calculate the costs and benefits for their own self-interest—that is, they must be able and willing to take the threat contained in the deterrence-based rule and use it to decide how they will act. Third, having done those calculations, the target must come to the conclusion that the costs of the contemplated offense, in terms of punishment, outweigh the benefits of the offense. Yet, as discussed below, these prerequisites commonly do not exist. Situations in which they all exist (a necessary prerequisite for any deterrent effect) are the exception rather than the rule.

Consider each of the three prerequisites in turn, to see the real-world complications that arise in trying to satisfy each. As to the first prerequisite—that the target must know the rule by which conduct is sought to be manipulated—the studies suggest that offenders commonly don't know the rule. How many people know whether their state has a felony murder and, if so, its terms? Whether their state has a "three-strikes" rule? Not many (even among readers of this volume, I would guess). What are the chances that a young man standing outside a convenience store contemplating a robbery will know the rules? Yet it is this person whose conduct the rules seek to influence.

One thing that helps us in this instance is that the more involved a person is in the business of criminality, the greater his incentive to actually learn the criminal law's rules. But what is known from studies is that even criminals commonly have no idea what the rule is and, even if they think they know, they often have it wrong.

Even if the target knows the rule, there can be no deterrent effect unless the person is able to take that information and use it to rationally guide his conduct.

The problem here is that the people most likely to be offenders are the people who are most likely to be bad calculators, or to be indifferent to future consequences. They are more likely to be under the influence of alcohol, drugs, anger, fear, group arousal, group identity shift, overimpulsiveness, mental illness, or a variety of other factors making them dysfunctional in their calculations. This is not true of every offender, of course. White collar offenders, for example, are much more likely to be the rational calculators that deterrence requires.

Even if the target knows the rule and is a rational calculator, however, there can be no deterrent effect unless the target perceives that the costs of the contemplated offense outweigh its benefits. As Bentham has famously suggested,[5] this perception is the product of three things: the probability of punishment, its intensity (its amount), and its timing (the delay of the punishment following the offense). Let's look at each of these components of the deterrence formula in turn.

The effect of probability of punishment on the deterrent effect gives us some reason to be concerned. While the results of animal studies should not be relied on too heavily, they can be useful in at least giving a hint at where potential problems may be, because many species share the physiological reactions of humans. So, for example, studies of rats suggest that deterrent effect drops dramatically as the punishment rate decreases below levels of high likelihood. Where most offenses have a punishment rate of 100 or 50 to 1, it should not be a surprise that this threat level may prove inadequate to deter.

The deterrence formula may be helped by the fact that people tend to exaggerate the likelihood of rare events. That's why people buy lottery tickets. However, the more a person is inclined toward criminality, the more he may have a special incentive to sort out what the real rate of punishment is, and thus may discover that it is quite low.

That people tend to exaggerate their own abilities also hurts deterrence. That is, an offender may hear that another burglar has been caught and punished but may discount the significance of this to him on grounds that he is a much better burglar than the other person. The unfortunate bottom line is found in studies like that by Anderson, who suggests that many if not most offenders think the threat of punishment sufficiently low as to be of limited relevance to them.[6]

Regarding the amount-of-punishment part of the equation, it seems clear that the system can, of course, impose punitive bite. What is less clear is whether it is possible to modulate the amount of punishment, as a deterrence-based system requires. There are a host of facts that make it difficult to predict and control the amount of punishment that will be felt and remembered.

One well-known complication is found in the human tendency toward discounting future benefits and costs. Thus, most people would prefer to take $100 in hand

---

[5] Jeremy Bentham, The Rationale of Punishment (R. Heward, ed. 1830) at ch. VI.

[6] See David Anderson, *The Deterrence Hypothesis and Picking Pockets at the Pickpocket's Hanging*, 4 Amer. L. & Econ. Rev. 295 at p.1 (2002).

right now rather than an absolute guarantee of $150 a year from now, even though they can't earn 50 percent annual interest.

Another complication comes from what one might call "learning the pain." Having trained rats to get food by pressing a bar, one can deter them from continuing to press the bar by applying an 80 volt shock. However, the application of a 60 volt shock is not likely to deter. The animal will simply take the pain to gain the food. If one gives a 60 volt shock (which the animal will accept), then a 70 volt shock (which the animal will also accept), *then* the 80 volt shock, the animal will not be deterred, because the two lower-intensity shocks have taught the animal that he can take the pain; thus the 80 volts no longer holds the intimidation value it had when applied as the starting point. Indeed, when increasing incrementally, the animal takes up to 300 volts before being deterred![7]

The larger point here is that the dynamic of deterrence can be a complex one. Another source of complexity is shown by subjective well-being studies. Whether a person wins the lottery or becomes a paraplegic in a car accident, it is not uncommon for the person to adjust his baseline perspective over time. The lottery winner is ecstatic for a while but commonly returns to his old cranky, unhappy self as his expectations adjust upwards. The same can happen in reverse for paraplegics. This is not good news for a deterrence regime, for it means that the bite of imprisonment is likely to dissipate over time, making each successive unit of imprisonment less painful even though the cost of each unit remains the same. This produces an increasing inefficiency as the permitted prison term gets longer.[8]

In fact, human nature makes things even worse for deterrence. "Duration neglect" studies suggest that it is the maximum intensity and the endpoint intensity that determine the remembered punitive bite, but that the duration of punishment is of relatively negligible effect.[9] This is particularly significant when combined with the point just noted—that the punitive bite of imprisonment naturally degrades over time. The longer the term of imprisonment, the lower the perceived endpoint intensity. Thus, a shorter term may be remembered as more painful than a longer term because the shorter term has a higher endpoint intensity (because it has not yet had time to adjust downward)![10]

Regarding the last component of the deterrence formula—the delay in punishment—consider another animal study.[11] Hungry dogs are given separate bowls

---

[7] Anthan Azran et al., Fixed Ration Punishment, 6 J. EXPER. ANAL. BEHAV. 141, at 144. (1963).

[8] For a graphical depiction of the failure of deterrence, see Robinson, *Ongoing Revolution*, *supra* note 482, at 1095–97.

[9] D. Redelmeier and Daniel Kahneman, *Patients' Memories of Painful Medical Treatments: Real Time and Retrospective Evaluations of Two Minimally Invasive Procedures*, 116 PAIN 3 (1996); Daniel Kahneman, *Evaluation by Moments, Past and Future,* in DANIEL KAHNEMAN & AMOS TVERSKY, EDS., CHOICES, VALUES AND FRAMES 693, at 698(2000).

[10] Shane Frederick & George Loewenstein, *Hedonic Adaptation in Well-Being: The Foundations of Hedonic Psychology* 302–29 (Daniel Kahneman, Ed Deiner, & Norbert Schwarz, eds., 1999).

[11] R. L. Solomon, L. H. Turner & M. S. Lessac, *Some Effects of Delay of Punishment on Resistance to Temptation in Dogs*, 8 J. PERSON. & SOC. PSYCH. 233 (1968).

containing good tasting food and bad tasting food. At a session after they have sorted out which is the good tasting food, they are allowed back into test room and immediately go for the good tasting food, but then are bonked on the nose with a newspaper by the experimenter (bonking being an experience that dogs do not like). Some dogs are bonked immediately, some after a 5-second delay, and some after a 15-second delay. When the dog is later allowed back into the room, one can see how the different delay periods affect the length of time it takes for them to return to the good tasting food. The dogs bonked after the 15-second delay take three minutes to try eating the good tasting food again. In contrast, those dogs bonked more quickly, after only a 5-second delay, take eight days before they risk eating the good tasting food again! Those bonked immediately take two weeks before they try again. Clearly, the timing of punishment can be highly influential on deterrent effect.

Given that in the criminal justice system punishment is almost always long delayed—on average 7 months after a guilty plea and 13 months after trial and conviction—one may worry that the delay can seriously undermine the deterrent effect. Again, the point here is simply that deterrence is a complex business with complex dynamics, and there are many ways in which deterrent effect can be lost.

Compare these difficulties in establishing the costs of crime—low probability and long delay—with the perceived benefits of a crime, which are likely to be perceived as having a high probability (because of the low capture rate) and an immediate tangible benefit.

This skepticism about the satisfaction of the three prerequisites for deterrence is compounded by additional independent concerns about complexity in the application of a deterrence program. The problem of substitution effects, for example, is well known. Even if a deterrence program is successful, it might simply drive offenders to commit more serious offenses, as Katyal has noted.[12] Adding to the problem are dynamic effects. By being successful in creating a deterrent effect, one is likely to necessarily alter the parameters of the deterrence equation for the future, as Bar-Gill and Harel have suggested.[13]

Ultimately, the difficulties of deterrence are shown in the aggregated-effect studies,[14] which use real-world experiments—such as gauging crime rates before and after a rule or policy change—to determine whether the rule or policy has had the desired deterrent effect. The studies are useful because even if it seems that the prerequisites for effective deterrence are not present, it might be that there nonetheless may be a deterrent effect that somehow operates in ways that social scientists do not yet understand.

---

[12] Neal Kumar Katyal, *Deterrence's Difficulty*, 95 MICH. L. REV. 2385 (1997).

[13] Oren Bar-Gill and Alon Harel, *Crime Rate and Expected Sanctions: The Economics of Deterrence Revisited*, 30 J. LEGAL STUD. 485 (2001).

[14] For a discussion of the studies, see ROBINSON, DISTRIBUTIVE PRINCIPLES, *supra* note ??, at pp. 50–58.

But the studies suggest just the opposite. That is, they seem to bear out the conclusion that effective deterrence is possible only if the prerequisites are satisfied, and that the prerequisites commonly are *not* satisfied. The studies show that even when reformers actively seek to increase deterrence, there is most commonly no effect, and where there is any effect it is at best near trivial and often unpredictable, sometimes increasing a particular sort of crime rather than reducing it.

This is not to say that deterrence can never be increased through the manipulation of legal rules. Under special circumstances—where all three prerequisites are satisfied—one can produce a modest deterrent effect, albeit one that can quickly fade. The ultimate conclusion, then, is not to reject deterrence as a distributive principle but rather to understand that it has specific requirements and has limited situations in which it can be effective. Its strengths and weaknesses might be summarized this way.[15]

TABLE 14. } Strengths & Weaknesses of Deterrence

DP	Strengths/Advantages	Weaknesses/Disadvantages
GD	• under right conditions can avoid crime • can have effect beyond offender at hand	• works only when prerequisite conditions exist, which may not be common: knowledge of the deterrence-based rule, capacity and inclination to rationally calculate one's own best interest, perception that costs of crime (probability x punishment) exceed benefits • can give punishment other than what is deserved
SD	• under right conditions can avoid crime by offender at hand	• works only on the offender at hand • works only when prerequisite conditions exist can give punishment other than what is deserved

2. REHABILITATION

There are reasons to be skeptical about rehabilitation as a distributive principle for criminal liability and punishment. First, such programs typically work only for limited kinds of offenses and offenders. When they do work, the effects tend to be quite modest. Perhaps even more problematic, if rehabilitation were the sole distributive principle for liability and punishment, the system would release all offenders who could not be rehabilitated—which would probably be the majority of those incarcerated today. Needless to say, this would likely be seen as unworkable by anyone, whether their interest is in crime control or in doing justice. It probably explains why no known system has ever used rehabilitation as its sole distributive principle. One might instead use rehabilitation as part of a hybrid distributive principle in conjunction with some other principal. For example, one might construct a hybrid distributive principle that relied upon rehabilitation but, if rehabilitation is not possible, reverts to incapacitation.

[15] For a fuller account *see* ROBINSON, DISTRIBUTIVE PRINCIPLES, *supra* note 483, at chs. 3 & 4.

On the other hand, rehabilitation might be a very good correctional policy. That is, one might want prison wardens and probation and parole officials to use rehabilitation programs as much as possible for those offenses and offenders where rehabilitation is, in fact, possible. Used under the right circumstances, it could well be a good investment. What is problematic is using rehabilitation as the basis for deciding who the criminal justice system should restrain and for how long. On the other hand, there may well be special value to rehabilitation apart from its crime-control potential. Most would agree that there is intrinsic value in helping people to change themselves to live more useful and satisfying lives to their full potential. Rehabilitation's strengths and weaknesses as a distributive principle are summarized in Table 15 below.[16]

3. INCAPACITATION OF THE DANGEROUS

Unlike deterrence and rehabilitation, there is no doubt that incapacitation can effectively control future crime. It does work. It is probably equally clear that there is general agreement that society has a right to protect itself by restraining dangerous persons, as it does now with the civil commitment of those who are mentally ill, who have contagious diseases, or who have a drug dependency.

The weakness of incapacitation comes from its use as *a distributive principle for criminal liability and punishment within the criminal justice system*. The problem is that the system, for good reasons to be discussed in a moment, continues to advertise itself as being in the "criminal justice" business, as if it was designed solely to punish people for past offenses. Thus, when the system is being used for preventive detention purposes—incapacitating persons in order to prevent future crimes that they might commit—it must "cloak" its preventive nature; it must continue to pretend that it is only bringing about justice for a past offense. And it is that preventive detention use of the criminal justice system, with its attendant "cloaking," that produces serious problems. To telegraph my conclusions: Such a practice undermines the system's predictive accuracy, which in turn reduces its preventive effectiveness and efficiency. At the same time, it increases the criminal justice system's unfairness to detainees and undermines the system's moral credibility with the community, which in turn reduces its normative crime-control effectiveness.

One may wonder: Why bother doing preventive detention within the criminal justice system? Why not do it as part of a separate, open, civil, preventive detention system that focus directly and openly on a person's dangerousness? There are good reasons why not; that is, system designers do have reasons for being attracted to preventive detention cloaked as criminal justice, rather than to open preventive detention.

The cloaking allows the system to avoid the limitations that logically follow preventive detention, such as the legal limitations that are put on civil commitment.

[16] For a fuller account, *see* ROBINSON, DISTRIBUTIVE PRINCIPLES, *supra* note 483, at ch. 5.

Cloaking preventive detention as criminal justice also has the benefit of reducing the visibility of the criminal justice system's shift away from deserved punishment. This is important because greater openness about this shift would tend to undermine the criminal justice system's "moral credibility," and thereby undermine its normative crime-control effectiveness.

While one can understand why such cloaking is attractive to system designers, the fact is that such cloaking is also seriously problematic for the effectiveness of preventive detention. Consider two examples. Where the goal is incapacitation of dangerous offenders through the criminal justice system, it is common to use a person's criminal history, rather than a direct assessment of their current dangerousness. This is because the former—past criminal history—appears to be related in some way to the offender's blameworthiness, and thus looks more like doing justice. Unfortunately, criminal history is a significantly less accurate predictor of future criminality than would be a direct clinical assessment of a person's dangerousness.

To give another example, when preventive detention is being done within the criminal justice system, it commonly uses determinate sentences, rather than release decisions contemporaneous (or nearly so) with release. That is, judges impose a sentence, including the release date, at the time of sentencing rather than delaying the decision until the time when release is contemplated. For cloaking purposes, this practice makes good sense: all of the factors affecting deserved punishment are available at the time of sentencing. If preventive detention is to be cloaked as doing justice, there is little justification for delaying the release decision. The difficulty with this cloaking practice is that making release decisions at the time of sentencing significantly reduces their accuracy for preventive detention purposes. It is difficult enough to predict future criminality at the time of release. It is much more difficult to accurately predict future criminality months or years or decades earlier, when the offender is initially being sentenced.

These kind of cloaking practices are bad for effective and efficient preventive detention because by reducing predictive accuracy, they provide less protection at greater cost. Relying upon criminal history as the stand-in for dangerousness, for example, means that dangerous persons can be released because of insufficient criminal history. Consider the case of stalking as a first conviction. If social scientists can reliably predict that the stalking will mature into greater violence, good prevention would favor detention—but the lack of criminal history would translate into immediate release.

At the same time, relying upon criminal history as the stand-in for dangerousness means that non-dangerous persons will be detained simply because they have a criminal history or because they were dangerous back when they were sentenced. The problem is apparent in the operation of "three-strikes" statutes. The common trajectory for violent offenders is increased violence in the late teens and twenties—the testosterone years—that trails off as the offender gets older. Thus, the focus on criminal history under "three strikes" means that the young offender runs free during his most violent time, as he is building his criminal history, then is imprisoned after he has finally reached his third strike—often as his violence is naturally tapering off. This, unfortunately, tends toward producing a collection of geriatric nonviolent detainees.

Not only is the cloaking of preventive detention as criminal justice bad for effective preventive detention, it is also unfair to detainees. By doing preventive detention under the guise of criminal justice, it avoids the limitations that logically should constrain it. Specifically, where the justification for detention is the prediction of future criminality, the system logically ought to have a principle of minimum restraint. That is, the preventive detention rationale justifies no more restraint than is necessary to protect society, which may mean the use of methods other than imprisonment. Preventive detention also logically means nonpunitive conditions, as is now the case with civil commitment of the mentally ill. It also means a right to treatment, if that treatment can reduce the need for further detention. It also means a right to periodic review. That is, the government ought to have to regularly show continuing dangerousness if it seeks to continue preventative detention. Finally, a preventive detention system logically would set some minimum decision standards—requiring, for example, some defined minimum likelihood of a violation, some defined minimum level of the harm seriousness threatened, and some defined minimum level of predictive reliability.

By using incapacitation as a distributive principle for criminal liability and punishment, all of these logical limitations called for by preventive detention system are avoided. If we are to have preventive detention—and there are good arguments for why society ought to be able to protect itself with such a system—it would be better for both society and for detainees to have that preventive detention done openly through a system of civil commitment rather than cloaked as a system of criminal justice.

Such an expansion of civil commitment system could be dangerous. Liberal democracies, and American values in particular, naturally want to put significant limits on the power of government to intrude in the lives of its citizens. Punishing criminals is one thing, but detaining people based only on a prediction of future criminality is another. However, the important point here is that our current practice of doing preventive detention cloaked as criminal justice creates the potential for greater abuse, not less. It avoids the scrutiny that an open preventive detention system would attract. It avoids the logical constraints to which preventive detention should be subject.

If one has any doubt about this, imagine the *Rummel* case coming before the Supreme Court as a preventive detention case rather than as a criminal justice case. Rummel was convicted of a third minor fraud and under a three-strikes statute was sentenced to life imprisonment. The Supreme Court held the sentence constitutional.[17] There are many good reasons not to constitutionally constrain the criminal justice sentencing process too tightly; criminal justice does sometimes need life imprisonment as a punishment. But if Rummel had come before the Court as a preventive detention case, which it was in reality because of its three-strikes predicate, one can imagine that it would not have passed the Court's laugh test. Is automatic life detention warranted

[17] Rummel v. Estelle, 445 U.S. 263, 285 (1980).

to avoid another minor fraud offense? I don't think so.[18] The strengths and weaknesses of incapacitation and rehabilitation as distributive principles for criminal liability and punishment are summarized below.

TABLE 15. } Strengths & Weaknesses of Rehabilitation and Incapacitation

DP	Strengths/Advantages	Weaknesses/Disadvantages
RH	• if successful, can avoid crime by offender at hand • may have value in itself, in making person's life better	• works only on the offender at hand • only modest success in only limited cases • can give punishment other than what is deserved • problematic as sole DP; must combine with another • forcibly changing person's nature may raise ethical questions about intruding upon personal autonomy
Inc	• no doubt that effective in reducing crime by offender at hand	• works only on the offender at hand • commonly inaccurate in predictions, which causes wasted costs and unjustified detentions • can give punishment other than what is deserved • can better reduce prevention costs, reduce damage to system's moral credibility, and increase accuracy by operating as open civil preventive detention system apart from CJ system

B. Normative Crime Control: Why People Obey the Law

Now consider empirical desert as a distributive principle for criminal liability and punishment. (This section is drawn primarily from portions of my article with John Darley, *Intuitions of Justice: Implications for Criminal Law and Justice Policy.*[19]) The case for the greater utility of law tracking lay judgments of justice emerges when one considers why most people generally "obey the law," even on occasions when law-breaking is unlikely to engage the criminal justice system's machinery of arrest, conviction, and punishment. Given the generally weak deterrent threat facing people,[20] why do the vast majority of societal members still act in a way consistent with the law? Social scientists have two answers: people obey the law because (1) they regard the law as representing the principles that moral people adhere to, and they are socialized in such a fashion as to want to live up to those moral rules; and (2) if people perceive that the community believes in the "righteousness of the law," they fear the disapproval of their social groups if they violate the law. In social science, these two factors are referred to as (1) "internalized behavior" produced by moral standards and rules that have been internalized by the individual in question; and (2) "compliance produced by normative social influence," generally involving concerns for the sanctions that others will inflict when one violates the accepted rules of conduct. Criminal law can have influence on people's conduct through both of these mechanisms.

---

[18] For a fuller account, *see* ROBINSON, DISTRIBUTIVE PRINCIPLES, *supra* note 483, at ch. 6.

[19] Paul H. Robinson & John M. Darley, *Intuitions of Justice: Implications for Criminal Law and Justice Policy*, 81 S. CAL. L. REV. 1, 18–31 (2007).

[20] ROBINSON, DISTRIBUTIVE PRINCIPLES, *supra* note 483, at ch. 3 & 4.

These two barriers to deviant behavior—internal moral sanctions and social sanctions—are analytically and often experientially separable, but in the longer term they converge. Children are trained by a powerful socialization process into internalizing the beliefs represented by the social norms of the culture to which they belong. People come to hold the moral standards of the cultures in which they are raised; internal moral standards and external norms generally have matching views of whether an action is right or wrong.

What is the evidence concerning crime prevention due to fear of social sanction or fulfillment of moral obligation? Previous studies have been scattered but supportive. Since many of the studies that provide evidence for the operation of social sanctions also report evidence about the role of internalized moral control in inhibiting criminal acts, evidence for both forces is reviewed simultaneously.

Harold Grasmick and his associates have done the most sustained work documenting the role of the informal determinants of law-abidingness. Their research consistently finds that fear of social disapproval and moral commitment to the law both inhibit the commission of illegal activity.[21] They comment that their "findings highlight the importance of internal control in producing conformity to the law."[22] Other researchers reach similar conclusions. Paternoster and Iovanni conclude that "the greatest effects on delinquent involvement are those from informal forces of social control."[23] Meir and Johnson conclude: "despite contemporary predisposition toward the importance of legal sanction, our findings are... consistent with the accumulated literature concerning the primacy of interpersonal influence" over legal sanction.[24] Tom Tyler's review of existing studies concludes, "Testing the ability of each of the attitudinal factors... to predict variance in compliance... the most important incremental contribution is made by personal morality."[25]

Are these normative forces relevant to criminal law? It is argued here that criminal law can harness these forces by enhancing its moral credibility with the community it governs, by earning a reputation as an authoritative and reliable source of the community views. A morally credible criminal law can have an effect in at least five different ways: by harnessing the power of social influence through stigmatization, by avoiding vigilantism, by avoiding resistance to and subversion of the criminal justice system, by earning a role in shaping societal norms, and by gaining compliance in borderline cases.

---

[21] Harold Grasmick & Donald Green, *Legal Punishment, Social Disapproval and Internalization as Inhibitors of Illegal Behavior,* 71 J. Crim. L. & Criminology 325 (1980).

[22] Harold Grasmick & Robert Bursik, *Conscience, Significant Others, and Rational Choice*, 24 Law & Soc'y Rev. 837, 854 (1990).

[23] Raymond Paternoster & Lee Ann Iovanni, *The Deterrent Effect of Perceived Severity: A Reexamination*, 64 Social Forces 751, 769 (1986).

[24] Robert Meir & Weldon Johnson, *Deterrence as Social Control: The Legal and Extralegal Production of Conformity*, 42 Am. Soc. Rev. 292, 302 (1977).

[25] Tom R. Tyler, Why People Obey the Law 60 (Princeton: 1990).

1. HARNESSING THE POWER AND EFFICIENCY OF NORMATIVE SOCIAL INFLUENCE THROUGH STIGMATIZATION

Actors generally feel the force of a social norm as an external force impinging on them. In this, it is not unlike the weight exerted by the general knowledge that a criminal deterrence system has a host of penalties that await transgressors. However, the sanctions feared for social norm transgressions are generally experienced as coming from the community. People obey the social norms of the communities in which their lives are located for a number of reasons. Violating those social norms may involve the loss of one's standing in the community gained from one's past achievements; losing the benefits that flow from valued relationships with others, since those bonds are now shattered; and suffering the shunning experienced by those who have become stigmatized within their communities. If one is thought to have committed a crime, one may lose one's job, ability to borrow money, ability to command trust from others, possible business partners, and diminished marriage prospects.[26]

Other scholars have made similar observations based on the concepts of social capital and reciprocal trust. They have noted that "generalized trust depends on the willingness of individuals to adhere to their community's social norms; moreover, trust and social capital are viewed as products of people's compliance with these social norms."[27] Increasingly, social scientists have come to recognize the social value of having a "reputation as trustworthy." An untrustworthy person cannot be counted on to do his share of the countless social exchanges that life in communities depends on. Thus, a person perceived as falling short of community norms can signal, among other things, an unwillingness to live up to future commitments he might make in exchange for the positive treatments that others might choose to grant him in the present. Criminal behavior, known to the community, even if not resulting in formal criminal liability, is a strong signal that a person is not one in which the community should reside trust or confidence.

Formalizing this general perspective, Eric Posner has created a signaling version of social norm theory. One obeys social norms in the present to signal to others that one will behave cooperatively in future social exchanges, and being included in these exchanges is critically important for one's own benefit. One attempts, in other words, to develop a reputation for normatively trustworthy behavior so that one can trade on or benefit from that reputation in the future.[28]

The core of the argument is this: people generally do not want to violate social norms, and if they think that criminal law accurately maps those social norms, they obey the law. A good deal of the criminal justice system's power to control conduct derives from the fact that ordinary members of the community will stigmatize violators of criminal laws—with some potential offenders this is a more powerful, yet

---

[26] Paul H. Robinson & John M. Darley, *The Utility of Desert*, 91 Nw. U. L. Rev. 453, 472–76 (1997).

[27] Jack Knight, *Social Norms and the Rule of Law: Fostering Trust in a Socially Diverse Society*, in Trust in Society 354–73 (Karen S. Cook ed., 2001).

[28] Eric Posner, Law and Social Norms 18–27 (2002).

essentially cost-free, control mechanism compared to the financial and social costs of using the criminal justice system of arrest, trial, conviction, and imprisonment. But notice that this wonderfully efficient result will come about only if violating a legal code is seen by the community as violating a social norm. The system's ability to stigmatize depends upon it having moral credibility with the community. That is, for a violation to trigger stigmatization, the law must have earned a reputation for accurately representing, from the community's point of view, what violations do and do not deserve moral condemnation. Liability and punishment rules that deviate from a community's shared judgments of justice undercut this reputation.

2. AVOIDING VIGILANTISM

Vigilantism may be the most dramatic reaction to a perceived failure of justice.[29] Vigilante justice, descriptively, refers to occasions in which groups of citizens come together to enforce rules that are not otherwise being enforced by the formal forces of the legal system. Historically, vigilante groups often sprang up in newly settled areas without real law enforcement mechanisms. However, vigilante action also occurs even when police and courts are available if citizens perceive that the criminal justice system is failing in its responsibilities to protect them from wrongful acts.

Some of these latter cases quite vividly make the reader understand the impulses that drive the citizens to vigilante action. In one case, occurring in 1981 in a small town in Missouri, a man had, for some years, been terrorizing the town, raping young girls, robbing farms for antiques, and blatantly intimidating anyone who accused him of crimes or might testify against him in the various trials in which he was charged with these crimes. (The story includes a lawyer who was constantly manipulating the laws to this person's advantage.) The police in this small town probably also were intimidated but certainly were unable to keep the man from crimes and intimidations. One day the man was standing watch out in his truck in front of the place of business of a grocer whom he had threatened with death. This proved to be bad timing on his part. At their wit's end about what to do, the townsfolk were meeting nearby, and a large number of them came out of their meeting to see the man sitting in his truck, intimidating the grocer. He was shot with several weapons and killed.[30] The circumstances suggest that the crime had been witnessed, but nobody could be found, then or ever, to report to authorities what they had witnessed.

This is a classic vigilante response to an obviously intolerable situation. As Peter French points out, three types of mental states drive the urge to action.[31] The first

---

[29] *See*, e.g., INFORMAL JUSTICE 25–40 (Dermot Feeman ed., 2002) (discussing vigilantism and "informal criminal justice" generally); *id.* at 99–134 (examining vigilantism more specifically in the context of South Africa); Elisabeth Ayyildiz, *When Battered Woman's Syndrome Does Not Go Far Enough: The Battered Woman as Vigilante*, 4 AM. U. J. GENDER & L. 141, 146 (1995) (discussing vigilantism and the place battered woman's syndrome fits into the concept).

[30] *See generally*, HARRY MACLEAN, IN BROAD DAYLIGHT (1990).

[31] PETER FRENCH, THE VIRTUES OF VENGEANCE 6 (2001).

is the deep and personal feelings the citizens have of being deprived, in this case of justice. The second is a long-held feeling of powerlessness, or in this case the shocking powerlessness of the law, which has failed over years, to do what is just. Finally, these two feelings generate further feelings of contempt, hatred, scorn, disdain, and loathing for the offender. These are powerful responses, and they motivate equally powerful actions.[32] In the case in which the legal system is tolerating some actions that citizens consider morally wrong, these cognitive/affective appraisals attach themselves differentially to the wrongdoer and the legal system. Hatred and loathing are directed toward the offender; contempt, scorn, and disdain toward the legal system that tolerates the offense. When the system punishes a citizen for some action that the community considers morally acceptable, reactions of sympathy and support are generated toward the unjustly punished person; and again, contempt, scorn, and disdain are generated toward the legal system, along with fear and anger.

3. AVOIDING THE RESISTANCE AND SUBVERSION PRODUCED BY A SYSTEM THAT IS SEEN AS DOING INJUSTICE OR FAILING TO DO JUSTICE

The resort to vigilantism is a dramatic reaction to the system's failure to do justice, one in which the disaffected persons move outside of the criminal justice system. But an analogous dynamic results, less dramatically but more commonly, when the criminal justice system itself intentionally deviates from community views of justice. In communities in which the liability and punishment rules regularly deviate from the consensus of the community members, those criminal law rules are diminished in their moral credibility. Concretely, the effective operation of the criminal justice system depends upon the cooperation or at least the acquiescence of those involved in it—offenders, judges, jurors, witnesses, prosecutors, police, and others. To the extent that people see the system as unjust or failing to do justice, as in conflict with their judgments about justice, that acquiescence and cooperation is likely to decline and even disappear. But more than that: to the degree that these deviations are frequent and morally consequential, active forces of subversion and resistance are generated in the community.[33]

There are, broadly, two ways that the criminal justice system may deviate from the community's judgments about appropriate criminal laws: by failing to punish actions that the community thinks are morally wrong and by punishing actions that the community regards as morally innocent. Depending on which of these

---

[32] *Id.*

[33] *See, e.g.*, Lewis R. Katz & Robert D. Sweeney, Jr., *Ohio's New Drunk Driving Law: A Halfhearted Experiment in Deterrence*, 34 CASE W. RES. L. REV. 239, 240 (1984) ("The frequency of drunk driving creates a tendency to view this criminal behavior without the condemnation warranted by its often tragic consequences. Until recently, the law's treatment of drunk drivers has been shaped by this tolerant attitude, and enforced and administered by police, prosecutors and judges affected by [leniency due to their own participation in drunk driving]").

intuitions is violated, the community may respond with different specific actions. If the law "allows" actions that the community regards as condemnable, then in some cases, the community will seek to mobilize informal methods that restrict and sanction these activities, as with the vigilantism discussed above. If, on the other hand, the law criminalizes actions that the community or segments of the community thinks are morally permissible, then it is likely that those actions will continue to be practiced by people but will "go underground." This in turn generates other consequences: the rise of entrepreneurs who profit by facilitating people's indulgence in those activities, venues in which those activities are practiced, pay to authorities willing to overlook the commission of these actions, and so on.

But in addition to these undesirable reactions attempting to engage or escape control mechanisms for these actions, when the criminal justice system is seen as out of tune with community sentiments, a less obvious but more common and troublesome reaction occurs in the loss of moral credibility that the justice system brings on itself. And in general, these reactions can be summed up as the justice system's loss of relevance as a guide to good conduct. Initially, the reactions may be limited to conclusions about the impropriety of the specific legal rule that offends the community's morality; but as the apparatus of the social control agents of the government, such as police and courts are mobilized to enforce the senseless laws; or as those forces seem to stand by passively as moral offenses are committed, there develops a generalized contempt for the system in all its aspects and a generalized suspicion of all of its rules. Deviations from what is perceived as deserved punishment, "empirical desert," may have consequences for the respect in which the criminal justice system is held.

> Just as the institution of the criminal law may be brought into disrepute by the too easy attribution of criminality in situations where the label criminal is generally thought inappropriate, so also may the institution be undercut if it releases as noncriminal those society believes should be punished. This does not mean that the criminal law may not be a means of educating the public as to the conditions under which moral condemnation and punishment is inappropriate. It does mean that the results may not depart too markedly from society's notions of justice without risking impairment of the acceptability and utility of the institution.[34]

Acts of vigilante violence, noted above, are at an extreme end of the scale of citizens' responses to what they perceive as failures of the justice system to stop violations of the core moral rules instantiated in legal codes, but a host of other less dramatic—but more common—forms of resistance and subversion have shown themselves when citizens perceive injustice. Jurors may disregard the jury instructions and punish or not punish acts according to their own judgments rather than the legal rules. Police officers,

---

[34] Joseph M. Livermore & Paul E. Meehl, *The Virtues of M'Naghten*, 51 Minn. L. Rev. 789, 792 (1967).

prosecutors, and judges may make up their own rules. Witnesses may lose any incentive to offer their information and testimony. And offenders may be inspired to fight the adjudication and correctional processes rather than participating and acquiescing in it.

Empirical studies support this. Research has found that Americans are likely to obey the law when they view it as a legitimate moral authority.[35] In turn, they are likely to regard the law as a legitimate moral authority when they in turn regard the law as being in accord with their own moral codes. As Tyler concludes, "the most important normative influence on compliance with the law is the person's assessment that following the law accords with his or her sense of right and wrong."[36]

As this in turn implies, people who come to believe that the legal codes are importantly deviant from their own moral codes feel lessened concerns with abiding by the law. Two recent experiments provide evidence for the beginnings of this rejection process in individuals who discover contradictions between the legal codes in force and their own moral intuitions of justice. In these studies, participants read about a case in which there was a mismatch between the laws in existence and the moral intuitions of the participants. The mismatch was one that many participants found shocking. It was derived from a real-world instance in which one young man dragged a young girl into a semiprivate space and raped and killed her. A friend, aware of the series of actions, took no steps to intervene or report the action to authorities that might have intervened. The watcher who did nothing and the murderer spent the next two days gambling in casinos, and on return home, the watcher bragged to friends about the crime. Since there was no law against the watcher's actions in the state in question, no legal action was brought against him.[37] Many respondents found the absence of a law criminalizing this conduct unbelievable.[38] The study of omission liability reported in chapter 12, section F similarly found that respondents generally punished actors who failed in a duty to rescue a person in distress, if the intervention could be achieved without serious inconvenience or danger to the potential rescuer, as it could have been in the case described here.[39]

Participants made aware of this and other unjust cases rated themselves significantly less likely to cooperate with police and less likely to use the law to guide their behavior after reading these intuition-violating cases.[40] More specifically, participants who had read cases in which the legal system behaved in ways counter to their

---

[35] *See* TYLER, *supra* note 498, at 68; see also chapter 9.

[36] *Id.* at 64; see also chapter 9.

[37] For a narrative describing the case facts and a discussion of the issues arising in it, *see* PAUL H. ROBINSON, CRIMINAL LAW: CASE STUDIES & CONTROVERSIES, 399–414 and *Teacher's Manual* (3rd ed. 2012).

[38] Janice Nadler, *Flouting the Law*, 83 TEX. L. REV. 1399, 1417 (2005).

[39] Chapter 12, section F.

[40] The contrast ratings were provided by control respondents who read similar stories but with endings that they perceived as just. For example, control respondents learned that the watcher was prosecuted as an accessory to the crime and received a one-year prison sentence. Janice Nadler, *Flouting the Law*, 83 TEX. L. REV. 1399, 1417 (2005).

moral intuitions rated themselves more likely to take steps aimed at changing the law (including replacing legislators and prosecutors and breaking the law while taking part in demonstrations), less likely to cooperate with police, more likely to join a vigilante or watch group, and less likely to use the law to guide behavior. Overall, participants appeared less likely to give the law the benefit of any doubt after reading cases where the law was at odds with their intuitions.[41] In another study, learning about a case in which a similar mismatch occurred on one law "caused participants to report a willingness to flout unrelated laws commonly encountered in everyday life as well as willingness of mock jurors to engage in juror nullification."[42] A more recent study on this issue is the subject of chapter 9.

These studies report the beginnings of the process within individuals of coming into contempt for legal codes when they learn about thirdhand examples of the legal system failing to do justice. But the community would also come into contempt for the justice system in the reverse case: where it criminalized actions that the community thought was morally acceptable. The United States "experiment" with the prohibition of the consumption of alcohol demonstrates what can be the end result of a catastrophic mismatch between elements of the legal codes and the moral intuitions of large segments of the population directly affected in their own lives by the codes. People continued to wish to drink, and the institutions that came into being to allow this were, of necessity, illegal. The inadvertent and unforeseen consequences of Prohibition included the rapid development of thriving criminal activity focusing on smuggling and bootlegging and the consequential clogging of the courts with alcohol-associated prosecutions.[43] Crime increased and became "organized," and crime mobs eventually engaged in criminal activities beyond those associated with alcohol consumption. Contrary to Prohibition's goal of eliminating corrupting influences in society, it increased those influences because it brought many persons into contempt for the moral correctness of one law, which generalized to the institutions enforcing this law, and eventually, to the legal code in general.

It has been suggested that the United States Congress has continued in similar "overcriminalization" practices. John Coffee asserts that "the dominant development in substantive federal criminal law over the past decade has been the disappearance of any clearly definable line between civil and criminal law."[44] He also concludes, with a note of anger, that "this blurring of the border between tort and crime predictably will result in injustice, and ultimately will weaken the efficacy of the criminal law as an instrument of social control."[45] This is so because "the factor that most distinguishes

---

[41] Erich Justin Greene, *Effects of Disagreements Between Legal Codes and Lay Intuitions on Respect for the Law*, 64 SCI. & ENGINEERING 2-B (2003).

[42] *See* Nadler, *supra* note 511, at 1399.

[43] Paul L. Murphy, *Societal Morality and Individual Freedom*, *in* LAW, ALCOHOL, AND ORDER: PERSPECTIVES ON NATIONAL PROHIBITION 67, 67–80 (1985).

[44] John Coffee Jr., *Does "Unlawful,' Mean "Criminal"? Reflections on the Disappearing Tort/Crime Distinction in American Law*, 71 B.U. L. REV., 193, 193 (1991).

[45] *Id.* at 193.

the criminal law is its operation as a system of moral education and socialization. The criminal law is obeyed not because there is a legal threat underlying it, but because the public perceives its norms to be legitimate and deserving of compliance.[46]

Coffee cites other scholars who have made similar points. "Our leading criminal law scholars—among them Henry Hart, Stanford Kadish, and Herbert Packer—have periodically warned of the danger of "overcriminalization"; namely, excessive reliance on the criminal sanction, particularly with respect to behavior that is not inherently morally culpable....All three agreed that a basic "method" distinguished the criminal law...including a close linkage between the criminal law and the behavior deemed morally culpable by the general community."[47]

This applies not only to cases where civil law and criminal law have become blurred, but also to many "moralistic" criminal prohibitions. In an op-ed essay in the *New York Times*, Charles Murray comments on a recent bill that has been passed and signed into law that "will try to impede online gambling by prohibiting American banks from transferring money to gambling sites." He first comments that this will cost those who passed the law a good many votes from online gamblers who think that what they do is morally allowable, but then he goes on.

> In the long term, something more ominous is at work. If a free society is to work, the vast majority of citizens must reflexively obey the law not because they fear punishment, but because they accept that the rule of law makes society possible. That reflexive law-abidingness is reinforced when the laws are limited to core objectives that enjoy consensus support, even though people may disagree on means.
>
> Thus society is weakened every time a law is passed that large numbers of reasonable, responsible citizens think is stupid. Such laws invite good citizens to choose knowingly to break the law, confident that they are doing nothing morally wrong.
>
> The reaction to Prohibition, the twentieth century's stupidest law, is the archetypal case. But the radical expansion of government throughout the last century has created many more.
>
> The temptation for good citizens to ignore a stupid law is encouraged when it is unenforceable. In this, the attempt to ban Internet gambling is exemplary. One of the four sites where I play poker has blocked United States customers because of the law, but the other three are functioning as usual and are confident that they can continue to do so. They are not in America, and it is absurdly easy to devise ways of transferring money from American bank accounts to institutions abroad and thence to gambling sites.
>
> And so the federal government once again has acted in a way that will fail to achieve its objective while alienating large numbers of citizens who see

[46] *Id.* at 193–94; TYLER, *supra* note 498 (using survey research to find that the public complies with the criminal law based not on its deterrent threat, but its moral legitimacy).

[47] *Id.* at 197–98.

> themselves as having done nothing wrong. The libertarian part of me is heartened by this, hoping that a new political coalition will start to return government to its proper functions. But the civic-minded part of me is apprehensive. Reflexive loyalty to the rule of law is an indispensable cultural asset. The more honest citizens who take for granted that they are breaking the law, the more their loyalty to the law, and to the government that creates it, is eroded.[48]

Resistance to particular laws occurs because they do not correspond with the prototype perception that the community holds of a moral offense of the sort worthy of treatment within the criminal justice system. The criminal law can most effectively maximize its moral credibility and thereby minimize resistance and subversion by adopting criminal rules that track shared community intuitions of justice. The danger of failing to harmonize criminal codes with community judgments of justice is that the law may lose credibility on a wide array of prohibitions if too many are perceived to be against notions of what is just.

4. HAVING A ROLE IN SHAPING SOCIETAL NORMS: THE PERSUASIVE POWER OF THE LAW

Perhaps the greatest utility of empirical desert comes through a more subtle but potentially more powerful path. As suggested above, the real power to gain compliance with society's rules of prescribed conduct lies not in the threat of official criminal sanction, but in the influence of the intertwined forces of social and individual moral control. The networks of interpersonal relationships in which people find themselves, the social norms and prohibitions shared among those relationships and transmitted through those social networks, and the internalized representations of those norms and moral precepts control people's conduct.

The law is not irrelevant to these social and personal forces. Criminal law, in particular, plays a central role in creating and maintaining the social consensus necessary for sustaining moral norms. In fact, in a society as diverse as ours, the criminal law may be the only society-wide institution that transcends cultural and ethnic differences. Thus, the criminal law's most important real-world effect may be its ability to assist in the building, shaping, and maintaining of these norms and moral principles. It can contribute to and harness the compliance-producing power of interpersonal relationships and personal morality.

In many discussions of the criminal justice system, it is noted that a characteristic that sets it apart from other societal institutions is that it has a monopoly on the legitimate use of force against citizens. Even if one grants the truth of this, it does not mean that the criminal justice system does not have the power to persuade and not just compel behavior. The criminal justice system, as an institution involving legislatures, legal philosophers, various criminological experts, and enforcement agencies, has the power to persuade citizens about the moral appropriateness of its enacted laws.

---

[48] Charles Murray, *The G.O.P.'s Bad Bet*, N.Y. TIMES, Oct. 19, 2006 at A27.

Social scientists know a good deal about persuasion, both in terms of how it succeeds and how it fails. Consider the criminal justice system as a "persuasive source." A large body of research suggests that a source that has certain characteristics has considerable power to persuade people of the correctness of its conclusions. Specifically, a source that is seen as legitimate in its authority, expert in its knowledge, and trustworthy in its motives, is highly persuasive.[49] If the criminal justice system, and more generally, the government's criminal liability and punishment rules, can be persuasive guides for conduct to citizens, the knowledge of "what the law says" can play a powerful role in the debates between groups of citizens about what the governing social norms should be.

5. GAINING COMPLIANCE AN BORDERLINE CASES

The criminal law also can have an effect in gaining compliance with its commands through another, related mechanism. If it earns a reputation as a reliable statement of what the community perceives as condemnable, people are more likely to defer to its commands as morally authoritative and as appropriate to follow in those borderline cases in which the propriety of certain conduct is unsettled or ambiguous in the mind of the actor. The importance of this role should not be underestimated; in a society with the complex interdependencies characteristic of ours, an apparently harmless action can have destructive consequences, and thus code drafters may "criminalize" the action. When the action is criminalized by the legal system, one would want the citizen to "respect the law" in such an instance even though he or she does not immediately intuit why that action is banned. Such deference will be facilitated if citizens are disposed to believe that the law is an accurate guide to appropriate prudential and moral behavior.

Social science research on "persuasion" supports this conclusion and illuminates the mechanisms of thought that bring it about. Lately persuasion researchers have distinguished between two types: one more analytic and direct, the other more peripheral and heuristic.[50] The latter is more relevant to our discussion here. This path often involves giving the person cues that lead her to believe that the action in question should be regarded as wrong or right, criminalized or decriminalized, without presenting the direct arguments why this should be so. It often relies heavily on the person's assessment of the source of the communication. Specifically, if the message comes from a credible and trustworthy source, people are likely to accept the rightness of the communication.[51] This is the immediate acceptance and obedience that Murray referred to as the "reflexive loyalty to the rule of law."[52]

---

[49] Richard Petty & John Cacioppo, Attitudes and Persuasion, Classic and Contemporary Approaches 62–69 (1996).

[50] Tilmann Betsch, Henning Plessner & Elke Schallies, *The Value-Account Model of Attitude Formation, in* Contemporary Perspectives on the Psychology of Altitudes 251, 252 (Geoffrey Haddock and Gregory Maio eds., 2004).

[51] Richard Petty & John Cacioppo, *The Elaboration Likelihood Model of Persuasion*, in 19 Advances in Experimental Social Psychology 123–205 (Lennard Berkowitz ed., 1986).

[52] Charles Murray, Op-Ed., *The G.O.P.'s Bad Bet*, N.Y. Times Oct. 19, 2006, at A27.

It is what the state relies on people giving when, for instance, the state passes security laws against "insider trading" of stocks based on news that is not yet known by the public. Without knowing quite why it is that "insider trading" is morally wrong, most of us accept the conclusion that it is wrong, because the relevant authorities have thought about it and assert that it is wrong. Or it is what we all count on when, as we travel down a highway that is new to us, we slow up when we see a sign saying "caution, blind curve," and count on others to slow up as well. It is, in one sense, "blind obedience," but it is extremely socially useful, and it functions based on attitudes of trust toward the source in turn based on past experiences of the source providing messages that turned out to be credible.

That citizens in general regard the law as a credible guide to how they ought to behave is shown by the responses of the random sample of Chicago citizens tested in Tyler's 1990 survey.[53] Eighty-two percent of the sample strongly agreed or agreed with the statement "disobeying the law is seldom justified," and 85 percent strongly agreed or agreed with the statement that "people should obey the law even if it goes against what they think is right."[54] However, it will be remembered that this survey also revealed that the people Tyler tested assigned a high degree of moral authority to legal codes, and it is this "moral credibility" that gives the law what social science calls its "informational influence": its power to bring about law-abiding behavior even when the citizens are unsure in their own minds that the behavior is correct.[55]

The connection between the criminal law's moral credibility and its crime-control effectiveness is not an entirely new idea. Johannes Andenaes remarks that "a certain degree of respect for the formal law is probably essential for the smooth functioning of society. Where it is lacking, law enforcement agencies play a role similar to that of an occupying army in foreign territory."[56] World War II helped create a popular view that violently opposing the rules imposed by an occupying army is not only not immoral, it is highly moral. When a criminal law offends the moral intuitions of the governed community, the power of the entire criminal code to gain compliance from the community is risked.

C. Deontological Desert and Empirical Desert

Section B makes the case for empirical desert as a distributive principle. As noted previously, there is considerable overlap between empirical desert and deontological desert, but they are different. Let me say more about their similarities and their differences.[57] Their differences are important because it is only empirical, not

---

[53] TYLER, *supra* note 498, at 46.

[54] *Id.*

[55] *Id.*

[56] JOHANNES ANDENAES, PUNISHMENT AND DETERRENCE 34 (1974).

[57] For a fuller account, *see* Paul H. Robinson, *Competing Conceptions of Modern Desert: Vengeful, Deontological, and Empirical*, 67 CAMBRIDGE L.J. 145, 148–155 (2008).

deontological, desert that triggers the crime-control effectiveness of enforced moral credibility with the community. Their similarities are important because the considerable overlap between them may prompt the supporters of deontological desert to accept empirical desert as perhaps the best practical approximation of deontological desert that they could hope to have operationalized.

1. TWO CONCEPTIONS OF DESERT

The deontological conception of desert focuses on the blameworthiness of the offender as drawn from the arguments and analyses of moral philosophy. "It is morally fitting that a person who does wrong should suffer in proportion to his wrongdoing. That a criminal should be punished follows from his guilt, and the severity of the appropriate punishment depends on the depravity of his act."[58] A key aspect of the deontological conception of desert is that it transcends the particular people and situation at hand and embodies a set of principles derived from fundamental values; principles of right and good; and thus will produce justice without regard to the political, social, or other peculiarities of the situation at hand. As Henry Sidgwick famously put it, moral judgments are made "from the point of view of the universe."[59]

Empirical desert, like deontological desert, similarly focuses on the blameworthiness of the offender, but in determining the principles by which punishment is to be assessed, it looks not to philosophical analyses but to the community's judgments of justice. The primary source of the principle, then, is empirical research into those factors that drive people's assessments of blameworthiness. The existing studies suggest that the variety of factors at work is as rich and varied as those at work in determining deontological desert.[60] The extent of the harm or evil plays an important role but is only one of a wide variety of factors, including many related to the offender's situation and personal capacities.

Also like deontological desert, empirical desert envisions a set of liability and punishment rules to be applied identically to all defendants; it is not the community's view of deserved punishment in a particular case that is relevant here. Further, in collecting data to construct the liability and punishment rules, real cases, especially publicly known ones, typically are not a useful source. People's views on such cases are commonly skewed by political or social context or by other factors, such as race, that all would agree have no proper role in setting principles of justice.[61] Instead, the community's judgments of justice must be derived from controlled social science studies that determine the factors that influence people's assessment of a violator's

---

58 J. Rawls, "Two Concepts of Rules, (1955) 64 PHILOSOPHICAL. REVIEW. 3, 5. Central here are the writings of Immanuel Kant. *See* "The Metaphysics of Morals" in H. Reiss ed. and H. B. Nisbet trans., *Immanuel Kant: Political Writings* (1991) p. 156.

59 H. Sidgwick, *The Methods of Ethics*, 7th ed., (London 1907) pp.420–21.

60 *See* chapter 17, section A.

61 *See* chapter 1, section C & shapter 2.

blameworthiness, not by asking people about abstract factors but rather by having them "sentence" a variety of carefully constructed variations of cases to see what factors produce what punishment differences among the scenarios.

2. WHERE THE TWO CONCEPTIONS AGREE

An important similarity between deontological and empirical desert is the lack of importance given to the absolute amount of punishment to be imposed.[62] For deontological and empirical desert, the absolute amount of punishment is of limited interest. Their central concern is the relative amount of punishment among cases of differing degrees of moral blameworthiness. They focus primarily on ensuring that the offender is given that amount of punishment that puts him in his proper ordinal rank among all cases of differing degrees of blameworthiness.[63]

While the absolute severity of punishment is not central to empirical or deontological desert, they might play some role in a society's setting its punishment continuum end point, but in doing so they operate differently than they do when performing their core function of establishing the proper ordinal rank of each case. In setting the punishment continuum end point, they might offer general guidance as to extremes that should be avoided, rather than to give guidance as the specific end point to pick. (It is in this limited sense that Norval Morris's "limiting retributivism" may have application.[64])

Another characteristic that deontological and empirical desert share is the significance given to punishment method. Neither insists that the punishment match the means by which the victim was made to suffer (as another conception of desert—vengeful desert—would). Deontological and empirical desert focus only on the amount of punishment—an amount that will put the offender in his proper ordinal rank according to his blameworthiness. As long as the total punitive "bite" of the punishment achieves this proper ranking, these conceptions of desert have little reason to care about the method by which that amount of punitive "bite" is imposed.[65]

While a variety of different sanctioning methods might be used, the offender should get punishment "credit" for each only in proportion to the punitive "bite" of that method. This requires, then, establishment of ratios between the different

---

[62] This is not the case with a third conception of desert, vengeful desert, whose focus is on this absolute amount of punishment: It must be similar in amount, if not also in means, to the suffering caused by the offense conduct. J. Dressler, *The Wisdom and Morality of Present-Day Criminal Sentencing*, 38 AKRON L. REV. 853, 860 (2005). For a modern defense of this "reciprocity principle," as it is sometimes called. *See* L. Crocker, *The Upper Limit of Just Punishment*, 41 EMORY L.J. 1059, 1065 (1992).

[63] A. von Hirsch, *Past or Future Crimes: Deservedness and Dangerousness in the Sentencing of Criminals* (New Brunswick 1985) pp. 39–46.

[64] Recall earlier discussion of Morris's theory in chapter 1, section B.

[65] *See*, for example, M. S. Moore, "The Moral Worth of Retribution, in Responsibility, Character and Emotions," in F. Schoeman (ed.), *Responsibility, Character, and the Emotions* (Cambridge 1988), p. 180.

punishment methods that reflect the differences in their punitive "bite." If the "bite" of one week in jail is equivalent to that of a month of weekends in jail or is equivalent to that of 80 hours of community service, these two conceptions of desert would be satisfied with any of these sentences, so long as that amount of punishment was the amount deserved given the offender's blameworthiness. The ideal equivalency table would be one that generates alternative sanctions about which an offender and a community are indifferent as to which is imposed.[66]

3. WHERE THE TWO CONCEPTIONS DISAGREE

While deontological desert and empirical desert have many similarities, they also have important differences. This is as one might expect, given that they are based on different notions of blameworthiness: reasoned analysis from principles of right and good versus people's shared judgments of justice. These differences in underlying criterion can produce important differences in the distribution of liability and punishment. For example, moral philosophers disagree about the significance of resulting harm—for example, whether to punish attempts the same as the substantive offense—and each side of the debate has plausible arguments to make. In contrast, all available data suggest a nearly universal and deeply held view among lay persons that resulting harm does matter, that it increases an offender's deserved punishment.[67] This is only one of a host of issues on which moral philosophy's analytic conclusions may vary from the empirical data on lay persons' judgments of justice.[68]

Perhaps even more important than such differences in blameworthiness judgments are the differences between the underlying theories that drive the two conceptions of desert and that thereby shape their application. In its most fundamental form, the difference is this: the special value of the empirical conception of desert is its utilitarian effectiveness in crime control; the special value of the deontological conception of desert is its ability to produce true principles of justice independent of personal or community opinion.

As has been argued in section B and will be confirmed by recent empirical studies in chapter 9, there are good reasons to suggest that there is great utility in a distribution of liability and punishment according to people's shared judgments of justice, perhaps greater than the utility of distributing liability and punishment in the traditional utilitarian manner (to optimize deterrence, rehabilitation, or incapacitation). No such utility arises from deontological desert. To follow it where it deviates from empirical desert is to undermine the law's moral credibility with the community,

---

[66] *See* Paul H. Robinson, *Desert, Crime Control, Disparity, and Units of Punishment*, in PENAL THEORY AND PRACTICE: TRADITION AND INNOVATION IN CRIMINAL JUSTICE, 93–107 (A. Duff eds. 1994).

[67] *See, e.g.*, chapter 12, section B; chapter 16, section D.

[68] For community views on a wide variety of criminal law issues, see Paul H. Robinson, *The Role of Moral Philosophers in the Competition between Philosophical and Empirical Desert*, 48 WM. & MARY L. REV. 1831–1843 (2007).

thereby undercutting its normative influence. Even if the philosophers who suggest that resulting harm ought to be irrelevant in assessing punishment were correct in their analysis, a criminal law based upon such a view would be seriously discredited in the eyes of lay persons, as an unreliable judge of the principles of justice.

But while empirical desert has the advantage of crime-control utility, its reliance upon the community's judgments of justice presents a serious disadvantage. The community's intuitions of justice could be wrong, even if there is a high degree of agreement about them. Empirical desert can tell us only what people think is just; only deontological desert can tell us what is actually just. Like slave owners in the Old South or anti-Semitic Germans before World War II, one may fail to appreciate the injustice of one's views until later, especially if one's views at the time are shared by a large number of other people. Even a popular liability or punishment rule may be unjust. Only deontological desert can spot these justice errors in people's justice judgments and can provide a conception of desert that transcends time, community, and culture. Only deontological desert can give us the means by which we can tell the truth of what is deserved, insulated from the vicissitudes of human irrationality.

D. Criticisms of Empirical Desert as a Distributive Principle

A variety of criticisms have been offered against using empirical desert as the distributive principle for criminal liability and punishment. Some have persuasive responses; others do not. A brief discussion of the most common criticisms may be useful here. The first two criticisms below have already been confronted, in chapters 1 and 2, so only a brief reminder is needed here. Several others require a more detailed response. This section is drawn primarily from portions of my article with John Darley, *Intuitions of Justice: Implications for Criminal Law and Justice Policy.*[69]

1. NOTIONS OF DESERT AS HOPELESSLY VAGUE

A common objection to any kind of desert as a distributive principle is its so-called vagueness. Some writers, such as Norval Morris,[70] may be willing to concede that desert is not a hopelessly vague concept—that it has some meaning but would make a related yet slightly different criticism: desert cannot specify a particular amount of punishment that should be imposed; it can only identify ranges of punishment that should not be imposed because they would be seriously disproportionate.

But as discussed in chapter 1, section B, such complaints are based in part on a failure to appreciate the specific demands of desert. Recall that part of the confusion

---

[69] Paul H. Robinson & John M. Darley, *Intuitions of Justice: Implications for Criminal Law and Justice Policy*, 81 S. Cal. L. Rev. 1, 18–31 (2007).

[70] Norval Morris, The Future of Imprisonment 75–76 (1974).

here arises from the failure to distinguish two distinct judgments: setting the end point of the punishment continuum and, once that end point has been set, ordering all cases along that punishment continuum. Every society must decide what punishment it will allow for its most egregious case, be it the death penalty or life imprisonment or 15 years. Once that end point is set, the process of distributing punishment requires only an ordinal ranking of offenders according to their blameworthiness. The result of that process is the specific amount of punishment needed to set the offender's offense at its appropriate ordinal rank according to its blameworthiness relative to all other offenses.

But this does not settle the vagueness issue. Some writers argue that even ordinal ranking is something that can be done only in the vaguest terms and that establishing specific rankings is impossible. The claim is that the ranking of offenses based on blameworthiness is beyond the ability of people's judgments of justice, because those judgments are too vague to do more than roughly distinguish between "serious" cases and "nonserious" cases and cannot provide the nuance needed to do more.

This is an empirical claim, and its does not match the empirical reality. As shown in chapter 1, section C, the evidence from a wide variety of empirical studies is quite clear: subjects display a good deal of nuance in the judgments they make. Small changes in facts produce large and predictable changes in punishment. Durham summarizes the surveys this way: "virtually without exception, citizens seem able to assign highly specific sentences for highly specific events."[71] The conclusion suggested by the empirical evidence is that people take account of a wide variety of factors and often give them quite different effect in different situations. That is, people's intuitions of justice are not vague or simplistic, as claimed, but rather quite sophisticated and complex.

2. HOPELESS DISAGREEMENT AS TO NOTIONS OF DESERT

The other common objection to using empirical desert as a distributive principle for criminal liability and punishment is the concern that, even if individuals may have a clear notion of what desert demands, there is simply no agreement among people. This objection was dealt with in chapter 2. Again, the common wisdom simply does not match the empirical reality. The extent of agreement on the relative seriousness of different cases has in the past been obscured by disagreements over the general severity of punishment or the punishment continuum end point. Further, some apparent sources of disagreement are misleading. For example, poor testing methods will predictably underestimate the extent of agreement. When a test scenario is written ambiguously so that different test participants perceive it differently, the existence of shared intuitions of justice itself will predict different

[71] Alexis M. Durham III, *Public Opinion Regarding Sentences for Crime: Does it Exist?*, 21 J. CRIM. JUSTICE 1, 2 (1993).

judgments among the participants. So too, when a case in the headlines has social or political implications, it is common that its relevant facts will be perceived differently by different people.

The studies discussed in chapter 2 show broadly shared intuitions that serious wrongdoing should be punished, as well as broadly shared intuitions about the relative blameworthiness of different cases. Recall the conclusion that there are stable, significant agreements as to the deserved degree of punishment merited by various criminal acts, and that these agreements exist across cultures. This is not to say that there are no disagreements among people's judgments of justice. As chapter 4 makes clear, people obviously do disagree about many things relating to crime and punishment. However, there does exist a core of issues on which there is enormous agreement across demographics.

3. PEOPLE INTUITIVELY ASSESS PUNISHMENT ACCORDING TO DETERRENCE OR INCAPACITATION

Another criticism leveled against empirical desert is that people's intuitions of justice are not distinct from conceptions of deterrence or incapacitation. That is, people make intuitive judgments of justice according to utilitarian models and not according to the desert model. However, several studies have examined the issue of what criteria people rely on when they make intuitive judgments of justice and found that it is desert, not deterrence or incapacitation, that drives people's assignments of punishment.[72]

The first set of studies explored the intuitive use of just deserts and incapacitation as models for judgments about justice. Participants were given 10 short descriptions of criminal cases, which were generated by combining five levels of moral seriousness, "case seriousness" (theft of a CD, theft of a valuable object, assault, homicide, and assassination) with two levels of perpetrator's criminal history, "case recidivism" (no prior history, history of actions consistent with the crime committed). Participants read each scenario separately and after reading were prompted to rate the case on two scales: first a seven-point scale of the severity of the punishment that should be imposed, ranging from "not at all" to "extremely severe;" and second a 13-point scale of criminal liability, ranging from "no liability" to "death penalty." After submitting their liability judgments on these scales, participants were asked to reconsider the scenarios and assign punishments from a just deserts perspective and from an incapacitation perspective, respectively. The just deserts standard instructed participants to assign "the just punishment that the criminal *deserves* for

---

[72] *See* John M. Darley, Kevin M. Carlsmith & Paul H. Robinson, *Incapacitation and Just Deserts as Motives for Punishment*, 24 L. & HUM. BEHAV. 659 (2000) [hereinafter *Incapacitation and Just Deserts*]; Kevin M. Carlsmith, John M. Darley & Paul H. Robinson, *Why Do We Punish? Deterrence and Just Deserts as Motives for Punishment*, 83 J. PERSONALITY & SOC. PSYCHOL. 284 (2002) [hereinafter *Deterrence and Just Deserts*].

the wrong he did," the incapacitation standard instructed participants to assign "a sentence long enough to protect society from further harms by this person."[73]

The results showed that participants were more responsive to case seriousness than to case recidivism. More importantly, participants' punishment assignments based on just deserts were closely aligned with their original intuitive decisions, while the punishments they assigned using the incapacitation model were not. "What this suggests is that the default perspective of sentencing is indistinguishable from the just deserts perspective, but that both are significantly different from the incapacitation perspective."[74]

Another set of studies explored participants' reliance upon a just deserts model as opposed to one of deterrence. In a series of related studies, participants were given criminal scenarios that varied on a two-by-two format: the scenarios included high and low desert situations (severity of offense, extenuating circumstances) and high and low deterrence factors (detection rate, publicity). Different variations of deterrence and desert factors were used, and participants were asked to rate the scenarios based on the same scales described above, along with study-specific questions including whether they endorsed or rejected general statements about the two theories, the moral acceptability of the crime committed, and how much resources should be expanded to either catch the perpetrator or prevent future occurrences.

The results of these studies reinforce the notion that people's intuitive default for assigning criminal liability is consistent with a just deserts model. While participants explicitly endorsed statements of deterrence justification for punishment, in fact, they meted out sentences "from a strictly deservingness-based stance."[75] All of the studies indicated that where an actor perpetrates an intentional harm on another, people assign that actor punishment in relation to the actor's deservingness, rather than out of concern for deterrent effect. While participants support the concept and goals of deterrence, this does not translate into differential assignments of punishment.

Finally, in a third experiment, the researcher used a "judgment tracing method" to examine whether punishment intuitions were based on just deserts considerations.[76] In this method, the respondent is initially told only, for instance, that an offender has embezzled a certain amount from his employer. It is the respondent's task to determine the appropriate sentence by examining in a self-selecting order various pieces of information about the crime. The researcher then examines the order in which the subject acquires the information, inferring that the most important information is acquired first. The information "bits" used in the study were either relevant to just deserts issues, incapacitation, or deterrence. Results showed

---

73 *Incapacitation and Just Deserts*, *supra* note 539, at 681.

74 Kevin M. Carlsmith, John M. Darley & Paul H. Robinson, *Why Do We Punish? Deterrence and Just Deserts as Motives for Punishment*, 83 J. PERSONALITY & SOC. PSYCHOL. 284, 667 (2002).

75 *Deterrence and Just Deserts*, *supra* note 539, at 295.

76 Kevin M. Carlsmith. *The Roles of Retribution and Utility in Determining Punishment*, 42 J. EXPERIMENTAL SOC. PSYCHOL 437 (2006).

that participants initially requested information related to desert considerations. Only later did some seek information relevant to incapacitation, and rarely sought deterrence-relevant information.

Subjects were asked their level of confidence in the punishment judgment at each point in their acquisition of information. Increments in the respondents' confidence in their proposed sentence for the crime were most influenced by the just deserts information. This effect could have occurred because the just deserts information was acquired first, when the respondents' uncertainly would have been maximal. However, in a follow-up study, this condition was removed, and the desert information continued to be the most effective in increasing the confidence of the respondents in their sentencing assignments.[77]

These studies, taken together, support the conclusion that lay judgments about punishment are based primarily on just deserts considerations.

4. EMPIRICAL DESERT AS INEVITABLY DRACONIAN

Some resistance to giving empirical desert a role in setting criminal liability rules comes from a line of reasoning that goes something like this: (1) I don't like many of the draconian modern crime-control reforms—such as the three-strikes statutes, lowering the age of prosecution as an adult, high penalties for drug offenses, the trend toward expanding the scope of criminalization to what had previously been regulatory offenses. (2) These reforms are the product of recent legislative actions that reflect the community's views. (3) Thus, giving explicit deference to empirical desert will only increase the influence of an apparent public preference for such draconian measures.

However, such reasoning both misconceives the nature of empirical desert and mistakenly assumes that modern American crime politics track people's judgments of justice. In fact, empirical desert has little, if anything, to do with people's views on the cases and issues in political debate, and modern American crime politics have just as little to do with people's judgments of justice. On the contrary, the modern crime-control reforms noted above seriously conflict with people's shared intuitions of justice. Chapter 9 presents empirical studies that demonstrate this point directly.

Empirical desert embodies those principles of justice that people intuitively rely upon in making judgments about relative blameworthiness, not their professed views on matters of public debate. The most reliable method for determining people's judgments of justice is giving a series of cases, seeing how they treat the cases differently, than deducing from the factual differences among the cases the factors that are shaping the person's judgments. It is how people actually assess blameworthiness that can be trusted, not the positions they take on abstract public debates. Further, people's political views or their reactions to the cases in the headlines commonly have little to do with their judgments of justice. Too often, a political position or a case in the

---

[77] *Id.* at 447.

headlines brings with it political baggage that colors people's views. Whether one supports or opposes the death penalty, for example, is an issue that people see as placing them in a larger complex of social and political dimensions, which involve much more than their judgments of justice.

Perhaps more importantly, the engine driving American crime politics is not people's judgments of justice. On the contrary, it is primarily crime-control theories, most notably deterrence and incapacitation, which commonly conflict with desert, deontological and empirical. Three-strikes statutes, lowering the age of prosecution as an adult, high penalties for drug offenses, expanding the scope of criminalization to what had previously been regulatory offenses, and other recent popular reforms are typically justified by their purported ability to reduce crime, not by a claim that they are necessary to do justice. The increased criminalization and penalties are justified as needed to produce a stronger deterrent threat. And the longer prison terms are said to more effectively incapacitate persons seen as likely to recidivate. Chapter 9 will demonstrate that these crime-control doctrines not only do not embody people's judgment of justice but seriously conflict with them.

5. EMPIRICAL DESERT AS POTENTIALLY IMMORAL

While empirical desert may not be hopelessly vague, the subject of eviscerating disagreement, or intolerably draconian, it is subject to a valid and important criticism: it is potentially unjust as a distributive principle. As touched on above at the conclusion of section C, while a community may share a view that certain conduct is moral or certain punishment is just, such shared views do not make it so. Recall the cases of slaveholders in the pre-Civil War South. Empirical desert can only tell us what people think is just. It cannot tell us what is actually just in a transcendent sense. That is a task for moral philosophers, in determining "deontological desert."

This is, of course, an objection to all utilitarian principles for the distribution of liability and punishment. They set as their guiding purpose not the doing of transcendent justice but rather maximizing utility, chiefly by reducing future crime. Among utilitarian principles, empirical desert may be the least objectionable on these grounds, for it may best approximate a distribution according to true moral blameworthiness. Nonetheless, it is conceptually and practically distinct from deontological desert and can fairly be criticized as at least potentially deviating from it.

To protect against a community's judgments of justice that are wrong, a system must look beyond the empirical desert the social scientists can discover, to the deontological desert of moral philosophy that will provide a transcendent check on the justness of its liability rules. Unfortunately, an examination of the modern methodology of moral philosophers suggests that they fail to appreciate the importance of the difference between deontological and empirical desert. They commonly rely heavily upon shared judgments of justice in their analyses, and thereby bias their conclusions in favor of principles of justice that match people's shared judgments of justice. That reduces the extent to which moral philosophy can be relied upon to provide the transcendent check that empirical desert needs.[78]

The current methodology of moral philosophers relies upon judgments of justice in a variety of ways. A standard analytic form, if not *the* standard form, among moral philosophers of today is to test variations in a series of hypotheticals according to the philosophers' own intuitions about the proper resolution of each, as a basis for building moral principles, as in Rawls's "reflective equilibrium."[79] The differences in the philosopher's judgments about the intuitively proper resolution of different hypotheticals are used as data points, as it were, from which philosophers derive a moral principle, which can in turn be tested and refined by testing that moral principle against the philosophers' intuitions in new sets of hypotheticals.[80]

But the methodological reliance on the philosophers' intuitions of justice creates a bias in favor of moral principles that are consistent with intuitions. Moral principles with reasoned support might fail to gain currency among philosophers or might be discarded, simply because philosophers as a group think their results inconsistent with their shared intuitions—a practical veto by philosophers' shared intuitions.[81]

Perhaps even more problematic than the tendency to rely upon shared intuitions of justice is the practical problem that arises from the well-known tendency of philosophers to disagree among themselves about many, if not most, things. How, as a practical matter, is a community to decide which group of philosophers to follow and which to reject? In other words, while moral philosophy might seem, as a theoretical matter, to provide a check on empirical desert, as a practical matter it may be nearly useless in this regard.

The failure of modern philosophy to provide a reliable guard against a community's shared but immoral intuitions of justice can make empirical desert both more and less attractive as a distributive principle. On the one hand, it means that moral philosophy is unavailable to provide the transcendent check on intuitions of justice that is needed. That makes empirical desert less attractive as a distributive principle. On the other hand, it means that deontological desert provides little or no advantage over empirical desert as a distributive principle. Thus, if empirical desert has any real competition, it is among other utilitarian theories. And among the utilitarian theories, empirical desert will be the one most likely to approximate true justice. It at least sets moral blameworthiness as its prime criterion, which no other utilitarian

---

[78] For a full discussion, *see* Robinson, *The Role of Moral Philosophers in the Competition between Deontological and Empirical Deserts*, 48 WM. & MARY L. REV 1831 (2007) [hereinafter Robinson, *Moral Philosophers*].

[79] JOHN RAWLS, A THEORY OF JUSTICE 48 (1971) (explaining that the best sense of justice is one which matches a person's judgments in reflective equilibrium—a state reached after consideration of various conceptions of justice).

[80] *Id.* For an example of moral philosophers using intuitive analysis of case hypotheticals as a standard method, *see* Leo Katz, *Incommensurable Choices and the Problem of Moral Ignorance*, 146 U. PA. L. REV. 1465, 1482–83 (1998).

[81] *See* Robinson, *Moral Philosophers*, *supra* note 544.

distributive principles do. At the same time, for all the reasons summarized in section B, it also will be the one most likely to reduce crime in the long run.

E. Conclusion

To conclude, some criticisms of empirical desert as a distributive principle for criminal liability and punishment, but not all, are unfounded. Arguments that intuitions of justice are hopelessly vague or the subject of eviscerating disagreement either fail to appreciate the rank-order method of desert judgments or simply make assumptions that are inconsistent with the empirical evidence. Similarly inconsistent with available empirical evidence is the claim that people's intuitions about justice are based on notions of deterrence and incapacitation or are draconian. On the other hand, it is fair to complain that following empirical desert does not guarantee that true justice, in a transcendent sense, will be done.

To return to the larger project, consider empirical desert as a distributive principle as compared to the other traditional alternatives. The strengths and weaknesses of deontological and empirical desert can be summarized in the table below, along with the summaries for the coercive crime-control distributive principles developed in section A.

TABLE 16. } Summary of Distributive Principles and Their Strengths and Weaknesses

DP	Strengths/Advantages	Weaknesses/Disadvantages
GD	• under right conditions can avoid crime • can have effect beyond offender at hand	• works only when prerequisite conditions exist, which may not be common: knowledge of the deterrence-based rule, capacity and inclination to rationally calculate one's own best interest, perception that costs of crime (probability x punishment) exceed benefits • can give punishment other than what is deserved
SD	• under right conditions can avoid crime by offender at hand	• works only on the offender at hand • works only when prerequisite conditions exist can give punishment other than what is deserved
RH	• if successful, can avoid crime by offender at hand • may have value in itself, in making person's life better	• works only on the offender at hand • only modest success in only limited cases • can give punishment other than what is deserved • problematic as sole DP; must combine with another • forcibly changing person's nature may raise ethical questions about intruding upon personal autonomy
Inc	• no doubt that effective in reducing crime by offender at hand	• works only on the offender at hand • commonly inaccurate in predictions, which causes wasted costs and unjustified detentions • can give punishment other than what is deserved • can better reduce prevention costs, reduce damage to system's moral credibility, and increase accuracy by operating as open civil preventive detention system apart from CJ system

DP	Strengths/Advantages	Weaknesses/Disadvantages
ED	• most likely to be seen as just punishment, which can increase criminal law moral credibility, thus crime control benefit	• may do injustice that is not apparent to the present community • failure to deviate from empirical desert misses special crime control opportunities that can arise when deterrence prerequisites are satisfied (e.g., high deterrent effect possible, reliable prediction of high probability of an offender's serious future offense)
DD	• does justice	• fails to prevent avoidable crime • difficulty in operationalizing because of common disagreement among moral philosophers

Empirical desert may offer the best balance of advantages over disadvantages. It may be preferable for both instrumentalist and deontological reasons. An empirical desert distribution would provide opportunities for deterrence, incapacitation, and rehabilitation, yet would avoid the crimogenic effect of undermining the criminal law's normative influence by conflicting with the community's judgments of justice. Empirical desert also may offer the best practical approximation of deontological desert—the closest to justice in a transcendent sense that we can hope to get. The fact we know empirical desert does not itself produce true deontological desert enables us to be on the lookout for issues on which community views of justice could be wrong, and to give those community views the scrutiny and criticism they deserve.

9}

Building Moral Credibility and the Disutility of Injustice

Chapter 8 argued that there is commonly greater utility in distributing liability and punishment according to people's shared judgments of justice than in distributing liability and punishment under the traditional coercive crime-control principles of deterrence, rehabilitation, or incapacitation.[1] Specifically, it argued that the extent of the criminal law's effectiveness in bringing the power of stigmatization to bear, in avoiding resistance and subversion to a system perceived as unjust, in facilitating, communicating, and maintaining societal consensus on what is and is not condemnable; and in gaining compliance in borderline cases through deference to its moral authority is to a great extent dependent on the degree to which the criminal law has gained moral credibility in the minds of the citizens governed by it. Thus, the criminal law's moral credibility is essential to effective crime control, and is enhanced if the distribution of criminal liability is perceived as "doing justice"—that is, if it assigns liability and punishment in ways that the community perceives as consistent with its shared judgments of justice. Conversely, the system's moral credibility, and therefore its crime-control effectiveness, is undermined by a distribution of liability that conflicts with community perceptions of desert.

This chapter presents a wide variety of studies that give empirical support to those theoretical arguments of the previous chapter. Even within the limits of how researchers can manipulate the system's moral credibility in a laboratory, the evidence shows that changes in the system's moral credibility produce changes in people's willingness to defer to the system's judgments and values, and to internalize them as their own. This chapter is drawn from portions of my article with Geoffrey Goodwin and Michael Reisig, *The Disutility of Injustice*.[2]

---

[1] For a fuller account, *see* PAUL H. ROBINSON, DISTRIBUTIVE PRINCIPLES OF CRIMINAL LAW: WHO SHOULD BE PUNISHED HOW MUCH? 175–210 (2008) [hereinafter ROBINSON, DISTRIBUTIVE PRINCIPLES]; Paul H. Robinson & John M. Darley, *Utility of Desert*, 91 NW. U. L. REV. 453 (1997) [hereinafter Robinson & Darley, *Utility of Desert*]; Paul H. Robinson & John M. Darley, *Intuitions of Justice: Implications for Criminal law and Justice Policy*, 81 S. CAL. L. REV. 1 (2007) [hereinafter Robinson & Darley, *Intuitions of Justice*].

[2] Paul H. Robinson, Geoffrey P. Goodwin, & Michael D. Reisig, *The Disutility of Injustice*, 85 N.Y.U. L. REV. 1942, 1997–2016 (2010).

A. Recent Empirical Studies on the Disutility of Injustice

This section describes two empirical studies whose results support the arguments made in chapter 8, section B. The studies were designed to test for evidence that a criminal justice system's reduced moral credibility produces disillusionment that, in turn, undermines the deference that moral credibility brings. Specifically, the studies examine whether knowledge of the extent to which existing criminal law doctrines deviate from ordinary judgments of justice can affect people's general respect for the law, as well as their intention to cooperate, support, and comply with it. The hypothesis tested in Studies A and B was that, where criminal law doctrines deviate dramatically from ordinary judgments of justice, such awareness of the law's predictable injustices and failures of justice could indeed negatively affect people's attitudes toward the law, as well as weakening their behavioral intentions to cooperate, support, and comply with it.

1. STUDY A DESIGN AND METHODOLOGY

In Study A, 59 subjects (34 female, 25 male; age range of 18 to 77) were tested using a simple pre-post design. Subjects were first asked a series of questions to assess their general attitudes and behavioral intentions with regard to the criminal justice system, which establishes their baseline responses. They were then exposed to a set of cases in which the criminal justice system in a hypothetical jurisdiction gave liability and punishment that was unjust: either too high or too low. All cases and results were real but not from any single jurisdiction. Subjects were then asked the same set of questions regarding their views to be answered on the assumption that they lived in that hypothetical jurisdiction. The question of interest was whether their answers on the questions (when subjects responded as if they were living in that hypothetical system) would differ from their earlier baseline answers (applicable to the criminal justice system in which they currently lived).

The eight questions of most interest for present purposes are reproduced in Table 17 below. A subset of these questions—Questions 1, 2, and 3—examines the extent to which people regard the criminal law as a reliable source of moral authority, whose norms they are likely to internalize. A second subset—Questions 4, 5, and 6—examines people's willingness to cooperate with and assist in the operation of the criminal justice system. For instance, these questions shed light on how willing people are to report conduct deemed criminal, even though it may not seem particularly condemnable to them. A third subset—Questions 7 and 8—examines people's intentions to comply with the criminal law's rules in morally gray areas. All questions were to be answered on a nine-point Likert scale, which asked subjects to rate their level of agreement with each statement, ranging from 1: "strongly disagree" to 9: "strongly agree," with interim points for "disagree," "agree," and "unsure." As is usual with such scales, most subjects avoided the extremes and answered within the range of 3: "disagree" to 7: "agree." The questions were presented at the beginning of the survey in a new random order for each subject.

TABLE 17. } Questions on the Effect of Moral Credibility of the Criminal Justice System

Question: Agree or disagree?
1. Life sentence means offense conduct must be heinous You see a story on the evening news about a prisoner who was sentenced to life in prison. Based on his extremely harsh sentence, you would conclude that the person must have committed a heinous crime and believe that he deserves the punishment that he got.
2. Law prohibition means posting false comments must be condemnable You learn from a newspaper story that posting false negative comments on another person's online profile site (e.g., Facebook) can count as an act of criminal libel. Based on the criminal law's prohibition of this act, you would consider it to be condemnable.
3. High sentence for financial maneuver means condemnable Your newspaper reports that a particular financial maneuver on taxes has just been made a crime and that the law has assigned it a very serious sentence of 28 to 32 years. Because the law assigns such a high sentence, you would conclude that the conduct must be morally condemnable and probably deserves such a sentence.
4. Report removal of arrowhead You learn of a person in your town who has illegally taken an arrowhead from an important historical site that he visited. It is illegal to take anything from the site. You would report the removal to the relevant authorities.
5. Give found handgun to police You are walking through an alley and find a handgun next to a sewer drain. You think it might not be safe for children to leave it there, but you worry that picking it up and carrying it to police might create problems for you. No one is around to see what you are doing. You would pick up the gun and take it to the police.
6. Report dog violation to authorities Your neighbor is a dog lover. He recently got three more dogs, for a total of six. The law only allows three dogs in a single home. You might report the neighbor's new dogs to the relevant authorities.
7. Go back and report your mistake to gas station While on vacation in a place that is distant from the one you live in, you drive off from a gas station without paying. You realize this later, but you also know that the employees could have no knowledge of your identity, and that you would not be traceable. You have the possibility to turn back and report your mistake, but you are somewhat concerned that this act itself would lead to some penalty. You would turn back or attempt to contact the gas station to correct for your mistake.
8. Go back and report your mistake to restaurant While on vacation in a place that is distant from the one you live in, you drive off from a restaurant without paying. You realize this later, but you also know that the employees could have no knowledge of your identity, and that you would not be traceable. You have the possibility to turn back and report your mistake, but you are somewhat concerned that this act itself would lead to some penalty. You would turn back or attempt to contact the restaurant to correct for your mistake.

The responses to these questions were used to establish a baseline. Subjects were then presented with seven real-world cases, for which pilot testing had shown that the liability or sentence actually given in the case deviated dramatically from ordinary intuitions. Several of these cases engage the modern crime-control doctrines described in chapter 7, section B. Subjects were instructed truthfully that all of the cases and sentences were real. They read each case in turn and assigned a sentence that they thought was appropriate, if any, from a drop-down menu of sentences.[3]

[3] The options presented to subjects were as follows: Death, Life, 30 years, 26 years, 22.5 years, 19 years, 15 years, 13 years, 11 years, 9 years, 7 years, 6 years, 5 years, 4 years, 3 years, 2.5 years, 2 years, 1.5 years, 1 year, 10.5 months, 9 months, 7.5 months, 6 months, 5 months, 4 months, 3 months, 2 months, 6.5 weeks, 5 weeks, 3.5 weeks, 2 weeks, 11 days, 1 week, 4 days, 1 day, Liability but no punishment, No punishment.

The actual sentences assigned to these cases were then revealed to the subjects,[4] with instructions reminding them that these sentences had all come from real-life cases. Out of the seven cases, five had real-world sentences much more severe than most people judged appropriate, whereas the remaining two received no sentence, though most people answered that a serious sentence should be imposed. For each case in turn, the actual sentence was revealed to the subjects, and the computer program that administered the survey also fed back the sentence that the subject had previously assigned. Subjects were asked to calculate the difference between the two sentences and to enter it on the screen. This exercise was a means of focusing the subjects' attention on the difference between their own intuitions and the sentences actually imposed in the hypothetical system. Subjects next responded to the same set of questions that were asked in the first part of the survey, set out in Table 17, and instructed to respond to those questions as if they were living in the hypothetical criminal justice system that had assigned the liability and sentences they had just seen.

The specific hypothesis was that learning about the injustices created by the current criminal justice system (described to subjects as a hypothetical system), including those described in chapter 7, section B, would undermine the system's moral credibility and have the detrimental effects on attitudes suggested in chapter 8, section B. The prediction was that when responding to questions about how they would think and act if they were living in the hypothetical system, subjects would be less inclined to defer to the criminal law or to internalize it and less inclined to cooperate and comply with it.

2. STUDY A RESULTS AND DISCUSSION

Subjects' average sentences were, as expected, dramatically different from the actual sentences imposed by the criminal justice system for each of the seven cases.[5] The data critical for the main hypothesis concerns the differences between the time 1 (pre-stimulation) and time 2 (post-stimulation) responses to the questions that asked about intentions and attitudes with regard to the criminal justice system. As Table 18 below shows, subjects' attitudes and behavioral intentions at time 2 shifted noticeably from what they had been at the time 1 baseline. For seven questions, responses moved reliably in the direction of decreased reliance on, and decreased willingness to comply and cooperate with the criminal law. For one question (#2), this decrement was only marginally reliable. Moreover, these shifts occurred with respect to each of the three areas of interest investigated: deference to the law in drawing conclusions about condemnability of conduct relevant to shaping norms, intention to cooperate with and assist the system, and intention to comply with it. The eight questions on which these shifts occurred, and the means for both time points, were as follows:

---

[4] Shown in column 4 of Appendix C.

[5] To see the figures from the study, refer to Robinson, Goodwin, & Reisig, *Disutility of Injustice*, *supra* note 548, at 2031.

TABLE 18. } Study A Pre- and Post-Stimulation Averages

Question	Baseline average	Post-stimulation average	Significance
1. Life sentence means offense conduct must be heinous	6.46	5.14	p<.001
2. Law prohibition means posting false comments must be condemnable	6.14	5.76	p<.07
3. High sentence for financial maneuver means condemnable	5.25	4.63	p<.02
4. Report removal of arrowhead	5.93	5.14	p<.01
5. Give found handgun to police	6.66	5.56	p<.001
6. Report dog violation to authorities	5.15	4.59	p<.01
7. Go back and report your mistake to gas station	7.05	5.69	p<.001
8. Go back and report your mistake to restaurant	7.15	5.71	p<.001

The size of these shifts was predicted by subjects' responses to the first general question about whether the hypothetical system assigned deserved punishments. For each of the eight items, the degree to which subjects saw the hypothetical system as assigning unjust punishments correlated with the size of their attitude shift from time 1 to time 2. These correlations are important because they show the link between individuals' general beliefs about the justness of the hypothetical system, and their more specific attitudes and intentions with regard to that system.

Study A shows how knowledge that a criminal justice system produces systematic injustices can produce negative attitudes toward that system. It also suggests that those negative attitudes can lead to diminished intentions to defer to, cooperate with, and comply with the law. The systematic changes in attitude and intentions observed between time 1 and time 2 occurred even with a relatively small sample size (N < 60), suggesting that the effects are not small.

However, the within-subjects design of Study A is open to a possible criticism concerning demand characteristics—that by asking the same questions twice, there may have been an implicit suggestion perceived by some subjects that the experimenters expected them to change their responses. While acknowledging this point, it is important to note that the subjects were participating in a web survey, and that they were entirely anonymous, which in contrast to a laboratory setting should diminish the implied pressure to respond in a way that is perceived to be desired by the researcher. Also clouding the effect is the fact that the "disillusioning cases" moved in both directions—some too harsh, some too lenient—making it less than obvious what change in responses the experimenters might be expecting. However, to more conclusively rule out this possibility, Study B was run that employed similar measures to those used in Study A, but with a between-subjects manipulation in which each subject would be asked the questions only once.

3. STUDY B DESIGN AND METHODOLOGY

The total number of 207 subjects (137 female, 70 male) were randomly assigned by the survey program to one of two groups. The experimental, or "high disillusioned" group (N = 108) was presented with the same series of seven real-world cases that were presented in Study A, in which the actual sentencing outcome deviates dramatically from ordinary intuitions. Subjects read each case, in turn, and assigned a sentence that they thought was appropriate, if any. The actual sentences imposed in these cases were then revealed, alongside subjects' own sentences. As in Study A, subjects were instructed that these cases and sentences were all real and that they should assume that they had all been given by a single, hypothetical criminal justice system. Subjects then responded to the same eight questions that were asked in Study A (see Table 17), which were presented in a new random order for each subject.

The "low-disillusionment" group (N = 99) followed the same procedure, except that the seven cases being "sentenced" by subjects were chosen so that the actual sentences given by courts in the cases accord more closely with ordinary lay intuitions[6]—that is, none of the cases engaged the application of one of the modern crime-control doctrines discussed in chapter 7, section B.

The hypothesis again was that exposure to the injustices and failures of justice created by the criminal justice system, including those created by the modern crime-control doctrines, would undermine the system's moral credibility and have the same detrimental effects shown in Study A. Thus, it was predicted that when reporting how they would think and act in the hypothetical criminal justice system, the high-disillusionment group would report less inclination to defer to and to cooperate and comply with it than the low-disillusionment group. The comparison between high- and low-disillusionment groups equates the procedures in the two conditions as closely as possible, and therefore allows for testing of the specific causal effect of disillusionment.

As in Study A, at the conclusion of the survey, subjects responded to a series of demographic items, as well as the same two questions that were asked of Study A subjects regarding their general impressions of the hypothetical criminal justice system.

---

[6] The cases were taken from an earlier study that is also reproduced in chapters 2 and 5. *See* Paul H. Robinson & Robert Kurzban, *Concordance and Conflict in Intuitions of Justice*, 91 Minn. L. Rev. 1829 (2007).

4. STUDY B RESULTS AND DISCUSSION

Subjects' average sentences in the high-disillusionment condition were dramatically different from the actual sentences imposed by the criminal justice system for each of the seven cases.[7] In contrast, for the low-disillusionment condition, the degree of discrepancy between subjects' sentences and the law's was much lower. Reflecting this condition difference, responses on the two general questions that asked about the hypothetical system showed that subjects in the high-disillusionment condition thought the system did a much poorer job in administering justice than did subjects in the low-disillusionment condition. The high-disillusionment group thought the system did a worse job in assigning deserved punishments, and also thought the system would have less credibility with its citizens. In both cases, the mean for the high-disillusionment group was significantly below the scale midpoint of 5, whereas the mean for the low-disillusionment group was significantly above the scale midpoint. The manipulation was thus sufficient to produce more negative attitudes about the hypothetical system among those in the high-disillusionment group.

The main question of interest was whether these negative general attitudes would translate into specific decreases in willingness to defer to this hypothetical system. The results are reported in the third and fourth columns of Table 19 below. As predicted, the subjects in the high-disillusionment group showed less deference to and less willingness to assist or cooperate with the criminal justice system than did subjects in the low-disillusionment group when responding to the test questions.

The second column in Table 19 compares these results to the results for the subjects in Study A, who responded to the same eight questions at the start of Study A, thus before any disillusionment. The means for this no-disillusionment group were statistically significantly different from the high-disillusionment cases in seven of the eight instances, and the difference was marginally significant for the remaining item (item #2, $p < .07$). The results summarized in Table 19 suggest that the greater

TABLE 19. } Study A Baseline and Study B Results

Question	Study 2a baseline No disillusionment	Study 2b Low disillusionment	Study 2b High disillusionment
1. Life sentence means heinous	6.46	6.59	5.35
2. Posting condemnable	6.14	5.38	5.59
3. Financial move condemnable	5.25	5.16	4.34
4. Report arrowhead	5.93	5.65	4.95
5. Turn in handgun	6.66	5.40	4.32
6. Report dogs violation	5.15	4.75	4.43
7. Return to gas station	7.05	6.63	5.63
8. Return to restaurant	7.15	6.47	5.84

[7] To see the figures from the study, refer to Robinson, Goodwin, & Reisig, *Disutility of Injustice*, *supra* note 548, at 2031–33.

the disillusionment, the less likely people are to cooperate with the criminal justice system and to defer to it as a moral authority that shapes societal norms and the internalization of norms.

What conclusion should be drawn from these results in relation to the crime-control costs of doing injustice? They would seem to suggest that there are clear benefits to be found in doing justice: greater assistance and cooperation with the criminal justice system, upon which the system much depends; and greater ability to harness the powerful forces of social influence and the internalization of norms to gain compliance in borderline cases and to shape norms where needed.

However, it might be argued, given what has been said in chapter 7, section D, about the distortions and imperfections inherent to public perceptions of crime and punishment, that instances of injustice and of failures of justice by the system may not be immediately and fully appreciated by the community. The fog of media errors and inaccuracies may protect the system's reputation even when it does not deserve it, and thus, there might not be a loss of moral credibility and its detrimental effects from deviating from desert.

Unfortunately, it seems unlikely that the fog of media reporting will so completely insulate the system such that it can freely do injustice and fail to do justice without concern that these imperfections will be revealed and undermine its moral credibility. Indeed, what seems likely is that, just as crime is news (thereby exaggerating the rate and nature of crime), instances of injustice and failure of justice are news. Even if the nature of the news coverage hides some portion of the deviations from desert, the more frequently and more seriously the system deviates from desert, the greater the chances that such deviations will come to light.

Worse, even very few disclosures have the potential to undermine the system's credibility. As discussed in chapter 8, section B, what is known about making and keeping reputations means that the system's intention regarding doing justice counts enormously.[8] While accidental or unavoidable injustices or failures of justice may be forgiven, if the system seems committed to trying to do justice, when revealed deviations from desert are intended by the system then even a single telling case can have detrimental consequences. The system's only protection is to indeed try to do justice as best it can, admitting that there are some limitations on how perfect it can be in practice.[9]

Studies A and B, which suggest that doing injustice and failing to do justice can undermine the criminal justice system's moral credibility, which in turn can lead to citizen reluctance to support, assist, and defer to the system, were conducted using data collected under controlled conditions for the study. One may wonder whether

---

[8] *See* Robinson & Darley, *Utility of Desert*, *supra* note 549, at 495–96.

[9] For an analysis of the various doctrines by which the criminal justice system regularly and intentionally deviates from desert, and a critique of the justifications offered in support of each doctrine of deviation, *see* PAUL H. ROBINSON & MICHAEL T. CAHILL, LAW WITHOUT JUSTICE: WHY CRIMINAL LAW DOESN'T GIVE PEOPLE WHAT THEY DESERVE (2005).

the same effects might be observed in data from large population samples collected by others. In an associated study,[10] information from existing national databases was used to see what, if anything, they might say about the hypothesis concerning the practical effects of a system's moral credibility on the effective operation of the criminal justice system. A possibility for relevant variables existed in one large national survey involving telephone interviews with Americans. Included in this database were people who recently participated in criminal court proceedings. Bivariate and multivariate statistical techniques were used to determine whether the observed results support the research hypothesis: as moral credibility increases, the willingness to defer to the courts to resolve a similar case in the future will also increase. The findings suggest that the dynamics from the experiment reported in Studies A and B also operate among people who have actual experience with the criminal courts. Put simply, if a person has a high level of confidence in the moral credibility of the criminal justice system, he or she will be more likely to defer to the system in the future.

B. Previous Studies

The conclusions reached in the recent studies described above are consistent with previous studies suggesting that conflicts between the criminal law's dispositional rules and the community's shared intuitions of justice have the sorts of detrimental effects described above. A number of studies have confirmed the existence of the relationship between an individual's disbelief in the morality of a particular law and his or her willingness to obey that law. Studies also show that the degree to which people report that they have obeyed a law in the past and plan to obey it in the future correlates with the degree to which they judge that law to be morally valid. Some studies also go further in showing how perceptions of injustice might lead to more generalized flouting of the law.

A number of studies have focused on how beliefs about the morality of a particular law can affect compliance with it. In one such study, by Grasmick and Green, a random sample of 400 adults was selected from the Polk City Directory and subsequently interviewed.[11] Information was gathered about the subjects' involvement in eight illegal activities—theft of property worth less than $20, theft of property worth more than $20, gambling illegally, cheating on tax returns, intentionally inflicting personal injury, littering, illegal use of fireworks, and driving under the influence. The respondents were then asked to estimate the perceived certainty of arrest, the perceived severity of punishment, and their moral commitment to adhering to the given legal rule. The researchers summarized their results by saying that "three independent variables—moral commitment, perceived threat of legal punishment and

---

[10] Robinson, Goodwin, & Reisig, *supra* note 548, at 2016–24.

[11] *See* Harold G. Grasmick & Donald E. Green, *Legal Punishment, Social Disapproval and Internalization as Inhibitors of Illegal Behavior*, 71 J. Crim. L. & Criminology 325 (1980).

threat of social disapproval—appear to constitute a concise and probably exhaustive set of factors which inhibit illegal behavior."[12]

Similarly, Jacob suggests a greater relation between compliance and a law's perceived moral correctness than between compliance and perceived likelihood of punishment for violating it. He randomly interviewed 176 people over the age of 18 from Evanston, Illinois, by allowing a computer to pick random phone numbers.[13] The respondents were interviewed regarding whether they sped on highways, had smoked marijuana, and whether they would shoplift a $50 item if no one was looking. Marijuana smokers were the most numerous, followed by speeders, followed by potential shoplifters. Two-thirds of respondents thought the 55 miles per hour speed limit was right, three-quarters agreed that the laws against shoplifting were correct, but only one-quarter thought the law against marijuana was correct. The results showed that for those who think the speeding laws are right, 62.3 percent comply, while only 9.8 percent who think it is wrong comply. Of those who think the marijuana law is just, 85 percent do not smoke marijuana. Contrastingly, only 36 percent of those respondents who think that the law is wrong complied with its ban on smoking. There was no statistical difference in shoplifting, which is evidence of high agreement that shoplifting is wrong. The researchers conclude that "[t]he relationship between compliance and legitimacy appears to be considerably stronger than the one between compliance and perception of severity or certainty of sanctions."[14]

Silberman conducted a similar study on 147 undergraduates at a small private university.[15] The students responded to whether they had ever committed certain moral or legal violations, such as assault, use of hard drugs, petty theft, vandalism, shoplifting, drunk and disorderly conduct, premarital sex, marijuana use, and drinking under age. The students then responded to questions regarding the morality of the act, the certainty of punishment, the severity of punishment, and peer involvement. One proposed hypothesis that was being tested was that "the higher the degree of moral support for the legal regulation of an offense or offenses, the lower probability that the offense or offenses will be committed." On the data, Silberman concluded that "[w]hen public sentiment disapproves [of a] given offense, it is relatively unlikely to occur. Similarly, serious criminal activity is less likely to occur among those who show a high degree of moral commitment, even though these individuals might commit less serious offenses," thus validating his hypothesis.[16]

The previous studies demonstrate that perceptions of the moral legitimacy of particular laws can affect compliance with them. Other studies have gone further in

---

[12] *Id.* at 334.

[13] Herbert Jacob, *Deterrent Effects of Formal and Informal Sanctions*, 2 LAW & POL'Y Q. 67 (1980).

[14] *Id.* at 70. *See also* Robert F. Meier & Weldon T. Johnson, *Deterrence as Social Control: The Legal and Extralegal Production of Conformity*, 42 AM. SOC. REV. 292, 301 (1977) (stating that "the belief that marijuana use is immoral . . . functions to inhibit marijuana use," while "legal threat . . . shows a measurable, but essentially trivial influence on marijuana use/nonuse.").

[15] Matthew Silberman, *Toward a Theory of Deterrence*, 41 AM. SOC. REV. 442 (1976).

[16] *Id.* at 457.

showing how perceptions of the immorality of a particular law, or of some act of the criminal justice system, can lead to more generalized effects on compliance. One in particular is a recent investigation by Janice Nadler that looked at how knowledge of injustices created by the criminal justice system can affect intentions to comply with the law.[17] In one study, subjects read mock newspaper stories describing legislation that was perceived as either highly just or highly unjust. Subjects in the unjust condition later reported greater intentions to engage in minor acts of lawbreaking, which were unrelated to the content of the unjust legislation, such as parking illegally, or making illegal copies of software. In a second study, conducted over the web, subjects acted as mock jurors and had to render a verdict in a fictional case in which the evidence pointed to a guilty verdict. Prior to this, they were exposed to a mock news story of a (real) crime in which the protagonist watched his friend abduct and rape a seven-year-old girl in a casino. The story had two versions—one in which the protagonist was described as being appropriately punished (just version) and another in which he was not punished at all (unjust version). In the ensuing mock trial scenario, with unrelated content, subjects who had seen the unjust news story were more likely to engage in juror nullification by rendering a Not Guilty decision.

A similar study by Greene presented cases including the one described in the Nadler study and also examined their effect on subjects' attitudes.[18] Greene reached similar conclusions to the ones arrived at by Nadler. More specifically, subjects who had read cases in which the legal system behaved in ways counter to their moral intuitions rated themselves "more likely to take steps aimed at changing the law, less likely to cooperate with police, more likely to join a vigilante or watch group, and less likely to use the law to guide behavior."[19] He further concluded that "overall, subjects appeared less likely to give the law the benefit of any doubt after reading cases where the law was at odds with their intuitions."[20]

These studies affirm the conclusion reached by our Studies A and B. Nadler's first study is closest to ours and is also her most conclusive. However, whereas Nadler's study only investigated issues of compliance, our studies have extended her result by showing effects not only on compliance, but also on cooperation and moral credibility.[21] The unjust primes in Nadler's studies were also somewhat fictionalized, whereas the primes in our studies were descriptions of real cases. Nadler's studies

---

[17] Janice Nadler, *Flouting the Law*, 83 TEX. L. REV. 1399 (2005).

[18] Erich J. Greene, Effects of Disagreements Between Legal Codes and Lay Intuitions on Respect for the Law (June 2003) (unpublished Ph.D. dissertation, Princeton University) (on file with Mudd Library, Princeton University).

[19] *Id.* at iv.

[20] *Id.* at v.

[21] Nadler's second study, on juror nullification, does investigate cooperation, but its results are not as easily interpreted as those of her first study, nor are they easily assimilated with our own results. The greater proportion of Not Guilty verdicts in the unjust condition were accompanied by diminished ratings of the defendant's guilt. This suggests that the unjust prime (the defendant who got off) may have produced juror nullification through shifting subjects' thresholds for criminal culpability, rather than through affecting their perceptions of the moral credibility of the criminal justice system.

are thus an important first step that our studies have extended. The conclusion we draw is that knowledge of systemic injustice can negatively affect not only compliance but also other relevant variables such as cooperation and moral credibility, and these effects can be produced simply through knowledge of several current criminal law practices.

A more recent study by Mullen and Nadler shows how the perception of moral illegitimacy in the legal system can increase rates of deviant behavior.[22] During the experimental session, 137 undergraduates read a newspaper article that summarized the legal trial of a doctor who allegedly provided an unlawful late-term abortion. Subjects were randomly assigned to read that the defendant was found "Guilty" or "Not Guilty." One week prior to this session, subjects had completed a questionnaire that assessed their attitudes about abortion, and these attitudes were used to predict the critical dependent variable, which was whether subjects failed to return (i.e., stole) the pen that was provided to fill out their questionnaire. After subjects completed all the studies, they were instructed to return their pen and an envelope containing their materials to designated boxes. The researchers numbered the identical pens with ink that was only visible under ultraviolet light. Therefore, subjects did not know that their pen was numbered, but the experimenter was able to identify the pens that were not returned at the end of each experimental session. The percentage of subjects who did not return the pen was substantially higher for those subjects who had strong pro-choice attitudes, and who were exposed to the guilty verdict—that is, those for whom the outcome clashed with their moral principles. The researchers interpreted these results as indicating that exposure to outcomes that are inconsistent with a person's strongly held moral beliefs increase the likelihood of their engaging in deviant behavior.[23]

Finally, peoples' common compliance with tax law raises interesting issues related to these points. Large numbers of American citizens pay their taxes, even though the penalty for tax evasion is not great and the probability of detection is trivial; therefore, the expected sanction is quite small.[24] For these reasons, many legal scholars believe that the threat of official sanction does not explain why such large numbers of citizens pay taxes.[25] A survey by Kinsey sheds some light on the underlying forces.[26] When people reported that a friend or coworker, after contact with the IRS, had been made to pay more taxes than they properly owed, the people thought the tax laws generally were less fair and were more likely to intend to cheat on their taxes in the future. Nadler, in reviewing the study, comments that "[t]he

---

[22] Elizabeth Mullen & Janice Nadler, *Moral Spillovers: The Effect of Moral Violations on Deviant Behavior*, 44 J. Experimental Soc. Psychol. 1239 (2008).

[23] *Id.* at 16.

[24] Eric Posner, *Law and Social Norms: The Case of Tax Compliance*, 86 Va. L. Rev. 1781, 1782 (2000).

[25] *Id.*

[26] Karyl A. Kinsey, *Deterrence and Alienation Effects of IRS Enforcement: An Analysis of Survey Data*, *in* Why People Pay Taxes: Tax Compliance And Enforcement 259 (University of Michigan Press 1992).

results of the tax study suggest that exposure to reports of an unjust legal outcome in a particular situation might lead to lower perceived fairness of the law more generally, which in turn can lead to noncompliance with the law in the future."[27] It would appear that one who sees tax law and the IRS as being just is likely to comply even though expected sanctions are small and unlikely.

Taken together, these studies complement the conclusions of Studies A and B that knowledge of systematic injustice produced by the criminal justice system, particularly when it is intentional, can have a range of deleterious effects on people's attitudes and on their behavior. People are less likely to comply with laws they perceive to be unjust. They may also be less likely to comply with the law generally when they perceive the criminal justice system to cause injustice. The studies have shown that these sorts of effects are not limited to compliance, but generalize to cooperation and assistance with the legal system, as well as to perceptions of its moral authority, which can affect its ability to harness the normative forces of social influence and the internalization of norms. The flip side, of course, is that if the criminal justice system reflects ordinary perceptions of justice, it can take advantage of a range of psychological mechanisms that serve to increase assistance, cooperation, compliance, and deference.

C. Conclusion

The studies reviewed here refute the apparent conventional wisdom of the past half century that it is cost free for the criminal law to deviate from desert in the pursuit of crime control through deterrence, incapacitation of the dangerous, and other such coercive crime-control programs. There are crime-control costs in deviating from desert that follow from the system's reduced moral credibility with the community it governs. And those crime-control costs must be taken into account in setting an effective crime-control program.

The power of the forces of normative social influence and internalization of norms shown here, together with the reasons to be skeptical of the crime-control effectiveness of the traditional mechanisms of coercive crime control, as discussed in chapter 8, section A, suggest that in the long run, doing justice may be the most effective means of fighting crime.

---

[27] Nadler, *supra* note 564, at 1409–10.

10 }

Deviations from Empirical Desert

Chapters 8 and 9 have made the case for using empirical desert as a principle for distributing criminal liability and punishment. Building the moral credibility of the criminal law by having it embody lay judgments of justice can harness the enormous power of social influence and internalized norms for crime-control purposes. However, it does not follow that it is never appropriate for a criminal justice system to deviate from empirical desert.

Some deviations from empirical desert are inevitable, as section A explains, suggesting that to promote moral credibility the criminal law ought to track community views whenever it does have the opportunity to do so, or at least to appreciate that there is a cost to deviation, which ought to be an important part in assessing whether a deviation can be justified.

Section B suggests that some apparent deviations may not be what they appear, but section C makes clear that other deviations are quite real and are likely to incrementally undermine moral credibility, albeit upon claims that the deviation advances some other important social interest. While there is crime-control utility in promoting moral credibility, the good utilitarian must remain open to the possibility that a deviation doctrine, while incurring a cost in marginally reducing the criminal law's moral credibility, nonetheless may generate a crime-control benefit that exceeds that cost. Further, it is simply not the case that crime control is the only or even the most important societal interest. Privacy, fairness, limitations on governmental power, proper allocation of governmental authority, and a variety of other interests might be judged sufficiently important to outweigh the crime-control interest furthered by empirical desert.

Nor is it the case that reformers must remain content with the community's existing judgments of justice. Adopting criminal liability and punishment rules that deviate from existing judgments of justice may be a necessary part of a social engineering program. Section D examines the challenges brought by such programs and advises reformers how they might most effectively change community views of justice.

Finally, section E introduces the literature suggesting that lay perceptions of fairness in adjudication procedures can build a sense of "legitimacy" in the criminal justice system, which may promote cooperation with and deference to the criminal justice system, in a dynamic that is parallel to that of the cooperation and deference promoted by the system's moral credibility earned through a reputation for producing just results. However, this practical value of fair procedures introduces the problem of conflict between procedural fairness and just results. Promoting legitimacy through fair procedures can sometimes undermine the law's moral credibility from just results. When such a conflict occurs, which goal should prevail?

A. Inevitable Deviations: The Problem of Moral Divisions within the Community

As chapter 4 makes clear, there is disagreement among members of the community on a variety of issues outside the "core" wrongdoing. It follows from what has been said in chapters 8 and 9 that this disagreement creates a risk to the law's moral credibility. Regardless of the criminalization rule that a society chooses, some group will disagree with the justness of the result. When a society contains groups with a strong and deeply felt moral disagreement, as ours does at this time on the morality of abortion, for example, the situation is destructive for the law's moral credibility and thus its power to gain compliance. More critically, one side will feel that the law is immoral, either because it criminalizes an innocent act, or because it fails to criminalize a morally abhorrent act—in this case fails to criminalize what is seen as a particular kind of murder. The "losing" side at this moment—those who wish abortion to be criminal—may lose respect for the legislative process; for the courts that enforce the laws; and eventually, for the legitimacy of the entire criminal law system.[1]

When one thinks that the law does not prohibit murder, one is inclined to "take the law into one's own hands," as can be seen in the case of a number of antiabortion activists. Note the sequence of steps in what might be called the radicalization of the "pro-life" individual. Perhaps it begins with picketing the abortion clinic and then moves toward more coercive forms of picketing that are arguably legal violations of the rights of others. For some, the line is crossed toward spraying noxious substances into the clinics at night—an undeniable and more substantial offense. The next step is setting fire to the abortion clinic, perhaps at night so "no one will get hurt," but certainly this is an act of arson and possibly life-risking. The final step in this process is death threats and even the murder of a doctor or nurse who performs abortions.

One might discount the danger of such moral disagreements on the ground that people who disapprove of a particular law—be it Prohibition or giving a right to an abortion—can distinguish this "bad" law from the remainder of the system. But the possibility for such compartmentalization of disrespect is limited; it is more likely to result in what might be called "the generalization of disrespect."

Consider the psychological processes that are begun when, for instance, a constitutional amendment prohibiting the use of alcohol is put in place. Examine the situation from the perspective of a person whose cultural traditions have a place for

---

[1] This section is drawn primarily from sections of Paul H. Robinson & John M. Darley, *The Utility of Desert*, 91 Nw. U. L. Rev. 453, 482–85 (1997).

alcohol consumption on certain occasions, and whose individual opinion supports such use. A law that criminalizes an activity, such as drinking, which I consider not immoral, may initially seem to me to be an isolated and aberrant one, and only the moral validity of that specific law will be denied by me. However, I cannot deny that it was a criminalization action taken by the same authorities that produced the entire criminal code, and I must now be willing to entertain doubts about the moral correctness of the criminalizing of the other activities that those authorities have chosen to sanction. By a process that is easily understood psychologically, if not logically, when the police apprehend me for violation of the drinking laws, I have a revelatory experience canceling the equation of all police actions with the apprehension of wrongdoers; and if the court system convicts, the hypocrisy that I feel that this court manifests will lead me toward generalization to other courts. If I become aware of another instance of the code violating my moral sensibilities, then all these generalizations and others are likely to occur. There is a natural process of spreading generalization of disrespect that the reader can intuit here.

The potential for the generalization of disrespect is even greater where the disapproval does not concern a particular controversial law. Where the system generates objectionable case results because of a highly publicized and controversial position, as with Prohibition or the right to an abortion, there is at least the potential to limit the system's discredit to the controversial law. But it is much more frequently the case that the cause of an objectionable result is not so apparent, and in these cases the compartmentalization of disrespect is essentially impossible. The criminal law may conflict with community views in an endless number of ways in its definition of offenses or general principles of liability. An objectionable definition of rape or a counterintuitive rule governing offense culpability requirements, accomplice liability, or causal accountability for a harmful result, or any of a wide range of the general rules relied upon in most cases, can generate an objectionable result.[2] Yet, the specific source of the perceived error will not be apparent to the observer, just the improper result. Without a segregable and visible "bad" law to blame, the observer can do little other than be suspicious of the entire enterprise.

That there exists such unavoidable risks of injury to the criminal law's moral credibility means that it is that much more important that the criminal law be formulated to maximize its moral credibility in all those respects that are within its control.

B. Right-Spirited Deviations: Promoting Justice in a Complex World

Some legal rules that deviate from desert are adopted out of fear that a more desert-based rule would be subject to easy manipulation and abuse, which ultimately would produce less justice, not more. That is, they depart from the abstract demands of justice for the

---

[2] See part III for a large number of examples of smaller points of disagreement between lay judgments and criminal law rules.

case at hand, but do so in order ultimately to advance the interests of justice generally. In the real world, we simply cannot achieve justice in every case: limitations of time, knowledge, and money prevent us from identifying and punishing every offender. Accordingly, we must make some compromises to try to achieve as much justice as we can with the time, knowledge, and money we have. Sometimes these require us to create rules that cut some corners in terms of desert—rules that we know will lead to distortions from the ideal of justice in some or even many individual cases but that we think will track the just result in the vast majority of cases, and will do so more efficiently than an ideal rule that did not cut corners. In the end, it is thought, these compromises will lead us to more real-world justice being done, rather than less.[3]

Frequently the accuracy of these rules, in terms of whether they really do lead to just results more often than unjust ones will be debatable, but the important thing is that the terms of the debate are clear. The debate involves a disagreement over practice rather than principle. The advocates as well as the opponents of these rules are trying to support the principle of desert-based punishment; they simply differ in their opinions of how to achieve that result given concerns about the relevant practical constraints.

There are three distinct practical-constraint rationales driving rules that deviate from desert. The first concern is that, in some situations, a pure desert-based rule would allow manipulation of juries into voting for improper acquittals. The rationale is used to justify the limitation or rejection of various exculpatory defenses or mitigation rules. A second rationale, at the root of such rules as statutes of limitation and the use of strict liability, reflects concerns about the reliability of evidence and the unavoidable difficulty of using fallible or incomplete evidence to prove a person's guilt or innocence with any certainty. A final concern touches practices such as plea bargaining and witness immunity that are predicated on the claim that, given constraints on available time, resources, and fact-seeking capacities, the system can maximize justice overall by making compromises in individual cases.

The concerns driving all of these deviating rules are ultimately empirical rather than philosophical in nature, as they rest on the premise that each such rule or practice advances justice more than would a rule that, in the abstract, might seem more just. That premise is an assertion about objective fact, capable of proof or disproof. For this reason, the appropriateness of any such deviations can, at least potentially, be determined through objective analysis. Accordingly, the debates about the validity of these deviating doctrines admit of definitive resolution. It is merely necessary to shift the focus of debate away from the abstract arguments of which legal academics are so frequently enamored and toward empirical research.

It must be acknowledged that these deviation rules risk undermining the system's moral credibility, and they ought to be maintained only if there is no other,

---

[3] For a full discussion of these kinds of deviations from desert, *see* Paul H. Robinson & Michael T. Cahill, Law without Justice: Why Criminal Law Doesn't Give People What They Deserve 27–88 (2005).

non-deviation means of achieving the objective. Under that principle, some of these deviation rules may fall. Some of these apparent deviation doctrines may be maintained, however, in part because the system can defend its reputation for doing justice by explaining why the apparent deviation in practice does greater justice overall. Good intentions count a good deal in setting reputation. Thus, it is meaningful that by these apparent deviations from desert, the system is *trying* to do justice, as best it can in a complex world.

C. Justifying Deviations from Empirical Desert

Other deviations from desert are motivated by goals other than doing justice in the larger picture. That is, the deviation might serve to promote some interest other than doing justice and building moral credibility. One can imagine several different kinds of situations in which one might justify deviating from empirical desert, even taking account of its virtues as a distributive principle. The point is, doing justice and effective crime control are not the only important societal interests. General principles of balance between the value of empirical desert and other interests might look like this:

> 1. *Primary Principle of Empirical Desert*. Formulate criminal liability and punishment rules and exercise adjudication discretion so as to most effectively build the criminal justice system's reputation within the community for being just. That is, distribute liability and punishment according to the relative blameworthiness of an offender based upon principles derived from the shared judgments of justice of the community that is to be governed by that law—empirical desert. Deviation from empirical desert is permitted in the three instances set out below.
>
> 2. *Inconspicuous Deviations*. Liability and punishment may deviate from empirical desert in order to advance any important societal interest if the deviation is sufficiently small that it will go essentially unnoticed and therefore will have little or no effect on the criminal justice system's moral credibility.
>
> 3. *Deviations to More Effectively Control Crime*. Taking full account of the difficulty in repairing damage to the system's justness reputation caused by deliberate injustice or deliberate failure to do justice, liability, and punishment may deviate from empirical desert if (a) the crime-control benefits from the deviation outweigh the crime-control costs, and (b) no non-deviation means of obtaining the crime control is possible. If more than one crime-control opportunity justifies deviation, liability and punishment should be distributed according to the opportunity with the greatest crime-control effect. (This justification for deviation is available to rule-making bodies, such as sentencing guideline drafters, but should be used only cautiously by individual sentencing judges.)

4. *Deviations to Advance Interests Other Than Crime Control.* Liability and punishment may deviate from empirical desert in order to advance an important societal interest, such as fairness, limitation on governmental power, privacy, or proper allocation of governmental authority, if the interest is more important than the resulting loss of effective crime control and if there is no other reasonable non-deviation means to advance it. (This justification for deviation is available only to rule-making bodies.)

The larger point is that, if reliance upon empirical desert is justified on utilitarian crime-control grounds, then its value might be overridden by other interests, both those that concern controlling crime as well as other societal interests. (Of course, if reliance upon empirical desert rests on other grounds, such as its value in reflecting democratic or other principles,[4] then this same analysis might not apply.) For a detailed discussion of the proposal, see my book *Distributive Principles of Criminal Law: Who Should Be Punished How Much?*[5]

1. DEVIATIONS TO MORE EFFECTIVELY CONTROL CRIME

Because empirical desert as a distributive principle is ultimately instrumentalist in its justification, it should take seriously opportunities to more effectively control crime than would a pure desert principle. Theoretically, a system might more effectively control crime, even in the long term, by permitting certain deviations from empirical desert where a valuable crime-control opportunity presents itself.

Of course, it may be that these opportunities will be rare. Rehabilitation and special deterrence opportunities might offer opportunities to prevent recidivism in the individual offender at hand. However, because the effect is only on the individual offender at hand, there is little likelihood that either principle will offer such striking gains as to outweigh the detrimental effects of undermining the system's moral credibility generally. Even a few cases can damage the system's reputation if it is seen as deliberately doing injustice or failing to do justice. Nonetheless, a good instrumentalist would not want to foreclose the possibility.

Incapacitation of the dangerous may be more likely to present substantial crime-control opportunities, because it is so effective at preventing future crimes by the individual offenders detained. But again, it does not follow that these opportunities will regularly justify deviation from empirical desert. Aside from the standard problem of undermining the criminal law's moral credibility, such preventive detention faces a different hurdle. A deviation from empirical desert can be justified only if the crime control it offers cannot be achieved through non-deviant means.

---

[4] *See, e.g.*, Andrew E. Taslitz, Empirical Desert: The Yin and Yang of Criminal Justice, *in* CRIMINAL LAW CONVERSATIONS 56, Robinson, Garvey & Ferzan eds., (2009); Adil Ahmad Haque, Legitimacy as Strategy, in *id.*

[5] PAUL H. ROBINSON, DISTRIBUTIVE PRINCIPLES OF CRIMINAL LAW: WHO SHOULD BE PUNISHED HOW MUCH? 248–54 (Oxford 2008).

In this instance, as chapter 8, section A.3 discusses, the possibility for *civil* preventive detention of dangerous persons, which indeed may be more fair and effective and less costly, means than incapacitation through criminal justice deviation from desert cannot be justified.

General deterrence, which can have effect upon an entire population of potential offenders, may be the more likely alternative distributive principle to present opportunities that would justify a deviation from desert. This is so because deviation from desert in a single case or a small group of cases might be enough to send an effective deterrent message to a very large group of potential offenders. On the other hand, as chapter 8, section A.1 discusses, it is likely that one or more of the three prerequisites for a deterrent effect will be missing, thereby subverting the possibility of such striking gains.[6] (Recall the three prerequisites for a deterrent effect: (1) the intended targets must be aware of the rule, directly or indirectly; (2) the intended targets must have the capacity and inclination to rationally calculate what is in their best interest; and (3) the target must conclude that the costs of committing the offense exceed its anticipated benefits, which may not happen when considering factors such as low capture rates and the tendency of people to discount future punishment.) Nonetheless, it seems likely that there may be some instances in which the prerequisites will be satisfied, and striking gains might be possible.

It should be cautioned, however, that satisfaction of the deterrence prerequisites is not itself enough to justify a deviation from desert. A deviation is justified only if the general deterrent effect would be so great as to outweigh even the long-term detriment to the criminal justice system's moral credibility that would result from such a deliberate choice to do injustice or to fail to do justice. Even a single well-publicized case (and recall that well-publicized cases are often the most useful for general deterrence) that conflicts with community judgments of justice can have a serious detrimental effect on the criminal justice system's reputation, because the deliberateness of the deviation reveals the system's lack of full commitment to doing justice.[7] Thus, the opportunities for a deviation from desert based on general deterrence, while likely to exist, may not be as frequent as one might expects.

Note that the statement of general principles at the start of this subsection expressed a preference for limiting such deviations to rule-making bodies, such as sentencing guideline drafters, urging that they be used only rarely and cautiously by individual sentencing judges. The point here is that such deviations have system-wide effects in undermining moral credibility, and generally it ought not be for an individual judge to decide whether the benefit outweighs that system-wide cost. This is a decision best left to system-wide decision makers. On the other hand, one would not want to foreclose the possibility if a special opportunity presents itself and the balance in favor of deviation is clear to all.

---

[6] *See* Robinson, Distributive Principles, *supra* note 579, at 24–49.

[7] *See id.* at 198–200.

2. DEVIATIONS TO ADVANCE INTERESTS OTHER THAN CRIME CONTROL

While debates about criminal law and punishment theory tend to focus on the interests of crime control and doing justice, clearly there are other important societal interests. For example, it is not just the end result of the criminal justice process but its fairness in reaching that result that can be important to society. (More on this in section E below.) Similarly, liberal democracies place a high value on limiting the power of government to intrude in the lives of its citizens. Privacy interests have come to stand on their own as a societal interest worth protecting. A society also may have strong interests in who within government exercises governmental power. For example, the legality principle reflects our preference for criminalization and punishment rules to be made by the most democratic branch of government, the legislature, rather than by either the judicial or executive branches.

Of course, articulating beforehand exactly which of these interests will trump doing justice and its crime-control benefits is an enormous project. It is a significant portion of the agenda of moral philosophy, constitutional theory, and political theory. The point here is simply to acknowledge that those debates are indeed relevant to the distribution of criminal liability and punishment.

The existence of a competing interest will not necessarily justify deviation from empirical desert, but the possibility must be examined. Nor does the existence of even a compelling competing interest necessarily justify deviation. Injustices or failures of justice are justified under the proposal only if there is no reasonable non-deviation means by which the compelling interest can be as effectively advanced.

The proposal limits this justification for deviating from desert to decisions by rule-making bodies, such as sentencing guideline drafters. It is not available to individual sentencing judges. The range of possible "interests other than crime control" is numerous, and the potential for mischief and disparity in application is great. Thus, it ought to be for criminal code commissions and sentencing guideline commissions to wrestle with the societal interests that compete with effective crime control, rather than individual judges in adjudicating individual cases. The importance of equality of treatment and the unfairness of having a disposition depend on the good or bad luck in the sentencing judge assigned leads to the proposition that all individual case dispositions ought to be bound by the same balance of interests—that struck by the rule makers.

D. Deviations to Change Social Norms: Altering Empirical Desert

If criminal law always tracks shared community views, then it becomes difficult, if not impossible, for social reformers to use criminal law to change existing moral norms.[8]

---

[8] Throughout, when using the term "norm," I mean "moral norm"—a shared understanding of what is properly held to be wrongful, not a common pattern of conduct.

Drunk driving and domestic violence, for example, are instances in which community views have changed over the past several decades, in part because criminal law got out in front of community views rather than strictly following them.

However, the social reformers' decision on whether to urge deviating from community views is not always an easy one. The deviation can have serious costs to a planned reform program, even as it can have benefits. Let me use as a case study the situation of rape law reformers. Assume you are a reformer who believes that men do not take sufficiently seriously the importance of ensuring clear and free consent before having intercourse. You might view current law and community views as problematic because they seem to accept in some ways the attitude of many of today's young man—who you think are insufficiently sensitive to the importance of clear and free consent. You might easily conclude that the criminal law's traditionally demanding culpability requirements allow young men's damaging insensitivities regarding consent to continue unabated.

With this view, in setting the offense culpability requirements for lack of consent, you would be likely oppose not only use of the higher culpability levels of purpose and knowledge, but might also be tempted to oppose use of the lower culpability levels of recklessness and negligence. The problem you see is that the definitions of recklessness and negligence commonly incorporate existing community standards by judging the young man's risk taking or inattentiveness by standards of "reasonableness." That standard has the effect of relying upon the existing norms that the reformer thinks are so troubling.

It is not hard to see, then, why the concerned rape reformer might be attracted to a rule of strict liability as to consent. She could very well argue that giving a defense to young men who have intercourse without consent, albeit mistakenly, only perpetuates the unacceptable existing norm. If the law is to get serious about social reform, intercourse without consent ought to be punished in all cases, the reformer might argue. Once young men understand this, they will have a strong incentive to become careful about consent.

1. THE IMPORTANCE OF MORAL CREDIBILITY TO SOCIAL REFORMERS

Unfortunately, things are not so simple for the reformers. The primary problem is this: it is social reformers, perhaps more than others, who very much need the criminal law to speak to the community with strong moral authority. If the criminal law is to have sufficient moral authority to prompt people to rethink their views on what to expect of young men, it must have earned that moral credibility with those it seeks to influence. Every deviation from desert the community perceives can incrementally undermine the law's moral credibility.

It is not that a criminal law must be perfect in tracking community views or lose all credibility. Some deviations from desert will be quickly and easily excused by the community because they are seen as unavoidable. The criminal law can do only so much in trying to accurately re-create the facts of a past event, especially in reference to culpable states of mind that may be difficult to be sure of even at the time. Also, as noted above, there are other important societal interests, such as fairness, that may call for deviating from desert. Doing justice, while it is an important interest to most people, is not the only interest. What a sophisticated criminal law can do is take every opportunity to build its moral credibility—building up its store of "credibility chips"—with an eye toward prudently spending those chips on those special occasions that it judges to be worth the expenditure in order to shift an existing societal norm. And if the effort is successful at shifting the norm, then the conflict with community views will fade away as community views change.

What guidance can one give the savvy social reformer about how to perform this balancing act of when to follow community views and when to deviate from existing views in order to lead them? First, it would seem appropriate to always try to avoid blatant and serious conflicts with the community's shared judgments of justice, that is, to avoid ever producing cases that will be perceived as instances of the criminal law intentionally doing what will be seen as serious injustice. That may mean, for example, that strict liability as to consent is a bad idea for the ultimate success of rape reform. Such a rule would invite serious liability for a mistake that could not have been avoided *even by the most thoughtful and careful person*. It also risks creating defendant martyrs, which will muddy the offender-victim distinction in such cases, hurting rather than helping the shift in community norms.

Second, it seems likely that the system ought to in all other instances try to track community views of justice in order to build up its reserve of "moral credibility chips." That is, it ought to avoid frittering them away with deviations from desert that have little payoff, such as doing what current law frequently does today in deviating from desert to advance general deterrence even when the prerequisites for effective deterrence are not likely to exist.[9] The central point here is that no deviation from desert should be tolerated unless the benefits from it are clear. Hopefully, the recent empirical work has at least discredited what was the common wisdom of the past 50 years—that deviations from desert are cost free.[10]

Finally, when reformers do decide to spend some of their credibility chips, they should do so carefully and thoughtfully. This means "picking your fights." Understand that one has limited and dearly earned chips to spend. Don't spend them now if one will regret not having them for a more important purpose later. In the context of rape reform, for example, this might mean adopting a culpability requirement as to lack of consent (that is, avoiding strict liability), but perhaps setting it lower than criminal law might normally set it. A negligence requirement would avoid the

---

[9] *See, .e.g.,* Paul H. Robinson, John M. Darley, *Does Criminal Law Deter? A Behavioural Science Investigation*, 24 OXFORD J. LEGAL STUD. 173 (2004); Paul H. Robinson & John M. Darley, *The Role of Deterrence in the Formulation of Criminal Law Rules: At Its Worst When Doing Its Best*, 91 GEO. L.J. 949 (2003); ROBINSON, DISTRIBUTIVE PRINCIPLES, supra note 579, at chs. 3–4.

[10] *See, e.g.,* Paul H. Robinson, Geoffrey P. Woodwin, & Michael Reisig, *The Disutility of Injustice*, 85 N.Y.U. L. REV. 1940, 2025–26 (2010).

perceived injustices likely to result from a strict liability standard, and would place at center stage the issue of what the society should reasonably expect of its young men with regard to assuring full and free consent. Thus, every case litigated in public would become not an opportunity for hand wringing about the injustice being done to young men who make honest mistakes, as strict liability would risk, but rather an opportunity to promote the public discussion about what should be considered "reasonable" in this context.

This does not mean that a few cases will produce a dramatic shift in societal norms. Norms are glacial—enormously powerful but slow moving. However, when norms are successfully shifted, conduct does change, and not just the conduct that is likely to be caught and prosecuted as a criminal offense. The power of social norms is one that will seep into the conduct of two people in an intimate setting, the facts of which neither would ever seriously think to make public, let alone to involve the criminal law. A changed internalized norm will change even that private conduct, which presumably is what the social reformer is seeking.

2. LIMITATIONS ON AND TECHNIQUES FOR CHANGING NORMS

An important caveat remains to be made: not every judgment about wrongdoing is open to easy modification by social reformers, at least not through techniques that would be permitted by liberal democracies. (A good deal of modification can be done through coercive indoctrination techniques that require serious intrusion into and control over a person's life.[11]) Our best guess of the intuitions of justice that, as a practical matter, cannot easily be modified are those on which there is an existing near unanimity as to their central aspects, part of the "core" of wrongdoing. This core includes aspects of physical aggression and theft.[12] Out from this "core," however, change is possible, probably including judgments about coercion to intercourse.

Appreciating the difference between intuitions that can be changed and those that cannot is important for reformers. First, as noted above, it can avoid a waste of resources in an effort toward an unreachable goal. (Those who seek to persuade people that they ought not want to punish serious wrongdoing, for example, are on a fool's mission.[13] Reformers who want real change, rather than just an excuse for fiery rhetoric, must focus on what is possible.)

Second, savvy reformers can use the unchangeable core for their own purposes, if they acknowledge it rather than fight it. For example, an effective technique aims toward building up (or tearing down) the strength of the analogy between the

---

[11] *See, e.g.*, Paul H. Robinson, "The Case of Richard R. Tenneson," CRIMINAL LAW CASE STUDIES 158–159 (West, 4th ed. 2009).

[12] *See* studies and findings presented in chapters 2 & 3. For more on this, refer to Paul H. Robinson & Robert Kurzban, *Concordance and Conflict in Intuitions of Justice*, 91 MINN. L. REV. 1829 (2007); Paul H. Robinson, Robert Kurzban, & Owen D. Jones, *The Origins of Shared Intuitions of Justice*, 60 VAND. L. REV. 1633 (2007).

[13] See chapter 11, section C.

unchangeable "core" and the norm out from the "core" that the reformers seek to modify. One can see this lesson at work in recent advertising campaigns, such as that of the music industry seeking to reduce the amount of unlawful downloading of music. A recent television campaign shows a person sneaking money from the pocket of a pleasant and hard-working musician. The message: unlicensed downloading of music is just like stealing. The campaign seeks to build the strength of the analogy between the core wrong of physical taking without consent and the unlicensed downloading of music. For rape reformers, the approach may suggest focusing public discussion and education on the impropriety of coercive pressure for sex—building the analogy between psychological coercion and physical coercion—and on the harmful effects of intercourse without consent—building the analogy to assault.

To conclude, the persons who ought to be most interested in criminal law routinely tracking community views are those who want to use the moral credibility thereby earned to bring about important changes in societal norms.

3. MANAGING BENEFITS VERSUS RISKS OF REFORM PROGRAMS: PERSUASION VERSUS CONTEMPT

The previous section explains the great potential value for bringing about social change that comes from building criminal law's moral credibility by normally tracking a community's judgments of justice. It is important to note, however, that attempts to change social norms also can create substantial risks—not only that the reform program will fail but that it will destroy the law's moral credibility, hurting not just its crime-control effectiveness but also its potential to help in other reform efforts. That is, sometimes the law can convince persons that they should respect and obey the provisions of the criminal code, and internalize those prohibitions as part of their own moral code. But at other times, a conflict between the legal code and individual moral intuitions can lead people to persevere in their own judgments and move toward contempt for the legal code.[14]

Social science research suggests that two factors are particularly relevant in determining whether an effort to change views will be persuasive: the credibility of the source that is attempting to persuade the individual who is the target of the message and the certainty or strength with which the target holds his or her own opinion. The two factors interact as follows: the higher the credibility of the source, the more likely the source's message is to persuade the target;[15] the more strongly

---

[14] This section is drawn primarily from Robinson & Darley, *Utility of Desert*, *supra* note 575, at 485–87.

[15] The credibility of a source of communication is generally thought to be a joint function of the source's expertise on the communication topic and the source's trustworthiness as a communicator. One reviewer concludes, "Few areas of research in social psychology have produced results as consistent as the findings that sources high in expertise and/or trustworthiness are more persuasive than those low in these qualities." Glen Hass, "Effects of Source Characteristics on Cognitive Responses and Persuasion," in COGNITIVE RESPONSES IN PERSUASION 141 (Richard Petty et al. eds. 1981).

or certainly held the original opinion, the less likely the target is to be persuaded to change his or her opinion.[16]

The application of these factors to the present issue is fairly direct. The source of the message is the legal code and the intentions and motivations of the drafters who stand behind it. The message is, in essence, that this or that action ought to be criminalized is wrong and deserves the specified level of punishment. When will the legal code as a source be regarded as credible? The conclusion previously developed here is that the legal code is credible to the extent that it has moral credibility. For the present discussion, two components of this credibility are important to note. First, the law's credibility is a function of the trustworthiness of its judgment. The law gains trustworthiness by assigning punishment in accord with the principles of justice of the person it is attempting to convince. Second, the law's credibility is a function of its perceived expertise, relevant in this instance when the law asserts that some conduct that is not obviously harmful should be treated as such because the conduct has less apparent but real harmful consequences. The law is saying, in essence, "Trust those of us who drafted the code. We have thought this through. This action is sufficiently harmful or evil that it deserves to be criminalized."

The other factor that influences whether the law will persuade or will draw contempt is the strength of the original opinion on the issue. When are individuals relatively certain of their opinions in the domain of criminal law? People are likely to be certain about the criminality of actions such as killing, arson, and theft—those offenses that historically have been referred to as malum in se, "actions that are wrong in and of themselves," and in particular the "core of wrongdoing" on which chapter 2 shows such wide agreement. Different people may have somewhat different mappings here; abortion is held to be wrong with great certainty by some. People in general can be expected to be less certain on the actions historically referred to as malum prohibitum and may have quite differential certainties produced by past personal histories. A parent whose child has been killed by a drunk driver is likely to hold, with a high degree of certainty, that drunk driving is a serious wrong.

Thus, the social science literature suggests five generalizations, most of which reaffirm conclusions developed in earlier sections. First, the credibility of the criminal law depends on it being perceived as a trustworthy guide to assigning liabilities according to the community's perception of which actions are moral, which are immoral, and how severely the immoral actions should be punished. Second, the higher the credibility of the law (that is, the greater its reputation for assigning liabilities according to perceived desert), the more persuasive it will be in convincing people of the correctness of its judgment, and thus, the more they will be inclined to behave in compliance with the law and internalize its judgments as morally appropriate. Third, since people are likely to be relatively less certain about malum

---

[16] Alice Eagly & Shelly Chaiken, The Psychology of Attitudes 429–30 (1993) (reviewing the theories that link attitude strength with resistance to change, and the evidence that supports those theories).

prohibitum offenses, the law will be more likely to convince people with regard to those offenses. Fourth, when the law condemns an action that a person is certain is not morally condemnable, or fails to condemn an action that a person is certain is morally condemnable, its credibility is, at minimum, put at risk, normally lowered, perhaps eventually destroyed, by the spreading processes of radicalization that have been suggested. Fifth, when the criminal law, asserting its expertise, criminalizes an act that is not obviously harmful, if people later discover that the act does not lead to the consequences that they generally regard as properly criminal, the law loses credibility, although not as decisively as in the fourth conclusion above.

Suppose that code drafters wish to adopt a specific proposal that is known to be in conflict with the moral intuitions of the community or a section of the community. They face a difficult but not impossible task; they must convince the community that the community's intuitions are wrong and that justice would be better served by distributing liabilities according to the new principle. From this point of view, they must engage in this persuasive task directly and forcibly and assess the success of their efforts. If they do not succeed in convincing the community, they then risk lowered credibility if they nonetheless adopt the proposal. When, as sometimes happens, the code provisions are adopted without this sort of educational debate, the potential for community contempt for the code has been established, and that potentiality is likely to become an actuality when the first publicized prosecution for violation of the new provision takes place.

The larger point here is advice for social reformers and for those who influence them: watch carefully at how successful a law change is in changing the community's views to match it. If the community's view changes, or at least is in the process of moving people's views in the desired direction, then all is well. But if the law change, after a fair period of time to gauge the community reaction, is not changing people's views, then the reform program ought to be quickly rethought and perhaps withdrawn and revised. Waiting until the conflict with community views has ripen into contempt for the law may do more harm than good, not only to the reform program at hand but to others as well that rely upon the law having the moral credibility to persuade.

E. Deviation to Promote Legitimacy

The "legitimacy" literature, championed by Tom Tyler,[17] shows a dynamic similar to that of empirical desert and moral credibility, as discussed in chapters 8 and 9. Just as a system's reputation for imposing just results can produce moral credibility, which in turn can promote cooperation and deference, so too can a system's earned

[17] *See, e.g.,* Tom R. Tyler & Yuen J. Huo, TRUST IN THE LAW xiv (2002); Tom R. Tyler, *ProceduralJustice, Legitimacy, and the Effective Rule of Law*, 30 Crime & Just. 283, 286 (2003); Tom R. Tyler, Why People Obey the Law (2006); Tom R. Tyler, *Legitimacy and Legitimation*, 57 Ann. Rev. Psych. 375–400 (2006).

reputation for being fair in its adjudication procedures produce "legitimacy" that promotes cooperation and deference. But while the dynamics may be analogous, they are distinctive. A procedurally fair system may generate seriously unjust results, and a procedurally unfair system may nonetheless produce just results. In short, the police practices, criminal adjudication procedures, and the criminal liability rules within a jurisdiction may be in very different states. Not only is it possible for fair practices and procedures and just punishment to be on different tracks, but sometimes they are on a collision course. Specifically, practices and procedures that advance fairness sometimes can undermine justice. And enforcement practices and adjudication procedures that would most effectively advance justice may be seen as unfair. When such a conflict between fairness and justice occurs, which should prevail? This section is drawn primarily from my article with Joshua Bowers, *Perceptions of Fairness & Justice: The Shared Aims & Occasional Conflicts of Legitimacy and Moral Credibility*.[18]

1. POINTS OF TENSION

Fairness and justice can have a variety of points of tension. Consider, for example, such stalwarts of the American criminal justice system as the prohibition against allowing prosecutors to rely on illegally seized evidence, or to retry acquitted defendants, or to delay trials as best suits effective prosecution. The rights against double jeopardy and to a speedy trial, as well as the exclusionary rule, all have been enshrined to some extent. Yet it may well be that the virtues that drive these procedural rules are not accuracy in truth finding or reliability in doing justice. On the contrary, each of these rules, and many others,[19] can easily frustrate justice.

The exclusionary rule can exclude reliable evidence that allows the perpetrator of even a serious offense to go free, a result that cannot help but draw the criminal justice system into disrepute, at least with regard to its commitment for doing justice. In the case of Larry Eyler, for example, police suspected Eyler of a string of gruesome killings of young gay men. When a state trooper just happened upon Eyler parked on the side of the highway preparing for another kill of a young hitchhiker, he became suspicious, called headquarters and heard of prior suspicions, and took Eyler to the station, probably saving the hitchhiker's life. A search of Eyler's vehicle turned up conclusive proof of his previous crimes, but the court excluded the evidence because the search was unlawful. Eyler was released to kill again, and, indeed, did so before subsequently being captured and convicted for the later crime.[20] Many may wonder whether this frustration of justice, together with its high cost in human life, is worth the benefits that the exclusionary rule offers.

---

[18] Joshua Bowers & Paul H. Robinson, *Perceptions of Fairness & Justice: The Shared Aims & Occasional Conflicts of Legitimacy and Moral Credibility*, 47 WAKE FOREST L. REV. 211 (2012).

[19] *See generally* Paul H. Robinson & Michael T. Cahill, LAW WITHOUT JUSTICE: WHY CRIMINAL LAW DOESN'T GIVE PEOPLE WHAT THEY DESERVE (2005) (cataloguing the variety of justifications for, and the doctrines used in deviating from desert).

[20] *Id.*, at 139–49, 157–59.

The double jeopardy bar may present a similar situation. In the case of Melvin Ignatow, for example, Brenda Schaefer was brutally raped, tortured, and killed by Ignatow and his former girlfriend. At trial, the girlfriend testified for the prosecution but came off as an unreliable witness, and Ignatow simply lied his way to reasonable doubt. He was acquitted. Ten months later, as the new owners of Ignatow's former house were putting down new carpeting, they found film taped inside a floor duct. When the film was developed, it provided a grisly record of Ignatow's horrendous offense, yet Ignatow could not be retried for the murder.[21] Again, this gross failure of justice is likely to undermine in many peoples' minds the system's commitment to doing justice.[22]

Or imagine that an Eyler or an Ignatow is released because of a speedy trial violation, or because a statute of limitations has run, or because the text of an offense statute was ambiguous (even though the defendant knew his conduct was wrong).[23] The fairness interests may be clear—speedy trial rights, statutes of limitation, and the legality principle are common and well established—but the justice costs can be significant.

Nonetheless, there are good reasons to insist on adhering to the conventional standards and rules that are premised on fairness concerns. First, and obviously, fairness is an important value in itself. But there are practical crime-control reasons beyond this, as Tom Tyler has argued.[24] A criminal justice that earns "legitimacy" by being seen as fair is one that can command greater deference. But one can say more. For example, the system's adherence to these fairness rules, even in such costly cases, advertises the extent of its commitment to them. Indeed, it is the costs of undermining justice in discrete cases that may do the most to advertise just how devoted the system is to these fairness interests. If the system is willing to follow such rules even when they undermine justice in such egregious cases, then citizens can have confidence that the rules certainly will be followed in the less egregious cases, which are more common. That demonstration of high commitment enhances the system's legitimacy, and with this comes the consequent benefits of greater deference and compliance.

However, one can imagine ways in which a society might strike a different balance between fairness and justice on these and other issues. A system might limit

---

[21] *Id.*, at 159–66, 169–70.

[22] For example, when law students are asked to judge what, if any, liability and punishment Ignatow deserves, 100 percent impose liability, with a mean and a mode of life imprisonment:

1% 1% 1% 2% 17% 67% 10%

no liability 1 day 2 wks. 2 mo. 6 mo. 1 yr. 3 yrs. 7 yrs. 15 yrs. 30 yrs. life death

liability but imprisonment no punishment Paul H. Robinson, Criminal Law Case Studies & Controversies, Teacher's Manual (2d ed. Aspen 2008).

[23] *See e.g.*, Keeler v. Superior Court, 470 P.2d 617 (Cal. 1970) (reversing murder conviction where statute did not unambiguously cover killing of fetus); Billingslea v. Texas, 780 S.W.2d 271 (Tex. Crim. App. 1989) (reversing abuse conviction where code did not provide adult son with duty to care for elderly disabled mother who was living in his home).

[24] Tom R. Tyler, Why People Obey the Law at 3 (2006).

application of the rules, perhaps by applying them less rigorously in case of serious offenses, as some have suggested.[25] Or a system might shift to alternative procedures that could as effectively advance fairness interests without jeopardizing justice—for example, by replacing the exclusionary rule with a robust civil-compensation or administrative-disciplinary regime that could punish police for unlawful searches of any individual (and not just of accused offenders).[26] Or a system might narrow application of rules and standards in circumstances where the threat of injustice is high, but the threat of unfairness is low. For example, the system might bar application of double jeopardy when a defendant's deceptive conduct helped generate the original acquittal.[27]

2. RESOLVING THE CONFLICT

Although a system should strive to realize both fair procedures and just results, this may not always be possible. When the two conflict, which objective ought to be achieved at the expense of the other? Resolving the deontological tensions between fairness and justice is a significant issue in moral philosophy, criminal procedure, and criminal law theory scholarship. The more narrower question addressed here is which value ought to be preferred where the goal is gaining deference to and compliance with the criminal justice system. To telegraph our conclusion: although legitimacy may be the superior value in discrete circumstances (as discussed below), moral credibility is more often to be preferred in the unfortunate circumstances where a system may optimize only one.

Overall, Tyler seems to concede that moral credibility has a much greater effect in shaping compliance than does legitimacy,[28] but no doubt things are more complex than an absolute preference for moral credibility. It may depend on the setting. In different contexts, one or the other justification carries potentially greater normative force. For instance, in the order-maintenance policing context, the state cannot rely on moral credibility, because many of the governing laws are borderline regulatory public-order crimes that lack inherent normative punch.[29] Instead, legitimacy is the sole source of genuine normative power. In fact, legitimacy may be the sole effective source of *any* power, because traditional carrots and sticks are particularly insufficient at deterring commonplace borderline crime. Police must necessarily be

---

[25] *See, e.g.,* United States v. Janis, 428 U.S. 433, 454 (1976) (If . . . the exclusionary rule does not result in appreciable deterrence, then clearly, its use in the instant situation is unwarranteded.

[26] *See, e.g.,* ROBINSON & CAHILL, LAW WITHOUT JUSTICE, *supra* note 592, at 149–55.

[27] *See, e.g., id.* at 167–68.

[28] Tyler reports the relative weight of the factors shaping compliance with the law as: morality 0.33, legitimacy 0.11, deterrence 0.02. TOM R. TYLER, WHY PEOPLE OBEY THE LAW (2006).

[29] William J. Stuntz, *Self-Defeating Crimes*, 86 VA. L. REV. 1871, 1894 (2000) ("The more "crime" includes things that only a slight majority of the population thinks is bad, the harder it is to sell the idea that "criminal" is a label that only attaches to very bad people.").

selective, because offenses of this kind are typically so prevalent.[30] This creates a further complication: selective enforcement may feed perceptions of bias and illegitimacy, which may generate more disobedience, which may lead to even more selective enforcement, which may further feed perceptions of illegitimacy. The situation is delicate and potentially counterproductive. Procedural fairness is left alone to do the heavy lifting without the backstops of moral credibility and instrumental deterrence; and the enforcement process, if perceived to be unfair, may succeed only in making the load heavier.[31] If nothing else, the potential for a negative feedback loop provides yet another powerful reason to reconsider the degree to which we rely on the criminal law to achieve regulatory ends.[32]

Comparatively, when it comes to *mala in se* crimes, even if the public were to perceive legal authorities to be somewhat illegitimate and even if an instrumental approach were unable to deter the rational bad actor, ordinary individuals would still tend to comply for the simple reason that ordinary individuals are not, in the main, bad actors. They obey murder statutes and cooperate with murder investigations and prosecutions (discounting, of course, fears of reprisal), because their moral aversion to homicide is that strong.[33] With serious *mala in se* crimes, moral credibility alone may prove somewhat effective, even with low levels of legitimate (or even much of any) enforcement.[34]

In sum, procedural fairness is more important to the enforcement of regulatory crime, while moral credibility is more important to the enforcement of conventional crime. This may be reason alone to emphasize moral credibility over legitimacy (in the event that a criminal justice system were competent to emphasize only one), because moral credibility operates best within the traditional criminal law domain of *mala in se* offenses, while legitimacy operates best in only regulatory domains in which state objectives might be achieved equally or nearly as well through civil law or other means.

The question comes down to which concept ultimately provides a better screen. For a number of reasons, we believe that moral credibility should be expected to more effectively motivate optimal deference. First, moral credibility entails a concrete assessment of the substantive law or enforcement effort at hand. Legitimacy, by contrast, entails institutional analyses that operate at higher levels of abstraction. To produce deference, then, legitimacy is mediated by a cognitive move: the prospective offender must contemplate illegal conduct, then consider what he thinks

---

[30] Tom R. Tyler, *Legitimacy and Criminal Justice: The Benefits of Self-Regulation*, 7 Ohio St. J. Crim. L. 307, 311–12 (2009) (noting that in circumstances where there is "insufficient risk to motivate compliance... the legal system benefits when people voluntarily defer to regulations... even when they do not anticipate being caught.").

[31] Stuntz, *supra* note 601, at 1894 (2000) (focusing on how criminalizing and criminally enforcing vice crimes may prove counterproductive).

[32] Robinson & Cahill, Law Without Justice, supra note 592, at 186–95.

[33] Stuntz, *supra* note 601, at 1800.

[34] *Id.* at 1871 ("The mass of the population avoids seriously bad behavior not because they know it can be found in the codes, but because they know the behavior is thought to be seriously bad.").

of the set of procedures used to enforce it, and then decide whether to engage in the forbidden conduct based on her feelings—not toward the law itself—but toward the system that prescribes it. For moral credibility to produce deference, the prospective offender need only contemplate the illegal conduct and then consider what he thinks of that conduct. The questions are discrete and coherent: Should I comply with *this* law? Is *this* law morally justified? Should I cooperate with *this* prosecution? Is *this* prosecution morally justified? We expect that an individual is likelier to refrain from behavior that she finds immoral than from behavior that she deems neither right nor wrong but that just so happens to be proscribed by legitimate authority.[35] As Sarah Lawsky has observed, "[A]ssessments of distributive justice might lead to compliance (or noncompliance) directly, without being mediated by an increased belief in legitimacy."[36] Indeed, studies have shown that "whereas assessments of procedural justice tend to influence views and beliefs, . . . assessments of distributive justice tend to influence behavior."[37]

Second, moral judgments are innately comprehensible. We are all social beings with moral compasses that we instinctively consult.[38] We require no auxiliary understanding to access perceptions of just deserts. But we must achieve a certain level of socialization for legitimacy to do its work. We must grasp the objectives, structure, and methods of a justice system and the implications of its procedural practices and strategic choices. For this reason, perceptions of moral credibility are not just easier to tap; they are likelier to be right. Fewer external variables cloud our moral valuations. By contrast, perceptions of legitimacy may fail to reflect reality in fact, because these perceptions may be based on incomplete or inaccurate information about supplementary matters of enforcement and adjudication. Indeed, the fact that perceptions of procedural fairness rely on more than intuition may explain the somewhat greater dissensus that we think we see on questions of procedural as opposed to distributive justice.[39]

Third, legitimacy is an umbrella concept that covers everything from discourteous to discriminatory behavior. And even if we lack a comprehensive rank ordering of legitimacy criteria, it simply stands to reason that mere rudeness is less likely to undermine deference than perceived immorality. Fourth, perceptions of procedural fairness are more likely to be socially constructed than perceptions of substantive justice. Therefore, the corrupt state may more easily manipulate the legitimacy project to serve its bad ends. In sum, moral intuitions pack more punch and, normatively, this is as it should be.

---

[35] See Linda Skitka, Christopher Bauman, & Brad Lytle, *The Limits of Legitimacy: Morality as a Constraint on Deference to Authority*, Presentation to 22nd Ann. IACM Conf. (June 15, 2009), *available at* http://papers.ssrn.com/sol3/papers.cfm?abstract_id=1493520.

[36] Sarah B. Lawsky, *Fairly Random: On Compensating Audited Taxpayers*, 41 Conn L. Rev. 161 (2008).

[37] *Id.*

[38] Paul H. Robinson & John M. Darley, *Intuitions of Justice: Implications for Criminal Law and Justice Policy*, 81 S. Cal. L. Rev. 1 (2007); chapter 1, section B.

[39] Robinson & Kurzban, *Concordance and Conflict*, *supra* note 586, at 1830.

11 }

Implications for Criminal Justice and Other Reform

Chapters 8 and 9 discuss the benefits that can flow from a criminal law that earns a reputation for doing justice. What reforms to current criminal law are needed to establish this moral credibility with the community the law governs? As section A reminds us, the most obvious and most important reform would be to bring criminal liability and punishment rules more in line with community views, perhaps starting with the modern crime-control doctrines shown to be points of serious conflict in chapter 7. A corollary to this is that the kinds of reforms that would be most damaging are those that seek to undermine the imposition of punishment generally, including, in some people's view, certain forms of the recently popular "restorative justice" programs, examined in section B.

Section C discusses reforms relating to existing doctrinal deviations from empirical desert, such as those examined in chapter 10, as well as other reforms of deviation doctrines that ought to be considered. The most important of these may be the sharpening of the criminal-civil distinction, discussed in section D.

Sections E and F give two examples of just how far empirical desert might take the criminal law beyond its present boundaries. Depending upon the empirical findings regarding community views, the law might formalize its recognition of some mitigation matters considered now only as discretionary matters of mercy, discussed in section E, and even might reconsider what in the past has been a bright-line prohibition of the law looking at how an offender came to be the person he is, examined in section F's discussion of the coercive indoctrination and "rotten social background" defenses.

A. A Central Concern for Doing Justice

The criminal law's power to nurture and communicate societal norms and its power to have people defer to it is directly proportional to its moral credibility. If criminalization or conviction (or decriminalization or refusal to convict) is to have an effect in the norm-nurturing process, it will be because the criminal law has a reputation for criminalizing and punishing only that which deserves moral condemnation, and for decriminalizing and not punishing that which does not. If, instead, the criminal law's reputation is one simply of a collection of rules, which do not necessarily reflect the community's perceptions of moral blameworthiness, then there would be little reason to expect the criminal law to be relevant to the societal debate over what is and is not condemnable and little reason to defer to it as a moral authority. What, then, are the requirements for a criminal law system to gain this credibility? How can this credibility be lost?

Enhancing the criminal law's moral credibility requires, more than anything, that the criminal law make clear to the public that its overriding concern is in being just. Therefore, the most important reforms for establishing the criminal law's moral credibility may be those to the rules governing which criminal liability and punishment are distributed, as discussed in several chapters of this part. The criminal law must earn a reputation for (1) punishing those who deserve it under rules perceived as just; (2) protecting from punishment those who do not deserve it; and (3) where punishment is deserved, imposing the amount of punishment deserved: no more, no less. Thus, for example, the criminal law ought to maintain a viable insanity defense that excuses those who are perceived as not responsible for their offenses and ought to avoid the use of strict liability (imposing liability in the absence of a culpable state of mind). (Two sections below consider whether the law should go even further to institutionalize mercy, discussed in section D, and to break the foundational assumption that criminal law will not ask how a person came to be who he or she is, in section E.) At the same time, it ought to limit, where possible, the use of non-exculpatory defenses.[1]

The point is that every deviation from the community's judgments of justice can incrementally undercut the criminal law's moral credibility, which in turn can undercut its ability to help in the creation and internalization of norms and its power to gain compliance by its moral authority. Contrary to the apparent view of past practice, deviations from desert are not cost free, and their cost must be included in the calculation when determining which distribution of liability will most effectively reduce crime. It is not enough to show, for example, that a general deterrence opportunity might have some positive effect. It must also be shown that the injustice produced by such an imposition of punishment will not have crime-control costs that will overwhelm any crime-control benefits.

B. Abolition of Punishment and "Restorative Justice"

If the central concern in establishing the criminal law's moral credibility is doing justice, it follows that the kinds of reforms that would be most damaging to the criminal law's moral credibility are those that seek to undermine the imposition of

---

[1] For a more detailed discussion of these and other related reforms, *see* Paul H. Robinson & Michael T. Cahill, Law without Justice: Why Criminal Law Doesn't Give People What They Deserve 183–85 (2005).

punishment generally. This follows directly from the finding, discussed in chapter 2, section A that lay persons almost universally judge that serious wrongdoing ought to be punished. Yet several academics and others have seriously argued for the abolition of punishment—that any punishment component included in the disposition of criminal offenders is probably primitive, certainly misguided, and should have no part in the criminal justice system. [2]

The movement to abolish punishment takes this view:

> At its core, criminal law is still based on the same repressive assumptions as the Inquisition from which it originates. From the beginning it has been seen to create problems instead of solving them. A penal reaction after the fact is not preventive but desocializes an ever-increasing number of people. Therefore it would be better to abolish penal means of coercion, and to replace them by more reparative means.[3]

What is it that should replace punishment, in the abolitionists' view?

> First, we should think of "conflicts," or "troubles," rather than "crimes"; abolitionists offer a critique not only of punishment but of the concept of crime as that which requires or merits punishment. Second, we should look for reparation, restoration, and reconciliation, not for retribution and punishment ("pain-delivery"); instead of inflicting penal pain on wrongdoers, as retribution or for deterrence, we should seek negotiated reparations for those who have been harmed, the restoration of relationships between the parties to conflicts, their reconciliation with each other and with the community.[4]

The most popular modern form of the abolitionist movement is the "restorative justice movement." (But not all "restorativists" support the abolition of punishment, as will be discussed.[5]) While it uses the term "justice" in its description, its platform is explicitly to reject the use of retributive punishment components, which most people would see as critical components to the practice of doing justice.[6] One of its originators, John Braithwaite, explains:

> Restorative justice is a process of bringing together the individuals who have been affected by an offense and having them agree on how to repair the harm caused by the crime. The purpose is to restore victims, restore offenders, and

---

[2] This section is drawn primarily from portions of my article with John Darley, *Intuitions of Justice: Implications for Criminal Law and Justice Policy*, 81 S. CAL. L. REV. 1, 11–18 (2007).

[3] Rene van Swaaningen, *What is Abolitionism?* in ABOLITIONISM: TOWARDS A NON-REPRESSIVE APPROACH TO CRIME (1986).

[4] R. A. Duff, *Penal Communications: Recent Work in the Philosophy of Punishment*, 20 CRIME & JUST. 1, 69–70 (1996). The passage continues in noting as well a preference for "informal, participatory methods of resolving conflicts." *Id.*

[5] Paul H. Robinson, *The Virtues of Restorative Processes, the Vices of "Restorative Justice*," 2003 UTAH L. REV 375, at 379 [hereinafter, Robinson, *Virtues*].

[6] *Id.* at 382.

> restore communities in a way that all stakeholders can agree is just. One value of restorative justice is that we should be reluctant to resort to punishment.... It involves rejection of a justice that balances the hurt of the crime with proportionately hurtful punishment.[7]

In fact, the "eye for an eye" notion of doing justice to which Braithwaite refers is rejected by most modern desert theorists, who take full account not just of the "hurt of the crime" but the characteristics and circumstances of the offender, and whose central distributive criteria is not the victim's hurt but rather the offender's blameworthiness.[8] But the pure form of "restorative justice" pressed by Braithwaite is one that rejects the notion of punishment on any grounds.

The suggestion here is that this is not a proposal that societies will or should adopt, for two reasons. First, a majority of individuals in the society would strenuously resist the abolition of punishment because the impulse to punish serious wrongdoing is deeply ingrained. Second, having punishment available to administer to norm violators greatly reduces the frequency of norm violations that occur. The assertion is not that the strikingly lengthy prison terms that the criminal justice system currently imposes on offenders, coupled with the "prisonization" that is inflicted on offenders in prisons, reduces the frequency of criminal violations that exist in society. Instead, the argument is that the absence of punishment mechanisms in a society would lead to a set of violations sufficient to threaten the existence of the society.

Proponents of abolishing punishment have on rare occasion addressed the empirical issue of whether it is indeed realistic to persuade people to no longer care about doing justice or the punishment of serious wrongdoing.

> Robinson...pleads in his conclusion for restorative justice to recognize and respond to the emotional need—"inherent in human nature"—that people have for retribution. Indeed I do suspect this is a desire deeply rooted in our biology that was probably once useful to the survival of peoples fighting off starvation by defending scarce assets of productive land. A person's deeply felt desires for retribution should be addressed openly in conferences. However, the restorativist's hope is that the conversation about the urge for retribution will result in it being transcended so that people can move on. The reason restorativists think this way is that they believe peoples' natural retributive urges are not healthy things to perseverate upon. Moreover, in the conditions of contemporary societies, as opposed to the conditions of our biological inheritance, retribution is now a danger to our survival and flourishing. It fuels cycles of hurt begetting

[7] John Braithwaite, *Symposium: The Future of Punishment: A Future Where Punishment is Marginalized: Realistic or Utopian?*, 46 UCLA L. Rev. 1727, 1743 (1999) [hereinafter Braithwaite, *Symposium*].

[8] *See* Paul H. Robinson, *Competing Conceptions of Modern Desert: Vengeful, Deontological, and Empirical*, 67 Cambridge L.J. 145 (2008); see also chapter 8, section C.

> hurt. It is hoped that conversations that allow a space for the consideration of healing will help people to see this more clearly.[9]

These are socially optimistic sentiments, but they are only intellectual ones. Braithwaite may be overoptimistic that his intellectual arguments about what would be good for people and society today—his hope to "help people see more clearly"—can undo the evolutionary and social function reasons that people have the intuitions of justice that they have.

Against the weight of the evidence showing how fundamental the desire to do justice is to human nature and how difficult it is to erase it, Braithwaite has little to offer:

> What is the proper punishment for a given type of crime? This question has obsessed the most distinguished philosophers of criminal justice. But it seems a silly question, for why should one assume that any punishment is the proper response to a crime? Why not assume that punishment is rarely the best way to respond to crime? The former assumption seems grounded in a failure of imagination and ignores the practices that citizens of all cultures utilize instead of punishment in responding to wrongdoing. We might do better to follow the lead of many Native American peoples who believe in putting the problem rather than the person at the center of this deliberation. The "right" punishment of the wrongdoer is rarely going to be the best solution to the problem.[10]

Is it the case that Native American peoples did not and do not believe in doing justice and do not regularly impose punishment for significant moral transgressions? A citation in support of this claim would be useful. There is no evidence of a society in which there are no intuitions of justice nor any use of punishment. Indeed, as a cross-cultural review of the existing studies confirms, humans across a wide range of cultures share the intuition that serious wrongdoing should be punished.[11]

Other societies than modern-day America may have more successful systems for the control of deviance, or may have better systems of inculcating moral rules into their citizens, so that the occasions for punishments may arise less often. However, even if this is true, it does not disprove the contention that they do have and use punishment when the occasional need arises.

Braithwaite is not the only restorativist to deny the empirical problem of making people not care about punishing serious wrongdoing:

> We frequently must set aside our natural human responses (for example, jealousy, lust, rage and anger) and adopt more considered and reflective

---

[9] John Braithwaite, *The Theory and Jurisprudence of Restorative Justice: Holism, Justice, and Atonement*, 2003 Utah L. Rev. 389, 407–08 (2003).

[10] John Braithwaite, *A Future Where Punishment is Marginalized: Realistic or Utopian?*, 46 UCLA L. Rev. 1727, 1743 (1999).

[11] *See* studies presented in chapter 2; Paul H. Robinson & Robert Kurzban, *Concordance and Conflict in Intuitions of Justice*, 91 Minn. L. Rev. 1829, 1852 (2007).

> dispositions, because of the harm which they cause. So too could it be argued. with intrinsic retributivism. Of course, it could be countered that as a psychological matter, our make-up is such that it is not possible to react in a manner other than to punish wrongdoers: inferring, therefore, that it is wasteful even to consider (other) justifications for punishment, since there is no point in arguing against that which cannot be curtailed. This, however, is repudiated by the sheer number of counter-examples where people bear no animosity towards those who have violated their important interests. Indeed, there have been loud calls for the abolition of punishment.[12]

Again, what exactly is being asserted here is puzzling. It is well worth considering "other justifications for punishment." Additionally, there are at least many examples "where people bear no animosity towards those who have violated their important interests," although in those cases those who violated have likely either provided accounts of why their violations were not exactly intentional ones, or provided recompense, or more likely both. However, this is a different claim than that one can identify societies that have as a matter of policy, eliminated punishments that serve a retributivist impulse and successfully maintained social control of wrongdoing.

There is, after all, an empirical question here. A recent study explored the acceptance of purely "restorative justice" practices in American society.[13] The researchers asked people to role play "referring judges" whose task it was to send specific offense cases to one of three alternative court systems. One system was described to respondents as a purely restorative system; another as a standard prison-focused system; and a third that included the restorative procedures, but also allowed for punitive alternatives.

Results indicated that the respondents were willing to send just under 80 percent of the less-serious cases to a purely restorative procedure, but as the seriousness of the crimes increased the respondents were more drawn to a restorative procedure that included the possibility of punitive measures being assigned. For mid-level serious crimes, about 40 percent were sent to pure restorative procedures and 40 percent to the mixed procedure. For high-seriousness cases, only about 12 percent of the cases were assigned to purely restorative procedures, and 66 percent to the mixed procedure.

Even these results may tend to exaggerate the willingness to forego punishment. One might conclude that "restorative justice" was accepted as an option for the less-serious cases only because the subject believed that the range of outcomes available in that process were sufficient to provide the punishment deserved. That is, just because a victim agrees to a disposition in "restorative" mediation does not mean that the disposition is not what the victim sees as deserved punishment. Whether it

---

[12] Mirko Bagoric & Kumar Amarasekara, *The Errors of Retributivism*, 24 MELB. U. L. REV. 124, 159 (2000).

[13] Dena M. Gromet & John M. Darley, *Restoration and Retribution: How Including Retributive Components Affects the Acceptability of Restorative Justice Procedures, Social Justice Research*, 19 SOC. JUST. RES. 4 (2006).

is or not will depend upon how strongly the particular victim at hand is committed to seeing justice done.

In one way, these results should please "restorative justice" advocates, for this is one of the first studies that demonstrates that people are accepting of a restorative justice system under some circumstances. However, the conclusion that is less palatable for them is "that in order for citizens to view a restorative justice procedure as an acceptable alternative to the traditional court system for serious crimes, the procedure must allow for the option of some retributive measures."[14]

I have argued elsewhere that restorative processes, such as victim-offender mediation and sentencing circles, are wonderful procedures that ought to be used much more extensively than they are today. A good many restorative inflictions such as hours of service to the victim have punitive elements. But, for more serious offenses, people will see justice as demanding more serious impositions that will require criminal justice system involvement if not available in the restorative process.[15]

There are a group of scholars, sympathetic to "restorative justice" practices, who reject the idea that retributive practices should be banned from procedures that seek restorative ends:

> By framing justice aims (or principles) and practices in oppositional terms, restorative justice advocates not only do a disservice to history, they also give a restricted view of the present. They assume that restorative justice practices should exclude elements of retribution; and in rejecting an "attitude of hostility," they assume that retribution as a justice principle must also be rejected.

When observing conferences, I discovered that participants engaged in a flexible incorporation of multiple justice aims, which included:

> 1. some elements of retributive justice (that is censure for past offences);
> 2. some elements of rehabilitative justice...
> 3. some elements of restorative justice..."[16]

R. A. Duff introduces a recent paper this way:

> My thesis can be stated quite simply. Our responses to crime should aim for "restoration," for "restorative justice": but the kind of restoration that criminal wrongdoing makes necessary is properly achieved through a process of retributive punishment. To put it the other way round, offenders should suffer retribution, punishment, for their crimes: but the essential purpose of such punishment should be to achieve restoration. To put it yet more simply, my slogan is "Restoration through retribution."[17]

---

[14] *Id.* at 395.

[15] *See* Robinson, *Virtues*, *supra* note 618, at 375.

[16] Kathleen Daly, *Restorative Justice: The Real Story*, 4 Punishment and Society 55, 58 (2002).

[17] *See* R. A. Duff, *Restorative Punishment and Punitive Restoration*, *in* Restorative Justice and the Law 382 (L. Walgrave ed., 2002).

To conclude, even if one were convinced intellectually that abolition of punishment was a desirable ideal, it is a reform that could never be successfully implemented, and it would be folly to try to do so. As chapter 2, section A makes clear, it is simply a reality that human beings will demand justice for serious wrongdoing and that the absence of a system that allows for the imposition of deserved punishment would produce intolerable consequences.

C. Reforms to Existing Deviations from Empirical Desert

Given what has been said in chapters 8 and 9, the variety of existing deviations from empirical desert, including those discussed in chapter 10, ought to be examined to determine whether their benefits exceed their costs and, if so, whether they can be modified or should be abandoned, or whether their benefits might be advanced through some non-deviating means.[18]

1. CRIMINAL JUSTICE REFORMS

Some of the deviation doctrines may no longer be valid on their own terms. For example, regarding statutes of limitation, there may have been a time when the trial process was inadequate to exclude evidence that was unreliable because it was too old. But with modern trial procedures that give defense counsel every opportunity to point out the weakness in the prosecution's evidence, there seems a less obvious need for a statute of limitations today. For a long time, there was little need to abandon the doctrine, however, because the proof beyond a reasonable doubt standard and the fact that the strength of a prosecutor's case tends to degrade over time, meant that prosecutors have little interest in pursuing old cases. But scientific advances, such as fingerprinting and DNA analysis, increasingly make it possible for prosecutors to present overwhelmingly reliable evidence in old cases. It may be no surprise then, that jurisdictions today are repealing or lengthening their statutes of limitation.[19]

But for many other doctrines of deviation, an awareness of their potential costs simply suggests that they be narrowed in some way or that their objectives be achieved in a way that does not deviate from community notions of desert. For example, rather than rejecting a mistake excuse for a reasonable mistake of law or permitting the use of strict liability, the system could avoid the potential for abuse and manipulation by simply shifting the burden of proof to the defendant.[20] Rather than rejecting legitimate excuse defenses out of fear that an acquittal will muddle the

[18] This section is drawn primarily from portions of my article with John Darley, Paul H. Robinson & John M. Darley, *Intuitions of Justice: Implications for Criminal Law and Justice Policy*, 81 S. CAL. L. REV. 1, 49–51 (2007).

[19] *See* ROBINSON & CAHILL, LAW WITHOUT JUSTICE, *supra* note 614, at 53–63 (describing a case that prompted Illinois to dramatically extend its statute of limitation for sexual assault).

[20] *Id.* at 205–09.

clarity of a prohibition, the system could create a verdict system that distinguishes between an acquittal that condones the defendant's conduct and an acquittal that condemns that conduct but excuses the actor.[21] Rather than imposing punishment that conflicts with community views of justice in order to rehabilitate, incapacitate, or deter, the system could impose the amount of punishment that is deserved but select a punishment method for doing so that best furthers these other crime-control goals. A wide range of punishment methods are available other than incarceration, many of which can more effectively serve these alternative purposes.[22]

The law's moral credibility also may depend upon procedural and institutional reforms that reinforce the criminal justice system's commitment to doing justice and avoiding injustice.[23] Some of these include less use of the exclusionary rule to exclude reliable evidence, less plea bargaining for reasons unrelated to genuine factual disputes, and the development of non-incarcerative sanctions that have sufficient punitive bite to inflict the amount of punishment deserved. Promoting the criminal justice system's moral credibility also might include such reforms as increased protection of inmates against prison violence; decreased use of dangerousness as a criterion in setting prison terms; and more vigorous training, discipline, and leadership to promote just dealings by prosecutor and police when dealing with citizens.[24]

2. EMPLOYING CIVIL RATHER THAN CRIMINAL PROCESSES

While criminal justice reforms are possible, it is likely that the most effective and most important reforms will not be those of the criminal justice system but rather reforms that shift the responsibility for advancing a societal interest away from the criminal justice system to another institution. For example, given that the penalties imposed by the criminal justice system for regulatory violations typically are only fines, there is little to gain by using the criminal justice system for such cases and much to lose. By using criminal conviction in cases obviously devoid of conduct that merits moral condemnation, such convictions only serve to dilute the condemnatory effect of criminal liability. In other words, the criminalization of regulatory violations undermines that very characteristic of criminal liability that such regulatory criminalizations seek to harness.[25] An analogous point might be made about the use of criminal liability for nonhuman legal entities such as corporations. Because legal fictions cannot make moral decisions, there is at least some question as to whether morally condemning a nonhuman entity tends to undermine the

---

[21] *Id.* at 210.

[22] For a general discussion of what a system like this might look like, *see id.* at 212.

[23] For a more detailed discussion, *see* ROBINSON & CAHILL, LAW WITHOUT JUSTICE, *supra* note 614; Paul H. Robinson, *Moral Credibility and Crime*, THE ATLANTIC MONTHLY 72 (Mar. 1995); Joshua Bowers & Paul H. Robinson, *Perceptions of Fairness & Justice*, *supra* note 591, at 57–61.

[24] For a discussion of the tension between justice and fairness, *see* chapter 10, section E.

[25] ROBINSON & CAHILL, LAW WITHOUT JUSTICE, *supra* note 614, at 218.

condemnatory value of criminal conviction.[26] Whether this is true or not will require empirical research into community reactions to criminal conviction of corporations. The more successful the personification of corporations in the lay person's mind, the more appropriate the use of criminal conviction to condemn illegal corporate conduct.

An even more important reform may be to use civil rather than criminal methods to control overzealous police and thereby avoid the costly deviations that arise from excluding reliable evidence because of police error or that arise from giving an entrapment defense to a career criminal looking for a crime opportunity. Administrative sanction of offending officers by citizen review boards or quick, easy, and substantial compensation of citizens whose rights are violated, or both, will avoid the deliberate deviations from desert that undermine the criminal justice system's moral credibility and may be more likely to provide an effective means of controlling police.[27]

Another important reform is to avoid the practice of using the criminal justice system as a mechanism of preventive detention. The practice is problematic because, by engaging in preventive detention of dangerous offenders while pretending it is punishment for past crimes, we end up not only with a criminal justice system that does not do justice but also with a preventive detention system that is both unfair and ineffective. This occurs because rather than looking directly and openly at the dangerousness of an offender, as an open preventive detention system would do, we have the criminal justice system look instead at his prior criminal record, for example, as a substitute for his dangerousness. But it is a poor substitute, one that produces both false positives, which wastefully and unfairly imprison nondangerous persons; and false negatives, which let dangerous offenders go free. And by using the criminal justice system for preventive detention, we pervert the procedures that ought to be in place when restrictions on liberty are based upon merely a prediction of future dangerousness. For example, in a criminal justice system designed to punish for a past wrong, there is little reason for the use of nonpunitive conditions, a principle of minimum restraint, periodic review of present dangerousness, or a preference for treatment of all detainees; yet these characteristics would logically govern in a preventive detention system. If we are indeed interested in preventively detaining dangerous offenders, it would be better for both detainees and for the community to do it openly in a civil preventive detention system.[28]

The larger point here is that, once it is understood that deviations from empirical desert have crime-control costs, the criminal justice system ought not permit such deviations unless it is clear that they provide some greater benefit in advancing crime control or some other core interest, and that there is no non-deviation means available to advance the interest.

---

[26] *Id.* at 192–95.

[27] *Id.* at 222.

[28] *See id.* at 225; Paul H. Robinson, *Punishing Dangerousness: Cloaking Preventive Detention as Criminal Justice*, 114 HARV. L. REV. 1429, 1429–55 (2001).

D. Sharpening the Criminal-Civil Distinction

The previous subsection notes the preference for using the civil rather than the criminal system when possible to advance societal interests that would require the criminal justice system to deviate from empirical desert. Of course, such reforms would have little effect if the law had come to blur the distinction between criminal and civil liability dispositions. Indeed, one of the most important structural reforms to enhance the criminal law's moral credibility would be to move in the opposite direction, to affirmatively sharpen the distinction between criminal and civil disposition.[29]

1. WHY HAVE TWO LEGAL SYSTEMS?: THE LAY PERSON VIEW OF THE CRIMINAL-CIVIL DISTINCTION

It may well be that criminal law seeks to blame, condemn, and punish, while civil law does not, but why should this difference in function call for a separate and distinct criminal system? Wouldn't it be more efficient to have a single system that avoids the complexity and wasteful duplication of two separate and distinct systems, a single system in which condemnation, punishment, and damages could be imposed when deserved and in which only damages could be awarded when condemnation and punishment are not deserved? And, given the great diversity of legal and societal cultures, wouldn't one expect that some societies would develop such a unitary system? Wouldn't one expect that some legal systems would use the criminal-civil distinction while others would not?

The answer is that the human desire to make moral judgments is universal,[30] as chapter 2 makes clear; that there is practical value in giving formal legal expression to this human desire; or as chapter 8 explains, and that a distinct criminal justice system is the only way to effectively express condemnation and to gain the practical benefits of doing so.

The first advantage of a separate system is its communication value. Most people have lives full of concerns and pressures having little to do with the law. If the legal system hopes to communicate with the average person, to say nothing of a less educated and less intelligent person, that communication must be clear and simple. By creating a special *criminal* label and widely disseminating the notion that this label has a different condemnatory meaning, the system enhances its ability to communicate a condemnatory message when it wishes to. Without a distinct criminal system, it would be more difficult to convey the message that some cases (that are now called criminal) signal condemnation while other cases do not.

---

[29] Much of this section is drawn from my article, Paul H. Robinson, *The Criminal-Civil Distinction and the Utility of Desert*, 76 B.U. L. Rev. 201, 202–212 (1996), and my article with John Darley, Robinson & Darley, *The Utility of Desert*, Nw. U. L. Rev. 479–82 (1997).

[30] The most readable full account of this and the reasons for it is found in James Q. Wilson, The Moral Sense (1993).

And it is not just the final verdicts in court cases that must be distinguished as criminal and noncriminal. If it were only an issue of distinct verdicts, one might try to do this within a single system with the use of distinct verdict labels. But it is the inquiry itself that people must know is a *criminal* inquiry. The system conveys messages to the public in the conduct that is selected for investigation or indictment or is brought to trial, for this may signal conduct that is in the zone of suspicion, conduct that people ought to know may attract the attention of the system. The criminal system also conveys messages by the cases that are not investigated; not indicted; not brought to trial; or end in acquittal at trial, for this can signal, depending upon the stage at which the inquiry is dropped, that the conduct is not within the suspicious zone; that it is within an exception (as with a justification of self-defense[31]); or that the conduct *is* a violation of a rule of conduct, but the offender is excused (as with the duress defense). The point is that only a separate and distinct criminal justice system can clearly signal that the inquiry in a given case is *criminal* in nature, with all the attendant meanings that this carries.

The duplication costs of distinct and separate criminal and civil systems are partially offset by the fact that the systems will in any case require different rules and procedures because of their different functions: the nature of the plaintiffs (public versus private); the recipients of a fine or award (public versus private); the availability of defenses, such as consent and de minimis defense; as well as the prohibition of insurance against criminal penalties; and the need for greater procedural safeguards for criminal liability. Other important differences that derive from their different functions also exist. For example, as noted above, the conditions for civil commitment ought not be as onerous as the conditions of criminal confinement, which is intended as punishment. Criminal commitment, as punishment for a past offense, logically can be for a fixed term, while civil commitment of a person on a claim of dangerousness logically requires periodic review to test for continuing dangerousness. While these many differences do not compel separate and distinct systems, they support the important communicative reasons for having two distinct systems.

2. THE DETRIMENTAL EFFECT OF BLURRING THE CRIMINAL-CIVIL DISTINCTION

It follows from what has been said above that an important structural reform will be to sharpen the criminal-civil distinction, which has grown increasingly muddled over the past two decades. Civil law has been "criminalized" with the increased use of punitive damages. But of greater concern is the "civilization" of the criminal

[31] I refer here only to the objective form of justification. The subjective form, what I would call mistaken justification, sends no such message. It is in part the important difference between these two messages that leads me to argue for an objective formulation of justification defenses, with a separate excuse defense for mistaken justification. *See* Paul H. Robinson, *Competing Theories of Justification: Deeds vs. Reasons*, in CURRENT PROBLEMS OF CRIMINAL THEORY (A.T.H. Smith & A. Simester, eds. 1995).

law: the tendency to criminalize actions that the community would not conceive of as condemnable conduct. As Jack Coffee has noted, there is a strong trend toward the criminalization of regulatory offenses, leading to the astounding number of some 300,000 federal "crimes."[32] The problem with this is that current law has extended criminalization beyond even the domain of traditional malum prohibitum offenses, to criminalize conduct that is "harmful" only in the sense that it causes inconvenience for bureaucrats. Thus, most federal regulations are now routinely converted to federal crimes to give the regulators greater leverage in enforcement. Of similar effect is the increased use of strict liability and vicarious liability,[33] common features of civil law but out of place in a criminal system.

A few concrete cases will make the point clear. As is well known, individuals and organizations are required to provide large amounts of information to federal, state, and local governments. Providing false information is sometimes a criminalized regulatory offense. If false information knowingly is supplied to evade pollution regulations, taxes, or safety precautions, then the community will agree that this is conduct worthy of criminalization. However, if erroneous information is provided unwittingly or if such information has little bearing on matters of importance, then the community is not likely to see the action as morally condemnable deserving criminalization. Or consider a case in which an employer inadvertently fails to put all required information in a federally required report (as opposed to knowingly putting false information in the report). This may arguably hurt society in some sense, but it is hard to see how; and even if it does, the degree of the injury is so infinitesimal that no one—even those who have full information about the need for the reporting requirement—would think the failure rises to the level of harm that deserves the moral condemnation traditionally associated with criminal conviction. If an adult-appearing 20-year-old, with high-quality forged ID papers, buys an alcoholic beverage from a harassed bartender, the community has trouble seeing the action as criminal, although a strict liability statute holds the bartender liable, and a vicarious liability statute holds the absent bar owner criminally liable.

The law cannot have moral credibility outside of a system with a clear criminal-civil distinction. Much of civil law is governed by principles unrelated to desert. While there is some disagreement on the issue, one might well justify, for example, a tort system that uses forms of strict liability or vicarious liability. Even if fairness were adopted as the primary distributive principle for tort liability, no one would claim that tort liability ought to be limited to cases where moral condemnation is appropriate. A mixed criminal-civil system, then, will inevitably have some cases where the result is driven by moral desert and others where it is not. It would be difficult, if not impossible, for such a system to build a reputation with the public as a system devoted exclusively to judging moral blameworthiness. Every instance of liability

---

[32] John C. Coffee, Jr., *Does "Unlawful" Mean "Criminal"?: Reflections on the Disappearing Tort/Crime Distinction in American Law*, 71 B.U. L. Rev. 193, 216 (1991).

[33] *See id.* at 210–15.

based upon non-desert criteria would undercut the system's moral credibility, and the "criminal" label could not be used as a clear signal that moral condemnation is deserved. In the cases where the criminal system wishes to wave the red flag of moral condemnation, it would have only an ambiguous pink flag at its disposal. The separation of the two systems, into criminal and civil, enables for the criminal law to focus exclusively on desert and, perhaps more importantly, to make clear to the public that it is so focused. It allows the "criminal" label to be a red flag.[34]

The current trend toward blurring the criminal-civil distinction is particularly foolish because it can provide little or no long-term gain, even with respect to the very cases brought within the expansion. First, cases of regulatory offenses, strict liability, and vicarious liability are just the types of cases where the likelihood of a prison sentence is remote;[35] the sentences typically are fines and restitution, the sanctions that are available at civil law. Thus, by criminalizing these offenses, access to more severe sanctions are not necessarily gained.

But, of course, access to more severe sanctions is not the reason that many have argued for the extension of the criminal law to these cases. More severe sanctions could be provided within the civil system. The arguments for such criminal expansion often focus upon the possibility for the moral stigma criminal liability brings that civil liability does not.[36] Obviously, stigmatization can have a substantial effect in shaping the conduct of potential offenders, but this attempted use of stigmatization is likely to be ineffective because it offends rather than educates the moral code of the community. Passing a statute that criminalizes new conduct does not itself cause that conduct to be perceived as immoral. As the previous discussion suggests, law does not create norms but only acts as a participant in the process by which consensuses are built. Making a regulatory violation a "crime" is not in itself likely to do much to cause people to attach stigma to liability for the violation. Making 300,000 regulatory violations "crimes" makes it even less likely that people will take the resulting liability as evidence that moral condemnation is deserved. Similarly, criminalizing actions that are offenses only from a strict or vicarious liability perspective fails to bring the stigmatization of criminality to bear on those violations. Far from being an independent and respected source of moral authority, a collection of laws of this sort becomes a pettifogging caricature.

---

[34] *See* Paul H. Robinson, *The Criminal Civil Distinction and Dangerous Blameless Offenders*, 83 J. Crim. L. & Criminology 693 (1993).

[35] The majority of regulatory offenses are misdemeanors, for which a serious prison term is not authorized. Even for the most egregious forms of these offenses, where danger to life or property is created, the likelihood of an incarcerative sentence is not high. In 1989, the number of convicted federal regulatory violators sentenced to prison was 37 agricultural, 22 antitrust, 2 labor, 24 food and drug. Table 5.17, Sentences imposed in cases terminated in U.S. District Courts, 1992 Sourcebook of Criminal Justice Statistics 488 (1993).

[36] *See* John C. Coffee, Jr., *"No Soul to Damn: No Body to Kick": An Unscandalized Inquiry Into the Problem of Corporate Punishment*, 79 Mich. L. Rev. 386, 424–34 (1981). *But see* Michael K. Block, *Optimal Penalties, Criminal Law and the Control of Corporate Behavior*, 71 B.U. L. Rev. 395 (1991).

More important, the expansion of criminal law to punish these various violations is not only ineffective but destructive. The more criminal law's stigmatizing effect is sought to be applied to non-condemnable conduct, the less stigmatizing effect there exists to apply. With each additional non-blameworthy use, the meaning of "criminal liability" becomes incrementally less tied to blameworthiness and incrementally less able to evoke condemnation. As each strict liability case, or vicarious liability case, or case of innocent or trivial conduct is criminalized, more and more people will conclude that the criminal law is being used not to reflect community notions of desert but rather as a tool of a powerful government to intervene destructively in the lives of ordinary people. Expanding the criminal law beyond the bounds of perceived desert weakens and then destroys the stigmatizing effect—the very effect that that expansion seeks to enlist. Eventually, criminal penalties for non-condemnable conduct cause the public to sympathize with the person charged, and to despise the legal system that brings the charge. And it is the credibility of the criminal law in general that may be destroyed. Criminal conviction for a violation that the community sees as non-condemnable affects not just the meaning of liability imposed for those offenses but the condemnatory message for all criminal convictions.

E. Expanding the Reach of Blamelessness: Exercising Mercy

With this general review of the kinds of reforms that might be called for to promote criminal law's moral credibility with the community it governs, this section and the next give two examples of just how far empirical desert might take the criminal law beyond its present boundaries. They illustrate that, if the criminal law were to commit itself to empirical desert, it might well generate formal excuse defenses substantially broader than current law. These examples certainly show how misguided is the once common concern, noted in section 8, section D.4 that empirical desert might naturally be too draconian in the liability and punishment it would impose.[37] (This section is just one example of the implications of the research on lay views on extralegal punishment factors described in chapter 21.)

1. THE NATURE OF MERCY

While mercy may not be something deserved by the recipient, it can be a clear virtue in those who give it. The forgiving victim shows herself to be a virtuous person. Indeed, it is because the victim has every right to demand just punishment of her victimizer that her foregoing that right has such emotional power. That exercise of

---

[37] Much of this section is drawn from my article, Paul H. Robinson, Mercy, Crime Control & Moral Credibility, in Merciful Judgment and Contemporary Society: Legal Problems, Legal Possibilities 101–03 (Austin Sarat ed. 2011).

forgiveness says something about the forgiver that makes her endearing. This type of mercy has come to be seen as a characteristic to emulate.

But note that the virtue of mercy is about the giver. It is a virtuous person that forgives her aggressor. It is not necessarily virtuous for one to forgive *another person's aggressor*. What virtuous sacrifice has this forgiver made? What right has this non-victim to forgive? If one has not been victimized, where is the virtue in forgiving? Thus, where is the virtue in a sentencing judge's forgiving an aggressor's harm of others?

Beyond abstract virtue, one might also observe that the exercise of mercy, compassion, and forgiveness are of practical value. One spouse's compassion in response to errors by the other can help build an enriching and enduring relationship. The same can be said for compassion between friends. Indeed, a world in which strangers show compassion to one another would be a better world for all. But, of course, this is true because there is no societal cost in such exercise of compassion. There might be a personal cost to the victim of the transgression who forgives, but that is a cost that the victim has chosen to suffer, which she ought to be free to do. However, where the exercise of compassion frustrates a criminal offender's receiving of the punishment he deserves, it can have serious *societal* costs, in both frustrating justice and promoting avoidable crime.

One may conclude that mercy has no proper place outside of the context of interpersonal relationships. An expression of mercy by an injured to her injurer is a quite different matter than the institutionalization of the failure to give truly deserved punishment by a criminal justice system. The practice is suspect not only because it is not the victim who is showing mercy and not only because such institutionalization creates societal costs (that do not occur in the context of private exercise of mercy), but also because, by codifying mercy, one creates an expectation, if not a right, which may well undermine the virtue of giving mercy—it is a virtue to give it precisely because it is not required.

2. LAY INTUITIONS ON XPFS AND THE PROBLEM OF UNDERMINING THE LAW'S MORAL CREDIBILITY

Having made the case for leaving mercy out of the criminal law, there is one theory, however, a utilitarian one at that, which might well urge formal recognition of formal mitigations that otherwise would be seen as appropriate only upon the discretionary exercise of mercy. To the extent that the community would want less punishment for certain kinds of offenders in certain situations—if they would want the criminal justice system to exercise what might normally be described as mercy—then empirical desert would urge recognition of a mitigation as a means of enhancing the criminal law's moral credibility with the community.

If the criminal law is to build moral credibility with the community it governs, it should regularly take account of extralegal punishment factors (XPFs) that have strong support in that community. This is not currently done. A criminal justice system that ignores such an XPF risks being seen as deaf to the community's views of proper punishment.

At the same time, maintaining the criminal law's moral credibility with the community also means avoiding reliance upon XPFs that the community rejects as irrelevant to proper punishment. Allowing decision makers to rely upon these XPFs risks undermining the criminal law's moral credibility and thereby risks undermining its ability to harness the powerful forces of normative and social influence.

The study of lay intuitions on XPFs described in chapter 21 reports a variety of results that might well be translated into punishment rules or practices. For example, according to lay intuitions, an offender's reaction to his own offense is an important consideration at sentencing, but his character or past actions are less so. Remorse, regret, and apology seem to mitigate punishment in people's judgments, but character on its own does not appear to be a powerful factor. For another example, the extent of an offender's suffering is an important consideration, and there seems to be substantial, consistent support for the idea that punishment ought to be tailored, if possible, to a defendant's unique circumstances, especially when he or those close to him may doubly suffer because of an official sanction. Still further, whether and to what extent a punishment factor should affect punishment often depends on the nature of the underlying offense. Judges, parole boards, or other sentencing officials who hope to track lay intuitions should think not only about the punishment factor presented to them but the nature of the underlying offense. In a number of situations, the underlying offense appears to alter the logic of mitigation or aggravation. Finally, lay intuitions seem to hold that punishment should more readily take mitigating XPFs into account when the underlying offense is not a serious one. The reverse, though, may not be true: lay intuitions do not increase the effect of aggravating XPFs when the underlying offense is more serious.

3. DISAGREEMENTS ABOUT XPFS AND THE PROBLEM OF DISPARITY IN APPLICATION

The research reported in chapter 21 has one other set of findings that have implications for moral credibility of the criminal justice system: there is enormous disagreement among people on the proper effect of many, if not most, XPFs. The criminal justice system can only discredit itself in the eyes of the community if it allows XPFs to be used without guidance that will assure some greater uniformity in application.

There exist a myriad of points in the criminal justice process at which a decision maker may choose to take account of, or to ignore, the existence of an XPF. A prosecutor may consider, or ignore, extralegal punishment factors when deciding to prosecute an offender or when negotiating a plea bargain. A judge may consider, or ignore, an XPF at sentencing, occasionally upon legal authority, but more typically in the exercise of her sentencing discretion. In some trials, XPFs may come out during trial testimony and may be taken into account, or not, by jurors in determining a trial verdict. And in some sentencing regimes,[38] juries also participate in the sentencing process and may consider, or ignore, an XPF in that context. Finally, parole boards and corrections officials may consider XPFs, or not, in deciding when to release an offender.

There seems to be general agreement among lay persons and academics that a central feature of fairness and justice is consistency in the application of punishment. Similar offenders committing similar offenses ought to receive similar punishment. One's punishment ought to depend upon one's offense, culpability, and capacities—not upon the luck, good or bad—of the decision maker one happens to draw. As the Senate Report to the federal Sentencing Reform Act of 1984 put it when creating the United States Sentencing Commission:

> Sentencing disparities that are not justified by differences among offenses or offenders are unfair both to offenders and to the public. A sentence that is unjustifiably high compared to sentences for similarly situated offenders is clearly unfair to the offender; a sentence that is unjustifiably low is just as plainly unfair to the public. Such sentences are unfair in more subtle ways as well. Sentences that are disproportionate to the seriousness of the offense create a disrespect for the law. Sentences that are too severe create unnecessary tensions among inmates and add to disciplinary problems in prisons.[39]

Yet, there are many XPFs on which there is enormous disagreement as to the propriety of their application, even when people are considering the exact same XPF for the exact same offense and offender.[40] In more than 20 percent of the cells in Table 96 (19 of 90), the subjects were almost evenly split, 40 to 60 percent or closer.[41] In more than a quarter of the cells (25 of 90), there is a dissent of more than a third of the subjects. In almost half of the cells (43 of 90), a quarter or more of the subjects are dissenting.

There is little reason to think that such high levels of disagreement on some applications of some XPFs disappear among the police, prosecutors, judges, jurors, parole boards, and other criminal justice system decision makers.[42] Yet, clearly it would be unacceptable if the chances that one's punishment depended on the luck of the draw of a decision maker at these levels.

---

[38] *See* Nancy J. King & Susan R. Klein, *Essential Elements*, 54 VAND. L. REV. 1467, 1510 (2001) (noting that by the mid-20th century 13 states continued to allow sentencing by juries).

[39] S. Rep. No. 98-225, at 45–46 (1983), *reprinted in* 1984 U.S.C.C.A.N. 3182, 3182–3562. See Michael M. O'Hear, *National Uniformity/Local Uniformity: Reconsidering the Use of Departures To Reduce Federal-State Sentencing Disparities*, 87 IOWA L. REV. 721, 729 (2002).

[40] For empirical evidence of communal disagreement regarding XPF, refer to Paul H. Robinson, Sean E. Jackowitz, & Daniel M. Bartels, *Extralegal Punishment Factors: A Study of Forgiveness, Hardship, Good-Deeds, Apology, Remorse, And Other Such Discretionary Factor In Assessing Criminal Punishment*, 65 VAND. L. REV. 737 (2012).

[41] *Id.* at 32, Table 4.

[42] As a general matter, there is disagreement between the population at large and sentencing officials on how strict the criminal justice system should be. *See* Stephanos Bibas, *Transparency and Participation in Criminal Procedure*, 81 N.Y.U. L. REV. 911, 928 (2006) (reviewing studies).

Indeed, even more egregious are situations where an offender falls under a decision maker holding an idiosyncratic view.[43] Imagine an offender being judged by a decision maker who falls into a small group of dissenters. More than half the cells (48 of 90) in Table 96 show a minority view of 25 percent or less. Some of the XPFs had a dissenting group as small as 6 percent.[44] A lack of guidance in the application of XPFs invites the problem explicitly noted by the Senate: an offender receiving "more favorable or less favorable treatment because he happens to be sentenced by a particular judge."[45]

The potential for disparity in application is exacerbated by the demographic differences in assessing XPFs.[46] While there is much agreement across demographics, there also is some disagreement. An offender's punishment ought not depend upon the particular demographic characteristics of the decision maker, be it sentencing judge, sentencing jury, or prosecuting attorney exercising discretion in striking a plea and sentence agreement.

Thus, if XPFs are to be relied upon in assessing punishment, there are good reasons to provide an articulation of rules governing their use or at least some informal guidance, both to better avoid abuse and to improve the uniformity in their application among different decision makers. For all offenders, punishment ought to depend upon the same set of factors relevant to the case, not upon the personal preferences and idiosyncrasies of the individual decision maker. Unjustified disparity in the imposition of punishment can only tend to undermine the system's moral credibility.

F. Breaking New Ground: Are We Responsible for Who We Are?

Empirical desert may take criminal law not only beyond its current mitigations, as the section above suggests, but also across a bright-line prohibition that the law has always treated as foundational: holding an offender accountable for his own beliefs and values. That bright-line prohibition has served to reject any defense for coercive indoctrination (or for "rotten social background") that may have contributed to an offense.[47]

Should coercive indoctrination (CI) or "rotten social background" (RSB) be a defense to crime? There seems little doubt that traditional excuse theory would

---

[43] For some compelling examples of this, see the cases of Serafini, Warfield, and Pennington described in Robinson, Jackowitz & Bartels, *XPFs*, *supra* note 653, at 56–57.

[44] *Id.* at 32, Table 4.

[45] Stephanos Bibas, *Transparency and Participation in Criminal Procedure*, 81 N.Y.U. L. Rev. 911, n.35 (2006) (citing S. Rep. No. 98–225, at 79).

[46] Robinson, Jackowitz, and Bartels, *XPFs*, *supra* note 653, at 39–50, Tables 9 & 10.

[47] This section is drawn mainly from portions of my article: Paul H. Robinson, *Are We Responsible for Who We Are? The Challenge of Criminal Law Theory in the Defense of Coercive Indoctrination and "Rotten Social Background,"* 2 Ala. Civ. Rts & Civ. Lib. L. Rev. 53 (2012).

suggest that they ought not be. Even more clearly, the modern coercive crime-control doctrines of general deterrence and incapacitation would not support an excuse in such cases.[48] On the contrary, persons whose CI or RSB incline them toward crime would be special targets for deterrent threats and incapacitative control by the criminal justice system. Normative crime control, under a distributive principle of empirical desert, in contrast, is less clear in its rejection of a CI or RSB defense. Its view would depend upon whether there is community support for such excuse.

What I mean by "coercive indoctrination" (CI) is changing a person's values or beliefs through coercive means.[49] Thus, a defendant who would not have committed the offense in question were he his "old self" might claim that he should get a defense since he acted only because of new beliefs and values forcibly imposed on him for which he ought not be held accountable. One could view "rotten social background" as a specialized form of CI. That is, one might argue that the offender's "rotten social background"—for example, growing up in a world of deprivation and violence—induced beliefs and values that inevitably caused the offense and that the offender would not have committed the offense but for his RSB.

1. TRADITIONAL EXCUSE THEORY AND THE INADEQUACY OF A "BUT FOR" CAUSE AS AN EXCUSE: JUDGE BAZELON IN *BRAWNER* AND *ALEXANDER*

Traditional excuse theory, reflected in the excuses of essentially all American jurisdictions, provides an excuse upon the satisfaction of two requirements: (a) a *disability* must cause (b) a recognized *excusing condition*.[50] In the excuses of insanity and involuntary intoxication, for example, (a) a mental disease or defect or involuntary intoxication must cause (b) the offender at the time of the offense to suffer sufficient cognitive or control dysfunction so as to be unable to sufficiently understand or control his offense conduct.[51] The first element, of a *disability*, requires a real-world abnormality or dysfunction. The second element, of a resulting *excusing condition*, requires a normative judgment that the extent of the dysfunction is sufficiently severe to render the offender blameless for his offense conduct. To give another example, the duress excuse requires that the offender (a) committed the offense under the effects of duress or coercion; and (b) that the coercion, in the

---

[48] *See id.* at 8.

[49] As Richard Delgado describes the concept:The victim of [coercive indoctrination] typically commits criminal acts fully aware of their wrongfulness. He acts consciously, even enthusiastically, and without overt coercion. Yet, in an important sense, the guilty mind with which he acts is not his own. Rather, his mental state is more appropriately ascribed to the captors who instilled it in him for their own purposes.Richard Delgado, *Ascription of Criminal States of Mind: Toward a Defense Theory for the Coercively Persuaded ("Brainwashed") Defendant*, 63 MINN. L. REV. 1, 11 (1978) (footnotes omitted).

[50] *See* Paul H. Robinson, *A System of Excuses: How Criminal Law's Excuse Defenses Do, and Don't, Work Together to Exculpate Blameless (and Only Blameless) Offenders*, 42 TEX. TECH L. REV. 259, 263 (2009).

[51] *See* MODEL PENAL CODE §2.08(4).

words of the Model Penal Code, was such that "a person of reasonable firmness in [the offender's] situation would have been unable to resist."[52]

It is obviously inadequate for a defense to show simply that the offender was acting under *some* coercion or had *some* mental illness or was involuntary intoxicated to *some* extent. An excuse is merited only if the *extent of the dysfunction meets a critical level*: such that the actor could not reasonably have been expected to have remained law-abiding. This is true even if the disability is a "but for" cause of the offense. The offender who steals perfume from the department store because his girlfriend threatens to break up with him if he does not, may well be able to claim that he would not have committed the offense *but for the coercion*, yet no one would seriously consider that the effect of the coercion was sufficient to merit an excuse. The same is true of the man who is involuntarily intoxicated by his friends and, in that state, has nonconsensual intercourse with a semiconscious coed. He may well be able to honestly claim that he would not have committed the offense conduct but for his involuntary intoxication, but whether he is entitled to an excuse requires us to know more about the actual effects of the involuntary intoxication on him at the time of the offense conduct. Was the effect simply a pleasant buzz and a minor loosening of restraints? Could we have reasonably expected him to have avoided the offense conduct despite the involuntary intoxication? Even if the offender would not have committed the offense *but for* the disability, he does not necessarily merit an excuse. The extent of the dysfunction—the extent of cognitive or control impairment—must be shown to have been sufficiently severe as to render him blameless for his offense conduct.

Judge Bazelon's support of the *Durham* "product test" for insanity[53] stands in direct conflict with these standard requirements for modern excuses. Bazelon sought to leave off the second element for an excuse, the requirement that the disability (such as mental disease or defect) cause a sufficiently dysfunctional effect so as to render the offender blameless for his offense conduct. He argued for an excuse upon a showing of a disability—upon a showing that the offender was mentally ill and would not have committed the offense if he were not—but without inquiring into the extent of the dysfunction or the extent of its effect in causing the offense. By dispensing with the excusing condition requirement, Bazelon's theory of excuses would seem to provide a defense to the mildly coerced thief and the involuntarily intoxicated rapist noted above, a difficult position to sustain.

In *United States v. Brawner*, the DC Circuit rejected Bazelon's *Durham* arguments, for predictable reasons similar to those above explaining the importance of the excusing condition requirement.[54] The blamelessness driving an excuse defense does not derive from the bare existence of an actor's disability or even from the fact that the disability may influence the actor's violation. The conclusion of blame-

---

52 *Id.* §2.09(1).

53 *See* United States v. Brawner, 471 F.2d 969 (D.C. Cir. 1972).

54 *See id.* at 977–79.

lessness comes from *the existence of the excusing condition*—the finding that the effect of the disability on the actor was so severe that we could not reasonably have expected him to have remained law-abiding. In control dysfunction cases, this requires a finding that the actor made *enough* of an effort to resist the temptation or compulsion. In cognitive dysfunction cases, it requires that the actor was *sufficiently* confused in his thinking, and therefore unsure about the nature or legality of his conduct—that he is not to be blamed for the violation. Yet it was this central excusing condition element that Bazelon sought to dispense with in his proposed, and rejected, "product test" for insanity.

This same error propels Judge Bazelon's judgment in *United States v. Alexander*, in which "rotten social background," rather than mental illness, was said to have caused the offender's offense conduct.[55] A group of unarmed marines in their dress white uniforms had stopped at a hamburger shop with a girlfriend after a celebration of their near completion of officer basic training. Alexander began staring at the marines, and when one of the marines returned the stare, Alexander approached and confronted the marines, leaning in and poking one in his name tag, calling them to come outside. When words were exchanged, Alexander and codefendant Murdock each pulled a handgun and began firing into the group, killing two of the marines.[56]

Murdock's claim was that he should be excused because his RSB had caused his offense conduct.[57] This is similarly the thrust of Richard Delgado's rationale for a RSB excuse.

> An environment of extreme poverty and deprivation creates in individuals a propensity to commit crimes. In some cases, a defendant's impoverished background so greatly determines his or her criminal behavior that we feel it unfair to punish the individual.... [B]lame is inappropriate when a defendant's criminal behavior is caused by extrinsic factors beyond his or her control.[58]

There is good evidence that an RSB can have potentially quite powerful effects. Murdock grew up nearly penniless in the violent, chaotic Watts section of Los Angeles. He was not responsible for being born into the situation. He had no obvious or easy means of escaping from it. On the other hand, not all people who grow up in such circumstances become violent criminals. That is, even admitting that environment can seriously influence the development of personality, the strength of that to influence the committing of the offense at hand is at best unclear. But most important, even if it could be shown that Alexander's RSB was a but-for cause of his shooting, the marines, such a but-for cause by itself is insufficient for excuse, just as it is in the insanity (or duress or involuntary intoxication) situation. To qualify for a defense under traditional excuse theory, Alexander would have to show that

---

[55] *See* 471 F.2d 923, 959 (D.C. Cir. 1973).

[56] *See id.* at 928–30.

[57] *Id.* at 959 n.100.

[58] Richard Delgado, *"Rotten Social Background": Should the Criminal Law Recognize a Defense of Severe Environmental Deprivation?* 3 LAW & INEQ. 9, 54–55 (1985).

the overwhelming effect of the RSB was such that we could not reasonably have expected him to have remained law-abiding, that he was blameless for his shooting of the marines.

2. COERCIVE INDOCTRINATION UNDER NORMATIVE CRIME CONTROL: THE CASE OF POW RICHARD TENNESON

If empirical desert were one's distributive principle, should CI or RSB be a defense? There is some evidence to support some kind of excuse defense in some such cases. Consider the case of Richard Tenneson, a 17-year-old American who was kidnapped and brainwashed by Chinese Communists while serving during the Korean War.[59] After being "treated" by the Chinese Communists, Tenneson was effectively converted into a full-blown Communist and denounced his American lifestyle. When the war ended, he chose to defect to Communist China. Several years later, when he finally decided that he would like to be repatriated to the United States, Tenneson found that he was facing charges of treason.

At the time, there was strong public support for the POWs like Tenneson who were seen as being "brainwashed" into becoming collaborators, even though aiding the enemy in a time of war was seen as an extremely serious offense. The support for Tenneson was not simply a product of the special wartime atmosphere. Even today, there is much sympathy for Tenneson. For more than a decade, other criminal law teachers and I have been asking first-year criminal law students to "sentence" Tenneson after reading the facts above. These are their cumulative responses:[60]

Seventy-nine percent of the people in the survey impose either no liability or no punishment. Only 13 percent impose a sentence of over a year. For the serious offenses charged, this suggests that the vast majority, 87 percent, think a significant mitigation appropriate, if not a complete excuse.

58%	21%	1%	1%	-	3%	5%	5%	4%	1%	-	1%	-
no liability	liability but no punishment	1 day	2 wks.	2 mo.	6 mo.	1 yr.	3 yrs.	7 yrs.	15 yrs.	30 yrs.	life imprisonment	death

Mean = 3.6 days

FIGURE 20. Tenneson Liability Survey

If coercive indoctrination renders a Richard Tenneson blameless for conduct induced by the indoctrination, ought not the criminal law take notice? Certainly if one were to adopt empirical desert as one's distributive principle for criminal

[59] For more detail about the case, see Paul H. Robinson, Would You Convict? Seventeen Cases that Challenged the Law ch. 5 (1999).

[60] Paul H. Robinson, Teacher's Manual for Criminal Law: Case Studies & Controversies (3d ed. 2012).

liability and punishment, then such lay intuitive support suggests that a CI excuse ought to be seriously considered. But despite the public support, no court has ever recognized a defense for coercive indoctrination.[61] (Patty Hearst, for example, when kidnapped by the Symbionese Liberation Army, was held liable for crimes she committed while supposedly transformed by the SLA into the revolutionary "Tanya.") Given the evidence of the power of coercive indoctrination, why such resistance in law to recognizing a defense?

Perhaps the concern is that, while cases like Tenneson ought to be excused, others, perhaps Hearst, ought not, because they simply are not sufficiently compelling to produce the same intuitive conclusion of blamelessness. But the proper response to that concern is not to reject a CI excuse entirely, for such an approach assures the conviction of some blameless offenders, like Tenneson, a result that would incrementally undermine the moral credibility of the criminal law. Enhancing criminal law's moral credibility with the community it governs requires an attempt to dissect the intuitions that support the excuse and to fashion an excuse formulation that limits the defense to the situations that prompt conclusions of blamelessness.

To do this properly would require an empirical study that maps the contours of lay intuitive support and constructs the defense formulation that best captures those lay intuitions of justice in CI cases. Without such research, one can only speculate, using one's own intuitions and perhaps extrapolations from related studies. If one were to make such a rough guess at what drives people's intuitions in such cases, one might construct as a starting point a CI excuse formulation that looked something like this:

An actor is excused for his conduct constituting an offense if:

(1) he was coerced to adopt beliefs and values that were not his own;
(2) by influences sufficiently strong that he could not reasonably have been expected to have resisted their effect, given his abilities and situation; and
(3) the nature of the coerced beliefs and values were such as to demand the offense; and
(4) the actor would not have committed the offense had he not been coercively indoctrinated with those beliefs and values, and could not reasonably have been expected to have avoided committing the offense.

Such a formulation might well give a defense to Tenneson but perhaps not to Hearst or in other cases, depending upon the exact facts.

3. TESTING THE LIMITS OF A COERCIVE INDOCTRINATION OR A "ROTTEN SOCIAL BACKGROUND" EXCUSE: THE CASE OF ALEX CABARGA

If the law were to recognize a CI excuse for Tenneson, how far beyond Tenneson's circumstances should it extend? And should it extend to RSB cases, where the

---

[61] Rebecca Emory, Comment, *Losing Your Head in the Washer—Why the Brainwashing Defense Can Be a Complete Defense in Criminal Cases*, 30 PACE L. REV. 1337, 1338 (2010).

indoctrination effect could be as powerful but is less of an explicit "indoctrination program" and more simply the daily influence of a horribly difficult life? Consider, for example, the case of Alex Cabarga, who had a seriously rotten social background.[62] Cabarga's parents permitted Luis "Tree Frog" Johnson, a transient living in an old school bus, to have intimate relations with their son from at least the age of 7. When Cabarga was 9, Cabarga's mother willingly gave custody over to Tree Frog even though she was aware of the intercourse. Tree Frog continued his abuse of Cabarga for many years. When Cabarga reached the age of 17, Tree Frog convinced him to kidnap a young girl, 2½ -year-old Tara Burke, whom they planned to induct into their small, incestuous family. Cabarga willingly assisted Tree Frog, and the pair abused Tara for 10 months before they were turned into authorities by another runaway they had picked up.

Alex's case has some similarities to Richard Tenneson's, but also some significant differences. Alex was never a prisoner as Richard was. On the other hand, Alex was a psychological captive of Tree Frog, especially after Tree Frog took parental custody. Indeed, 9-year-old Alex was considerably younger and more vulnerable when given to Tree Frog than was 17-year-old Richard when he became a POW.

Alex's greater vulnerability was effectively exploited by Tree Frog. Note the similarity between Tree Frog's treatment of Alex and the Communist captors' coercive indoctrination of Richard. Tree Frog created isolation and control by living in a bread van from which there was no escape from his constant attention, and a nomadic existence that prevented Alex from developing relationships with persons other than Tree Frog. In other words, Tree Frog's program followed many of the standard elements of the first phase of coercive indoctrination: physiological debilitation through reduced food, which served in addition as a means of control; and creation of constant background anxiety through the constant fear of abuse and denial of food.

There was little need for the other elements of the indoctrination scheme—the degradation of Alex's preexisting self and the required performance of symbolic acts of self-betrayal, betrayal of group norms, and confession. At age nine, Alex had almost no preexisting self, and that which did exist had so internalized the counterculture norms of his parents and their social group that the violation of traditional norms was a virtue.

Would Alex qualify for a coercive indoctrination defense under the formulation set out above? Cabarga does seem to have been indoctrinated by beliefs and values that were not his own, as required by (1). And it seems clear that Alex would not have committed the offenses but for Tree Frog's (and his parent's) indoctrination, and, given his age and situation, it might not have been reasonable to expect him to have resisted, satisfying (4). Further, Tree Frog's indoctrination was indeed focused on committing just those offenses with which Cabarga is charged, the requirement in (3). Finally, one might conclude that the younger, more vulnerable Alex could not reasonably have been expected to have resisted Tree Frog's indoctrination any more

[62] For more detail, see Robinson, Would You Convict?, *supra* note 672, at ch 5.

than POW Richard could have been expected to have resisted his captors', as (2) requires.

If there is some suspicion on this last point, or point (4), it is that as Alex grew older, at 17 or 16 or earlier, he should have had the strength of character to see the wrongfulness of what he was doing and to break off from Tree Frog. But that assumes Alex had some internal normative conflict over what he was doing, which goes back to the lack-of-anchor problem. Certainly most 17-year-olds would be repulsed by the conduct. And clearly Alex knew that what he was doing was wrong, at least in the sense that he knew society strongly disapproved of it. After all, he and Tree Frog actively hid what they did. But, in Alex's upbringing, that social disapproval meant that it was the "right-thinking" thing to do.

But still, Alex must have known it was wrong in a deeper moral sense. He, better than anyone, knew how it felt to be the object of such manipulation and abuse from Tree Frog. Better than anyone, he understand what Tara endured. On the other hand, Alex *had* chosen to stay with Tree Frog despite the abuse.

There is a complex dynamic at work. Abused children often abuse their own children. Fraternity pledges often willingly endure abuse to become a member (and, in turn, abuse the members of the next year's pledge class). Army recruits, like Richard, volunteer for the abuse of boot camp (and may well aspire to become abusing drill instructors themselves). Knowing the sting of abuse does not always give an understanding of how wrong it is; it sometimes seems only to devalue its wrongfulness, to desensitize the abused to the wrongfulness of abuse.

Could Alex reasonably have been expected to have resisted Tree Frog's indoctrination? Could he have been expected to have spontaneously walked away to start a new life for himself? People will disagree on this; it is not entirely clear. But it seems clear that, in judging Alex, the law cannot retain moral credibility if it ignores the indoctrination that brought Alex to the offenses.

In the survey, over half of the people impose either no liability or no punishment.[63] Only 18 percent impose a sentence of 3 years imprisonment or more. Even among those who impose imprisonment, however, the terms are dramatically less than one might expect for such a collection of serious offenses; only 8 percent suggest prison terms of 15 years or more. (About a fifth of the people surveyed would subject Cabarga to detention for as long as he is dangerous but would not impose criminal liability.) Apparently Alex's history does serve as a substantial mitigation to most people and as a complete excuse from punishment for a majority (55 percent).

Alex, in fact, was charged by prosecutors with the same range of offenses as Tree Frog. At trial, the prosecution case was based primarily on the pictures and movies taken by Tree Frog. The law had not changed since Richard Tenneson's time two decades before. Coercive indoctrination was neither a defense nor a mitigation. Alex was convicted of all offenses and sentenced to 208 years in prison. (At the same

---

[63] ROBINSON, TEACHER'S MANUAL, *supra* note 673, at 92.

26%	29%	-	-	1%	1%	3%	5%	5%	4%	2%	2%	19%
no liability	liability but no punishment	1 day	2 wks.	2 mo.	6 mo.	1 yr.	3 yrs.	7 yrs.	15 yrs.	30 yrs.	life imprisonment	**

** no punishment, but civil preventive detention for as long as he is dangerous

Mean = 10.1 days

FIGURE 21. Sentencing Survey for Alex Cabarga

time, the board of the California Victims of Crime Program concluded that Alex was a victim of Tree Frog's abuse; found Alex eligible for aid under the program; and agreed to pay $10,000 toward his psychiatric counseling, the same amount that victim Tara received.)

4. "ROTTEN SOCIAL BACKGROUND" AND EMPIRICAL DESERT

Tenneson is a classic CI case. Cabarga is a somewhat atypical CI case, resting as it does more on a horrible RSB than on a formal indoctrination program, but a case that seems plausibly analogous to CI. The strength of the analogy between the two cases illustrates the potential strength of the analogy between CI and RSB generally. That is, once one goes beyond the official *indoctrination program* in Tenneson to the less formal *indoctrination effect* that occurred in Cabarga, it seems hard to exclude from the analogy any other influential factor that shapes beliefs and values, no matter whether it was formal or informal, intended or accidental, whether it was the product of one person or group or an entire society, or whether it was executed in a bread truck or on the mean streets. That is, if sympathy exists for Tenneson and Cabarga, then that same sympathy should exist for any offender who can show he has been similarly coercively and involuntarily indoctrinated into committing an offense.

Yet simple RSB—that is the influence of a terribly difficult life of privation and violence but without an identifiable protagonist, like a Tree Frog, who is attempting to manipulate the defendant—does not have the intuitive sympathy offered a Cabarga, let alone the strong support offered a Tenneson. What might explain the lack of support for an excuse for a "simple RSB," as it might be called?

One difficulty may be skepticism about whether one's general environment alone is so overwhelming as to undermine one's normal ability to shape one's own beliefs and values. Many people—including people with RSBs—will point out the obvious: that the vast majority of people with RSBs do not become criminals.[64] That so

[64] The criminogenic effects of a RSB remain unclear, in part because RSB remains a vague sociological concept. Still, the literature may be read to suggest that certain variables related to having a RSB, while correlated with criminality, have inconsistent effects on criminality, often having no effect on females (or whites). *See, e.g.,* Beverly Rivera & Cathy Spatz Widom, *Childhood Victimization and Violent Offending*, 5 VIOLENCE & VICTIMS 19, 30 (1990); Jeffrey R. King et al., *Neighborhood Effects on Crime for Female and Male Youth: Evidence from a Randomized Housing Voucher Experiment,* 120 Q.J. ECON. 87 (2005); Cesar J. Rebellon, *Reconsidering the Broken Homes/Delinquency Relationship and Exploring Its Mediating Mechanism(s)*, 40 CRIMINOLOGY 103, 125 (2002).

many people with RSBs internalize appropriate norms would seem to suggest that the power of the indoctrination is something less than overwhelming. On the other hand, most prisoners in Tenneson's situation did not betray their country by adopting the ideology of the enemy, yet Tenneson gets sympathetic support.

Part of the skepticism about an excuse for simple RSB may stem from a judgment that the kinds of beliefs and values with which one is indoctrinated by RSB are not beliefs and values that themselves compel lawbreaking in the way that Tenneson's captors or Cabarga's custodian shaped their indoctrination to achieve the specific goal of engaging in conduct that was an offense. That is, an RSB may have a serious influence on beliefs and values, but those beliefs and values do not seem to clearly lead to criminality, such as the shooting of insufficiently respectful marines, as occurred in *Alexander*. Alexander may well have been a different person than he otherwise would have been if he had not had an RSB, but it is hard to see how that RSB compelled his killings. What may seem more plausible to people is that his offense conduct was as much a product of his own selfishness, arrogance, and pride as it was a product of anything his RSB created in him. (Note that Alexander would not seem to satisfy the requirements of the CI defense proposed above.)

A different sort of skepticism may arise from the implications of giving Alexander an excuse. There is an enormous lay intuitive commitment to the notion that people normally operate with free will: that people are generally responsible for who they are.[65] It is this foundation that supports the essentially universal human intuition that serious wrongdoing deserves punishment.[66] Cases like *Tenneson* do not seriously threaten this conception of people's accountability for who they are. The circumstances of Tenneson's "brainwashing," as it was called back then, were so unusual and so apart from the nature of people's daily lives that they could easily shift the blame for the offense to the effects of having been "brain washed." Giving an excuse to Tenneson seems to have few implications for offenders other than prisoners subjected to official indoctrination programs.

In this respect, even the *Cabarga* case raises some suspicion, although it might be tolerable. While Cabarga's situation is quite bizarre and not likely to be replicated, his case does illustrate a certain ambiguity as to where the line should be drawn, for the case is not qualitatively different from the many other difficult life situations in which people suffer. As sad as it is, Cabarga's "social background" is just the extreme of a genre of bad situations in which people are raised. A bread truck is not a prison camp, and a twisted hippie's malevolent teachings are not an enemy's indoctrination program. Tenneson does seem to have had an experience that is qualitatively different from the average life, while Cabarga might be seen as having had one that

---

[65] *See* Eddy Nahmias et al., *Surveying Freedom: Folk Intuitions about Free Will and Moral Responsibility*, 18 PHIL. PSYCHOL. 561, 571 (2005).

[66] *See* Paul H. Robinson & Robert Kurzban, *Concordance and Conflict in Intuitions of Justice*, 91 MINN. L. REV.1829, 1872 (2007).

was only quantitatively different, albeit an extreme. It is perhaps for this reason that people's intuitions are somewhat less sympathetic for Cabarga than for Tenneson.

By these measures, one would expect little if any intuitive support for Alexander or any other simple RSB offenders. A rotten social background is likely to be seen as the tragic reality of many people's unfortunate life. As bad as such a life may be, it is only quantitatively different from the struggles, disappointments, temptations, deprivations, and outrages that most people experience in their daily lives. It is worse, but it is not qualitatively worse. If the base intuitive assumption is that people are responsible for who they are, then the circumstances of a simple rotten social background itself may not be so unique as to override an intuitive assumption.

PART } III

The Content of Lay Judgments of Justice

Part I discusses the existence and nature of lay persons' judgments of justice, while part II shows why these lay judgments are important to criminal law. This part takes up the challenge of sketching just what our judgments of justice are, especially as they relate to the matters on which the criminal law must formulate liability and punishment rules. As will become clear, the formal criminal law rules track community views in many ways but also diverge in many ways. Chapter 7 has already shown serious conflicts between certain popular modern crime-control doctrines (many of which are discussed here as well) and lay judgments of justice. Part III considers the full array of legal issues that a criminal law must address.

Chapters 12 and 13 examine community judgments regarding rules of conduct: doctrines of criminalization, which define offenses; and doctrines of justification, which define when a violation of an offense prohibition is justified. Both are important for telling the community ex ante what the law expects of them.

If a conduct rule is violated, the law must judge whether there was sufficient blameworthiness in the violation such that the actor deserves condemnation or punishment. Chapter 14 examines the doctrines of culpability, which require a particular culpable state of mind with regard to the offense elements at the time of the offense. Even if the offender has the necessary culpability—he did *intentionally* kill the victim—the law will excuse the offender if his impaired capacities or his situation means that he could not reasonably have been expected to have remained law-abiding. This may occur, for example, because of the offender's insanity, immaturity, duress, or involuntary intoxication. The community's view on such excuse doctrines is examined in chapter 15.

If it is determined that criminal liability should be imposed, the law must determine the general extent of the punishment or its "grade." In the community's view, what factors affect a punishment's grade and how? Chapter 16 examines lay judgments on a variety of topics related to grading, including the actor's culpability level, the strength of the causal connection between his conduct and the prohibited result, and the commission of other offenses by the same person.

Finally, chapter 17 steps back from the examinations of the previous chapters and discusses the patterns observed in those studies of where lay notions of desert diverge from the legal rule. It concludes, among other things, that while small discrepancies may be fixed by jury action, the better approach would be reform of the criminal code to better reflect community views, for the reasons laid out in part II.

Before beginning the presentation and discussion of the research, sections A and B of chapter 12 describe and illustrate the methodology used in the studies reported throughout part III.

12 }

Rules of Conduct: Doctrines of Criminalization

Doctrines of criminalization answer the question: what conduct should be prohibited? Criminal law must tell people ex ante the rules of conduct that are commanded of them. The law also must tell people the relative seriousness of different violations, because some rules require people to distinguish violations according to their relative seriousness—for example, many justification defenses allow the violation of a prohibitory norm but only if the violation avoids a greater harm or evil. If the law is to have its guidance on such matters reflect the community's views, what should its rules look like?

Most people would agree that homicide, rape, theft, and so on ought to be criminalized. Some current offenses, like price-fixing, are less intuitively improper conduct. The common law distinguished the former kind of offense, called "malum in se" offenses, from the latter kind, called "malum prohibitum" offenses. Malum prohibitum offenses may seem somewhat artificial in what they prohibit; however, there is likely to be some consensus on the value of their ultimate objectives—in this instance increasing the competitiveness of the market. Some people might disagree that the particular offense formulation is the best means of achieving the ends, but few would dispute that the criminalization helps toward the goal and that the goal is desirable.

A significant potential for disagreement does exist, however, with regard to "victimless crimes," such as prostitution, gambling, or distribution of certain drugs. The criminalization of such conduct is designed in part to enforce the community's conceptions of morality. However, as the 1920s "Prohibition" and its failure illustrate, different groups may have different conceptions of what constitutes immoral conduct. As the community consensus on a morality issue fades, so can consensus on the laws that enforce it. As one would expect from current culture, there is lack of consensus on the enforcement of laws against what seem to be victimless crimes such as prostitution.[1]

There is an existing literature on people's views on malum prohibitum offenses.[2] This chapter concerns itself with more difficult and less studied issues. A complete

---

[1] *See, e.g.,* M. Levi & S. Jones, *Public and Police Perceptions of Crime Seriousness in England and Wales*, 25 British J. Crim. 234 (1985).

[2] *See*, e.g., Thorsten Sellin & Marvin E. Wolfgang, The Measurement of Delinquency 268 (1964); Jeffrey A. Roth, *Prosecutor Perceptions of Crime Seriousness*, 69 J. Crim. L. & Criminology 232 (1978); Joseph E. Jacoby & Francis T. Cullen, *The Structure of Punishment Norms: Applying the Rossi-Berk Model*, 89 J. Crim. L. & Criminology 245, 263 (1998).

statement of law's prohibitions includes not just the prohibited conduct itself but also what might be called secondary prohibitions built upon it, and the nature of those rules may be more complex. The law clearly should and does prohibit the (unjustified) killing of another, but should it also prohibit attempting such a killing, creating a risk of causing another's death, assisting another in such a killing, causing another's death through an omission? And, if so, what form should these secondary prohibitions take—at what point does conduct become a criminal attempt or criminal assistance; at what point does a risk created become a criminal risk? What are community views on these more complex liability rules? These are the subject of this chapter, which is drawn primarily from portions of my work with John Darley in *Justice, Liability & Blame: Community Views and the Criminal Law.*[3]

A. Research Methodology in Testing Lay Judgments of Justice

Before beginning the review of the research, let me describe in this section, and illustrate in the next one, the methodology that was used and the reasons for it. (There are important variations on this methodology that are better for other kinds of research. See, for example, the methodological note in chapter 21, section C describing the variation used there and used in the study described in chapter 7.)

The most promising method to test lay judgments about justice is what might be called "scenario" research. Subjects are presented with a short description of a person's conduct and are asked whether and, if so, how much liability and punishment the actor should receive for the conduct. Subjects are then given another scenario and assess liability and punishment for that actor, then another scenario, and so on. These scenarios are varied by the researchers in accordance with the theories being tested, and the researcher examines the differences among the liabilities assigned by subjects to each scenario.

Rather than having the subjects assign ratings to what can quite quickly become a large number of differing scenarios, why not just ask the subjects whether they think a particular rule formulation is appropriate? It is because psychologists have discovered that subjects often do not have mental access to the principles and processes they use to make decisions, and thus cannot accurately articulate those principles. Instead, researchers present subjects with various cases to judge and infer their judging principles from the resulting patterning of responses between the different cases.

To illustrate the method, consider the study of the objective requirements of attempt liability. How much conduct toward an offense must a person perform to be liable for a criminal attempt? The law has used a variety of tests. If one were to construct a criminal code that best captured peoples intuitions, which test would it adopt?

[3] Paul H. Robinson & John M. Darley, Justice, Liability & Blame: Community Views and the Criminal Law chs. 1 & 2 (1996).

Subjects first read a paragraph of core information describing the background of the various scenarios. Next, they read a specific scenario and are asked to assign a liability to the perpetrator described in it. The base scenario reads as follows:[4]

> Ray, a locksmith, recalls working on a safe in a coin shop. The safe was kept in a back room and always contained valuable coins. Ray thinks about how easily he could sneak into the back room during normal business hours and "crack" the safe. Ray decides that he will rob the safe in the coin shop. Before he does anything to prepare for the robbery, Ray tells a friend that he has decided to rob the safe.

In this version of the scenario, the actor, Ray, performs no act toward commission of the robbery. He only thinks about it. This establishes a useful point of comparison to other scenarios in which Ray does more toward committing the offense.

Another scenario uses the same situation but has Ray completing the offense:

> Ray, a locksmith, recalls working on a safe in a coin shop. The safe was kept in a back room and always contained valuable coins. Ray decides that he will rob the safe in the coin shop. To make sure that the safe is still there, Ray goes to the coin shop to check out the situation before the robbery. The next day Ray goes to the coin shop and meets the old man who owns it. While the owner helps another customer, Ray slips into the back room and cracks the safe. Ray slips away with a briefcase full of valuable coins. That night Ray tells a friend about what he did, and his friend tells the police. The next day two policemen search Ray's home with a search warrant, find the coins, and arrest him.

This scenario provides the point of comparison at the other end of the spectrum of conduct: the completed offense. A variety of other scenarios test interim points along the spectrum from "thought only" to "completed offense" and are likely to give liability scores that are speculated to fall between these two "control" scenarios.

No doubt some people will give higher punishment for all the scenarios than other people. In cases involving killings, for example, some people may give the death penalty, while others who are opposed to its use will not. But using the experimental design chosen, it is possible to functionally exclude from the analysis whether the subject is a generally harsh or easy sentencer, which is not the focus. The focus is in the *difference* in liability between specific scenarios, not the absolute amount of liability attached to any scenario.

As noted above, scenarios differ in ways designed to elicit any differences in liability that subjects might attach to differences in the actor's objective conduct. Thus, the scenarios were constructed so the actor, Ray, in the objective requirements of attempt study, engaged in conduct that would just satisfy one legal test for attempt but not another. For example, in one scenario, Ray's conduct satisfies

---

[4] *See id.* at 229–231.

the Model Penal Code's "substantial step" test, which generally allows the earliest assignment of liability of any of the various formulations:[5]

> Ray, a locksmith, recalls working on a safe in a coin shop. The safe was kept in a back room and always contained valuable coins. Ray decides that he will rob the safe in the coin shop. To make sure that the safe is still there, Ray goes to the coin shop and checks out the situation before the robbery. Ray tells a friend what he has decided to do.

In another scenario, Ray goes further and satisfies the requirement of the common law "dangerous proximity" formulation:[6]

> Ray, a locksmith, recalls working on a safe in a coin shop. The safe was kept in a back room and always contained valuable coins. Ray decides that he will rob the safe in the coin shop. To make sure that the safe is still there, Ray goes to the coin shop and checks out the situation before the robbery. Ray tells a friend about his plans to rob the safe the next day. His friend tells the police. The next day Ray goes to the coin shop and slips into the back room, where he begins to crack the safe. Before Ray is able to open the safe, however, two undercover policemen burst into the room and arrest him.

A series of other scenarios have Ray engaging in conduct that satisfies some other formulations. By looking at the subjects' liability and punishment responses, one can see which test best corresponds to their lay intuitions of the minimum requirements for attempt liability.

Notice that the goal was to vary the scenarios only with respect to the element that is relevant to the theoretical comparison in question. The subjects perceive the different scenarios as having the same overall characteristics, so that any differences in liabilities assigned can be attributed to the one characteristic that is varied between the contrasting scenarios—in this study, the extent of the actor's conduct toward the offense. More on the difficulties of scenario design will be assessed below.

The task of each subject, then, in response to each scenario, was to assign a degree of liability and punishment to the protagonist in the scenario—in their view, to assign punishment to a wrongdoer. Subjects did this by marking their judgment on the scale shown below.

no liability	liability but no punishment	1 day	2 wks.	2 mo.	6 mo.	1 yr.	3 yrs.	7 yrs.	15 yrs.	30 yrs.	life imprisonment

FIGURE 22. Punishment Scale

[5] *See* Model Penal Code §5.01(1)(c) (1985).

[6] *See* Robinson & Darley, *supra* note 682, at 8.

As one can see, subjects may choose among assigning no criminal liability to the protagonist; liability but no punishment; and 11 levels of punishment, ranging from one day in jail to the death penalty.

Notice that the length of the prison sentence increases differentially as the assigned punishments increase. For instance, an assignment of punishment level two is an assignment of 14 days in prison, an increase of only 13 days over punishment level one. An assignment of punishment level nine is a 15-year increase from the punishment represented by level eight. The scale was constructed in this way for two reasons: First, and primarily, because the differences correspond to the differences in grading categories used in typical American criminal codes. Second, because the differences correspond, roughly at least, to what ordinary people perceive as equal differences between sentences. Thus, these sorts of differences are the ones available to code drafters when they decide how to grade an offense, the ones juries and judges must deal with when sentencing a convicted offender, and perhaps the ones that come to the minds of citizens when they read and think about criminal sentences.

In designing the scenarios, the task was to create as many scenarios as were needed to provide a reasonably complete test of the issues that were being investigated in the particular study. In the attempt study referred to above, for example, it was found that 11 scenarios were needed. This included the 2 control scenarios, 4 scenarios each embodying one of the major formulations of the objective requirements of attempt, and 5 more scenarios testing an additional issue—the effect on liability and punishment of the actor's renunciation at various points in the process. The scenarios are described in Table 23.

Pilot testing indicated that for most studies, 10 to 14 scenarios could be read and evaluated by a subject in approximately one-half hour. The subjects were able to maintain concentration during this time; their reports indicated that they found the task quite interesting, and were intrigued by thinking about what differences in cases "made a difference" to them.

All of the subjects responded to all of the cases. In the experimental design literature, this is referred to as a "within-subjects" design. This design focuses the subjects' attention on the differences between the scenarios. The danger is that the subjects may think that the existence of a difference implies an instruction from the researcher that the difference should "make a difference," that it should provoke different liability assignments from the subject. To counter this possibility, subjects were told that the researchers did not expect that different scenarios necessarily should get different liability judgments, and they were to give the researcher their own judgments about what differences mattered. Looking over the individual responses, it was found that the subjects did rate some cases alike as to the liabilities they generated.

As is usual in these designs, the order in which the cases were given to the subjects was randomized. To make the subjects' contrast task simpler for them, cases with one dimension of variation were grouped together. The order of cases within those groups was randomized, as was the order in which the groups were presented.

TABLE 23. } Attempt Scenarios

Scenario Number, Description (Abbreviation)	Summary	Comment
1. The actor only thinks about robbing the safe and decides to do so. He takes no action toward committing the crime. (TH)	Only thinks about offense	No test would assign liability.
2. After deciding to rob the shop, the actor goes to the coin shop to make sure the safe is still there. (SS)	Substantial step test satisfied	Actor is liable under this test because "reconnoitering" (casing) the shop is a substantial step.
3. After deciding to rob the shop, the actor makes a special tool to the crack the safe with. (EQ)	Unequivocality test satisfied	The actor is liable under this test because action manifests criminal intent.
3a. The actor cases the shop and meets the owner while he does so. Out of pity for the owner, he gives up his plan to rob the safe. (EQR)	Renounces after reaching point of unequivocality	The Model Penal Code (MPC) allows a defense if an actor's renunciation of criminal intent is "complete and voluntary." No liability if this defense is available.
4. Having told a friend he intends to rob the shop, the actor drives there. Before he can get to the shop he is stopped by police, who were informed of his intent by the actor's friend. (PD)	Probable desistance test satisfied	Without outside interruption, the actor would have completed the offense. Actor is liable under this test.
5. The actor is in the process of cracking the safe in the coin shop when he is stopped by two undercover policemen. (PX)	Dangerous proximity test satisfied	Actor is liable because the offense is nearly completed.
5a. When he is in the shop and about to crack the safe, the actor feels pity for the shop owner and decides not to rob the safe (PXR)	Renounces after reaching point of dangerous proximity	MPC allows a defense when actor renounces his criminal intent "completely and voluntarily." No liability if this defense is available.
5b. When he is in the shop and about to crack the safe, the actor stops because he sees a policeman in the front of the store and he fears getting caught. (FR)	Desists out of fear after dangerous proximity	Actor is allowed no renunciation defense because renunciation was not voluntary. Actor is liable for full attempt.
6. The actor completes the robbery and returns home with the coins. (CP)	Offense complete, no renunciation	The actor is liable for the completed offense.
6a. The actor completes the robbery and returns home. On the way home, he feels pity for the shop owner and returns the coins to the safe. (CPR)	Renounces after offense is complete	Actor is liable for completed offense because renunciation defense not available.
6b. The actor completes the offense, feels pity for the shop owner, tries to return the coins to the safe, but is caught by police. (UNR)	Renounces, but is unsuccessful at "undoing"	Actor is liable for the completed offense because renunciation defense unavailable.

Randomization prevents results from being dependent upon the order in which the scenarios were judged.[7]

One further methodological matter deserves additional attention: scenario design. As is apparent, the "scenarios" are glorified versions of the hypotheticals

[7] For a more detailed discussion of the methodology, *see* Robinson & Darley, *supra* note 682, app'x. at 217–28.

that criminal law professors have so long employed as a form of argument and analysis. But the scenarios are different in an important way, and that difference highlights the danger of the analysis-by-hypothetical that many law professors and moral philosophers so often practice.[8]

When people make blameworthiness judgments, they take into account an astonishing variety of factors. Small facts of every sort can make a difference to a person's determination of blameworthiness. Given this kind of intuitive sophistication, it should be no surprise that in order to make intuitive blameworthiness judgments, people want to know the "story." They want and need some basic sense of who the people are and what has happened. Most important for these purposes, if the scenario does not give them the basic relevant facts, readers often fill in the missing important details on their own, drawing upon what "usually" is the situation or what "probably" happens in such a case, extrapolating from the facts they are given. Because everyone's life experience is different, different people may "fill out" the story with different details. The fewer details the scenario provides, the more the reader is left to fill in. Thus, the variability of the "stories" that different readers envision is at its greatest when the scenario is at its shortest.

For scenario drafters, this malleability of the scenario's meaning is a major headache. It makes drafting scenarios a difficult undertaking. After a set of scenarios is prepared, isolating the factors to be tested and varying them appropriately among the different scenarios, it must be field tested to determine how the scenarios are actually perceived by subjects. During this field testing, subjects commonly are not even asked the ultimate question, "how much liability do you think is appropriate?" Instead, they are asked a series of questions about what the scenarios say. For example, "according to the scenario, did Abel intend to cause the harm?" or "how harmful was the conduct?"

These "manipulation checks," as they are called, tell the designer whether the scenario is being perceived as intended. If it is not, the facts are then manipulated in a way that the designer thinks will produce the desired perception, and the instrument is retested in the field. Without the quality control measure of manipulation checks, one can never know whether the subject's reaction to the scenario is a reaction to the scenario intended by the designer or a reaction to a different situation, constructed from the subject's special reading and extrapolation of the facts.

As noted, the less information the scenario provides, the more the subject must "read in" to compose a mental picture with enough information to make a meaningful judgment of blameworthiness. It is for this reason that the argument-by-hypothetical, as practiced by many law professors and moral philosophers, is a particularly dangerous exercise because the hypotheticals tend to be thin on facts, inviting more uncontrolled and unknown information to be "read in."

---

[8] For a more detailed discussion, *see* Paul H. Robinson, *Some Doubts About Arguments by Hypothetical*, 88 CAL. L. REV. 813 (2000).

Consider some examples of common problems for scenario designers. Below are two straightforward hypotheticals, the results of which the study wants to compare to test the subject's intuition, in this instance, about the role of harm in assessing blame:

1. X hits Y. Y is injured.
2. Z hits Y. Y dies.

What should be the extent of liability for X and for Z?

It would seem that any difference in liability between the two hypotheticals should demonstrate the role of resulting harm, yes? No.

Subjects commonly read in different degrees of intentionality depending on the facts of the story. They may read in greater intentionality in the case of a death than in the case of an injury. The reader may assume that because Y died from Z's hit but not from X's hit, Z hit with a greater determination to cause Y's death, whereas X may have only intended to cause injury. The reader could make this kind of determination without really thinking about it, in the course of making a good faith intuitive judgment of blameworthiness. Under these circumstances, any difference in liability between the scenarios may be because of the difference in perceived intentionality rather than the difference in resulting harm.

One could adjust the hypotheticals to better control the perception of intentionality:

1. Intending to kill Y, X hits Y. Y is injured.
2. Intending to kill Y, Z hits Y. Y dies.

What should be the extent of liability for X and for Z?

In fact, it is not always sufficient to simply tell the subject the fact you want them to perceive. Especially when that fact is something as subjective as intention, as opposed to extent of harm, the subject may find the stated fact unbelievable and discount it.

But assume your manipulation check confirms that your revision has succeeded in controlling the subject's perceptions of intentionality. Can you assume that any difference in liability between the two hypotheticals then springs from the difference in resulting harm? Not necessarily. A reader may well assume that, even if the intentions of the two are the same, Z's hit involved greater force than X's. After all, Y died from Z's hit but not from X's. Upon this reading, any liability difference reported for the two hypotheticals is of little value. Greater liability for Z than X might reflect the subject's view that resulting death deserves more punishment than resulting injury, all other things being equal. But it also might reflect the subject's view that, while actual resulting harm is irrelevant, the greater force used by Z deserves greater punishment. Or, it might reflect some unknown combination of these two views.

Assume you try to avoid this problem by explicitly describing the force used in each case:

1. X hits Y with a stick that is one inch in diameter, breaking the stick in half. Y is injured.
2. Z hits Y with a stick that is one inch in diameter, breaking the stick in half. Y dies.

What should be the extent of liability for X and for Z?

Does a comparison of the blameworthiness of X and Z now depend entirely on the difference of resulting harm? Not necessarily. For example, subjects commonly take account of subsequent results when they judge the extent of a prior risk. If a result actually occurs, the subject is more likely to rate its probability of occurring, as judged at an earlier time, as higher than in the case where the risked harm does not in fact result. In other words, the benefit of hindsight commonly alters a subject's perception of what the extent of risk must have been. Thus, any difference in liability may be due in part, or in whole, to the subject's perception that X and Z have created different degrees of risk. The subject may assume that, while X and Z have used the same amount of force, each struck Y somewhat differently, in ways that would create different degrees of risk of death. Any difference in liability between the two hypotheticals, then, might be the result of either the perceived difference in risk created or the difference in resulting harm, or of some unknown combination of the two.

The larger point here is that there is a clear need to test how scenarios are perceived before assuming that they will be read and understood in the way the researcher intends. By pretesting how a scenario is perceived, and manipulating it until it is perceived in the way that tests the issues desired, the designer can have greater confidence that the resulting pattern of liability does result from the differences being tested, not from some unseen, inadvertent difference perceived by the subjects. Unfortunately, such "manipulation checks" are very time and resource consuming. They often take many times longer than the final testing itself, so there is great temptation for a researcher to cut corners with them.

B. An Illustration: Testing the Objective Requirements for Attempt Liability

To illustrate how this scenario-variation methodology plays out in practice, consider further the study about the objective requirements for attempt liability. The study examines those cases in which an individual takes steps toward committing a crime but does not actually commit it. Thinking about committing a crime is not itself a crime. However, at some point in a person's course of conduct, after the initial thought but before actual commission of the offense, the person becomes criminally liable.

The history of Anglo American criminal law reveals that at one time or another the law has used several remarkably different definitions of the point at which a person's preparation becomes a criminal attempt. State laws still disagree on this issue. The underlying practical considerations are twofold. On the one hand, the law does not want to assign liability to a person who has not committed a crime and, in the final event, would not do so. On the other hand, the law wishes to be able to "head off" crimes before they are committed and to punish those who have manifested their intention to commit them. On a more theoretical level, there generally is thought to be insufficient moral blameworthiness in pure thoughts to support criminal conviction and condemnation. However, at some point between the thought and the completed offense, sufficient blameworthiness does attach. Thus, there is the need to define a category of criminal attempt.

In such cases, because the harm or evil of the actual offense has not occurred, the liability assigned to attempt is termed "inchoate liability." In most current legal codes, inchoate liability leads to less punishment than would be given if the same offense had been completed, but there is some controversy on this point. The Model Penal Code (MPC), the provisions of which have served as a model for code reform in three-quarters of the U.S. states, generally grades an attempt the same as the completed offense. Most jurisdictions, however, have been reluctant to adopt the MPC's inchoate grading provision.

The older common law legal tests for determining when a person's conduct reaches the point of criminal attempt tend to be quite demanding, in the sense that they require the person to come close to committing the crime before attempt liability is imposed. Under the "dangerous proximity" test, a common formulation, a person typically has to reach a point where the offense is likely to be completed successfully. Arrest before this point does not result in liability. An example of dangerous proximity was set forth above. A locksmith, Ray, decides to rob a coin shop safe he recently worked on. He goes back to the shop and confirms that the safe is still there. He then tells a friend of his plan to rob the coin shop the next day. Unbeknownst to the locksmith, his friend notifies the police. The next day, the locksmith goes to the coin shop and begins to crack the safe. Suddenly, two police officers burst in and arrest him. Although the locksmith has not completed the robbery, he has come dangerously close to completion; his conduct satisfies the requirements of the dangerous proximity test, thus making him liable for attempt.

The dangerous proximity test reflects a view that the moral blameworthiness sufficient for criminal condemnation does not arise until the actor is dangerously close to committing the offense. This test seeks to balance the two practical considerations mentioned above in a specific way—to allow some opportunity for successful intervention by those who would prevent the crime but delay the point of liability until the time when completion is a real danger. The dangerous proximity test is somewhat pragmatic in that it does not ask complex questions about what can be inferred about the person and his intentions. It simply requires citizens to avoid bringing plans for criminal activities to a point at which they could be successfully completed.

The most common test in modern American codes, however, is the "substantial step" test, as formulated in MPC section 5.01(1)(c).[9] Rather than focusing on how close the person has come to completion of the offense, as the dangerous proximity test does, the substantial step test focuses upon how far the person has moved toward committing the offense after forming the intention to commit the offense. Any "substantial step" in the direction of commission is adequate, assuming the person's intention to commit the offense is clear and unequivocal. This test typically imposes liability at an earlier point in the steps toward commission than does the dangerous proximity test. It reflects a claim that the moral blameworthiness required for criminal condemnation attaches earlier. It also alters the balance of interests between the individual and society toward the interests of society by reducing an individual's opportunity to desist on his own in favor of allowing earlier intervention.

The 11 variations of the attempt scenario, and the legal test to which each corresponds, are set out in Table 23 above. The initial core scenario, in which the person only forms the intent to commit the crime, is shown in row (1). The substantial step scenario, in which the person returns to the shop to see if the safe is still there, is shown in row (2). Brief characterizations of the other scenarios are given in the "description" column of the table. The "summary" column of Table 23 gives a summary description of each scenario. These are used to identify each scenario in subsequent tables. The "comment" column gives further explanation of the legal treatment of the case.

After reading each scenario, subjects indicated what criminal liability, if any, they would assign to the locksmith. The liability results of the study are reported in Table 24. Columns (d) and (e) summarize the liability that would be assigned to the scenario by the common law and the MPC, respectively. (The focus for this illustration will be on the different liabilities assigned to the various attempt scenarios. The reader may consult the original study for a discussion of the effects of renunciation and the related act of desisting out of fear of being apprehended.[10])

Table 24 arrays the various scenarios from top to bottom in terms of the general progression of how close they come to the actual commission of the crime. In the first scenario, row (1), the individual develops an intention to commit the crime and does not progress further. In the last scenario, row (6), the individual actually commits the crime.

Adjacent to the scenario descriptions are three columns indicating related but different ways of analyzing the degree of liability that the respondents assign to the perpetrator whose actions were described in the specific case under discussion. Column (a) reports the average amount of liability assigned to the perpetrator on the 11-point scale discussed above. Subjects who assign no liability or liability without punishment are included in this calculation as assigning a liability of zero. Column (b) reports what percentage of the respondents chose "No Liability" for the

---

[9] Model Penal Code §5.01(1)(c) (1985).

[10] *See* Robinson & Darley, *supra* note 682, at 23–26.

TABLE 24. } Liability for Various Degrees of Conduct toward a Completed Theft Offense

	(a)	(b)	(c)	(d)	(e)
Attempt Scenarios	**Liability**	**% No Liability (N)**	**% No Liability or No Punishment (N+0)**	**Common Law Result**	**Model Penal Code Result**
1. Thought only (TH)	1.46	65	77	No liability	No liability
2. Substantial step (SS)	1.54	50	73	No liability	Attempt liability[a]
3. Unequivocality (EQ)	1.81	42	65	—[b]	Attempt liability[a]
3a. Renounces	0.38	85	92	No defense	Complete defense
4. Probable desistance (PD)	1.88	27	62	—[b]	Attempt liability[a]
5. Dangerous proximity (PX)	5.35	0	0	Attempt liability	Attempt liability[a]
5a. Renounces	0.69	46	85	No defense	Complete defense
5b. Desists out of fear	1.58	35	65	No defense	No defense
6. Completed offense (CP)	6.12	0	0	Full offense liability	Full offense liability
6a. Renounces and "undoes"	3.23	12	27	No defense	No defense
6b. Renounces but unable to "undo"	5.35	0	4	No defense	No defense

Liability Scale: N = No criminal liability, 0 = Liability but no punishment, 1 = 1 day, 2 = 2 weeks, 3 = 2 months, 4 = 6 months, 5 = 1 year, 6 = 3 years, 7 = 7 years, 8 = 15 years, 9 = 30 years, 10 = life, and 11 = death

[a]An attempted theft under the Model Penal Code is graded the same as a completed theft.

[b]This depends upon which of the common-law tests is applicable in the jurisdiction.

locksmith, roughly equivalent to a jury verdict of "not guilty." Column (c) reports what percentage of respondents chose either the "No Liability" or "Liability But No Punishment" options of the scale. This gives the percentage of subjects who would impose no punishment on the defendant. This percentage will always be equal to or higher than the percentage shown in column (b) because it includes the subjects reported in column (b) and the subjects who report that they judge that the perpetrator deserves criminal liability but does not deserve any punishment. Columns (d) and (e) characterize the treatment of the offense given by various legal formulations.

Figure 25 presents a visual representation of the liability means that are presented in column (a) of Table 24. Figure 26 presents the percentage of respondents choosing "No Liability" or "Liability But No Punishment" that are presented in columns (b) and (c) of Table 24. In these figures, only a subset of the cases are included (excluding scenarios with renunciation or desistance) to highlight specific important conclusions to be extracted from these results. The letters along the horizontal axis of each figure correspond to the abbreviations assigned to each scenario in Table 24.

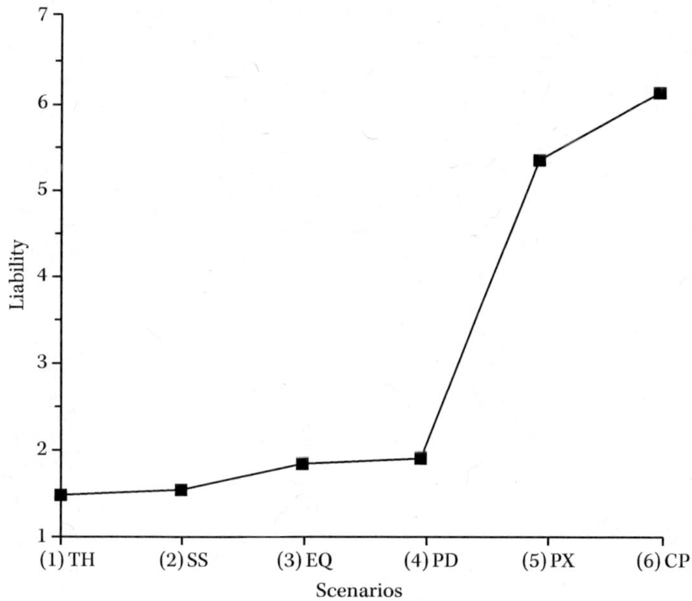

FIGURE 25. Liability for Various Degrees of Conduct toward Theft

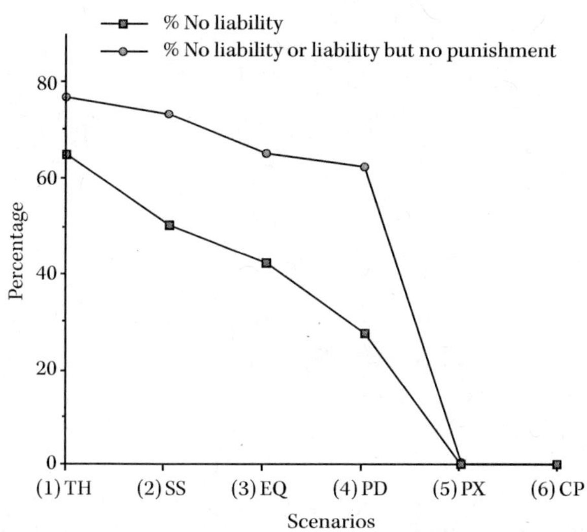

FIGURE 26. Percentage of Subjects Assigning No Liability or Liability But No Punishment

In Figure 25, the vertical axis represents the subjects' judgment as to liability amount. The higher the point, the more severe the sentence. In Figure 26, the vertical axis represents the percentage of respondents assigning no liability, or assigning either no liability or no punishment to the defendant; the higher the point, therefore, the fewer the people who would impose liability or punishment for the attempt.

With that explanation, let us turn to the results of the study.[11] Look at the result for scenario (1) in Figure 25. It appears that even thinking about committing an offense generates on average some assignment of liability. Recall that this is the case in which the locksmith forms a settled intention to rob the coin dealer but takes no further steps to do so. Looking at Figure 26, scenario (1), we notice that 65 percent of the subjects assign no liability, and therefore 35 percent of the subjects do impose liability in this scenario where the person only thinks about committing the offense and forms the settled intent to do so. However, about one third of those imposing liability (13 percent of all subjects) assign no punishment.

The intention of a person to commit an offense has been shown to be a powerful determinant of liability in other contexts. It should be no surprise to see that the person's intention alone has some effect in generating judgments of liability by a minority of the subjects. Here, a commonly unnoticed property of scenario research may create a difference between the result found and a result that would be likely to emerge from an actual court process. The scenarios were written "from the eye of God," as it were, and give the readers access to the inner workings of the person's mind. Thus, the subjects were able to believe unequivocally that a person has formed a settled intent to commit a crime. In the real world, it would be extraordinarily difficult to establish intention with such certainty in the absence of any conduct and, as a result, more difficult to carry through a successful prosecution of the individual, even if the law permitted it.

The scenarios in which the dangerous proximity test criteria are not met are scenarios (1) through (4). Notice that these scenarios correspond with very low assignments of liability, and the line connecting them in Figure 25 is essentially flat, which suggests that respondents are seeing these cases as alike in the degree of liability they generate. In scenario (5), in which the criteria for "dangerous proximity" are met, the liability ratings of the subjects suddenly are much higher. This suggests that dangerous proximity best reflects what the respondents perceive to be the critical point after which attempt liability should be assigned.

Figure 26 shows us that between 65 percent and 27 percent of the subjects indicate no liability in the first four scenarios, where the defendant does not reach the point of dangerous proximity. However, this percentage drops to 0 percent in the scenarios where the dangerous proximity test criteria are met, scenarios (5) and (6), a difference that is statistically significant ($p < .01$). Even more strikingly, the percentage of subjects who would impose no liability or no punishment ranges between 77 percent and 62 percent for scenarios (1) through (4), but drops to 0 percent for scenarios (5) and (6) ($p < .01$). The results reveal a relatively dramatic difference in the subjects' view of the scenarios where the dangerous proximity test is not met, scenarios (1) through (4), and those where it is, scenarios (5) and (6). This suggests that of the available tests, the common law's dangerous proximity test, as applied to this case, seems to best reflect the views of a majority of the subjects.

---

[11] *See id.* at 21–27.

The respondents assign different liabilities for attempts than for completed crimes: the liability mean for the dangerous proximity scenario shown in Table 24, row (5), 5.35 (1.8 years), is significantly lower than that for the completed offense in row (6), 6.12 (3.4 years). This result is consistent with the traditional grading of attempt as less serious, and inconsistent with the MPC's grading of attempt as the same as for the completed offense. The MPC's grading of attempt seems all the more incongruous when the liability for a completed offense, 6.12 (3.4 years), is compared to that for the MPC's test for attempt, the "substantial step" test, 1.54 (7.5 days). While the MPC dictates that a person held for attempt is liable at a grade equal to that for the full offense, a majority of the subjects (73 percent, row (2) column (c)) think that no punishment is appropriate for a mere "substantial step."[12]

The liability results of the study might be summarized in psychological terms as follows. In the view of the subjects, punishment ought not be imposed until a person has reached a point of dangerous proximity to completion of the offense. Further, the level of punishment for attempt ought to be significantly less than that for the completed offense.

With respect to legal applications this study sought to determine which of the tests for the objective requirement of attempt best reflects the community's view. In the scenarios where the person has gone just far enough to satisfy the substantial step test, the unequivocality test, or the probable desistance test, a strong majority of subjects would impose either no liability or no punishment. However, in the scenarios where a person satisfies the common law's dangerous proximity test, a dramatic shift in opinion occurs: all of the subjects would impose both liability and punishment. This would seem to suggest that if the community's view were to be the guiding principle in the definition of the offense, criminal codes should revert to the common law's dangerous proximity test. If early intervention by law enforcement is desired to increase the effectiveness of crime prevention, legislation could create authority to intervene without holding the person liable for an attempt to commit the substantive offense or holding the person liable only at a low level. Liability might be imposed at a fixed misdemeanor level, for an offense of "Preparing to Commit an Offense" or something of such nature.

C. Desistance, Renunciation, and Undoing in Attempt

If a person engages in conduct that is enough to constitute a criminal attempt as described above, is there any means by which he can then stop his conduct and thereby avoid all criminal liability? Relatedly, can a person escape criminal liability by voluntarily "undoing" his offense after it is complete?

The effect of a person's voluntary desistance has received different treatment at different times and in different jurisdictions. The older common law treated attempt

---

[12] Chapter 6 in JUSTICE, LIABILITY, AND BLAME: COMMUNITY VIEWS AND THE CRIMINAL LAW provides an examination of matters of proper grading.

no differently than a substantive offense in this regard; once the elements of the offense were satisfied, there was no "undoing" the offense. Attempt liability was imposed no matter what the person did after passing the point where his preparation became a criminal attempt. The Model Penal Code introduced a renunciation defense to attempt and other forms of inchoate liability, which provides a complete defense if the actor's desistance is complete and voluntary. The defense is not available if the actor renounces out of fear or delays the planned attempt until a later date.[13] The defense is provided in part because the Code's substantial step test moves the point of criminalization so much earlier in the chain of events. Combined with the Model Penal Code's grading of attempts as equal to the completed offense, the substantial step test would mean that once an actor takes a substantial step toward commission that he has no incentive to stop, his liability will be that of the completed offense whether he completes the offense or not. The common law and modern codes that maintain a grading difference, in contrast, have a built-in incentive to desist at any point before completion of the offense. Thus, they have no practical need for a renunciation defense. It has been retained in most jurisdictions, however, including those that grade inchoate offenses less than completed offenses, perhaps because voluntary renunciation is thought to reduce a person's blameworthiness.

Compare these legal rules to the results of the study reported in section B. The scenarios presenting an individual's voluntary desistance from committing the crime or the renunciation of it after completion are presented in scenarios (3a), (5a), and (6a). Figure 27 presents the data for these scenarios. In that figure, bar graphs are presented, with each scenario involving renunciation shown paired with its non-renunciation equivalent.

Look first at the left-hand pair of scenarios, which are the cases in which the individual takes an unequivocal step in the direction of the crime. Clearly, renunciation reduces the assigned penalty, but notice that the respondents assign very little penalty in the first place to that case (1.81; 11.4 days), so one ought not make much of this result. Looking next at the case where renunciation comes after dangerous proximity (case (5a), the second pair of bars), note that the judgments of the subjects conflict with aspects of both the common law and the Model Penal Code doctrines. While the common law does not provide a defense when a person renounces after satisfying the dangerous proximity test, the results indicate a sharp decrease in punishment assigned. Referring back to Table 24, 85 percent of the subjects think no punishment is appropriate in this renunciation case while no subject thinks no punishment is appropriate for the individual who reaches the level of dangerous proximity and does not renounce the attempt; that is, it seems that the majority of subjects view renunciation even after taking the dangerous proximity step, the step that they think generally created an attempt offense, as a legitimate defense. Unlike the common law, the Model Penal Code does provide a defense in such a case, if

[13] Model Penal Code §5.01(4).

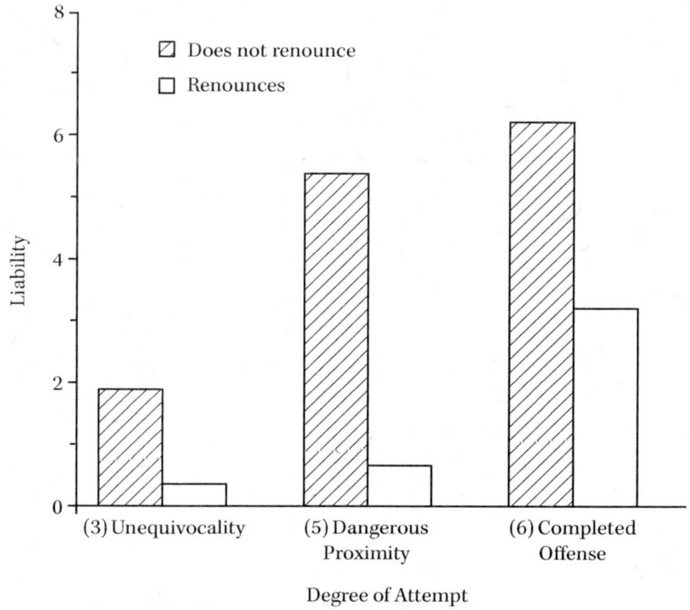

FIGURE 27. Effect of Renunciation in Reducing Liability

the renunciation is complete and voluntary, and this seems to fit the subjects' intuitions; if the locksmith decides not to commit the crime for his own reasons, very low liability is incurred.

This result is somewhat ironic. As noted previously, the common law recognized no renunciation defense. The Model Penal Code introduced the renunciation defense. Why? The drafters realized that they were essentially required to create it to avoid a problem created by their other planned changes. Specifically, the early intervention authorized by their "substantial step" test means that a person who is in the early stages of committing a crime is liable. This, combined with the Model Penal Code drafters' grading of attempts as the same as the substantive offense, means that a person who has taken a substantial step toward a crime is liable for the full penalties for the commission of that crime. Thus, there is no incentive for "the rational criminal" who has taken a substantial step to stop before commission of the crime; surely a socially undesirable reinforcement contingency! Here, again, is the problem: if the person who begins a crime is liable at a grade equal to the full substantive offense, he or she has little reason to stop once his or her conduct constitutes an offense. Because the "substantial step" test for commission is satisfied early in the process, this incentive to continue kicks in early. Thus, the renunciation defense is provided to give attempters a reason to stop, right up until the moment before the offense is complete. If one rejects the Code's equal grading provision and "substantial step" provision, as the test subjects appear to do, the reasons that led to the creation of the renunciation defense in the Model Penal Code disappear. Yet the data suggests that the subjects would keep such a defense. Thus the Code's defense is supported by the subjects but apparently for reasons other than the Code's.

Note that the effect of renunciation on liability according to the subjects is significantly less after completion of the offense than before, as illustrated by the third pair of bars. The assigned liability drops from 6.12 (3.4 years) for the un-renounced completed offense, case (6); to 3.23 (2.8 months) for the completed but renounced and "undone" offense, case (6a). The Code also gives significance to the point of completion. More so; it denies a defense for renunciation after the offense is complete. That the subjects give a significant mitigation even after the offense is complete may reflect a view that such renunciation undercuts the resoluteness with which the person held his original intent, and therefore retroactively alters their assessment of his original culpability. As discussed below, an alternative explanation arises from the absence of the harm of the offense.

Where the person desists after satisfaction of the dangerous proximity test, not because of a change of heart but rather out of fear of getting caught, the liability assigned by subjects increases, from liability of 0.69 (less than 1 day) to a still modest 1.58 (8.8 days). (Please refer back to Table 24 for these comparisons, rows (5) and (5b), column (a)). A good majority of the subjects, 65 percent, still think no punishment is appropriate (column (c)), although 65 percent would assign liability (column (b)). The Model Penal Code joins the common law, however, in barring a defense on these facts. The absence of the harm or evil of the completed offense appears to have a greater effect on the subjects than it has in the legal doctrine.

The subjects' focus upon the occurrence of the harm or evil of the offense also is highlighted by their response to the case of the person's renunciation after completion of the offense. That the person "undoes" the harm (returns the stolen goods) does not exempt him from liability from the subjects (see the last pair of bars in Figure 27) but significantly reduces his punishment from 6.12 (3.4 years; 100 percent imposing punishment) to 3.23 (2.8 months; 73 percent imposing punishment). Notice also that where the person, as above, renounces after completion but is unable to "undo" the offense, liability is much closer to the un-renounced complete offense than it is to the renounced complete offense. The renouncing thief who cannot "undo" his offense is given 5.35 (1.8 years; 96 percent imposing punishment).

Further results suggest that occurrence of the harm or evil is not the only influential factor; remorse also counts. In fact, the two may be equally influential. (Again, please refer to Table 24 for these comparisons.) Note that the liability means are the same in the dangerous proximity attempt scenario (scenario (5)) and the completed offense scenario where the person would like to but is unable to "undo" the offense, scenario (6b) 5.35; 1.8 years. In the former case, the person has the evil desire to commit the offense but has not caused the harm of the offense. The latter has the harm of the offense but a change of heart leading the person to want to "undo" the offense. These liability means differ significantly from other scenarios in crucial ways: they are each significantly lower than the liability assigned the successful, unrepentant actor (scenario (6), 6.12; 3.4 years), where the harm exists in the absence of any remorse; and both means are higher than in the scenarios where (i) renunciation occurs before completion (scenarios (3a) and (5a) 0.38 and 0.69, respectively; both less than one day), and (ii) renunciation occurs after completion (scenario (6a), 3.23; 2.4 months). This patterning of results suggests that both the occurrence of the harm and the perpetrator's remorse about that occurrence matter to the respondents.

Finally, it is important to note that subjects frequently select the "liability but no punishment" option in this study. (Figure 26 presents this rather dramatically.) This option is used not only in the case of renunciation and desistance immediately after the point of dangerous proximity but also where the person satisfies an attempt test short of dangerous proximity. (Compare columns (b) and (c) for scenarios (2), (3), and (4) in Table 24) These results may suggest that the subjects think it important to disapprove of the person's conduct (and thus a majority would impose liability in each case: 50, 58, and 73 percent, respectively; these percentages are obtained by subtracting the tabled percentages from 100 percent) but are hesitant to impose punishment in the absence of sufficient proximity to the harm or evil of the offense. The subjects may want to disapprove of the person's conduct and intention but, because they ultimately see insufficient blameworthiness, are hesitant to impose punishment.

D. Creating a Criminal Risk

Just as someone may be liable for attempting to cause a prohibited harm, so too may one be liable for creating a risk of causing a prohibited harm even if the harm does not come about. Not every risk created is a criminal risk. Current codes typically limit liability to substantial risks of harm. Legal codes set a minimum standard of criminal risk to distinguish those risks to be regarded as criminal from those that are not. Where to set the minimum standard is a complex question for legal code drafters, but most are in agreement that the ultimate judgment of criminality of the risk is a product of, among other things, the seriousness of the harm risked, the probability of the harm occurring, and the purpose of the conduct. For example, one may create a high risk of getting a passerby wet in the way one sets a lawn sprinkler, but the seriousness of the harm risked may be sufficiently low so as not to make this a criminal matter. Whenever one drives a car, one risks causing death to pedestrians, but the likelihood of killing one is low enough, and the purpose of the conduct valuable enough, that the simple act of driving is not considered a criminal risk.

Thus, an assessment of whether someone creates a criminal risk depends in large measure on the degree of harm and the probability of the harm occurring. This study sought to determine what minimum level of potential harm and degree of risk the community believes is necessary for assignment of criminal liability. In addition, it tried to determine what interaction, if any, may exist between these two factors.

The study hoped to determine whether these factors affected liability independent of what respondents believe to be the person's "culpable state of mind" as to causing the prohibited result. To do this, it was necessary to counter a common psychological tendency of individuals reading descriptions of cases. If a person is described as creating only a slight risk of harm, it might commonly be thought that he or she is at most simply aware of such risk. By comparison, observers may think that a person who creates a great risk of harm is more than just "aware" of that risk; the person may be seen as at least knowing and perhaps in some sense intending that such harm will come about.[14] Thus, if one compares a case where a person creates only a small risk to a case where he creates a high risk, greater liability assigned in the latter case may be a function of a belief that the person has a more culpable state of mind in the latter.

The study attempted to hold constant the person's culpable state of mind in order to determine whether increased degree of risk and increased potential harm would show the aggravating effects that the code suggests, without the possibility that subjects would infer a higher culpable state of mind of the person when the person took greater risks. To accomplish this, a scenario was created that could simply specify the person's state of mind and set the person's state of mind at "purposeful." This means that the conclusions will be limited to cases in which some degree of harm was intended.

This study presented the respondents with the following core case. A wife, wishing to kill her spouse, puts poison into his breakfast food. In different versions of the case, the poison (unbeknown to the wife) if ingested, would produce only slight stomach cramps (slight injury); cause material and substantial damage to the digestive tract (moderate injury); or alternatively, and as planned, cause death (high injury). The risk of harm was varied by altering the likelihood that the husband would actually eat the poisoned food.

Table 28 reports liability ratings assigned in each scenario, along with percentages of respondents who chose "No Liability" and percentages of those choosing either "No Liability" or "Liability But No Punishment."

Note that all variations of the scenario produced some assignment of liability; no respondents recommend "No Liability" in any of the scenarios. This suggests that, while the extent of harm risked and the probability of its occurrence may be relevant to grading, no minimum level of potential harm or minimum probability is required before liability can be assigned. Or, if there is such a minimum, it is below even the lowest levels of harm and probability tested here. Presumably, the person's intention to commit the offense and the poisoning of the cereal, without more, are sufficient for criminal liability. This is consistent with the results of the attempt study discussed previously.

---

[14] Marylee Karlovac & John Darley, *Attribution of Responsibility for Accidents: A Negligence Law Analogy*, 6 Soc. Cog. 287 (1988); Baruch Fischhoff, *Hindsight Does Not Equal Foresight*, 1 J. Experimental Psychol. 288 (1975).

TABLE 28. } Liability for Creation of Risk

Scenarios	(a) Liability	(b) % No Liability (N)	(c) % No Liability or No Punishment (N+0)
SLIGHT RISK			
1. Slight injury	6.61	0	10
2. Moderate injury	7.48	0	2
3. High injury	8.24	0	0
MEDIUM RISK			
4. Slight injury	6.93	0	10
5. Moderate injury	7.71	0	0
6. High injury	8.51	0	0
HIGH RISK			
7. Slight injury	7.39	0	7
8. Moderate injury	8.00	0	2
9. High injury	8.95	0	0
ACCOMPLISHED			
10. Slight injury	7.33	0	7
11. Moderate injury	8.17	0	0
12. High injury	9.81	0	0

Liability Scale: N=No criminal liability, 0=Liability but no punishment, 1=1 day, 2=2 weeks, 3=2 months, 4=6 months, 5=1 year, 6=3 years, 7=7 years, 8=15 years, 9=30 years, 10=life, and 11=death

Because of this, most of the results of this study concern issues of grading, which is the subject of chapter 17, but they will be reviewed here in preparation for that more complete discussion. Figure 29 suggests that as either the probability of injury or the severity of the risked injury increases, the liability assigned to the risk-taker increases.

Interestingly, the interaction between these two factors is statistically significant. This result suggests that the probability and harm variables, taken together, have effects on judgments of liability that are not equivalent to the sum of their independent effects. Specifically, in Figure 28, one sees that scenario 12 draws an assignment of liability that is considerably more severe than the others (and thus may be the cell that makes the interaction significant). Respondents were particularly severe in assigning liability to the case in which the wife intends to kill her husband and actually does so. She planned to murder her husband, successfully does so, and gets a sentence that corresponds to nearly life imprisonment.

With the exception of this particular case, however, one is struck by the general continuity of the respondents' judgments. As either the probability or the severity of the harm risked increases incrementally, so too does the liability judgment in an essentially continuous fashion.

Are the respondents' reactions consistent with the criminal codes? Only in a broad sense. Because all of the scenarios described an individual who was purposeful as to

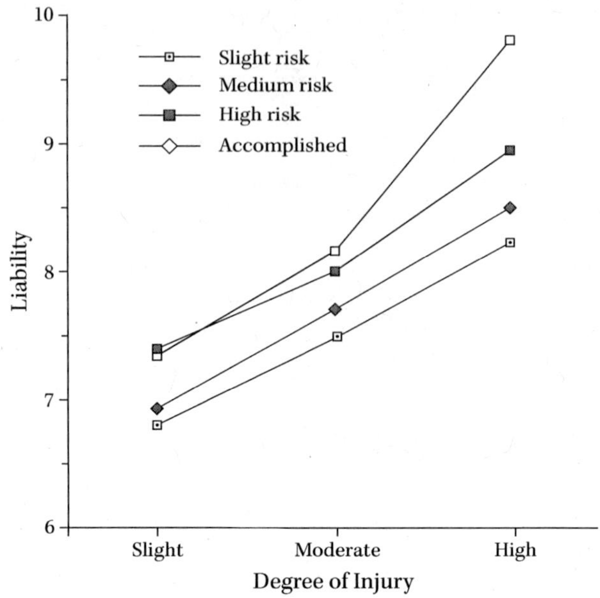

FIGURE 29. Liability as a Function of Risk and Injury

committing the crime, the Code would treat all of the scenarios as ones of attempted murder, without making distinctions depending on the probability of the harm or the severity of harm risked. The respondents, in contrast, alter their sentences depending on these factors, and do so in a nontrivial way. First, they assign greater liabilities as a function of the degree of risk. (This is shown by the consistent differences in elevation of the high, moderate, and slight risk lines of Figure 29.) In other words, the respondents judge that the actual risk created is relevant to their liability judgments. This is consistent with their tendency to be more harm oriented than the Code, with the harm being seen in the creation of ex ante risk. Second, as the quite steep slopes of the four lines of Figure 29 show, they also base their liability judgments on the amount of injury that is intended. Again, their judgments are based on the extent of the risk actually created; not just that intended. This issue and its implications will receive a fuller discussion in chapter 17.

What remains to be investigated are those cases in which an individual creates a risk of a serious harm with a high probability, but does so at a much lower level of culpability (for instance, recklessly or even negligently). How would liability be assigned to those cases? It would be for this sort of case that the Code drafters might have expected an assignment of criminal liability only if the harm was severe and likely. Another useful study would test scenarios in which the person intentionally creates only a risk of harm and which vary the extent of harm risked. This would reveal whether the subjects punished intentional risk creation of different extents of harm differently. Much remains to be studied in this area.

E. Objective Requirements of Complicity

One can be held accountable for another person's conduct if one is judged to be "an accomplice" of that other person. This study examines the objective requirements of "complicity": that is, the requirements of what a person actually must do in order to be liable as an accomplice.

What sorts of actions has the law treated as sufficient for complicity? To be an accomplice at common law, a person had to assist or encourage the perpetrator in some way. Two general ways of engaging in complicity were thereby recognized: first, by giving encouragement to another to commit a crime, one may cause or reinforce another's settled intention to commit the crime; second, by giving assistance, one not only implies encouragement, but more strongly causally contributes to the commission of the offense. Note that the common law did not require that the action of the accomplice be necessary for commission of the offense; one could be an accomplice by standing watch even though nobody came or being prepared to drive a backup getaway car even though it was not needed. Similarly, encouraging a principal to commit a crime engenders liability whether or not that encouragement was necessary for the commission of the crime.

It was not enough at common law, however, that a person tried to assist or encourage the perpetrator if the person was unsuccessful in assisting or encouraging. If the person provided neither actual assistance nor actual encouragement (for example, because his unsuccessful attempt to assist was unknown to the perpetrator), he was not liable as an accomplice.

The Model Penal Code drafters found this exemption for an unsuccessful attempt to assist inappropriate; they broadened the scope of complicity by assigning liability to an actor's unsuccessful attempt to encourage or assist. A person need simply "aid or agree or attempt to aid" the perpetrator to be held liable as an accomplice.[15]

Where complicity liability is established, the actor is held liable for the full offense. Unlike inchoate offenses, such as attempt, where the actor commonly is held liable for a lesser grade than the offense attempted, complicity is a means of establishing full offense liability. Thus, from the law's view, an accomplice has the same liability as the perpetrator.

This study sought to test the subjects' view of the minimum amount that a person could contribute in encouraging or assisting an offense to be held criminally liable for it. It also sought to test whether the subjects would alter the degree of the liability they imposed according to the person's degree of contribution to the offense. Few codes take degree of contribution into account in setting the grade of an accomplice's liability, but such a scheme has been introduced, albeit with relatively broad categories, in the United States Sentencing Commission Guidelines.[16]

---

[15] Model Penal Code 2.06(3)(a)(ii).

[16] *United States Sentencing commission Guidelines Manual* (1994) §§3B1.1 and 3B1.2.

The study presented subjects with a series of scenarios, each of which presented a different degree of contribution to a killing, including scenarios where the person attempted but failed to assist. In order to test whether the subjects' view depended upon the actual occurrence of a resulting harm, such as death (other studies, for instance those in chapter 10, section C, have shown that resulting harm is a powerful determinant of liability and punishment), several of the scenarios presented instances where the principal actor, the "perpetrator," was not successful in his attempt to kill.

The core of these scenarios involve an unhappily married woman who "longs for her husband's death, which would make her a rich widow." A friend of the wife is aware of her feelings and assists or tries to assist her in various ways to bring about her husband's death. These various ways form the variation in the scenarios. The wife eventually kills her husband or attempts to do so and fails. In Table 30, the three "murder fails" cases are indicated by the bold facings of the scores assigned and the "a" following the scenario number.

The variations in the actions of the friend are shown in the different rows of Table 30. Column (a) shows the liability assigned to the wife for her actions. As can be seen, she is assigned a liability of 10 or above when the murder succeeds, which is the equivalent of a life sentence. When her actions fail to kill her husband, her liability drops to about 7.5 (11 years). This pattern repeats itself for the subjects giving lesser sentences for an attempt than for a completed crime. In the specific description of the failed attempt, it is reported that the wife "shot at her husband but missed." Therefore, no wound is inflicted. The respondents could read the miss as signaling that the wife is conflicted in her purposes. These two facts may help explain the considerable reduction in sentence for the wife in the three no-death scenarios.

Next examine the central question of the study, which is the liability assigned to the accomplice. In scenario (1), the male friend is described as realizing that "if she did decide to do it, he would be willing to help her," but before he can communicate this to her, "she shoots her husband dead." Look at columns (b), (c), and (d) for row (1), in which the liability assignments to the complicit friend of the wife are tabled. In this instance, no liability is assigned to the friend. As before, the subjects were asked various questions about how they perceived the case. The exact questions are given in the key to the table, and the subjects' numerical responses tabled in columns (e) and (f). As column (e) of scenario (1) indicates, the respondents judged that the accomplice approved of the wife's actions, a rating of between 8 and 9 where 7 indicates agreement with the statement and 9 indicates strong agreement. (Notice, while attention is directed to column (e), that in all cases the respondents see the friend as approving of the wife's actions, so that can be taken as established for the discussion of all cases.) As column (f), row (1) indicates, the respondents are clear that the friend "does not help (the wife) at all."

In other scenarios described in this and other chapters, the respondents assign some liability if they decide that the individual has formed a settled intention to commit a crime and acts upon that intention. But here they assign no liability to

TABLE 30. } Liability as Related to Object Requirements of Complicity

	Wife	*Accomplice*				
	(a)	*(b)*	*(c)*	*(d)*	*(e)*	*(f)*
Scenarios	*Liability*	*Liability*	*% No Liability (N)*	*% No Liability or No Punishment (N+O)*	*Accomplice Approves Killing*	*Accomplice's Role*
1. Only thinks of helping	10.15[a]	0.00[e]	100	100	8.24	1.00
2. Failed attempt to help	10.15[a]	1.15[e]	68	85	8.71	1.44
2a. Failed attempt to help/Murder fails	**7.79[b]**	**0.82[e]**	**65**	**88**	8.61	1.56
3. Encourages/No help	**9.59[a]**	**4.15[d]**	12	38	8.75	2.59
4. Minimal help	10.03[a]	6.15[c]	6	21	8.74	4.71
4a. Minimal help/ Murder fails	**7.47[b]**	**4.88[c,d]**	**6**	**24**	8.64	4.21
5. Substantial help	10.12[a]	9.18[a]	0	0	8.94	5.44
6. Necessary help	10.06[a]	9.32[a]	0	0	8.94	6.41
6a. Necessary help/ Murder fails	**7.71[b]**	**7.29[b]**	**0**	**0**	**8.94**	6.00
7. Unique and necessary help	10.15[a]	5.44[c,d]	9	32	8.21	5.03
8. Masterminds	9.97[a]	9.18[a]	0	3	8.88	7.47

Liability Scale: N=No criminal liability, 0=Liability but no punishment, 1=1 day, 2=2 weeks, 3=2 months, 4=6 months, 5=1 year, 6=3 years, 7=7 years, 8=15 years, 9=30 years, 10=life, and 11=death.

Key to column heads:
(e) The accomplice approves of the wife killing her husband: 1=strongly disagree, 3=disagree, 5=unsure, 7=agree, 9=strongly agree.
(f) The accomplice's role in the crime can best be described by which of the following statements?

1. The accomplice does not help the wife at all.
2. The accomplice attempts to help the wife but is unsuccessful in the effort.
3. The accomplice and the wife reach an agreement that she is going to kill her husband.
4. The accomplice provides minimal help to the wife.
5. The accomplice provides substantial help to the wife.
6. The accomplice's assistance is necessary if the wife is going to kill her husband.
7. The accomplice provides unique help that is necessary for the wife to kill her husband.
8. The accomplice masterminds the crime.

Note: Superscript letters indicate significance at the $p < .05$ level by a Newman-Keuls test. Matching superscripts indicate means that are not statistically significantly different from each other. Means are compared within columns only.

the accomplice who decides he would be willing to help. What might cause this difference? There are two possibilities. Deciding that one is willing to help in the commission of a crime is one step removed from deciding to commit the crime, and that step might have been sufficient to make a difference to the subjects. Alternatively, "realizing that one would be willing to help" may be read as a less settled and formed intention than, for instance, the intention formed in the attempt case of chapter 10, section A, where the person plans to rob the safe.

Look next at the scenarios tabled in row (2) and (2a), in which the friend attempts to help the wife kill her husband but fails to do so even though the murder is accomplished (2) or not accomplished (2a). (The attempt to help is unknown to the wife.) These are examples of cases in which the accomplice provides no real assistance or encouragement of any kind. That individual gets a very low assignment of liability, next lowest to the liability assigned to the individual who only realizes that he would help. This result is dramatically different from the Code's imposition of full offense liability for such a failed attempt to assist.

In the "encourages" scenario tabled in row (3), the person has agreed with the wife that she should go ahead with her plan to murder her husband. Note from column (f) that respondents tend to agree that the two of them have reached an agreement that she will kill her husband. This "giving of encouragement" is recognized by both the common law and the Model Penal Code as filling one of the tests for accomplice liability, and is seen by the subjects as requiring the assignment of some liability, although not a high amount. (Such agreement also would satisfy the test of liability for conspiracy liability, which the Model Penal Code sets at the same grade as the substantive offense but which most jurisdictions grade less than the full offense.)

The liability assigned the friend, 4.15, is equivalent to a sentence of about seven months. But notice that about 38 percent of the respondents think that, whether they find the person guilty or not, the person does not deserve any time in jail. Again, this seems significantly less than the punishment provided by the Code. (However, the extent of the code-community difference may not be as great in other "agreement" cases. In this scenario, the wife is described as already having decided to murder her husband, so the agreement of the friend is probably not seen as necessary to her decision although it undeniably reinforces it.)

Reading through the table reveals the great variation of perceived deserved punishment for an offender and his accomplice based on the scenarios surrounding a given offense. With this in mind, look at the patterning of the liability judgments. The eight murder scenarios describe what was hoped would be seen as an increasing degree of help and encouragement to the wife in her plan to kill her husband. The check on the manipulation questions help show whether the subjects perceive the scenarios as planned. In the "failed attempt to help" scenarios, rows (2) and (2a), the friend overhears the wife confide her plan in her sister, and attempts to meet the wife to supply the necessary gun. However, before he reaches her, she has already shot at her husband. Respondents see this as midway between providing no help and an attempt to provide help that is unsuccessful, ratings of 1.44 and 1.56 respectively in column (f). In the minimal help scenarios, rows (4) and (4a), the wife has formed the plan to shoot the husband, and the friend tells her where to buy the gun. Obviously, his agreement with the plan is implicit in that action. Respondents see this as providing somewhere between minimal and substantial help; ratings of 4.71 and 4.21 respectively, when 4 equals minimal help, and 5 equals substantial help. In scenario (5), the friend gives the wife his gun with which to shoot the husband, thus providing substantial help, and she uses the gun to kill her husband. (The scenario in which the friend gives substantial help and she shoots at her husband and misses was not presented to the subjects.) The respondents agree that he, in fact, provides substantial help (column (f), a rating of 5.44 where 5 equals substantial help). In scenarios (6) and (6a), the friend provides necessary help. The wife has been unable to obtain a firearm and is given one by the friend. She then confesses that she does not know how to shoot it and he teaches her how. The respondents see this as hoped, giving ratings of 6.41 and 6 respectively, where 6 equals necessary help.

In scenario (7), the friend provides what was considered to be unique and necessary help; he alerts the wife to the fact that her husband, suspicious of her intentions, is fleeing town, and she goes home and kills him before he can leave. But row (f) indicates that the subjects do not see the case as hoped, instead they see him as providing only substantial help.

In scenario (8), the friend is described as a business partner of the husband, who will be relieved of debt if the husband dies. Knowing that the wife is unhappy with her husband, he provides her with a plan in which she can shoot her husband and make it look like an accident. She follows the plan and kills her husband. While this is labeled as the "mastermind" scenario, about half the respondents agree (column f) that he "mastermind's the crime," while the other half report that he "provides unique help that is necessary if the wife is to kill her husband."

So with the rather unique exception of scenario (7), the subjects see the role of the accomplice about as hoped. What differences did this make to their liability assignments? Comparing the liability ratings of 11 cases is not an easy matter, but Figures 31 and 32 should help.

Figure 31 is designed to enable one to examine the effects of increasing the degree of the accomplice's complicity in committing the crime on the liability he is assigned. In this figure, all of the cases in which the wife successfully kills her husband are charted (except scenario (7), the one that the subjects saw the scenario differently from what was intended), and the cases in which the wife fails to kill the husband are eliminated; these will be considered later. As the involvement of the friend moves from failed attempt, to minimal, up through masterminding of the crime, the liability ratings of the respondents increase. That is, the liability assignments to the friend increase as his causal involvement in the incident increases. Interestingly, the liability assignments do not seem to increase once the complicit individual has reached the level of substantial involvement in the killing. For cases of substantial involvement, necessary involvement, and masterminding the crime, the respondents assign a sentence of about 30 years in prison. This suggests that substantial assistance is something of a threshold after which greater assistance is of little consequence to liability. The flattening of the graph at a level lower than the liability assigned to the perpetrator (9.18, 9.32, and 9.18 for accomplice vs. 10.12, 10.06, and 9.97 for perpetrator) also confirms that the subjects see reduced liability as appropriate for the accomplice, as compared to the perpetrator, apparently without regard to how active a role the accomplice has played, at least on these facts.

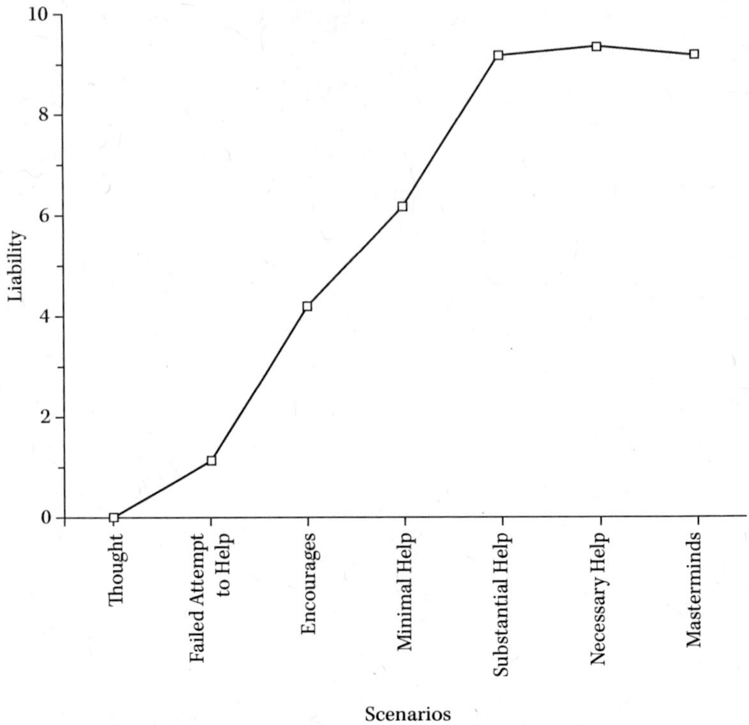

FIGURE 31. Liability Assigned to the Accomplices as a Function of His Involvement

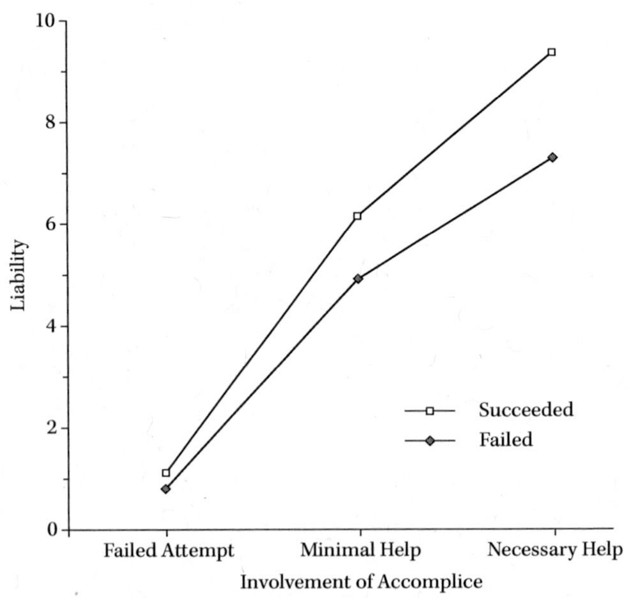

FIGURE 32. Effects of Success or Failure of Killing on Liability for the Accomplice

The "mastermind's" scenario hints at the possibility of a limit for the grade reduction for accomplices. The liability assigned to the masterminding friend is high, above 30 years in prison, but still below that assigned to the wife. Yet, as a glance at Table 30 will confirm, the liability assigned to the wife is lower than it is in cases in which she acts more independently. It is interesting to note that some of the responsibility for the crime might be shifted away from the wife here—this is the only scenario in which she receives less than a life sentence for her actions. As her accountability for the death is reduced, one might expect the mastermind's to increase, perhaps eventually eliminating the usual accomplice grade reduction.

Now, turn to the case in row (7), which is labeled "unique and necessary" help. Recall that the case is not perceived by the subjects as providing unique and necessary help; this would have been a rating of 7 in column (f). Instead it is perceived as simply providing substantial help to the wife, 5.03 where 5 equals substantial help. Future research will need to create a case in which subjects perceive that unique and necessary help is given by a complicit individual to see if such approaches the liability given a mastermind, as it would be predicted. However, it is interesting to contrast the liability assignment of case (7) with that of case (5), in which the respondents do perceive that, as hoped, substantial help was given. Case (5) gets a significantly higher liability assignment (a sentence of over 30 years), than does case (7) (a sentence of only about two years), even though both are roughly matched on what is known of the nature of the respondents' perceptions of the complicit individual's involvement in the case. This suggests that the respondents may be considering some as of yet undiscovered factors that are influencing their decisions, and future research should discover what they are.

Next, what difference does it make to the accomplice's liability whether the wife successfully kills her husband or shoots and misses? This is answered in Figure 32, which examines the three pairs of cases in which the friend fails in his attempt to help, provides minimal help, or provides necessary help, and the woman succeeds in killing her husband or fails. As the figure shows, the respondents consistently give a somewhat reduced liability to the accomplice friend in the cases in which the perpetrator wife fails to kill her husband. (That is, the "failed" line is consistently lower that the "succeeded" line.) As previously mentioned, there is a general tendency of the respondents to follow this pattern: to give reduced sentences when the harm of the offense does not actually occur. This is on first glance consistent with the Model Penal Code's treatment of such cases. While the accomplice's failed attempt to assist is treated the same as successful assistance, the perpetrator's failure to commit the crime does affect at least the label that is given to the accomplice's liability: his liability is only that of complicity in an attempt rather complicity in the full offense. Recall, though, that what the Code gives with one hand, it takes away with the other. While most jurisdictions give a somewhat reduced grade for attempt liability, the Code grades attempts the same as the substantive offense, so that no reduction in accomplice liability would be achieved.

To summarize, the results of this study are generally what intuition would have led one to expect. The greater the degree of help provided by the accomplice, where help is conceived of on a rough continuum beginning with encouragement and ending with planning direction, the greater the liability assigned to the accomplice.

First, the significance of these results for various code formulations is support for the common law rule and against the Model Penal Code in the debate between the two on whether actual assistance is required for accomplice liability or whether an unsuccessful attempt is sufficient. The subjects tend to agree with the common law formulation that requires actual encouragement or assistance.

Second, the gradations in liability assigned by the respondents to the person, depending on his degree of assistance in the crime, represent a pattern that will be seen repeatedly in the data and one that frequently contradicts the legal system's tendency to treat various actors who play "supporting roles" in the commission of a crime as equally complicit with the individual who commits the crime. In the eyes of the respondents, complicity is a matter of degree. However, within legal codes it is often treated as an all-or-nothing issue. If one fails to qualify as an accomplice, there is no liability; if one is an accomplice, full liability for the offense is imposed, equal to that assigned the major actor in the crime. The respondents persist in making finely graduated distinctions. This gradation of liability is what the sentencing guidelines attempt to provide, at the level of actual sentences assigned to accomplices.[17]

Finally, the subjects seem to disagree with the Code's view that an accomplice's liability ought to be the same grade as the perpetrator's liability. This is true even where the degree of assistance is very high, even essential to successful commission of the offense. The subjects would give a minimum of one grade reduction to accomplices as most jurisdictions do for attempt liability.

F. Omission Liability

The definitions of substantive offenses, together with the secondary prohibitions of attempt, risk creation, and complicity, discussed above, give a complete account of what a person must not do. But the rules of conduct enforced by the criminal law occasionally require that a person perform specific conduct. People must pay taxes, register for the draft, obtain a license to engage in certain regulated activities, and so forth. While this book does not fully address it here, subsequent study should examine whether current codes accurately map the conduct that the law ought to require upon pain of criminal liability for failure to act. Are some failures currently punished by legal codes perceived by the community as of insufficient seriousness for liability? Ought the criminal law to create duties to act in situations not now required?

One aspect of the present study focused on the practice of current codes in imposing the same degree of liability on a person who commits an offense through affirmative action as on a person who commits an offense through omission of a legal duty.

---

[17] *United States Sentencing Commission Guidelines Manual* (1994).

The law sees as equivalent, for example, affirmative conduct causing a death and an omission to perform a legal duty that results in a death, all other things being equal.

Another aspect of the present study focuses upon the most controversial instance of the law's failure to create a legal duty to help where another person is in danger of serious injury or death. Anglo American law has generally resisted imposing liability for a person's failure to act to help a stranger in distress. Under current doctrine, liability may be imposed for an omission to help only if the person has a specific duty to act,[18] and such duties are relatively rare and narrowly defined. For example, consider the case of a person who comes upon a drowning person whose life could be saved merely by throwing a nearby life preserver. The law imposes a duty to assist the drowning man, and thus imposes liability if one does not assist, only if the person has one of several defined relationships to the endangered person. The most common sources of a duty to rescue are the duty of a parent to protect his or her child and a duty created by virtue of contractual agreement between parties, for instance when a swimming club hires a person to serve as lifeguard. A duty to rescue also may be created if one undertakes to help a person in distress, which may signal to others that the situation is under control, and then fails to help, thereby leaving the person less likely to be assisted by another. Once one assumes the responsibility to rescue, even voluntarily, one has a legal duty to carry it to completion.[19]

But if none of these relationships exist, the law holds that the person is under no obligation to help. Thus, in the case of the drowning individual, the person who knows of danger and can avert it generally has no duty to do so. This is so even if the act of helping, such as throwing the life preserver, presents no danger or even inconvenience to the person, even if the person knows that the person otherwise will drown, and even if he knows that he can save the person by this simple act. Because the person has no duty to act, he has no criminal liability for failing to do so.

The debate on this issue has an old and distinguished history. Several commentators have criticized the restrictive view of omission liability. Livingston, for example, argues that one should have a legal duty to act to save a stranger if it can be done without personal danger or pecuniary loss.[20] Such proposals to create a general duty to rescue have been criticized, in turn, as being too broad. Macauley argues that "there may be extreme inconvenience without the smallest personal danger, or the smallest risk of pecuniary loss."[21] More generally, proposals to create a general duty to rescue are thought by many to go beyond the appropriate realm of criminal liability, into the sphere of moral accountability:

> It is, indeed, most highly desirable that men should not merely abstain from doing harm to their neighbors, but should render active services to their

---

[18] *See e.g.*, Model Penal Code §2.01(1).

[19] *See* Paul H. Robinson, Criminal Law Defenses §87(b)(3) & (4) (West 1984).

[20] Edward Livingston, A System of Penal Law, Code of Procedure, ch. II, art. 12–13 (1833).

[21] Thomas Babington Macauley, A Penal Code: Prepared by the Indian Law Commissioners 53–45 n.M (1837).

> neighbors. In general however the penal law must content itself with keeping men from doing positive harm, and must leave to public opinion, and to the teachers of morality and religion, the office of furnishing men with motives for doing positive good. It is evident that to attempt to punish men by law for not rendering to others all the service which it is their [moral] duty to render to others would be preposterous. We must grant impunity to the vast majority of those omissions which a benevolent morality would pronounce reprehensible, and must content ourselves with punishing such omissions only when they are distinguished from the rest by some circumstance which marks them out as peculiarly fit objects of penal legislation.[22]

While an omission to act may not be morally correct, the argument goes, it is not the sort of thing that ought to generate criminal liability other than in exceptional circumstances.

This is the prevailing view that is instantiated in the laws of society, although there are occasional exceptions. Despite such general reluctance to create omission liability, a few states have enacted a limited general duty to rescue, typically limiting the duty to cases of serious danger to the victim where the rescuer need not endanger him or herself.[23] The statutes also tend to provide only minor penalties.

The omission study presented below sought to test the community's views on whether criminal liability and punishment are appropriate for a failure to rescue a stranger and, if so, to determine how the assignment of liability and punishment may vary with different levels of danger or inconvenience. It also examined the community's views of the comparative liability for a commission and an omission where one of the traditional sources of duty—parental or contractual relationship or assumption of responsibility to rescue—does exist. Subjects were given a series of scenarios involving one actor pushing another into the water in circumstances in which it is apparent that the victim will likely drown if not rescued. Another actor observes this but fails to act to rescue the victim. For the first subset of scenarios, (1) to (4) in Table 33, a flotation device is present; all that is necessary for the bystander to do is to throw it to the victim. For the second set, (5) to (8), since the study was interested in whether the respondents would require action of a bystander of a more major sort, it is necessary for the bystander to swim to the aid of the victim. The bystander is described as a strong swimmer. The respondents were asked to rate the liability that they would assign both to the perpetrator (who affirmatively pushes the victim into the water) and the nonacting bystander. The scenarios differed in the relationship between the bystander and the victim and in the degree of danger or inconvenience that rescuing would impose on the bystander. The results are shown in Table 33.

The first point of interest is a global one: when compared with the liability judgments for the person who created the danger, the liability judgments for the

---

[22] *Id.* at 55–56.

[23] *See, e.g.,* R.I. GEN. LAWS §11–56–1; WIS. STAT. ANN. §940.34.

TABLE 33. } Liability for Commission and Omission

	Commission			*Omission*			
	(a)	*(b)*	*(c)*	*(d)*	*(e)*	*(f)*	*(g)*
Scenarios	*Liability*	*% No Liability*	*% No Liability or No Punishment*	*Liability*	*% No Liability*	*% No Liability or No Punishment*	*Model Penal Code Result (for omission)*
1. Stranger	8.55	0	0	2.93[a]	21	52	No liability
2. Parent	8.66	0	0	5.10[b]	7	31	Same liability as commission
3. Contract	8.62	0	0	6.21[b]	0	10	Same liability as commission
4. Assumption	8.62	0	0	5.55[b]	3	24	Same liability as commission
5. Stranger—high danger	8.66	0	0	0.97[a]	55	86	No liability
6. Stranger—low danger	8.61	0	0	2.41[a]	21	62	No liability
7. Stranger—high inconvenience	8.66	0	0	3.64[a]	14	43	No liability
8. Stranger—low inconvenience	8.59	0	0	3.79[a]	14	41	No liability

Liability Scale: N=No criminal liability, 0=Liability but no punishment, 1=1 day, 2=2 weeks, 3=2 months, 4=6 months, 5=1 year, 6=3 years, 7=7 years, 8=15 years, 9=30 years, 10=life, and 11=death.

Note: Superscript letters indicate significance at the $p < .05$ level by a Newman-Keuls test. Matching superscripts indicate means that are not statistically significantly different from each other. Means are compared within columns only.

bystander's failure to act are greatly mitigated. Liability and punishment for the person who pushes the victim into the water and thereby causes the death through commission, column (a), is constant through all scenarios, at approximately 8.6 (24.4 years). For the bystander who does not help, liability and punishment for failing to rescue is consistently significantly less. This is most easily seen by scanning column (d), which tables the liability assigned to the person who fails to help; at no point does that liability even approach that assigned the person who commits the act.

The mitigation from full liability is given even where the bystander has a legal duty to act, as in scenarios (2) through (4). (In one instance, the bystander is a parent of the victim; in the second instance he has a contractual obligation to rescue because he is a guard at the site; and in the third case the actor tells another that he will rescue, thus assuming the obligation.) Even in these duty scenarios, omission liability—5.10 (1.2 years) to 6.21 (3.8 years)—is significantly lower than commission liability for the same death—8.6 (24.4 years).

The results shown in Table 34, which reports the respondents' perceptions of various aspects of the state of mind of the person who fails to rescue, suggest that part of the difference in liability that the subjects assign to the perpetrator and the bystander might be partially due to perceptions that the two actors have different culpable states of mind as to causing the death. The respondents judge that the individual who pushes the victim into the water wants him to drown, while the individual who fails to help him is not seen as wanting the victim to drown. (For the omission actor, these ratings range between 3.38 and 4.76, with a rating of 3 meaning the respondents "disagreed" with the statement that the individual wanted the victim to drown and a rating of 5 indicating "unsure.") Still, as column (c) shows, the respondents agree that the potential rescuer is practically certain that the victim would drown. This suggests that the respondents give a liability discount to the person who fails to help, as compared to the person whose act of commission created the situation in the first place, even though they do regard the omission as blameworthy.

Returning to considerations affecting the level of liability assigned, as Table 34 shows, subjects clearly do distinguish between the stranger (no-duty) scenarios, (1) and (5) through (8), and the duty scenarios, (2) through (4). In the latter, a large majority of subjects impose liability and punishment (93 to 100 percent). These

TABLE 34. } Respondents' Perceptions of Commission and Omission Cases

	Commission		*Omission*			
	(a)	*(b)*	*(c)*	*(d)*	*(e)*	*(f)*
Scenarios	*Knowledge*	*Purpose*	*Knowledge*	*Purpose*	*Inconvenience*	*Danger*
1. Stranger	6.48	5.86	6.71	3.45	1.48	1.45
2. Parent	6.41	6.10	7.28	4.17	1.21	1.28
3. Contract	6.45	6.03	6.90	4.28	1.48	1.24
4. Assumption	6.55	5.97	6.66	4.76	1.21	1.31
5. Stranger—high danger	6.48	6.03	6.72	3.38	5.21	6.93
6. Stranger—low danger	6.45	6.00	6.79	4.10	4.03	4.55
7. Stranger—high inconvenience	6.48	5.83	6.79	4.28	4.59	2.45
8. Stranger—low inconvenience	6.62	5.86	6.69	4.21	3.21	2.34

Key to column heads:

Statements *(a)* through *(d)* were responded to on a scale where 1=strongly disagree, 3=disagree, 5=unsure, and 9=strongly agree.

(a) The actor is practically certain that the victim will drown.
(b) The actor wanted the victim to drown.
(c) The potential rescuer is practically certain that the victim will drown.
(d) The potential rescuer wanted the victim to drown.
(e) To what extent would it have been inconvenient for the potential rescuer to help the victim? 1=not at all inconvenient and 9=extremely inconvenient.
(f) To what extent would it have been dangerous for the potential rescuer to help the victim? 1=not at all dangerous and 9=extremely dangerous.

results confirm the importance of the legal doctrine's consideration of whether a legal duty exists and suggest that the community sees the same sorts of relationships as creating this duty to rescue as does the Code. Thus, the study results suggest that violation of a duty is recognized by the community as grounds for assigning a person criminal liability. However, the liability scores assigned in the duty cases are by no means as severe as those that the Code would assign in the same cases. The Code's penalties for omission would be the same as those assigned for commission of the act, which in the scenarios would be punishment levels of approximately 8.6 (24.4 years). Consistently the subjects assign liability levels well below this, ranging from 5.1 to 6.2 (1.2 years to 3.8 years).

It is not the case that the subjects are lenient in all of their judgments. In contrast to the legal duty scenarios, subjects appear to be stricter than the Code in cases where no legal duty exists. In all scenarios where a bystander fails to rescue a stranger, except the one involving high danger to the rescuer, a majority of the subjects would impose criminal liability in such cases (from 79 to 86 percent). Even in the high danger scenario, 45 percent would impose liability. Yet, the legal doctrine imposes no liability where no duty to rescue exists. In the eyes of the respondents, absence of a duty does not exempt a person from liability for failing to save a stranger's life. As the responses to scenarios (5) through (8) show, the respondents think that a bystander, who can swim, should swim to the rescue of a drowning individual and should be criminally liable if he does not.

In saying this, it is not meant to deny that the subjects make some carefully nuanced qualifications of the duty to rescue a stranger. The results of these four non-duty scenarios are illustrated in Figure 35. This figure has arrayed the four scenarios in terms of the sacrifice required of the possible helper, with the incon-

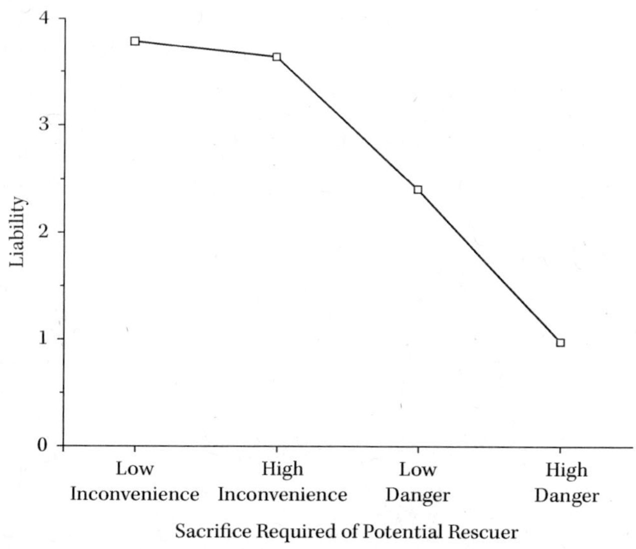

FIGURE 35. Liability as a Function of the Degree of Sacrifice Necessary to Rescue

venience cases assumed to require less sacrifice. Notice that the respondents lower their liability judgments as the inconvenience and particularly the danger to the potential rescuer increases; the less the inconvenience or danger to the bystander in attempting a rescue, the more the liability he incurs for not doing so. (An analysis of variance indicates that the degree of either danger or inconvenience makes a reliable difference in the respondents' assignment of liability. As the figure also indicates, the danger that exists for the potential helper mitigates the respondents' condemnation of him for not intervening more than does the inconvenience.)

But details of the patterning aside, the respondents see a very far-reaching duty to intervene, one that generally goes beyond the views encapsulated in codes. In the high danger case, involving the necessity to jump into shark-infested waters to attempt the rescue, row (5) of Table 34, 45 percent of the subjects assign liability to the person who chooses not to help, although the punishments assigned in this case were low.

The Code-community difference in the no-duty cases is not as great, however, when one focuses upon punishment rather than liability. Many subjects impose liability but no punishment (compare columns (e) and (f) of Table 34). In the two danger scenarios, only a minority of subjects impose punishment: 38 percent in the low-danger scenario, 14 percent in the high-danger scenario. There is a possible pattern here, in which the respondents are using an assignment of criminal liability to censure conduct, without wishing to impose an actual punishment on the censured individual. In the no-danger cases, where a majority of subjects do impose punishment, the degree of punishment is not high, ranging from 2.93 (7.4 weeks) to 3.79 (5.2 months).[24]

To summarize, the results of this study indicate that the subjects would support a system in which causing a death by omission receives some liability, but less liability and punishment than if the death were caused by commission, all other things being equal. Some support for the standard legal distinctions is found: failing to save a life in the absence of relationships that the law suggests create a duty to act receives less liability and punishment than where a duty exists. Where no duty exists, the degree of liability and punishment is reduced as the degree of danger or inconvenience to the rescuer increases. Still, only in the case of high danger is the potential rescuer free from liability, and only in the case of noticeable danger is the potential rescuer free from punishment. Inconvenience never exempts the potential rescuer from liability, but the degree of his punishment is low. These results appear to support the few American state statutes that create a limited duty to rescue strangers from serious threats.[25]

When a person fails in a legal duty to rescue, created by contractual agreement, parental relationship, or voluntary assumption of responsibility, the subjects impose significantly lower liability than current doctrine would. Apparently, causing a death

---

[24] This generally corresponds to the penalty range provided in the Rhode Island and Wisconsin duty rescue statutes cited above, which make the failure to act a "petty misdemeanor" (six months maximum) and a "Class C misdemeanor" (fine not to exceed $500, or imprisonment not to exceed 30 days, or both), respectively.

[25] See statutes cited in footnote 23.

by omission is judged less blameworthy than causing the same death by commission (with the same state of mind concerning whether the individual was likely to die). Current doctrine imposes full liability for the substantive offense, while the subjects discount liability for omission. The findings suggest that code drafters provide significant grade reductions where liability is based upon a failure to perform a duty.

Finally, the respondents make nuanced distinctions between similar but not identical cases. For instance, the subjects vary the amount of liability assigned according to the nature of the circumstances that create the duty to rescue. A continuum of accountability also exists, in the context of rescue of a stranger, where liability varies with the degree of danger or inconvenience.

G. Secondary Prohibitions: A Summary

The four studies reviewed above suggest that secondary prohibitions are indeed a rich source of disagreement between community views and criminal codes. Codes frequently impose liability where the subjects would not impose liability, or at least would impose considerably less. For instance, the subjects find the dangerous proximity test embodied in the common law a better trigger for attempt liability than the substantial step test of the Model Penal Code. Further, the respondents give more weight to the renunciation of a criminal attempt even when that attempt has progressed far enough to trigger criminal liability. Unsuccessful attempts to encourage or assist in a crime seem to the subjects to call for little or no liability, more in keeping with the common law treatment of these unsuccessful attempts than the Code treatment, which would impose full offense liability. Also, a person who intends murder, but creates only a slight risk of causing a slight harm, receives a sentence that is greatly reduced from the Code's treatment of the act as attempted murder. An accomplice to a crime receives higher liability as his contribution to the crime increases, but the level of liability does not rise high enough to equal the liability assigned the principal criminal, as the Code provides. A person who has a duty to rescue and fails in that duty is liable, but not for murder, which is the liability that the Code would assign.

In other instances, the respondents impose liabilities greater than that imposed by legal codes, or assign liability in cases in which the codes assign none. Some degree of liability is assigned to individuals who develop a settled intention to commit a crime, a case in which the codes assign none, for instance. The respondents would impose some liability on persons who fail to assist a person in distress, even though the codes do not.

It is worth commenting further on this last result. Except in limited cases, American legal codes impose no omission liability on one who fails to help another in distress, even when that help would be easy to give. The respondents disagree with this; they impose some degree of liability in those situations. The liability they impose is small, and they frequently suggest a verdict of "liability but no punishment." This suggests that they would support the broadening of duty to assist laws. It also suggests that they are discriminating between two functions of liability assignments: two functions that are sometimes not differentiated. First and foremost in the minds of legal thinkers, the criminal justice system assigns punishments. But it also communicates a community's message of what is desirable and undesirable conduct, and it may have been this second message that the respondents were attempting to send when they assigned this sort of liability.

The above discussion focuses on liability discrepancies between code and community standards in individual cases; it is also possible to focus on the difference in patterning of responses across cases and the associated differences between code and community. Examining those differences highlights what might be called the underlying conceptual differences between code and community standards. One very apparent pattern of differences is worthy of note. The respondents consistently assign reduced liabilities to individuals who play secondary roles in the commission of a crime, even when the code would assign those individuals liabilities equivalent to the principal. In addition, and closely connected with this, reduced liability is assigned for the violation of secondary prohibitions such as attempt by the respondents even when the Code would assign liabilities equivalent to those assigned for the commission of the primary prohibited act.

Finally, one other overarching pattern in the respondents' system of judgment requires marking. The community is more "harm oriented" than is the Model Penal Code. That is, their liability judgments are more affected by whether a given harm actually comes about. A person intends to poison another. If she succeeds, she receives a severe sentence; if she fails, she receives a reduced sentence, graded by the respondents based upon the degree of actual harm done to the victim. A wife intends to kill her husband and shoots at him. If he is killed, a severe sentence results; if not, a much less severe sentence is given. In contrast, the Model Penal Code looks to the intent of the harm-doer, and assigns sentences to that harm-doer that generally set the liability at the level that would be given for the successful accomplishment of the crime intended.

13 }

Rules of Conduct: Doctrines of Justification

When should it be lawful to engage in conduct that normally would constitute a violation of criminal law? The law recognizes that in some instances a greater harm can be avoided or a greater good can be achieved by allowing a person to engage in conduct that normally would be a violation. Burning another person's property is a violation, but it is to be tolerated (even encouraged) if the burning acts as a firebreak to save a town. Striking another person without consent is a violation but is permitted if a police officer finds it necessary in order to overcome resistance to a lawful arrest. While shooting another person normally would be illegal, it may be justified if it is a necessary defense against unlawful force. The doctrines defining when conduct constituting a violation is nonetheless lawful are known as justification defenses. They are permissive only. They tell people when they will be permitted to act in violation of the doctrines of criminalization; they do not require one to act.

The criminal law recognizes a number of justification defenses. Self-defense and defense of property, studied here, are examples of defensive force justifications, which allow a person to defend him or herself or property against an aggressor's threat. Law enforcement officials' authority includes the use of nondefensive force, such as the right to use force to arrest a violator. An officer or a private citizen in some cases (also studied here) may use force to effect an arrest even if the violator is no longer presenting a threat. Other justification defenses allow for nondefensive use of force by, for example, teachers, prison guards, military personnel, parents and legal guardians punishing children, persons responsible for maintaining order in public vehicles, doctors treating patients, and persons acting under a judicial order. As shall be seen, the law's requirements for all justification defenses are analogous in several respects. Basically, they require that the force used be the minimum necessary to avoid the threatened harm or to further the defined interest. They also require that the amount of force used not be disproportionate to the value of the interest to be protected or furthered.[1]

The following studies examine not only the rules of justified conduct but also the rules governing the effect of a person's mistake as to whether his conduct is

---

[1] *See* Model Penal Code art. 3; Paul H. Robinson, *Criminal Law Defenses: A Systematic Analysis*, 82 Colum. L. Rev. 1999 (1982).

justified. There is some controversy over whether it is proper to use of the label "justified" when describing such mistake cases,[2] but this is not relevant to our current task. The discussion below will distinguish conduct that is actually justified and conduct that the person only mistakenly believes is justified.

Unlike some of the other areas discussed in part III, there are a few studies in the psychological literature bearing on ordinary people's perceptions of the legitimacy of justifications for acts that would otherwise generate liability. Darley and Zanna, for instance, have demonstrated that even young children are capable of recognizing and granting validity to some of the most common classes of justifications recognized by the legal system.[3]

The studies reported in this chapter measure the extent that community judgments fit the patterns of justifications given validity within legal codes. They are drawn primarily from portions of my work with John Darley in *Justice, Liability & Blame: Community Views and the Criminal Law*.[4]

A. Use of Deadly Force in Self-Defense

The law allows a person to use force, even deadly force on occasion, to defend himself. What otherwise would be murder (intentional killing) is fully exculpated as long as the conditions of self-defense are met. It is universally required that the use of force in self-defense be necessary. This notion of "necessity" means that if less force would be adequate for defense, then the force used is not necessary and therefore not justified. If a person can protect himself by using no force at all, then any use of force is unnecessary. Thus, law typically obliges a person to retreat before using deadly force if he can do so in safety. The law limits the duty to retreat, however, by not requiring retreat from one's home or work place, on the theory that such retreat would expose the person to greater danger. A second, equally important condition of self-defense requires that the person's use of force take account of the seriousness of the threat. That is, even if force is necessary to protect a person, she is not justified in using deadly force to protect against a kick in the shin. This required proportionality between the nature of the threatened harm and the nature of the defensive force is manifested in the law's limitation of the use of deadly force to instances where serious bodily injury is threatened.

A person may fail to meet some of the conditions for the use of deadly force in self-defense, yet, receive a defense or mitigation if he or she (mistakenly) believes that the conditions are satisfied. For example, a person who mistakenly but reasonably believes that he cannot safely retreat, nonetheless will receive a defense for the use

---

2 *See* Paul H. Robinson & Michael Cahill, Criminal Law §8.5 (2d ed. 2011).

3 John Darley & Mark Zanna, *Making Moral Judgments*, 70 Am. Scientist 515 (1982).

4 Paul H. Robinson & John M. Darley, Justice, Liability & Blame: Community Views and the Criminal Law ch. 3 (1995).

of deadly force in self-defense. Similarly, a person who mistakenly but reasonably believes that an attacker is threatening serious bodily injury will also be entitled to a defense. If the person's mistake is culpable (reckless or negligent), some jurisdictions deny a defense while others impose reduced liability. If a person is reckless as to the existence of a serious threat, for example, he may be liable for manslaughter rather than murder if he kills in mistaken self-defense. If his mistake is negligent, liability for negligent homicide may follow. If his mistake is reasonable (nonnegligent), he may have no liability.[5] If a person accurately perceives the situation but is mistaken as to what the law permits, his mistake does not provide a defense or mitigation. Thus, there is no defense for a person who mistakenly believes that he is justified in law in killing an attacker who does not present a serious threat.[6] The law also denies a defense to a person who provokes an attack in order to kill the attacker in self-defense.[7]

As is obvious, the law's self-defense rules are detailed and complex. The self-defense study sought to examine the community's views on the use of deadly force in self-defense and to compare it to the legal doctrine's rules and conditions. The core of the scenario is this: A man who legally carries a gun for protection is walking on a deserted street in a city at night. He is accosted by another man, under various circumstances, and shoots the other, killing him. The liability results may be summarized as follows.

To begin discussion of these results, look first at the boundaries of liability established by the two "control" cases shown in the first and second rows of Table 36. The control scenario in the row (2) of the table involves a case in which a person is attacked with a deadly weapon and responds by killing the attacker. These results confirm that subjects give a defense to a person who kills under conditions that satisfy the legal requirements for self-defense. First, the assignment of liability was vanishingly low, an average of 0.14, which scales to well below one day in jail. Of the respondents, 71 percent gave no liability; 97 percent gave no liability or no punishment.

For a killing that meets none of the doctrine's requirements for justification, the control scenario in row (1) establishes the baseline liability, of 7.97 (15.0 years). This result surprised the researchers because this level of liability is noticeably less than the liability typically given to murderers by other respondents in the other scenarios that have been presented or will be presented later. A possible interpretation does exist after studying the data. In this case, a person is approached by a beggar and shoots the beggar. Apparently, what to the researchers seemed a trivial annoyance (being pestered by a beggar who persists in requesting money after he is turned down by the other) led the subjects to see the person as less blameworthy than the typical murderer; that is, the pestered person is seen as less blameworthy

---

[5] Model Penal Code §3.09(2).

[6] *Id.* at §3.09(1)(b).

[7] *Id.* at §3.04(2)(b)(i).

TABLE 36. } Self-Defense Liability

	(a)	(b)	(c)	(d)	(e)	(f)
Scenarios	*Liability*	*% No Liability (N)*	*% No Liability or No Punishment (N+0)*	*Model Penal Code Result*	*"Force Was Reasonable"*	*Maximum Force Permissible*
1. Killing, no self-defense	7.97	3	9	Liable for murder	2.20	2.34
2. Killing, self-defense. Knows deadly force is not necessary because:	0.14	71	97	Complete defense	7.97	7.83
3. Unarmed attacker	6.66	6	14	Liable for murder	2.97	3.54
4. Could retreat	4.63	23	40	Liable for murder	4.06	4.46
5. Could retreat from home Believes deadly force is necessary but:	0.77	43	86	Complete defense	6.20	7.00
6. Mistaken as to threat	1.40	31	80	Complete defense or mitigation	5.89	5.31
7. Mistakenly believes retreat not possible	0.49	54	94	Complete defense	6.86	6.77
8. Actor provokes attack. Believes deadly force is not necessary but:	6.40	6	17	Liable for murder	5.11	4.31
9. Mistakenly believes deadly force legal	6.71	3	17	Liable for murder	2.74	3.20

Liability Scale: N=No criminal liability, 0=Liability but no punishment, 1=1 day, 2=2 weeks, 3=2 months, 4=6 months, 5=1 year, 6=3 years, 7=7 years, 8=15 years, 9=30 years, 10=life, and 11=death.

Key to column heads:
(e) The amount of force the actor used was reasonable under the circumstances: 1=strongly disagree, 5=unsure, and 9=strongly agree.

(f) What is the maximum amount of force that someone should be able to use to protect themselves in this situation? 0=no force, 2=risk of bodily injury, 4=bodily injury, 6=serious bodily injury, 8=serious bodily injury with risk of death, and 10=death.

than one who actively seeks out another and initiates the killing encounter. There is, unfortunately, the possibility that the respondents "read into" the case some degree of threat in the beggar's behavior, or believed that the person felt such a threat.

As previously mentioned in the other scenario studies described elsewhere in this book, higher degrees of liability are assigned to persons who commit murders (averaging around 10, which scales to life imprisonment); thus, one would not conclude that people take a particularly lenient view of murder in general. What the unforeseen low sentence for killing the beggar suggests is that future research should examine the minimum threat that people view as giving a person warrant for a defensive response. The context may also be important in assessing the level of threat. A behavior that signals possible menace on a subway platform may not do so on a sunny small-town street. And the context is perhaps one that is perceived as dangerous by the respondents: a deserted city street at night. Regardless, the finding that some people consider the approach of a beggar a mitigation for shooting that beggar is an alarming finding.

Turn next to the liability assignments given in scenarios (3) through (9). It appears that the respondents believe that a killer with some claim to self-defense, whether or not that claim is granted validity by the legal codes, should receive a mitigated punishment. The liability assignments in all of the noncontrol cases are lower than that given for the baseline case in row (1).

In these other scenarios, the general pattern suggests that assigned liability is a function of the seriousness of the threat to the attacked individual. Where the person knows the attacker is unarmed, and thus his deadly force is not necessary, row (3), subjects impose liability of 6.66 (5.8 years). This is less, although only marginally significantly less, than the control scenario of row (1) where no or a very ambiguous threat exists, suggesting that a person is judged increasingly less blameworthy as the degree of threat increases. As Figure 37 shows, the subjects appear to see a continuum of degree of liability based upon the degree of threat. While further studies should investigate the exact nature of this relationship, it is important to note a contradiction with the legal code. The legal doctrine adopts a simple cutoff when there is no belief of threat. If serious bodily injury is threatened, a complete

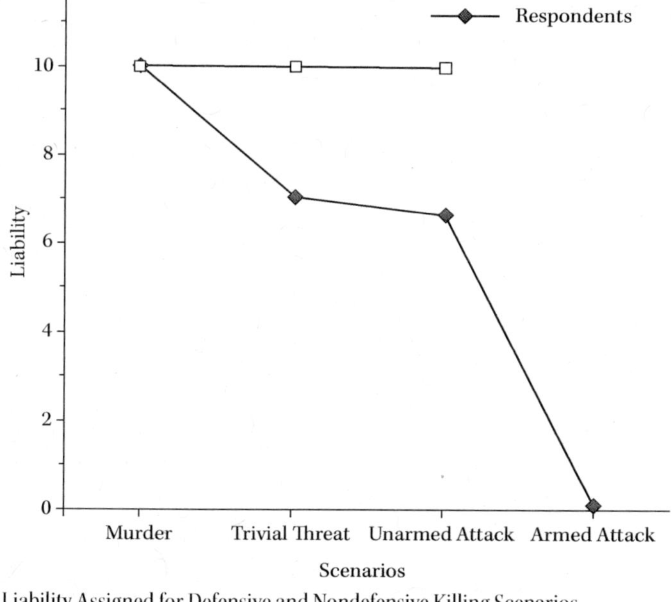

FIGURE 37. Liability Assigned for Defensive and Nondefensive Killing Scenarios

defense is given. If less than serious bodily injury is threatened, murder liability is imposed assuming the subject did not believe that he was threatened. The law's treatment and the liability judgments given by the respondents are shown in Figure 37, and the contrast can be clearly seen.

Further, as the degree of the perceived threat increases, the amount of force the subjects authorize also increases. The subjects' views on the maximum force that they think permissible in the situation are shown in Table 36, column (e). In the control scenario shown in row (2), when the other individual attacks, the subjects judge that it is appropriate to respond with force that risks "serious bodily injury and risk of death," 7.83 on the force scale. In the cases tabled in rows (5), (6), and (7), in which the person is attacked by a man wielding a knife, the respondents also agree that the maximum force allowable in self-defense is also high, judgments of 7.00, 5.31, and 6.77 respectively, as shown in column (f). In the other cases, they judge that the maximum force that would be appropriate in self-defense to be equal to or below that which would cause bodily injury but not serious bodily injury to the attacker. The case in row (8), in which the person kills an individual that he provoked into attacking him, is a complex case which will be expounded upon below. Note for now that the force that would be reasonable to use is rated at 5.11.

Notice, from Table 36, that these ratings of the maximum force allowable are consistent with the subjects' judgments of liability, and probably provide the basis for those judgments. To visualize this comparison, look to Figure 38. It orders, along the horizontal axis, the scenarios in the order of the maximum force that the respondents would allow in self-defense (the maximum force is given along with the scenario identification), and the vertical axis shows the degree of liability assigned to the killer. Note the close relationship. If the respondents judge that rather low amounts of force were appropriate in self-defense, then the person who kills the other is given the maximal sentence that the respondents assign. If they judge that more force is allowable, they reduce the sentence to the individual who kills the other, and in the final four cases, in which they report they would tolerate a response that involves serious bodily injury to the attacker, they give the defender quite low liability assignments. This suggests that the respondents are arriving at some global judgment, based on the set of facts they read, about what would constitute a reasonable action in the case, comparing the person's action and judging liability from the degree of discrepancy. Again, this view contrasts with the simple cutoff approach of current codes. Under the Model Penal Code, for example, only a threat of serious bodily injury or greater justifies the use of deadly force; a lesser threat justifies only the use of force short of deadly force.

An interesting code-subject discrepancy is found in scenarios involving possible retreat. Americans, stereotypically support people "standing their ground," and the subjects in this study seem to want them to even when the legal codes say they should not. That is, when a person's use of deadly force is unnecessary because he could safely retreat, the "could retreat" case of row (4), the subjects mitigate liability while the Code does not. As Table 39, column (f) reveals, subjects agree that the

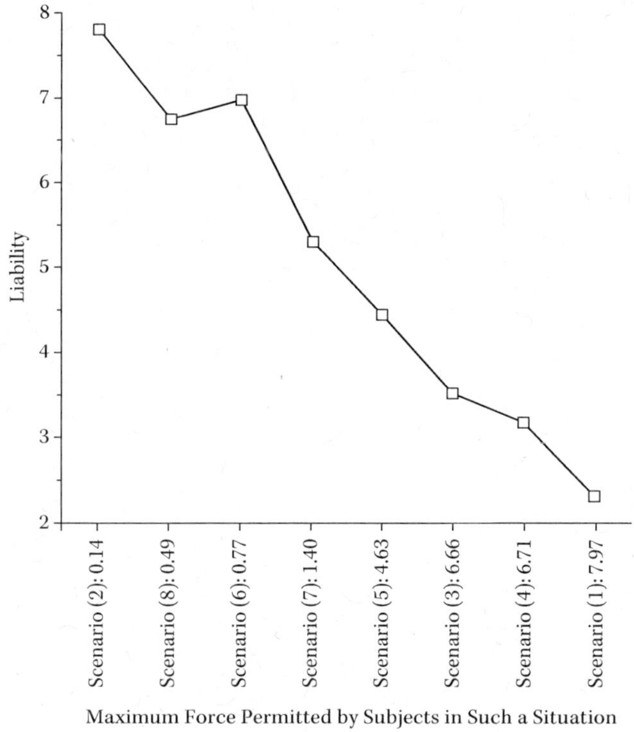

FIGURE 38. Liability as a Function of Maximum Force Allowed

person could retreat, but as Table 36, row (4), column (a) reveals, the liability mean of 4.63 (9.6 months) reflects a sentence considerably less than the liability for murder that the doctrine imposes. Apparently some subjects are unsure about whether retreat should be required at all: 23 percent give no liability; 40 percent give either no liability or no punishment. While a numerical majority appear to support the retreat rule, they support it as a basis for liability significantly short of what the Code assigns to that case, which is liability for murder.

Consistent with the subjects' equivocal support for the retreat rule, a large portion of the subjects agree with the Code's view that a person ought not be required to retreat from his own home, even if he knows that he can do so safely (the "retreat from home" case of row (5)). Table 39 shows the respondents' ratings of the cases on the various dimensions of perception that they were asked about. From Table 39, column (f), it is clear that they only rather grudgingly agree that retreat was possible. As shown in Table 36, 43 percent give no liability in such a case. Similarly, a person who mistakenly believes that it is impossible to retreat, row (7), receives almost no liability (.49) from the respondents. The subjects also agree with the codes in giving a defense to a person who incorrectly, but honestly, believes that his use of deadly force is necessary, rows (6) and (7). This occurs both where the person is mistaken as to whether the attacker threatens serious bodily injury, e.g., as to whether

TABLE 39. } Subjects' Perceptions of Self-Defense Cases

	(a)	(b)	(c)	(d)	(e)	(f)	(g)
Scenarios	*"Risk of Bodily Injury"*	*"More Force Than Necessary"*	*"Could Have Safely Delayed"*	*"Intended to Shoot"*	*"Believed Force Necessary"*	*"Could Retreat in Safety"*	*"Unaware Could Retreat"*
1. Killing, no self-defense		7.51	7.57	6.63			
2. Killing, self-defense. Knows deadly force is not necessary because:		2.23	2.40	5.03			
3. Unarmed attacker		7.51	7.34	6.43			
4. Could retreat		6.60	5.57	6.46		6.23	
5. Could retreat from home Believes deadly force is necessary but:		5.37	4.77	6.11		5.49	
6. Mistaken as to threat		5.66	5.51	5.83	6.71		
7. Mistakenly believes retreat not possible		4.09	4.17	5.46			7.51
8. Actor provokes attack. Believes deadly force is not necessary but:	7.43	6.60	5.77	6.57			
9. Mistakenly believes deadly force legal		7.69	7.26	7.17	4.49		

Key to column heads:
Statements *(a)* through *(e)* were responded to on a scale where: 1="strongly disagree," 5="unsure," and 9="strongly agree."

(a) The force the person used...created a risk of causing serious bodily injury.
(b) The person could have effectively protected himself by using less force.
(c) The person could have effectively protected himself if he delayed the use of force.
(d) The person intended to shoot the person he shot.
(e) The person believed that the amount of force was justified/necessary to protect himself.
(f) The person could have avoided the threat by retreating out of his house in complete safety.
(g) The person was unaware that he could retreat.

he is armed, row (6), and also occurs where the person is mistaken about whether he can retreat in safety, row (7). The former result suggests some empathy for the person who must decide under difficult circumstances whether to shoot. The latter result, commented on before, is predictable, given the subjects' weak support for the retreat rule. Many jurisdictions permit a defense only if the person's mistake is reasonable; an unreasonable mistake gives murder liability. Other jurisdictions allow a mitigation for an unreasonable mistake. The scenario used in the study gave no facts to suggest that the mistake is culpable, and columns (e) and (f) of Table 36 suggest that the respondents see the use of a serious degree of force as acceptable in these situations. Thus, the no liability result seems consistent with the Code's complete defense for a reasonable mistake. One might speculate that the low liability scores, given where the person's mistake might have been interpreted as culpable, suggests that the codes should give at least a mitigation for a culpable but honest mistake. A future study might test subjects' reactions to various levels of culpability in making a mistake as to a justification.

It may be that the respondents are attempting to understand what a reasonable person would infer from the actions of the attacker, and therefore, what latitude of action they will allow to the defender. On this account, if the attacker commits certain actions, those may trigger an inference by the attacked individual that leads him or her to respond with deadly force. This inference may be incorrect, but the attacked individual is given a great deal of leeway in making it. Unless the inference is conspicuously egregious, the fact that it is made, and acted on, is largely the attacker's problem. Putting this another way, it is the privilege of the attacked individual not only to judge what force is sufficient to deal with the present level of force that the attacker is using, but also to judge what level of force the attacker might escalate to in the immediate future. Fists may be all that is in play at the moment, but will knives or guns come into play next?

The subjects also agree with the Code in rejecting a defense for a person who mistakenly believes that he is legally authorized to use deadly force against an unarmed attacker (row (9), Table 36). The liability mean, 6.71 (5.9 years), is not statistically different from that assigned to a person, using similarly unnecessary force, who does not believe that his use of deadly force against an unarmed attacker is lawful (row (3), 6.66; 5.8 years). This is an interesting result and one that will be seen again. It suggests that respondents believe that it is widely accepted that one should not kill an unarmed attacker. A mistaken belief that the law allows such an attack does not excuse it. Having said all of this, future research, in which, for example, it is more clear that the person knew his conduct to be unlawful, will be necessary to confirm these conclusions.

In the scenario in which the person provokes the threat that requires defensive force, row (8), the respondents assign a high degree of liability but the Code's liability exceeds that of the subjects. The provoked-attack liability scenario has a liability mean of 6.40 (4.6 years), which suggests that the subjects see clear blameworthiness in the person but not of the level of a murderer, as the Code provides, or perhaps not even of the level of a killing upon a trivial threat (7.97; 15 years). Further research is necessary to illuminate the parameters of this complex issue. As indicated earlier, the respondents see that great force was appropriate once the attack by the provoked person was launched (Table 36, column (e), 5.11, where 4 equals bodily injury and 5 equals serious bodily injury). Intuitively, one would expect that if an individual attacks another in response to a mild provocation, killing the mildly provoking attacker would be seen as less warranted than if the provocation is more complete and violent. Here is the intuitive rule that is working: if I say something to you that is only mildly provoking, and you then come at me with dagger drawn, I will be assigned relatively low liability for killing you before you kill me. My mild provocation does not warrant your overblown response; you are the primary cause of your attack on me. However, if my provocation to you was really quite intense, then I have some causal responsibility for your attack on me, and bear some liability for killing you to head off your attack. Perceivers of these situations are likely to be attempting to unravel the familiar question of "who really started it."[8] There is also a question of what, exactly, the one who provokes the attack intends to do when attacked. If the respondents perceive, as in the formulaic cowboy movie, that the fast-drawing villain provokes the innocent, slow-drawing citizen into "drawing," with the certainty of outdrawing him and intending to kill him, then they see it as murder and are glad when the hero does in the villain in the last reel. Fascinating questions lie here for future research.

To summarize, it appears that the subjects' judgments are complex, and in many instances they agree with the pattern of distinctions made in the Code. The subjects generally decline to punish in the instances where the Code gives the person a defense: where he knows he could retreat in safety but is in his home, where he mistakenly but honestly believes serious bodily harm is threatened, and where he mistakenly but honestly believes that he cannot safely retreat. Similarly, the subjects impose significant liability in instances where the Code would deny a defense: when the person knows the attacker is unarmed, when he knows he can retreat in safety, or when the person provokes the attack to justify his subsequent use of force.

On the other hand, a second element in the patterning of the subjects' responses is evident: a tendency to give lesser punishments than the Code would assign. The subjects and the Code disagree on the extent of liability that should be imposed where the person acts in self-defense but knows that deadly force is unnecessary or provokes the attack. The subjects' disagreement with the Code is particularly striking in the case in which it would be possible for the person to retreat from the threat. While the Code denies a defense in these instances, leaving the person liable for murder, the subjects impose liability akin to manslaughter or, in the case of failure to retreat, something less. Apparently the subjects see a clear and significant distinction between an unjustified killing in self-defense and an intentional killing where no attack exists. A self-defense provision that mirrors the subjects' views would mitigate liability for even unjustified killings in a self-defense setting. The significant agreement that does exist between the subjects and the Code may be the result of community views manifesting themselves in the centuries of common law development, upon which most of these rules are based. It may not be that the detailed rules are intuitive but rather that both the subjects' views and the Code's rules result from application of a few basic principles, such as the requirements that the defensive response be necessary and proportional.[9] It also is possible that the

---

[8] Barbara Carpenter & John Darley, *A Naive Analysis of Counteraggression*, 4 Personality & Soc. Psychol. Bull. 68 (1978).

[9] For a discussion of these general principles and how they are manifested in the Code's detailed rules, *see* Paul H. Robinson, Criminal Law Defenses §131(c) & (d) (1984).

rules of the legal code, which once may have been alien to the moral codes of the governed, over time became accepted moral principles. Morality can shape the law, but the law also can shape morality.[10]

B. Use of Force in Defense of Property

The criminal law typically allows a person to use force in the protection of property. As with self-defense, the force used must be necessary to protect the property, both in the amount of force used and in its timing; that is, no lesser force and no delay in the use of force would have provided adequate protection. The force used also must be generally proportionate to the threat. Thus, the use of deadly force is usually prohibited to protect property alone, even if such deadly force is the only means by which the property can be protected. As with self-defense, when a person makes a mistake as to the necessity for the use of force, he nonetheless may get a mitigation or defense, depending on the culpability level of his mistake. All jurisdictions give a defense for a reasonable mistake. Some give no defense for an unreasonable mistake; others give a mitigation in degree of liability. No mistake as to the illegality of using deadly force in protection of property is grounds for a defense.

The defense of property study sought to test the current defense of property rules against the subjects' assignment of liability in analogous defense of property situations. Subjects were given seven scenarios in which the person uses force to defend against an attempt to steal his motorcycle. One scenario presented a baseline case in which necessary, non-deadly force is used, which would receive complete exculpation under current doctrine. The other six scenarios presented variations in which the person deviates from the baseline case in one or more ways, typically in violation of one of the limitations on the use of force to defend property. The liability results are shown in Table 40. Notice that column (e) reports the liability assigned to the person who attempts the theft. As one would expect, the thief is assigned some liability, and it is roughly constant across the cases.

With respect to perceptions of the use of necessary non-deadly force (as can be seen from the results in row (1)), the subjects agree that complete exculpation was appropriate. Eighty-nine percent of the respondents judge that no liability should be assigned to the property defender; the remaining 11 percent assign liability but no punishment.

Examine next scenario (2), in which the force is labeled "questionably necessary." In this scenario, the description read as follows: "Joe punches the man, believing at the time that it is necessary. Joe's wife begins to yell at Joe that the man was small and not very muscular and Joe probably could have scared him off with a yell. Joe later realizes that his wife was right." Here too essentially no liability is imposed by the subjects on the property defender.

---

[10] Thomas Andrew Green, Verdict According to Conscience (University of Chicago Press 1985).

TABLE 40. } Liability for the Use of Force in Protection of Property

	(a)	*(b)*	*(c)*	*(d)*	*(e)*	*(f)*
Scenarios	*Liability*	*% No Liability (N)*	*% No Liability or No Punishment (N+0)*	*Model Penal Code Result for Defender*	*Liability for Thief*	*Maximum Force That Should be Permitted*
1. Necessary force	0.00	89	100	Complete defense	4.58	3.80
2. Questionably necessary force	0.00	77	98	Unclear[a]	4.70	3.91
3. Necessary force applied by device	0.19	77	93	Complete defense[b]	5.11	3.91
4. No imminent threat (perceived as not immediately necessary)	0.48	48	82	Unclear[c]	4.14	3.36
5. More than necessary force by choice	0.14	55	93	No defense; liable for simple assault, a misdemeanor	4.05	3.41
6. Deadly force, knowing not lawful	2.56	21	46	No defense; liable for	5.39	4.32
7. Deadly force, mistakenly believing it lawful	2.63	18	48	aggravated assault, a second-degree felony	5.45	4.25

Liability Scale: N=No criminal liability, 0=Liability but no punishment, 1=1 day, 2=2 weeks, 3=2 months, 4=6 months, 5=1 year, 6=3 years, 7=7 years, 8=15 years, 9=30 years, 10=life, and 11=death.

Key to column heads:
(f) What is the maximum amount of force that someone should be permitted to use to protect his property in this situation? 0="no force," 2="risk of bodily injury," 4="bodily injury," 6="serious bodily injury," 8="serious bodily injury with risk of death," and 10="death."

[a]This scenario was intended to present the case of a mistaken actor. Such an actor might get a defense under current law, especially if his mistake was reasonable; he might only get mitigation if his mistake was not reasonable. In fact, the scenario was perceived as a case of necessary force, for which the actor would have a defense under current doctrine.

[b]If the scenario had been perceived as the device creating a substantial risk of serious bodily injury, as was intended, there would be no defense. But no such risk was perceived by the subjects. See column *d* of Table 3.6. In a case of no risk of serious bodily injury, a complete defense is available.

[c]An "imminent *threat*" was required by common law; modern codes such as the Model Penal Code require only that the "*force used* be immediately necessary."

In Table 41, respondents' perceptions of various aspects of the scenarios are shown. Examining the ratings on the questions concerning whether more force than necessary was used, column (a); and whether the force could have safely been delayed, column (c), the respondents seem to be giving the benefit of the doubt to the person of row (2). That is, they are not convinced that the person used more force than necessary or that the use of force could be delayed. Given the particular scenario, in which the defender realizes only later that the force he used was not necessary, this seems a reasonable set of perceptions and liability assignments.

TABLE 41. } Subjects' Perceptions of the Use of Force in Protection of Property

Scenarios	*(a)* "More Force Than Necessary"	*(b)* "Actor Believes Less Force Ineffective"	*(c)* "Could Have Safely Delayed"	*(d)* "Force Used Created Risk of Death"	*(e)* "Amount Reasonable Under Circumstances"	*(f)* "Believes Lawful to Create Risk of Death"
1. Necessary force	3.16		3.16	2.86		
2. Questionably necessary force	3.70	5.66	3.84	3.25		
3. Necessary force applied by device	3.75		3.50	3.52		
4. No imminent threat (perceived as not immediately necessary)	5.75		5.61	3.42		
5. More than necessary force by choice	5.59	4.57	5.45	3.74		
6. Deadly force, knowing not lawful	5.48		4.39	7.41	4.00	3.95
7. Deadly force, mistakenly believing it lawful	5.41		4.34	7.70	4.70	6.41

Key to column heads:
Statements *(a)* through *(f)* were responded to on a scale where: 1="strongly disagree," 5="unsure," and 9="strongly agree."

(a) The actor could have effectively protected his property by using less force than he did.
(b) At the time when the actor hits the man, the actor believes that less force would be ineffective to protect his property.
(c) The actor could have effectively protected his property if he delayed his use of force.
(d) The force that the actor used created a risk of causing the man's death.
(e) The amount of force the actor used was reasonable in light of the situation.
(f) The actor believes that he is legally entitled to use force that risks causing the thief's death.

In case (3), the owner has rigged a protective device to the motorcycle so that if anyone tampers with the ignition, an explosion that fires a beanbag is triggered. In this case, the thief fiddles with the ignition, and the device is triggered, breaking the thief's nose. This began a probe of the reactions of the respondents to "spring guns" and "man traps," the use of which is significantly limited by law.[11] Their use is a complex area of the law because it is hard to predict the degree of harmful consequences of these devices for the thief or the nature of the existing threat when the device is triggered. Also, they can cause injury when no threat to person exists, because the owner of the trap is not present. Subjects seem to read this case as within the bounds of acceptability: they disagree that it was more force than was necessary, Table 41, column (a), and do not agree that it created a risk of death, column (d). Ninety-three percent of the respondents assign no punishment to the

[11] *See* Model Penal Code §3.06(5).

person who set the device. Future research ought to examine how respondents feel about setting more lethal traps for thieves.

Examining next scenarios (4) and (5), there is a continuation of the general pattern of lenient treatment of the person protecting his property. In case (4), where the force used in defense is described as not clearly necessary, 82 percent of the respondents assign no punishment to the force user. There, the thief agrees to leave when Joe yells at him, but makes clear he has an imprint of the keyhole and will return for the motorcycle. Joe resorts to force in order to retrieve the imprint. Scenario (5) sought to make it completely clear that the force used was knowingly more than was necessary. "Joe realizes that he can simply scare the man away by yelling at him. He nonetheless approaches the man and punches him in the face." Nonetheless, even in this scenario, 93 percent of the respondents impose no punishment on the person.

For each scenario, respondents were asked to indicate the degree to which they agreed with the statement that "the person could have protected his property by using less force than he did" (tabled in column (a) of Table 41). An examination of the respondents' ratings here suggests the thinking that may lie behind their rather permissive stance on punishment: they are not convinced that more than necessary force had been used. Thus, even when a scenario explicitly describes the force as unnecessary, the subjects generally are unconvinced. In this scenario (5), subjects' ratings on the necessity of the force used average 5.59, less than one point above the scale midpoint of 5, column (a), indicating that they are unsure that the force was more than was necessary. It may be here that the subjects are taking the role of the person whose property is threatened and concluding that they would not require that his cognitions be perfectly clear, or his responses perfectly measured, when he is in the stressful circumstances of an ongoing theft. Further, there may be an element of calculation that involves the value of the property at risk; a motorcycle is a relatively costly object, and a punch on the nose not too high a price for the attempted thief to pay.

Consistent with the tendency to see non-deadly force as necessary, the subjects generally fail to impose liability even where they see the force as possibly unnecessary. Even in the last scenario quoted above—where the subjects fall somewhere between "unsure" and "agree" as to whether the amount of force used was unnecessary—55 percent of the subjects think that no liability was appropriate, and 93 percent think that no punishment was appropriate.

Summing up, this initial look at the five scenarios involving non-deadly force, a considerable majority of the subjects would impose no liability in any of the scenarios. Eight-two percent or more would impose either no liability or no punishment. Overall, this might suggest that the subjects are not concerned with the many distinctions that the Code uses and that they generally approve of the use of non-deadly force in the protection of property, whether necessary or not.

Examining the matter more closely, however, some evidence hints that subjects do take into account the necessity for the use of force in assessing the proper degree of liability. The two cases perceived as the weakest cases for necessity are scenarios (4) and (5), with 5.75 and 5.59 indicating slight agreement with the "unnecessary amount" manipulation check, Table 41, column (a) quoted above, as compared to means of 3.16, 3.70, and 3.75 for the other non-deadly force scenarios, which indicate disagreement with the statement that unnecessarily strong force was used. These same two cases have the lowest "no liability" percentages, 48 and 55 percent, respectively. But this seems at best weak support for the necessity principle, which is seen as fundamental to the legal doctrine. Recall that current doctrine treats the use of nonnecessary force as a basis for denying any mitigation or defense to the property defender. The respondents rather obviously treat it differently, as a factor determining liability. And the average liability of less than one day in jail, 0.48 and 0.14 respectively, that they impose for using more than necessary force is considerably less than would be imposed by current legal codes, which would treat the case as one of simple assault with a maximum sentence of one year.[12]

Rather than focusing on the necessity of the force, the subjects seem to rely more heavily on the reasonableness of the amount of force in light of the seriousness of the threat, what the doctrine calls the proportionality of the force, as a basis for determining liability. Where the aggressor makes a single threat to take property, as in the first five scenarios, the subjects see the "maximum amount of force that someone should be able to use to protect his property in this situation" as approximately constant. (See Table 40, column (f), ranging from 3.36 to 3.91, where 4 equals bodily injury). The amount of force that they think ought to be permitted increases slightly in the remaining two scenarios, however, where the thief persists after repeated efforts by the owner to discourage him are unsuccessful, rows (6) and (7), 4.32 and 4.25. As previously noted, it would be interesting to determine in future research whether the maximum amount of force perceived as appropriate in defense would increase with the value of the property defended. If the individual was a store owner defending his goods, would subjects see a greater degree of force as reasonable than if he were only defending some inexpensive piece of property? This question remains to be answered.

The tendency to see (or claim to see) the person's use of force as necessary, despite objective appearances to the contrary, does not appear to exist in the deadly force scenarios. The two deadly force scenarios, (6) and (7), involve the following core: a thief is detected attempting to steal a motorcycle, and the owner attempts to get him to stop. The thief persists, and the owner gets a gun and shoots him. The respondents are told that the thief is wounded but not killed. Given the persistence of the thief in the face of several attempts to stop him, the shooting seems to have portrayed force that, at least some, might see as necessary, but it brought manipulation-check responses of 5.48 and 5.41 (Table 41), suggesting that subjects as a group are leaning slightly toward agreeing that the force is unnecessary or are at best unsure that it is necessary. Examining column (f) of Table 40, one sees that the respondents think force that causes bodily injury, but not serious bodily injury,

[12] *See* Model Penal Code §§211.1 & 6.08.

is the appropriate maximum to use on the persistent thief, and from column (d) of Table 41, that they agree that the actual force used, the gunshot, created a risk of death, and therefore was, by inference, more than the maximum allowable force. This is confirmed by column (e) of Table 41.

In these cases where deadly force is used, the percentage of subjects who impose no liability drops to 21 and 18 percent. The liability means correspondingly increase, from between 0 and 0.48 (less than a day) to 2.56 and 2.63 (about 5.6 weeks). Thus, the thief's greater aggression may justify the use of greater defensive force, but the use of deadly force will result in a considerable increase in liability. While the use of unnecessary force in defense of property is generally approved of by respondents, this principle has a limit: the majority of subjects think that the person's resort to use of a deadly weapon is unjustified. A majority of the respondents think it wrong to shoot the person attempting the theft of the motorcycle. Interestingly, they are not moved by being told that the person mistakenly thought that the shooting was lawful, row (7). This suggests that people see a clear moral issue here: one should know better than to shoot in defense of that sort of property.

These findings tend to support the Code's prohibition against the use of deadly force in defense of property, but it also must be pointed out that there are vast differences between the way the respondents view the use of deadly force in defense of property, and the way that it is treated by the Model Penal Code. Indeed, almost half of the subjects (46 and 48 percent) would impose no punishment even in the cases of deadly force in the protection of property. Also significant is the fact that the liability means of 2.56 and 2.63 imposed by the subjects represent average sentences of 5.6 weeks, not the one-to-three-year minimum, ten-year maximum sentence provided by the Model Penal Code.

Scenario (6) may be the most revealing in what it shows us about people's judgments:

> Joe arrives home to find a man attempting to steal his motorcycle. [Next are described a number of attempts by Joe to stop the thief, through which the thief persists in his attempts to steal.] While Joe believes that it may not be lawful to use a gun to prevent the theft of a motorcycle, he sees no other way to stop the man. He goes to his house just a few steps away, retrieves his gun, returns and shoots the man. The man survives and is later taken into custody by the police.

The subjects indicate that the maximum amount of force that should be permitted to protect property in this situation is 4.32 (Table 40, column (f)), approximately enough force to result in bodily injury (4 equals bodily injury, 6 equals serious bodily injury, 8 equals serious bodily injury with risk of death). And the subjects clearly perceive of Joe's conduct as creating a risk of death. Yet, despite Joe's failure to limit his conduct as the subjects would want, 46 percent of the subjects believe that either no liability or no punishment is appropriate. Of those who believe that punishment is appropriate, 74 percent would impose a sentence of one year or less.[13] This is strikingly different than the Code treatment of the offense; the Code treats it as aggravated assault, a second degree felony with a maximum sentence of 10 years.

To summarize, even where the force used in defense of property is unnecessary or disproportionate, according to legal codes, the vast majority of subjects impose no punishment. The subjects also show a tendency to interpret a person's conduct as necessary to defend his property even in instances where such a conclusion is difficult to support on the objective facts. As with self-defense, the defensive nature of the person's situation appears to have a significant effect on the subjects' judgment. Even where the person's defensive response is knowingly improper—that is, he knows that the law does not justify his conduct—the subjects significantly reduce the person's liability. Again, the subjects appear to distinguish a person who improperly defends his property from a person who uses the same force in other than a defensive context. This argues in favor of providing reduced grades of liability for those who err in defending against an attack. It remains a question for further research as to whether the value of the property being defended enters into the respondents' calculus.

If the legal code were modeled after the subjects' responses, it would give a complete defense for non-deadly force, necessary or not, used in the defense of property. The use of deadly force would be disapproved of but would result in low liability and punishment if the force appeared to be necessary (and the thief is not actually killed). In further research it would be important to address the question of what "philosophies" lie behind the judgments of individuals. Are there some individuals who believe that even deadly force is allowable in the defense of property? Does this belief reflect the view that the criminal justice system has become ineffective in defending property? The results may well be consistent with a public that is angry with what they see as the criminal justice system's failure to protect. "At the very least," the argument might go, "if the system will not protect my property, I should be permitted to do what is necessary [and perhaps more] to protect it myself."

C. Citizens' Law Enforcement Authority

Citizens sometimes seek to exercise the authority of a law enforcement officer, as when they attempt to apprehend a person who has committed a crime against them. If the use of force is defensive in any way—for example, an aggressor is attacking them or attempting to take their property—a citizen can rely on a defensive force defense, such as self-defense or defense of property, which frequently permits the use of greater force than would the normal authority granted to a citizen enforcing

[13] This percentage was calculated from data not presented in Table 40.

the law. If the use of force is not defensive but offensive in an effort to apprehend—for example, after a rape or after property damage has been caused—a citizen nonetheless has a right to use some degree of force to apprehend and restrain the offender.[14]

Exercise of a citizen's law enforcement authority is subject to several limitations. A citizen is never justified in using deadly force to arrest an offender (unless he does so in assisting a peace officer and meets other special conditions).[15] A person may use non-deadly force only to the extent that it is immediately necessary to effect a lawful arrest. If he is mistaken in some respect, for instance about whether the person he is attempting to arrest is the actual perpetrator of the crime, he may nevertheless be entitled to a defense if his mistake is reasonable. If it is unreasonable, some jurisdictions deny any defense or mitigation while others permit mitigation. In the latter jurisdictions, if the person recklessly or negligently injures an innocent person, for example, he may be liable for an offense of recklessness or negligence, as the case may be.[16] The Code does not alter the degree of non-deadly force permissible according to the seriousness of the offense for which the arrest is made; in all cases, the force must be just that which is necessary to effect the arrest.

The citizens' law enforcement authority study sought to test the current doctrine's rules on such authority against the community's views. Subjects were presented with scenarios involving the use of deadly and non-deadly force by the victim to restrain an offender after a rape and after a property damage offense (setting the victim's car on fire). Notice that in both cases the offense is already complete at the time force is used; thus it is not a case of self-defense or defense of property. The deadly force scenarios depict the victim as shooting the fleeing offender with a handgun and killing him; the non-deadly force scenarios involve the use of a stun gun, which would temporarily immobilize the offender, but not inflict lasting injury. In some scenarios the person stuns or kills the offender, and in others the person stuns or kills an innocent person that she mistakes for the offender. The subjects were asked, as usual, to determine how much liability, if any, the person should receive. They were also asked how much force a person in such a situation should have been able to use, column (e) of Table 42, and whether the actual force used created a risk of death, column (f). The results are as follows:

Notice first that the subjects see the differences between the use of the stun gun and the handgun as was expected. They agree, as column (f) shows, that the handgun creates a risk of death, 7.92 on the average (not surprising, since they were told that the person using it shoots and kills the fleeing individual), and the stun gun does not create a risk of death, 2.83 on the average.

Look next at the liability judgments. Examine first the patterning of the liability assignments in the four cases in which the citizen uses force to apprehend the indi-

---

[14] Model Penal Code §3.07(1).

[15] *Id.* at §3.07(2)(b).

[16] *Id.* at §3.09(3).

TABLE 42. } Liability for Exercise of Citizens' Law Enforcement Authority

	(a)	(b)	(c)	(d)	(e)	(f)
Scenarios	*Liability*	*% No Liability (N)*	*% No Liability or No Punishment (N+0)*	*Model Penal Code Result*	*Maximum Force That Should Be Permitted*	*"Force Used Created Risk of Death"*
Rape—Deadly force:						
1. Actual offender	0.21	65	90	Liable for murder	7.55	7.87
2. Mistaken identity	1.27	13	68	Liable for murder	6.87	7.82
Rape—Nondeadly force:						
3. Actual offender	0.00	83	100	Complete defense	6.85	2.92
4. Mistaken identity	0.35	30	83	Complete defense[a]	6.49	2.82
Property destruction—Deadly force:						
5. Actual offender	2.60	33	45	Liable for murder	4.39	8.08
6. Mistaken identity	3.27	8	43	Liable for murder	3.92	7.92
Property destruction—Non-deadly force:						
7. Actual offender	0.00	70	100	Complete defense	4.07	2.67
8. Mistaken identity	0.62	23	80	Complete defense[a]	4.00	2.90

Liability Scale: N=No criminal liability, 0=Liability but no punishment, 1=1 day, 2=2 weeks, 3=2 months, 4=6 months, 5=1 year, 6=3 years, 7=7 years, 8=15 years, 9=30 years, 10=life, and 11=death.

Key to column heads:
(e) What is the maximum amount of force that a person should be permitted to use to detain an offender in this situation? 0=no force, 2=risk of bodily injury, 4=bodily injury, 6=serious bodily injury, 8=serious bodily injury with risk of death, and 10=death.
(f) The force used was likely to cause death or bodily injury: 1="strongly disagree," 5="unsure," and 9="strongly agree."
[a]This assumes that the actor was not reckless as to injuring an innocent person. If the individual was reckless, the person could be liable for assault under MPC §§ 3.09(3) and 211.1(1).

vidual who actually committed the crime, scenarios (1), (3), (5), and (7). While the difference in liability assigned to the individual who uses deadly force, scenarios (1) and (5), is slightly higher (0.21 and 2.60; less than one day and 5.6 weeks) than the zero liability assigned to the person who uses non-deadly force, scenarios (3) and (7), what is most striking, as noted in the previous study, is the tendency to assign very low degrees of liability no matter what degree of force is used. The most dramatic difference between the subjects and the Code is in the deadly force scenarios. A strong majority (65 percent) would allow the use of deadly force by the citizen to apprehend the rapist, or at least would not punish such conduct. If added to this group are the respondents who find the defendant guilty but would impose no punishment, it would include 90 percent of the respondents. The Code, in contrast, denies a defense (or a mitigation) and thereby holds the person liable for murder.

Only in the case of the use of deadly force to apprehend an individual who has injured property alone is there any meaningful assignment of liability by a majority of respondents (67 percent); apparently there the use of force that has the potential to kill the offender exceeds the respondents' perceptions of the allowable level of force. Still, the average liability imposed, 2.60, translates to a sentence of 5.6 weeks for an act that the legal code would treat as murder, a vast difference.

Does this pattern of results change in the scenarios in which the person stuns or kills another person who is not the actual person who committed the crime, and is instead mistaken for that person by the person? Not very much changes in the liability ratings. Examine the four cases in which the person mistakenly uses force to apprehend an individual who did not in fact commit the crime, in scenarios (2), (4), (6), and (8). Look ahead now to Table 44 and notice, in column (d), that the respondents judge that the person is unaware of the possibility of making this mistake. The person is not, therefore, seen as lashing out at anybody in the vicinity; the force is directed at the individual whom the person thinks committed the crime.

The Model Penal Code's treatment of mistake does not match that of the subjects in several important respects. The Code does give a defense to the person who mistakenly injures an innocent person with non-deadly force, and a majority of the subjects would impose no punishment in such a case (83 percent in the rape arrest, 80 percent in the damage arrest). On the other hand, a vast difference exists between the Code and community in the mistaken deadly force scenarios, (2) and (4). Here the Code permits no defense[17] and imposes liability for murder. But the percentage of subjects who would impose no punishment, column (c) of Table 42, is substantial: 68 percent in the rape case and 43 percent in the property destruction case. The no punishment percentage is not dramatically different between the mistake and no-mistake scenarios (68 percent vs. 90 percent in the rape arrest scenarios, 43 percent vs. 45 percent in the damage arrest scenarios); but the percentage of subjects who would impose no liability, column (b), is significantly lower where the person has mistakenly killed an innocent person (13 percent vs. 65 percent in the rape arrest scenarios, 8 percent vs. 33 percent in the damage arrest scenarios). One interpretation of this is that the mistaken killing is disapproved of, and the person's conduct is judged to warrant the formal disapproval of the legal system, in the form of a "guilty" verdict, but not to warrant a prison sentence for the person. This "liability but no punishment" response, by now familiar to the reader, is discussed further in the concluding chapter of this book.

The low liability ratings of the person in the mistaken use of deadly force scenarios are striking. Figure 43 presents this graphically; in reading it one ought to remember that the legal code would treat the deadly force cases as murder and assign a liability of around 10. Only when the person mistakenly kills an innocent person in an attempt to arrest the person who set fire to her car do a majority of

[17] Model Penal Code §3.07(2)(b).

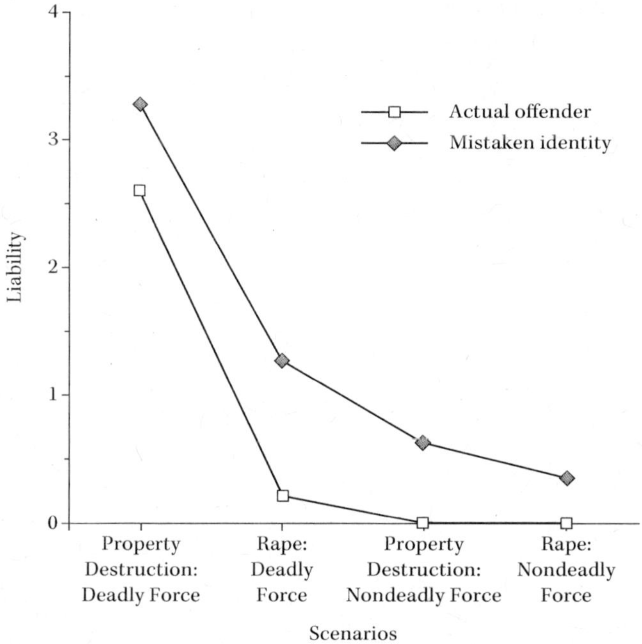

FIGURE 43. Effect of Use of Deadly and Non-Deadly Force on Liability for Exercise of Citizens' Law Enforcement Authority

subjects (57 percent) impose punishment. Even in this case, however, the liability means suggest that the punishment imposed is relatively minor: 3.36 (3.6 months), where an innocent person is mistakenly killed. This is considerably less than the potential life (or death) sentence that a person could receive for murder under the Code. In the scenarios, the mistake is what arguably might be described as "reasonable"; the person is at least not egregiously wrong in assuming that the person whom he or she harmed was the actual perpetrator. In future research, the plausibility of the case of mistaken identity should be varied, and one would expect that at some point this variation would make a difference. In the present case, however, it is only the combination of mistaken identity and the application of deadly force that receives any substantial penalty, and still nowhere near the penalty that would be given by the legal code.

What can be learned from the patterns of the subjects' perceptions of the cases, which might reveal the grounds for their relatively lenient judgments? Three sets of perceptions stand out. First, given that the perpetrator is fleeing, respondents feel that immediate action is required to apprehend him if he is to be apprehended, as Table 44, column (a) shows. Second, and particularly in the case of the fleeing rapist, no less harmful action would successfully apprehend the perpetrator, column (b). What the respondents clearly see is the dilemma that was sought to be created: a perpetrator of a crime is fleeing, and will escape unless the victim uses the only

TABLE 44. } Subjects' Perceptions of the Exercise of Citizens' Law Enforcement Authority

	(a)	*(b)*	*(c)*	*(d)*
Scenarios	*"Immediate Action Required to Detain"*	*"No Less Harmful Means to Detain"*	*"Intended to Shoot the Person Shot"*	*"Aware of Risk of Mistaken Identity"*
Rape—Deadly force:				
1. Actual offender	7.62	6.62	7.74	3.08
2. Mistaken identity	7.42	5.57	3.20	3.12
Rape—Nondeadly force:				
3. Actual offender	7.40	7.32	7.82	3.20
4. Mistaken identity	7.41	7.15	2.97	3.03
Property destruction—Deadly force:				
5. Actual offender	6.41	4.58	6.82	3.62
6. Mistaken identity	6.27	4.70	3.50	3.17
Property destruction—Nondeadly force:				
7. Actual offender	6.69	6.26	7.46	3.16
8. Mistaken identity	6.87	5.97	4.10	3.37

Key to column heads:
Statements *(a)* through *(d)* were responded to on a scale where: 1="strongly disagree," 5="unsure," and 9="strongly agree."

(a) If the victim did not act immediately, she would not have been able to detain the offender.
(b) There was no less harmful way, given the facts in this scenario, for the victim to successfully detain the offender.
(c) The victim intended to shoot the person she shot.
(d) Before she shot, the victim was aware of a significant risk that the person she was about to shoot may not be the offender.

resource at her disposal to stop him, which is the gun. Third, as mentioned before, the subjects always judge that the victim is quite unaware of the risk that she has mistakenly misidentified the individual whom she shoots as the true perpetrator of the crime, column (d). These three perceptions, taken together, suggest that the victim of the crime is seen by the respondents as responding reasonably to the event.

Recall the Code's treatment of the force allowable as it relates to the seriousness of the offense committed. The Code gives the same liability for use of force in the rape scenarios as it gives for use of the same force in the property damage scenarios, suggesting that it does not find it appropriate to allow greater latitude to a citizen apprehending an individual who has committed a more serious crime. As is shown by their ratings of the maximum force allowable in the various cases, Table 42, column (e), the respondents deeply disagree. The subjects approve the use of greater force for arrest after the more serious rape offense than after the less serious damage offense. After rape, the average maximum force permitted is 6.94, with 6 equaling serious bodily injury and 8 equaling serious bodily injury with risk of death; after setting fire to a car, the property destruction case, the average maximum force is 4.10, with 4 equaling bodily injury. These results suggest that the subjects would have the law vary the degree of force permitted according to the seriousness of the underlying offense. The subjects would authorize something between serious bodily injury and risk of death to effect the arrest of a rape offender, but only bodily harm for arrest of an offender who causes property damage.

To summarize the general findings on force in citizen arrests: the subjects agree with the Code's defense for a citizen's use of non-deadly force to effect an arrest. They disagree, however, with the Code's position that a citizen may not, independent of an officer, use deadly force. Most would approve the use of deadly force to arrest a fleeing rapist. A large minority would take the same view even if the offender is fleeing from a property damage offense.

In general, the subjects are much more forgiving than the Code of a person's mistakes in using deadly force to affect a citizen's arrest. The Code imposes murder liability if the person kills an innocent person. A strong majority of the subjects, in contrast, impose no punishment even where the citizen kills an innocent person in trying to stop a fleeing rapist. Only where an innocent person is killed in an attempt to stop an offender fleeing from a property damage offense do a bare majority of subjects judge punishment to be appropriate and, there, liability is a few months rather than the murder liability that the Code provides. As the above discussion demonstrates, the difference in views between the rape and property damage cases reveals that many subjects take into account the seriousness of the offense in judging the amount of force permissible to make an arrest, while the Code does not.

These results are surprising. Although intuitively it was expected that the respondents might judge the use of force by citizens to apprehend criminals more leniently than does the legal code, it was not expected the overwhelming magnitude of the differences found. It was expected that the use of deadly force would be more widely condemned where, as here, the damage is already done and the force is being used aggressively (rather than defensively) to arrest the offender. This seems especially true where only damage to property is involved, but while the respondents do assign more liability to that case than to others, the liability assigned is very low.

D. Justification Defenses: A Summary

The three studies above examine community views on three kinds of situations in which an individual has a justification for the use of force: when the force is used in self-defense, in defense of property, or to apprehend a person fleeing from a crime he has committed. In all of these studies, the community judges that these justifications are more compelling than what the legal codes are willing to grant. Respondents frequently assign no liability in cases to which the code attaches liability. Even when respondents assign liability, they typically assign considerably less punishment than would be suggested by codes. This discrepancy is least evident in the justifications provided by claims of self-defense. In defense of self, the Code allows force, even deadly force, to be used in a number of cases. The differences between community standards and criminal codes become more apparent when what people think is justifiable in defense of property is examined, and even more apparent in the cases involving a citizen who uses force to apprehend a criminal fleeing a crime, or to apprehend a person thought to be a criminal fleeing a crime. Community standards, as evidenced by the respondents, are willing to tolerate the use of more force than the Code permits, and assign lesser sanctions to the use of force even in the instances in which they judge that some blame accrues.

What can be said to explain this sharp contrast between community standards and criminal codes? One obvious possibility springs to mind. Criminal codes are formulated with the often implicit presupposition that there is a reasonably effective criminal justice system in place. In the assumptive world of the code drafters, people who commit crimes have a high likelihood of getting caught, convicted, and punished with due severity. But this is not what many modern day individuals believe to be the case. The subjects may feel that the criminal justice system is not likely to apprehend criminals, convict them when it apprehends them, or justly punish them when it convicts them. They may feel that the criminal justice system is failing in its role of protecting citizens. The present results may stem from a general sentiment that when the criminal justice system does a poor job in punishing offenders it is appropriate for individual citizens to do more in defense of self and property and in law enforcement. The more ineffective the system is seen to be, the more people may be willing to let victims take matters into their own hands.

If this is the explanation for the results, it is a sad and troublesome one. The strength of the differences between community standards and legal code results that are found would indicate, at a minimum, that large segments of the population are deeply dissatisfied with the criminal justice system. These observed discrepancies may illustrate one of the "hidden costs" to policies that fail to provide adequately funded police forces, or to court systems that fail to punish blameworthy offenders.

14 }

Principles of Adjudication: Doctrines of Culpability

When is violation of a legal conduct rule blameworthy? Once the criminal law defines the conduct that is prohibited and required, it must be determined whether a person who violates those rules should be punished and, if so, how much. Even if a person violates a criminal law conduct rule, it does not follow that liability is appropriate, especially if the law tracks community views. The condemnatory nature of criminal law requires that if the person's violation is blameless, he ought to be free from liability even though he may well have caused the prohibited harm or evil.

To assure the minimum level of blameworthiness, the law requires proof of a person's culpability as to each element of an offense. Thus, the "intruder" in your basement is criminally liable only if he knows it is another's house that he is entering. If, because all of the row houses are identical and he just moved in next door, he enters your basement garage honestly believing it to be his own, his trespass may be a violation of the rules of conduct but may not be a sufficiently culpable violation to merit the condemnation of criminal conviction.

Modern criminal codes classify a person's culpability with regard to the circumstances or results that make his conduct criminal into one of four levels: purpose, knowledge, recklessness, or negligence. A person can bring about an outcome "on purpose," meaning that he or she fully intends that the particular consequence happen. For example, I may set a bomb, hoping and intending to injure the people in the area. Alternately, the injury can be brought about knowingly but not purposefully. When I blow up a safe to steal the contents, I may know that the blast will injure people on the adjacent floors, but it is not my purpose to do so; all things being equal, I would prefer that they not be injured. Alternatively, I may be only reckless as to the blast injuring others. That is, I may be aware of a risk of causing injuries but disregard the risk. Finally, I may be unaware of a risk that people may be injured but should have been aware—a reasonable person would have been aware—in which case the law judges me negligent as to causing the injuries.[1]

[1] Model Penal Code §2.02(2); Paul H. Robinson & Jane Grall, *Element Analysis and Defining Criminal Liability: The Model Penal Code and Beyond*, 35 STAN. L. REV. 681 (1983).

Generally, a minimum of recklessness as to each objective element is required for criminal liability, given the rather severe penalties that the system imposes, as compared to the civil justice system. Thus, a person must be aware of a substantial risk that his conduct may obstruct a highway, or that the property he is taking belongs to another, or that the garage he enters is not his own, in order to incur criminal liability. This preference for recklessness as the normal minimum culpability required for criminal liability is expressed by provisions like the Model Penal Code's, which "reads in" recklessness whenever an offense definition is silent on the required culpability as to an offense element.[2]

Several of the earlier studies in this book have touched on culpability issues. For instance, the study in chapter 12, section B shows that a person who forms a settled intent to commit a crime is assigned some liability. The study in chapter 12, section D found that where a person's purpose is to kill another, even though the action taken runs only a slight risk of bringing about a slight harm, the respondents judge the person to be highly culpable. These findings give some preliminary indications that culpability is not only a prerequisite for liability but also a powerful determinant of the degree of liability.

This chapter is drawn primarily from portions of my work with John Darley in *Justice, Liability & Blame: Community Views and the Criminal Law*.[3]

A. Offense Culpability Requirements and Mistake/Accident Defenses

The definition of an offense typically includes the requirement that a person's conduct cause a specified harmful result or that the conduct be performed under specified circumstances that make it harmful or evil. Offense definitions are constructed from these three kinds of objective elements: conduct, results, and circumstances.[4] A result element might be something like the requirement in arson that a building be damaged. A circumstance element might be the requirement that the building be a dwelling and that it belong to another person (specific required characteristics of the nature of the damage) or the requirement in rape that the intercourse be without the consent of the victim or the requirement in so-called "statutory rape" that the partner be underage (an existing circumstance at the time of the conduct). A conduct element might be the requirement of intercourse in rape or of setting a fire in arson. In some instances, the definition of an offense does not require a specific kind of conduct. Homicide offenses prohibit any conduct that causes a death. Property destruction offenses frequently require only that the person engage in any conduct that causes the prohibited damage.

---

[2] Model Penal Code §2.02(3).

[3] Paul H. Robinson & John M. Darley, Justice, Liability & Blame: Community Views and the Criminal Law ch. 4 (1995).

[4] Model Penal Code §1.13(9).

Satisfaction of all of the objective elements of an offense definition is required for liability for the offense. Burning a dwelling that is your own property is not arson. Having intercourse with a woman who consents is not rape. Of course, such conduct may render a person liable for another offense, if his conduct satisfies the elements for that other offense. Intercourse with someone who consents is not rape but may be statutory rape if the person is underage.

In addition to the objective elements of an offense definition, modern codes require proof that a person has a specified culpability level as to each objective element of an offense.[5] That is, it is not enough for criminal liability that the person's conduct caused destruction of another's dwelling or that the person had intercourse with another person without her consent. The person must be shown to have been culpable as to the fact that the person was not consenting to intercourse or that the property belonged to another (and even that the property was a "dwelling," if that is an objective element of the offense).

Just as all objective elements must be proven to establish liability, so too must each culpability requirement as to each objective element be proven. Where a required culpability element is not proven, the person is given a defense frequently called a mistake defense, especially where the missing culpability concerns a circumstance element.[6] That the person made a reasonable "mistake" as to the female's age, for example, means that he did not have the culpability of negligence as to the female being underage that some statutes require for statutory rape. Where a person lacks the required culpability as to a required result, in contrast, ordinary language might refer to the case as one of "accident." Where a person has no reason to be aware that his storage of a friend's goods creates a risk to his neighbor's house, he is faultless as to causing damage to the neighbor's house if the goods turn out to be dangerous chemicals that explode because improperly stored. The reasonableness of the person's conduct in causing the "accident" means that the offense's requirement of negligence as to causing damage is not satisfied.

As one can imagine, the process of drafting a criminal code requires thousands of decisions as to the level of culpability that should be required as to each objective element of each offense. Each decision determines the kind of mistake or accident that will provide a defense to the offense. The drafters must determine what minimum level of culpability should be required as to each element of each offense. By what process and under what guiding principles should these decisions be made? Should a person's liability be increased if he or she has a greater culpability than the minimum required?

The culpability requirements study below sought to determine the community's views of the appropriate level of culpability that should be required for various kinds of elements of various kinds of offenses. Subjects were given scenarios containing instances of unconsented-to intercourse, statutory rape, and property damage

---

[5] *Id.* at §2.02(1)&(3).

[6] *Id.* at §2.04(1).

offenses involving damage to a dwelling or to unimproved property. The property damage offenses have a clear result element, while the rape offenses have circumstance elements, lack of consent or minimum age, which are central to liability. Some of the property scenarios focus upon the person's culpability as to causing the harmful result, others on his culpability as to the fact that the property belongs to another.

The six base scenarios—mistake as to causing damage to a house, mistake as to causing damage to unimproved property, mistake as to ownership of the house damaged, mistake as to ownership of the unimproved property damaged, mistake as to lack of consent to intercourse, mistake as to age of the underage partner—were each presented in four variations. In each scenario, the level of culpability of the person's mistake varied—among knowledge, recklessness, negligence, and faultlessness. In this study, unlike some of the others conducted, the respondents were essentially told that the action was knowing, reckless, negligent, or faultless rather than giving them circumstances and hoping that they inferred the proper state of mind. For instance, in the case of property damage where the person was to be faultless as to the property being that of another, the respondents were told that the person was told by his lawyer that the property was his. In the corresponding negligence case, respondents were told that, while the person did not realize that title to the property has not yet come to be his, a reasonable person would have realized this. (Because these matters were specified directly, and because these respondents had so many cases to judge, the respondents were not asked questions about how they perceived the various elements of the case. Research carrying these topics further might give more subtle information about culpability and include the manipulation check questions.)

The liability results for each of these 24 variations are shown in Table 45. The table gives the complete results of the study and is not easy to follow. Therefore, presented are several figures that clarify various aspects of the data.

Within each of the six scenarios, the differences in liability assignments due to the different levels of culpability suggest the general importance of the assessment of culpability in the assignment of criminal liability and punishment. This result emerges very clearly in Figure 46, which graphs liability assignment as a function of the person's level of culpability.

Subjects perceive the four variations of each scenario as presenting distinguishable cases, where liability and punishment increase as the manipulated level of culpability increases. The consistent slopes of the lines graphing the six cases make this very clear. Further, the patterns of liability shown in Figure 46 suggest a special significance in the distinction between recklessness and negligence (that is, between conscious versus inattentive risk taking). Visually this is shown by the fact that the slope of the line connecting the reckless and negligent cases is always more sharp than the slopes of the lines connecting the other cases. This effect on the subjects' liability assignment of the reckless-negligent distinction would seem to support the Model Penal Code's special treatment of recklessness as the normal minimum culpability requirement.[7]

---

[7] *Id.* at §2.02(3).

TABLE 45. } Liability for Mistake/Accident

	(a)	*(b)*	*(c)*	*(d)*
Scenarios: Element of Offense and Actor's Culpability	***Liability***	***% No Liability***	***% No Liability or No Punishment***	***Model Penal Code Result***
1. As to causing damage to house:				
a. Knowing	6.21	0	0	Second degree felony [§220.1(1)(a)]
b. Reckless	5.08	0	10	Third degree felony [§220.1(2)(b)]
c. Negligent	2.22	8	55	Third degree felony[b] [§220.3(a)]
d. Faultless	1.25	30	75	No liability
2. As to causing damage to unimproved property:				
a. Knowing	5.54	0	3	Misdemeanor[a] [§220.3(a)]
b. Reckless	4.31	3	18	Misdemeanor[a] [§220.3(a)]
c. Negligent	1.75	15	65	Misdemeanor[a] [§220.3(a)]
d. Faultless	0.95	38	83	No liability
3. As to house belonging to another:				
a. Knowing	5.77	0	3	Second degree felony [§220.1(1)(a)]
b. Reckless	5.31	0	3	Third degree felony [§220.1(2)(b)]
c. Negligent	3.62	0	28	No liability
d. Faultless	3.26	8	38	No liability
4. As to unimproved property belonging to another:				
a. Knowing	4.92	3	10	Misdemeanor[a] [§220.3(a)]
b. Reckless	4.49	3	13	Misdemeanor[a] [§220.3(d)]
c. Negligent	3.10	3	38	No liability
d. Faultless	2.44	10	50	No liability
5. As to victim's lack of consent in rape:				
a. Knowing	6.60	5	8	First degree felony [§213.1(1)(a)]
b. Reckless	5.55	3	15	First degree felony [§213.1(1)(a)]
c. Negligent	3.82	13	33	No liability
d. Faultless	0.26	78	90	No liability
6. As to victim being underage in statutory rape:				
a. Knowing	5.28	3	8	Third degree felony[c] [§213.3(1)(a)]
b. Reckless	3.97	8	23	Third degree felony [§213.3(1)(a)]
c. Negligent	1.38	33	73	Third degree felony [§213.6(1)]
d. Faultless	0.51	65	88	No liability

Liability Scale: N=No criminal liability, 0=Liability but no punishment, 1=1 day, 2=2 weeks, 3=2 months, 4=6 months, 5=1 year, 6=3 years, 7=7 years, 8=15 years, 9=30 years, 10=life, and 11=death.

[a]Assumes property damage between $100 and $5,000.

[b]Assumes property damage in excess of $5,000.

[c]Assumes that the defendant is at least 18 years old (4 years older than the 14-year-old victim).

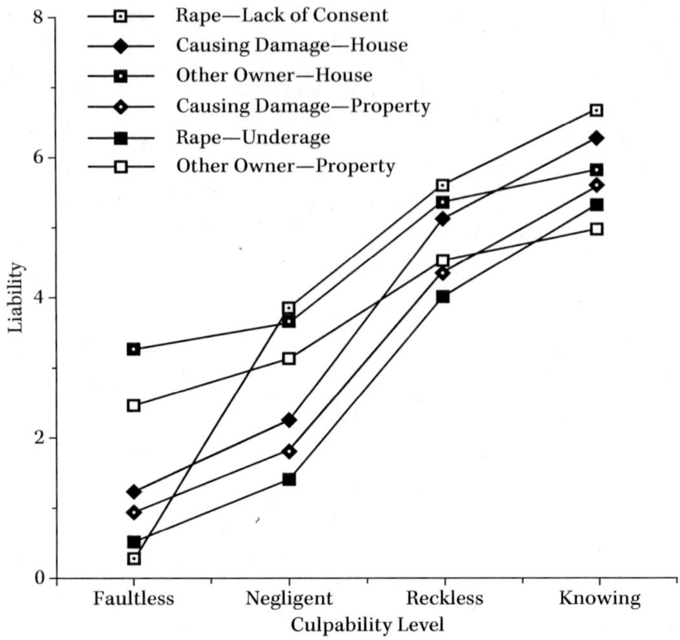

FIGURE 46. Liability as a Function of Culpability Level

However, a further examination of Figure 46 suggests a result that is not always in accord with penal codes. The difference between the average liability assigned by the respondents for reckless and knowing culpability suggests that the higher culpability—knowing—might properly be reflected in an offense definition that grades the knowing violation one grade higher than the reckless violation. (Each unit on the liability scale represents a difference in punishment that commonly is equal to one offense grade.) The Model Penal Code treatment of offenses, shown in column (d) of Table 45, sometimes but not always makes grading distinctions according to the reckless-knowing distinction. In the case of damage to the neighbor's house, knowingly causing the damage is a second degree felony while recklessly causing the damage is only a third degree felony, a grading similar to the ones that the respondents imposed. However, in both the damage to unimproved property and rape cases, in which the Code does not assign a different level of liability to the knowing and reckless commission cases, the respondents would do so. The responses of the subjects, if modeled in the code, would assign a higher degree of liability to the knowing versus reckless commission of all offenses.

In fact, on examination, the Code's differing grading of the culpability levels for the various offenses generates more inconsistencies with the subjects' tendency to have culpability alter grade in all offenses. Look first at the Code's treatment of various levels of culpability as to causing damage, in Table 45, rows (1) and (2). The Code's treatment of knowingly and faultlessly causing damage to a dwelling tracks that of the subjects'. A knowing violation is one grade higher than that for a reckless violation; a faultless violation is exempt from liability (Table 45, row (1).) The Model Penal Code scheme deviates from the subjects' view in that it fails to lower liability for cases of negligent damage. Indeed, it imposes the same degree of liability (third degree felony) for negligent violations as for reckless violations, contradicting its own general tendency to draw the line between reckless and negligent culpability.

The Code's treatment of analogous cases of damage to unimproved property, Table 45, row (2), is also divergent from the subjects' views. As above, a negligent violation is a basis for liability under the Code, while the subjects would considerably reduce the liability of the person in that case. Knowing and reckless violations are not distinguished in the Code; they are treated the same as a negligent violation. They are distinguished by the respondents, as the line in Figure 46 marked "causing damage-property" makes clear.

The Code's scheme also is divergent from the subjects' views in its treatment of mistakes as to ownership, in Table 45, rows (3) and (4). It gives no liability in cases of negligent and faultless mistake as to ownership, where the subjects give liability, albeit low liability, as is shown in Figure 46.

Turning to an examination of the rape cases, presented in Table 45, rows (5) and (6), what can be said about the respondents' perceptions of the two rape scenarios? Refer back to Figure 46, looking at the topmost line representing the lack of consent case. The Code's treatment of mistake as to consent in rape also is divergent in several respects from the views of the respondents. The subjects treat the degree of culpability as a graded consideration, assigning a higher degree of liability as the offense progresses from negligence with respect to consent, through recklessness, through knowing.

In contrast, the Code, as is shown in Table 45, column (d), imposes no liability for a negligent mistake, while the subjects' liability mean, shown in column (a) is 3.82 (5.2 months). The Code does not distinguish reckless and knowing errors, grading both as first degree felonies; the subjects impose greater liability for a knowing error, 6.60 (5.4 years), than for a reckless error, 5.55 (2.2 years).

A more exaggerated form of this difference appears in the liability patterns for statutory rape, the case in which the victim is described as being under the statutory age of consent. The Code treats knowing, reckless, and negligent errors as to the victim's age as the same grade. The subjects make significant distinctions between them all. The majority of subjects, 73 percent, would impose either no liability or no punishment where the person is negligent as to age, as is shown in Table 45, row (6)(c), column (c), but the Code treats this as a third degree felony.

The rape results reveal that the subjects tend toward setting different minimum levels of culpability for the two different cases. In statutory rape, a majority of the subjects impose no punishment on a person who is faultless or negligent as to the victim's age. In rape, in contrast, only faultlessness as to the victim's lack of consent draws no punishment from a majority of subjects; negligence as to lack of consent is no defense in the view of most subjects. This suggests that the subjects perceive the minimum culpability requirements of these two offenses somewhat differently, and intuitively one sees why they make the particular distinctions that they do.

If one were to draft a statutory rape provision using the intuitions contained in the respondents' judgments, one would grade the offense as a continuous function of the degree of culpability of the offender, rather than, as the Code currently does, as a dichotomous function, with negligent and higher degrees of culpability all assigned a third degree felony grade.

Many of the above results can be summarized as follows: the results generally support the Code distinction that draws a sharp line between reckless and negligent commission of an offense. However, and frequently counter to the Code, the respondents also distinguish between knowing and reckless commission and between negligent and faultless commission. They assign differing liabilities, in other words, to all of the different levels of culpability. This is an important result but a somewhat predictable one; it is the result that one would have intuited. But certain of the other results confront us with a data pattern that were not expected (or, at least, did not expect to be so strong in effect as to be evident from the data). If confirmed in further research, it would reveal an important code-community disagreement.

To see evidence of the disagreement, turn back to Figure 46. Specifically, look at the liability for damaging a house and damaging unimproved property. In each of those cases, two culpability elements pertained to the same offense. In the case of a house, refer to the lines Causing Damage—House and Other owner—House in Figure 46. (Recall that the person has some reason to believe that he himself has bought the house.) Then consider property damage by referring back to Causing Damage—Property and Other Owner—Property, again in Figure 46. Notice that the line graphing liability as a function of culpability as to the property belonging to another, is flatter in slope than is the line graphing liability as a function of culpability as to causing damage. What this means is that in each instance, where the culpability as to ownership is varied, the range of liabilities, 5.77 (2.6 years) to 3.26 (3.2 months) for house and 4.92 (11.4 months) to 2.44 (4.4 weeks) for property, is noticeably less than the range of liabilities when the culpability as to damage is varied, 6.21 (3.8 years) to 1.25 (4.9 days) for house and 4.92 (11.4 months) to 0.95 (1 day) for property. This suggests that the person's culpability as to causing damage is a stronger determinant of his liability, in the respondents' minds, than is his culpability as to another's ownership.

This seems to give objective evidence of the somewhat vague feeling shared by many criminal law practitioners and scholars that some objective elements within an offense definition are more important than others in assessing blame. . While both "causing damage" and "property of another," and culpability as to each, are required elements of the damage offenses, culpability as to "causing damage" and culpability as to "property of another" appear to play different roles in the determination of liability and punishment. "Causing damage" appears to be a primary determinant, a core element, while "property of another" appears to be a more collateral element, which establishes a minimum background condition. The implications of this will be discussed further in the summary below.

One last result is worthy of note. Chapter 16 will comment more on the task of the comparative grading of offenses. Note here that the respondents saw the various offenses described to them in this study as differentially serious in nature. The differences in elevation between the lines in Figure 46 illustrate a pattern that makes good intuitive sense. Look simply at the treatment of the various crimes committed knowingly. As one might expect, the rape scenario, where another person is harmed, shows the highest liability, 6.60 (5.4 years) for knowing culpability; followed by the scenario of damage to a dwelling, 6.21 (3.8 years), where people might be endangered. Damage to unimproved property, 5.54 (2 years), and consensual intercourse with a minor, 5.28 (1.6 years), are viewed as slightly less serious offenses.

To summarize, the culpability requirements study sought to determine the community's views of the degree of liability that ought to be assigned to various levels of culpability required for different kinds of elements for three kinds of offenses. Culpability elements of offenses serve two distinct functions: defining the minimum requirements for liability and distinguishing different grades of a single offense. The research results give some insight into how the subjects would have each function performed.

The most interesting finding pertains to the minimum requirements for liability. In setting the minimum requirements for liability, and also in grading offenses, it appears that some culpability elements are considerably more significant than others. For example, in an offense of causing damage to property, a person who is faultless or only negligent as to causing the damage (while knowing it is another's property) receives no punishment from a majority of subjects. Where the person is faultless or negligent as to the property being that of another (while knowing that he is destroying the property), in contrast, a majority would impose punishment. The respondents seem to be suggesting that, at least in the specific case of storing potentially dangerous material, which was the way the elements in these scenarios were manipulated, the person needs to recognize an obligation to assess the danger potential of what is being stored. It is of some concern, but to a lesser degree, that the person figures out who owns adjacent property. A sturdy component of common sense commends itself to the attention here. A person first needs to figure out the damage-causing potential of his or her actions. To whom, exactly, the potential damage might occur is an important but secondary question. Thus, in formal terms, the study suggests that the person's culpability as to the potential for causing damage is more influential on the subjects' decision to impose liability than the person's culpability as to the property being that of another. The same pattern is seen at the high culpability levels; higher culpability as to causing damage increases punishment significantly more than higher culpability as to it being property of another.[8]

This pattern suggests the need to distinguish between elements when defining the minimum requirements for liability. If one were to follow the subjects' intuitions, the minimum culpability as to causing damage may properly be set higher than the

[8] See Table 45, rows (1)–(4), columns (a)–(c).

minimum culpability as to the property belonging to another. Further, differences in levels of culpability as to causing damage should make a larger difference in the liability grading of an offense then culpability as to ownership. This illustrates one of the dangers of a provision like Model Penal Code §2.02(4), which applies a stated culpability term in an offense to all objective elements. It tends to apply the same culpability requirement to both "core" elements—such as causing damage—and "collateral" or "background" elements—such as ownership by another.

But what constitutes a core versus collateral element? The research results suggest that this is not an easy question. The results reveal different patterns of weighing culpability elements, depending on the circumstances of the crime. These are complex considerations that merit further investigation.

With respect to the second function of culpability requirements, to distinguish grades within the same offense (as in homicide), the subjects appear to make significant liability distinctions on this basis across the range of culpability levels. The difference in assigned punishment between a person who is knowing and one who is reckless frequently is greater than what constitutes the difference between offense grades in American criminal codes. Also, the respondents generally distinguish between the other levels of culpability as well; they generally assign increasing levels of liability as the level of culpability rises from negligent, to reckless, to knowing, to purposeful. As suggested, these patterns of liability assignments are significantly different than those provided by the Model Penal Code. First, few offenses in the Code, other than homicide, contain grades dependent upon culpability level. Indeed, most offenses are not defined to have more than a single grade. This may have been an attempt by the Code to preserve the sentencing discretion of judges. The fewer the grades of an offense provided in the Code, the greater the flexibility of the judge to rely upon distinctions of his or her own choosing in imposing sentence. The shift to more articulated sentencing rules in the 30-plus years since the drafting of the Model Penal Code may suggest that it is time to have the Code make more distinctions in grading offenses. Certainly, degrees of an offense based upon the person's level of culpability would provide a refinement that would better mirror the community's liability and punishment judgments. If code drafters want the criminal code to follow community views, it would be useful to do studies of this sort to determine where the community sets the minimum culpability levels for different elements of different offenses and whether increased culpability over this minimum ought to give rise to a higher grade of liability.

B. Culpability Requirements for Complicity

Liability for complicity requires that a person assist another in the commission of an offense. The precise nature of the conduct requirement for assistance is examined in the objective requirements of complicity study reported in chapter 12, section E. In addition to this objective requirement, current doctrine requires that a person have a defined culpable state of mind as to providing such assistance in commission of the offense.

Just as criminal liability is inappropriate for an inadvertent commission of an offense, liability is inappropriate where one inadvertently assists another in the commission of an offense. Thus, the Model Penal Code requires that at the time of assisting the perpetrator, the accomplice must be acting "with the purpose of promoting or facilitating the commission of the offense."[9] A proposal to require "knowledge" rather than "purpose" was rejected by the full membership of the American Law Institute. The requirement of "purpose" was judged preferable and was said to continue the long-standing common law rule.

The phrase "purpose to promote or facilitate the commission of the offense" is ambiguous on an important point, however. Does the very demanding "purpose" requirement apply only to the person's culpable state of mind as to assisting ("promoting or facilitating") the perpetrator's conduct, or does it apply as well to all elements of the substantive offense, such as "purposeful" with respect to the prohibited results of the person's conduct? If it applies to all elements of the substantive offense, the effect is dramatic—it makes complicity very difficult to establish, essentially limiting it to cases where the accomplice wanted not only the offense conduct to occur but also wanted any required results to occur or circumstances to exist. For example, statutory rape typically requires no more than negligence as to the partner being underage. Where a person purposely assists conduct that in fact constitutes statutory rape, can he defend by saying that he only thought it probable (reckless) that she was underage but did not know or did not necessarily want or hope that she was underage? If complicity liability requires purpose as to all offense elements, anything less than purpose as to underage will provide a defense. For another example relating to a result element, the offense of endangerment requires that the perpetrator be at least reckless as to creating a risk of death. Where a person purposely assists conduct that constitutes endangerment (dumping hazardous chemicals near a playground, for example), can he defend by saying that he knew that the conduct he was assisting would create a risk of death but he did not necessarily want it to? If complicity liability requires purpose as to all offense elements, anything less than purpose as to creating the risk of death will provide a defense.

This was the ambiguity at issue in *Etzweiler v. State*,[10] for example, where the defendant was charged as an accomplice to a killing caused by a drunk driver. The defendant clearly had "purposely" assisted his drunk friend to engage in the conduct consisting the offense, driving; he gave his drunken friend the keys to his car. It was not clear, however, that Etzweiler was "purposeful" or even "knowing" as to his conduct creating a risk of death. At most, one might conclude that by giving car

---

[9] Model Penal Code §2.06(3)(a).

[10] *Etzweiler v. State*, 125 N.H. 57, 480 A.2d 870 (N.H. 1984); *see also* State v. Rivera, 27 A.3d 676 (N.H. 2011) (confirming New Hampshire's rule that a person may be held liable as an accomplice for reasonably foreseeable consequences of the defendant's conduct).

keys to his obviously intoxicated friend he was "reckless" as to the resulting death; that is, at the time of giving the keys, he was aware of a substantial risk that a death could result.

The justices of the New Hampshire Supreme Court in *Etzweiler* disagreed over the proper interpretation of the state code's "purpose" requirement for complicity, which was modeled in large part on the Model Penal Code. A majority of the court held that the purpose requirement had the effect of elevating all culpability requirements of the homicide definition to purposeful for the accomplice. Thus, while manslaughter normally requires only recklessness as to causing a death, complicity in manslaughter requires that the accomplice be purposeful as to causing the death (even murder liability requires only knowing as to causing death). Some common law cases came to a similar view that the culpability requirements for complicity in an offense are "elevated" over those of the substantive offense itself. Other common law cases essentially came to the view of the dissenting judges, a view sketched out below.

The dissenting justices in *Etzweiler* concluded that complicity's purpose requirement only requires that the complicit individual be purposeful as to assisting the perpetrator's conduct—that is, purposely giving the friend the car keys with the purpose of allowing him to drive the car. The culpability requirements of the substantive offense—recklessness as to causing death, for manslaughter—are not elevated to purpose for complicity liability. Under the latter view, a person can be an accomplice to manslaughter by purposely assisting another to engage in conduct that the accomplice is aware creates a substantial risk of causing death (i.e., is reckless as to causing death). The Model Penal Code drafters make it relatively clear that they support this "no-elevation" view, at least with respect to result elements as in *Etzweiler*.[11] The complicity culpability study sought to test the subjects' view on the importance to liability of an accomplice's culpability as to assisting and culpability as to the elements of the substantive offense.

The study involved the same core description of an individual who makes his car keys available to an intoxicated friend. The six scenarios presented variations on the *Etzweiler* situation. Two individuals arrive at the plant where they work. Because one friend is intoxicated, the other is driving. The intoxicated friend announces his plan to borrow the car to race home to pick up something he needs for work. The area through which he will drive is crowded with workers arriving for their shift at the plant. In some cases, the nonintoxicated individual is described as sure that the drunk friend will kill people if he drives; in the other cases, only aware of the possibility that the drunk friend might kill people. Thus, the study attempted to make clear that the state of mind of the complicit individual was knowing or reckless as to causing the resulting deaths, an element that it seemed was likely to be an important one to the respondents. The drunk obtains access to the car keys, heads home, and kills two workers just coming to work through the factory gate.

---

[11] *See* Model Penal Code §2.06(4).

The study manipulated the description of the circumstances of the drunk driver's obtaining the car keys of his friend to create the perceptions that the accomplice is either purposeful, knowing, or reckless as to his drunk friend taking his car keys to drive while intoxicated. In the purposeful case, he willingly hands the friend the keys. In the knowing case, he first urges the friend not to drive, then reluctantly hands over the keys. In the reckless case, he refuses his friend but then leaves the keys in a place where his friend can find them, even though it crosses his mind that the friend might take them.

The results of the study are presented in Tables 47 and 48. Table 47 includes the liability assigned to the accomplice. Table 48 presents the respondents' perceptions of the accomplice's and the perpetrator's state of mind with respect to the various elements of the situation.

First let us look at some general aspects of the data patterns. Notice first the commonsense result, tabled in Table 47, column (a), that the liability of the individual who drives while drunk and kills others is high; translated into years, the sentence is from 11 to 14 years. This is as one would expect. The perpetrator, while drunk, is not so drunk that he can't pressure the accomplice to give him the keys, make his way to the car, start it up, and drive off. As column (i) of Table 48 indicates, the respondents see the driver as somewhere between unaware and aware that

TABLE 47. } Liability as Related to Culpability Requirements for Complicity

	(a)	*(b)*	*(c)*	*(d)*	*(e)*	*(f)*
Scenarios	*Driver Liability*	*Accomplice Liability*	*% No Liability (N)*	*% No Liability or No Punishment (N+0)*	*Result Under MPC (& Etzweiler dissent)*	*Result Under "Elevation" View (Etzweiler decision)*
Purposeful as to assisting driving:						
1. Knowing as to causing death	7.76	4.50	8.8	29.4	Murder	No liability
2. Reckless as to causing death	7.65	3.56	8.8	44.1	Manslaughter	No liability
Knowing as to assisting driving:						
3. Knowing as to causing death	7.82	3.56	5.9	38.3	No liability	No liability
4. Reckless as to causing death	7.68	2.74	14.7	50.0	No liability	No liability
Reckless as to assisting driving:						
5. Knowing as to causing death	7.50	1.82	17.6	67.6	No liability	No liability
6. Reckless as to causing death	7.74	1.68	23.5	70.6	No liability	No liability

Liability Scale: N=No criminal liability, 0=Liability but no punishment, 1=1 day, 2=2 weeks, 3=2 months, 4=6 months, 5=1 year, 6=3 years, 7=7 years, 8=15 years, 9=30 years, 10=life, and 11=death.

TABLE 48. } Subjects' Perceptions as to Culpability Requirements for Complicity

Scenarios	(g) *Accomplice's State of Mind as to Driving*	(h) *Accomplice's State of Mind as to Causing Death*	(i) *Perpetrator's State of Mind as to Causing Death*
Purposeful as to assisting driving:			
1. Knowing as to causing death	3.09	2.59	1.29
2. Reckless as to causing death	3.21	1.97	1.26
Knowing as to assisting driving:			
3. Knowing as to causing death	2.82	2.47	1.29
4. Reckless as to causing death	2.59	2.00	1.32
Reckless as to assisting driving:			
5. Knowing as to causing death	2.21	2.24	1.29
6. Reckless as to causing death	2.03	1.91	1.35

State of Mind Scale: 1=negligent, 2=reckless, 3=knowing, and 4=purposeful.

Key to column heads:
(g) State of mind as to driving:

1. The accomplice was unaware of a substantial chance that the driver would drive the car.
2. The accomplice was aware of a substantial chance that the driver would drive the car.
3. The accomplice was practically certain that the driver would drive the car.
4. The accomplice hoped or wanted the driver to drive the car.

(h) State of mind as to causing death:

1. The accomplice was unaware of a substantial chance that the driver would kill someone.
2. The accomplice was aware of a substantial chance that the driver would kill someone.
3. The accomplice was practically certain that the driver would kill someone.
4. The accomplice hoped or wanted the driver to kill someone.

(i) Perpetrator's state of mind as to causing death:

1. The driver was unaware of a substantial chance that he would kill someone.
2. The driver was aware of a substantial chance that he would kill someone.
3. The driver was practically certain that he would kill someone.
4. The driver hoped or wanted to kill someone.

his driving has a substantial chance of killing somebody. Second, notice that the driver's liability is constant through all scenarios; it is not affected by variations in the state of mind of the accomplice, and again this is as one would expect. Third, note that in each instance, the liability of the accomplice, shown in column (b), is significantly less than that for the perpetrator. This reiterates the pattern where accomplices are given a significant discount in liability, as compared to the perpetrator. The doctrine, remember, holds an accomplice liable at the same grade as the principal.

Examine next the questions that enable us to see how the respondents perceive the accomplice's state of mind in the different scenarios. These are tabled in columns (g) and (h). Respondents give their answers on a four-point scale, with four indicating a rating of "purposeful" and three a rating of "knowing." (See the key to Table 48 for the full description of the questions.) Look first at the numbers tabled in column (g) for the first two cases, which are found in row (1) and (2). Respondents see the accomplice as closer to knowing (3.09 and 3.21, with 3 equals knowing) than to purposeful as to having the friend drive the car, where it was hoped that the accomplice would be perceived as purposeful, and slightly below knowing in the knowing scenarios of rows (3) and (4) (2.82 and 2.59). The reckless conditions, rows (5) and (6), are perceived about as intended (2.21 and 2.03, with 2 equals reckless).

Examine next the question concerning the accomplice's state of mind with respect to the killing that eventuated, column (h); there one sees a similar effect. The reckless scenarios, rows (2),(4), and (6) are perceived roughly as expected, 1.97, 2.00, and 1.91 respectively, where 2 equals reckless. The knowing scenarios are perceived at an intermediate state between knowing and reckless (2.59, 2.47, and 2.24). This last result is mildly troublesome; it means that the dimension of variation that was designed to be most important, which was the state of mind with respect to the killing, is not perceived by the subjects as varying across the full range that was expected. Keep this in mind as we interpret the data; found differences in liability scores are likely to be of a lesser magnitude that they might be if the full range of culpability had been achieved on both the elements of culpability.

As can be seen from the graph of the results shown in Figure 49, the punishment assigned to the accomplice is affected by his state of mind, both with respect to the degree of deliberateness that he shows in giving his friend the car keys when he knows it is his friend's intention to drive, and what he knows about the risk that driving creates. The line labeled "knowing" is the line graphing the results for the accomplice who knows that if the drunk friend drives, people will be killed; the

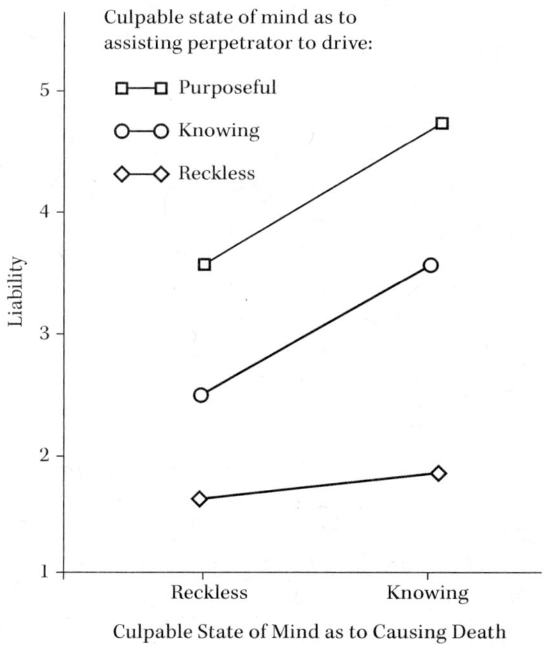

FIGURE 49. Liability as a Function of Accomplice's Culpability as to Resulting Death

"reckless" line graphs the results for the accomplice who thinks people might be killed but disregards that risk. Statistical analyses confirm what the figure reveals: First, the accomplice is judged more liable if his conduct in turning over the keys is purposeful with respect to assisting his friend's driving (although recall that the respondents see it as intermediate between purposeful and knowing), less liable if his action is knowing as to assisting, and least liable if his conduct is simply reckless in that respect. Second, the accomplice is held more liable if he is knowing (although recall that the respondents see it as intermediate between knowing and reckless) as opposed to only reckless with respect to the risk of killing others. The figure hints that the accomplice's state of mind with respect to risk of killing another becomes less important when he is only reckless with respect to giving the perpetrator access to the car keys, but the interaction term of the analysis of variance, which tests the reliability of that difference, does not reach significance. Further research might examine this possibility.

At the higher levels of culpability with respect to assisting, the magnitude of the two effects looks about the same. Knowing versus only reckless assistance as to the death causes a difference of about one grade, and the state of mind with respect to assisting the perpetrator also causes a difference of about one grade. Recall that the prediction about the relative magnitude of these two effects; culpability with respect to causing death, ignored in the MPC, would be the more major determinant of liability. But recall also that there was a possible reason why this might not show up in the results: the manipulation of culpability with respect to causing a death was not entirely successful, leading to a range restriction on that dimension. Given the significant grade difference that derives from only a slight difference in perceptions of culpability as to result, one might speculate that the effect of culpability as to death is indeed the strong influence that was predicted. But a more complete test of this conclusion will have to await further research.

To summarize, first, and as we have seen before, the respondents are making essentially continuous judgments when the code makes dichotomous ones. Next, the subjects can and do see the difference between the two culpability issues that this study presented to them, and these two dimensions of culpability make a difference in their liability assignment. This suggests that both of these issues should be addressed within the legal provisions dealing with complicity liability.

Next, consider how the results bear on the various formulations of the doctrine in *Etzweiler*. To do this, recall the discussion of the interpretation of the requirement of "purposefulness." In one view, the "elevation" view, the accomplice needs to be purposeful as to bringing about the prohibited result; in this case the accomplice would need to be purposeful in bringing about the eventual outcome of death. As column (h) shows, not even the highest three cases, (1), (3), and (5), meet this criterion, and yet significant liability is assigned to the accomplice in each of those three cases. Obviously the respondents do not hold the interpretation that purposefulness with regard to causing death is essential for liability. In fact, they do not even require knowledge for liability; they assign significant although reduced criminal liability to an accomplice who is merely reckless, not even knowing, with respect to the death that eventuated. (See the bottom line of Figure 49.) However, notice also that the accomplice's state of mind about the death, when it is reduced from knowing to reckless, does cause respondents to assign considerably less punishment. (This is shown by the difference between the two lines of the figure.)

The subjects' disagreement with the "elevation" view is shown starkly in Table 47; that view would assign liability in none of the cases presented to subjects, column (f), yet the subjects assign liability in all cases. Subjects are assigning punishments to accomplices who are knowing or even only reckless with respect to the criminal outcome in instances in which the elevation view would assign no liability. From the point of view of the respondents, the culpability requirement as to result should not be elevated to purposeful as the *Etzweiler* majority did and others would require; instead the offense should be graded according to the degree of culpability that the person shows.

Even the non-"elevation" view of the Model Penal Code, shown in column (e), that the accomplice need merely to be purposeful with respect to assisting the conduct that in fact causes the death, does not entirely accord with the subjects' judgments. Accomplices who knowingly rather than purposefully commit the act of assistance draw punishment, rows (3) and (4) of the table, sentences corresponding to more than 4 months and 6 weeks, respectively. Accomplices who merely recklessly assist draw reduced but still some sentences from the respondents, rows (5) and (6) of the table, sentences of about 11 days and 9 days, respectively.[12]

Remember that the respondents do not see the "purposeful" cases as being completely purposeful. Yet, even though there was not full success in producing cases that the subjects read as creating accomplices who are purposeful with respect to causing death, that variable makes a considerable difference in the liabilities that the subjects assign. This suggests that the variable might emerge as even more determinative of liability assignments in future studies. If this proves to be the case, then it would strengthen the argument for recognizing culpability as to causing death as the primary determinant of liability.

From the point of view of the respondents, the Code is wrong to set purpose as the minimum requirement for culpability as to assisting. The results support a tentative draft proposal that was voted down by the full Institute that would have required only knowing as the minimum requirement for assisting. Further, even if only knowing was required as to assisting, the Code would differ from the respondents' judgments because it would exclude liability in cases of recklessness as to assisting. Finally, the respondents would also view the Code deficient, as a grading matter, because it fails to adjust grade according to culpability level.

---

[12] However, and interestingly, notice that, as shown in column (d) of Table 47, around 50 percent of the respondents would assign the "liability but no punishment" verdict in these cases. Again, they use this particular verdict, which condemns conduct but does not incarcerate individuals, for the person who recklessly leaves car keys around for a drunken friend to take.

So the subjects assign liability, although reduced liability, in knowing and reckless cases of assistance, and the Code does not. What might explain this difference? One rather speculative possibility exists. The legal code seems to begin by taking for granted that the central question is whether the accomplice should be regarded as committing the same offense as that with which the perpetrator is charged. In other words, is the crime committed by the "assister" the same as the crime committed by the perpetrator? Not surprisingly, the Code sets quite high standards for a "yes" answer to that question. Judging by the reduced liability ratings that they give, the subjects do not ask themselves the same question. They do not ask, in the present case, "Is the accomplice guilty of manslaughter?" They instead express the view that an individual who contributes to the commission of a crime by another deserves some punishment. The more purposeful that contribution, both in terms of facilitating the actions of the perpetrator and being aware of the perpetrator's criminal purposes, the higher the liability incurred. But, even when the accomplice is merely reckless in his or her contributions to the offense, some liability is incurred, although eventually it may result in nothing more than a condemnation rather than incarceration.

There are some hints that legal code drafters have recognized this point. Some states have created an offense called "criminal facilitation" that punishes at a lower level than is assigned to the perpetrator of the offense, but also requires less in the way of culpability. This would approximate the liability pattern assigned by the respondents.

C. Voluntary Intoxication

When a person voluntarily becomes intoxicated and commits an offense both in that state and as a result of it, the assignment of liability is complicated by two competing factors. On one hand, because of his intoxicated state, the person may not be aware of the nature or consequences of his conduct. For example, his conduct may create a risk of causing another's death, but because of his intoxication he is unaware of the danger. This absence of awareness of risk normally would bar liability for reckless homicide (manslaughter) because recklessness requires such awareness. The first study in this chapter confirms the importance of such culpability requirements to a finding of blameworthiness. On the other hand, that the person intoxicated himself voluntarily makes it less clear that he should qualify for mitigation; many would say that he should not benefit from a dysfunction that he himself causes. Obviously the issue is a complicated one.

Current criminal law doctrine typically responds to this dilemma with the following rule: if a person is culpable as to becoming intoxicated, he will be treated, for the purposes of assessing liability, as if he were aware of a risk (i.e., is reckless as to an offense element) even though, because of his intoxication, he in fact is not aware of the risk. A fixed minimum requirement of culpability as to becoming intoxicated (negligence, in the Model Penal Code §2.08(5)(b)) thus establishes whether a person falls under the rule that imputes awareness of risk (recklessness) to the person. This means, for example, that a person who negligently becomes intoxicated and thereafter kills another with no culpability as to the killing due to his intoxication will be held liable for reckless homicide (manslaughter) under the Model Penal Code.

Given this approach by current law, the primary focus of inquiry in investigations and trials is on whether the person has the minimum required culpability as to becoming intoxicated. A higher culpability as to becoming intoxicated—recklessly, knowingly, or purposely—does not increase the person's liability. Nor do different levels of a person's pre-intoxication culpability as to committing the offense have a bearing on his liability. In concrete terms, this means a person may be only negligent as to becoming intoxicated, but that the law will impute recklessness to him or her, even recklessness as to causing death. The liability here may seem more than is deserved.

At the same time, an individual who for some reason desires to harm another, gets intoxicated and does so, is given the same liability treatment as an individual with no desire to harm another, but who gets intoxicated and does so. This seems counterintuitive; an individual who has some reason to know that he might be violent when intoxicated would seem to have more reason to avoid getting intoxicated, and perhaps to warrant more condemnation if he does get intoxicated and commit the crime.

The voluntary intoxication study sought to test the community's support for the rule that, as long as the minimum of negligence as to becoming intoxicated is met, a fixed level of culpability, that of recklessness, will be imputed to a person who lacks a culpable state of mind because of voluntary intoxication. The study also sought to test whether some instances exist in which the respondents judge that the level of culpability imputed under the rule should be higher or lower than the recklessness that present law provides. Specifically, the study examined variations on the example above, in which before becoming intoxicated individuals have various levels of culpability as to causing another's death while intoxicated.

It was speculated that a person's pre-intoxication level of culpability as to the offense elements (causing another's death) would be seen as properly influencing the intoxicated offender's liability. That is, as a person's pre-intoxication culpability as to the offense increases, so too would the degree of liability assigned to him. A person who has no reason to think that he might cause a death while intoxicated (this is where the conditions are labeled "faultless as to causing a death") would be given less liability than a person who becomes intoxicated while aware of a risk that he might cause a death while intoxicated (reckless), who in turn would be given less liability than a person who becomes intoxicated wanting and hoping to cause a death (purposeful). In commonsense terms, a person who is aware that he becomes violent when drunk ought to be held to higher liability than one who is not.

Current doctrine does not take account of a person's pre-intoxication culpability as to causing harm; it focuses only upon the pre-intoxication culpability as to becoming intoxicated and upon the culpability as to the offense elements at the time of the conduct constituting the offense. This is odd; it was speculated that a person's pre-intoxication culpability as to the offense would have greatest effect on liability and that culpability as to becoming intoxicated would have less effect and further, that the latter probably would not operate simply as the minimum level requirement that current doctrine gives it.

The study presented subjects with two control scenarios containing cases of a purposeful and a reckless un-intoxicated killing, which would be murder and manslaughter, respectively, under current law. It then presented nine test cases that varied the person's culpability as to becoming intoxicated (pre-intoxication, obviously) and the person's pre-intoxication culpability as to causing a death while intoxicated. In each scenario, the person is described as sufficiently intoxicated so that he lacks awareness of the consequences of his conduct at the time of the killing. He is at the time of the killing, therefore, only negligent with respect to the killing but the legal codes will impute to him recklessness as to causing the death. Thus the code treatment of all of these cases is alike—manslaughter.

A few comments on the scenarios will be useful. The core of the scenario described an individual who is angry with his roommate for attracting the affections of his girlfriend. In the control murder scenario, included to determine what liability the respondents would assign to an act of murder involving no intoxication, the perpetrator returns home and beats the roommate, who later dies from the beating. The liability assigned here is 9.54, between a 30-year sentence and life imprisonment. In the control reckless killing scenario, he plans only to severely beat his roommate but not kill him. He beats him, this time with a lead pipe about the head, and the roommate later dies from the beating. Again, no intoxication is involved. The liability assigned here is, on the average, 30 years in prison: high compared to some of the other cases reported. It is almost certainly high because beating another individual with a lead pipe about the head is an action that is highly likely to cause death. In the comparisons below, it is well to remember that the sentence assigned this manslaughter is relatively high. In future research it would be worthwhile to create a reckless killing case that involves an act that is less certain to bring about death.

A closer description of the various noncontrol scenarios is in order here. When the scenarios involved a pre-intoxication purpose to kill, the person plans to kill his roommate and gets drunk while waiting to do so. In the pre-intoxication reckless killing scenarios, he plans only to severely beat his roommate. In the faultless killing scenarios, he is angry with his roommate but plans no assault on him and does not kill the roommate; instead he kills an individual with whom he is drinking. As for his culpability as to becoming intoxicated, in the scenarios presenting purposeful intoxication, he drinks in order to get intoxicated. In both the reckless and negligent conditions he is taking medication for a back condition. In the reckless scenario, he thinks that alcohol might interact with his medication to make him severely intoxicated, but he drinks anyway. In the negligent condition, he never reads the warning label on his medication and is unaware of any possibility that the medication will react with alcohol to produce severe intoxication, although the warning label clearly states this. In both scenarios, when the person drinks, the medication interacts with the alcohol and he gets very drunk, where the alcohol alone would not have produced such an effect.

Before examining the liability results, let us examine how the respondents actually perceive the various kinds of culpability that were intended. Notice first the three farthest right-hand columns of Table 50, (d), (e), and (f). These tell us how

TABLE 50. } Liability for Voluntary Intoxication

	(a)	*(b)*	*(c)*	*(d)*	*(e)*	*(f)*
Scenarios	*Liability*	*% No Liability (N)*	*% No Liability or No Punishment (N+0)*	*Culpability as to Intoxication—Pre-intoxication*	*Culpability as to Killing—Pre-intoxication*	*Culpability as to Killing at Time of Killing*
Controls:						
1. Purposeful killing	9.54	0	0			1.71
2. Reckless killing	9.02	0	0			3.14
Pre-intoxication purposeful killing:						
3. Purposeful intoxication	9.89	0	0	1.59	1.07	1.83
4. Reckless intoxication	9.78	0	0	2.37	1.37	1.96
5. Negligent intoxication	9.46	0	2	3.26	1.28	2.17
Pre-intoxication reckless killing:						
6. Purposeful intoxication	8.82	0	0	1.80	3.37	3.52
7. Reckless intoxication	8.56	0	0	2.44	3.76	3.67
8. Negligent intoxication	8.37	0	0	3.61	3.85	4.07
Pre-intoxication faultless killing:						
9. Purposeful intoxication	8.38	0	2	1.65	4.29	3.80
10. Reckless intoxication	8.02	0	4	2.50	4.39	3.80
11. Negligent intoxication	7.89	0	7	3.57	4.52	3.91

Liability Scale: N=No criminal liability, 0=Liability but no punishment, 1=1 day, 2=2 weeks, 3=2 months, 4=6 months, 5=1 year, 6=3 years, 7=7 years, 8=15 years, 9=30 years, 10=life, and 11=death.

Key to column heads:
(d) Culpability as to intoxication, pre-intoxication. Before becoming intoxicated, the actor:

1 = wanted to become intoxicated.
2 = was practically certain that he would become intoxicated.
3 = was aware of a substantial risk of becoming intoxicated and most people would have been aware of the risk.
4 = was not aware of a substantial risk of becoming intoxicated but most people would have been aware of the risk.
5 = was not aware of a substantial risk of becoming intoxicated and most people would not have been aware of the risk.

the subjects perceive the various kinds of culpability that were thought to be relevant to their judgments. Column (d) tables the answers to the question concerning how culpable the individual is as to getting intoxicated; that is, how deliberately he goes about getting drunk. The element of the story that was included about getting intoxicated had the desired effect to some extent. When the individual was described as purposefully setting about getting drunk, the subjects see this as more purposeful than the individual who only recklessly sets about getting drunk. Those who negligently get drunk are seen as even less purposeful than those who recklessly set about getting drunk. However, the differences are not as extreme as one would expect. In the cases designed to be purposeful, for instance, the subjects tended to see as somewhere between purposefully and knowingly getting drunk (the average is 1.68, where 1 equals purposeful and 2 equals "practically certain he would become intoxicated").

In column (e), the subjects' ratings of the degree to which they see the perpetrator's culpability as to the killing as purposeful can be seen. As expected, in the story in which the perpetrator is described as having formed a plan to kill the other, the perpetrator is always seen as planning the killing, but this is less so when he only plans to beat the other (reckless), and not at all when the scenario describes him as having no intention of killing another. The right-hand column, column (f), tables the degree to which the subjects see the perpetrator as purposeful in killing the roommate at the time that of the killing. The results indicate that subjects see differences in intentionality here. The results would have been simpler if there had been a stable perception of purpose. This creates a complexity that will be discussed later.

Examining next the data on liability assignments from the various experimental conditions, shown in column (a) of Table 50, one notices first that all of the assignments of liability are consistently high; 7.89, the lowest sentence translates to a sentence of 14.2 years. The generally high scores reflect the propensity of people to incarcerate someone who beats another over the head with a lead pipe.

Next, examine the differences in liability judgments caused by the variations in the different kinds of culpability, a task facilitated by examination of Figures 51 and 52. The differences between the liability assigned to the various cases that differed with respect to the purposefulness of causing the death before becoming intoxicated are statistically significant, suggesting that the subjects see a person's pre-intoxication culpability as to causing a death as a significant and important determinant of liability. The importance of the differences that pre-intoxication culpability makes is shown visually in Figure 51.

Also confirming this is the fact that liabilities assigned in the reckless and faultless cases of pre-intoxication culpability are statistically and significantly lower than the results in the control murder scenario, while the results in the purposeful case are not. (These numbers are pooled across the three levels of purposefulness with respect to intoxication). This suggests that the subjects see the cases of pre-intoxication purpose as similar to murder but pre-intoxication recklessness or faultlessness as less serious than murder. Suggesting a similar conclusion is the fact

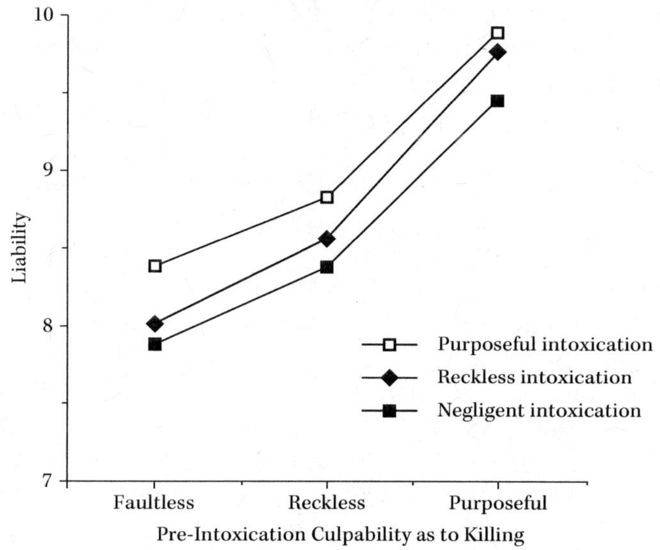

FIGURE 51. Liability as a Function of Pre-Intoxication Culpability as to Killing

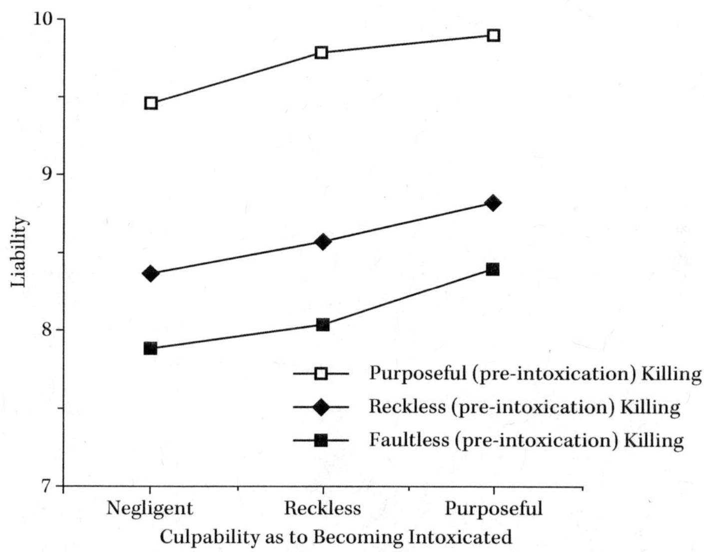

FIGURE 52. Liability as a Function of Pre-Intoxication Culpability as to Becoming Intoxicated

that the liability assigned to the person who plans to kill the other and then purposefully gets drunk while waiting to do so are statistically significantly higher than the results for the manslaughter control; two of the three liability assignments in the reckless case are not statistically different from the manslaughter control; all of the liability assignments in the faultless cases are statistically significantly lower than the manslaughter control.

All this suggests that the subjects see a pre-intoxication purpose to kill another, followed by a deliberate attempt to get drunk, followed by killing the other, as more serious than manslaughter; they see pre-intoxication recklessness as similar to manslaughter; and they see pre-intoxication faultless as less serious than manslaughter. In sum, a person's pre-intoxication culpability as to causing death is not only a highly influential determinant of liability but, indeed, is viewed by the subjects as being similar in effect to a person's culpability as to causing death at the time of the offense in the non-intoxication (control) cases.

The liabilities assigned in the "faultless" killing scenarios, which are graphed as the "faultless killing" line of Figure 52, might strike the reader as high. But consider the facts. In those variants of the scenario the person, upset with his roommate, goes out with friends and drinks. One of the friends assists him home, and the person "loses control and starts striking [the friend] with a lead pipe. [The friend] later dies from the beating." The preexisting condition of anger is likely to affect the subjects' judgments here: one should not drink when in a hostile state. Also, and again, those who beat people about the head with a lead pipe are persons whom one would want to incarcerate. Still, the person who is nonnegligent (i.e., faultless) as to causing a death before his intoxication is given less liability than the manslaughter case; the average sentence is about 20 years. However, it is still a substantial amount.

Recall that the legal codes place considerable emphasis on the person's culpability for getting intoxicated. What are the subjects' judgments about that dimension of variation? They were told that the perpetrator, awaiting the return of his roommate, becomes intoxicated either deliberately or recklessly, or he drinks and is unaware that it will interact with the medication he is taking, and so becomes drunk negligently. As Figure 52 shows, this makes a difference in the liability judgments of the respondents in the way that one would expect, but the difference is of a lesser magnitude than the difference caused by the pre-intoxication culpability as to the killing, a fact that is visually revealed by the flatter slopes of the lines in Figure 52. Look again at Figure 51, which graphs the person's liability as a function of the degree of culpability represented in his pre-intoxication plans to kill another. Obviously, as the steepness of the slopes of the lines suggests, pre-intoxication culpability is a greater determinant of the respondents' assignment of liability than is culpability as to getting intoxicated.

Still, the statistically reliable effect for culpability as to getting intoxicated suggests that the subjects see a person's level of culpability as to becoming intoxicated as a small but relevant factor in determining the person's liability for a death caused during the intoxication. The subjects do perceive that the person's intoxication comes about purposefully, recklessly, or negligently as their responses in column (d) of Table 50 indicates. They moderate their sentences slightly, depending on the level of this culpability, but are not much moved by these distinctions.

This minimal adjustment of sentences is still worth noting, given that the subjects do not see the person's culpability as to being intoxicated in the various conditions as differently as has been hoped. Examine the ratings of the cases in which it was expected that the subjects would perceive the person as negligent with respect to getting drunk, the cases in which the medication he took for back problems interacted with the alcohol to cause the drunkenness. Instead of negligence, the subjects saw the person as reckless, perhaps reasoning that anyone who is taking medications must be aware of at least a risk of serious intoxication through interaction of medication and alcohol. These are the cases shown in rows (5), (8), and (11); the average culpability as to intoxication rating is 3.48, meaning that he is seen as between being aware of the risk and not aware, but most persons would be aware of the risk.

Even though range restricted, the alteration of liability judgments caused by the person's level of culpability for getting intoxicated is inconsistent with the doctrine's treatment of a person's culpability as to becoming intoxicated as a simple "trigger," a minimum requirement, rather than as a liability factor. It is true that the legal code would impose similar liability for manslaughter in all of the scenarios given that all of the actors are at least negligent with respect to becoming intoxicated, while the subjects grade the punishment as a close function of the specifics of the circumstances. In a broader sense, however, the results generally fit with the code's rule. All of the persons are at least negligent with respect to getting intoxicated, and all are assigned sentences within one grade of that assigned to the individual in the control scenario who commits manslaughter. The generally high level of liability assigned to all appears to support the doctrine's selection of negligence (rather than recklessness, for example) as the trigger point for the attribution of liability equivalent to manslaughter.

Concerns that negligence as to becoming intoxicated might be too low a level on which to impose liability cannot be perfectly tested in the study since the respondents see the person who was intended to be negligent as about midway between negligent and reckless, as shown in Table 50, column (d), rows (5), (8), and (11). Still, they impose significant liability even on a person they see as near negligent, who lacks awareness of the consequences of his conduct at the time of the killing. This suggests that negligence is not seen by the respondents as too low a level to set as a requirement for liability.

This discussion signaled previously that something about the subjects' perceptions of the culpability of the person as to causing death at the time of the killing needs to be said, and it turns to that topic now. Returning to the table of results, notice the data on the culpability of the person as to causing death at the time of the killing, column (f). An interesting set of attributions emerge for those persons, rows (3), (4), and (5), who had previously planned to kill their roommates and then get intoxicated for whatever reason. Note that the average score for culpability at the time of the killing for these persons hovers around 2, meaning that the respondents see them as knowing with respect to killing their roommate at the time of the killing, even though they were described as so drunk that "at this point [he] could barely stand. His thought processes and vision are severely impaired." Although it was expected that the subjects would see this individual as less aware of the consequences of his actions, and thus less culpable as to causing death at the time of the killing, what the respondents may be suggesting with their high ratings of purposefulness makes psychological sense: if I plan to kill somebody, and then get drunk, my intent is preserved almost no matter how much the drink impairs my motor, thought, and perceptual systems. We see people as able to cling to their central intents under these conditions, and we assign punishments that are as high as when they commit the act without drinking. Future research will need to determine whether it is possible to separate these two kinds of culpability in the minds of perceivers.

To summarize, in the subjects' view, the factor that is highly determinative of liability is the person's pre-intoxication culpability as to committing the offense. A person who becomes intoxicated—purposefully, recklessly, or negligently—and at the time of becoming intoxicated is purposeful as to causing death, is treated by the subjects as a murderer and, as mentioned above, is seen as having a highly culpable state of mind as to the killing at the time he causes the death. A person who is reckless as to whether he will cause a death as shown by his plans to severely beat another individual, becomes intoxicated either purposefully, recklessly, or negligently, and while intoxicated beats and kills the other, is assigned liability similar to one committing reckless homicide (manslaughter). In the faultless cases, the person, upset because his roommate stole his girlfriend, drinks with friends and beats and kills the friend who helps him home. He too receives quite high sentences, although ones that are diminished from the reckless and purposeful cases.

These results suggest that there are occasional differences between the respondent's moral intuitions and most codes, but that these differences are not as great as in some other cases that have been considered. Certainly the codes' positions are consistent with the subjects' view in the cases where a person culpably intoxicates himself and, before his intoxication, has no purpose as to causing another's death. He is treated as liable for manslaughter by most codes and nearly so by the subjects.

The major difference between the code and community arises in the consideration of the person's pre-intoxication degree of culpability as to causing death. This makes a great deal of difference to the respondents and none in the codes. For instance, when a person is purposeful as to causing death before he becomes intoxicated, the subjects would impose liability for murder while the codes' voluntary intoxication provision imposes liability only for manslaughter. That is, the codes, counterintuitively, do not discriminate the case of the individual who is purposeful about killing another beforehand, and then gets drunk and kills from the individual who has no such pre-intoxication purpose. But, as has been suggested elsewhere, the codes do not prevent a prosecutor from using as the basis for homicide liability the person's conduct in becoming intoxicated and his culpable state of mind as to causing death at that time.[13] Such a theory of prosecution would produce the murder liability that the subjects impose.

---

[13] Paul H. Robinson, *Causing the Conditions of One's Own Defense: A Study in the Limits of Theory in Criminal Law Doctrine*, 71 Va. L. Rev. 1 (1985).

Higher culpability than negligence as to becoming intoxicated generally has some but not a major effect in increasing the liability assigned by the subjects, and is given no such effect in the legal codes. Apparently culpability as to getting intoxicated is only slightly a determinant of degree of liability but serves mainly to provide a fixed minimum requirement for liability. Codes could be altered to give a slightly higher degree of liability for greater culpability in becoming intoxicated, or this factor could be taken into account as a factor in sentencing.

D. Individualization of the Objective Standard of Negligence

The Model Penal Code's culpability distinctions—distinguishing among being purposeful, knowing, reckless, and negligent as to causing a result or as to the existence of a circumstance—have been confirmed by several studies as reflecting decreasing levels of blameworthiness as perceived by the respondents. All other things being equal, as the level of a person's culpability decreases, so too does the level of assigned liability. The higher culpability levels of purposeful, knowing, and to a lesser extent reckless focus primarily on the person's conscious state of mind as to causing the harm. The person may desire, know of or risk the harm respectively. The lowest level of culpability, negligence (and recklessness to a lesser extent), relies not upon a person's conscious wrongdoing but rather upon a person's need to pay adequate attention to whether his conduct creates an unacceptable risk of harm. This means that judgments about a person's negligence must involve a different sort of consideration than judgments of purposeful or knowing harm doing; such judgments must consider what a person "should" have known or reasoned out. A person parking a car on a hill should think of the possibility of the car overcoming its brakes and rolling downhill; a person shooting at a deer in a backyard should realize that the bullet could hit something other than the deer.

In these negligence cases, where the person may have no consciousness of the circumstances or consequences that make his or her conduct criminal, the law assesses the person's blameworthiness by comparing his or her attention (or inattention) to that of a "reasonable" or "prudent" individual in the same circumstances. The reasonable, prudent individual knows that cars roll and bullets carry. It is for this reason that, within legal circles, negligence is said to be based on an objective standard, rather than the subjective inquiries into this particular person's exact state of mind that is characteristic of inquiry into higher culpability levels.

Thus, a person's unawareness of the risks of harm his action creates is culpable if the "reasonable person" would have been aware of those risks. Obviously, the phrase reasonable person does not give a precise standard. Rather, it provides a jury or judge with a mechanism for thinking about whether the person is blameworthy. The reasonable person is not the average person, statistically. Rather, it necessarily represents a composite of those traits that the community sees as making up a person who is perceived as reasonable. That is, it embodies the community's judgment of how the prototypical person can properly be expected to behave, not necessarily a prediction of how the average person actually would behave, an inquiry that would leave the standard of care hostage to the percentage of sociopaths in the community. Nor is the reasonable person standard the same for every person and all situations. Modern criminal codes ask a jury to imagine a reasonable person in the actor's situation. Would the reasonable person have been unaware of the risk, as the person was? More in a moment on what kinds of circumstances and characteristics are taken into account in putting the reasonable person "in the actor's situation."

The judgments of improper risk taking can be relatively refined. For example, in the case of driving, some driving may be negligent while other driving is not. A person may well drive in a manner that creates a greater risk than is acceptable. Even if the driver is not conscious of the unjustified risk he is creating—he did not look at his speedometer to see his speed and did not notice the "school zone" signs and the children just getting out of school—he nonetheless may be blamed for his inattentiveness to the risk he creates. A reasonably careful driver would have been aware of the risk; this driver should have been aware. His failure to do so is judged to be blameworthy and an adequate basis for criminal liability.

The criminal and civil aspects of the legal system divide the responsibility for the punishment of negligence in an interesting way. Not every deviation from the reasonable person standard is sufficiently condemnable to merit criminal liability. Unlike civil liability, where the issue is who among the parties should suffer the loss that has occurred, criminal liability is not appropriate simply because a harm has occurred, and the defendant caused it by conduct that was not entirely reasonable. Criminal negligence requires a sufficient degree of unreasonableness to merit condemnation. Thus, the Model Penal Code requires proof that the person's risk taking is a "gross deviation" from the standard of care of a reasonable person. Therefore, the criminal justice system, which is set into action by representatives of society rather than the injured party, and which has at its disposal society's most severe penalties, deals with those cases of negligence in which the negligent action is grossly out of line with societal standards. Less-flagrant cases can be pursued within the civil justice system, in which the penalties normally involve financial recompense for the damages done.

These aspects of criminal negligence are relatively well accepted and clearly expressed in the statutes and cases. One final aspect is more problematic. Early legal tests defined the negligence standard in purely objective terms, or so it was thought. The particular characteristics of the person—whether he or she was unusually stupid or distracted—were irrelevant. But there has also been a tradition of uneasiness with the absolute application of this standard; to many commentators it seems to be unrealistic and unfair to some violators. A person with mental retardation or a physical handicap, for example, presents a relatively obvious case of one who cannot meet a fixed objective standard that the vast majority of persons can meet. To impose criminal liability on such persons when it is beyond their ability to meet the objective standard is to violate the primary principle that criminal liability ought to be imposed only where the person is blameworthy for the violation. One cannot be condemned for failing to do something that one is incapable of doing.

In response to this very fundamental problem, some modern codes seek to partially individualize the objective reasonable person standard.[14] The person is held to the standard of a reasonable person possessing attributes modified to reflect some attributes of the defendant that may make it difficult for him to meet the objective standard. Thus, the mentally handicapped person, judged under the standard of the reasonable person similarly handicapped, would not be held liable for failing to perceive a risk that a person with such a mental handicap could not reasonably have been expected to perceive in the same circumstances. Yet, the handicapped individual might be held liable, despite his handicap, for a failure to perceive very obvious and serious risks that someone like him could be expected to perceive and avoid.

The weakness in this policy lies in the difficulty of determining which characteristics ought to be recognized as potentially altering the reasonable person standard. Mental retardation might be an easy and obvious reason to reduce our expectations of a person, but what of the parent upset over recent news of a child's death? Should our expectations be adjusted for a person's age, gender, cultural background, religious beliefs, genetic makeup? At some point, individualization of the objective standard runs the danger of rendering it a subjective standard that every person will meet because we have so individuated the reasonable person as to make him or her identical to the specific individual. Even a callous ego maniac will be judged nonnegligent if his failure to perceive risks to others is judged by the standard of an equally callous and ego-maniacal reasonable person. Even more complicated considerations also arise. For example, if we are to recognize factors that lower our legal expectations, should we similarly recognize factors that raise our expectations? Should smarter, stronger, more coordinated people be held to a higher standard because, with the same effort, they can do better than the average person?

A similar challenge arises in judging a person's recklessness. A person may be aware of a risk he or she creates yet disregard that risk as reasonable under the circumstances. The standard of culpable recklessness determines whether a person acts reasonably when he disregards a given risk. Again, the system must ask what circumstances and characteristics of the person it is fair to superimpose upon the reasonable person in creating a standard by which to judge the blameworthiness of the person's disregard of the known risk. Are these circumstances and characteristics of a person different from those that are properly taken into account when judging the reasonableness of a person's failure to perceive a risk in negligence?

Neither the Model Penal Code nor the existing literature give a coherent theory for determining which characteristics or attributes of a person ought to be used to individualize the reasonable person standard and under what circumstances.

---

[14] See Model Penal Code § 2.02(2)(d).

Indeed, the Model Penal Code drafters essentially admit that the matter is beyond their current ability to sort out. The Code allows judges and juries to make an ad hoc determination of which attributes to consider. It does so by providing that a person is to be judged by the standard of care of a reasonable person "in the actor's situation." The commentary notes:

> There is an inevitable ambiguity in "situation." If the person were blind or if he had just suffered a blow or experienced a heart attack, these would certainly be facts to be considered in a judgment involving criminal liability, as they would be under traditional law. But the heredity, intelligence or temperament of the person would not be held material in judging negligence, and could not be without depriving the criterion of all its objectivity. The Code is not intended to displace discriminations of this kind, but rather to leave the issue to the courts.[15]

The present study sought to begin the inquiry into which attributes ought to be taken into account in judging a person's failure to be aware of or his conscious disregard of a risk. Because no existing literature or case law proposes a general theory or principal that can be tested, this study attempts the very preliminary step of identifying attributes that might be seen by people in the community as either mitigating or aggravating criminal negligence liability. From this initial sampling, it was hoped that the responses might show a pattern that could be used to develop hypotheses and that those hypotheses might then be tested in subsequent studies.

The methods used in this study were somewhat different from the ones to which the reader has become accustomed. Subjects were first asked to assign liability and punishment to each of three base scenarios, each of which presented a situation of risk: an omission resulting in property damage, an omission resulting in death, and a commission resulting in death. The omission resulting in property damage is depicted by an apartment house owner who does not maintain the property well, and thus it catches fire. This scenario, shown in row (3) of Table 53, drew an average liability rating of 2.61, five to six weeks in jail. In the omission resulting in death case, row (2), a caretaker of a child pays insufficient attention to symptoms of the child's illness and fails to seek medical attention for the child, who dies. This was assigned a liability of 4.92, between 10 and 11 months in jail. The commission resulting in death case of row (1) involves a hunter who, in a remote wilderness area, shoots into the bush at a noise he hears, and kills another hunter, earning a liability rating of 3.98, about 6 months in jail. Notice the subjects' responses to the question, tabled in column (d), about whether the incident occurred because of something the person did, row (1); or failed to do, row (2). Obviously the two acts of omission were seen as omissions. The act that is labeled "commission" was rated nearer an act of omission, as shown in Table 53 row (1), column (d), and that puzzled the researchers until they talked to some of the subjects who read the case who said

[15] Model Penal Code §2.02 comment 4, 242 (1985).

TABLE 53. } Liability and Culpability in Core Cases

	(a)	(b)	(c)	(d)	(e)
Scenarios	*Liability*	*% No Liability (N)*	*% No Liability or No Punishment (N+0)*	*Commission or Omission?*	*Culpability Level*
1. Commission: Death	3.98	2	32	1.73	4.00
2. Omission: Death	4.82	5	29	2.00	3.87
3. Omission: Property damage	2.61	7	44	2.02	4.07

Liability Scale: N=No criminal liability, 0=Liability but no punishment, 1=1 day, 2=2 weeks, 3=2 months, 4=6 months, 5=1 year, 6=3 years, 7=7 years, 8=15 years, 9=30 years, 10=life, and 11=death.

Key to column heads:
(d) Please indicate whether you think the incident occurred because of:

1=something the actor did.
2=something the actor failed to do.
3=some cause unrelated to the actor's conduct.

(e) At the time of the incident, the actor:

1=wanted the other to die.
2=was practically certain that his action (or inaction) would cause serious injury or death.
3=was aware of a substantial risk of serious injury or death.
4=was not aware of a substantial risk but should have been.
5=was not aware of a substantial risk and a reasonable person would not have been aware of such a risk.

that they thought the hunter "had failed to take proper precautions," which was what they were rating rather than the act of shooting. Given this, the "commission" label for the case will continued to be used. Now notice the row (e) ratings. They hover around 4, which was a rating of "was not aware of a substantial risk but should have been." This suggests that the respondents saw the cases as instances of negligence, as was hoped.

Each subject then was asked to consider whether each of 14 actor characteristics would make a difference in the liability they had assigned to the base scenarios. The 14 actor characteristics were selected from those that were thought to be most likely to give some kind of reaction, either mitigating or aggravating. Frequently, the characteristics included the two extremes of a single continuum, for example, higher and lower than average intelligence, advanced and subnormal training, old age and youthfulness. Subjects were asked to indicate for each variation whether, if the person possessed this characteristic, they would alter the punishment assessment they gave in the base scenario. A nine-point scale allowed subjects to indicate less liability (1), no change (5), or more liability (9). Table 54 needs to be read differently than the other tables that have been presented. A rating that hovers around 0 means that the respondents, on the average, did not think that characteristic either lowered or raised the liability assigned to the person in the original case. Ratings that differ from 0 by about 0.7 are reliably different from 0, meaning that a rating of -0.7 or lower indicates a tendency on the part of the respondents to want to lower the liability assigned to the negligent individual in that case, and a rating of +.0.7

or higher indicates that the average respondent thinks that possession of that characteristic warrants an assignment of more liability.

Before looking at the ratings, a bit needs to be said about how the specific stories that the subjects read were created. The specifics of the story that created, for example, lack of cultural knowledge, needed to vary depending on whether the story was about a failure to perceive a child's illness or the precautions to keep a building from burning. Similarly, different past upbringings would lead to knowing little about hunting or child care. The case writers simply tried to create individuating information that fit the general category and seemed to them to be both plausible and a potential source of reasons to individuate. For these reasons, the labels that are assigned to the various conditions creating the different cases are rather approximate ones, and one would want to interpret the results with considerable tentativeness.

Looking at Table 54, notice first that subjects do not often give ratings that deviate far from zero; that is, they rarely find that a particular characteristic is a reason to sharply increase or reduce the liability they assigned to the perpetrator of the original scenario. (Those that are statistically significant in the table are starred to call them to your attention.) Given that the stories were created in way that was expected to give room for individuation, this is an interesting fact. The respondents, like the code drafters, seem cautious about individuating the objective standard of negligence.

TABLE 54. } Factors in Individualization of Negligence Standard

	Scenarios		
	(a)	*(b)*	*(c)*
Actor Characteristics	*Commission: Death*	*Omission: Death*	*Omission: Property Damage*
1. Old age	−0.3	−0.4	0.0
2. Advanced experience	0.6	1.6*	1.8*
3. Genetic irregularity	−0.5	−0.9*	−0.7*
4. Upbringing (knowledge)	1.5*	−0.2	−0.3
5. Below-normal intelligence	−0.2	−1.4*	−0.7*
6. Religion (knowledge)	0.2	−0.2	0.0
7. Above-normal intelligence	0.6	0.8*	0.6
8. Upbringing (environment)	0.7*	−0.3	−0.1
9. Lack of knowledge (culture)	−0.3	−1.7*	−1.0*
10. Substandard education	−0.4	−0.3	−0.2
11. Cultural norms	−0.8*	−0.1	−0.5
12. Recent upset	−0.4	−0.4	−0.5
13. Religion (norms)	0.2	0.0	−0.1

*These items are statistically significantly different ($p < .05$) from the liability assigned to the person who did not have the named condition.

Note: The characteristic of "immaturity" is not included in this table's analysis.

However, in several instances the subjects do individuate. The results suggest that some actor characteristics do, in the subjects' view, affect a person's liability for inattention to risks. In each scenario, two or more characteristics showed statistically significant differences in each direction from the "no change" point on the scale, (0). In the hunter scenario, Table 54 column (a), an individual whose upbringing was such as to make him knowledgeable about hunting was judged more liable for shooting at a noise in the bushes. On the other hand, an individual whose cultural norms do not include care with guns is judged as less negligent. For the apartment house owner, Table 54 column (c), coming from a cultural background in which persons have little or no knowledge of the risks of particular materials catching fire, caused respondents to reduce liability, while having experience at building care increased it.

The respondents saw a number of factors as increasing or mitigating liability in the case of the child caregiver who failed to take the child for medical attention, Table 54 column (b). This makes sense if one notes that the case is a more complex one than the other two, involving recognizing complex cues of the infant's distress. Immaturity, below normal intelligence, genetic irregularity, and a lack of knowledge of children all decrease liability. Having above-average intelligence or past experience with children increases liability for failing to get medical treatment for the infant.

It is also possible to ask which individuating characteristics the respondents give weight to across the scenarios. This is a difficult generalization to make. The following is tentatively suggested: in each of the cases, having relevant experience with the situation is seen as increasing liability for behaving negligently within it. Having a genetic defect or a culturally established lack of knowledge about the hazards often reduces liability. But the results suggest that the characteristics appropriate for individuating the reasonable person standard vary with the factual situation, confirming the code drafters' assessment that this is a complex problem and suggesting that perhaps they were right to leave this to the ad hoc determination of courts. Further study may reveal a pattern to the kind of characteristics judged influential on liability in different kinds of situations. Or perhaps the jurisprudential literature will develop a hypothesis that can be tested.

To summarize, in several ways, the present results do produce some insights. They confirm that some individuation of the objective standard is consistent with the community view. Also, they suggest an answer to the question of whether individuation ought to increase as well as decrease our expectations of persons. The subjects clearly believe that it is appropriate to elevate the standard of care required of an experienced person, and occasionally of a person who is above average in intelligence as well.

Furthermore, although the Code drafters in the official commentary quoted above specifically exclude the characteristics of subnormal intelligence or genetic defect as reasons to lower the standard, the respondents occasionally use information about these characteristics to reduce the liability they assign. One might think that within the legal system, given that it generally is left to the juries to decide on the particular ways that they will individuate the reasonable person standard, these cases of reduced liability can be accommodated. Unfortunately, this is not entirely true. It is the judge who decides whether evidence of a particular characteristic will be allowed to be introduced into evidence, so jury intuition on this point is not a safeguard, because the jury may never hear about relevant factors. The fact that the Code's official commentary specifically excludes low intelligence as an individuating factor is particularly troublesome for this reason. A judge may well feel bound to follow the commentary and exclude such evidence, while the respondents report that it is a factor on which they would individuate the standard. Were the court system willing to individualize the objective standard of negligence to the degree reflected in these results, it would be possible to call the jury's attention to the general possibilities of individuation, perhaps using these specific examples.

E. Summary

In the study of the culpability requirements for various offenses, first, the law's tendency to make a major differentiation between reckless and negligent commission of an offense was generally confirmed. The subjects make major differences in their liability assignments depending on whether the individual is reckless with respect to the various elements specified as relevant by the code or merely negligent. However, unlike the standard treatment of the codes, which with the exception of homicide generally assigns no higher liability for an offense committed knowingly or purposefully than one committed recklessly, the subjects do assign higher liability for higher culpability than recklessness. The subjects also distinguish recklessly committed offenses from negligently committed ones, but unlike the general code treatment, sometimes assign significant liabilities to negligently committed offenses. In general, to model the respondents' judgments, code drafters should consider more frequently having the code make a distinction in the grade of the offense depending on the degree of culpability of the offender, rather than dichotomizing judgments between only two particular levels.

Of course, it is possible that judges accomplish one of these results in their sentencing decisions, by giving longer sentences to individuals who they see as filling the requirements for purposeful commission over and above knowing commission. However, given the current tendency to move toward more articulated sentencing rules that remove discretion from judges, it strikes us that it might be better to have this result included in code formulations, or at least embodied in sentencing guidelines, rather than being left to the discretion of the individual judge. Also, since cases of negligent commission in current code treatment typically do not trigger liability, these cases do not reach trial, and the respondents judge that they should.

A similar result emerged when we examined the culpability requirements for complicity. The codes set purposefulness as to assisting as the minimum requirement for complicity, but the respondents are willing to assign liability to a person who knowingly assists, or even one who recklessly assists. The respondents assign different and lower levels of liability as the culpability level decreases, which again suggests that the community would support a difference in grading of the offense depending on degree of culpability.

For the cases of voluntary intoxication, a pattern of judgments that was broadly consistent with the legal treatment of the cases in one respect was found. Codes commonly use negligence as the trigger point for the attribution of liability, and so do the subjects, thus supporting the codes' adoption of that standard rather than one triggered by a higher degree of culpability. However, the respondents are considerably influenced by the degree of pre-intoxication culpability that the person had with respect to commission of the offense, while codes, counterintuitively, do not consider that factor.

A person is negligent if he or she disregards possible risks that a reasonable or prudent individual would consider. Traditionally codes have treated this as an objective standard, not to be varied as a function of, for instance, the lower intelligence of the person whose conduct is being judged. However, some modern codes have moved in the direction of individualizing the standard, based on some of the characteristics of the individual, but have not provided a coherent theory of how to determine which should be taken into account. Instead, judges (and, to a lesser extent, juries) are allowed to determine what attributes of the person should be considered. Without a theory to test, the researchers conducted a study that was to some extent a "fishing expedition," seeking to discover what attributes the subjects considered to be appropriate grounds for individualization of the reasonable person standard. As the reader will recall, the results were complex, and instances of both lowered and raised standards were found. This suggests that the modern trend toward individualizing the objective reasonable person standard has support among the community. The absence of an obvious pattern tends to confirm the practical need to leave the individualizing determination to ad hoc judgment with little principled guidance. At the same time, the dangers inherent in this lack of a guiding principle are illustrated by the Model Penal Code commentary's exclusion of a characteristic, low intelligence, which the subjects think is relevant in assessing the appropriate degree of liability. Because judges control the evidence that a jury will see, jurors may never know of characteristics or circumstances that might alter their assessments of liability.

15}

Principles of Adjudication: Doctrines of Excuse

The doctrines of excuse ask the question: when is a rule violation blameless? That a person satisfies the culpability requirements of an offense typically will be enough to establish the blameworthiness that makes criminal liability appropriate. However, this conclusion of blame may be rebutted by showing that, at the time of the offense conduct, the person suffered a disability that makes him not responsible for the offense. The insane arsonist may have intended to burn the building, as the culpability requirements of arson require, yet his insanity may render him blameless for his conduct. A person may be excused through any of a number of general disability excuse defenses—such as insanity, immaturity, involuntary intoxication, or duress. While the law and the community commonly assume sanity, maturity, sobriety, and absence of coercion, in the unusual case, a person may suffer a disability and its effects may be such that he or she cannot reasonably be expected to have avoided the criminal violation.

Reduced expectations of an offender who suffers from some sort of disability or abnormality have been hinted at in previous studies, notably the study on the individuation of standards for negligence (chapter 14, section D) in which the respondents were willing to require lowered standards of care from individuals suffering from various disadvantages. Another class of excuses, "mistake excuses," look not to a person's abnormality but, on the contrary, to the reasonableness of his mistake as to an aspect of the circumstances, which would render his conduct noncriminal if the mistaken circumstances actually existed.

Below is a selection of studies regarding community views on various doctrines of disability excuses. This chapter is drawn primarily from portions of my work with John Darley in *Justice, Liability & Blame: Community Views and the Criminal Law*.[1]

A. Insanity

Previous psychological research has asked many questions about the insanity defense, but two seem particularly germane. The first question is dealt with in surveys focusing on people's estimates of the fairness and effectiveness of the insanity defense as

[1] Paul H. Robinson & John M. Darley, Justice, Liability & Blame: Community Views and the Criminal Law (1995).

an instrument of public policy. These surveys have proven quite useful in comparing attitudes toward the insanity defense across different segments of the general population. For instance, Pasewark and colleagues have used this approach to compare lay persons' and legislators' estimates of how frequently defendants enter an insanity plea.[2] They found that while legislators' estimates of the frequency of cases of the insanity plea were substantially more conservative (i.e., fewer) than those of lay community members, both groups vastly overestimated the frequency and the success rate of insanity pleas. This overestimating tendency has been confirmed in more recent studies; people generally assign a much greater role to the insanity defense than it truly plays in the workings of the criminal justice system.[3] This finding is interesting in the present context, in that it suggests that most individuals, concerned not to overapply the defense themselves, will be relatively reluctant to grant validity to mental illness as a reason for excusing from criminal liability.

Surveys and experiments that attempt to discover lay definitions of insanity constitute the second approach that previous research has taken to studying the insanity defense. These studies have focused on the implications of lay definitions of insanity for the decision-making processes of juries. One conclusion has been that instructing jurors in simulated trials to apply different legal code tests of insanity makes remarkably little difference in the verdicts that jurors ultimately reach.[4] This suggests that various individuals hold their own views of what constitutes insanity, and that they do not modify these views in the direction of code formulations, even when instructed to do so during their participation in simulated trials. In other words, lay definitions of insanity appear strong enough to override the specifications of the legal code in determining the Not Guilty by Reason of Insanity (NGRI) verdict.

One study has tested lay understandings of legal definitions of insanity directly.[5] This survey was conducted in the week following the announcement of an NGRI verdict in the case of John Hinckley, Jr., the man who attempted to assassinate U.S. President Ronald Reagan in 1982. During this week, Americans were exposed to unprecedented amounts of information and debate about the insanity defense. Consistent with previous research, Hans and Slater found that the majority of their respondents were still unable to accurately report the legal test for insanity that was being applied to Hinckley. A substantial proportion of respondents (23 percent) volunteered the definition: "Don't know what you're doing."[6]

---

[2] Richard A. Pasewark & Mark L. Pantle, *Insanity Plea: Legislator's View*, 136 AM. J. PSYCHOL. 222 (1979); Richard A. Pasewark & Deborah Seidenzahl, *Opinions Concerning the Insanity Plea and Criminality Among Patients*, 1 BULL. AM. ACAD. PSYCH. & LAW 199 (1980).

[3] Valerie P. Hans, *An Analysis of Public Attitudes Toward the Insanity Defense*, 24 CRIMINOLOGY 393 (1986).

[4] Norman J. Finkel, *Insanity of Trial*, in 8 PERSPECTIVES IN LAW AND PSYCHOLOGY (B. D. Sales ed., Plenum Press 1988).

[5] Valerie P. Hans & Dan Slater, *"Plain Crazy": Lay Definitions of Legal Insanity*, 7 INT'L J. LAW & PSYCH 105 (1984).

[6] *Id.* at 107.

The interesting question is the degree to which ordinary persons spontaneously use standards for judging mental illness that are in rough accord with those that the legal system suggests are relevant, a question that is not answered by the research cited above. What distinctions, then, are made by standard legal codes? Within the legal system, mental disease or defect can affect a person's criminal liability either (1) by negating (i.e., making it impossible for the prosecution to prove) a culpable state of mind that is required by the definition of the offense charged, or (2) by satisfying the conditions of a general insanity defense. The latter, the general insanity defense, operates without regard to the elements of the offense charged. If the conditions of the insanity defense are met, the person escapes criminal liability, whatever the offense. Rather than focusing upon the person's actual state of mind as to the offense elements, the insanity defense focuses upon the person's general capacity for normal mental and emotional functioning. This study tests the goodness of fit between community standards and the provisions of the general insanity defense.

The common law recognized an insanity defense under what is called the McNaughten test, which provides a defense if the person was laboring under such a defect of reason due to mental disease that he did not know the nature or quality of the act he was doing; or, if he did know, did not know that what he was doing was wrong.[7] The test focuses exclusively upon the person's cognitive (as opposed to control) dysfunction and requires a very high, if not absolute, degree of loss of function. The person must "not know" the nature of his conduct or that it is wrong. In contrast, the cognitive dysfunction prong of the Model Penal Code's more modern formulation (called the "ALI test" because the American Law Institute authored the Model Penal Code) sets a somewhat lower standard of dysfunction: it requires only that the person lacked "substantial capacity" to "appreciate" the criminality or wrongfulness of his conduct.[8] The Code's language permits the defense upon less dysfunction; cognitive function only need be impaired, not lost.

Many jurisdictions adopting the McNaughten test have added an alternative ground of exculpation: even if the person knows the nature of what he is doing, and that it is wrong, he nonetheless is excused if he has so far lost the power to avoid doing the act in question that his free agency is at the time destroyed.[9] This introduces the possibility of a defense upon a pure control dysfunction, with a person's cognitive functioning intact. Like McNaughten, however, this "irresistible impulse" test, as it is called, is stated as absolute in its demands. The person must have no power to control his conduct; his free agency must be "destroyed." Under the control prong of the Model Penal Code's ALI test, in contrast, the person need only lack "substantial capacity" to conform his conduct to the requirements of law.[10]

[7] McNaughten's Case, 8 Eng. Rep. 718, 722 (1843).

[8] Model Penal Code §4.01(1).

[9] *See, e.g.,* Parsons v. State, 81 Alaska 577 (D. Alaska 1887).

[10] Model Penal Code §4.01(1).

Absence of control is not required for the Code's defense; substantial impairment of control is sufficient.

These two distinctions—cognitive versus control, and complete loss versus substantial impairment of function—represent the major distinctions among the most common American formulations of the insanity defense. Some jurisdictions still use just the McNaughten test—requiring high cognitive dysfunction. Some adopt McNaughten and add the irresistible-impulse test as an alternative ground of defense—thus requiring either high cognitive or high control dysfunction. The Model Penal Code's ALI test has been adopted in many jurisdictions. It requires only substantial impairment of either cognitive or control functioning. Some jurisdictions, such as the federal system, have recently dropped the control prong of ALI and kept the cognitive prong. Rather than reverting to McNaughten entirely, they have retained the ALI test's substantial impairment approach.[11] Public disillusionment and dissatisfaction have led a few jurisdictions to drop the insanity defense altogether.[12]

The insanity study sought to determine whether the subjects would give a general defense because of a person's insanity, whether they recognize the validity of the cognitive versus control distinction that the doctrine uses; and which of the tests, if any, best reflects their views. In the core of the story presented to subjects, an individual, who is characterized with various details that suggest insanity, picks up an object that is nearby, such as a baseball bat, a mallet, or a rock, and hits another person with it, killing that other person. Because the writers of these cases wanted to make the mental dysfunction of the person vivid, they created scenarios that differed from one another in several different ways. What is important here, therefore, are the respondents' perceptions of the kind and degree of mental dysfunction experienced in each case.

When examining the subjects' perceptions of the degree and kind of insanity that was conveyed by the scenarios, one discovers that their perceptions are somewhat different than they had been expected to be. The cases and the way they are perceived are shown in Table 55.

The first two columns, (a) and (b), show the subjects' ratings of the degree to which the perpetrator suffers from a substantial or complete control dysfunction. The right-hand three columns, (c), (d), and (e), report the subjects' perceptions of the degree of cognitive dysfunction. The questions on cognitive dysfunction are more numerous because, as noted about cognitive dysfunction, the legal doctrine distinguishes between cognitive dysfunction of two sorts: first, one may be unaware of the nature of one's conduct (unaware that the thing one is hitting is a person); and second, even if one is aware of the nature of the conduct, one may be unaware of the wrongfulness of the conduct (unaware that hitting another is

---

[11] 18 U.S.C. §17. For a description of which states have adopted which formulation, *see* Paul H. Robinson, Criminal Law Defenses §173(a) nn.1-5 (West 1984).

[12] *See id.* at n.5 (Idaho, Montana, and Utah have abolished their insanity defense; Connecticut has reached essentially the same result through other means).

TABLE 55. } Respondents' Perceptions of Cognitive and Control Dysfunctions

	Control Dysfunction		*Cognitive Dysfunction*		
	(a)	*(b)*	*(c)*	*(d)*	*(e)*
Suggested Scenario Label	*Substantial*	*Complete*	*Substantial*	*Unaware of Nature of Conduct*	*Unaware of Wrongfulness*
4. High control, low cognitive	7.58	7.39	3.05	2.76	2.71
5. High control, low cognitive	7.29	6.61	2.95	2.50	2.74
6. Medium control, high cognitive	4.47	4.74	7.68	7.97	7.58
7. Low control, high cognitive	3.79	3.89	6.82	3.29	6.68

The questions asked whether the respondent 1="strongly disagreed," 5=was "unsure," or 9="strongly agreed" that the actor had a substantial or complete control or cognitive dysfunction. The exact questions are shown in Table 5.4 and correspond to each of the five lettered columns of this table. The questions tabulated here are the common-language formulations.

wrongful). Therefore, questions about both of these sorts of dysfunction were included.

The results indicate that respondents are able to competently distinguish cognitive from control dysfunction, a fact that lends some support for the use of this distinction by the doctrine. As can be seen from rows (4) and (6), the test was generally successful in creating perceptions of high dysfunction, whether cognitive or control. Subjects read the case tabled in row (5) as being a case of high control dysfunction; and the case in row (6) as having a fairly high degree of cognitive dysfunction. Looking at these degree-of-dysfunction ratings, one is struck by the fact that there are two conditions in which the control dysfunction is judged to be high, and the cognitive dysfunction moderately low, and two conditions in which the cognitive dysfunction is judged high and the control dysfunction low or moderate. Therefore, in the analyses of liability judgments, each member of each pair is treated as to some extent a replication of the other, although trying to be sensitive to the differences between the pair. These are the scenario descriptions represented in the "suggested labels" column of Tables 55 and 56.

One more result depicted in Table 55 is worth interpreting. The two different aspects of cognitive dysfunction have a complex relation with each other. As said above, one can be aware of the nature of one's conduct but unaware of the wrongfulness of the conduct. It looks like this is the way that the subjects treat this situation, as the doctrine suggests. Scenario (7) is perceived by them as being a case in which the person is aware of the nature of his conduct, column (d), but unaware of its wrongfulness, column (e). As column (c) shows, they agree that this individual has a substantial degree of cognitive impairment. Note that if one is unaware of the nature of one's conduct, that one will of course be unaware of its wrongfulness, but not the reverse. The categories—aware of nature of conduct and wrongfulness—are serial in relation rather than alternative.

TABLE 56. } Liability as Related to Insanity

	(a)	(b)	(c)
Suggested Label	*Liability*[a]	*% No Liability (N)*	*% Civil Commitment*
Control Conditions:			
1. Murder	10.42	0	
2. Self-defense	0.11	79	
3. Mistaken identity	7.79	0	
Experimental Conditions:			
4. High control, low cognitive	1.89 (19%–8.29)	81	81
5. High control, low cognitive	3.00 (34%–9.25)	66	66
6. Medium control, high cognitive	0.64 (8%–5.67)	92	92
7. Low control, high cognitive	1.65 (16%–9.00)	84	84

Liability Scale: N=No criminal liability, 0=Liability but no punishment, 1=1 day, 2=2 weeks, 3=2 months, 4=6 months, 5=1 year, 6=3 years, 7=7 years, 8=15 years, 9=30 years, 10=life, and 11=death.

[a]Civil commitment cases are included as 0 in calculating these means. The numbers in parentheses indicate the percentage of respondents who assigned criminal liability and, of those, the average liability they assigned.

In Table 56, the usual liability results are shown in columns (a) and (b). Before examining the liability ratings for the mental illness cases, a note on the comparison cases is in order. The comparison cases are shown in rows (1), (2), and (3). The case in row (1) involves a person who, because he is angry at another, goes to that person's house and bludgeons him to death, a straightforward murder; and notice, from column (a), that it commands a sentence of somewhere between life imprisonment and the death penalty. Row (2) shows the liability assigned to a convenience store owner who defends himself from a knife-carrying robber by pulling a nightstick from under the counter and striking the robber, who is lunging at him with a knife. The robber is killed. This seems a straightforward case of self-defense, and the respondents judged the case accordingly. The third comparison case, row (3), involves again a convenience store owner who chases a robber and misidentifies another individual as that robber. The misidentified individual and the owner get into a fight, the owner uses the nightstick that he is carrying, and the misidentified individual eventually dies of his injuries. The liability assigned to this case is high. This provides an indication of the respondents' views about the wrongfulness of a mistake as to what the person thinks is justified force. The subjects' response is notable because the mistake is in some sense similar to the sorts of mistakes that the mentally dysfunctional persons make in the test cases.

There is one additional result in column (a) that is worth explaining. Notice that a new column (c) appears in this table, the percentage of subjects who assign civil commitment to the perpetrator. In the real world, the choice facing judges and juries in insanity cases is not simply criminal liability or no criminal liability. A special verdict of not guilty by reason of insanity is available where an insanity plea is made, and this disposition generally leads to civil commitment, not to immediate release into society. Because of this fact, subjects were given the option to recommend this course of handling the mental illness cases, and even to suggest a term of the civil commitment. They were given this option as a way of assuring that those who are concerned about community safety more than anything else would feel that the civil commitment system would provide this assurance and that they need not impose criminal liability on someone who they thought might not deserve it in order to assure the community's safety. The ability to specify not just civil commitment but also a term of years thus makes the civil option equally effective at protecting the community as the criminal option did. Thus, those who give the criminal option would be those who are doing so because they believe that the person really deserves the condemnation and punishment of criminal conviction. Notice that many of the subjects choose this civil commitment option; the percentages tabled in column (c) are 66 percent or higher.

The first result to notice from these various liability judgment comparisons is the global one. Perpetrators who are judged to be suffering from a high degree of dysfunction, whether that dysfunction is of the cognitive or conduct control sort, are normally not assigned criminal liability. In other words, the subjects do grant validity to a defense of insanity and sharply reduce the liability assigned to a person who commits a crime while mentally ill; in making this judgment, they are in general accord with the way that the criminal codes treat such cases. Typically, more than 70 percent of the respondents assign no criminal liability to such cases.

This result has special implications for the current controversy over whether the insanity defense should excuse only for cognitive dysfunction or whether control dysfunction also should provide a defense. Recall that the federal system, and several states following its lead, recently has reverted to a cognitive-only test, denying any defense for a control dysfunction. The respondents would most likely disagree with this change. In scenario (4), which is perceived as showing high control and low cognitive dysfunction, 81 percent of the respondents impose no criminal liability (in scenario (5), similarly perceived, 66 percent). Scenario (7), perceived as the reverse, low control and high cognitive, has about the same percentages of respondents giving no criminal liability, 84 percent. This suggests that both cognitive and control dysfunctions can support an insanity defense in the community's eyes. This conclusion is also supported by the results in scenario (6). Where medium control and high cognitive are perceived, 92 percent give the defense, noticeably more than the 84 percent who give the defense in scenario (7) for low control and high cognitive. Control dysfunction can support a defense; the greater the perceived control dysfunction the greater the likelihood of a defense. Of course, these respondents do judge that civil confinement is appropriate for the insane individual; they do not wish to release him into the community. Indeed, if the length of the period of confinement recommended by the respondents was tabled, without respect to whether it was civil or criminal confinement, one would see that the time period of incarceration recommended was reasonably constant across cases. The respondents seem to be making a complex judgment here. As is well understood in legal circles, there are a number of reasons why one incarcerates a person: because the person is blameworthy and deserves the sentence is one; to incapacitate the person so no further crimes will be committed is another. Respondents wished, given the alternatives presented to them, to punish the non-insane with a prison sentence and to incapacitate the insane for a long period of time, an option that in our current system looks remarkably like prison.

Return now to the criminal liabilities assigned to the cases in which possibly insane persons were depicted as bringing about death. Column (a) shows the criminal liabilities assigned. The number not in parentheses is the liability assignment normally tabled; it is the average liability assigned by all respondents, treating those who assigned no liability, no liability or punishment, or civil commitment, as assigning a criminal liability of zero. The number in parentheses is the average liability assigned by those who imposed criminal liability. (To make the reader's task easier, the two numbers are actually tabled. The first is the percentage of respondents who assigned criminal liability. The second is the average liability assigned by those persons. So, for instance, reading (4) one sees that 19 percent of the people assigned criminal liability in that scenario, and their average liability was 8.29). This new average liability number reveals that those subjects, a minority of respondents in each case, who don't exculpate the offender for reasons of insanity, judge that quite high sentences are appropriate. And notice that this is true for all of the insanity cases shown in rows (4) through (7). Even within this minority group, however, liability differences do exist. Also, slightly fewer respondents assign criminal liability to the two high control dysfunction cases than the two high cognitive dysfunction cases. Further research will need to be done to determine the persistence and importance of these differences, and the degree to which they will transcend the specifics of the scenarios that written to create each case.

One more question in this study can be addressed: what is the respondents' understanding of the legal code's wordings of the various formulations of the insanity defense? For each scenario, the respondents were asked to estimate the degree to which the individual in the scenario fit the various formulations of the insanity defense. This was done in two ways: first, in the best commonsense translation of the legal code concept, Table 57 column (a); and, second, in the exact wording of the legal code formulation, Table 57 column (b). For example, respondents were asked the degree to which the reader agreed with the statement that the perpetrator "did not realize that striking the victim with the baseball bat was wrong," and the statement that the perpetrator "was laboring under such a defect of reason due to mental disease that he did not know that what he was doing was wrong."

Table 58 shows the average responses of the respondents to these questions, and more importantly, shows the correlations between the pairs of equivalent questions. As will be seen from the table, the correlations are generally high, averaging 0.86 in scenario (4), 0.85 in scenario (5), dropping to 0.58 in scenario (6), and returning to 0.84 in scenario (7). These high correlations are interpreted to mean that in this context the subjects saw the paired questions as having about the same meanings. This conclusion of the essential interchangeability of the two forms of the questions is

TABLE 57. } Questions for Common and Legal Language Formulations

Dimension of Perceived Dysfunction	*(a) Common Language Formulation*	*(b) Legal Language Formulation*
1. Unaware of nature of conduct	Because of mental illness, the actor did not realize that he was striking the tenant with a baseball bat.	The actor was laboring under such a defect of reason due to mental disease that he did not know the nature or the quality of the act he was doing.
2. Unaware of wrongfulness	Because of mental illness, the actor did not realize that striking the tenant with a baseball bat was wrong.	The actor was laboring under such a defect of reason that he did not know that what he was doing was wrong.
3. Substantial impairment of appreciation of wrongfulness	Because of mental illness, the actor's ability to understand the wrongfulness of his conduct was substantially impaired.	As a result of mental disease or defect at the time of his conduct, the actor lacked substantial capacity to appreciate the criminality or the wrongfulness of his conduct.
4. Complete loss of control	Because of mental illness, the actor lacked any ability to stop himself from striking the tenant with the baseball bat.	Because of the duress of mental disease, the actor had so far lost the power to avoid doing the act in question, as that his free agency was at the time destroyed.
5. Substantial impairment of control	Because of mental illness, the actor's ability to stop himself from striking the tenant with the baseball bat was substantially impaired.	As a result of mental disease at the time of his conduct, the actor lacked substantial capacity to conform his conduct to the requirement of the law.

supported by the general close agreement between the average scores on each of the two equivalent questions. (The comparison across rows between columns (a) and (b) shows this.) This suggests that, on the one hand, it would not be wrong in the criminal justice system to use the ordinary language formulations of the questions that the jurors are instructed to decide in determining whether a specific individual meets the legal criteria for insanity. On the other hand, it also suggests that the people who were given these scenarios, and by extension, jurors, are able to understand and apply the somewhat ponderous legal wordings of the various formulations of insanity as well. This does not contradict the findings of other research, discussed earlier, that showed that people were unable to reproduce the legal system definitions of insanity.

To summarize, recall the discussion of the treatment that would be given to each case by various formulations of the current law. For the moment, assume that the typical judgments in every scenario are of "not guilty," as in fact they are. If this is assumed, interestingly, both the formulation of insanity contained in the Model Penal Code and the formulation under the McNaughten-irresistible impulse test accurately fit the pattern of the respondents' judgments, while the formulations of the McNaughten rule and the recently passed federal statute do not match the respondents' judgments. Specifically, the last two formulations do not grant a defense when the person is laboring under a control dysfunction, while the respondents do see control dysfunction as establishing a defense of insanity. Thus, the two formulations that grant validity to the insanity defense based on either a cognitive or a control

TABLE 5.8. } Respondents' Perceptions of Cognitive and Control Dysfunction: Agreement with Common and Legal Language Formulations

		(a)	(b)	(c)
Scenario	*Dimension of Perceived Dysfunction*	*Common Language Agreement*	*Legal Language Agreement*	*Correlation**
4. High control, low cognitive	1. Unaware of nature of conduct	2.76	3.42	0.79
	2. Unaware of wrongfulness	2.71	2.97	0.87
	3. Substantial impairment of appreciation of wrongfulness	3.05	3.29	0.86
	4. Complete loss of control	7.39	7.13	0.94
	5. Substantial impairment of control	7.58	7.47	0.86
5. High control, low cognitive	1. Unaware of nature of conduct	2.50	3.24	0.84
	2. Unaware of wrongfulness	2.74	3.08	0.90
	3. Substantial impairment of appreciation of wrongfulness	2.95	3.21	0.86
	4. Complete loss of control	6.61	6.42	0.83
	5. Substantial impairment of control	7.29	6.84	0.83
6. Medium control, high cognitive	1. Unaware of nature of conduct	7.97	7.71	0.48
	2. Unaware of wrongfulness	7.58	7.63	0.34
	3. Substantial impairment of appreciation of wrongfulness	7.68	7.50	0.57
	4. Complete loss of control	4.74	4.42	0.68
	5. Substantial impairment of control	4.47	4.61	0.85
7. Low control, high cognitive	1. Unaware of nature of conduct	3.29	4.16	0.77
	2. Unaware of wrongfulness	6.68	6.68	0.74
	3. Substantial impairment of appreciation of wrongfulness	6.82	7.16	0.89
	4. Complete loss of control	3.89	3.63	0.85
	5. Substantial impairment of control	3.79	4.26	0.95

Note: The exact wordings of these questions are shown in Table 5.4. Question 1 is tabulated in column *d* of Table 5.1, question 2 in column *e*, question 3 in column *c*, question 4 in column *b*, and question 5 in column *a*. Respondents were asked whether they 1="strongly disagreed," 5=were "unsure," or 9="strongly agreed" with the common and legal language formulations that correspond with each of the five dimensions of perceived dysfunction for each of the four scenarios presented here.

*All of the correlations shown in column *c* are statistically significant ($p < .05$).

dysfunction are the ones that best match the judgments of the respondents. Further, the subjects were able to distinguish cognitive from control dysfunctions, lending some support for the use of this distinction by the doctrine. As the history of the doctrine might predict, cognitive dysfunctions appear to provide persuasive excuses to more of the subjects than do control dysfunctions.

Further examination of the data suggests another rather tentative conclusion. Examine again the degree of the subjects' agreement with the dysfunction statement for scenarios (6) and (7), tabled in column (c) of Table 55. Although the subjects are in strong agreement with those dysfunction statements, they are by no means in total agreement with them. This supports the Model Penal Code's formulation of the cognitive dysfunction rule, which requires only that the person lack "substantial capacity" to appreciate the criminal wrongfulness of his conduct. This accesses the defense when cognitive functioning is impaired, rather than totally lost, a judgment with which the respondents seem to be in accord. Further research will test whether a cognitive dysfunction that respondents judge as establishing a lack of substantial capacity to appreciate the criminal wrongfulness of his conduct is sufficient to cause those respondents to grant the insanity defense.

Further research also will be necessary to provide more support to the conclusions sketched above. Since the respondents perceive all of the cases as containing a high level of either control or cognitive dysfunction, further testing is necessary to determine what degree of each dysfunction is required before support for the defense appears. It would also be useful to determine whether respondents use the defense in an essentially dichotomous way, granting it standing as a complete defense after it rises above a certain level, or continuously scale their liability judgments to the degree of dysfunction that they detect. The former is the process that most closely matches those contained in all of the legal formulations.

In current society, there is a great deal of controversy about the insanity defense. As noted, many individuals feel, probably inaccurately, that it is used often and has the effect of "letting off" many blameworthy persons. Given this is so, it is worth noting that a strong majority of the subjects still excused a person who bludgeoned his victim to death if they saw that perpetrator as genuinely dysfunctional because of mental illness. It may be that much of the controversy about the insanity defense is generated in circumstances in which the average reader of the publicity about a case sees the perpetrator as having only a modest degree of dysfunction, not enough to trigger the defense, whereas the jurors see a degree of dysfunction sufficient to trigger the defense. Still, one should also note that those minorities of the respondents who did find criminal liability appropriate assigned quite lengthy sentences.

B. Immaturity and Involuntary Intoxication

As the discussion of the previous study on insanity reviews, where a person commits an offense under the influence of some significant dysfunction of his capacity to control his conduct or to understand the nature of his conduct, the criminal law frequently recognizes an excuse that provides a defense. In addition to mental illness, the law excuses for dysfunctions that arise from either involuntary intoxication or immaturity (or, as shall be seen in the next study, from duress).

Current legal codes typically use a person's chronological age as conclusive evidence that the person is too immature to understand or control the harmful and criminal nature of his or her conduct.[13] The study sought to test the subjects' willingness to excuse persons because of their immaturity, as evidenced by their chronological age. A harm was described and then described as committed by individuals of various ages. No other information accessing an excuse was given, so if respondents gave lesser sentences to the younger offender, they did so solely because of the differential inferences they drew from the offender's age.

The defense of involuntary intoxication in legal theory works through mechanisms similar to those used for the defenses of insanity and immaturity, as described in the previous study concerning insanity. Chapter 14, section C discussed the legal theory relating to voluntary intoxication. If a person voluntarily becomes intoxicated, his intoxication has a limited effect, if any, in mitigating his liability. Where a person's intoxication is involuntary, however, liability may be eliminated or mitigated in two ways, parallel to those seen for mental illness. First, the resulting dysfunction from involuntary intoxication may provide a defense if it negates a culpable state of mind required by the offense definition. Second, the condition may excuse if it satisfies the conditions of the general involuntary intoxication defense, notwithstanding that the elements of the offense are satisfied. Those conditions typically are analogous to the conditions required by a jurisdiction's particular formulation of the insanity defense.[14] As with insanity, the most common defense formulations use the McNaughten test, McNaughten plus the irresistible impulse test, or the ALI test. The differences among these tests arise from the distinctions between cognitive and control dysfunction and between loss versus impairment of function, as described in the insanity study above.

This study attempted to see the degree to which the immaturity and involuntary intoxication defenses recognized by the legal doctrine exculpate and involve similar underlying mechanisms of exculpation. To examine community views on the general involuntary intoxication defense and its effect on a person's liability, subjects were given five homicide scenarios intended to depict a person who suffers from the following dysfunctions, respectively: high cognitive only, low cognitive only, high control only, low control only, and low cognitive plus low control. To examine community views on the doctrine's immaturity defenses, three scenarios presented cases in which the person engages in similar conduct under similar circumstances (but without being under the influence of any intoxication). In these cases, it is the person's age that is varied, from 10 to 14 to 18 years of age. Finally, there was a control comparison case to establish the penalty these respondents would give to the perpetrator of a similar homicide who suffered from no dysfunction.

In the control case and the three age-related cases, the core scenario is this: two brothers have a history of antagonism. After an argument, one waits until the other is asleep and kills him by dousing him with kerosene and setting him on fire. In the involuntary intoxication scenarios, the respondents were told that the cause of the involuntary intoxication is an unexpected interaction between two medications

---

13 Model Penal Code §4.10.

14 Model Penal Code §2.08(4).

that the person is taking: a medication to control long-term pain and a medication described as an over-the-counter drug for treatment of a cold. (By describing it as an over-the-counter-medication, the researchers attempted to create the perception that people would regard it as generally safe and unlikely to enter into side-effect interactions with other medications.) The prescribing physician had not mentioned the possibility of drug interaction side effects, and the person had not thought to ask about them. The core of these stories had the involuntarily intoxicated person killing the victim by suddenly dousing him with kerosene and setting him on fire. The kind and degree of the resulting dysfunction were manipulated both by a description of the person's resulting mental experiences and the later testimony of a physician about what dysfunction the particular drug interaction would cause. Thus, the study attempted to create perceptions that the involuntary intoxication experienced by the person brought about high or low cognitive or control dysfunctions.

Look first at the five cases, tabled in rows (2) to (6) of Table 59, those that involve involuntary intoxication. The involuntary intoxication cases are more closely analogous to the insanity cases of the previous study. For these cases, the civil commitment of the perpetrator was not an option that made sense within the judicial system, and was not given to the respondents as an option. First, and obviously, the sentences are greatly reduced from the control case of murder, as is revealed by an examination of column (a). Second, both cognitive and control dysfunction appear to support a defense. This is similar to the conclusion of the insanity study. Third, statistical analysis reveals that the high and low dysfunction cases differ reliably,

TABLE 59. } Liability as Related to Immaturity and Involuntary Intoxication

	(a)	*(b)*	*(c)*	*(d)*
Scenarios	*Liability*[a]	*% No Liability (N)*	*% No Liability or No Punishment (N+0)*	*% Civil Commitment*
Control:				
1. Murder	10.42	0	0	
Involuntary intoxication:				
2. High control	5.00	7	44	
3. High cognitive	3.84	23	52	
4. Low control	6.19	0	26	
5. Low cognitive	6.83	0	20	
6. Low control and cognitive	6.93	7	20	
Immaturity:				
7. 10-year-old	4.84 (53%–8.94)	47	47	47
8. 14-year-old	6.66 (77%–8.77)	23	23	23
9. 18-year-old	8.70 (90%–9.26)	7	10	7

Liability Scale: N=No criminal liability, 0=Liability but no punishment, 1=1 day, 2=2 weeks, 3=2 months, 4=6 months, 5=1 year, 6=3 years, 7=7 years, 8=15 years, 9=30 years, 10=life, and 11=death.

[a]Civil commitment cases are included as 0 in calculating these means. The numbers in parentheses indicate the percentage of respondents who assigned criminal liability and, of those, the average liability they assigned.

with the high dysfunction cases of rows (2) and (3) receiving lower criminal liabilities than the low cases of rows (4), (5), and (6). The type of dysfunction, cognitive versus control, is not found to produce reliable differences. The interpretation that arises from this, then, is that people do assess cases of involuntary intoxication in terms of the degree of dysfunction that they bring about, and those perceptions of the dysfunctions cause them to reduce the liability they assign to the person.

Before taking this conclusion at face value, look at the respondents' actual ratings of the degree of dysfunction brought about by the different scenarios, which are shown in Table 60. As column (b) indicates, the respondents certainly see the person in all of these scenarios as being intoxicated by the drug. They see him as much less intoxicated in scenario (6), and since that involves low degrees of dysfunction this is appropriate. And, as column (c) indicates, they agree that he is not responsible for being drug intoxicated in all of these scenarios.

Next look at the individual scenarios and see what conclusions that can be extracted from them. The information tabled in columns (d) through (h) shows how these cases are perceived in terms of cognitive and control dysfunctions, with columns (d) through (f) concerning cognitive dysfunction and (g) and (h) concerning control dysfunction.

TABLE 60. } Subjects' Perceptions of Immaturity and Involuntary Intoxication Cases

	(a)	*(b)*	*(c)*	*(d)*	*(e)*	*(f)*	*(g)*	*(h)*
Scenarios	*Age*	*"Intoxicated"*	*"Intoxication Involuntary"*	*"Unaware of Actions"*	*"Unaware of Wrongfulness"*	*"Understanding Impaired"*	*"Not Able to Stop"*	*"Ability to Stop Impaired"*
Involuntary intoxication:								
2. High control		7.19	6.13	3.77	3.87	4.90	6.03	6.42
3. High cognitive		7.90	6.52	7.00	7.10	7.13	6.74	7.10
4. Low control		6.90	6.03	3.71	3.55	5.13	4.74	5.58
5. Low cognitive		8.26	8.45	6.39	7.10	8.00	6.84	7.39
6. Low control and cognitive		6.42	5.97	4.06	4.32	5.48	4.58	8.19
Immaturity:								
7. 10-year-old	10.19	–	–	2.58	2.90	3.61	2.58	3.35
8. 14-year-old	14.13	–	–	1.74	1.90	2.42	2.00	2.19
9. 18-year-old	17.87	–	–	1.39	1.32	1.39	1.42	1.48

Key to column heads:
All statements were responded to on a scale where: 1="strongly disagree," 5="unsure," and 9="strongly agree."

(b) The actor was drug intoxicated at the time he performed the offense.
(c) The actor, if drug intoxicated, was not responsible for being drug intoxicated.
(d) Because of drug intoxication, the actor did not realize that he was committing the offense.
(e) Because of drug intoxication, the actor did not realize that committing the offense was wrong.
(f) Because of drug intoxication, the actor's ability to understand the wrongfulness of his conduct was substantially impaired.
(g) Because of drug intoxication, the actor lacked any ability to stop himself from committing the offense.
(h) Because of drug intoxication, the actor's ability to stop himself from committing the offense was substantially impaired.

In the high control dysfunction case, row (2), respondents agree that the individual is tending toward being unable to stop, column (g), and is also impaired in his ability to stop, column (h). They also see the individual as being moderately cognitively aware; that is, they disagree that he is unaware of his actions, column (d), unaware of the wrongfulness of those actions, column (e), and that his ability to understand the wrongfulness of his actions is substantially impaired, column (f). In this condition, it is reasonable to say that the respondents perceive that the individual has a modest degree of cognitive impairment and a higher degree of control dysfunction; in other words, that scenario is not inaccurately described as a "high control, low cognitive dysfunction" cell. Persons perceived to have that level and kind of dysfunction get a considerable reduction in sentence; certainly as compared to the control case of murder, but also as compared to the low dysfunction cases. However, the sentence of 5 (about one year in jail) is some distance from the sentence of no liability that many of the legal codes would give to an individual who has that dysfunction. Still, the respondents grant some considerable degree of validity to a defense based on a control dysfunction, which suggests that the legal codes that include a control prong in their formulations accurately represent community standards.

Look next at scenario (3), which attempted to create perceptions of a high cognitive dysfunction, an unawareness of the meaning or the wrongfulness of the harmful actions, and a low degree of control dysfunction. The respondents' ratings of the two questions on unawareness and the third on whether the individual is impaired in his ability to perceive the wrongfulness of his actions all are high; clearly the case is perceived, as intended, as one of high cognitive dysfunction. But the high ratings on the questions about whether the individual is able to stop the wrongful act indicate that the respondents see this case as one of high control dysfunction as well as high cognitive dysfunction. This means that this study was even less successful in creating a clear case of high cognitive dysfunction coupled with low control dysfunction than in the insanity case discussed previously. (Recall that there it was demonstrated in that case that subjects do considerably reduce sentences for individuals who have high cognitive and moderate control dysfunctions.) Notice here that this individual gets a low sentence, of 3.84, corresponding to a prison term of about five and one half months, which is the lowest sentence given to the various cases of involuntary intoxication. This makes sense, since they see this individual as impaired on both prongs of the defense.

The fact that the present case of high cognitive dysfunction was also read by the respondents as having a high control dysfunction may reveal something interesting about their "theories of mental dysfunction." Intuitively, a person who is thinking so oddly as to be unaware of the wrongfulness of killing somebody may be seen as not able to stop the action because he sees no moral need to stop it. To put it another way, a person who is unaware of his own actions and their wrongfulness has a cognitive dysfunction that may be seen by the respondents as also creating a control dysfunction. A similar pattern showed up in the insanity cases, in which the individual who is seen as highly cognitively dysfunctional is also seen as having a substantial although not complete conduct dysfunction (see Table 55, row (6)).

Examining the three cases that were intended to communicate low dysfunction of various specific sorts, shown in Table 60 rows (4) to (6), one notices that the respondents in fact perceive those cases as involving moderate levels of dysfunction of a rather generalized sort. That is, the scenario (4) and (6) descriptions caused the respondents to perceive a moderate degree of both control and cognitive dysfunction, as is shown in columns (d) through (h). Intuitively in keeping with this, they do reduce the sentences given to those individuals as compared to the control case of murder (Table 59, row (l), sentence of 10.42, above life imprisonment) or the case in which an 18-year-old, non-intoxicated individual committed the same act (row (9), liability of 8.70, over 25 years in prison). But the sentences are by no means minor ones, ranging around 5 years in prison, and relatively low percentages of the respondents assign no liability or punishment in these cases.

There is one anomaly that cannot currently be explained. In the "low cognitive" impairment scenario of row (5), the respondents perceive that individual as having a considerable degree of both control and cognitive impairment, yet gave that individual a relatively high sentence. Further research will be needed to clarify this finding. It is possible that the subjects saw something in the specifics of the description that led to this odd result.

Still, with some tentativeness, one can derive a conclusion relevant to code drafters. Involuntary intoxication seems to be analyzed by the respondents as analogous to mental illness; they analyze it using the same concepts of control and cognitive dysfunction that they employ for analyzing mental illness. This supports the common practice of providing analogous conditions of exculpation in the involuntary intoxication and insanity defenses.

Some general comments may be in order on the exact circumstances that created the involuntary intoxication in the core scenario. Recall that the individual is taking a long-term drug for the control of pain, has not been warned by the physician as to the possibility of side effects, and takes an over-the-counter medication that, in interaction with the pain medication, triggers the mental dysfunction. This case seems fairly far toward one end of a continuum of what a sensible person should know about what might happen to his or her mental state as a consequence of certain actions. The actor is relatively justified in not realizing in advance that the particular drug combination would produce mental dysfunction. In contrast, consider the case of the individual who is taking some long-term medication, ingests random handfuls of mixed street drugs to experience a new and different high, and kills others while suffering a temporary mental dysfunction caused by the interaction of the medication and the street drugs. That individual may be recognized as equally in the grip of a mental dysfunction when he killed, but may draw judgments of considerably more liability from respondents, because he ought to have known that the drug-ingesting action would have mind-altering consequences of a potentially dangerous nature. In other words, that case may be treated as one of voluntary intoxication. Recall that, in the voluntary intoxication study, the respondents judge that an offense committed while intoxicated generates more liability the more purposeful the individual is about achieving a state of intoxication. A similar dynamic may be at work in cases of involuntary intoxication in which the person should be aware of the possibility of becoming intoxicated.

What can be said about the respondents' judgments of liabilities and associated perceptions of the immaturity cases? Returning to Table 60, consider next the set of scenarios, shown in rows (7), (8), and (9), that varied the age of the person. Notice, first, the "age" column (a) of the table; clearly the readers notice and can accurately report the age of the different persons in the scenarios. Look at the various columns (d) through (h), which report the degree of awareness the person has about the consequences and the wrongfulness of his actions. In general, the results track the age of the person, so the youngest person is seen as less aware of the wrongfulness of his actions and the likely consequences of his actions. He is less aware, but by no means unaware: all of the ratings stay well on the "aware" side of the scale midpoints.

Next, notice the civil commitment column (d) of Table 59. For the cases involving underage perpetrators, the respondents were asked if they would recommend some alternative, non-prison form of dealing with the offender, as is sometimes available in the juvenile criminal justice system. Notice that some of the respondents do indeed recommend this form of treatment for the underage offender; the younger the person, the higher percentage of those recommending it. For the 10-year-old person, almost half of the respondents recommend this form of treatment.

Next, notice the liability ratings assigned to the differently aged persons reported in Table 59. The parenthesized numbers of column (a) report the percentage of respondents imposing criminal liability and the average sentence given by those who choose to impose criminal liability. Relatively severe sentences are given, and age makes little difference in this. This is surprising, and it will be interesting to see if this result holds up in future research. However, tentatively, the following is an interpretation: the younger the perpetrator, the higher percentage of respondents that want that person to receive treatment that is alternate to criminal incarceration; however, for the minorities who see criminal sentences as appropriate, youth does not decrease the duration of the sentence. There are two possible interpretations for this: those minorities see criminal incarceration as an appropriate vehicle for reform of the young individual, or they see him as just as incorrigible as an older person would be.

To summarize, the involuntary intoxication scenarios involved an interaction between a prescribed and an over-the-counter drug. One would want to have cases about other forms of involuntary intoxication before coming to any firm conclusions. That said, involuntary intoxication does seem to be judged by principles similar to those used for the general defense of insanity. However, the respondents are noticeably less willing to treat involuntary intoxication as a complete defense; it mitigates liabilities, but the liabilities assigned are still reasonably high. Further research is needed to determine whether this is the case in all instances of involuntary intoxication, or was specific to the cases created.

The younger the offender, the higher the percentage is of the respondents who want the offender to be treated by some alternative to the normal criminal justice system. However, for any of a number of reasons that have been discussed, those who want the offender retained in the criminal justice system are willing to give him sentences of over 20 years in length. Much depends on the degree of rationality that the respondents attribute to the offenders, and that may not correlate well with the age of the offender. Much remains to be explored here in further research, and notice that the criminal justice system is in a somewhat unsettled state with regard to the treatment of youthful offenders.

C. Duress and Entrapment Defenses

In legal codes, the defense of duress exculpates a person whose conduct otherwise would create liability. Here, unlike the insanity, immaturity, and involuntary intoxication defenses, the focus is not directly on the dysfunction caused, but on the external pressures on the individual that might create reasons why he or she engaged in the otherwise punishable conduct. These pressures normally arise from the improper actions of other people and create such a force that even a reasonably resolute person, subject to those pressures, might succumb to them. The bank manager who lets the burglars into the bank vault after hours because the burglars have kidnapped his family and he believes that they will harm his family if he does not let them in, is an example of an individual who acts under coercion. The external pressure may cause coercion that, in turn, one might guess, causes an impairment of control analogous to the impairments excused under insanity or immaturity defenses. Statutes typically require that the force exceed a given level and reach a level of sufficient coerciveness to render the person blameless, before a defense is available. Frequently the definition of that level involves the familiar legal fiction of the "reasonable person." Under the Model Penal Code, for example, the force must be such "that a person of reasonable firmness in [the actor's] situation would have been unable to resist."[15]

The case of the "entrapped individual" is sometimes thought to share a similar philosophical grounding; an individual who would not otherwise have committed the criminal act is led by abnormal circumstances into doing so. The possibility of entrapment arises when an agent of the government somehow lures or entices an individual into committing a crime. At the highest level of generalization, the entrapment doctrine gives a person a defense if a government agent induces or persuades him to commit the offense. But as intuition would lead one to expect, entrapment statutes typically have additional limitations and restrictions that are taken into account. The defense is limited to instances of improper entrapment by a police officer, typically undercover; the same inducement by a private individual is not a defense. The inducement or persuasion of entrapment is not as compelling as

---

[15] Model Penal Code §2.09.

the coercion typical of duress and does not seem to so clearly remove blame from the acting individual.

The entrapment defense is almost unique to the United States, and within this country there is a great deal of variety among the different jurisdictions in defining it. The debated differences center around defining it in an appropriately limited way. Two general approaches are common. What may be called the "subjective formulation" of entrapment requires that the person be induced on this occasion to commit the offense by the police agent, and that the person is not otherwise predisposed to commit the offense. Thus, a career drug dealer cannot get an entrapment defense, under a subjective formulation, even if the instant transaction was induced or encouraged by a government agent, because the previous transactions demonstrate predisposition.

The first type of entrapment formulation is subjective. Note that somewhat counterintuitively, the subjective formulation of the entrapment defense does not have a specific requirement for the amount of pressure or enticement that was brought to bear on the person. As long as the person is not predisposed to commit the offense, any amount of pressure or inducement that successfully causes the person to commit the offense will provide a defense. The subjective approach focuses on both the police and the person and requires two conditions for the defense to be successful—improper police conduct (conduct that would have caused a person not predisposed to commit the offense) and no predisposition by this defendant.

A second common approach of entrapment defenses is what may be called the "objective formulation." Under this approach, the focus does not include the person—whether he was predisposed to commit the offense—but rather the focus is exclusively upon the propriety of the government agent's conduct. Of course, the subjective approach also focuses on one aspect of the police officer's conduct—is the conduct such that it would cause a person not predisposed to commit the offense to do so? The difference is that the objective approach is such that it does not ask, in addition, whether this particular person was in fact predisposed to commit the crime.

A career drug dealer may get an entrapment defense under the objective formulation if the government agent's conduct is "improper." What conduct is "improper?" Under the Model Penal Code (which uses such an objective formulation), for example, a government agent acts improperly and may generate an entrapment defense for an offender if he induces an offender to commit an offense by:

> (a) making knowingly false representations designed to induce the belief that such conduct is not prohibited; or (b) employing methods of persuasion or inducement that create a substantial risk that such an offense will be committed by persons other than those who are ready to commit it.[16]

Note that the objective formulation seems somewhat more inconsistent with people's intuition. The first clause of the statute requires only that the false

[16] Model Penal Code §2.13(1)(a) & (b).

representation be designed to induce a belief that the conduct was not prohibited. The second clause requires only that the methods create a risk of inducing a person not ready to commit the offense to commit the offense. Thus the statute does not require that the actual offender be brought to the belief that the action is legal, or actually have been persuaded or induced to commit the offense. That is, the person need not actually be induced by the agent; he need only have committed the offense in response to certain actions on the part of the agent. For instance, a government agent may tell a habitual drug dealer that it is not illegal to sell a certain sort of drug. The dealer may know full well that it is illegal and yet escape liability for the act of selling the drug under the objective formulation of the defense.

It may be apparent by now that the entrapment defense is not, strictly speaking, an excuse that exculpates the person. It permits the person to escape from liability, but does so for a variety of reasons relating to fairness and deterring governmental overreaching rather than the person's lack of blameworthiness. This is true of the subjective formulation as well as the objective formulation. No minimum coerciveness of the inducement is required. Nor is the defense available if the person succumbs to inducement from a private citizen, even where the same inducement from a government agent would give a defense.

The present study tested cases involving both duress and entrapment. First, it sought to determine whether the subjects would recognize a duress defense for coerced conduct and, if so, how much coercion would be required to evoke the defense. Second, and considerably more tentatively, it explored the related questions of entrapment. It sought to determine whether the subjects would recognize a defense under the various conditions of entrapment suggested by different formulations of the defense. That is, it sought to determine whether the subjects would see entrapping conditions as exculpating the person or, alternatively, whether they might reduce the person's liability because they saw mitigating if not exculpating conditions. It sought to examine as well whether the respondents' views correspond better with one or the other of the two formulations of the entrapment defense.

The study gave subjects duress scenarios with varying levels of coercion, and also scenarios involving entrapment with and without predisposition of the offender, with and without improper inducement by a government agent, as well as variations substituting a private citizen for the agent. The core scenario involved an individual who agrees to transport eight ounces of cocaine for another individual. The respondents were asked to tell the researchers the degree to which they saw the person as being personally disposed to commit the crime that he commits; to rate the amount of coercion they saw exercised on the person; whether a person of reasonable firmness would be coerced or induced to commit the offense; and the degree of impropriety of the inducements that are held out to the person in committing the crime, as well as an assessment of the punishment that the person deserves, if any.

As to the duress defense, notice first that in the control case of row (1) of Table 61, in which the person commits the crime, transporting cocaine, with no degree of duress or inducement, the liability imposed is 5.52, corresponding to a sentence of

TABLE 61. } Liability and Subjects' Perceptions as Related to Duress and Entrapment

	(a)	*(b)*	*(c)*	*(d)*	*(e)*	*(f)*	*(g)*	*(h)*
Scenarios	*Liability*	*% No Liability (N)*	*% No Liability or No Punishment (N+0)*	*Amount of Coercion*	*"Reasonable Person Coerced"*	*"Predisposition"*	*"Improper Inducement"*	*"Reasonable Person Induced"*
1. Control—no duress or inducement	5.52[a]	0	3	–	–	5.58	–	–
Duress scenarios:								
2. High coercion	2.29[c]	9	50	8.21	6.31	2.32	8.09	6.32
3. Low coercion	3.65[b]	3	24	6.29	4.88	3.68	7.53	4.82
Entrapment scenarios:								
4. No prior record—agent	2.44[c]	21	50	7.62	6.06	2.79	8.18	5.91
5. Prior record—agent	6.24[a]	6	9	3.65	4.38	6.91	6.03	4.50
6. No prior record—buddy	3.50[b]	3	26	7.12	5.41	2.65	7.62	5.18

Liability Scale: N=No criminal liability, 0=Liability but no punishment, 1=1 day, 2=2 weeks, 3=2 months, 4=6 months, 5=1 year, 6=3 years, 7=7 years, 8=15 years, 9=30 years, 10=life, and 11=death.

Key to column heads:
Statements *(e)* through *(h)* were responded to on a scale where: 1="strongly disagree," 5="unsure," and 9="strongly agree."

(d) How much coercion (i.e., pressure or force) did the actor feel, from the accomplice, to commit the offense? (1=no coercion; 9=extreme coercion).
(e) The amount of coercion (i.e., pressure or force) from the accomplice on the actor would have been enough to cause a reasonable person in the actor's situation to commit the offense.
(f) The actor is generally inclined to commit an offense like this even if no one encouraged him to do so.
(g) The accomplice used methods of persuasion or inducement on the actor, to get him to commit the offenses, that were improper.
(h) The accomplice used methods of persuasion or inducement on the actor, to get him to commit the offenses, that would have caused a reasonable person to commit the offense.

Note: Superscript letters indicate significance at the $p < .05$ level by a Newman-Keuls test. Matching superscripts indicate means that are not statistically significantly different from each other. Means are compared within columns only.

approximately two years. For contrast, take the most extreme duress case, that of high coercion in row (2). In this case, an individual with no prior record transports the cocaine for an individual who threatens to kill his family if he does not do so. This high-coercion duress scenario gave liability results that are much lower than the control case, suggesting that the respondents see a considerable mitigation in this case; the average liability assigned, column (a), is 2.29, a sentence of 3.8 weeks. Notice also that 50 percent of the subjects assign no punishment to the offender.

As the degree of coercion decreases (the low coercion case of row (3)), the subjects produce a liability result that is between that of the high coercion and the control cases, of 3.65, corresponding to 4.4 months. An examination of the distribution of the results provides no evidence of bimodality, which would have supported a "threshold" notion of coercion. It appears that here, the respondents are making continuous judgments of liability when the legal system imposes a threshold concept by requiring a fixed minimum coercion for a complete defense. The respondents see degrees of coercion when the legal system wishes to see either coercion or no coercion.

Examine next the ratings on the perceptions of the coercion cases shown in rows (d) through (h). In the case of high coercion, respondents are in agreement that the coercion is indeed high (column (d), 8.21 on a scale on which 9 equals extreme coercion), and they are in agreement with the statement that it is sufficient coercion to cause any reasonable individual to succumb to it, column (e). (But notice that the extent of the agreement is not strong but 6.31, where 5 equals unsure and 7 equals agree. Respondents mention such options as reporting the threat-making individual to the police.) The case of "low coercion," which involves a person smuggling cocaine because he would lose his job as a truck driver otherwise, is read by the subjects as moderate to high coercion, as indicated by their column (d) rating of 6.29 (on a 9 point scale) and they are generally unsure whether it is enough coercion to get a reasonable person to comply with the request, column (e), averaging 4.88, quite near the "unsure" response. This suggests, in future research, cases of very low coercion be included, in order to test the lower limits of the respondents' perceptions. There may be cases in which subjects recognize that some degree of pressure has been exerted, yet do not grant the defense of coercion. However, note the unexpectedly high level of coercion necessary to exculpate the defendant. Even the actor who experiences high coercion receives no punishment from only 50 percent of the subjects! This is puzzling because the facts described in this scenario appear to be highly coercive, the respondents see them as highly coercive, and yet the person does not receive complete exculpation.

Still, the degree of coercion that they perceive operating on the person makes a difference in the liabilities that the respondents assign. There is a second line of evidence that coercion makes a difference to the respondents. Look within the low coercion condition, in which perceptions of whether a reasonable person would have been coerced into committing the crime are tabled, column (e). The extent to which the individual subject judges that the degree of coercion would cause a reasonably firm individual to succumb to the pressure and the degree of liability assigned to the person correlate strongly. The lesser the degree of coercion that the respondent sees exerted on the person to commit the criminal action, the longer sentence he or she imposes for committing that conduct.

Look next at the psychologically more complicated situation of entrapment to see if one can discern a pattern in the respondents' judgments. In scenario (4), the driver, who has no prior record of offenses, is approached by an undercover government agent, who was previously acquainted with him in the military service. The person is put under pressure by the agent to transport drugs. Scenario (5) is the same, except the readers were told that the person had prior convictions for transporting and was looking to get back into the drug business. The liabilities assigned to the two cases are significantly different; the liability assigned the person with the prior record is as high (indeed, higher) as the liability assigned to the individual who commits the act with no inducement. Compare this result with that suggested by the objective formulation, which relies solely on the propriety of the behavior of the government agent. Quite clearly, the objective method does not accord well with the subjects' intuitions. For the objective formulation, the past convictions are irrelevant; what is critical is that the government agent approached the person, and in some sense "lured" him into the behavior. Yet, for the respondents, prior convictions are critical; the individual with a prior record is assigned a mean sentence of about 4 years, exceeding that assigned to the control condition, while the individual with no prior record is assigned a sentence that is sharply lower, between 4 and 5 weeks in prison.

The reason for this difference is probably found in the respondents' perceptions of the degree to which the criminal action resulted from the predispositions of the person. Refer to column (e) in which subjects were asked whether they agree that "the individual generally is inclined to commit an offense like this even if no one encouraged him to do so."[7] When the person has a prior history of similar offenses, the respondents read the person's current criminal action as springing from his predispositions, and they think that the coercion would not have worked with a reasonable person, column (e); they judge the criminality of the person accordingly. In contrast, when the person is a first-time offender, as shown in row (4), the coercive force of the inducements provided by the agent is seen as much more strong, and the assigned liability is accordingly reduced. What has happened here is psychologically interesting; the discovery of prior convictions has caused the respondents to see the entire scenario quite differently.

This is not to say that there is no concern that government agents are involved in the inducement process or are acting improperly. A slightly greater mitigation of liability is given in the case of identical inducements by a government agent, row (4), than by a friend of the person, row (6), and the percentages assigning no punishment, shown in column (c), are much greater. However, an examination of the various other ratings of the two cases suggests that this may not be due to the fact that the inducer is a government agent; instead it may be because, knowing that the inducements came from a government agent who can be expected to be more skilled at the "inducement game," the amount of the coercion contained in the inducement is read by the subjects as slightly higher, the degree to which a reasonably firm person would succumb to them slightly higher, and so on.

Whatever the source of this slight difference in liabilities assigned an individual who succumbs to identical pressures from a person who is either a friend or a police agent, the finding tends to undermine the validity of the entrapment defense generally—both the objective and the subjective formulations. The defense is available only for inducement by a police agent, yet the subjects see the police versus non-police source of the inducement as not a major determinant of liability.

Much about the objective formulation is untested in this study and awaits further research. One would want to create cases in which the government agent entrapped but was not perceived as coercing the person. Also one would want the government agent to violate one of the objective formulation's prohibitions, such as telling the person that the action was not illegal.

The subjective formulation of entrapment is this: a person, who is not predisposed to commit the offense, is induced (not coerced, as in the duress defense) to commit the offense by inducements offered by a police officer that would have induced a reasonable person to do the same. On initial examination of the data, the subjective formulation of the entrapment defense corresponds better to the subjects' view than the objective formulation. Scenario (4), the first of the three entrapment cases, draws an average liability assignment from the subjects of 2.44 (4.9 weeks), and the person is perceived, as column (f) shows, as not predisposed to commit the crime. Further, subjects tend to agree, as shown in column (h), that a reasonable person would have been induced to commit the crime. Scenario (5), in which the person, who has a prior record, is seen as predisposed and the inducement is seen as not sufficient to cause a reasonable person to commit the crime, draws a sentence higher than the comparison condition of scenario (1)! Further analysis confirms that the degree of perceived inducement matters. Within the condition, tabled in row (4), in which the government agent entices the person, the more the respondent sees the actions of the agent as providing an inducement that would sway a reasonable person to commit the crime, the lower the degree of liability he or she assigns to the person.

Note that even the subjective formulation of entrapment does not find full support among the subjects as a defense. The individual with no prior record who is lured by the government agent into committing the crime gets a liability rating of 2.44 (about 5 weeks in jail). This assignment of some liability on the part of the respondents suggests that they do not think that a complete defense should be available in entrapment cases, which is what current doctrine provides, but rather that only a mitigation is appropriate. And recall also that the subjective defense, like the objective defense, stresses the importance of the inducer being a police agent, while the subjects give only minor weight to that distinction.

It is tempting to ask whether, in terms of community standards, there should be an entrapment defense at all. One of the questions that awaits further research is whether one might explain the entrapment mitigations found here as reflecting the subjects' assessment of the degree of duress-like coercion that existed in the entrapment cases. Some of the results suggest that the subjects may recognize entrapment as a defense only to the extent that it would give a defense or mitigation under a duress defense (albeit a duress defense altered to take account of degree of coercion and to give mitigations for coercion that does not exculpate.) If this were so, then, if one were to reform the criminal law doctrine to conform to the subjects' views, one would expand the duress defense to provide a mitigation (but not a complete defense) in cases of high to moderate coercion. Having done that, one might then abolish the entrapment defense as unnecessary.

To summarize, this study confirms that in fact people do mitigate and exculpate for coercion. If duress is perceived, liability is lowered. An individual who is under quite high duress to commit a crime receives a significant reduction in liability, but does not, as one might have expected, have his liability reduced to zero. The frequent use of the "liability but no punishment" option suggests that the respondents want to make clear that they are not condoning the conduct, but such disapproval of the conduct does not take away from their willingness to exculpate the person. Recall that unlike insanity, which has a special verdict that signals the reason for the acquittal, a duress acquittal under the current system leaves the message about the conduct ambiguous. Thus, one would expect more resort to this particular verdict of, essentially, "rule violation but no punishment," here than in insanity cases. The use of this response shows no ambivalence about exculpating the person, it is suggested, but rather ambivalence about apparently approving the conduct.

With respect to entrapment, the study found that both of the standard formulations, which emphasize the importance of the inducement coming from a police agent, and the particular conduct of the police agent, do not have much effect on the liability judgments of the subjects. Instead the subjects tend to give a defense to the degree that they think the person is strongly coerced, and the degree to which they think a reasonably firm person would also be induced to commit the crime. Thus, if the community's view was to be followed, the entrapment defense would disappear as a separate defense and be subsumed under the duress defense.

D. Summary

This chapter examines community views on disability excuses, finding that there are some broad conclusions to be made in the area but that there is also more to be explored. The disability caused by mental incapacity is recognized by the respondents as a valid reason to exculpate a person. Formulations of mental incapacity that recognize both a control and cognitive deficit are the preferred ones; the respondents seem to judge that dysfunction of either type is a valid trigger for exculpation. The greater the dysfunction, the greater the likelihood of a defense. And respondents seem satisfied with a substantial rather than a complete dysfunction as establishing exculpation.

Involuntary intoxication is analyzed in legal codes on principles similar to the ones used for the analysis of mental illness, and this seems appropriate to the subjects. They show a similar pattern of liability for involuntary intoxication as for insanity: they recognize both cognitive and control dysfunctions as an excuse; and the greater the dysfunction, the greater the likelihood of excuse.

Duress scenarios, the data reveals, are recognized as providing at least a mitigation of liability for offenses, and the degree of mitigation is a function of the degree of coercion the respondents see in the particular situation. Whether duress can provide a complete excuse awaits further research. Code formulations of the entrapment defense require that it be given only when a police agent supplies the inducement that leads the person to commit the crime and the respondents did not see the importance of this requirement. Instead, they seemed to judge these cases using considerations similar to the ones they used in the duress cases, leading to the consideration of the possibility that the entrapment defense might properly disappear as a separate defense, and be subsumed under the duress defense.

The respondents often deal with their complex judgments about many of these excuse cases by giving a response that signals that they do wish to disapprove of the conduct, but they do not wish to do more than symbolically punish the person.

16 }

Principles of Adjudication: Doctrines of Grading

Doctrines of grading ask the question: what degree of punishment is deserved for a blameworthy violation? A legal code's grading of the seriousness of a blameworthy violation appears in two forms: within offenses and between offenses. Within a general offense such as rape or theft, the code often makes some distinctions about the differential seriousness of different kinds of rapes, or thefts. Different levels of punishment are attached to these different grades of offense. Also, different types of offenses are given different grades, reflecting the relative seriousness of rape as compared to theft, for example. This chapter, which is drawn primarily from portions of my work with John Darley in *Justice, Liability & Blame: Community Views and the Criminal Law*,[1] considers both kinds of grading judgments.

A. Grading Distinctions among and within Offenses

Earlier chapters have highlighted several studies about peoples' views of the relative seriousness of different criminal conduct.[2] In Blumstein and Cohen's 1980 survey, for example, respondents were asked to assign the length of a prison sentence that "best fits the seriousness of the offense."[3] The results indicated that the offense seriousness was seen as follows, from least serious to most serious: simple assault, larceny, drunk driving, receiving stolen property (television), fraud (supplying false information on a loan form), possessing a gun without a license, burglary, auto theft, sodomy, robbery, cocaine use, aggravated assault, heroin possession, prison escape, Medicaid fraud, subjecting employees to unsafe working conditions, armed robbery, cocaine sales, rape, assault with intent to kill, manslaughter, second degree murder, and first degree murder.

---

[1] Paul H. Robinson & John M. Darley, Justice, Liability & Blame: Community Views and the Criminal Law ch. 6 (1995).

[2] *See* e.g., chapter 2, section C & chapter 4, section B (presenting studies where people ranked various crimes based on seriousness); chapter 12, section B (examining peoples' views on seriousness of different versions of attempt when applied to a specific hypothetical crime).

[3] Alfred Blumestein & Jacqueline Cohen, *Sentencing of Convicted Offenders: An Analysis of the Public's View*, 14 L. & Soc. Rev. 223, 229 (1980).

Rossi and others conducted a more comprehensive study in 1972,[4] largely replicating an earlier study by Sellin and Wolfgang.[5] The results of the 140 offenses, with a score of 9 being most serious, are presented in the table below.

The issue of grading within offenses has already been touched upon. The factors that establish the minimum requirements for criminalization and for liability provide the starting point for grading within an offense. They establish the require-

TABLE 62. } Average Seriousness Ratings Given to 140 Offenses in Baltimore Survey

Rank	Crime	Mean	Variance
1	Planned killing of a policeman	8.474	2.002
2	Planned killing of a person for a fee	8.406	2.749
3	Selling heroin	8.293	2.658
4	Forcible rape after breaking into a home	8.241*	2.266
5	Impulsive killing of a policeman	8.214	3.077
6	Planned killing of a spouse	8.113*	3.276
7	Planned killing of an acquaintance	8.093	3.273
8	Hijacking an airplane	8.072	2.776
9	Armed robbery of a bank	8.021	8.020
10	Selling LSD	7.949	3.048
11	Assault with a gun on a policeman	7.938	3.225
12	Kidnapping for ransom	7.930	3.844
13	Forcible rape of a stranger in a park	7.909	3.737
14	Killing someone after an argument over a business transaction	7.898	3.536
15	Assassination of a public official	7.888	5.400
16	Killing someone during a serious argument	7.867	3.663
17	Making sexual advances to young children	7.861	3.741
18	Assault with a gun on a stranger	7.847*	2.172
19	Impulsive killing of a spouse	7.835	3.952
20	Impulsive killing of a stranger	7.821*	3.429
21	Forcible rape of a neighbor	7.778	3.726
22	Impulsive killing of an acquaintance	7.717	4.205
23	Deliberately starting a fire which results in a death	7.707	4.189
24	Assault with a gun on a stranger	7.662**	2.976*
25	Manufacturing and selling drugs known to be harmful to users	7.653	3.280
26	Knowingly selling contaminated food which results in a death	7.596	5.202
27	Armed robbery of a company payroll	7.577	3.080
28	Using heroin	7.520	4.871
29	Assault with a gun on an acquaintance	7.505	3.482
30	Armed holdup of a taxi driver	7.505	3.336

(*Continued*)

[4] Peter H. Rossi et. al., *The Seriousness of Crimes: Normative Structure and Individual Differences*, 39 AM. SOC. REV. 224 (1974).

[5] *See* THORSTEN SELLIN & MARVIN E. WOLFGANG, THE MEASUREMENT OF DELINQUENCY (Patterson Smith 1975).

Rank	Crime	Mean	Variance
31	Beating up a child	7.490	3.840
32	Armed robbery of a neighborhood druggist	7.487*	3.221
33	Causing auto accident death while driving when drunk	7.455	3.904
34	Selling secret documents to a foreign government	7.423*	5.722
35	Armed street holdup stealing $200 cash	7.414	3.633
36	Killing someone in a bar room free-for-all	7.392	4.637
37	Deliberately starting a fire in an occupied building	7.347	5.177
38	Assault with a gun on a spouse	7.323	4.650
39	Armed robbery of a supermarket	7.313	3.911
40	Assault with a gun in the course of a riot	7.245	3.218
41	Armed hijacking of a truck	7.198	3.866
42	Deserting to the enemy in time of war	7.194	4.673
43	Armed street holdup stealing $25 in cash	7.165	4.431
44	Armed robbery of an armored truck	7.163	5.210
45	Spying for a foreign government	7.135	7.024
46	Killing a pedestrian while exceeding the speed limit	7.122	3.964
47	Seduction of a minor	7.021	5.729
48	Beating up a policeman	7.020	5.734
49	Selling marijuana	6.969*	7.216
50	Father-daughter incest	6.959	7.112
51	Causing the death of an employee by neglecting to repair machinery	6.918	4.556
52	Breaking and entering a bank	6.908	4.641
53	Mugging and stealing $25 in cash	6.873*	5.305
54	Selling pep pills	6.867	5.683
55	Cashing stolen payroll checks	6.827	4.784
56	Mugging and stealing $200 cash	6.796	5.051
57	Causing the death of a tenant by neglecting to repair heating plant	6.704	6.314
58	Killing spouse's lover after catching them together	6.691	7.695
59	Blackmail	6.667	5.122
60	Advocating overthrow of the government	6.663	7.715
61	Neglecting to care for own children	6.660	6.977
62	Forcible rape of a former spouse	6.653	6.394
63	Manufacturing and selling autos known to be dangerously defective	6.604	5.968
64	Beating up a stranger	6.604	5.379
65	Using LSD	6.557	7.479
66	Driving while drunk	6.545	6.006
67	Practicing medicine without a license	6.500*	6.908
68	Burglary of a home stealing a color TV set	6.440*	5.048
69	Knowingly passing counterfeit money	6.392	5.220
70	Beating up someone in a riot	6.368	5.788
1	Performing illegal abortions	6.330	5.723
2	Passing worthless checks for more than $500	6.309	5.119
3	A public official accepting bribes in return for favors	6.240	6.467
4	Employee embezzling company funds	6.207*	5.030

(*Continued*)

Rank	Crime	Mean	Variance
5	Knowingly selling stolen stocks and bonds	6.138*	4.960
6	Refusing to obey lawful order of a policeman	6.118*	5.806
7	Burglary of a home stealing a portable transistor radio	6.115*	5.871
8	Theft of a car for the purpose of resale	6.093*	5.085
9	Knowingly selling defective used cars as completely safe	6.093	5.023
0	Burglary of an appliance store stealing several TV sets	6.062	5.371
1	Looting goods in a riot	6.043	5.052
2	Knowingly selling stolen goods	6.021	4.463
3	Leaving the scene of an accident	5.949	6.620
4	Printing counterfeit $10 bills	5.948	6.820
5	Shoplifting a diamond ring from a jewelry store	5.939	5.466
6	Mother-son incest	5.907	9.189
7	Theft of a car for joy-riding	5.876	6.047
8	Intimidating a witness in a court case	5.853	4.850
9	Brother-sister incest	5.825	8.709
0	Knowingly selling worthless stocks as valuable investments	5.821	5.021
1	Beating up a spouse	5.796	7.051
2	Selling liquor to minors	5.789	7.572
3	Burglary of a factory stealing machine tools	5.789	5.317
4	Using stolen credit cards	5.750	5.832
5	Using pep pills	5.656	9.512
6	Joining a riot	5.656	6.750
7	Lending money at illegal interest rates	5.653	5.775
8	Knowingly buying stolen goods	5.596	5.794
9	Refusal to serve when drafted in peace time	5.535	8.863
0	Resisting arrest	5.449	6.271
1	Impersonating a policeman	5.449	7.405
2	Using false identification to obtain goods from a store	5.438	6.628
3	Bribing a public official to obtain favors	5.394	6.198
4	Passing worthless checks involving less than $100	5.339*	5.921
5	Desertion from military service in peace time	5.323	7.526
6	Under-reporting income on income tax return	5.305	6.321
7	Willfully neglecting to file income tax returns	5.157*	6.470
8	Soliciting for prostitution	5.144	7.687
9	Proposing homosexual practices to an adult	5.140	9.361
0	Overcharging on repairs to automobiles	5.135	6.455
1	Shoplifting a dress from a department store	5.070	6.308
2	Beating up an acquaintance	5.032	5.644
3	Driving while license is suspended	5.031	7.988
4	Pouring paint over someone's car	4.938	7.449
5	Shoplifting a pair of shoes from a shoe store	4.990	6.781
6	Overcharging for credit in selling goods	4.970	6.213
7	Shoplifting a carton of cigarettes from a supermarket	4.969*	6.793
8	Smuggling goods to avoid paying import duties	4.918	5.618

(*Continued*)

Rank	Crime	Mean	Variance
9	Killing a suspected burglar in home	4.868*	8.930
0	False claims of dependents on income tax return	4.832	6.801
1	Knowingly using inaccurate scales in weighing meat for sale	4.786	5.902
2	Refusal to make essential repairs to rental property	4.781	6.678
3	Engaging in male homosexual acts with consenting adults	4.736	9.396
4	Engaging in female homosexual acts with consenting adults	4.729	9.042
5	Breaking a plate glass window in a shop	4.653	6.697
6	Fixing prices of a consumer product like gasoline	4.629	6.069
7	Fixing prices of machines sold to businesses	4.619	6.218
8	Selling pornographic magazines	4.526	7.826
9	Shoplifting a book in a bookstore	4.424*	6.551
0	Repeated refusal to obey parents	4.411	9.074
1	Joining a prohibited demonstration	4.323	6.486
2	False advertising of headache remedy	4.083	7.972
3	Refusal to pay alimony	4.063	6.670
4	Refusal to pay parking fines	3.583*	6.475
5	Disturbing the peace	3.779	7.174
6	Repeated truancy	3.573	7.658
7	Repeated running away from home	3.571*	6.342
8	Loitering in public places	3.375	8.111
9	Refusal to answer census taker	3.105	7.329
0	Being drunk in public places	2.849	6.021

NOTE: Scores have a range of 9 (most serious) to 1 (least serious).

*Crimes rated by all members (200) of the Baltimore sample.

**This offense was inadvertently repeated (see crime rank No. 18), indicating that differences in scores as much as .185 can be obtained through response unreliability.

ments for the lowest grade of any given offense. The determination of higher grades of the offense then requires consideration of various other factors. Nearly all jurisdictions recognize several grades of homicide: negligent homicide, manslaughter (paradigmatically reckless homicide), and murder (intentional homicide). It is also common to distinguish even within these categories. Some jurisdictions may recognize two grades of murder and of manslaughter, first and second degree. Thus, first degree murder might be reserved for the most brutal forms of murder. Other offenses also have higher grades contained within their definitions, such as aggravated assault. Rape may have three or four grades, the term "rape" sometimes being used only in relation to the most serious.

A second sort of question involves what might be called "comparative grading" across different offenses. This describes judgments about the seriousness of a particular offense in comparison to other offenses. Murder intuitively seems a more serious offense than rape, that seems a more serious offense than theft, and the criminal codes recognize this by classifying murder as a higher grade offense than rape and rape a higher grade than theft, with a corresponding classification of each of the grades within each general offense.

Questions of offense seriousness and grading have become more important of late because of the move to standardize sentences by creating sentencing guidelines that judges must follow when they sentence convicted criminals. Factors that were once left to be considered by the sentencing judge in a highly discretionary judgment of how much punishment ought to be imposed, are now articulated and given defined weight under modern sentencing guidelines. So, offense grading principles, historically important in constructing criminal codes, have become important in the sentencing context.

The criminalization doctrines identify many of the most important factors in assessing the degree of punishment a person deserves, and thus what one might call the comparative grading of the offense, because they define the harm or evil of the offense. Interestingly, they frequently have done so by appeal to human intuition, although others have suggested that comparative grading is derivable from some more logical, less intuitive, analysis. Regardless of presumed source, it usually comes out that human safety is more important than the safety of property; intercourse with a 9-year-old is a more egregious wrong than intercourse with a 16-year-old. Assessing the relative seriousness of an offense requires an assessment of the relative value of the full range of interests protected by the criminal law. Criminal law theorists have only recently attempted to formulate principles for determining the relative seriousness of violations, having relied previously on appeals to shared intuitions within the culture.[6]

The grading task for the code drafters, then, is twofold: to distinguish among distinct grades of an offense, specifying minimal requirements for the crime; and specifying the circumstances that will produce a more aggravated version of that crime; and also to put these individual crimes into some comparative relationship of seriousness. Many of the studies reported earlier in this book give a hint at the kinds of factors that are relevant to these tasks.

First, the greater the seriousness of the harm caused, the higher the grade assigned to the offense. "Seriousness" can be an intuitive notion, and people can differ on how "serious" a particular offense like theft is, but it is clearly a notion that occupies a central place in a code's grading of offenses. Crimes in which life is risked or lost consistently receive more severe sentences than what one cannot help call "lesser crimes." As seen in the study on offense culpability requirements, in section A, people regard a sexual offense, in which an individual who did not consent to intercourse is raped, as more serious than setting fire to a dwelling, in which a person could conceivably be harmed; and setting fire to a dwelling, in which a person could conceivably be harmed, as more serious than setting fire to a similar site in which people would

---

[6] *See, e.g.,* JOEL FEINBERG, HARM TO OTHERS: THE MORAL LIMITS OF CRIMINAL LAW (Oxford University Press 1984); Andrew von Hirsch & Nils Jareborg, *Gauging Criminal Harm: A Living-standard Analysis,* 11 OXFORD J. LEG. STUD. 1 (1991).

not be dwelling. Second, similar notions of seriousness define the grades within a category of offense. The risk-of-harm study[7] showed that subjects increase liability as the extent of the harm risked increases.

The operating principle used to grade across and within offenses appears to be the same: the greater the harm caused or risked the greater the liability, all other things being equal. Later in this chapter, a study concerning sexual offenses that shows just how refined the community's judgments can be in distinguishing among actions judged to be of different seriousness is reported. It also shows that the general principle of "greater harm means greater liability" applies as well to offenses, like many sexual offenses, which are defined in terms of the immorality of the conduct rather than the harmfulness of the results of those actions.

A second powerful influence in grading is the person's culpability level. Several studies in the previous chapters have demonstrated that greater culpability in producing a fixed level of harm generally means greater liability. For instance, recall that greater liability is assigned to the accomplice who has greater culpability as to the perpetrator's offense or as to assisting a perpetrator.[8] Also recall the greater liability assigned to the individual who purposefully sets out to become intoxicated before he kills another, as compared to the individual who only knowingly or recklessly does so.[9] This chapter refines that picture with a study of felony murder, a doctrine frequently criticized as deviating from the normal principles of culpability.[10] The results suggest that the subjects make relatively refined judgments about culpability.

A third influence on grading is the actual presence of the harm or evil of the offense and the strength of the person's causal connection to it. This is a related but distinct factor from the nature of the harm or evil noted above. There it was said that, for instance, intentional killing is perceived as more serious than theft, and is therefore graded more seriously. The point here is that, within the realm of intentional killings, an actual killing is assigned more liability than an unsuccessful attempt to kill. The attempt study above demonstrates this point.[11] This notion is refined in this chapter by showing that resulting harm provides increased liability, but only if the harm is sufficiently causally connected with the person's conduct. A study of subjects' reactions toward different causal connections to a resulting death, reported in this chapter, shows that the stronger the causal connection with a resulting harm, the greater the increase in liability because of that resulting harm. This result was signaled in the objective requirements of complicity study, in chapter 12, section E. Complicity is a form of causing an offense by another person. The complicity study suggested that the greater the degree of the accomplice's causal contribution to the offense, the greater the accomplice's liability.

---

[7] Chapter 12, section D.

[8] Chapter 14, section B.

[9] Chapter 14, section C.

[10] See chapter 7, section B, 6.

[11] See chapter 12.

A fourth contributor in setting a person's ultimate punishment is the number of offenses for which he is to be punished. Consider the example of a headline that reads, "Burglar Who Committed 20 Burglaries Finally Caught." Obviously whether the burglar actually did commit the 20 offenses requires judicial determination, but suppose the system determines that he did. Somehow this must be reflected in the sentence the burglar receives. This goes somewhat beyond the issue of offense grading, but it is an essential part of setting the general range of punishment, the goal of the grading determination. A study reported in this chapter investigates a few of the basic principles involved in determining the range of punishment for multiple offenses.

B. The Seriousness of the Offense: Sexual Offenses

One of the major tasks of a criminal code is to identify the most significant factors that affect the seriousness of a criminal action and to define offenses in a way that incorporates these factors. The first study in this section examines the grading of offenses within the category of sexual offenses. These offenses were selected because, intuitively, some of the judgments encased within some legal codes on these issues seemed "out of kilter" with the ways that modern people seem to think about these offenses.

Sexual offenses, as they are defined by the Model Penal Code, are defined and graded around several central distinctions. For example, forms of forcible intercourse generally are treated as more serious than forms of consensual but unlawful intercourse, such as consensual intercourse with an underage partner. Within each of these groups, forcible and consensual intercourse, the Code adds several grading refinements, and it is here that the Code may contradict community standards. Forcible intercourse is deemed less serious if the victim is a voluntary social companion on the present occasion or previously permitted the person sexual liberties.[12] Forcible intercourse is judged to be still less serious (indeed, is not a sexual offense but only simple assault) if the aggressor and the victim are married[13] or living together as married.[14] On the other hand, if the same forcible intercourse occurs between a homosexual couple living together as married, it is not judged to be as serious as rape, because the relationship between the parties is not given legal standing in the Code.[15]

Cases of consensual intercourse similarly are distinguished in seriousness according to several factors. Intercourse with a partner under 16 ("statutory rape") or with a mentally disabled female who is "incapable of appraising the nature of her conduct" is judged less serious than forcible rape, but more serious than

[12] Model Penal Code §213.1(1).

[13] *See* Model Penal Code §213.6(2).

[14] Model Penal Code §213.1(1)&(2).

[15] Rape and gross sexual imposition are offenses only where the victim is a female. Model Penal Code §213.1(1)&(2). This is also true of statutory rape. *Id.* at §213.3(1).

consensual intercourse by a female with a retarded male or consensual intercourse with a person who is in the person's legal custody (such as a prisoner is to a jailer). It is a complete defense to several offenses, including statutory rape, which the victim previously engaged promiscuously in sexual relations with others.[16]

The sexual offenses study sought to test the offense distinctions used in the Model Penal Code against the community's views by presenting a series of scenarios, each of which embodies one of the Code's distinctions. In this study, the different scenarios were allowed to vary more widely in their circumstances than had been the case in many of the other studies discussed above, because the researchers hoped to lend overall plausibility to each case. Thus, occasionally differences in the scenarios may not be central to the legal issues being pursued. When that is the case, this section will comment on it. The results are described in Table 63.

The control case of "stranger" rape involves a woman who is followed as she leaves her health club, forcibly detained in a deserted parking lot, and forced to have

TABLE 63. } Liability for Sexual Offenses

	(a)	*(b)*	*(c)*	*(d)*
Scenarios	*Liability*	*% No Liability (N)*	*% No Liability or No Punishment (N+0)*	*Model Penal Code Result*
Forcible intercourse:				
1. Stranger	7.84[a]	0	0	First degree felony [§213.1(1)(a), rape]
2. Date	7.26[a,b]	26	29	Second degree felony [§213.1(1)(a)&(ii), rape]
3. Live together	6.27[b,c]	26	31	Misdemeanor [§2.11(1)(a), simple assault]
4. Married	5.88[c]	53	66	Misdemeanor [§2.11(1)(a), simple assault]
5. Homosexual	5.58[c]	53	66	Second degree felony [§2.13.2(1)(a), deviate sex by force]
Consensual intercourse:				
6. Statutory	2.29[d]	18	55	Third degree felony [§213.3(1)(a), statutory rape]
7. Statutory—prior promiscuity	2.39[d]	21	53	Complete defense [§213.6(3)]
8. Mentally handicapped female	1.97[d]	34	63	Third degree felony (§213.1(2)(b), gross sexual imposition]
9. Mentally handicapped male	1.37[d]	37	74	Misdemeanor [§213.4(2), sexual assault]
10. Female in jail	1.82[d]	37	63	Misdemeanor [§213.3(1)(c), seduction]

Liability Scale: N=No criminal liability, 0=Liability but no punishment, 1=1 day, 2=2 weeks, 3=2 months, 4=6 months, 5=1 year, 6=3 years, 7=7 years, 8=15 years, 9=30 years, 10=life, and 11=death.

Note: Superscript letters indicate significance at the $p < .05$ level by a Newman-Keuls test. Matching superscripts indicate means that are not statistically significantly different from each other. Means are compared within columns only.

[16] Model Penal Code §§213.1(1)(a) & (2)(b), 213.3(1)(a), 213.4(2) & (8), 213.6(4).

sexual intercourse by a man who threatens to kill her if she screams or resists him. This act, as you can see from Table 63, row (1), column (a), receives a sentence of 7.84 units, which corresponds to 13.4 years. Examine next the "date" case in row (2) perpetrated by an individual who was out on a date with a woman, returned with her to her apartment, and raped her there. The forcible intercourse mitigation that the Code recognizes for a voluntary social companion appears only as a slightly lower liability mean for that scenario than the control scenario, 7.84 vs. 7.26 (13.4 years vs. 9.4 years).

This interpretation of the difference is complicated by the fact that the respondents perceived a higher, although not significantly different, degree of consent on the part of the woman to the intercourse in the date scenario, and also attribute a higher degree of causation to her as well. Examine Table 64, rows (1) and (2) of columns (b) and (c) for these results. In future research, a date rape versus a stranger rape comparison should attempt to create similar perceptions of consent and causation in both

TABLE 64. } Subjects' Perceptions of Sexual Offenses

	(a)	*(b)*	*(c)*	*(d)*	*(e)*	*(f)*
Scenarios	*"Actor Forced"*	*"Victim Consented"*	*"Victim Caused"*	*"Victim Should Have Struggled More"*	*"Victim Acted Morally Inappropriately"*	*"Victim Capable of Consent"*
Forcible intercourse:						
1. Stranger	8.18^{a}	1.37^{c}	1.82	2.55	1.47	
2. Date	8.13^{a}	$1.87^{b,c}$	2.47	2.97	1.89	
3. Live together	$7.79^{a,b}$	2.32^{b}	3.95	2,97	2.87	
4 Married	$7.82^{a,b}$	2.18^{b}	3.95	2.95	3.11	
5. Homosexual	7.00^{b}	2.26^{b}	3.50	3.97	3.76	
Consensual Intercourse:						
6. Statutory	2.16^{c}	7.70^{a}	5.16		5.32	5.37
7. Statutory—prior promiscuity	2.26^{c}	7.63^{a}	5.71		5.47	5.55
8. Mentally handicapped female	3.05^{c}	6.95^{a}	4.05		3.37	
9. Mentally handicapped male	2.82^{c}	7.08^{a}	3.89		3.45	
10. Female in jail	2.57^{c}	7.22^{a}	3.86		3.89	

Key to column heads:
All statements were responded to on a scale where: 1="strongly disagree," 5="unsure," and 9="strongly agree."

(a) The actor forced the victim to have sexual intercourse with him.
(b) The victim consented to have sexual intercourse with the actor.
(c) The victim's behavior caused the actor's actions.
(d) The victim should have struggled harder to prevent what happened.
(e) The victim acted in a way that is morally inappropriate.
(f) The victim was capable of meaningfully consenting to sexual intercourse.

Note: Superscript letters indicate significance at the $p < .05$ level by a Newman-Keuls test. Matching superscripts indicate means that are not statistically significantly different from each other. Means are compared within columns only.

instances, and see if any reduction of sentence for the offender remains. Still, even if the subjects see greater consent in the date context, they see it as having only a slight effect on liability, not enough to support the grading difference assigned to the two cases by the Code drafters. It may well be that perceptions of the meaning of accepting an invitation to a date may have altered from those held at the time the Code drafters were working. Perhaps the point to extract is that community standards can change over time, and legal codes might properly change with them. The hint of a discovered difference between the two cases, if it can be replicated in future studies, provides some support for the grading difference that the legal code assigns to the two cases, but even so the extent of the Code's difference in treatment between the two (maximum of life for first degree versus maximum of 10 years for second degree) is much more of a difference than is justified in the subjects' view.

In the next two cases, the rape occurs between people who have been cohabiting. The woman tells the man with whom she has been living, row (3); or to whom she has been married, row (4), that she is leaving him and does not want to see him anymore. The conversation takes place in their residence and she asks him to sleep in a different room or at a relative's home. Angered, the man comes into the bedroom, and they begin fighting. Then, the man forces the woman to have sex and threatens to kill her if she screams or resists. Notice that the rejection of the man creates the possibility that the respondents would perceive the rapist as in the grip of an emotion and perhaps reduce the sentence assigned for that reason.

Notice first, in Table 64, column (a), that the respondents perceive that these rapes involved the use of considerable force, but a little less force than in the stranger and date rape cases. They also perceive, column (b), a low degree of consent on the part of the victim, but significantly more consent than in the stranger rape case. This may provide at least a partial account of why the subjects' liability means for stranger rape, shown in column (a) of Table 63, 7.84 (13.4 years), and date rape, 7.26 (9.4 years), are noticeably higher than those for a couple living together, 6.27 (4.2 years), or for a married couple, 5.68 (2.4 years). But even with this possibility, the differences in liability are not nearly so great as the Code provides when the aggressor and victim are married or living together: from first or second degree felony for rape of a stranger to a misdemeanor for forcible intercourse with a legal or common law spouse (treated as simple assault, for which the maximum is one year). This seems to suggest that a reexamination of the Code is in order.

If the Code regards forcible sexual intercourse between a couple who are married or living together as significantly less serious, this seems a judgment that is no longer in tune with the way people think. If the Code lowers the degree of the offense because the drafters were attributing an automatically higher degree of consent to the woman, this too seems inappropriate. Sadly, in recent decades, evidence has revealed that spouses do batter, abuse, and rape their spouses without regard for the spouse's consent. The issue of consent is a judgment best left to the jurors who are privy to the details in each specific case.

The greatest difference between the Code's and the subjects' views of the forcible intercourse scenario arises where the aggressor and victim are a homosexual couple living together. In this scenario, row (5), the circumstances are the same as in the married couple scenario. One individual announces he wishes to end the relationship; angered, the other forcibly rapes him, threatening to kill him if he resists or screams. The subjects see the case as meriting essentially the same degree of punishment, 5.58, as that given in the case of forcible intercourse between a married couple, 5.68. The Code, in sharp contrast, treats the married heterosexual case as a misdemeanor, simple assault (not a sexual offense), and the homosexual case as a serious sexual offense, deviant sexual intercourse by force, a second degree felony. Clearly, a good deal of the reason for this difference is that the respondents see the case of rape within marriage as much more serious than does the Code. A further reason is that the respondents are not assigning an increment in liability for the belief that the homosexual intercourse is "deviant" while the Code appears to.

Disparities between the Code and the subjects also exist in the consensual intercourse scenarios. The two cases at issue here are the "statutory" and the "statutory with prior promiscuity" cases tabled in rows (6) and (7). In both, a 14-year-old girl initiates sexual intercourse with a teenage boy. In the latter, she has a reputation for prior promiscuity. The Code gives a complete defense to the third degree felony of statutory rape for a victim's prior promiscuity, while the subjects see no significance in an underage victim's prior promiscuity assigning 2.29 and 2.39 to (6) and (7) respectively. The mean sentence in both cases is a bit less than 4 weeks, and over half of the subjects would assign no punishment. Given the specifics of the case, that the girl is 14, near the age of consent and initiates the intercourse, that the other participant is a teenage boy, and that there is no suggestion of violence, the respondents do not regard the case as particularly serious whether or not there is prior promiscuity on the part of the girl. Notice that in these two scenarios, and these two scenarios only, the respondents agree with the statement that the victim brought about the intercourse, column (c) of Table 64. They also agree strongly that she had consented to it, as shown in column (b); a sensible judgment since they were told that the girl had initiated it. However, note the sharp difference in the relatively lenient sentence that the subjects assign (2.29, 3.8 weeks) and the third degree felony liability (a five-year maximum) that the Code assigns in the case of the individual who has intercourse with a non-promiscuous 14-year-old girl. The respondents do not see this particular case of statutory rape as serious.

The Code classifies consensual intercourse with an underage female and with a mentally handicapped female as the same grade, and the subjects agree. The liability difference between the two cases is not significant. Here it is important to say more about the specifics of the mentally retarded case. The degree of mental handicap is probably perceived by the subjects as mild, since the woman is described as able to attend physical therapy sessions at a local health club, and the case description made clear that the handicapped individual initiates the sex act with the man. The respondents clearly perceived, column (b) and (c) of Table 64, that these circumstances, taken jointly, warrant the inference that the handicapped individual plays a considerable causal role in bringing about the intercourse, and certainly "consents" to the intercourse.

In these circumstances, the respondents do not view the male's participation in this case of intercourse as particularly blameworthy. This does not mean that people will never see intercourse with a mentally handicapped person as serious; another set of circumstances would probably lead to an inference of more serious wrongdoing. For instance, one would expect that a person who is extremely mentally handicapped would not be perceived as able to give meaningful consent to intercourse. However, the results do suggest that people are capable of making quite nuanced judgments in this area and resist seeing statutory rape, or intercourse with a mentally handicapped other, as always as serious as a third degree felony.

One obvious limitation on the results ought to be mentioned here; in the case of consensual intercourse with an underage person, the underage person is a 14-year-old teenager, and is likely to be seen by the respondents as fairly adult in her decision-making capacities. Were the victim to be younger, one would expect that the subjects would see the offense in a more serious light. (So would the Model Penal Code; if the victim is less than 10 years of age, the Code moves the grade up to the same grade as for forcible rape of a stranger—first or second degree felony.[17]) Similarly, the mentally handicapped person also seems to be perceived as competent enough to give consent. However, the contradiction between the respondents' judgments on these two cases and the Code remains. The implications of these differences will be discussed below.

Turning to the mental handicap case tabled in row (9), a female has sexual intercourse with a mentally handicapped male, under the same circumstances as the previously described case in which the male has intercourse with a handicapped female shown in row (8). In the case tabled in row (10), a female prisoner has sexual intercourse with one of the guards. The guard has supervisory responsibility over the woman, but there is no suggestion in the scenario that he has used his power to coerce the woman into intercourse. The Code differentiates between these three cases. Under the Code, consensual intercourse with a mentally retarded female is classed as a third degree felony, while the same conduct with a mentally handicapped male or with a person for whom the person has custodial supervision is a misdemeanor. The subjects, in contrast, do not distinguish significantly between these three forms of consensual intercourse. Nor do they assign significant sentences to any of them; all persons receive a mean sentence of less than two weeks in jail and between two thirds and three quarters of the respondents assign no jail term at all.

In these three cases, the respondents see the victim as giving consent to the intercourse. As an examination of the ratings in the "consent" column for these cases reveals, in all of these cases the respondents give responses to the consent question (Table 64 column (b)) that suggest they see the individual as consenting to the

[17] Model Penal Code §213.1(1)(d).

intercourse. An underlying issue here that code drafters might raise is the degree to which the consent is freely and competently given, or perhaps a reasonable person's readings of the perceptions of the perpetrator on this issue. The Code may treat other cases involving prisoners or mentally retarded individuals differently because they regard those cases as involving a lower degree, or otherwise flawed case, of consent. If this is so, then code drafters might consider making the degree and quality of consent the explicit focus of the judicial inquiry rather than imputing different degrees of consent to the different categories of sexual offenses. Alternatively, this may be one of those cases in which there is a reasoned set of valid considerations for having the legal code contradict the initial judgments of respondents, in which case it would be useful to articulate them.

Another important aspect of the results overall is that some major differences appear in punishment assignments between groups of the subjects. More specifically, the results reflect a dramatic disagreement in the amount of punishment imposed in the consensual intercourse scenarios. A majority of subjects would impose no punishment in any of the scenarios (6) through (10) (see the no punishment column, (c), of Table 63). The examination of the distribution of punishment given by the subjects suggests two distinct camps of opinion among the subjects. While a majority of subjects impose no punishment, the subjects that do impose punishment impose liability in the 4 to 6 range (4 equals six months; 6 equals three years); no one in the study assigned punishment in the in-between range of 1 to 3. One would have expected more sentences in this range if the distribution was of the typical normal curve pattern.

Obviously, this finding arises mainly from the cases in which the lower liability assignments were made. This is one of the few times in the studies in which it was found that subsets of subjects saw the situation differently. The grounds for this result will need to be addressed in future research. One obvious hypothesis, that males and females are seeing the situation differently, seems not to be the case.[18] A related possibility is that a small subset of the sample regards sexual congress with an underage or mildly retarded other as a serious offense while most others do not.

To summarize, the results of the sexual offenses study suggest that the subjects agree with some of the distinctions contained in the Code but not others. Of the scenarios tested, all forms of forcible intercourse are viewed by the subjects as more serious than any form of unlawful consensual intercourse. However, the subjects do not recognize the Code's significant reduction in liability for forcible intercourse with a social companion, nor do they provide as much reduction as the Code does for forcible intercourse with a spouse. The Code uses a marital-like relationship of a heterosexual couple to give a greater mitigation in the seriousness of forcible intercourse than the subjects would. Yet, at the same time, the Code disregards a

---

[18] Because the subject matter suggested that males and females might give different responses, the data also was analyzed for such differences. No statistically significant difference was detected between the responses of male and female subjects (12 men, 27 women).

marital-like relationship of a homosexual couple, treating the offense as if it is one between strangers, while the subjects would treat the case as analogous to that of a married couple. These differences between the Code and the subjects may reflect a change in public attitudes since 1962, when the Code was promulgated.

The subjects see as less serious than the Code does all forms of consensual intercourse, and most of the Code's distinctions in this area are not particularly significant to the subjects. Consensual intercourse with someone under 16 is seen as only slightly more serious than other forms of consensual intercourse. Contrary to the Code's rule, prior promiscuity of the underage partner is judged as having no mitigating effect, although there is the possibility that this is true because the sentence assigned the nonprior promiscuity is so low as not to be much reducible. In the context of consensual intercourse as well, the distinctions that the Code uses—prior promiscuity of a statutory rape victim, female versus male mentally retarded victim—and its more serious treatment of all forms of unlawful consensual intercourse, may reflect public opinion as it was before 1962. Nearly five decades have passed since then, and public opinion has shifted. Even in the several years since this data was collected, state code reforms have nearly eliminated use of the Model Penal Code's spousal exception to rape as well as other traditional formulations of sexual offenses. Thus, state legislatures appear to have been sensitive to the changing public views revealed here and have reformulated their codes accordingly.

Another more complex explanation of the differences between the Code and the subjects' responses is that the Code standards were based on a mix of two considerations: first, assumptions about what the degree of consent was likely to have been, as inferred from the nature of the existing relationships between the two individuals; and second, notions concerning "a husband's rights" and the "unnaturalness" of any homosexual relationship. It would be useful, in future research, to see if individuals who differ on these attitudes also differ in their liability assignments to specific rape scenarios. It would probably be useful, to the degree to which codes were based on what seem today to be outmoded notions, to revise the Code to reflect changes in community views. If codes are instantiating notions about what degree of consent assumed to exist in different relationships, it might be better to deal directly with consent issues in the context of the specific trial rather than infer them from relationships.

Should the Code be drafted in terms of the ultimate issue of effective consent, rather than using substitutes for consent such as age, mental retardation, or position-of-power disadvantage? In an age in which sexual harassment is a commonplace issue, this is a remarkably timely question. Some might suggest that these objective substitutes are needed because a person uses them to know whether the partner is capable of, and in a position to, give effective consent. In this way one avoids punishing persons who are honestly mistaken about effective consent. But an alternative approach to protect these same persons from liability is available: to rely on culpability requirements to exculpate for a mistake. To be logically consistent, however, this might mean that the culpability requirement would need to be restored for statutory rape, for example, from which it frequently has been removed.

This section has offered the suggestion that community standards about sexual offenses may have changed over the past few decades. Not all offenses are likely to be the subject of significant changes in public opinion, but a mechanism ought to exist that will detect such changes and signal a need for reexamination of the offense definitions. This is one important function of increased social science research on community views of criminal liability and punishment.

C. The Culpability of the Person: Felony Murder

One person causes the death of another. As common intuition suggests, the legal codes concern themselves with exactly how this came about, and assign different degrees of liability depending on the answer. Specifically, the standard grading differences among homicides tie the degree of liability to the level of a person's culpability as to causing the death. Recall that a person who purposely or knowingly causes a death is liable for murder; one who recklessly causes a death is liable for manslaughter; one who negligently causes a death is liable for negligent homicide; and the grade of the offense in each instance is diminished.[19]

When an accomplice aids in the homicide, similar considerations of culpability are used. Specifically, the culpability level as to causing death of a person who assists the principal (an "accomplice") is determinative of the degree of liability. Like the principal, an accomplice who is purposeful or knowing as to death is liable for murder; one who is reckless is liable for manslaughter; one who is negligent is liable for negligent homicide.[20]

But for a certain kind of homicide, the consideration of either the principal's or the accomplice's degree of culpability abruptly stops, and any homicide is considered to call for the penalties assigned for murder. This is the case when the homicide occurs during the commission of a felony. Most jurisdictions have a special doctrine, called the felony murder rule, which holds a person liable for murder, without regard to his level of culpability as to causing the death, if he causes the death in the course of a felony. Thus, a negligent killing that would otherwise be punished as negligent homicide is treated as murder if it occurs during a robbery.[21] A second aspect of the felony murder rule applies this aggravation of culpability to accomplices as well. Thus, an accomplice in a robbery is liable for murder, although he assists a principal who is only negligent as to the killing and is himself (the accomplice) only negligent as to such a death.[22]

Initially, one intuitively sees the point of this. Assume I am robbing a bank and aim to fire a warning shot into the floor but have used such a powerful pistol that

---

[19] *See, e.g.,* Model Penal Code §§210.2(1)(a), 210.3(1)(a), 210.4(1).

[20] *See, e.g., id.* at §2.06(3)(a)(ii)&(4).

[21] *See, e.g.,* Ca. Penal Code §189 (West 1994); 18 Pa. Stat. Ann. §2502(b) (West 1994); N.Y. Penal Law §125.25(3) (McKinney 1994).

[22] *See, e.g.,* 18 Pa. Stat. §2502(b); N.Y. Penal Law §125.25(3).

the shot ricochets and, to my surprise, kills an innocent customer. One sees the force of the claim that I have committed an offense more serious than a negligent homicide. I have created a situation fraught with danger and should pay the price when the potential harm is realized. Still, one also sees why the case is still distinguishable from intentional killing, murder, in a way that suggests lower liability.

The felony murder rule is even broader in some jurisdictions, and it seems to move farther away from community intuitions. Some jurisdictions hold felons liable for a death caused by an innocent person resisting the intended felony.[23] Thus, where a person who is being robbed draws a gun and accidentally kills an innocent bystander, the robbers are held liable for murder for the killing of the bystander by the robbery victim. A specific case will make the operation of the rule clear, and also help explicate why it causes uneasiness. Two thieves have tunneled into a bank vault and are surreptitiously hauling away cash. Alerted by a silent alarm, private security forces rush to the scene. Unfortunately, two groups of security forces are alerted, and both rush to the scene. In the confusion, security force A shoots and kills a member of security force B. The thieves, neither of whom is armed, are charged with murder. Now clearly, they have created the occasion for the accident, and are in some very basic and central way responsible for the outcome, but it does not seem intuitively obvious that the right decision is to assign them the same penalty one would assign a thief who actually shoots the security guard.

The Model Penal Code drafters disapproved of the felony murder rule, even in its most narrow form. They substituted an evidentiary presumption, rebuttable by the defendant, that if a killing occurs in the course of a felony, the felons are presumed to have caused the death "recklessly under circumstances manifesting an extreme indifference to the value of human life," which it defines as adequate culpability for murder.[24] Commentators similarly criticize the felony murder rule and have applauded the Model Penal Code's rejection of it.[25] Both code drafters and commentators argue, in part, that the rule fails to accurately assess the felon's degree of blameworthiness. That is, they concur with the lay assessment of the blameworthiness of the individual, who admittedly caused the state of affairs that led to the death, but did so in a way distinguishable from prototypical case of murder.

Interestingly, this is one of the instances in which the code drafters and the commentators have had little effect on state criminal codes. The enduring popularity of the felony murder rule is reflected in the fact that while over two thirds of the states have recodified their codes to adopt the Model Penal Code's general structure, a majority have insisted on reinserting felony murder. Could this be because of a misunderstanding of community standards about this issue? Does the community wish to impute the penalties for murder in the cases discussed? Or, might

---

[23] *See, e.g.*, Jackson v. State, 286 Md. 430, 408 A.2d 711 (1979).

[24] Model Penal Code §210.2(1)(b).

[25] *See, e.g.*, George P. Fletcher, *Reflections on Felony-Murder*, 12 Sw. U. L. Rev. 413 (1980); Maynard E. Pirsig, *Proposed Revision of the Minnesota Criminal Code*, 47 Minn. L. Rev. 417 (1963).

those legislators be wrong in believing that their constituents would insist on such a rule? There are reasons for such a rule. A broad felony murder rule, while in some general sense unjust, is a useful additional deterrent that makes felons more careful during the commission of a felony, or better yet, makes them not commit the felony in the first place. Relatedly, it does give the prosecution a heavy weapon to bring into play during pretrial maneuvering on crimes in which a death has occurred; various individuals who have played some subsidiary role in a crime that has led to death can be threatened with murder liability if they do not cooperate with the prosecution.

Below is an examination of the community view on the various possible instances in which the felony murder rule could come into effect, and then about a discussion of the reasons for the rejection of the Model Penal Code position.

Subjects in the study were presented with a variety of felony murder scenarios and three control cases. The control cases give the baseline liability the respondents assign for standard murder, row (1) of Table 65; for manslaughter, row (2) and for negligent homicide, row (3). The liability or punishment that results in the felony murder scenarios can then be compared to the three controls to determine which the subjects see each felony murder scenario as more akin to: murder, manslaughter, or negligent homicide. The results are shown in Table 65.

Look first at the control scenarios in rows (1) through (3). These were used to ascertain subject's opinions on punishment for basic cases of purposeful, reckless, and negligent killing in order to compare with the various felony murder scenarios. These provide reference points against which one can evaluate the sentences assigned in the various cases of felony murder.

On to the felony murder cases. The felony murder scenarios are complex and differentiated in specific ways. In order to facilitate better understanding of the results, this section will walk through them in detail. Begin with cases (4) through (7), all of which share a common core. Two men set out to rob a liquor store, carrying guns. One or both of them plans to shoot the owner if he does not turn over the cash fast, or one or both does not plan to shoot the owner but simply to menace him with what the person thinks is an unloaded gun. The owner is slow about turning over the cash, and one of the robbers, labeled the principal or "shooter," shoots him. This is true even if the principal did not plan originally to shoot the owner. This creates four cases in which the principal does shoot the owner: The principal did or did not plan to shoot the owner, the accomplice did or did not plan to shoot the owner. In the cases in which the person, whether principal or accomplice, did not plan to shoot the owner, one would think that he would be perceived as negligent with respect to causing death and perhaps draw a reduced sentence. For all of these cases, the felony murder rule grades the offense as murder.

Look at the liability data of column (a). There are a number of questions that one can ask of this data. In each case, the perpetrator, purposefully or negligently, is the one that shoots the owner; the accomplice does not. Does this perpetrator-accomplice distinction make a difference in liability assignments given by the respondents?

TABLE 65. } Liability for Felony Murder

	(a)	(b)	(c)	(d)	(e)	(f)	(g)
Scenarios	*Principal Liability*	*Accomplice Liability*	*Defender Liability*	*Culpability of Principal*	*Culpability of Accomplice*	*Culpability of Defender*	*Legal Treatment Under Felony Murder Rule*
1. Purposeful killing	10.39[a]	10.39[a]		1.64			Murder
2. Reckless killing	9.08[b,c,d]	9.08[a]		3.29			Manslaughter
3. Negligent killing	4.58[f]	4.58[d]		4.00			Negligent homicide
4. Purposeful shooter, purposeful co-felon, owner victim	10.11[a,b]	9.56[a]		1.43	1.54		Murder
5. Negligent shooter, negligent co-felon, owner victim	8.78[c,d]	7.31[a]		3.86	3.91		Murder
6. Purposeful shooter, Negligent co-felon, owner victim	10.08[a,b,c]	6.92[b]		1.76	3.83		Murder
7. Negligent shooter, purposeful co-felon, owner victim	8.53[d]	9.11[a]		4.00	2.19		Murder
8. Purposeful but innocent shooter, purposeful co-felon, felon victim	(killed)	5.25[c,d]	0.69		2.11	1.97	Murder*
9. Purposeful but innocent shooter, negligent co-felon, felon victim	(killed)	4.97[d]	0.67		3.71	2.11	Murder*
10. Negligent but innocent shooter, purposeful co-felon, felon victim	(killed)	5.39[c,d]	0.51		1.89	3.69	Murder*
11. Negligent but innocent shooter, purposeful co-felon, owner victim	6.83[e]	6.64[b,c]	0.33	1.83	1.72	4.08	Murder*

Liability Scale: N=No criminal liability, 0=Liability but no punishment, 1=1 day, 2=2 weeks, 3=2 months, 4=6 months, 5=1 year, 6=3 years, 7=7 years, 8=15 years, 9=30 years, 10=life, and 11=death.

Note: Superscript letters indicate significance at the $p < .05$ level by a Newman-Keuls test. Matching superscripts indicate means that are not statistically significantly different from each other. Means are compared within columns only. In addition, no subjects gave either No Liability (N) or Liability but No Punishment (0). The columns indicating (N) and (N+0) have therefore been left out of this table, as all percentages were 0. Culpability of principal (column *d*), accomplice (column *e*), and defender (column *f*) were scored on the following scale:

1 = The actor wanted to kill the victim (purposeful).
2 = The actor was practically certain that his conduct would cause the victim's death (knowing).
3 = The actor was aware of a substantial risk that the victim would be killed (reckless).
4 = The actor was not aware of a substantial risk that the victim would be killed but should have been aware (negligent).
5 = The actor was not aware of any substantial risk that the victim would be killed and a reasonable person in his situation would not have been aware of such a risk (faultless).

*Only under the broader forms of the felony-murder rule, where the rule is applied to killings by nonfelons.

Reviewing Table 65, it clearly does. As can be clearly seen, the perpetrator receives a higher sentence. The principal, even though he sometimes does not plan to do so, does pull the trigger and shoot the owner; the accomplice, even though he sometimes plans to do so, does not. The legal doctrine, in contrast, fails to recognize such mitigation for an accomplice. Standard complicity rules, such as those in the Model Penal Code, hold the accomplice liable as if he were the principal; the respondents do not. This result is consistent with the "complicity discount" that has been seen in other studies: for instance, the objective requirements of complicity study in chapter 12, section D and the culpability requirements of complicity study in chapter 14, section B. However, in a more global sense, the respondents and the various versions of the code are in accord: all give a very high sentence to both the principal and the accomplice.

Another useful question to ask is whether the state of mind as to causing death with which the two robbers enter the situation makes a difference to the respondents. Variations in the story made the accomplice or the principal either negligent as to the death because he has no plan to shoot, or therefore purposeful as to causing death because he plans to shoot.

Looking back to Table 65, it is obvious that state of mind matters. Comparing, for instance, the principal in (4) with that in (5), it is clear that those who plan to kill receive higher sentences than those who do not plan to kill.

The graph in Figure 66 shows the results of the four felony murder cases described in scenarios (4) through (7) in Table 65. Our examination can be brief, because the graph indicates that the individual cases are rated about as expected, based on the

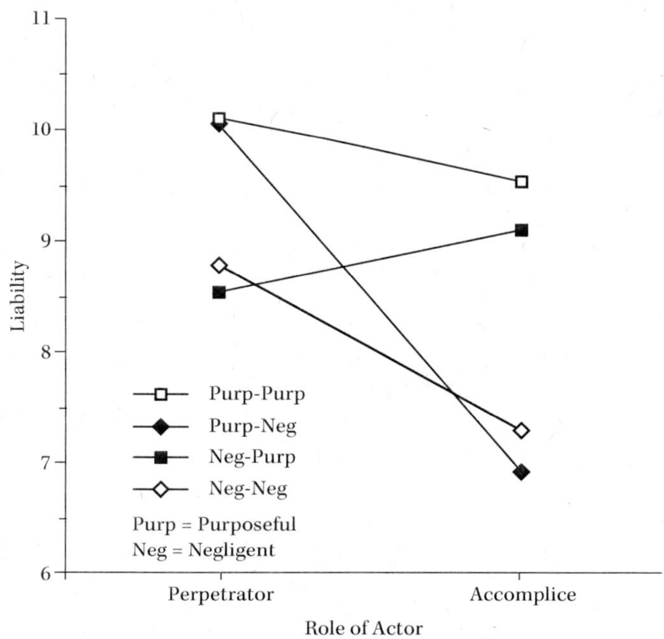

FIGURE 66. Liability as a Function of Role and State of Mind as to Killing

two rules articulated: the shooter gets a higher liability than the one who does not shoot, and a person who plans to shoot gets higher liability than one who does not plan to shoot. The figure legend indicates first, whether the principal is purposeful or negligent with respect to the shooting; and second, whether the co-felon is purposeful or negligent with respect to the shooting. Thus, for instance, the line labeled "P-N" is the one that graphs the results of the case in which the principal plans to shoot and the accomplice does not.

Three of the lines give a lower sentence for the accomplice, as one would expect from the joint operation of the two rules. The only case in which the accomplice draws a higher liability than the principal is the one in which the principal does not plan to shoot and the accomplice does plan to, which is the case in which one would expect this reversal to happen. This being the case, it is fair to summarize the results as follows: respondents assign more liability to the principal than to the accomplice, probably reflecting a tendency to punish more heavily the individual who does the actual shooting. They also give less liability to a person, principal, or accomplice, who they know does not intend to shoot if the store owner resists. These two effects, combined, give the accomplice who does not plan to shoot a considerable drop in liability from the other cases.

Recall a point that was made before. It is worth noting that the scenarios were such as to give the respondents confidence in the belief that one of the robbers really does not intend to shoot. Subjects were straightforwardly told this in the scenario. Notice that the culpability ratings shown in Table 65, column (d) for the felon; and in column (e), for the accomplice, indicate that the subjects believed what they were told. And the culpability ratings do make a difference; they predict the liability ratings assigned to the two individuals. An actual robber, trying to convince an actual jury of that lack of intention, might have considerable difficulty in doing so and therefore often may be treated as a purposeful murderer. Still, the pattern of responses of the respondents argues that the accused should at least have the chance to try to convince the jury of his intentions. More generally this pattern of differences between the felony murder rule and the subjects' responses echoes the commentators' criticisms of the rule and the Model Penal Code's rejection of it in its current form.

Here is how one would formulate the rule that might underlie the respondents' judgment. Notice that the penalties assigned the negligent persons were reduced, but not reduced to the level of the grade given the negligent individual who kills another while cleaning his gun. The baseline for negligent homicide is 4.58 (9.6 months), while the subjects' sentences for negligent principals are 8.53 (22.5 years) and 8.78 (27.0 years), and for negligent accomplices are 6.92 (6.6 years) and 7.31 (9.4 years). These sentences are sufficiently greater than the baseline for a negligent killing to suggest that there is some support for the notion at the heart of the felony murder rule: that a killing in the course of a felony ought to be punished more severely than it would be without the felonious context. This suggests that the subjects, like the legislators, are assuming that committing an armed robbery, for example, creates a risk of causing death of which the person must be aware. The data pattern suggests that, from the respondents' view, the felony murder rule is on the right track but simply goes too far. The subjects would support a felony murder rule that significantly aggravates negligent killings during a robbery, but only to the level of manslaughter for principals and to something less than that for accomplices, not to murder as the current doctrine does. In other words, they would support a "felony manslaughter rule" with a standard "accomplice discount."

Next there are the cases of (8) through (10), in which a bystander to the robbery shoots and kills the principal felon. In these cases, the wife of the store owner, who is hidden from view, shoots the principal felon. The principal felon is dead, thus escaping any jail sentence; the question asked is always what sentence should be given to the accomplice. As noted previously, some jurisdictions extend the felony murder rule to killings committed by innocent persons defending against the felony, imputing the killings to the felons, as murder. In case (8), the wife purposefully shoots the felon, and the accomplice had planned to shoot the store owner if he did not respond quickly. In scenario (9), the wife purposefully shoots the felon, and the accomplice had not planned to shoot the store owner. In scenario (10), the wife accidentally shoots, and the accomplice had not planned to shoot. Obviously, it would be possible to intuitively order the cases. One might expect that the accomplice who had planned to shoot would get a higher sentence than either of the accomplices who had not planned to shoot and that the purposeful choice of the wife to shoot might further lower the liability assigned the accomplice.

In fact, no such differences appeared. The subjects' liability assignments hovered around 5.20, a sentence of about one year for all cases, with no statistical significance among them. One way of saying what this means is that the subjects do not spontaneously impose the level of liability that the most extended form of the felony murder rule provides in these cases. Intuitively, the respondents might condition their liability ratings on the fact that a bystander shoots the felon and do not attempt to reason through the somewhat complex possible interpretations of the various intentions that exist in the accomplice.

The lower level of liability assigned the accomplice in these cases of killings of the felon by an innocent does not differ significantly from the baseline for a negligent killing, 4.58 (9.6 months). It is possible (some would say, likely) that standard homicide grading would impose liability for negligent homicide in such cases. That is, it is likely that a jury would conclude that a robber who enters a store with his gun drawn is at least negligent as to causing a death regardless of who shoots who (i.e., he should have been aware of a substantial risk that his conduct would cause a death). If this is true, then the liability levels given by the subjects in cases of killings of co-felons by innocents may be obtained in settings in which the code is applied without the felony murder rule. The rule is needed, in the subjects' view, only in cases of negligent killings of innocents by felons. And there, the subjects would prefer that the rule only aggravates liability to manslaughter (reckless homicide) at most, and in most cases to something considerably less.

Next, it is useful to examine the somewhat baroque case, scenario (11), in which a bystander attempts to stop the robbery and clumsily shoots the owner of the store instead. In this case, although the felon is actually purposeful or knowing as to planning to cause a death, the subjects put his liability for the killing by an innocent of another innocent at 6.83 (6.2 years), significantly less than the liability for murder. Indeed, such liability is significantly less than the liability imposed on the purposeful accomplice in the analogous situation, scenario (7), where a negligent principal kills the innocent, 9.11 (9 equals 30 years; 10 equals life). The fact that the killing is actually done by an innocent person, not the principal or an accomplice, appears to matter a great deal to the subjects.

To summarize, this study confirms that subjects, like current legal doctrine, aggravate the liability of a person who kills during a felony over what it would be if not committed during a felony. They punish a person's negligent killing during a robbery at a liability level similar to a reckless killing in a non-felonious context. If one brandishes a gun during the course of a robbery, and it goes off accidently and kills an innocent, the subjects are not particularly sympathetic to the view that this is equivalent to accidentally discharging a gun and killing another. But according to the subjects, current doctrine goes too far, for it punishes such a negligent killing as if it were murder, while the subjects would prefer manslaughter. So, the subjects would support a "felony manslaughter rule."

The complicity aspect of the felony murder rule reflects similar differences. Like the doctrine, the subjects punish the accomplice for more than negligent homicide when the perpetrator kills during a felony. But while the doctrine treats the accomplice exactly like a murderer, the subjects impose liability somewhat less than they would for manslaughter. The lesser liability of the accomplice is significant. It reflects the view of the subjects, manifested in several studies examined above, that the accomplice generally deserves less liability than the perpetrator, all other things being equal. If the code were to adopt a standard "accomplice discount," felony murder accomplices could remain within the rule; the accomplice would be held at some level of liability less than that of the "felony manslaughter" perpetrator.

The vicarious aspect of the felony murder rule—holding a felon liable for murder for a killing by the intended victim of the felony or some other bystander—has even less support among the subjects than the aggravation and complicity aspects of the rule. When the victim kills an accomplice, the liability imposed by the subjects on the surviving accomplice is not significantly more than that imposed for a negligent homicide, far from the murder liability imposed by the felony murder rule in some jurisdictions. When an innocent person is killed by the robbery victim, the accomplice's liability is slightly more than that for negligent homicide but still nowhere near manslaughter liability. This result is likely under normal homicide grading; thus, the subjects would see no need for extension of the special rule to these cases.

To conclude, it is possible that a jury might reach the same conclusions as the subjects even without a felony murder rule, by seeing culpability in the creation of a situation in which the likelihood of a killing is brought about. It may be, as suggested earlier, that it is this perception of blame for creating the dangerous situation that generates the subjects' responses. Such increased liability is possible, if not likely, under the normal graded homicide offenses, and its likelihood is increased if the Model Penal Code's evidentiary presumption approach is used. The Code, recall, uses the fact of the felony as grounds to create a presumption of "recklessness manifesting extreme indifference to the value of human life," which is defined as sufficient culpability for murder; the defendant can rebut this presumption. One might argue, then, that these results argue against the continuing need for a felony murder rule. On the other hand, the results suggest that a form of a felony murder rule might be unobjectionable—and, thus, if politically demanded, might be continued—if revised to better reflect the subjects' views, which call for lower liability levels.

A rule that mirrors the subjects' views would aggravate a negligent killing by a felon in the course of a felony to reckless homicide (manslaughter), not murder. No special complicity rule would be required; accomplices would receive the normal complicity discount, which varies with the level of the accomplice's culpability and degree of contribution. A felon might be liable for killings by an intended victim of the felony, at the level of negligent homicide, but not under a special rule for killings during a felony.

D. The Strength of the Person's Connection with the Prohibited Result: Causation Requirements

A person acts, intending a result that is prohibited, such as another's death. Through some chain of circumstances, the result intended occurs, but not exactly in the way intended by the person. Should one hold the person liable for that result? This situation is a familiar one to fans of courtroom drama. I don't intend to kill Jones but only put him in hospital with a minor wound. The hospital, due to some medical ineptness, causes Jones's death. Have I committed murder? I shoot at Jones and miss, but he dies of fright induced by the noise of the shot. Have I murdered him? Alternatively, intending to kill my rival, Smith, I administer a slow-acting poison to him. Before it acts, the third rival, Clark, kills Smith with a fast-acting bludgeon. What is my liability? Philosophers have posed these and similar cases for generations to explore the limits of moral sanctions; the study posed some similar cases to a set of the respondents.

Current criminal law doctrine typically imposes two requirements for a person to be held causally accountable for a result. First, the person's conduct must have been necessary ("but-for" cause) for the result to occur: "it is an antecedent but for which the result in question would not have occurred."[26] Second, even if the person's conduct is a necessary cause of the result, the nature of the connection between the conduct and the result must be sufficiently close and direct; the result must not be "too remote or accidental in its occurrence to have a [just] bearing on the person's

[26] Model Penal Code §2.03(1)(a).

liability or on the gravity of his offense."[27] Where these two requirements—termed factual causation and legal causation, respectively—are not met, a person cannot be held accountable for the result and, typically, is liable only for an attempt to commit the substantive offense (or, in some instances, has no liability).

The traditional doctrinal position is to require a necessary cause. During the Model Penal Code debate, it was argued that an alternative, less demanding ground for causal accountability be permitted, requiring only that the cause be "a substantial factor in producing the result," a formulation even less demanding in many ways than a sufficient cause requirement. The members of the American Law Institute rejected the sufficient or substantial cause formulations instead adhering to the traditional requirement of a necessary cause.[28] This means that, in the case described above, in which I poisoned Smith but Clark bludgeoned him to death before the poison acted, I would not be liable for murder (but would be liable for attempted murder). Although the poison eventually would have killed Smith without additional assistance or intervention, and thus fits the definition of a sufficient cause, it was not a necessary cause: Smith would have died when he did from the beating by the subsequent person, even if he had never been poisoned. One goal of the causation study was to examine which of these two tests—necessary cause or sufficient cause—best represents the community's view of a prerequisite for casual accountability.

A second concern of the causation study was the effect of the strength of the relationship between a person's necessary cause and the prohibited result—the so-called legal cause requirement. This is the question that arises in the example described above in which I set out to murder Jones, but only wound him, and some other events such as carelessness in the hospital, bring about his death. The test of the legal cause requirement in current doctrine is relatively vague (the result must not be "too remote or accidental in its occurrence to have a just bearing on the actor's liability"). Yet much depends upon the application of this standard, specifically, the difference between liability for the full substantive offense and liability for an attempt (or, in some cases, escape from all liability). The study sought to test various factors that might affect the community's liability judgment in such cases of potentially "remote" or "accidental" results. An identification of relevant factors, it was felt, might lead to formulation of a more specific standard or might guide decision makers in applying the present vague standard.

In summary, the causation study sought to determine which of the two factual cause tests—necessary cause or sufficient cause—best reflects the community's view of a prerequisite for causal accountability. A second goal was to examine the effect of the strength of the relationship between a person's necessary cause and the prohibited result—the legal cause requirement.

The respondents were first presented with two control scenarios that establish liability baselines for a clear, direct, and immediate killing, in row (1) of Table 67;

---

[27] *Id.* at §2.03(2)(b).

[28] *See id.* at §2.03(1)(a).

TABLE 67. } Liability as Related to Causation

Scenarios			Principal		Second Actor or Accomplice	
		(a)	(b)		(c)	(d)
		Liability	Legal Code Result		Liability	Legal Code Result
1.	Murder, control	9.89[a]	Murder		8.89[b]	Murder
2.	Attempt, control	7.25[e]	Attempted murder		6.67[e]	Attempted murder
3.	Subsequent killer	9.47[a]	Attempted murder		9.89[a]	Murder
4.	Allergy	8.75[b]	Murder		7.97[c]	Murder
5.	Careless nurse	8.33[b,c]	Murder or attempt (jury)		7.58[c,d]	Murder or attempt (jury)
6.	Accident on way to hospital	8.03[c,d]	Probably attempted murder		7.36[d,e]	Probably attempted murder
7.	Construction accident	7.36[d,e]	Attempted murder		6.75[e]	Attempted murder

Liability Scale: N=No criminal liability, 0=Liability but no punishment, 1=1 day, 2=2 weeks, 3=2 months, 4=6 months, 5=1 year, 6=3 years. 7=7 years, 8=15 years, 9=30 years, 10=life, and 11=death.

Note: Superscript letters indicate significance at the $p < .05$ level by a Newman-Keuls test. Matching superscripts indicate means that are not statistically significantly different from each other. Means are compared within columns only.

and a failed attempted killing, in row (2). The various other scenarios can then be compared to the control cases to see if the assignment of liability in each instance is more akin to the case where causal accountability for the death is clear or more akin to the case of no causal accountability, where only attempt liability is imposed. Examining Table 67, one sees that the liability assigned to the murder in the first scenario is high, 9.89, just slightly less than life imprisonment. Second, notice that the attempted murder scenario drew an average sentence of 7.25 (9.4 years). This finding in itself is significant for the topic of this chapter because it shows just how important the actual occurrence of the resulting harm is for the respondents' grading of it.

First, look at the necessary versus sufficient cause debate. In the scenario (3), labeled "subsequent killer," the first person inflicts a wound sufficient to kill but, before the victim can die from this wound, the second person, unaware of the prior attack, shoots and immediately kills the victim. This scenario is equivalent to the earlier example where I poison Smith, but Clark bludgeons him to death before the poison takes effect. Recall that the necessary cause requirement of the legal code is not satisfied in this scenario. The first person's conduct is sufficient to cause the death but is not necessary; the victim would have died exactly when he did from the conduct of the second person.

The subjects found the first person warranted a high degree of liability. The subjects imposed upon the first person liability very close to that imposed in the direct-killing control case (sufficient but not necessary cause, 9.47, vs. 9.89 for the murder control of row (1)). Unlike the attempt control where they imposed 7.25, the subjects imposed 9.47 years in this case. Thus, where a person's conduct is sufficient to cause death but is not necessary for the death, the subjects impose liability only slightly less than for conduct that is both necessary and sufficient to cause death.

Obviously, the respondents are much closer to a formulation that treats either necessary or sufficient actions equally as examples of murder than they are to the code formulation in which one is treated as murder and the other as only attempt. Here the study has found a substantial difference between results dictated by criminal codes and demanded by community standards. This is particularly ironic because the Code drafters apparently thought they had to preserve the necessary cause test because the necessary cause test was so well entrenched in the popular psyche. But, having said this, note that column (e) of this scenario, row (3), indicates that subjects were unclear that the act of the first person was not necessary for bringing about the death; instead their ratings hovered around the neither agree nor disagree point on the scale. Further research will need to see if the punishment equivalent to murder is given for actions clearly seen as not necessary but sufficient to bring about death.

Consider next the "legal cause" requirement, which holds that the connection between the person's conduct and the result must be close and direct for liability to be incurred. Four scenarios, (4) through (7), involving an attempted homicide, were used to present various situations that were thought might raise legal causation issues. In all of these scenarios, two persons go to the victim's house to kill him. The first person shoots at the victim, either missing or only wounding him, while the second person serves as a lookout. The scenarios differ in the way in which the death of the victim ultimately results. Two occur when the man is wounded and is being treated in the hospital. The victim dies from an allergic reaction to a drug given during initial treatment of the wound, row (4). Alternatively, death results from the careless actions of a nurse during initial treatment, row (5). In a third case, death of the wounded individual results from a traffic accident that occurs while the victim is on the way to the hospital for follow-up treatment, and this occurs two months after the shooting, row (6). In the fourth case, the shooters miss their intended victim, and he flees from them. His death results from a construction crane accident that occurs during his flight, row (7). The liabilities assigned the persons in these cases and the respondents' perceptions of the cases are shown in Table 68.

The major task is to analyze these results for what they say about the respondents' perceptions of legal cause. Before that analysis, consider the liabilities assigned to the perpetrator and to the individual who plays a lesser role in the incident. To realize all of the complex causal connections that were to be tested, it was necessary to have two individuals involved in the commission of the act. The liability assigned to the second person, who functioned as lookout, in contrast to that assigned the first person, supplies another chance to examine the effect of criminal role. To examine that, Figure 69 graphically plots the liability assigned to the perpetrator and the lookout.

As the figure shows, the liability scores assigned to the perpetrator and the lookout are consistently quite different; the liability assigned to the individual who

TABLE 68. } Subjects' Perceptions of Causation

		(e)	*(f)*	*(g)*	*(h)*
Scenarios		*"Actor's Act Necessary"*	*"Actor's Act Sufficient"*	*"Actor Intended Death"*	*"Accomplice Intended Death"*
1.	Murder, control	7.86[a]	8.22[a]	8.56[a]	7.75[b]
2.	Attempt, control			8.17[b]	7.92[b]
3.	Subsequent killer	5.74[c]	7.78[a]	8.31[a,b]	8.36[a]
4.	Allergy	7.20[a,b]	5.22[b]	8.08[b]	7.83[b]
5.	Careless nurse	6.91[a,b]	4.81[b]	8.08[b]	7.72[b]
6.	Accident on way to hospital	4.37[d]	4.83[b]	8.03[b]	7.69[b]
7.	Construction accident	6.34[b,c]	4.81[b]	8.11[b]	7.81[b]

Key to column heads:
All statements were responded to on a scale where: 1="strongly disagree," 5 ="unsure," and 9="strongly agree."

(e) The victim's death would not have occurred but for the actor's conduct.
(f) The actor's conduct was by itself sufficient to cause the victim's death.
(g) The actor intended to kill the victim.
(h) The accomplice intended that the actor kill the victim.

Note: Superscript letters indicate significance at the $p< .05$ level by a Newman-Keuls test. Matching superscripts indicate means that are not statistically significantly different from each other. Means are compared within columns only.

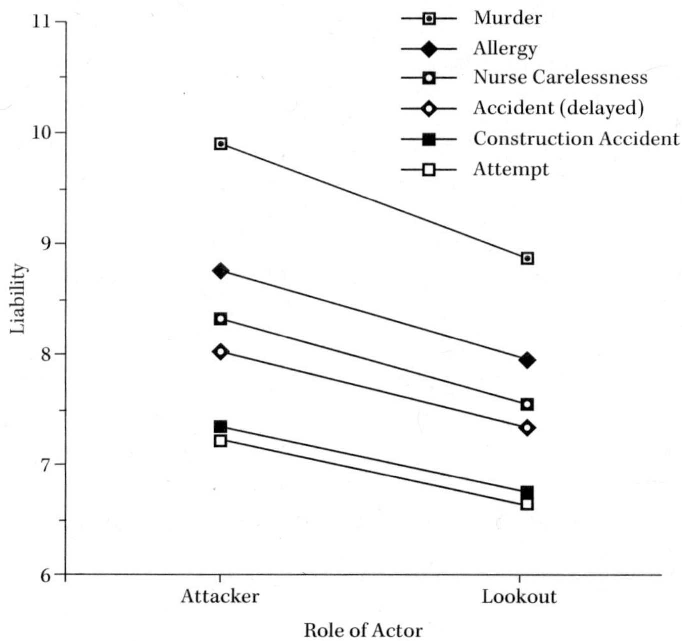

FIGURE 69. Liability for Perpetrator and Lookout in Causation Scenarios

fulfills only the lookout function is consistently lower than that assigned the major perpetrator.

This is consistent with the "accomplice discount" seen in other studies. In these cases, in which the second individual serves only as a watch-keeping accomplice, the codes regard both as equally liable for the murder. Given the results that emerge so clearly from Figure 69, and the results of the two earlier complicity studies, the community standard is in significant disagreement with the codes, in that a lesser degree of liability, reflected in a lesser prison term, is given the accomplice.

Notice that scenario (3) is omitted from the figure and this discussion. In that scenario, the second person, unaware of the first person's actions, steps in and kills the wounded victim. Therefore, the killer is not an "accomplice" but rather an independent perpetrator, who is appropriately assigned murder liability by the subjects.

There were several cases in which the perpetrator's conduct was seen by the respondents as necessary but not itself sufficient to cause death. These were the scenarios shown in rows (4), (5), and (7) of Table 68 involving first, the injection of a drug to which the victim (and almost nobody else) is allergic; second, the wounded victim dying in hospital because of a careless injection of a wrong medication; or third, the victim, shot at and missed by his attackers, fleeing the scene and being killed in a freak construction accident some blocks away. Actually, as an examination of columns (e) and (f) suggest, the respondents see the perpetrator's conduct as necessary to bring about death, column (e), but are unsure whether it is sufficient or not, column (f). Their sufficiency ratings hovered near 5, the neither agree nor disagree option. As the liability results of column (a) show, the subjects in these cases impose liability on the person, but at a reduced level. The liability ratings for those three cases averages 8.15 (18 years), reduced from the murder case of row (1), 9.89 (life), but above the attempt control case of row (2), 7.25 (9.4 years). In previous studies it is frequently seen that an act that harms is given a higher liability than an act that intends harm but fails to bring it about. In this study, the construction crane scenario of row (7) is seen as an attempt to kill that does not come off. Notice that column (a) shows that it gets a considerable reduction in liability. With that case eliminated, the average of the two remaining "necessary but uncertain about sufficient" cases rises to 8.54 (22.5 years) almost perfectly halfway between murder and attempt.

Compare these results to the independent persons case of row (3), in which the first person's action is sufficient but not clearly necessary to bring about death. The comparison suggests that the subjects would accept either a necessary or a sufficient cause as an adequate minimum requirement for causal accountability. Again, this is a rather tentative suggestion; future research that presents cases in which it is established that the actions are clearly not sufficient, or clearly not necessary, will be needed to test it further. Notice also the result of row (6), in which two months after the original shooting, the victim is killed in a traffic accident while returning to the hospital for postoperative treatment. The respondents are puzzled about whether the person's conduct is either necessary, column (e), or sufficient, column (f), to bring about death, but they gave the person a sentence above that given to a person who only attempts murder. This suggests that subjects are willing to assign considerable liability even when they are puzzled about necessary and sufficient conduct.

Return to the question of legal causation. The point at issue here is whether and when an outcome of a chain of events is so remote, in any of the various senses of "remote," that the respondents do not see the perpetrator as having the normal liability for the outcome, even if that was the outcome intended. When a person's conduct is necessary but not seen by the respondents as sufficient, the cases in rows (4), (5), and (7), the subjects impose significantly less liability than they do for the straightforward murder. Yet current doctrine typically would impose full liability for a murder in such a case.

More generally, the drop in liability assigned to the complex causal scenarios of rows (4) to (7) hints that the test scenarios sometimes include factors that make subjects further discount a person's causal accountability for the resulting death. Figure 70 attempts to examine this by graphing the liability assigned to the principal in each of the four test scenarios. The top line on the graph shows the liability assigned by respondents to the case of murder, the bottom line shows the liability assigned to attempted murder. What one would expect from the doctrine of legal causation is that some of the scenarios should be assigned murder liabilities, and others abruptly dropped to the liability assigned the attempt case. Obviously this does not happen.

Factors that seem to make a difference include whether the risk that comes to fruition is one that commonly results from the conduct (compare allergic reaction,

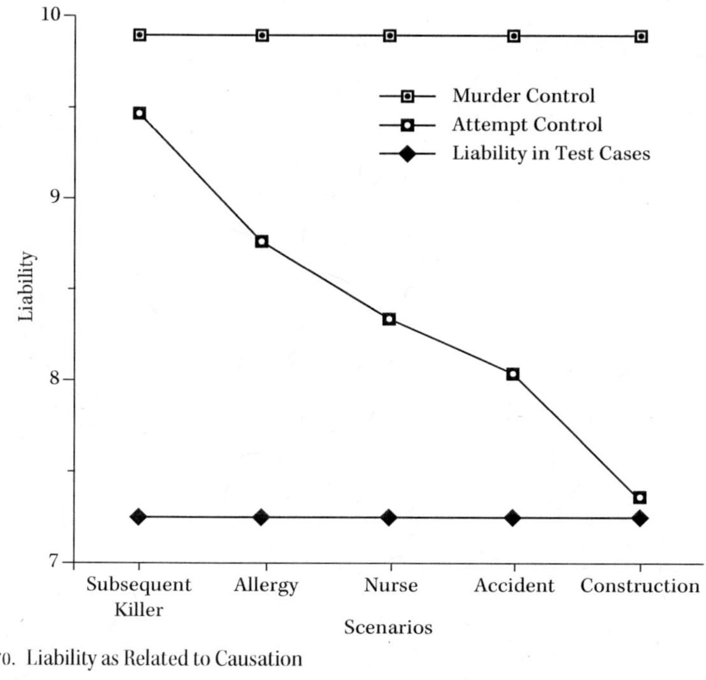

FIGURE 70. Liability as Related to Causation

8.75 (27 years), to construction accident cause, 7.36 (10.2 years); the presence of a subsequent volitional person contributing to the result (compare allergic reaction, 8.75 (27 years), to careless nurse, 8.33 (19.5 years); and the remoteness of the result in time and place from the person's conduct (see death by accident two months later when returning to the hospital for treatment, 8.03 (15 years)). Further studies could establish the factors that contribute to a perception of remoteness and the relative effect of the different factors on liability. It may be that the subjects are reaching their judgments of liability via the mediating inference of remoteness, or some alternate reasoning model may be needed. Or one may need a reasoning model that includes both remoteness of result and necessary versus sufficient causal contribution to the death.

Notice the pattern of the results. The liability of the perpetrator in the test scenarios, other than the construction-crane accident, is statistically significantly different than his liability in the control scenarios concerning murder and attempt—lower than the liability for murder but higher than the liability for attempted murder. This suggests that the subjects see the circumstances as reducing but not eliminating the person's accountability and liability for the death. In other words, the subjects see causal conditions as presenting a continuous rather than a dichotomous relationship with liability. The legal rules, in contrast, set causation as a minimum requirement, which when met establishes liability for the full offense (in this case, murder) and when not met defaults the case to one of attempt.

Therefore, and as common sense suggests, the degree of perceived liability generally lessens in a graduated way as the causal connection between the person's conduct and the result becomes weaker. Furthermore, many of the factors that one might guess would add to a result's "remote or accidental" nature do serve to reduce the liability that the subjects impose. An unusual event, such as an allergic reaction to a drug during treatment, reduces liability. A subsequent person's carelessness reduces liability even further, as does a significant time delay between the conduct and the result. Notice also, however, that no simple rule summarizes the results; the construction accident takes place within minutes of the attempted murder but receives lower liability assignments that do other scenarios in which the death-causing incident is much more delayed in time from the murder attempt. Therefore, unless the relevant factors and their interrelation can be more clearly explicated, it may be that code drafters will want to leave this particular determination to juries, rather than attempt to codify it.

To summarize, as to the factual cause issue, the findings are inconclusive. The subjects gave liability almost equal to murder in the sufficient cause scenario, which would suggest that the codes' necessary cause test was too limiting. But the analysis also suggests that the subjects were unclear as to whether the cause in that scenario was a necessary cause.

These results suggest that the extent of a person's liability is reduced as the result becomes more "remote or accidental" in relation to the person's conduct. This result is at significant variance with the current treatment in the modern codes. Subjects do not seem to conceive of the causation issue in the dichotomous way that the doctrine treats it. They do not see causal accountability as a yes-no issue but one with a continuum of accountability. As a person's degree of accountability increases, so does his liability, from attempt liability up to liability for the full substantive offense. This is one of several examples of current doctrine's tendency to treat continuous functions as dichotomous.

E. Punishment for Multiple Offenses

Current law has some considerable difficulty in determining the appropriate range of punishment for multiple related offenses. If a single instance of theft deserves a punishment of x amount, how much punishment is deserved if the offender is convicted of two identical but separate instances of such theft? Traditionally, judges sentence such an offender separately for each of the two offenses, then determine whether those sentences are to run concurrently or consecutively. Concurrent sentences are served at the same time; consecutive sentences are served one after the other. This leads to the odd result that a person who, for example, carries out two burglaries, and gets a two-year sentence for each to be served concurrently, serves only two years. Concurrent sentences are rightly criticized because they trivialize the second (and all subsequent) offenses. If consecutive sentences are imposed, the burglar would have his two sentences served one after the other, for a total jail term of four years. Consecutive sentences are criticized on the ground that two identical offenses by the same offender do not necessarily deserve twice the punishment as a single offense.

The theory behind this latter claim is somewhat unclear. It may stem, in part, from the fact that the punishment deserved for an offense is based only in part on the harm caused, such as the deprivation of the owner of his property. The person's willingness to violate the announced rules of society may be part of the foundation for punishment, and this factor is already taken into account in the sentence for the first offense. In any event, there seems to be some general sense that additional punishment is deserved for each additional offense but that the additional amount deserved is less than that for the first offense. There seems to be some feeling, specifically, that a third, fourth, fifth, or further offense ought to each give rise to additional punishment but that in each instance the amount of the punishment ought to be less than the additional punishment assigned for the previous offense. This multiple offense discount notion is instantiated in the United States Sentencing Commission Guidelines. Each additional offense is punished, although with increasingly reduced penalties. (The Sentencing Commission guidelines use a formula that takes account as well of different seriousness levels of the different offenses, establishing the baseline with the most serious offense and adding on penalties for additional offenses by considering offenses in their decreasing order of seriousness.)[29]

[29] United States Sentencing Commission Guidelines Manual §§3D1.1–3D1.5.1.

The "multiple offense discount" may well describe what sentencing judges would like to do, but their options may be limited by the consecutive versus concurrent options discussed earlier. (One somewhat manipulative way around this, reported by some judges, is to give the defendant more than the offense deserves on one or both of the counts, then have the sentences run concurrently.)

Given these competing models of multiple offense sentencing, it seemed useful to have some empirical data on what ordinary people think on the issue, and the present study set out to collect it. The multiple offenses study sought to determine whether the subjects concur with the general notion of a multiple offense discount for multiple offenses subjected to sentencing at the same time.

The study also sought to investigate the significance of the time interval between multiple offenses (all of which occurring before conviction for any one). It was speculated that the closer in time the offenses occurred, the more the subjects would treat them as a single offense and therefore impose proportionally less increase for each subsequent offense. The longer the period of time between the multiple offenses, the more the subjects would be likely to treat them as entirely independent offenses deserving entirely independent, nonoverlapping penalties. It might even be the case that they would begin to see the offender as a habitual offender and assign harsher sentences for the second offense than for the first.

The study also sought to determine whether the operative principles are different for offenses against a person, such as assault, than for offenses against property, such as theft. One might speculate that offenses against property, where the harm can more easily be reduced to a monetary form, may well be thought of in those terms only. They might follow a principle that allowed a simple accumulation of the monetary value of all the property taken. In other words, while two assaults may be viewed as entirely separate offenses for which a substantial add-on is appropriate for multiple violations, multiple theft offenses might be viewed as no different in seriousness than a single theft offense where the value of the property taken equals the sum of the values for the multiple offenses. This is the approach taken by the United States Sentencing Commission Guidelines: if the nature of the harm of multiple offenses is such that it simply can be aggregated, as in theft or fraud, then the amounts are aggregated and treated as a single offense of this amount.[30] Thus, the guidelines take different approaches to aggregable and non-aggregable offenses. They suggest a very different patterning of additional penalties for multiple theft offenses than for multiple assault offenses. Even the treatment of theft, an aggregable offense, does not really give full value to each additional dollar of theft, since the grading of theft itself provides a discount for each additional dollar stolen, but does ignore whether the total loss is caused by one theft or by many. This seems inconsistent with the general principle that every new offense should count for something additional—not just in recognition of greater harm but also in recognition of an additional violation

---

[30] *Id.* at §3D1.3(b).

of the legal rules. Non-aggregable offenses such as assault, on the other hand, would be expected to generate more substantial add-on sentences.

Other possible hypotheses might suggest other patterns of multiple offense sentencing. The researcher thought it best first to do the study, and then let its results guide further theorizing. Two sets of scenarios were set up. In the core assault scenario, an individual who had been angered by a coworker or workers at an office where he used to work returns to the office, armed with a baseball bat and breaks several bones of the coworker or workers. In the core theft scenario, the thief, waiting until no one is around (and thus by inference avoiding needing to use violence on anybody who observes him) steals a 55-gallon drum from a gas station to resell it, or steals several drums from several gas stations.

To study the effects of the time interval between the multiple offenses, several cases in which two persons are assaulted or two drums are stolen were created, and the interval between the events is either nearly zero (the previously described scenarios), two weeks, or two years in length.

The liability results are tabled in Table 71. As with other tables that have been presented in which multiple comparisons are possible, it is difficult to extract them from the table. Perhaps the main point to extract from the table is that no respondent thinks that no liability is appropriate; only very few assign liability with no punishment; and when this assignment is made, it is almost always in the theft cases.

TABLE 71. } Liability for Multiple Offenses

	(a)	*(b)*	*(c)*
Scenarios	*Liability*	*% No Liability (N)*	*% No Liability or No Punishment (N+0)*
Single day—Assault:			
1. 1 victim	5.85	0	0
2. 2 victims	6.17	0	15
3. 4 victims	6.76	0	0
4. 7 victims	7.10	0	0
Single day—Theft:			
5. 1 item	3.17	0	0
6. 2 items	3.95	0	5
7. 4 items	4.37	0	2
8. 4 items/1 victim	3.54	0	10
9. 7 items	4.68	0	2
Two-week interval:			
10. Assault, 2 victims	6.41	0	0
11. Theft, 2 items	4.10	0	5
Two-year interval:			
12. Assault, 2 victims	6.59	0	0
13. Theft, 2 items	4.15	0	7

Liability Scale: N=No criminal liability, 0=Liability but no punishment, 1=1 day, 2=2 weeks, 3=2 months, 4=6 months, 5=1 year, 6=3 years, 7=7 years, 8=15 years, 9=30 years, 10=life, and 11=death.

As previously explained, the various comparisons to make are difficult to make from an inspection of the liability table. It seemed useful to present them graphically. First, look at the major question of this study, which involves the patterns of changes in liability when the number of offenses increases. Figure 72 graphs all of the cases of theft or assault in which the multiple thefts or assaults occurred immediately one after the other.

First notice that the liability assigned for any assault is always greater than that assigned for any theft. This is exactly as expected from both intuition and the criminal code; harming another person is more serious than stealing an oil drum.

Notice, second, that both curves have the general property that matches the predicted intuitions of the subjects and is built into the federal sentencing guidelines for non-aggregable offenses. The greater the number of offensive actions, the greater the sentence grows, but it does not do so in a linear fashion. Instead it follows the general rule of adding a decreasing increment for each additional offensive action.

However, the results do not support the aggregation side of the United States Sentencing Commission Guidelines approach. Under the guidelines, theft is aggregable; assault is not. Therefore, under the guidelines each additional theft would get even less additional increment; each would be treated as providing no more punishment than if the person took the two drums from the same gas station in a single theft. The sharp increase in sentence for the thief for the theft of the second drum suggests that subjects do not follow this rule. Future research, in which the scenarios compare the theft of x drums from different stations with the theft of x drums all at once, will clarify this even further.

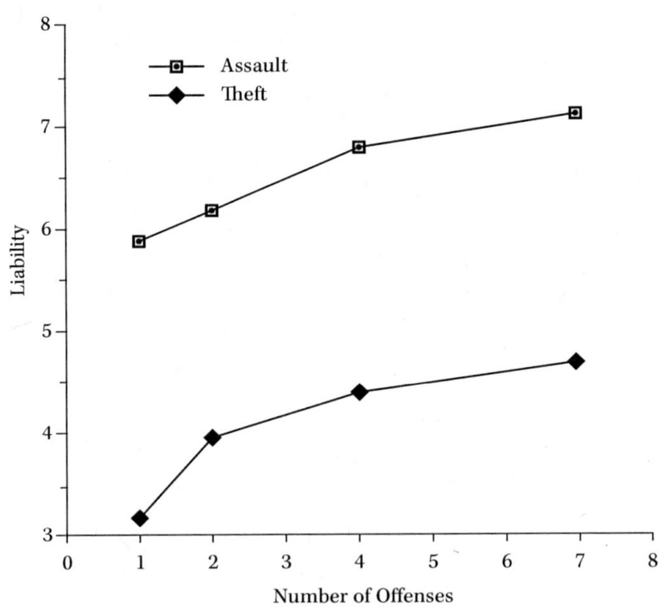

FIGURE 72. Total Liability as a Function of Number of Offenses (no time delay)

The statistical term that tests whether the two curves differ in shape from one another is marginally significant. The explanation might lie partially in the previously mentioned very sharp increase in liability assigned the thief who robs two gas stations of one drum each rather than one total. The respondents might have seen the first theft as somewhat impulsive, while two or more thefts reveal a continuing and calculated willingness to commit crimes.

Turn now to the effect that a time delay between offenses has on the sentencing patterns of the respondents. Figure 73 shows the effect of time delays between a first and a second offense on liability for the two offenses. (The figure graphs the total liability for the two offenses.) As can be seen, the time delay does seem to make a difference; the longer the time between the two offenses, the more severe the sentence for the pair of them, and this is confirmed by the statistical test. However, it is also important to note that, compared to many of the other differences found between scenarios in other chapters, the differences graphed here are not large or dramatic. Respondents assign only mildly more severe sentences the longer the delay between the incidents for which they are sentencing the individual. It may well be that this is because the longer the period of time between the multiple offenses, the more the subjects would be likely to treat them as entirely independent offenses deserving entirely independent, nonoverlapping penalties, as suggested earlier. The best description of these results is this: increasing the interval between offenses slightly increases the liabilities assigned.

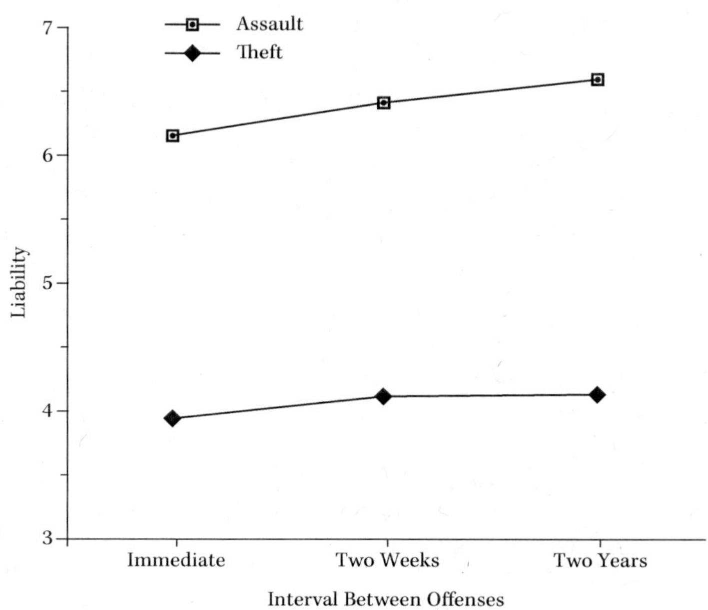

FIGURE 73. Total Liability as a Function of the Interval between Two Offenses

It seems that the respondents do what a great deal of research on person attribution processes suggests that they would, which is to treat information about a person's actions as providing information about his underlying dispositions.[31] In this instance, if a person does something once, a number of possible explanations are available for that action, including situational pressures rather than underlying dispositions. The thief of an oil drum could have been under some extraordinary pressure, for instance needing medicine for his child, that caused him to steal; and the person who assaults another could have been assaulting a coworker who harassed him. However, if the person commits essentially the same act in different situations, then one is likely to conclude that the act is dispositional; that the person is a thief or a habitually violent person. What the data pattern suggests is that the time separation between the two acts is read as suggesting that the two situations are in fact different.

To summarize, the respondents do function the way that societal intuitions suggest and as the general, non-aggregated aspect of the federal sentencing guidelines articulate. They give a more extended sentence for two crimes than one, but generally not one that doubles the sentence that would be given for the first offense. They do not follow the strictly additive pattern characteristic of consecutive sentencing, or the pattern of no increase in sentence that would be dictated by a concurrent sentencing philosophy. Their sentencing pattern is in accord with the principle suggested earlier: that the punishment deserved for an offense is based only in part on the harm caused, such as the deprivation of the owner of his property. The person's willingness to violate the announced rules of society may be part of the foundation for punishment, and this factor is already taken into account in the sentence for the first offense.

The respondents do not agree with the aggregation rules provided by the sentencing guidelines. Within those guidelines, theft is an aggregable offense, and a number of thefts of one item draw the same penalty as one theft of the same total number of items. The respondents assign a sharply increased penalty to the second theft. In further disagreement with the sentencing guidelines, although slight differences emerged between the pattern of sentencing for multiple assault and multiple theft cases, the small variations do not suggest any major differences in the respondents' sentencing "philosophies" in those two kinds of cases.

What remains to be explored in future research is the set of conditions under which a pattern of multiple offenses leads respondents to move from a model in which each additional offense is punished, although with increasingly reduced penalties, to one in which the "habitual offender" concept comes into play. The latter may apply when an individual who has served a sentence for an offense repeats the crime. The "psychological logic" would then be that the sentence for the first offense did not deter and a longer one is required. An alternative explanation is that, having once been officially sanctioned, greater punishment is called for with the second

---

[31] Edward Jones & Keith Davis, *From Acts to Dispositions: The Attribution Process in Person Perception*, in 2 ADVANCES IN EXPERIMENTAL SOCIAL PSYCHOLOGY (Academic Press 1965); Harold H. Kelley, *Attribution Theory in Social Psychology*, in 15 NEBRASKA SYMPOSIUM ON MOTIVATION (D. Levine ed., University of Nebraska Press 1967).

offense because the subsequent violation is a greater challenge to the authority of the criminal law. Consider yet, one more explanation: the subjects are making the inference that a person who commits the same sort of crime after a delay is predicted to be more likely to commit future crimes, and one might expect this to find its way into individuals' sentencing patterns. Subjects might be exercising the incapacitation function of punishment, locking away a person who is likely to commit future offenses. Future research could sort out some of these issues.

F. Summary

In several of the cases considered in this chapter, it was found that the respondents' intuitions about the appropriate grading for different variants of offenses differ from those reflected in the legal codes. For instance, in sexual offenses, the respondents regard forcible rapes as generally of similar grades regardless of the existence of various kinds of prior relationship between the individuals involved, while the Code sharply conditions the offense grade as a function of prior relationship. With regard to felony murder, the respondents preferred a "felony manslaughter rule" with a standard "accomplice discount" rather than the law's imposition of murder liability for all participants (and, in some jurisdictions, all variations of involvement by innocents and of felons). When this or another community-code discrepancy was discovered, it was helpful to consider what principles of judgment might be underlying the subjects' responses, and also to discuss the implications of the discrepancy for code alteration, where there might have been a case for consideration of that.

In sum, it is clear that the respondents are in accord with the general tendency in the legal codes to distinguish grades of offenses within and between offenses. For instance, they clearly distinguish different levels of sexual offenses, although not always exactly in the ways suggested by the legal codes. Interestingly, in the case of felony murder, in which, probably for policy reasons, the codes emphatically reject the idea of grading within felony murder and treat all cases as murder, the respondents do distinguish grades within that offense, assigning lower sentences to felons whose causal connection with the resultant death is more remote. Similarly, in the causation study, they graded murder differently with different causal connections to a death, specifically assigning lower sentences to persons who intended to kill but did not succeed in directly doing so, although death eventuates by means of a later chain of events. The general notion of grading offenses is recognized as a basic and appropriate code function, both in the eyes of the respondents and legal codes.

However, it is worth noting that the grading of offenses registered by the subjects is done in a somewhat different manner than codes generally accomplish it. The codes tend toward dichotomous grading: a botched attack on another's life which through a chain of circumstances leads to that other's death is either causally closely enough connected to the death, in which case it is murder, or not closely enough connected, in which case it is only an attempt. In contrast, the respondents provide more continuous judgments; for instance, judging that the attempted murderer's victim who dies only through a chain of events after the attempt warrants a sentence lower than a straightforward murder, but higher than that given for an attempt.

A different but related point is the tendency of some codes, including the Model Penal Code, to recognize too few categories of offenses, as compared to the refined intuitions of the respondents. Most jurisdictions have adopted a grading scheme that uses more than the five grades of the Model Penal Code,[32] but even seven or eight grades could not give expression to the rather nuanced judgments that the respondents made. The effect of this shortage of grades means that even where the codes properly identify a relevant mitigating or aggravating factor, they frequently must give it more or less effect in grading than it merits. The respondents agreed with the Model Penal Code, for example, that absence of a prior sexual relationship aggravates liability for rape but the Code's one grade difference for those two cases, the minimum distinction it can make, significantly exceeds the difference in grade that the respondents would give. This argues for codes with more grades into which offenses can be categorized.

The special problems of sentencing multiple offenses also suggest a structural change in current doctrine. Presently, multiple offenses typically are dealt with either by concurrent sentences, which impose no additional sentence for the second offense; or by consecutive sentences, which effectively double the penalty. The respondents assign sentences for a second offense that add to but do not double the sentence for the first offense; and continue this pattern for further offenses. This approach matches at best one aspect of the United States Sentencing Commission guidelines and the model provided by these guidelines may move the legal doctrine in this direction.

[32] The United States Sentencing Commission Guidelines recognize 43 "offense levels." United States Sentencing Commission Guidelines Manual, ch. 5, Pt. A (1994).

17 }

Law-Community Agreement and Conflict, and Its Implications

Chapters 12 through 16 have said a great deal about the content of community judgments of justice regarding a wide variety of liability and punishment issues and compared those judgments to the existing legal doctrine. The criminal law does often agree with community intuitions, as discussed below in section A. However, as section B demonstrates, the criminal law also often conflicts with lay judgments of justice, reaffirming what chapter 7 showed previously with regard to popular modern crime-control doctrines. Building on chapter 8's discussion of the "utility of desert," this chapter has more to say about the implications of these conflicts. The chapter is drawn primarily from portions of my work with John Darley in *Justice, Liability & Blame: Community Views and the Criminal Law*.[1]

Section C explains that the community and the law often differ not just in their result but in their general approach to assessing liability. For example, criminal law often views criminal liability as a dichotomous issue, while the community sees the same liability issue as one of placement along a continuum. That is, while law defines criteria to toggle between no liability and full liability, the community commonly looks to factors that serve to aggravate or mitigate.

Section D examines the interesting attraction that test subjects had for using the "liability but no punishment" option commonly given to them in the research studies. The popularity of this unique response reveals important insights about people's judgments about justice.

Finally, section E considers whether the use of a jury system has implications for our research findings here. Certainly, the use of jurors as decision makers makes familiarity with lay judgments of justice an important matter for lawyers and judges. Would not all parties want to better understand what drives the judgments of jurors? But one also might wonder whether the ability of juries to nullify—to ignore the law—makes irrelevant a concern for legal doctrine, and law-community conflict in particular. An analysis suggests not. Getting the doctrine right remains essential. Even if juries know of their power to nullify, which commonly they do

[1] Paul H. Robinson & John M. Darley, Justice, Liability & Blame: Community Views and the Criminal Law ch. 7 (1995).

not, the legal rules they take an oath to follow still have a significant effect on their decisions. And, of course, the vast majority of criminal cases are decided without juries.

A. Law and Community Commonly Agree

The results of the studies reported in chapters 12 through 16 confirm that many aspects of current doctrine mirror community views, including several important foundational principles upon which the doctrine is based. One foundational principle is that the degree of criminal liability should depend to a considerable extent on the culpability level of the person in violating the law. With this principle, the subjects were in agreement. The degree of a person's culpability for a violation, ranging from negligent through purposeful commission, consistently made a difference in the penalties that the subjects assigned. This emerges most clearly from the offense culpability requirements study, but also emerges indirectly in many other studies as well.

Similarly, the subjects recognized and granted validity to the various "excusing conditions" recognized in the law. For instance, debilitating abnormalities in an offender's capacities, from mental illness, for example, can indeed serve to exculpate a person, even for the most serious offense. Still further, the studies found broad support for the recognition of justification defenses. If the person's conduct is justified in any of several ways that the law now recognizes, the subjects do not punish what normally would be an offense.

The studies also support many specific aspects of current doctrine, including provisions that have been criticized by some commentators. For example, causing a death during a felony is treated by the subjects as more blameworthy than causing the same death in otherwise similar circumstances. Negligence as to becoming intoxicated is accepted by the subjects as an adequate basis to impose liability for many offenses committed while intoxicated, as it is in many legal codes. The subjects understand and use current doctrine's distinction between cognitive and control dysfunctions in excuses.

B. Law and Community Also Commonly Disagree

However, the studies also demonstrate that the subjects' views commonly conflict with current law. How can these differences be generally characterized? How would criminal law need to be changed to better track community views?

Empirical research suggests there are factors currently used by the doctrine that are not relevant to the community's assessment of blameworthiness. The sexual offenses study, for example, reveals instances in which the Model Penal Code, which was drafted in the late '50s, no longer reflects community social mores. The subjects do not treat consensual intercourse with an underage teenage partner as the very serious offense that the Code does; they give no mitigation because of prior promiscuity of an underage partner, as the Code does; they do not give the significant mitigation to forcible rape that the Code gives where the victim is a voluntary social companion. Recall that if subjects see the violated individual as the non-consenting victim of a sexual assault, they regard the act as incurring approximately equal liability whether or not the rapist had a previous relationship with the woman. This is an area in which the opinions of society have genuinely changed. In fact, current state codes now reflect this change in public opinion; most have recently dropped the spousal exclusion, the voluntary social companion mitigation, and so on.

Research also can suggest factors that the community view would add to the law's assessment of liability. The culpability requirements study, for example, reveals that subjects impose significant increases in liability for a person's increased culpability over the minimum required for the offense. As the person moves from negligent to purposeful commission of the same offense conduct, the subjects assign greater punishment in response to this heightened culpability. Yet, with the exception of homicide and a few other offenses, most codes typically define each kind of criminal conduct as an offense with a single grade, defined only by certain minimum culpability requirements, usually recklessness. If the law is to mirror community views, the culpability study suggests that offenses be defined to include multiple grades according to the person's culpability level. The specific suggestion here is that code drafters consider increasing the grade of the crime as a function of the culpability of the perpetrator, rather than using recklessness as the trigger for a single grade of offense.

Empirical studies have the potential to not only identify when an additional offense element is needed but also to guide drafters in formulating the elements, as in selecting the level of culpability to require as to which element. The culpability study illustrates that the subjects have specific views on what the minimum level of culpability ought to be and how much liability ought to increase for increases in a person's culpability. Recall that this judgment was a relatively complex one, with culpability as to different elements—for example, "core" elements versus "collateral" elements—having different effects.

In addition to identifying needed elements or setting culpability levels, empirical research can help choose between alternative formulations of an offense or even suggest new formulations or criteria. The attempt study, for example, challenges the Model Penal Code's formulation of the objective requirement for attempt. While modern doctrine imposes attempt liability as soon as a person takes a substantial step toward commission of an offense, 77 percent of the subjects would impose no punishment in such a case. Instead, the subjects generally support the older common law tests for attempt. The law-community discrepancy here is an interesting one, and one that raises pertinent issues in the policy debates. Given the current climate of worry about criminal acts, the law is moving in the direction of criminalizing relatively small steps toward the commission of crimes. To protect the law's moral credibility, lawmakers ought to make clear their valid reasons for the shift to requiring less conduct than the community might.

As noted earlier, the studies show agreement with the law's tendency to treat a killing that occurs in the course of a felony as deserving more blame than the killing would in non-felonious circumstances. Although this generally is true, the felony murder study reveals that the common formulations of the rule do not reflect popular sentiment. This makes all the more puzzling the rule's continuing political vitality despite its extensive criticism by scholars. Subjects tended to punish most accidental killings during a robbery as less serious than manslaughter, while many if not most codes would punish those killings as murder. Some aspects of the rule are clearly less popular with the subjects than others, suggesting a means by which the rule could be reformed. For instance, subjects do not follow the logic of assigning murder to the robber when, during the course of the robbery, a bank guard shoots another of the robbers.

A reconstruction of the rules to reflect community views is possible. Felony murder could be retained for killings that directly result from the action of the perpetrator and perhaps his accomplices, given the utility of holding participants in the crime responsible for the actions of their fellows. Alternatively, some might use the results to support abolition of the special rule in favor of reliance upon the usual homicide doctrines with the addition of certain evidentiary presumptions, as the Model Penal Code attempts but which most states have rejected. That is, if a death occurs during the course of a felony, the perpetrators would be presumed to have caused that death with recklessness as to causing death and with extreme indifference to the value of human life that warrants a murder penalty, and it would be the task of the defense to rebut this presumption with evidence showing that their conduct was not reckless or did not manifest extreme indifference to the value of human life.

Another use of the empirical research might be to set or adjust the grades of offenses. For example, if the felony murder doctrine is not to be abolished or reformulated, the research suggests that at very least, its liability grades should be reduced. A "felony manslaughter rule" might be more appropriate than the felony murder rule.

A more fundamental grading issue is illuminated by the attempt study. Some codes, like the Model Penal Code, impose the same level of liability for an attempt as for the offense that is attempted;[2] but a majority of codes provide a standard discount for attempt liability. The subjects support the majority rule here.[3] This sheds some light on a dispute in the literature over people's intuitive notions as to whether actual resulting harm should increase liability.[4] It suggests that resulting harm does

[2] *See* Model Penal Code §5.05(1).

[3] *See* the requirements for attempt in chapter 12, section B.

[4] *Compare* John H. Mansfield, Comment, *Hart and Honore, Causation in the Law*, 17 VAND. L. REV. 488 (1964), *with* Stephen J. Schulhofer, *Harm and Punishment*, 122 U. PA. L. REV. 1497 (1974).

increase a person's assessment of deserved punishment, to the point that even liability for a completed offense sometimes is reduced if the person is able to undo the harm that has been done. This evidence has implications for the formulation and grading of all offenses, as well as for doctrines of liability such as complicity. It suggests that codes ought to distinguish and punish more severely instances where the prohibited harm actually occurs or the prohibited conduct is actually consummated, as compared to instances where the harm or evil is only intended.

The studies also suggest different grading than current law for most of the doctrines that concern errors in justification. If a mistake as to a justification does not give a defense, it ought to at least mitigate liability, according to the subjects. This will be considered in more depth in chapter 20.

The general area of justification for actions otherwise prohibited is an interesting one from the perspective of law-community clashes. Review for a moment the findings on the degree of violence that the community finds appropriate in defense of self or property or to bring about a citizen's arrest. The shared theme here is the degree to which the average citizen can take the law into his or her own hands. Recall that the subjects were willing to approve the use of a good deal more force that the law would permit, and the use of force in a good many more cases that the law would allow.

Several possible explanations for this exist. First, many of the subjects may see the criminal justice system as failing to keep its side of the social contract, failing to apprehend criminals or get them to jail when they are caught or sentenced. If this is the case, have they, therefore, reverted to a vigilante notion of justice, in which any individual is entitled to take almost any step necessary to protect his or her property or person? To the degree that this is the case, it represents a complex problem for lawmakers. To what degree can or should the law be formulated to represent people's views about a perceived or actual breakdown of the criminal justice system? This seems a particularly acute question for the case of force allowable in carrying out a citizen's arrest. The subjects seem to be saying that a person who uses a high degree of force in these circumstances, even unnecessary or disproportionate force, should receive only relatively minor punishment for doing so. Again, what may be going on here is that subjects may perceive the existence of a crime crisis in society. People may believe that the overtaxed police departments have a low likelihood of apprehending a thief or the court system of appropriately punishing him if apprehended. If so, they may believe that the violent acts of the theft victims are the only punishment a perpetrator is ever likely to receive, and therefore victims are appropriately empowered to deliver this punishment.

A second explanation of the results also is possible. People may rely upon a different set of principles than those that the law reflects for judging appropriate defensive force. For instance, the legal code formulation seems to require some apparently complex calculations on the part of the attacked person, about exactly what an attacker intends and what is the minimum force sufficient to thwart those intentions. People may regard it as inappropriate to require an attacked individual to make these judgments in what they imagine as a rapidly occurring and emotionally terrifying situation such as an assault or a robbery.

The above cases raise the possibility that subjects would approve of alterations in the law that decriminalize certain acts or reduce the liability assigned to them. However, in other cases, the subjects seem to be calling for the criminalization or more serious treatment of actions that the law does not criminalize or to which the law assigns relatively minor penalties. The studies sometimes suggest that new offenses be created or that liability be expanded from its current scope. The omission study, for example, reveals that about 80 percent of the subjects would impose liability for a person's failure to rescue a stranger when such can be done with no danger to the person. Current doctrine, recall, imposes no duty to rescue in such a case, and therefore imposes no liability for failing to do so, no matter how minor the inconvenience.

C. Binary versus Category Judgments: Legality and Normative Power in Code Drafting

As interesting as the specific law-community comparisons is, the documentation that the process by which subjects assess liability is different from the way in which current doctrine conceptualizes the issue. Where the doctrine treats a factor as setting a fixed minimum requirement for full liability, the subjects frequently see the same factor as aggravating or mitigating the degree of a person's liability and punishment. For example, while the doctrine treats complicity as a means of establishing full liability for the substantive offense, the subjects generally consider an accomplice to be less blameworthy than the principal and reduce the accomplice's liability accordingly. A similar general "discount" in liability is seen in cases of omission. While the doctrine holds a person fully liable for the substantive offense if he satisfies the requirements of omission liability, the subjects significantly reduce a person's liability if he commits an offense by omission from what it would be if he committed the same offense by commission. Reacting intuitively, the community's views may seem to be more rational than the law's treatment here. In a failure to rescue case, the law's assignment of no penalty to the person who fails to rescue, and assignment of a penalty equivalent to murder or manslaughter if certain complex conditions about the assumption of duty are met, seems initially too lenient and then too harsh.

The definition and grading of attempt conduct similarly demonstrate this difference between the law's and the respondents' treatment of liability. The law defines a particular point, during the preparation and conduct toward an offense, as the moment when liability attaches. The subjects, in contrast, see increasing liability as the person gets closer to committing the offense.

The law's tendency to dichotomize signals a serious and pervasive flaw in current law, from the subjects' perspective. The doctrine more often than not sees a fact as either establishing liability or not. The subjects, in contrast, frequently see a continuum of blameworthiness and liability. A fact more frequently contributes to an increment or decrement in liability judgment than it produces a complete assignment of liability or total escape from liability.

One might initially think that this difference simply reflects the practical limitations of a criminal code: it can be so detailed in its liability and grading rules and no more. However, the law commonly does take account of just the kind of grading differences that the subjects are urging. Codes sometimes, too rarely from the subjects' perspective, vary the degree of a person's liability with his level of culpability. The law's culpability spectrum is not strictly continuous. Instead it sorts all offenses into four discrete levels of culpability. However, it is a practical and useful approximation of a continuum.

In most other instances, however, current doctrine fails to acknowledge continuums that the subjects clearly support, and where it is well within the law's ability to adopt grading rules that would at least attempt to approximate a continuum. In complicity, for example, not only do the subjects give a liability discount to the accomplice, which the law does not; but they vary the extent of the discount with the extent of the accomplice's contribution to the offense. Similarly, in attempts, the extent of the attempter's discount will depend in part on how far he has gone toward completion of the offense. In omissions, the extent of liability depends on the degree of danger or inconvenience a person would suffer to undertake the rescue. In causation, liability varies with the strength of the causal connection between the person's conduct and the result. The law, in contrast, sets a maximum degree of tolerable remoteness between the person's conduct and the result, in time, place, or strength of causal chain. If this maximum amount is not exceeded, the person is fully accountable for the result. The subjects, in contrast, see degrees of liability according to the degree of remoteness.

Obviously, a criminal code cannot take account of the infinite continuum over which many factors may range. However, it is not unrealistic to expect a code to recognize that these factors are relevant to determining liability—that is, to recognize some kind of discount—and to attempt a rough approximation of their varying effect. This can be done in the same way that modern codes approximate the harm and culpability continuums, by defining a few large categories for each of the most relevant factors. Such a rough approximation of a continuum generally is sufficient for the criminal code's role of indicating a range for the extent of punishment. More refined distinctions can be made in the sentencing process.

Is it not the case that all such distinctions could be reserved for the sentencing process? It would be a mistake to push over to the sentencing process the responsibility for making such rough approximations of highly relevant factors, especially when such determinations can effectively be made by a code. First, as a matter of principle, the purposes supporting the legality principle,[5] as well as modern notions

---

[5] *See* Paul H. Robinson, Criminal Law §2 (3rd ed. 2012).

of due process, prefer that the most significant determinants of liability be considered at the liability stage, where the jury can make the determination under the normal rules of trial procedure. To leave such determinations to the discretionary sentencing stage is to devalue legality, the jury system, and due process unnecessarily. Second, at the level of practice, jurors are more likely to abide by their legal instructions to the extent that those instructions reach results that they regard as fair outcomes. To fail to have verdicts that match the general range of punishment deserved is to invite jury dissatisfaction and resistance.

D. Criminal Liability without Punishment

In many of the studies, the subjects impose criminal liability on a person but then impose little or no punishment. Such is the subjects' view where the person is intent on crime but his conduct falls short of dangerous proximity of completion, where the person satisfies the objective elements of an offense but is faultless as to one or another element, where the person fails to rescue the stranger because of danger (or inconvenience), where the person mistakenly or improperly uses deadly force in self-defense, unnecessary force in protection of property, or excessive force or force against the wrong person in attempting to detain an offender.

This practice by subjects may seem somewhat odd. If the person's conduct is serious enough to merit the condemnation of criminal conviction, why should the person be free from punishment? One explanation is that the subjects want to express their disapproval of the person's conduct but feel that the person is not sufficiently blameworthy to be punished for the conduct. If one takes a once-popular view among academics that saw the only role of the criminal law as deterring criminal behavior, this response by the subjects makes very little sense. Liability is taken as a judgment that application of deterrent punishment is appropriate, yet no such application is made. However, if one sees the criminal law as having dual roles, of both announcing rules of proper conduct and adjudicating violations of those rules; and further, sees desert as the primary guide for assessing punishment, then this sort of judgment of "improper conduct, no punishment" makes good sense. It is the mechanism by which the subjects seek to achieve the sometimes conflicting functions of law: judging the propriety of the conduct as a signal to others in the future, and judging the blameworthiness of the defendant at hand for his past violation.

Notice that in each instance in which "liability but no punishment" is commonly given as a response, the person's conduct is arguably inappropriate although the actor is not held to be terribly blameworthy. In the omission cases, for example, in which an individual fails to rescue a drowning man although he could do so without great danger, the subjects often assign a verdict of "liability but no punishment." Here the subjects seem to be saying that this is conduct that they want to disapprove of, but the individual does not deserve a term in jail. The subjects use the condemnatory function of the legal system in a way that makes perfect sense if one sees that ordinary people take the law as having moral force to exert on the citizen. They are saying that these sorts of behaviors are morally inappropriate, without feeling that the person under the circumstances ought to be punished for the conduct. In doing so, they are acknowledging what has become one of the major messages of the discussion: that the law is seen as having moral force by the citizens of the state, and that moral force operates independently of the state's coercive force.

Still, imposing criminal liability in such a case, in one sense, perverts the function of criminal conviction. If the person is not sufficiently blameworthy, why should he or she suffer the condemnation of a criminal conviction? The answer may be found in the limited options available in the criminal law. The law provides no opportunity, other than through criminal conviction, for a person's criminal conduct to be disapproved. The subjects are caught in a difficult situation. To decline to impose liability is to seemingly approve of conduct of which they in fact disapprove. On the other hand, to impose liability is to blame a person whom they see as not warranting the blame they hand out. The liability but-no punishment option may seem an attractive compromise in such a situation.

In the end, however, the liability but-no punishment option may be just that—a compromise—rather than an accurate expression of the subjects' or jurors' feelings. The fact is that such a practice imposes the stigma of criminal liability, albeit without punishment, on persons who do not deserve it. This is not only unfair to the person and unsatisfying to the subjects and jurors but also undermines the effective operation of the criminal law. If the law's role is to do justice, it fails in that function when an insufficiently blameworthy person is convicted. That no punishment is imposed only minimizes the extent of the injustice. Also, of course, when juries convict, they cannot control whether the judge will exercise the no punishment option.

The difficult situation and the undesirable compromise arise because the criminal law has the two important but distinct functions noted above, each of which has its own special demands. These two functions—announcing ex ante public rules of conduct, and assessing ex post individual blame in adjudication of a violation—have very different doctrinal foundations. The rules of conduct function give the general population ex ante direction as to what they can, must, and must not do. The principles of adjudication function gives decision makers (i.e., prosecutors, juries, and judges) guidance in assessing ex post the blameworthiness of an individual's violation of the rules. When the doctrine tries to serve both of these functions with the same provisions, one or the other of the functions suffers. In this instance, an offender is convicted to assure that the proper signals are sent to disapprove of the conduct—the rules of conduct function is satisfied—yet a blameless or insufficiently blameworthy offender suffers the condemnation of conviction; the adjudication of blame function is perverted. In other instances, the reverse perversion occurs.[6]

---

[6] *See generally* Paul H. Robinson, *Rules of Conduct and Principles of Adjudication*, 57 U. Chi. L. Rev. 729 (1990).

The solution to the subjects' dilemma and the law's injustice is to allow subjects and jurors to disapprove of the person's conduct without condemning the person. This requires the use of trial verdicts that allow a distinction between an acquittal based on approval of the person's conduct and an acquittal based upon a person's blamelessness for admittedly improper conduct. As developed elsewhere, the available trial verdicts might be: "no violation," "blameless violation," and "guilty" (blameworthy violation).[7]

E. The Jury as a Resolver of Law-Community Conflicts

Is it possible that the elaborate focus on law-community comparisons misses the point? One could argue that the discussion above reflects a misunderstanding of the functioning of the legal system and ignores the presence of the jury as a mechanism that modifies the results produced by a mechanical application of the law where community standards would be seriously violated. Juries have been known to come to verdicts that seem far from the ones that would be required by an exact application of the law, choosing instead, for instance, to find an individual not guilty of the offense or guilty of a lesser offense that provides the reduced punishment that the jurors see as appropriate.

Instructive here is the case of "the subway vigilante," Bernhard Goetz, who shot several persons whom he believed were beginning to mug him during his ride on the subway in New York. Goetz was approached and surrounded by four African American men: Darell Cabey, Barry Allen, Troy Canty, and James Ramseur. They were all high school dropouts with criminal records. Their aggressive and somewhat threatening behavior caused the 15 to 20 other passengers on the subway to move to the other end of the car. Canty and Allen asked Goetz for $5, and Goetz then saw one of the other two men reach into his pocket, which appeared to be bulging. It was later determined that the men were carrying sharpened screwdrivers. Goetz asked them to repeat their request, which they did. Cabey later admitted that they were intending to rob Goetz because "he looked like easy bait." After the second request, Goetz pulled his gun and fired rapidly at them, hitting each at least once. He then saw Cabey sitting near the conductor's cab, and said "You seem to be doing all right. Here's another," and shot him. Canty, Allen, and Ramseur eventually recovered from their serious injuries, while the shooting paralyzed Cabey and caused brain damage. Goetz was found not guilty of any serious charges by a jury, even though his actions seemed to clearly violate what the law allows in self-defense. Similarly, battered women who finally kill their abusive husbands have been acquitted by juries even though strict application of the self-defense formulation would allow no defense.

---

[7] For a more detailed account and a more intricate proposal, *see* Paul H. Robinson, Natasha R. Goldstein, & Peter D. Greene, *Making Criminal Law Codes Functional: A Code of Conduct and a Code of Adjudication*, 86 J. Crim. Law & Criminology 304, 327 et seq. (1996).

Certainly, within the Anglo Saxon legal system, the jury emerged with what is called "jury nullification" as one of their accepted, if not encouraged, functions. Historically this was not always the case; the jury was not always given leeway to make these sorts of adjustments. Early in the history of the emergence of the jury, there were cases in which the civil authorities, outraged at a particular verdict of a jury, threw the members of the jury in jail. But quite early in the development of the jury, jurors became immune from this kind of retrospective punitive evaluation of their verdicts. This gave the jury the possibility of refusing to find individuals guilty even when the law would have found them guilty, or of finding guilty unpopular individuals who were charged with offenses they might not have committed. Interestingly, Green's analysis of jury deliberations occurring in the 12th century showed that jurors actually did use their nullification powers to find innocent various of their neighbors who had harmed or killed others in what the jurors regarded as an act of self-defense, even though the act did not meet the strict requirements that the law set for self-defense.[8]

The legal requirements at that time were not dissimilar to what they are now, requiring that the attack be imminent and that retreat from the attack be impossible. Facts damaging to the claim of self-defense, therefore, were that the attacker was wounded in the side or the back, since then his attack could not have been in progress, or that the incident took place in an open field or some other location from which it should have been possible to flee the attack. Coroner's reports often attested to the awkward presence of these facts in specific cases. But during the jury deliberations (as inferred from the facts as they were described in the jury reports), wounds that the coroner had described as located in the back or side of the attacker crept around to the front, and what were described as open fields were found to contain ditches, dikes, hedges or other obstacles that made retreat from the attack more plausibly impossible.[9] Juries have nullified the mechanical operation of the law in the 12th century, in the 20th century, and no doubt every century in between. By doing so, they bring community standards to bear in a context that gives them no apparent role.

However, relying on the jury to nullify the normal operation of the law in cases of law-community discrepancies does not seem to be an entirely satisfactory mechanism for adjudicating differences. First, it is unlikely to consistently work in a way that provides fairness across cases. One jury, somehow aware of its power to nullify, does so. Another jury, unaware of its power to do so, or more cowed by the authority of the court, does not. One of the accused goes to jail, the other goes free. What frequently happens is that this discrepancy, now personalized in the form of two individuals, is publicized, drawing attention to the unfairness of the legal system in a vivid and personal way.

Second, as discussed earlier, for the law to criminalize certain actions that people regard as morally acceptable, even though juries at least sometimes do not convict,

---

[8] Thomas Andrew Green, Verdict According to Conscience (University of Chicago Press 1985).

[9] *See id.* at ch. 8.

is to give a signal that damages peoples' respect for the justice system, and thus likely impairs its moral credibility. Third, as pointed out by Green, if juries systematically provide this kind of "safety valve" function for the law, they reduce pressure for a change in the legal rules that would move the law in the direction of better rendering community standards. In the extreme case, they stultify legal change.

Further, the jury's nullification ability is effective only as far as their power extends, in the assignment of liability. The jury's power only works in one direction; they can with their verdict minimize the extent of punishment that a person can receive, but they cannot assure that a judge will sentence a person to the full punishment that their verdict calls for. Finally, and relatedly, many of the legal positions that are shown to conflict with community views are instantiated in sentencing guideline systems. Most of what has been said about "missing discounts" and dichotomous rather than continuous treatment in the law applies equally to existing sentencing guidelines. While sentencing judges might share the jury's desire to deviate from the formal demands of the law, and might regularly have done so through the exercise of sentencing discretion, that possibility is lost when articulated sentencing rules deviate from community views.[10] For all of these reasons, then, it seems preferable to have community standards reflected in the law when it is appropriate to do so.

[10] For a general discussion of how sentencing systems might be constructed to better capture the subtleties of community views, *see* Paul H. Robinson, *A Sentencing System for the 21st Century?*, 66 Tex. L. Rev. 1 (1987).

PART } IV

Empirical Studies of Lay Judgments of Justice as a Law and Policy Tool

Part III showed how empirical studies can reveal the liability and punishment rules of lay persons, which can serve as a guide to criminal law's rules for the reasons detailed in part II. A criminal code drafter could use these studies and others like them to construct a code that tracked community views. But as part IV seeks to illustrate, research studies of lay judgments of justice have other uses as well, such as explaining historical shifts in liability rules, judging the strength of competing criminal law theories, and giving guidance in the exercise of judicial discretion.

Chapter 18 examines the claimed shift from the common law's objective view of criminality to modern criminal law's more subjective one. Does the change in doctrine reflect such an objective-to-subjective change in the way modern people think about criminal liability? Which way of thinking best tracks modern community views? Chapter 19 considers the ever-interesting offense of blackmail. Criminal law scholars have offered a half dozen or more alternative explanations of what drives the formulation of the offense. The research presented tests which of these theories best approximates lay judgments on the issue. Chapter 20 examines competing conceptions of justification defenses—the "deeds" theory versus the "reasons" theory—and tests which theory better reflects lay judgments. Finally, chapter 21 looks at a wide variety of factors that have been used or urged for use as factors in discretionary sentencing. Would lay judgments of justice take such factors into account? What level of agreement or disagreement exists for their use? If they do reflect shared community views, should their use or their rejection be formalized to promote greater uniformity in application?

The larger point here is that whenever doctrinal, theoretical, or policy analysis have reason to take account of lay judgments of justice—which part II suggests ought to be often—an empirical issue is raised, which can be authoritatively resolved through proper research. The four studies described here illustrate not only the breadth of issues on which such research can be useful but also the variety of research methods and designs that can be used in answering the empirical question.

18 }

Explaining History: Shifting Views of Criminality

Some of the more intriguing questions in criminal law examine the collection of doctrinal changes that occurred in the shift from the common law to modern criminal codes. Is there a meaningful pattern to the changes, and can one articulate a theory that explains why these set of changes came about together? Was there a change to the underlying theory of criminalization; and, if so, what was the nature of the change?

Section A describes a claim that the doctrinal changes show a coherent pattern, one that reflects a shift in the dominant view of what makes something criminal—what George Fletcher calls the shift from a "traditionalist" to a "modernist" view of criminality. Fletcher's claims are, in part, empirical in nature—that the doctrinal shift reflects a change in the way people think about criminality—and section B shows how the theory can be tested empirically.

The results of an empirical study reported in section C suggest that there is indeed a coherent pattern to the doctrinal shifts in the many different doctrinal areas, supporting Fletcher's speculation, but also suggests that the view of modern lay persons does not match what Fletcher describes as the "modernist" view. Rather, modern lay persons appear to take a subjectivist (what Fletcher calls a "modernist") view of criminality when making liability judgments but take an objectivist (what Fletcher calls a "traditionalist") view of criminality when making grading judgments. Thus, the empirical findings support the general insight that the changes reflect a coherent pattern, but suggest that the shift to a subjectivist view of criminality occurred only with regard to liability determinations and not with regard to grading. This chapter is drawn primarily from my article with John Darley, *Objectivist Versus Subjectivist Views of Criminality: A Study in the Role of Social Science in Criminal Law Theory.*[1]

[1] Paul H. Robinson & John M. Darley, *Objectivist Versus Subjectivist Views of Criminality: A Study in the Role of Social Science in Criminal Law Theory,* 18 Oxford J. Legal Stud. 409 (1998).

A. Theories for a Pattern of Criminalization Difference between Common Law and Modern Codes

Many changes from common law doctrine to modern criminal codes are easily explainable as responses to changing conditions. As societal interdependencies grew, so did the variety of ways in which a person could harm society, its institutions, or other persons. Thus, new offenses were created, and old offenses altered to take account of new harms. For example, most modern criminal codes contain white collar business crimes and special organized crime offenses that did not exist at common law. Other modern criminal code changes are simply attempts to make criminal law clearer and more comprehensive, as the legality principle demands. Thus, modern codes typically define commonly used terms, limit the number of culpability levels by carefully defining offenses, and codify a comprehensive set of defenses. The changes of greatest interest to criminal law theorists, however, have been those that suggest some kind of paradigm shift in defining the core of what constitutes "criminality," that is, changes that suggest that the foundational substance of the law, not just its form or application, has changed.

1. A DOCTRINAL SHIFT IN VIEWS OF CRIMINALITY FROM COMMON LAW TO MODERN CODES?

Consider the different views of criminalization that might be suggested by the following comparisons. The common law recognized an unconvictable perpetrator defense to complicity, under which the accomplice escaped liability if the perpetrator was unconvictable (because the perpetrator lacked the culpability required for the offense, for example).[2] Modern codes typically reject such an unconvictable perpetrator defense, arguing that an accomplice's liability ought to depend upon what the accomplice did and the accomplice's state of mind, and that the perpetrator's defense ought not alter the accomplice's liability.[3]

In the context of conspiracy, the common law defined the agreement requirement as two or more persons agreeing. Not only did the defendant have to agree with another, the other person genuinely had to agree back.[4] Agreeing with an undercover agent, for example, did not constitute an adequate agreement for conspiracy liability. Modern codes typically drop this "bilateral" agreement requirement for conspiracy and simply require that the actor have agreed with another, termed a "unilateral" agreement requirement.[5]

---

[2] Regina v. Richards, [1974] 1 QB 776 (CA, Crim Div).

[3] *See*, e.g., Model Penal Code §2.06(7); *see also* Regina v. Cogan & Leak, [1976] 1 QB 217 (CA, Crim Div).

[4] *See, e.g.,* Archbold v State, 397 N.E.2d 1071 (Ind. App. 1979).

[5] *See, e.g.,* Model Penal Code §5.03(1)(a)&(b); Model Penal Code §5.03 cmt. 398–402 (1985). *See also* People v. Schwimmer, 66 A.D.2d 91, 411 N.Y.S.2d 922 (1978), *aff'd*, 47 N.Y.2d 1004, 420 N.Y.S.2d 218, 394 N.E.2d 288 (1979).

In the context of attempts, the common law permitted a defense if an actor attempted an offense that, unknown to the actor, was impossible to complete under the circumstances as they actually existed. Thus, the actor who purchased goods believing them to be stolen could not be held liable for an attempt to receive stolen goods where the goods purchased were not, in fact, stolen.[6] Modern codes, in contrast, reject an impossibility defense to all forms of inchoate liability. An actor's liability is to be determined from the point of view of the actor, under the circumstances as the actor believed them to be.[7] If the actor believes that the goods are stolen, he can be held liable for an attempt to purchase stolen goods.

Also in the context of attempts, the common law adopted a variety of tests for determining whether an actor's conduct had moved from mere preparation to criminal attempt. The tests had in common their focus on how close the actor had come (his or her "proximity") to completing the offense.[8] Modern codes, following the Model Penal Code, look instead at how far the actor has gone from the start of the offense conduct. Once a "substantial step" is taken, the actor has shown a willingness to act upon the actor's intention and, therefore, the actor's conduct is deemed adequate for a criminal attempt.[9] Asking a secretary to type a letter that is the first of several steps in an elaborate fraud scheme, for example, would not constitute an attempt at common law, but could constitute a "substantial step" sufficient for liability under modern codes.

One may note from these examples that the common law is consistent in imposing liability only in the instance where there actually (objectively) exists the danger of the offense harm or evil: by requiring an attempt possible of completion and, in the context of conspiracy, a true agreement between two conspirators, for instance. One might term this an objectivist view of criminality, which sees the gravamen of an offense as its objective harm or evil. It focuses upon whether the actor's conduct came close to bringing about the harm or evil of the substantive offense. Where the potential for the harm or evil exists only in the actor's mind, as is the case in impossible attempts, liability is inappropriate. Hence, the common law rule giving a defense for instances of legal impossibility.

Modern codes, in contrast, are willing to impose liability when the actor believes that he or she is committing or participating in a criminal offense. Under what might be called this subjectivist view of criminality, the focus is not on the harm or evil of the offense but upon the actor's subjective culpability in attempting to bring it about. Coming close to a substantive harm or evil is not required. The question is whether the actor has gone far enough to demonstrate that his or her intention is fully formed and resolute, hence the requirement of a "substantial step." Similarly,

---

[6] *See, e.g.,* People v. Jaffe, 185 N.Y. 497, 78 N.E. 169 (1906).

[7] *See*, e.g., Model Penal Code §5.01(1)(a).

[8] *See, e.g.,* Commonwealth v Peaslee, 177 Mass. 267, 59 NE 55, 57 (1901) ("[A] mere collection and preparation of materials in a room for the purpose of setting fire to them, unaccompanied by any present intent to set the fire, would be too remote.").

[9] *See, e.g.,* Model Penal Code §5.01(1)(c).

while the actor's attempt may be impossible, it nonetheless may be adequate to show the actor's willingness to commit the offense.

The same common law objectivist and modern code subjectivist conflict occurs in determining the importance that attaches to the close risk or actual occurrence of the offense. A logical extension of the subjectivist view of criminality suggests that there ought to be little or no significance given to whether the harm or evil of an offense actually occurs. If the primary focus of liability is the actor's subjective culpability, the important facts are what the actor has done in furtherance and as expression of that culpability (and the level of the actor's culpable state of mind at the time of the offense). Whether the harm or evil intended or risked actually occurs does not alter the actor's subjective culpability.

The objectivist view, in contrast, would insist on greater punishment where the harm or evil occurs, for it is the gravamen of the offense. While the objectivist might be persuaded to impose liability on the actor who comes close to bringing about the harm or evil, it seems clear that the objectivist would think that still greater liability is due where the harm or evil in fact occurs.

Thus the subjectivist-objectivist perspectives generate important differences in the criminal rules governing grading of offenses. As it did with regard to minimum requirements for liability, the Model Penal Code generally takes a subjectivist view of criminality in grading. With a few exceptions, the Code's view is that the actual occurrence of a harm and evil ought not be significant. The actor's liability ought to depend only on the actor's culpable state of mind manifested in conduct. The most important provision implementing this view with respect to grading is Model Penal Code section 5.05(1), which grades inchoate offenses as follows:

> Except as otherwise provided in this Section, attempt, solicitation and conspiracy are crimes of the same grade and degree as the most serious offense which is attempted or solicited or is an object of the conspiracy. An attempt, solicitation or conspiracy to commit a [capital crime or a] felony of the first degree is a felony of the second degree.[10]

Thus, except for attempted murder and attempted aggravated rape, all other attempts—for example, attempted arson, attempted sexual assault—are graded the same as the completed offense. The traditional view, reflected in the objectivist common law, was to punish the inchoate offense less than the completed offense.[11]

Similarly reflecting the Model Penal Code's subjectivist grading philosophy is the Code's complicity provision, which treats unsuccessful attempts to aid a perpetrator as complicity, for which full substantive liability is imposed.[12] The Code's provision holds an actor as an accomplice if he "aids or agrees *or attempts to aid*"

---

[10] Model Penal Code §5.05(1).

[11] *See, e.g.,* 2 James Fitzjames Stephens, A History of the Criminal Law of England 224 (1883) (attempt to commit any felony was misdemeanor).

[12] *See* Model Penal Code §2.06(1), (2), (3)(a)(ii).

in the commission of an offense.[13] Thus, an unfulfilled agreement or unsuccessful attempt to assist or encourage is graded the same as the substantive offense. The actor who agrees to stand watch for a perpetrator bent on arson is liable for arson even if he gets the date confused and does not show. In other words, inchoate complicity is punished not as inchoate liability but as full substantive liability. At common law, an unsuccessful attempt to aid would not constitute complicity in the substantive offense.[14]

2. OBJECTIVIST VS. SUBJECTIVIST (TRADITIONALIST VS. MODERNIST) VIEWS OF CRIMINALITY

To oversimplify, the distinction between what is called an "objectivist" and a "subjectivist" view of criminality might be stated this way: the objectivist view maintains that the occurrence of the harm or evil defined by the offense is highly relevant; the subjectivist view maintains that such harm or evil is irrelevant and only the actor's culpable state of mind regarding the occurrence of the harm or evil is important.

The labels tend to overstate a rather subtle distinction. The "objectivist" or "harmful consequences" view is not so objective as to require that the harm or evil of the offense actually occurs in order to impose liability. The objectivist imposes liability for inchoate conduct, as for example, when the actor comes close to bringing about a real offense harm or evil. In turn, the "subjectivist" view is not so subjective as to only require a culpable state of mind. An intention alone is insufficient for liability; some act is required to prove the actor's willingness to act upon, or externalize, his or her subjective culpability.[15] While the occurrence of the harm or evil may not be important to the subjectivist, the nature of the harm or evil intended or risked is important to determine the degree of the actor's culpability. Intending to cause death is more serious than intending to rob someone.

George Fletcher has noted a similar distinction between the common law and modern codes and labeled the opposing views as "traditionalist" and "modernist."[16] Common law is said to reflect the objectivist view of the view of the traditionalists, where the gravamen of an offense is its resulting harm or evil. The modernist subjectivist view of criminality, in contrast, focuses upon the actor's culpable state of mind toward bringing about the offense harm or evil, without regard for whether the harm or evil actually occurs. Fletcher explains:

> The traditionalists root their case in the way we feel about crime and suffering. Modernists hold to arguments of rational and meaningful punishment.

---

[13] Model Penal Code §2.06(3)(a)(ii) (emphasis added).

[14] STEPHENS, *supra* note 794, at 234–37.

[15] For further discussion of this function of the act requirement, *see* Paul H. Robinson, *Should the Criminal Law Abandon the Actus Reus—Mens Rea Distinction?*, in CRIMINAL LAW: ACTION, VALUE AND STRUCTURE (S. Shute, J. Gardner, & J. Horder eds.) (Oxford, 1993).

[16] GEORGE P. FLETCHER, A CRIME OF SELF DEFENSE: BERNHARD GOETZ AND THE LAW ON TRIAL 64 (1988).

> Despite what we might feel, the modernist insists, reason demands that we limit the criminal law to those factors that are within the control of the actor. The occurrence of harm is beyond his control and therefore ought not to have weight in the definition of crime and fitting punishment. The tension between these conflicting schools infects virtually all of our decisions in designing a system of crime and punishment.[17]

Recall the comparison of common law and modern code rules relating to minimum requirements. Each of these common law rules reflects a "traditionalist" common law consistent in imposing liability only where an offense harm or evil or a credible danger of one actually exists. Completion of an attempt must be possible and must almost materialize; a conspiracy must be a true agreement between two actual conspirators; an accomplice must actually assist a real perpetrator. Where the potential for the harm or evil exists only in the actor's mind or is remote or speculative, traditionalists view the assignment of liability as inappropriate.

The subjective modernist view focuses upon the actor's intention to bring about the offense harm or evil. An actor need not come close to a substantive harm or evil of the offense; he need only engage in some conduct, a "substantial step," toward that end, to demonstrate his willingness to act upon his intention. Completion of an attempt need not be possible, provided that the actor thinks it is possible. The coconspirator need not actually agree with the actor, provided that the actor thinks he does. The perpetrator need not actually commit an offense, provided that the accomplice thinks that he will.

As Fletcher conceives of it, a person is either a traditionalist or a modernist. One either thinks that the occurrence of harm or evil is important to criminal liability, as the common law makers apparently did; or one thinks that it is not, as modern code drafters apparently do. While the distinction—what is called an objectivist versus a subjectivist view of criminality—is valuable Fletcher's characterization of it is unnecessarily dichotomous. His traditionalist-modernist distinction is misleading because it incorrectly suggests that one must be either an objectivist or a subjectivist on all issues. In fact, it is possible to be a subjectivist on some issues but an objectivist on others. Specifically, it would be logically coherent to advocate a subjectivist view of the minimum requirements of liability but simultaneously to take an objectivist view of grading.

In fact, this is what ordinary people do. Thus, this argument about legal doctrines is carried out in an unusual way. This study empirically investigates the liability assignment rules held by ordinary people in the community. From the community's view of liability and punishment, the common law's objectivist view was too demanding in setting the minimum requirements of liability, as in defining inchoate offenses. At the same time, subjectivist modern codes miss the mark when they take a subjectivist view in grading, as in ignoring the significance of resulting harm and

---

[17] *Id.*

evil. By demonstrating this, this chapter will have demonstrated that the distinction is an important one to make.

3. TESTABLE EMPIRICAL ISSUES

The disagreements here are to some extent empirical disagreements about how people think. With the help of social science, one can collect and analyze data that may sketch real answers. The discussion raises these testable empirical issues:

(1) Do people take an objectivist view, as the common law did, on both grading and minimum requirements issues, or do they prefer a subjectivist view, as modern criminal codes seem to? That is, are people of today Fletcher's "traditionalists" or, as Fletcher would seem to predict by his labeling, "modernists"?

(2) Are people consistent in the view they take? That is, do they stick to an objectivist view, or a subjectivist view, in a variety of situations? Or do they switch back and forth in a way that suggests that they cannot properly be characterized as taking either view?

(3) If people are not consistently "traditionalists" or "modernists," as Fletcher predicts, is there nonetheless a discernible pattern in their use of an objectivist or a subjectivist view? Do people take a subjectivist view in judging the minimum requirements for liability and an objectivist view in grading, as hypothesized? Or does the pattern follow a different principle? Or, is there no underlying pattern to peoples' liability preferences, as some writers would seem to expect?

B. Identifying Objectivist versus Subjectivist Views of Criminality

Using a scenario research methodology similar to that used in the studies in part III, a variety of scenarios were prepared that focused on the differences between the two—that is, scenarios to which an "objectivist" and a "subjectivist" would respond differently. By comparing the actual responses of the subjects against these benchmarks, one can determine whether a subject's response reflects an objectivist or subjectivist view of criminality, or something else. The scenarios used range from a the control case, scenario 1, in which an actor shoots and kills a victim down through various scenarios that test people's intuitions relevant to the subjective-objective dichotomy. The first eight scenarios all represent hypothetical situations that would obviously merit punishment, but the grading is unclear while the latter scenarios deal with whether the minimum requirement for liability has been met. A short description of the scenarios appears in the table below.[18]

[18] A fuller account of these scenarios is available in Robinson & Darley, *Objectivist Versus Subjectivist*, *supra* note 784, at 421–27.

TABLE 74. } Identifying Objectivist and Subjectivist Responses

Scenario	Objectivist will say:	Subjectivist will say:
	GRADING CASES	
1. Shoot to kill and kill—completed conduct murder—control	1. Murder control case	1. Murder control case
2. Shoot to kill and miss—completed conduct but failed attempt	2. Reduced grade	2. Same grade as completed offense in no. 1
3. Aiming gun but intervention before shoots—proximity but incomplete conduct	3. Perhaps further reduction from no. 2 because further from completed offense	3. No reduction, as in no. 2
4. Agrees with another that they will kill the victim, they go to look for a gun—bilateral conspiracy, no completed offense	4. Probably less liability than no. 3 (and possibly even less than no. 9), because far from completed offense	4. No reduction, as in no. 2
5. Gives gun to person fighting with victim hoping will kill, perpetrator does then shoot and kill—complicity in murder	5. Murder, but reduce liability to the extent that causal contribution is seen as less	5. Same grade as perpetrator in no. 1
6. Gets gun to help person shoot to kill, but person never receives gun, perpetrator has to find his own gun, then shoots and kills—failed complicity, successful offense	6. Reduced grade, perhaps even more reduction than in no. 5, because no causal contribution	6. Same grade as completed offense in no. 1
7. Shoots at target, knowing there might be persons in the overshot zone, kills—manslaughter	7. Reduced grade from no. 1 (because of reduced culpability, R rather than P)	7. Same as objectivist: reduced grade from no. 1 (because of reduced culpability, R rather than P)
8. Shoots at target, knowing there might be persons in the overshot zone, but luckily none endangerment	8. (Further) reduction from no. 7, MINIMUM REQUIREMENTS CASES	8. Same grade as no. 7
9. Gets gun with intention to go kill but fails—substantial step, incomplete conduct	9. Complete defense	9. p-sbj—no reduction, as in no. 2; o-g-sbj—reduction greater than in obj. no. 2 or 3
10. Shoots as in no. I but person turns out to be a life-like dummy of the intended victim—completed conduct, factually impossible attempt	10. Tempted to give complete defense, but perhaps some reduced liability because the appearance of an attempt can be a societal harm in itself	10. p-sbj—no reduction, as in no. 2; o-g-sbj—reduction, as in obj. no. 2
11. Same as no. 4 but other is undercover officer—unilateral conspiracy, no completed offense	11. Complete defense	11. p-sbj—no reduction, as in no. 4 (same grade as no. 2); o-g-sbj—same reduction as in obj. no. 4
12. Smuggles cocaine—control case for no. 13	12. Smuggling control case	12. Control
13. Believes smuggling cocaine but only talcum powder—completed conduct, legally impossible attempt	13. Complete defense	13. p-sbj—no reduction from no. 12; o-g-sbj—reduction, proportionate to that in obj. no. 10
14. Gives gun to person fighting with victim who then kills, as in no. 5, but perpetrator turns out to be a person who is acting and killing in self-defense—assisting unconvictable perpetrator	14. Complete defense	14. p-sbj—no reduction, as in no, 5; o-g-sbj—reduction in obj. no. 2 plus reduction in obj. no. 5

o-g-sbj = objectivist-grading subjectivist.

C. The Results

The liability results of the study are reported in Table 75. The second column reports for each scenario the mean of subjects' responses assigned to that scenario. Each point on the scale corresponds to about one grade in the average American criminal code grading scheme. For scenario 1, the straight murder case, liability is predictably with a mean of 10.10. Using this as a reference, one can see whether subjects impose less liability in other cases and, if so, how much less.

1. ISSUES OF OFFENSE GRADING

Consider the first eight scenarios, in which everyone would agree that some liability is appropriate; the only issue is what degree of liability should be imposed. Those who take a subjectivist view of grading offenses will regard scenarios 2 through 6 as

TABLE 75. } Liability Results and Their Objectivist-Subjectivist Implications

Scenario	Mean	Grading (G) or minimum requirements (MR) case?	Consistent with objectivist view?	Consistent with subjectivist view?
(1) Murder	10.10	—	—	—
(2) Completed conduct attempted murder	8.38	G	Yes	No
(3) Incomplete conduct (proximity) attempt in murder	7.33	G	Yes	No
(4) Bilateral inchoate conspiracy	6.06	G	Yes	No
(5) Complicity in murder	8.60	G	Yes	No
(6) Failed complicity in murder	6.35	G	Yes	No
(7) Manslaughter (reckless homicide)	7.15	G	Yes	Yes
(8) Endangerment	5.28	G	Yes	No
(9) Incomplete conduct (substantial step) attempt to murder	5.73	MR	No	Yes (obj-grd)
(10) Completed conduct factually impossible attempted murder	7.94	MR	Yes	Yes (obj-grd)
(11) Unilateral inchoate conspiracy	6.29	MR	No	Yes (obj-grd)
(12) Smuggling cocaine	7.40	—	—	—
(13) Legally impossible attempt to smuggle cocaine	5.06	MR	No	Yes
(14) Mistaken belief of complicity in murder	9.0	MR	No	Yes (obj-grd)*

abj-grd = subjectivist of the objectivist-grading type.

* But see text discussion concerning scenario 14.

equivalent to murder. In all of them, an intent was formed and displayed, and the intent was to do murder. Those taking an objectivist view, in which the occurrence of harm and other considerations are taken into account, will see these offenses as calling for less liability than the prototypical murder case.

The results of the study tell a simple story: the objectivist view of grading is the one adopted by the subjects. In all of the comparison cases, the liability assignments are lower than that assigned to the murder scenario. In scenario 2, the completed-conduct attempted murder case, subjects impose liability of 8.38. The absence of intended harm, which is the only difference between scenario 1 and scenario 2, generates a reduction in liability of about 1.7 grades (a "no-harm discount" as it might be called).

Scenario 3 is an attempt case, like scenario 2, but one in which the conduct is not complete; the actor is stopped before he can shoot, what the common law called a "dangerous proximity" attempt. The subjects give a liability of 7.33, a further discount from the failed attempt in scenario 2, where the actor shoots and misses. It appears that the subjects are giving an additional discount because the actor is farther from commission of the offense; this might be called an "incomplete-conduct discount." Tentatively, think of this discount as being added to the no-harm discount.

Scenario 4 is the bilateral inchoate conspiracy. The subjects give a reduction in liability, to 6.06, well below the murder scenario of 10.10. The liability assigned scenario 4 is also below the liability assigned to scenario 3. This latter difference may represent an additional incomplete-conduct discount thought appropriate because the conduct is even farther from the completed offense than in scenario 3's dangerous proximity attempt.

In scenario 5 the actor is only complicit in murder; the murder occurs but he is an accomplice rather than the perpetrator of the murder and is assigned a liability of 8.60, considerably lower than the liability assigned the murderer in scenario 1. Such a "complicity discount" is consistent with an objectivist view of criminality; the actor appears to have less of a causal responsibility for the death.

Scenario 6, assigned a liability of 6.35, presents the case of failed complicity in murder. The subjects give a substantial reduction, not only reduced from the liability of scenario 1 but also from the liability imposed in scenario 2, completed-conduct attempt, and that imposed in scenario 5, complicity. But such greater reduction is entirely consistent with an objectivist view of criminality. The actor is not only in the role of accomplice rather than perpetrator, as in scenario 5, but he also has no actual causal connection with the death; his conduct only constitutes an attempt, as in scenario 2. Interestingly, it appears that the no-harm discount and the complicity discount work additively to provide a cumulative reduction in punishment.

In scenarios 7 and 8, the intent to kill present in other scenarios is absent; instead the actor is only reckless as to causing the death. In scenario 7, the reckless homicide case, the subjects impose liability of 7.15, a reduction from the straight murder case in scenario 1. As noted in part B, it was not expected that the contrast between this scenario and the murder scenario would distinguish between an objectivist and a subjectivist view of criminality by the subjects; both views would give reduced liability because of the actor's reduced level of culpability. These results confirm the prediction of an "unintended-result discount."

The comparison of most interest for scenario 7 is with scenario 8. Scenario 8 is the same as scenario 7 except that the harm risked does not come about. The subjects reduce liability from the 7.15 of scenario 7, to 5.28. This seems to provide not only an unintended-result discount but also the no-harm discount that seen in scenario 2. Again, the two discounts appear to be additive.

For grading issues, the patterning of the subjects' responses to these scenarios is quite consistent and strongly suggests that they take an objectivist view of criminality on issues of grading; resulting harm and the extent of causal contribution to the harm are highly relevant to their assignment of liability.

2. ISSUES OF OFFENSE MINIMUM REQUIREMENTS

Now consider the remaining scenarios, in which the issue is the minimum requirements of criminal liability. Recall that in these cases, there is argument by some that no liability should be imposed. The objectivist holds that if there was no actual danger of harm occurring, then no liability ought to generated, even though the actor intended harm. The subjectivist holds that when a settled intent to do harm is formed, liability ought to be generated. The pure subjectivist would have the same degree of liability imposed no matter whether the harm actually occurs and no matter the actor's causal contribution to it, if any. As noted above, however, the objectivist-grading subjectivist concedes that the liability generated ought to depend upon whether the harm actually occurs and the extent of the actor's causal connection to the harm.

In these minimum requirements comparisons, the subjects show themselves to be subjectivists, rather than the objectivists they were when considering the grading scenarios. More precisely, they show themselves to be, as a group, objectivist-grading subjectivist. That is, they take a subjectivist view of minimum requirements but, in imposing that liability, they reveal their objectivist approach to grading.

Scenario 9 is the substantial step attempt case. The subjects' assigned liability averaging 5.73, sharply reduced from the relevant contrast case of murder. The fact that any liability is assigned is inconsistent with the objectivist view, which would have given a complete defense and therefore assign no liability because there had not yet been any real danger of the offense being committed. No liability would have been the actual result of application of the common law test in such a substantial step case.

The reduced liability assigned by the subjects is consistent with the objectivist-grading subjectivist's view. It seems to reflect a no-harm discount and, because the offense is so far from completion, a double incomplete-conduct discount. This case is even more distant from a completed offense than the proximity attempt in scenario 3, hence liability is even lower than the 7.33 in that scenario. This supports the theory that the subjects as a group are objectivist as to grading, but subjectivist as to minimum requirements. If their subjectivist minimum requirements are met, they shift to their objectivist view to determine how much liability to impose.

Scenario 10 is the completed-conduct factually impossible attempt scenario—the actor shot a wax dummy in the head, mistaking the dummy for his enemy. Recall that this is a case where objectivists will be torn, just as early common law gave a complete defense but later permitted reduced liability. It probably will not surprise the reader to learn that the subjects assigned an average liability of 7.94, which is certainly generally inconsistent with the early common law position of giving a defense, although one subject gave liability but no punishment. The rather high average liability assigned in this condition is perhaps something more than one might expect from an objectivist. However, it is entirely consistent with the objectivist-grading subjectivist, who after determining that liability is appropriate because of the actor's externalized intent, reverts to an objectivist view in determining the amount of liability. In comparison to the completed-conduct (possible) attempt of scenario 2, which received a liability of 8.38, the results here hint at the subjects providing an additional discount, beyond that for no harm; they seem to be giving a discount that takes account of the factual impossibility of actually causing the intended harm. However, the reliability of the difference between these two cases is marginal ($p = .07$).

Scenario 11 is a unilateral inchoate conspiracy case; the coconspirator is an undercover police officer. The subjects give liability of 6.29. This is inconsistent with the objectivist view, which would give a complete defense. The imposition of liability by the subjects is consistent with the objectivist-grading subjectivist's view. Again it does not follow the pure subjectivist pattern of having no reduction in liability from the prototypic murder case. Instead, it reflects the view of a subjectivist who, after determining that the minimum requirements of liability are satisfied, shifts to an objectivist view in judging the amount of liability to impose. The extent of liability is slightly below that imposed in scenario 9 ($p = .03$); both deserve a no-harm discount as well as a double incomplete-conduct discount. Conspiracy to murder is not murder.

An interesting comparison for the unilateral conspiracy case is scenario 4, an analogous conspiracy case, but one in which the coconspirator is real and not a police officer. The status of the coconspirator is irrelevant to the subjectivist, because it is outside of the knowledge of the actor. The subjects assigned nearly equivalent liability to the two cases (actually slightly but not reliably higher for the unilateral conspirator) which is what one would expect from a subjectivist view.

Scenarios 12 and 13 involve a drug smuggling offense rather than murder, and thus are not to be compared to any of the other scenarios. In scenario 12, the offender smuggles cocaine and receives a liability of 7.40. In scenario 13, which is identical but for the fact that unknown to the actor, the powder he smuggles is not illegal drugs but talcum powder, liability drops to 5.06. The fact that substantial liability is imposed by the subjects is inconsistent with an objectivist view, which would give a complete defense. The subjects' response is consistent with an objectivist-grading subjectivist view. The reduction seen here is similar to the no-harm plus impossibility reduction that seen in scenario 10, a bit more than two grades. Again, the pure subjectivist would give no reduction.

Scenario 14 is the case that seemed to try the subject's analytic thinking (or possibly their patience) the most. Recall that the case involves a belief by the actor that he is being an accomplice to murder, when it turns out that he is actually giving a gun to a person who uses it to kill another in self-defense. The subjects assign a liability of 9.0. This is inconsistent with the objectivist view, which would give a complete defense because the case is analogous to that of a legally impossible attempt in the sense that the actor mistakenly believes that the circumstances are such that he is committing an offense when in fact he is mistaken about the circumstances. From the objectivist perspective, his conduct is entirely lawful; it is only from his mistaken view of the circumstances that his conduct would be seen as an offense But neither does the case seem to be graded according to the objectivist-grading subjectivist's view, which was reflected in all of the previous cases. Under that view, the actor probably would have been entitled to both a complicity discount and a no-harm discount, in other words, liability in the range of 7 rather than the 9.0 that the subjects in fact assign. That is, subjects are treating the death as an actual harm for which the actor deserves punishment, rather than a justified harm that was entirely lawful.

How did the subjects think about this case? The researchers were sufficiently interested in determining this when they asked 10 new subjects to react to this case along with scenario 5, the case of complicity to murder. Recall that in both cases the actor gives the perpetrator a gun intending to assist the perpetrator in murdering the other. In both cases the other is killed; in one it turns out to be in self-defense, and murder in the other. But, the two cases are identical from the perspective of the actor being focused on here. Subjects made their liability assignments and were interviewed about how they saw the two cases. Subjects had trouble with this comparison, because they were torn between the two conflicting considerations, considerations that they recognized and articulated. Because they were compelled by the fact that the act was an identical one from the perspective of the actor, 2 of the 10 subjects gave the two cases identical and high liabilities. The other 8 subjects recognized this, but also recognized that the resultant killing was self-defense in one case, and reduced the liability they assigned (usually a one-grade reduction, occasionally a little more) without being able to articulate a reason for this other than they thought the actor should "get a little reduction" from the prototypic case. The force of the subjectivist perspective is revealed here, but the typical result makes the case inconsistent with the pure subjectivist view, which would be to give no discount. Instead, the subjects reverted to the objectivist view in grading.

To review these minimal requirement contrasts, the subjects as a group take the objectivist-grading subjectivist view, using subjectivist criteria to determine whether liability to be imposed but reducing that liability as a grading objectivist would, giving discounts for no harm, complicity, impossibility, incomplete conduct, and unintended consequences.

3. AN ANALYSIS OF RESPONSE PATTERNS OF INDIVIDUAL SUBJECTS

The previous section has examined the responses of the subjects as a group, and that examination has painted a relatively clear picture of the subjects as objectively grading subjectivists. Yet, treating the subjects as a group might hide important differences among the subjects as individuals. For example, is the group mean the result of a majority of objective-grading subjectivists outvoting a minority of pure subjectivists or pure objectivists? Or perhaps, the objective-grading subjectivists were not really the bulk of the group; perhaps the means simply reflected shifting majorities among polar opposites of pure subjectivists and pure objectivists. In fact, an examination of the subject's responses as individuals reveals a picture that is slightly different in important ways.

Most of the grading scenarios still suggested a strong objectivist view. The vast majority of the subjects gave reduced liability (compared to the control case of scenario 1) in scenarios 2, 3, 4, 6, and 7: 90, 98, 98, 96, and 98 percent of the subjects, respectively. Of course, this means that up to 10 percent of the subjects gave no reduction, the subjectivist view.

The subjectivist view, while still a minority view, seemed to be stronger in two scenarios in particular. In scenario 5, complicity in murder, only 65 percent of the subjects gave reduced liability; thus 35 percent thought the complicity ought to be equivalent in liability to murder. Also interesting is scenario 8, endangerment, in which 58 percent of the subjects gave reduced liability, but 42 percent did not. That 42 percent of the subjects did not reduce liability is a bit of a surprise. No jurisdiction grades endangerment, simple risk creation, the same as manslaughter, recklessly causing a death. Neither of these results was predicted. It would be interesting to learn more in future research about that substantial minority of the subjects who disagreed with the majority view and who believed that complicity and lack of harm from risk taking ought not reduce liability.

The minimum requirements scenarios also offered some surprises when the individual subject responses were examined. A majority of subjects performed in a way consistent with the picture offered by the means analysis above. That is, a majority of subjects showed a subjectivist view in imposing liability but switched to an objectivist view in grading. However, a few pure objectivists did exist. In each of the minimum requirements scenarios, a few subjects assigned either a rating of "no liability," or "liability but no prison sentence."

In scenario 9, the substantial step murder attempt, four persons, or eight percent of the sample, showed an objectivist assignment of no liability; three others generated the complex judgment that the attempter was liable, but should be assigned no punishment. In scenario 11, the unilateral inchoate conspiracy, three subjects assigned no liability and two more assigned liability but no punishment, a total of 10 percent of the subjects. Perhaps most interesting, in scenario 13, the legally impossible attempt to smuggle cocaine (that was actually talcum powder), a majority imposed a substantial punishment, but 23 percent (11 people) gave the objectivist response: six said no liability and five gave no punishment. In its weakest showing, the objectivist-grading subjectivist view was held by only 77 percent of the sample.

One more aspect of the data warrants examination. Do the individual subjects show a consistent view in their responses? That is, if an individual gives, for instance, an objectivist response to one scenario, is he or she also likely to give an objectivist response to other scenarios? The answer is "yes"; the data indicate moderate consistency among subjects. As mentioned before, seven subjects gave the pure objectivist response to the minimum requirements scenario 9. All of the subjects who gave a pure objectivist response to scenario 10 and 11 were drawn from that group of seven. Five out of that seven also gave the pure objectivist response to scenario 13. Clearly, a small subset of the sample tended toward objectivist responses on minimum requirement scenarios. These might be called "pure objectivists" because, like the majority, they also gave objective responses in the grading scenarios.

Did the study find any "pure subjectivists," persons who gave not only the usual subjectivist responses to minimum requirements cases but also to grading cases? Yes. One consistent subjectivist and other occasional subjectivists were identified. That is, one subject assigned liabilities identical to the liability he gave to the murder case to scenarios 2, 3, 4, 9, 10, and 11! As far as this subject was concerned, shooting to kill and missing, or aiming the gun and being stopped by a security guard, or shooting a wax doll mistaken for the target ought to generate the same liability as killing, as should conspiring to kill the other, whether unilateral or bilateral, and as should buying a gun for the purpose of killing the other. Four other subjects joined this one, thus 10 percent of the sample, in assigning similar liabilities to the murder scenario and the shooting to kill but missing scenario (scenarios 1 and 2). Four different subjects joined the first one, again, 10 percent of the sample, in assigning an identical liability to murder and shooting a wax figure mistaken for the target (scenarios 1 and 10).

To summarize, while the vast majority took an objectivist view of grading, a small minority took a subjectivist view in some cases (only one subject was consistently a grading subjectivist). Two of the grading scenarios (complicity and endangerment) revealed a more substantial minority of grading subjectivists. While the vast majority of subjects took a subjectivist view of minimum requirements (with objectivist grading again, of course), a small minority of pure objectivists seemed to exist.

D. Implications

Recall the questions presented at the conclusion of section A. The reader now knows from the description of results that most lay persons today are neither "modernists" or "traditionalists," as Fletcher seems to assume, and certainly they are not "modernists" as that label predicts. There does appear to be a consistent pattern in the typical subject's views: a subjectivist view in judging the minimum requirements of liability, but a shift to an objectivist view in assessing the proper grade of an offense. This was the pattern that was hypothesized.

When it comes to setting the minimal requirements for conduct to count as a crime, the vast majority of subjects take a subjectivist view: A person who intends to commit a crime and carries out conduct toward the direction of committing that crime, is assigned criminal liability, even when the crime and the harm does not ensue and even when it would have been impossible to ensue.

In determining how much liability to impose upon the offender, however, the subjects were acutely sensitive to such considerations as whether the harm actually occurred, whether the actions intended to bring about that harm were complete or incomplete, and the strength of the actor's causal connection with the harm, including whether the actor was the perpetrator or only an accomplice. They certainly did not agree with the core proposition of the subjectivist view on grading, that forming an intent to commit harm is always morally equivalent to causing that harm, and should generate equivalent liability.

To give a better sense of the patterning of the subjects' judgments, this part sketches a set of liability assignment rules that are consistent with the findings and that produce liability assignments similar to those given by the subjects. (As the empirically trained reader will recognize, it is always the case that a number of conceptual models can be generated that could fit the existing data patterns.) The proposal is that the liability assignment process would begin with the concept of the prototypical crime, in this case murder, and the appropriate sentence for that crime. The differing sentences for prototypes of differing crimes is not something investigated in detail in the present research, but the idea is generally accepted. Some offenses are more "serious" than others and deserve higher sentences. As was discussed in chapter 16, section A, murder deserves a greater punishment than theft, or as in the study, murder deserves and gets a higher punishment than cocaine smuggling.

Various classes of deviations from the prototype would cause a reduction in sentence. In this study, which considers cases that lie on the borderlines between some of the most complex issues in criminal law theory, it was found that five kinds of discounts were sufficient to represent all of the deviations from prototype: a no-harm discount, an incomplete-conduct discount, a complicity discount, an unintended-result discount, and an impossibility discount. Table 76 shows how these five discounts, combined in different ways, can account for the variations in means seen in the subjects' liability responses.

The apparent additive nature of the various discounts is an interesting implication of this study's results, and future research might test it further. Are such "discounts" additive in other situations? Is the proportion of discount similar in different situations, or is it entirely situationally dependent? Although this study was not designed for the purpose, it might be interesting to try to examine these questions with the current data.

By comparing cases which differed only on one of the kinds of discounts, one can examine the magnitude of the discount that the subjects judged appropriate. Column 3 of Table 76 lists some of the comparisons possible. For some of the discounts, more than one estimate of the discount from the data can be derived. For instance, the nonoccurrence of the harm, what Table 76 refers to as the "no-harm discount," can be estimated by contrasts between scenarios 1 and 2, but also by scenarios 5 and 6, and scenarios 7 and 8. If there are multiple estimates of a discount, they averaged them. These average discount estimates are shown in Table 77, column 5.

As can be seen when multiple estimates are possible, the different estimates of the discounts vary considerably. This suggests the first conclusion: something about the specific circumstances in which the discount is instantiated seems to make a difference in the degree of sentence reduction from the prototype that the subjects

TABLE 76. } A Discounting Model of Grading

Scenario	Mean	Implication of comparisons
(1) Murder	10.10	[control case]
(2) Completed conduct attempted murder	8.38	vs. (1): no-harm discount
(3) Incomplete conduct (proximity) attempt in murder	7.33	vs. (1): no harm + incomplete-conduct discount vs. (2): incomplete-conduct discount
(4) Bilateral inchoate conspiracy	6.06	vs. (1): no-harm + double incomplete-conduct discount vs. (3): additional incomplete-conduct discount
(5) Complicity in murder	8.60	vs. (1): complicity discount
(6) Failed complicity in murder	6.35	vs. (1): no-harm + complicity discount vs. (5): no-harm discount (no causal connection with harm)
(7) Manslaughter (reckless homicide)	7.15	vs. (1): unintended result discount
(8) Endangerment	5.28	vs. (1): unintended result + no harm discount vs. (7): no harm discount
(9) Incomplete conduct (substantial step) attempt to murder	5.73	vs. (1): no-harm + double incomplete-conduct discount vs. (2): double incomplete-conduct discount vs. (3): incomplete-conduct discount
(10) Completed conduct factually impossible attempted murder	7.94	vs. (1): no-harm + impossibility discount vs. (2): impossibility discount
(11) Unilateral inchoate conspiracy	6.29	vs. (1): no-harm + double incomplete-conduct discount vs. (4): analogous discounts
(12) Smuggling cocaine	7.40	[control case]
(13) Legally impossible attempt to smuggle cocaine	5.06	vs. (12): no-harm + impossibility discount
(14) Mistaken belief of complicity in murder	9.0	vs. (5): similar means, suggesting that only complicity discount given (no no-harm discount given)*

TABLE 77. } Estimate of Discount Size

Discount	Estimate 1	Estimate 2	Estimate 3	Average
No-harm	1.72 (1 v 2)	0.25 (5 v 6)*	1.87 (7 v 8)	1.28
Complicity	1.50 (1 v5)			1.50
Unintended result	2.95 (1 v 7)			2.95
Impossibility	2.34 (12 v 13)	0.44 (2 v 10)		1.39
Incomplete conduct	1.05 (2 v 3)	1.27 (3 v4)	1.6 (3 v 9)	1.31

* This is a scenario where the harm does occur, but the actor has no causal connection to it. Perhaps this difference is important to the subjects.

NB: The parentheticals indicate the two scenarios whose liability results are compared in order to generate the value of the discount.

assigned; the amount of a discount given seems to be to some extent situationally dependent. What variations in circumstance "make a difference" to the subjects is a question for further research; the study reported here, it will be recalled, was not designed to quantify discounts.

Another conclusion suggested by Table 77 is that four of the five discounts each seem to be of approximately the same amount, something more than one but less than two. Remember that each point on the liability scale represented approximately one offense grade in a typical American criminal code, and that the difference between points was different; the higher on the scale the greater difference, each point essentially doubling the punishment. The similarity in the amount of the discounts in light of the exponential nature of the scale seems to confirm that people tend to think in punishment differences in such exponential terms. The unintended-result discount was much larger than the others, suggesting that the absence of intention was a more powerful discount than the other sources of discount presented in the scenarios.

To test the effectiveness of the "discounting" system as a model for the subjects' responses, the actual results were compared against the results that would be generated by a system that used only the hypothesized discounting system. For example, in a very rough approximation, one could assign each discount a value of 1.5 points on the liability scale (representing a point somewhere between one and two, as four of the five discounts seem to fall). Applying this value to the scenario formulae given in Table 76, column 3, the results are represented by the line labeled "1.5 grade" on Figure 78.

For a slightly more accurate model, single discount estimates developed in Table 77 were used. These average values, different for each kind of discount, were then used in the formulae in Table 76, column 3. For instance, scenario 11, as contrasted to scenario 1, receives both a no-harm and a double incomplete-conduct discount. The average no-harm discount is 1.28; the average incomplete-conduct discount is 1.31, doubled it is 2.62. Next those two discounts were summed, and subtracted the result from the 10.10 liability assignment given to scenario 1, giving a predicted liability of 6.20. (The actual liability given by subjects for the scenario was 6.29.) The

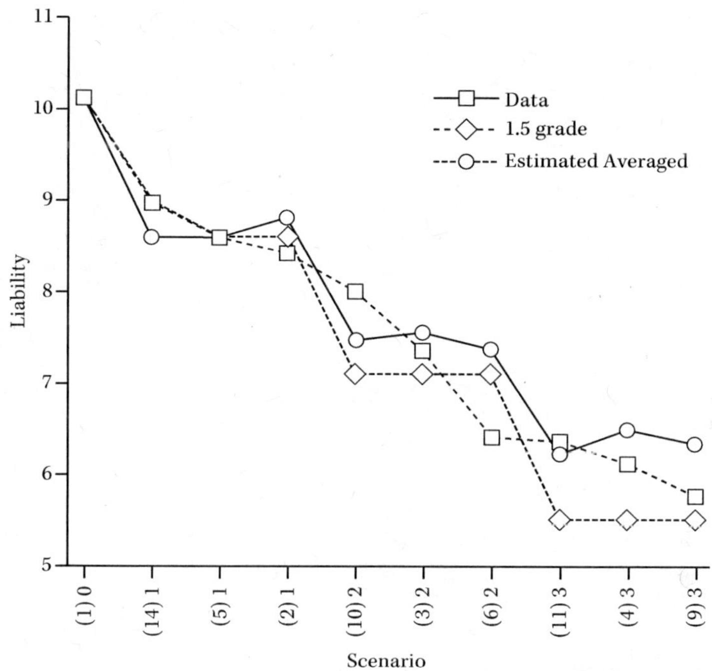

FIGURE 78. Discounting Models for Murder Cases

results of this process, done for all of the scenarios, are shown by the line labeled "estimated averaged" in Figure 78.

There are several results to notice from this figure. Initially puzzlingly, even for the model that estimated each discount separately, there is occasionally a noticeable difference in the liability assigned by it to the scenarios with single discounts from the liability actually given by the subjects. This is because the modeled liabilities are sometimes averaged ones, and as noted above, they differ from the specific ones assigned to specific instances. So, for instance, the estimated average model prediction for scenario 2 somewhat underestimates the actual discount the subjects gave that case.

Overall, the degree to which either version of the additive discount model does a good job of modeling the data is striking. Again, the study was not designed to derive a model for the psychological processes the subjects used to generate their liability judgments. However, the discounting model receives sufficient support from after-the-fact modeling to warrant testing in future research. Its central notion, that liabilities are generated by considering crime prototypes, and the number of differences between the actual case and the prototype, represented in terms of five discounting principles, seems intriguing. If validated, it is a formulation that could be used to generate a viable and conceptually understandable set of sentencing guidelines.

E. Conclusion

The results have implications for current criminal law, but there are limitations to the conclusions that one can properly draw.

1. LIMITATIONS OF THE STUDY

To begin, the limits of the generalizations that can be drawn from any one study, and particularly the one study done, must be acknowledged. Four potential limitations are important to note. First, while the wish was that the results be about different liability views toward crimes in general, the subjects were presented with scenarios about mainly, but not solely, one crime, the crime of murder. This deliberate choice postulated that murder is a crime likely to attract the most severe liability judgments from subjects, and it was beneficial to give room for large changes in liability judgments if the circumstantial variations were perceived by subjects as major mitigations. These major mitigations were found; some subjects judged the protagonist "not guilty" in some scenarios and imposed life sentences in other scenarios. Still, the patterning of judgments in which the core crime is other than murder needs to be explored.

Second, and closely related to the first point, the scenario for the factually impossible attempt case is only one such scenario, but there could be a family of such cases. Again and of course, the study was created in this specific way because researchers found these conditions most relevant to the question. The perpetrator shot at a wax dummy made to look like the intended victim because the police were concerned about possible attacks on the intended victim. The goal was to compare this scenario to others in which the actor similarly intended harm and acted to cause it. Certainly, a very different liability assignment would be given to an impossible attempt case in which the perpetrator made a wax dummy of the intended victim and shot or stabbed it, thinking that somehow this would kill the victim, as in voodoo cases. Further research, driven by theoretical considerations for varying the exact content of the scenarios, will extend the generalizations that can be made and certainly qualify them in interesting ways.

Third, a within-subjects research design was employed; each subject rated every scenario. In this sort of design, the subjects can become aware of the theoretical issues that generated the differences among the scenarios. The subjects were instructed that the researchers did not always expect differences between stories to produce differences between their liability judgments, and the reader will recall that subjects did not always treat different scenarios differently; subjects sometimes rated two scenarios as deserving identical liabilities. Still, it is possible that subjects who are alerted to a particular distinction then decide the distinction is important, but would have not have found it important without being alerted to it. Future research, using designs in which a single subject responds to a single case or a limited number of cases, can investigate this latter possibility. For this first exploration of the topic, the advantages of the within-subjects design were judged, and particularly its unparalleled ability to detect the pattern of judgments given by each individual subject, great enough to make its use appropriate.

Fourth, one can raise concerns about the degree to which the sample of subjects does a good job of standing in for the vast population of citizens whose views are relevant to the debate among the issues that are discussed. But the question here is different from the standard questions regarding sample size and populations. In the standard survey, one wishes to generalize about, for instance, what percentage of the population will assign the death penalty to the perpetrator of the murder described. To establish that percentage accurately, large and carefully stratified samples are necessary. That is not the sort of generalization these tests were meant to draw. Instead, the research was concerned with the patterning of the different liability assignments made by each individual, and the similarity of the resulting pattern across individuals.

There is evidence about both sorts of differences among the subjects, because two different sorts of people responded to the scenarios: students and jury qualified residents of the town. A difference of the first sort was actually found; students tended to assign slightly more lenient punishments than did citizens. But there was not a difference of the second sort; the pattern of differences in the liability assignments did not differ between students and citizens. This possibility of analyzing patterns is provided by the within-subjects character of the experimental design, and represents a strength of that design. Again, future research will search for important differences in patterning among broad samples of subjects, perhaps following up on the discovery of what seemed to be a small but interesting group of people who gave strong objectivist responses throughout and another group that gave subjectivist responses throughout.

2. IMPLICATIONS FOR EXISTING CRIMINAL LAW

If the preceding characterization of present lay judgment is correct, and if the criminal law ought to mirror the shared intuitions of justice of the community, then both common law rules and modern criminal codes are flawed in that they deviate from the subjects' intuitions. First, the results suggest that the common law doctrines no longer reflect community views, if they ever did. Most importantly, the doctrines that define the minimum requirements of liability at common law draw that liability too narrowly, excluding from liability a variety of actors who today's lay persons see as deserving of criminal liability. The actor whose attempt conduct falls short of "dangerous proximity," the actor whose criminal agreement is only "unilateral" (such as conspiracy with an undercover agent), and the actor who mistakenly believes that he or she has committed an offense (such as mistake of existing circumstance, e.g., belief that the talcum powder was drugs), would all ordinarily receive a complete defense at common law, but the subjects thought that some liability and punishment was appropriate.[19]

---

[19] *See, e.g.,* Table 75, col. 2, rows 9, 11, and 13, respectively.

On the other hand, the results suggest that modern codes also miss the mark on important issues. Modern codes generally do a good job in determining the cases in which to assign liability but fail to acknowledge the importance of many factors that lay persons today think important in determining the amount of punishment deserved. In particular, modern codes sometimes fail to adjust offense grade according to whether the offense harm actually occurs, how far the actor's inchoate conduct has proceeded toward the completed offense, whether the offender was only an accomplice rather than a perpetrator, and whether the offense contemplated by the actor was possible for him or her to actually commit, when the subjects clearly would.[20]

It may well be that individual judges sharing community intuitions will use their sentencing discretion to override the grading distinctions of the code and impose a sentence that reflects the community's view of criminality. This is not an appropriate solution to the problem of improper code grading for several reasons. First, many sentencing judges may not share the intuitions of the community.[21] Spending one's days watching a parade of criminals appear for sentencing may well alter one's views of proper punishment to be imposed. Second, even if all judges did share the community's objectivist view of grading, the availability of sentencing discretion creates other serious problems. It is out of recognition of these problems that the United States is presently in the midst of a wave of sentencing reform manifested primarily in the introduction of sentencing guidelines that reduce judicial discretion.

The press for sentencing guidelines comes from several concerns. Perhaps most important, unguided sentencing discretion is likely to generate disparate sentences in similar cases. Different judges have different sentencing philosophies. Some may think general deterrence the most important goal to pursue in a case; another may think rehabilitation the most important goal in an identical case. Still another may think the potential for future offenses is the most important factor in the same case; still another may think that the punishment deserved for this offense is central in determining the sentence. Other judges may look at the same facts and conclude that some combination of these factors and goals is the best criterion for determining the sentence. Without commitment to a single sentencing theory for a particular kind of case, it seems hard to see how the sentences of different judges could be similar.[22] A further concern about unguided sentencing discretion is the potential for abuse of that discretion, including abuse by the use of improper factors or by conscious or subconscious expression of racial, religious, gender, or other bias.

The trend in modern code drafting, evidenced in the Model Penal Code, is to move toward a subjectivist view of both minimal requirements and grading. These

---

[20] *See, e.g.,* Table 75, col. 2, rows 2, 3, 5, and 10, respectively.

[21] Research has demonstrated that sentencing judges hold sentencing-relevant attitudes that differ considerably from other segments of the population. *See* John Hogarth, Sentencing as a Human Process 138–48 (1971).

[22] For a further discussion of the point, *see* Paul H. Robinson, *Hybrid Principles for the Distribution of Criminal Sanctions*, 82 Nw. L. Rev. 19–42 (1987).

two tendencies taken together, achieve a sentencing philosophy that is simple to apply, but rather draconian in effect, and quite strongly in conflict with the sentencing patterns shown by the subjects. The subjects did not treat cases of an externalized intent to commit a crime as equivalent in liability to cases in which the commission of that crime was completed. Instead they were influenced in their liability judgments by variations in the objective circumstances surrounding the crime: the extent of the actor's causal contribution, how close to completion of the offense the actor came, and the occurrence of harm.

This means that a jurisdiction that moves toward the subjectivist sentencing philosophy of the Model Penal Code is a jurisdiction that moves away from law that embodies the moral intuitions of its citizens. This does not seem to be a very wise move to make, for three related reasons. First, for those who think that just deserts represents the preferred mode of distributing criminal liability, the intuitions of the community have a considerable claim to be considered when codes are adopted, and without evidence, any code adopted is unable to give standing to these community intuitions. The code drafters often refer to their speculations about community moral intuitions, indicating that they do think them relevant, and often get them wrong.

Second, as chapters 8 and 9 suggest, there is a utilitarian argument for having legal codes that in the main model community intuitions. Where the criminal law commands the respect of the community it governs, the law's moral credibility itself provides a reason for law abidingness.[23]

Third, as other studies have demonstrated, people tend to assume that legal codes conform to their moral intuitions.[24] This is not a surprising result if one asks what information people have available for inferring the content of codes; they have very little information other than their own intuitions: very little information is made public about the content of criminal codes, and very little attempt is made by code drafters to educate the public about code content. If the codes are in fact far distant from the moral judgments that people use to intuit the content of criminal codes, then people will be seriously confused about the actual content of the codes. This means that a counterintuitive law, unpublicized, fails to serve its ex ante function. It does not provide a clear guide according to which people can govern their conduct in the future.[25]

Earlier, a trend toward articulated sentencing rules was noted. As sentencing rules have clearly become more articulated and less discretionary, it becomes more important for those rules to reflect the objectivist-grading intuitions of the community.

---

[23] *See* chapter 10, section A (discussing the dangers of failure to align punishment with desert); Paul H. Robinson & John M. Darley, *The Utility of Desert*, 91 Nw. L. Rev. 453 (1997); Tom Tyler, Why People Obey the Law 19 (Princeton University Press 2006).

[24] *See, e.g.*, John Darley, Catherine Sanderson & Peter LaMantia, *Community Standards for Defining Attempt*, 39 Am. Behav. Sci. 405 (1996).

[25] For a discussion of the criminal law's ex ante rule articulation function, *see* Paul H. Robinson, *Rules of Conduct and Principles of Adjudication*, 57 U. Chi. L. Rev. 729, 730–33 (1990).

Sentencing guidelines that embody the subjectivist views of grading typical of many modern criminal codes—such as provisions setting the grade of inchoate conduct as the same grade as that for the substantive offense—would generate sentences likely to undercut the criminal justice system's moral credibility with the public. There is a need for more articulated sentencing criteria, but that improvement increases the need to insure that the system's rules more accurately reflect the community's views than they have in the past.

For all of the reasons detailed, one cannot yet assume that the results pattern is a perfect representation of community sentiments, although it would be surprising to discover that it was seriously deviant from them. But assuming that the results hold in future research, for all of the reasons just presented, adopting a criminal code that mirrors them should be advocated; adopting a criminal code that matches the moral intuitions of the community it governs is necessary. That entails adopting a criminal code that reflects the subjectivist views of criminality in the definition of minimum requirements for a crime and the objectivist views of criminality in the assignments of grading liability levels. Such a community standards-based approach would produce a consistent and coherent code that would increase the system's reputation for doing justice, which in turn eventually would serve to reduce crime.

19}

Testing Competing Theories: Blackmail

The crime of blackmail, a wonderfully curious offense, has long been the favorite of clever criminal law theorists. It criminalizes the threat to do something even if that something it is not criminal in itself. There exists a rich literature on the issue, with many prominent legal scholars offering their accounts. Each theorist has his own explanation as to why the blackmail offense exists. Most theories seek to justify the position that blackmail is a moral wrong, and claim to offer an account that reflects widely shared moral intuitions. But the theories make widely varying assertions about what those shared intuitions are without any evidence to support the assertions.

Section A summarizes the competing theories. Section C presents the results of an empirical study designed to test those competing theories to see which best accords with prevailing sentiment. Using a variety of scenarios designed to isolate and test the various criteria different theorists have put forth as *the* key to blackmail, the study reveals which of the various theories of blackmail proposed to date best reflect lay people's judgments.

Blackmail is not only a common subject of scholarly theorizing, but also a common object of statutory prohibition. Every American jurisdiction criminalizes blackmail, although there is considerable variation in its formulation. Section B reviews the American statutes and describes the three general approaches these provisions reflect. The empirical study of lay intuitions then allows an assessment of which of these statutory approaches best captures the community's views, thereby illuminating the extent to which existing law generates results that resonate with, or deviate from, popular moral sentiment.

The analyses provide an opportunity to critique the existing theories of blackmail and to suggest a refined theory that best expresses lay intuitions. The project also reveals the substantial conflict between community views and much existing legislation, indicating recommendations for legislative reform. The chapter is drawn primarily from my article with Michael Cahill and Dan Bartels, *Competing Theories of Blackmail: An Empirical Research Critique of Criminal Law Theory.*[1]

---

[1] Paul H. Robinson, Michael T. Cahill, & Daniel M. Bartels, *Competing Theories of Blackmail: An Empirical Research Critique of Criminal Law Theory*, 89 Tex. L. Rev. 292 (2010).

A. Competing Theories of Blackmail

Theories of the proper basis for the criminal prohibition against blackmail differ profoundly from one another. One reason for this is that, unlike many other crimes, it is not entirely clear whom (if anyone) blackmail harms or victimizes. On one level, the "victim" of a blackmail threat seems to be the person receiving the threat, who is forced to pay money (or give up something else of value) to prevent the blackmailer from carrying out the threat. Some theories of blackmail are based on this notion that the threat recipient is properly seen as the crime's victim, discussed in subsection 1.

Yet, being blackmailed is arguably *less* harmful to that "victim" than if the blackmailer were simply to perform the threatened activity without first making the threat, as the blackmailer is entirely at liberty to do. If the recipient of the threat accedes to the blackmailer's demand, presumably he does so because he finds that preferable to having the blackmailer carry out the threat, as would occur if the demand were rejected. He is therefore in a better situation by virtue of having the option to pay than he would be if the blackmail threat—or, as it could also be seen, the blackmail *offer*—were never made. Some theories, following this logic, conclude that the true victim of blackmail is some other party who, because of the blackmail transaction, is losing access to what the blackmailer would provide that party (typically information) if the blackmailer could not extract value from the threat recipient by engaging in blackmail instead. Subsection 2 discusses these theories.

Some theories do not depend on any claim that individual cases of blackmail necessarily harm anyone at all. Rather, they defend the criminalization of blackmail on the ground that if blackmail were legal, some overall social harm would ensue, such as a general loss of privacy or an inefficient allocation of resources to investments in protecting secrets. These theories are not included in the empirical survey because their premises are such as to make them unconcerned with whether any particular case of blackmail, or even the practice of blackmail as a whole, is wrongful or merits blame. Accordingly, these theories make no claim about relying on (or being able to predict) popular views as to when blackmail deserves punishment.

Even without their explicit reliance on lay intuitions of justice to justify themselves, it might nonetheless be interesting to see whether such economic theories accord, or conflict, with lay intuitions. However, the nature of such theories, at least as expressed in the current literature, lacks sufficient content to actually formulate an offense. That is, these theories may offer a basic explanation of why some form of blackmail offense should exist, but they typically do not say with any precision what such an offense should look like. These theories are discussed more fully in subsection 3.

Finally, there is the position that the criminalization of blackmail lacks any sound basis and is therefore inappropriate, a position discussed in subsection 4.

1. THEORIES OF BLACKMAIL AS A CRIME AGAINST THE THREAT RECIPIENT

Two major theories of blackmail see it as fundamentally a crime that victimizes the person being threatened. The first view, set forth at different times and in somewhat different variations by Mitchell Berman and Leo Katz, claims that blackmail is truly a species of extortion, that is, a threat to engage in a wrongful act. Accordingly, the putative blackmail "paradox" vanishes, because both the act and the threat are wrongful. The second view, espoused by George Fletcher, finds blackmail to be a harm to the recipient not by virtue of the threat per se, but because of the threat's potential for repetition, which creates the possibility that the recipient will be forced into an ongoing relationship of subordination to the blackmailer.

a. The Wrongful Intention Theory. Over a series of articles, Mitchell Berman has elaborated and slightly refined what he calls the "evidentiary" theory of blackmail.[2] For Berman, blackmail is wrongful if and only if it would be wrong for the blackmailer to carry out the threatened act. Where the threatened act is inherently harmful or wrongful, as where one threatens to injure another (unless paid), the threat presents a routine case of extortion, for which it is relatively easy to justify assigning blame or punishment. Yet even where the threatened act is not wrongful per se, it might also be wrongful based on the actor's culpability in performing it—and this, Berman claims, is the case with blackmail. Further, Berman contends that the threat itself provides evidence of the blackmailer's culpability, that is, evidence that he knows carrying out the threat will harm the recipient and that, were he to carry out the threat, he would be doing so for that very reason. In earlier writings, Berman described the offender's culpability as rooted in his motivations; in more recent work, Berman discusses culpability in terms of the offender's knowledge and beliefs.[3]

Berman's explicit goal for his theory is that it should track common intuitions regarding blackmail as closely as possible: he is engaged in a process of "reflective equilibrium" in which the general theory is meant to track general intuitive reactions to specific cases.[4] (Berman also thinks this process of rationalizing and seeking to track common moral intuitions is the norm for blackmail theorists.[5])

Somewhat like Berman, Leo Katz advances a test for blackmail that asks whether the threatened activity is itself wrongful.[6] The harm of blackmail, for Katz, is in forcing the recipient of the threat to choose between two "immoralities," namely, facing the prospect of (1) having to pay for the blackmailer's silence, or (2) having

---

[2] *See* Mitchell N. Berman, *The Evidentiary Theory of Blackmail: Taking Motives Seriously,* 65 U. Chi. L. Rev. 795 (1998); Mitchell N. Berman, *Meta-Blackmail and the Evidentiary Theory: Still Taking Motives Seriously,* 94 Geo. L.J. 787 (2006); Mitchell N. Berman, *On the Moral Structure of White Collar Crime,* 5 Ohio State J. Crim. L. 301, 322–25 (2007).

[3] *See* Berman, *Evidentiary Theory*, *supra* note 810, at 828–29 & n. 118.

[4] *See id.* at 799–800.

[5] *See id.* at n. 7.

[6] *See* Leo Katz, *Blackmail and Other Forms of Arm-Twisting,* 141 U. Pa. L. Rev. 1567 (1993).

the blackmailer carry out the threat. Importantly, and again similar to Berman's view, carrying out the threat might be "immoral" not only because of its objective harmfulness, but also because of the blackmailer's motivations—such as a spiteful or vindictive decision to expose a secret in retaliation for not having one's demand satisfied.[7]

Like Berman, Katz explicitly relies on moral intuitions that he expects readers to share and seeks to generate a theory of blackmail that accords with those intuitions. For example, he rejects Richard Epstein's social harm account of blackmail on the ground that it does not reflect "our instinctive revulsion at the practice."[8] He summarizes his own account as capturing conduct that is "deemed by us a very major wrong."[9]

Both Berman and Katz, then, think blackmail is wrongful if and only if carrying out the threat would be wrongful. They also have detailed and nuanced views of what would make a threat, or any other conduct, wrongful—and on this broader score, their views sometimes (though not often) differ from one another. Importantly, however, their broader views about wrongfulness are not directly relevant to the project at hand. The present task is to determine the extent to which their view of when and why blackmail specifically is wrongful tracks common lay views of that same issue. As to blackmail in particular, Berman and Katz take the same position: the wrongfulness of blackmail depends on the wrongfulness of the threatened act. Significantly, this view of blackmail could be "right" (in the sense of tracking lay intuitions) even if neither Berman nor Katz is "right" in his broader positions as to what makes actions wrongful. In other words, if lay people consistently give the same answer to the questions (1) "is this blackmail?," and (2) "would carrying out this threat be wrongful?," then they are employing the Berman/Katz approach to blackmail, even if they do not share Berman's or Katz's views regarding *why* carrying out the threat would be wrongful. If the driving criterion behind lay assessments of blackmail is rooted in a moral assessment of the wrongfulness of carrying out the threat, then lay intuitions agree with Berman and Katz about blackmail, even if they disagree about other aspects of moral theory.

b. The Continuing Domination Theory. George Fletcher has put forth a theory according to which blackmail is wrongful because it creates a relationship of "dominance and subordination" between the blackmailer and the recipient of the threat.[10] What distinguishes blackmail from other situations of hard bargaining between parties to a transaction is the potentially ongoing duration of the threat: it may involve not just one demand of money for silence, but repeated demands, as the blackmailer remains privy to the damaging information and can continue to

[7] *See id.* at 1598 (noting case where threatened act "is immoral only because, if it were to be done, it would be done for purely retaliatory reasons—retaliation for [the victim's] refusal to pay").

[8] *Id.* at 1578.

[9] *Id.* at 1615.

[10] *See* George Fletcher, *Blackmail: The Paradigmatic Crime,* 141 U. Pa. L. Rev. 1617 (1993).

extract money or other value from the threatened party. Like Berman, Fletcher's theory aims to track shared views of what constitutes blackmail, explicitly seeking "reflective equilibrium" between theory and intuition, which Fletcher describes as "a convincing fit between... agreed-upon outcomes... and general principles that can account for those outcomes."[11]

One issue Fletcher does not fully address is whether the threatened act must involve a certain degree of coercion or whether the blackmailer's demand must reach a certain magnitude for the threat to create a relation of dominance and subordination. As to the first of these, Fletcher seems to answer in the negative, as he thinks a proposal can be viewed as blackmail whether it is considered a "threat" or an "offer."[12] Elsewhere Fletcher seems to suggest that only certain kinds of demands qualify for blackmail, however, as he asserts that "no one can dominate someone else by asking for money to do or not to do that which is in one's recognized domain of freedom.... [T]here is no blackmail in demanding payments to do or not to do that which one has a right to do."[13] Yet that statement surely cannot be accurate as written, for any classic case of informational blackmail presents a situation where the blackmailer has the "freedom" or "right" to disclose the information rather than seeking payment, and the recipient of the threat has no legal or moral "right" to prevent that disclosure (in the case of disclosure of a crime, quite the contrary). It's equally clear that Fletcher himself views such cases as blackmail.[14] As to the magnitude of the demand, Fletcher asserts only that a "minimal" demand does not reach the level of blackmail, though he acknowledges that "[e]xactly what is required, however, is not clear."[15]

2. THEORIES OF BLACKMAIL AS A CRIME AGAINST THIRD PARTIES

Two other theories of blackmail view it not as a crime against the recipient of the threat, but as a crime against whoever would have received the blackmailer's information had the blackmail not taken place. Joel Feinberg conceptualizes this view in terms of the moral duties of the blackmailer to the other party. James Lindgren describes it in terms of the third party's authority to regulate or discipline the threat recipient directly, which the blackmailer is usurping for personal gain.

a. The Breach-of-Duty Theory. Joel Feinberg's test for blackmail asks whether, even holding aside the existence of the threat, the blackmailer's disclosure or nondisclosure of the information would be wrongful.[16] If the blackmailer has a duty to disclose the information, then it is improper for the blackmailer to violate that duty

---

[11] *Id.* at 1617.

[12] *See id.* at 1623 ("I am skeptical about whether a coherent account is available for these parallel distinctions between threats and offers and between nonproductive and productive exchanges.").

[13] *Id.* at 1627–28.

[14] *See, e.g., id.* at 1618–19.

[15] *Id.* at 1627.

[16] *See* JOEL FEINBERG, HARMLESS WRONGDOING 211–13, 238–76 (1990).

and keep silent in exchange for money. For example, withholding disclosure of the threatened party's criminal activity would be wrongful, because one has a moral duty to report crimes; hence nondisclosure of criminal activity in return for money would be blackmail.[17] On the other hand, if the blackmailer has a duty *not* to disclose the information, then it is improper to threaten disclosure.[18] (Such threats fall within the category of extortion—the threat to do an act that is itself impermissible—whose prohibition is relatively noncontroversial.) Yet where the person is allowed, but not obliged, to disclose the information, the conditional threat to do so is not blackmail for Feinberg.[19] In short, Feinberg takes seriously the so-called paradox of blackmail—its apparent willingness to punish a threat to perform conduct that would itself be permissible absent the threat—and maintains that law should only sanction the threat where it would also sanction the threatened conduct.[20]

Whether Feinberg's theory depends on the breach of a *legal* duty or a *moral* duty is not always clear. For example, Feinberg posits a duty to report crimes to the police, though he recognizes "[t]here is admittedly a problem about the precise status"[21]—legal or moral—of that duty, and concludes that "our political system... clearly imposes a *civic duty*... to cooperate with law enforcement, even when that duty is not specifically enforced by the criminal or civil law."[22] Such a "civic duty" is enough for Feinberg to find that its violation, in return for pay, is blackmail. Feinberg is also willing to allow the criminal law's blackmail prohibition to rest on duties imposed under civil law,[23] such as the tort law governing invasions of privacy.[24] Further, Feinberg makes a normative argument that civil law *should* recognize additional duties, such as a defamation claim for some truthful statements,[25] whose threatened violation would then also support blackmail liability.[26] It seems fair to say, then, that for Feinberg a threat can be considered blackmail if it implicates the violation of a duty that *is* or *could be* legitimately imposed by law. Such a violation could arise from the satisfaction of the blackmailer's demand (preventing disclosure of information he had a duty to disclose), or its non-satisfaction followed by the carrying out of the threat (leading to disclosure of information he had a duty *not* to disclose).

---

[17] *See id.* at 241–45.

[18] *See id.* at 249–58.

[19] *See id.* at 245–49.

[20] *See id.* at 240 (noting need to avoid paradox).

[21] *Id.* at 243.

[22] *Id.* at 244.

[23] *See id.* at 253 (asserting that "[t]he important point is that "the law"... imposes a duty," not whether the legal duty is criminal or civil).

[24] *See id.* at 250–51 (looking to tort law of privacy invasions as support for duty not to threaten disclosure of information that would damage another's reputation).

[25] *See id.* at 254–56 (supporting recognition of such a legal claim).

[26] *See id.* at 254 ("It is open to the liberal, however, to argue that there *ought* to be a civil remedy for such moral wrongs, so that he can argue for criminalization... without being thwarted by the paradox of blackmail.").

This category of legitimate (actual or potential) legal duties is similar to, but distinct from, the notion of a moral duty. Some behavior might be seen as immoral but outside the proper scope of law; as Feinberg says of the case where one knows of another's adultery, even if disclosing the adultery might be the right thing to do, "no *law* requiring or forbidding his disclosure would be justified."[27] Feinberg's general sense of when criminalization is justified is driven by a liberal demand for some demonstration that the law would prevent harm or offense to others.[28] Yet Feinberg's discussion of adultery blackmail, criminalization of which Feinberg personally opposes, also indicates his willingness to defer to shared community judgments about the proper scope of law's reach:

> Surely most of those who advocate criminalization of adultery blackmail would not also advocate legislation making it an independent crime to inform betrayed spouses; nor would they advocate prior legislation making it a legal *duty* to inform betrayed spouses. They cannot have it both ways. *Either* the blackmailer should have a duty to inform (or a duty not to, as the case may be) in which case it would be consistent to prohibit him from threatening to violate that duty unless paid off, *or* he should have no legal duty one way or the other, in which case it would be incoherent to punish him for threatening to do what is within his legal rights.[29]

If Feinberg's empirical assertion about public views as to prohibiting disclosure (or nondisclosure) of adultery were shown to be wrong, presumably he would change his position about the propriety of criminalizing adultery blackmail. Accordingly, for Feinberg, whether the law should prohibit a threat (i.e., treat it as blackmail) depends on whether the law should also prohibit doing the threatened act. If not—if the person making the threat "should have no legal duty one way or the other"—then the threat is not blackmail.

As with the wrongful intention theory, then, it is possible for subjects to agree with Feinberg about the proper criterion for blackmail but to disagree about how to employ that criterion in particular cases. For the Berman/Katz theory, it is possible to agree with the position that threats should constitute blackmail if and only if they are "wrongful," but to disagree with the theorists' own broader views about what is "wrongful." So too here, it is possible to disagree with Feinberg as to the proper scope of shared underlying legal obligations, while agreeing that blackmail should apply only to threats that entail violation of those obligations.

Thus, like other theorists, Feinberg makes an appeal to shared intuitions in justifying the criminalization of blackmail as a general matter, and his own account of

---

[27] *Id.* at 249 (emphasis in original).

[28] *See id.* at 275 ("I don't see how a coherent criminal code based on liberal principles...can prohibit people from offering, in exchange for consideration, not to do what they have an independent legal right (but no legal duty) to do.").

[29] *Id.* at 249.

blackmail in particular. He posits the existence of wide consensus as to the wrongfulness of the blackmailer's conduct:

> It is a free-floating evil, many people would judge, that *he* [the blackmailer] should make a big gain as a byproduct of someone else's crime or indiscretion, that he should profit unproductively from others' wrongdoing. That his gain is unjust seems clear.[30]

Feinberg also maintains that his own account of blackmail would prohibit "precisely those actions that common sense most insistently demands should be criminal."[31] At the same time, what dictates the contours of Feinberg's view is not an appeal to popular moral intuition, but an effort to develop an understanding of blackmail consistent with liberal principles. Indeed, Feinberg's desire to embrace such principles and avoid what he considers genuinely "paradoxical" cases of blackmail leads him to develop a theory that excludes cases commonly thought to be paradigmatic examples of blackmail, such as the threat to expose another's adultery.[32]

b. The Usurping Authority Theory. For James Lindgren, the "victim" of blackmail is not the recipient of the threat, but some third party whose interests the blackmailer is exploiting or suppressing. In the typical case of a conditional threat to disclose information, the wrong consists of the blackmailer's usurping or "leveraging" the interests of the party entitled to the information: law enforcement authorities, a wronged spouse, etc.[33] In a nutshell, for Lindgren, the wrong of blackmail is that the "blackmailer is negotiating for his own gain with someone else's leverage or bargaining chips."[34] Lindgren offers this account of blackmail in an effort to track common intuitions, describing his project as seeking to "meaningfully distinguish" between "large classes of threats that nearly everyone agrees ought to be illegal and other large classes of threats that nearly everyone agrees ought to be permitted."[35]

Whether the blackmailer is "leveraging" another's position or "using another's chips" can be determined by examining the nature of the blackmailer's demand. If the blackmailer is merely replicating the demand the other party would make if that party had the information, then no blackmail exists.[36] Even if the demand is not exactly what the other party would seek, so long as the maker of the threat is "trying in good faith" to benefit the other party rather than himself, Lindgren expresses "doubt that anyone would consider" the threat to be blackmail.[37] But if the person

---

[30] *Id.* at 239.

[31] *Id.* at 276.

[32] *See id.* at 245–49.

[33] *See* James Lindgren, *Unraveling the Paradox of Blackmail,* 84 COLUM. L. REV. 670 (1984); James Lindgren, *Blackmail: An Afterword,* 141 U. PA. L. REV. 1975 (1993).

[34] *Id.* at 702.

[35] *Id.* at 680.

[36] *See id.* at 714 (asserting there is "no blackmail" if "[t]here is a perfect congruence between the advantage sought . . . and the leverage used").

[37] *Id.* at 715.

"requests something in return for suppressing the actual or potential interests of others," the request is blackmail.[38]

3. THEORIES OF BLACKMAIL AS A SOCIETAL HARM

Some theories supporting the criminalization of blackmail are unconcerned with its moral status. For these theories, the prohibition of blackmail is justified not because blackmail is wrongful, but because it is harmful (some would say "costly") to society. These theories do not focus on the harm an individual act of blackmail might cause the recipient of the threat, but on the overall social costs that would arise from the improper behavioral incentives legalized blackmail would create. Some writers view these costs in terms of the unproductive efforts of would-be blackmailers, some in terms of the excessive privacy investments required of would-be blackmailees; but the shared underlying perspective is that blackmail's legal status should depend on a societal cost-benefit analysis rather than a moral inquiry.

A host of commentators have provided such a law-and-economics analysis of blackmail according to which it is properly criminalized because it leads to inefficient allocation of resources.[39] These analyses are interested only in contemplating the overall effects of legalizing or criminalizing blackmail on incentives to ferret out secrets, to overinvest in security, or to engage in fraud. They are uninterested in generating a formulation of blackmail that achieves the "right" or fair result in individual cases. Rather, according to this approach and its underlying concerns, the quality of a given formulation of blackmail would be assessed in terms of its likelihood of achieving the "optimal" or efficient overall societal level of blackmail, that is, the level at which the marginal costs of preventing blackmail exceeded the marginal costs of the blackmail itself. They are not concerned with the morality *vel non* of blackmail—indeed, some of these accounts raise the suggestion that blackmail might also have some efficiency-related *benefits* as a form of private law enforcement.[40]

Like the law-and-economics theorists, Jeffrie Murphy has offered an account focused on the general incentives that would arise if blackmail were legal.[41] Murphy's account is slightly distinct in its concern with the value of individual privacy. While the economic account is mostly concerned with the prospect of wasted or unproductive efforts to obtain information, Murphy is concerned with the likelihood of

---

[38] *Id.* at 672.

[39] *See, e.g.*, Ronald H. Coase, *The 1987 McCorkle Lecture: Blackmail*, 74 VA. L. REV. 655 (1988); Richard A. Epstein, *Blackmail, Inc.*, 50 U. CHI. L. REV. 553 (1983); Douglas H. Ginsburg & Paul Schectman, *Blackmail: An Economic Analysis of the Law*, 141 U. PA. L. REV. 1849 (1993); William M. Landes & Richard A. Posner, *The Private Enforcement of Law*, 4 J. LEGAL STUD. 1 (1975); Richard H. McAdams, *Group Norms, Gossip, and Blackmail*, 144 U. PA. L. REV. 2237 (1996); Richard A. Posner, *Blackmail, Privacy, and Freedom of Contract*, 141 U. PA. L. REV. 1817 (1993); Steven Shavell, *An Economic Analysis of Threats and Their Illegality: Blackmail, Extortion, and Robbery*, 141 U. PA. L. REV. 1877 (1993).

[40] *See* Landes & Posner, *supra* note 847, at 42–43.

[41] *See* Jeffrie G. Murphy, *Blackmail: A Preliminary Inquiry*, 63 MONIST 156 (1980).

privacy invasions and seems to think such invasions are inherently problematic. At the same time, Murphy would grant an exception allowing the blackmail of public figures, presumably because the information obtained from investigations of public figures would be more socially useful than information about purely private figures. In the end, then, Murphy seems to be addressing a set of cost-benefit tradeoffs, involving investments in obtaining or protecting secret information, similar to the typical economic theory.

Theorists of this type typically set themselves the task of merely justifying the blackmail prohibition's existence rather than specifying its proper scope. For economists, voluntary transactions, seemingly undertaken for mutual gain, are generally thought to be desirable; and their prohibition, as in the criminalization of blackmail, therefore stands in need of some explanation. Having given the explanation, however, law-and-economics accounts of blackmail typically do not proceed to elaborate as to the particular shape the blackmail offense should take. The implication is that, once the cost or externality that justifies blackmail's prohibition has been identified, the definition of blackmail should be whatever minimizes (or produces the socially optimal level of) that cost. The perspective operates on the level of curtailing social harms rather than responding to individual acts of wrongdoing.

Among theorists of this variety, Joseph Isenbergh stands out in offering an account of blackmail that specifies which particular cases of blackmail should be criminalized and which should not.[42] He attempts to determine "what information is more valuable kept private and what information is more valuable disclosed."[43] Describing the threat recipient, blackmailer, and third party entitled to the information as *A*, *B*, and *C*, respectively, Isenbergh suggests the possibility of limiting the blackmail prohibition to two sets of cases: "1) information, however acquired, held by *B* concerning a prosecutable crime or tort committed by *A* against *C*; and 2) information acquired by *B* outside a prior course of dealing with *A*."[44] Isenbergh later elaborates on the second category, pointing out that the relevant distinction is "between information already held by *B* (or obtained fortuitously) and information generated by *B*'s special efforts for the purpose of blackmail."[45] Isenbergh then posits that situations where *A* and *B* "have a preexisting relationship" are more likely to involve "information obtained fortuitously" in the course of the relationship, whereas situations where *A* and *B* have "no prior course of dealing" are more likely to involve "information deliberately farmed" and should hence be discouraged via legal sanction.[46] Even for the cases Isenbergh recognizes as undesirable blackmail, however, it is worth noting that he does not advocate direct criminalization as the best legal response. Rather, Isenbergh would favor making the blackmail transaction

[42] *See* Joseph Isenbergh, *Blackmail from A to C,* 141 U. Pa. L. Rev. 1905 (1993).

[43] *Id.* at 1927.

[44] *Id.* at 1908.

[45] *Id.* at 1929.

[46] *Id.* at 1930.

legally unenforceable and, in the first category of cases, also making *B* legally complicit in *A*'s criminal or tortious wrongdoing.[47]

4. THEORIES OF BLACKMAIL AS NON-CRIME: THE ABOLITIONIST POSITION

A final possible response to the blackmail "paradox" is to conclude that its only proper resolution is to decriminalize blackmail, thereby eliminating the paradox. Some libertarian theorists have defended the position that criminalizing threats to engage in lawful activity is an impermissible infringement on the freedom to engage in voluntary transactions, hence an unjustifiable exercise of criminal authority.[48]

Russell Christopher has offered a variation on this claim by introducing the concept of "meta-blackmail": the conditional threat to make a blackmail threat.[49] Christopher claims that there is no clear way to determine how meta-blackmail should be treated relative to blackmail itself—whether it should be punished more seriously, less seriously, or the same—and asserts that therefore the only way to avoid logical inconsistency, or at least even thornier puzzles than the paradox of blackmail itself, is to decriminalize blackmail (and hence meta-blackmail also).[50]

In this case, the abolitionist position is easily testable: if subjects reject the prospect of punishment in all scenarios of putative blackmail, then their moral intuitions would track the conclusion that blackmail should be abolished, and if not, then lay intuitions would contradict the abolitionist proposal. It should also be noted, however, that a disagreement between lay intuitions and these accounts would not necessarily undercut the relevant theorists on their own terms. The libertarian position rests on a broader understanding that the proper scope of criminalization is very narrow and fails to justify a prohibition against blackmail even if blackmail is a moral wrong.[51] Christopher does not purport to offer a moral refutation of the criminalization of blackmail, but what he says is a logical one.

---

[47] *See id.* at 1928–29.

[48] *See, e.g.*, Murray N. Rothbard, Man, Economy, and State 443 n.49 (1962); Walter Block, *Berman on Blackmail: Taking Motives Fervently*, 3 Fla. St. U. Bus. Rev. 57 (2003); Walter Block, *The Case for De-Criminalizing Blackmail: A Reply to Lindgren and Campbell*, 24 W. St. U. L. Rev. 225 (1997); Eric Mack, *In Defense of Blackmail*, 41 Phil. Stud. 274 (1982); Ronald Joseph Scalise, Jr., Comment, *Blackmail, Legality, and Liberalism*, 74 Tul. L. Rev. 1483 (2000).

[49] *See* Russell L. Christopher, *Meta-Blackmail*, 94 Geo. L.J. 739 (2006); Russell L. Christopher, *The Trilemma of Meta-Blackmail: Is Conditionally Threatening Blackmail Worse, the Same, or Better than Blackmail Itself?*, 94 Geo. L.J. 813 (2006).

[50] *See* Christopher, *Meta-Blackmail*, *supra* note 857, at 747–48 ("Resolving the trilemma of meta-blackmail either forces the decriminalization of blackmail or adds considerably to the already difficult puzzles to be surmounted in justifying the criminalization of blackmail.").

[51] *See* Christopher, *Meta-Blackmail*, *supra* note 857 (noting basis for libertarian position and asserting that it rests on fairly straightforward, easily articulated and understood, major premise that overwhelming majority of contemporary theorists of criminal law simply reject).

B. Statutory Approaches

While each United States jurisdiction has a criminal provision prohibiting traditional blackmail,[52] there is no single statutory approach used by a majority of states; and even within any given approach, a close comparison of any two blackmail statutes is likely to reveal some differences. However, the range of differences might be summarized as moving along two dimensions: first, the breadth of the range of demands criminalized; second, the breadth of the exceptions (or special defenses) to the crime.

On the first dimension, blackmail statutes can be categorized as either having a broad range of prohibited demands,[53] or a narrow range.[54] "Narrow definition" statutes address only threats made to obtain property or pecuniary value. "Broad definition" blackmail statutes cover those threats and also threats made to coerce action on the part of the victim or some third party.

The second dimension of blackmail is somewhat more complex: statutes can be categorized as having broad exceptions, narrow exceptions, or no exceptions. "Broad exception" statutes generally hold that the blackmailer can escape liability in some cases where she is acting with limited purpose to make the other party correct a wrong, desist from misbehavior, refrain from taking responsibility for which she is not qualified, or other similar situations.[55] These statutes commonly impose additional requirements on the actor and her behavior before she can make use of the exception.[56] "Narrow exception" statutes generally hold that the blackmailer may be excepted only if she is acting to recover restitution for harm done or to recover compensation for property taken or services rendered.[57] Finally, "no exception" statutes provide no explicit provisions recognizing exceptions to the blackmail offense.[58]

Relying upon these two dimensions of blackmail formulations creates four major categories into which all 52 blackmail statutes fall:[59] broad-broad, broad-narrow, narrow-narrow, and "other." (There are narrow-broad statutes—a narrow definition

---

[52] The standard blackmail case is one in which an actor threatens to disclose a damaging secret if the victim does not pay her some amount of money.

[53] Jurisdictions with broad ranges of prohibited demands include AK, AR, CO, CT, DE, FL, HI, IL, IN, IA, KS, KY, MD, MA, MI, MN, MO, MT, NJ, NM, NY, NV, ND, PA, RI, TN, TX (note that TX utilizes a common law duress offense to punish acts equivalent to blackmail), VT, WA, WI, and WY.

[54] Jurisdictions with narrow ranges include AL, AZ, CA, DE, GA, ID, LA, ME, MS, NE, NH, NC, OH, OK, OR, SC, SD, UT, VA, WV, and the federal government.

[55] *See, e.g.,* Model Penal Code §212.5(1)(d); *cf.* N.D. Cent. Code §12.1-17-06. Jurisdictions with broad exceptions to the blackmail offense include AK, CA, CT, HI, KY, NJ, NY, NC, ND, OH, OR, PA, and WA.

[56] For example, the MPC requires that an actor limit her purpose to compelling the "good" action, that the action coerced be reasonably related to the circumstances involved, and that the actor believes the accusation or secret revealed to be true. Model Penal Code §212.5(1)(d).

[57] Jurisdictions with narrow exceptions to the blackmail offense include AL, AZ, AR, CO, DE, DC, FL, GA, ID, IL, IN, IA, LA, ME, MD, MA, MI, MN, MS, MO, MT, NE, NH, NM, RI, TN, SD, TX, UT, VT, and WI.

[58] Jurisdictions with no exceptions to the blackmail offense include KS, NV, OK, SC, TX, VA, WV, WY, and the federal government.

[59] The 52 statutes are the codes of each of the 50 states plus the federal code and the District of Columbia code.

of the crime, with broad exceptions—but the narrow definition means that the broad exceptions are never really used, so they are effectively the same in their operation as the narrow-narrow statutes.)

Nine jurisdictions follow the Model Penal Code's broad-broad approach to blackmail by prohibiting threats made to coerce action or to take property, and providing either explicit or implicit exceptions to the crime for actors who commit the offense in the course of an attempt to make the victim behave in a way reasonably related to the circumstances that were the subject of the threat.[60] While these jurisdictions generally follow the MPC's statutory language, there is some variation; Washington, for example, prohibits seeking "property or services" but specifically mentions sexual favors as being included in the definition of "services."[61] Other jurisdictions are not so explicit. Additionally, there is some variation in the defined exceptions to the crime. Most broad-broad jurisdictions employ the MPC's formulation, but some limit the applicability of the exception to certain situations, and others (most significantly North Dakota) significantly broaden the MPC's exception.

Eighteen jurisdictions take the broad-narrow approach, criminalizing threats designed to coerce action or to take property, but providing an exception only to actors who make the threat in order to recover restitution for harm done, or to gain compensation for services rendered or property owed.[62] These statutes exhibit significantly more terminological and structural variation than do the broad-broad statutes; some are simply MPC-style provisions with narrower exceptions, some are uniquely drafted but part of a modern code structure, and others are common law-style provisions. Some broad-narrow statutes ban an extensive list of threats,

---

[60] AK, CT, HI, KY, NJ, NY, ND, PA, and WA. A typical broad-broad statute would be similar to Pennsylvania's:

> (a) Offense defined.—A person is guilty of criminal coercion, if, with intent unlawfully to restrict freedom of action of another to the detriment of the other, he threatens to:
> (1) commit any criminal offense;
> (2) accuse anyone of a criminal offense;
> (3) expose any secret tending to subject any person to hatred, contempt or ridicule; or
> (4) take or withhold action as an official, or cause an official to take or withhold action.
>
> (b) Defense.—It is a defense to prosecution based on paragraphs (a)(2), (a)(3) or (a)(4) of this section that the actor believed the accusation or secret to be true or the proposed official action justified and that his intent was limited to compelling the other to behave in a way reasonably related to the circumstances which were the subject of the accusation, exposure or proposed official action, as by desisting from further misbehavior, making good a wrong done, refraining from taking any action or responsibility for which the actor believes the other disqualified.

18 Pa. Cons. Stat. Ann. §2906.

[61] Wash. Rev. Code §9A.56.110.

[62] AR, CO, DE, FL, IL, IN, IA, MD, MA, MI, MN, MO, MT, NM, RI, TN, VT, and WI. Broad-narrow statutes can be constructed in a number of ways. One of the simplest is Tennessee's:

> (a) A person commits extortion who uses coercion upon another person with the intent to:
> (1) Obtain property, services, any advantage or immunity; or
> (2) Restrict unlawfully another's freedom of action.
>
> (b) It is an affirmative defense to prosecution for extortion that the person reasonably claimed:
> (1) Appropriate restitution or appropriate indemnification for harm done; or
> (2) Appropriate compensation for property or lawful services.

Tenn. Code Ann §39-14-112; *see also* D.C. Code Ann. §22-3252; Mich. Comp. Laws §750.213.

while others are much more limited. Nonetheless, these statutes are appropriately grouped because all prohibit threats seeking action *or* property, but only provide an offense exception if the actor is seeking property to which she has some legal right.

Sixteen jurisdictions take the narrow-narrow approach, criminalizing threats made to gain property, and provide an offense exception only where the actor makes an otherwise-prohibited threat in order to recover restitution for harm done, or to gain compensation for services rendered or property owed.[63] As with the broad-narrow jurisdictions, these statutes exhibit considerable variation in statutory language and organization. Many are codified as extortion statutes, but are intended to cover the traditional blackmail crime also.

In the "other" category are nine jurisdictions that appear to have no exceptions to their blackmail laws.[64] Four have broad prohibitions,[65] and five have narrow prohibitions.[66] Texas appears to punish traditional blackmail via the common law; a line of cases exists to explain the state's treatment of the offense.[67]

---

[63] AL, AZ, DE, GA, ID, LA, ME, MS, NE, NH, SD, and UT are "true" narrow-narrow states. CA, NC, OH, and OR have narrow prohibitions but seemingly broad exceptions.Narrow-narrow statutes, like broad-narrow statutes, do not share a general pattern as do most broad-broad statutes. However, Arizona's theft by extortion statute is typical of those jurisdictions with a narrow demand language and a narrow affirmative defense:A. A person commits theft by extortion by knowingly obtaining or seeking to obtain property or services by means of a threat to do in the future any of the following:

1. Cause physical injury to anyone by means of a deadly weapon or dangerous instrument.
2. Cause physical injury to anyone except as provided in paragraph 1 of this subsection.
3. Cause damage to property.
4. Engage in other conduct constituting an offense.
5. Accuse anyone of a crime or bring criminal charges against anyone.
6. Expose a secret or an asserted fact, whether true or false, tending to subject anyone to hatred, contempt or ridicule or to impair the person's credit or business.
7. Take or withhold action as a public servant or cause a public servant to take or withhold action.
8. Cause anyone to part with any property.

B. It is an affirmative defense to a prosecution under subsection A, paragraph 5, 6 or 7 that the property obtained by threat of the accusation, exposure, lawsuit or other invocation of official action was lawfully claimed either as:

1. Restitution or indemnification for harm done under circumstances to which the accusation, exposure, lawsuit or other official action relates.
2. Compensation for property that was lawfully obtained or for lawful services.

ARIZ. REV. STAT §13-1804.

[64] Jurisdictions with "no exception" blackmail statutes have varied approaches. Kansas's blackmail statute is simple:

Blackmail is gaining or attempting to gain anything of value or compelling another to act against such person's will, by threatening to communicate accusations or statements about any person that would subject such person or any other person to public ridicule, contempt or degradation

KAN. STAT. ANN. §21-3428. Other "no exception" statutes vary. *See,* e.g., OKLA. STAT. tit. 21 §60-1488; 18 U.S.C. §973.

[65] KS, NV, OK, and WY.

[66] SC, TX (per precedent), VA, WV, and the federal government.

[67] "Any coercion of another, either mental, physical, or otherwise, causing him to act contrary to his own free will or to submit to a situation or conditions against his own volition or interests, constitutes "duress"...The law condemns and the courts will grant relief against all character of duress." Hailey v. Fenner & Beane, 246 S.W. 412, 41213 (Tex. Civ. App. 1922).

C. Testing Community Views

To test which of the theories and statutory schemes best capture lay intuitions about the conduct that should be criminalized, subjects were given a series of scenarios designed to focus on the differences among the theories. As to each scenario, a test document asked whether such conduct should be criminalized. To be sure that subjects were perceiving the scenarios as intended, a second test document performed a "manipulation-check," asking for details about subjects' perception of each scenario, specifically questions testing what the subject perceived with regard to each of the factors that were being manipulated to test the different theories. The subjects' criminalization responses were then compared to those predicted by each theory, and each statutory approach, to determine which best reflected the subjects' views.

1. DESIGN AND METHODOLOGY

A total of 129 subjects recruited via flyers and a Listserv were interviewed in a laboratory in exchange for $4. The study subjects ranged in age from 18 to 58 and were diverse in gender, ethnicity, education, and economic standing. Each questionnaire presented subjects with the same 11 scenarios, reproduced in Table 79, which were constructed to highlight the differences among the theories being tested. Two versions of the questionnaire were administered, which varied the order of presentation of the 11 scenarios. Presentation order did not significantly affect any of the results reported.

As is apparent, each of the scenarios involves two main characters, Victor and Brian. In each case, Brian is the potential blackmailer, who threatens Victor, the potential victim, and demands, in return for not carrying out the threat, some action or other compensation. The threat and the demand in each scenario are different, and each scenario generates a different pattern with respect to whether it satisfies the criteria of each of the theories.

The first and second scenarios are designed for quality control purposes. The first scenario is a classic case of blackmail for which all theorists and all statutory schemes would impose blackmail liability. Scenario 2 provides an example of the reverse case, one in which all theorists and all statutory schemes would agree that no blackmail liability should exist. If a subject were to give an incorrect answer to either or both of these screening questions, that subject would be segregated from the bulk of the subjects and not included in the analysis of survey results.

To be sure that the subjects were in fact perceiving the scenarios in the way that each was intended, the manipulation-check questionnaire asked each subject whether he or she perceived certain facts or conclusions about each scenario, specifically those facts or conclusions that served as the criteria for each theory. The standard template for each manipulation-check question for each of the four theories are set out in Table 80. However, each manipulation-check question was in fact individualized to reflect the facts of each scenario. A six-point no-yes (ranging from

TABLE 79. } Text of Scenarios

1. Pay or Report Crime. Brian learns that Victor has killed a man and tells Victor he will report the crime to the authorities unless Victor pays him $1,000.

2. Pay or Face Lawsuit. Victor, driving negligently, seriously damages Brian's car in an accident. Brian tells Victor that he will sue him in court, where he can collect the cost of repairs, unless Victor pays him the $1,000 that the repairs will cost

3. Sober Work or Expose Drinking. Brian discovers that his factory coworker, Victor, has a drinking problem, which explains his frequent absences and tardiness and might also create a risk in the workplace. Victor is worried that if management finds out, he will lose his job under the company's "zero tolerance" policy, which mandates dismissal of anyone found to have an existing drinking problem. Brian says he will report Victor's drinking problem to management unless Victor promises to show up sober every day to work, join an alcohol abuse treatment program, and make a donation to a charity fighting alcohol abuse.

4. Pay or Reveal Recipe. Victor owns a bakery known for its cupcakes, which are very popular despite their high price. Brian discovers that the cupcakes are actually made using a cheap store-bought cake mix and frosting. Though Victor has never made any false claims about how his cupcakes are made, he knows his business will be ruined if the truth is revealed. Brian threatens to make the cupcake "recipe" public unless Victor pays him $10,000.

5. Pay or Publish Book. Brian, a literature professor, has spent considerable time conducting research for a biography of Victor, a famous author. His research has turned up information that would destroy Victor's reputation. Despite what he has learned, Brian admires Victor and does not wish to cause him harm, but he also thinks it would be inappropriate to publish a biography that does not accurately present what he knows. Accordingly, he contacts Victor and says he will discontinue his biography project if Victor pays him the $4,000 that will properly compensate Brian for his expenses and the work he has already done.

6. Pay or Expose Cheating. Brian and Victor are taking the examination to enter the police academy. All applicants sign a promise not to cheat and to report those who do. Authorities aggressively prosecute cheating but only if there is hard evidence, such as the "cheat sheet" used during the exam. During the exam, Brian sees and picks up Victor's "cheat sheet." He says he will give it to the authorities unless Victor pays him $500. If Victor pays, Brian will give the "cheat sheet" back, and no action of any kind against Victor will be possible.

7. Withdraw or Expose Cheating. Brian and Victor are taking the examination to enter the police academy. All applicants sign a promise not to cheat and to report those who do. Authorities aggressively prosecute cheating but only if there is hard evidence, such as the "cheat sheet" used during the exam. During the exam, Brian sees and picks up Victor's "cheat sheet." Victor is remorseful about the cheating but does not want to face legal action. Brian says he will expose the cheating unless Victor withdraws his application to the police force, so that he cannot actually benefit from this instance of cheating. If Victor does so, Brian will give back the cheat sheet, and no action of any kind against Victor will be possible.

8. Cut Tree or Publish Photos. Brian, Victor's neighbor, thinks that Victor's expensive and exotic tree is an eyesore. Brian has asked Victor to cut the tree down but Victor has refused to do so. Using a special telephoto lens, Brian takes photos of Victor in his home having sexual intercourse and tells Victor that he will post them on the Internet unless Victor agrees to cut down the offending tree. If Victor does cut it down, Brian will hand over the negatives and the only copy of the photos.

9. Pay or Report Smoking. Brian and Victor work for a nonprofit anti-smoking organization. Teresa, the current head of the organization, has made clear that she expects all her employees to not smoke, even though this was not an explicit condition for their employment, because she views smokers as insufficiently committed to her organization's mission. However, Teresa is permanently leaving the organization and her replacement, Tina, does not care whether her employees smoke outside the workplace. A few days before Teresa's departure, Brian runs into Victor at a restaurant. Victor is halfway through a cigar. He asks Brian not to tell Teresa, because he knows that if she finds out, her last act as head of the organization will be to fire him. Victor tells Brian that he loves his job, though he also enjoys smoking on occasion. Brian says he will tell Teresa immediately unless Victor pays him $1,000.

10. Pay or Report Crime. Brian doesn't like Victor. When he learns that Victor has killed a man, he tells Victor that he will report the crime to the authorities unless Victor pays him $1, as a way of forcing an admission of guilt. Brian might then choose to use this information against Victor in the future.

11. Pay Penalty or Foreclose. Brian is the banker who oversees Victor's home mortgage loan. He is also in love with Victor's wife. Victor has missed several mortgage payments, and Brian has been authorized by his bosses to either arrange a refinancing of Victor's loan, or to impose a substantial one-time penalty on Victor for missing payments. Brian imposes the penalty against Victor — which Brian assumes Victor cannot pay — with the threat that the bank will foreclose on Victor's house in the absence of payment. Brian believes if Victor

TABLE 80. } Manipulation-Check Questions for Criteria of Each Theory

a. **Wrongful Intention**. If Victor refuses Brian's offer, and Brian carries out the threat, would his primary reason for acting be wrongful? (+ = liability) *[a1: Berman] [& finding demand is substantial = a2: Katz]*

b. **Offer to Violate Legal Duty**. If another person knew what Brian knows, should the law require that the person do [or: forbid the person from doing] what Brian threatens to do to Victor, or face legal liability? (+ = liability) *[Feinberg]*

c. **Continuing Domination**. If Victor agrees to the demand, would Brian retain the power to make additional demands based on the same threat on a future occasion? (+ & finding demand is substantial = liability) *[Fletcher]*

d. **Leveraging Another's Influence**. If an interested third party learned what Brian knows, would the third party's reaction be to want something different from what Brian demands that Victor do? (+ = liability) *[Lindgren]*

* Scenario #2 required a special *d* question because the standard *d* question above assumes that there might be an interested third-party, but scenario 2 was constructed to not have one. Thus, we needed to confirm that the subjects perceived this to be the case and asked: Is there an interested third party who should more properly be exercising the authority that Brian is exercising when he threatens Victor? (If you think that Brian is threatening to use authority that properly belongs to him alone, select -3, -2, or -1.) (- = no liability.)

-3 meaning clearly no to +3 meaning clearly yes) scale was used for all 44 of these questions (one question for each of the 4 theories' criteria for each of 11 scenarios).

Following these four manipulation-check questions, three additional questions were asked with regard to each scenario. One asked whether the threat was substantial—an additional element of two of the theories (Katz's and Fletcher's). The two other questions asked about the extent of the harm that would be caused if the Brian did as he threatened and about the wrongfulness of the victim's conduct that Brain was threatening to expose. Again, each of these three questions was customized to the facts of the scenario.

The last two questions were asked to test whether these variables might play a role in the subjects' criminalization decisions. Notice that all three of these questions asked not merely for a binary response (e.g., wrongful or not wrongful) but for a quantitative measure of the factor, which could then be used to see if it correlated with subjects' criminalization decisions.

The "correct answers"—that is, those sought by the researchers to assure subjects were perceiving each scenario as intended—are set out in Table 81 below. In the liability questionnaire, after each scenario was presented, participants were asked whether or not Brian should be held criminally liable for his threat.[68]

2. THEORY PREDICTIONS

Each theory predicts a different pattern of criminalization results for the 11 scenarios, as summarized in Table 82 below. By comparing these predictions to the participants' actual preferences, as done in subsection 82 below, it is possible to determine

[68] For more details on the methodology and design, *see* Robinson, Cahill & Bartels, *supra* note 809, at 314–22.

TABLE 81. } Manipulation-Check "Correct Answers"

#	Scenario Q:	WI	BD	CD	UA	SD
1	Pay or Report Crime	+	+	+	+	≥ 2
2	Pay or Face Lawsuit	-	-	-	-*	≥ 2
3	Sober Work or Expose Drinking	-	-	-	+	≥ 2
4	Pay or Reveal Recipe	+	-	+	+	≥ 2
5	Pay or Publish Book	-	-	+	+	≥ 2
6	Pay or Expose Cheating	+	+	-	+	≥ 2
7	Withdraw or Expose Cheating	-	+	-	+	≥ 2
8	Cut Tree or Publish Photos	+	+	-	+	≥ 2
9	Pay or Report Smoking	+	-	-	+	≥ 2
10	Pay or Report Crime	+**	+	+**	+	<3**
11	Pay Penalty or Foreclose	+	-	-	-	≥ 2

Key: *WI* – Wrongful Intention Theory of Berman and Katz
BD – Breach of Duty Theory of Feinberg
CD – Continuing Domination Theory of Fletcher
UA – Usurping Authority Theory of Lindgren
SD – substantial demand (2 or less suggests subject thought Brian's demand was not substantial)

+ = 'yes' response – = 'no' response

* Question *d* for scenario 2 asks the preliminary question of whether there is an interested third party, to which we expect the answer to be "no," thereby obviating the need to ask subjects the question that is used in all other scenarios.
** In scenario 10, question *e* we expect to confirm that subjects do not see the threat as substantial, thus barring liability under theories *WI-K* and *CD* even though the liability requirements for those theories are otherwise satisfied.

TABLE 82. } Criminalization Predictions for Each Theory

Scenario	*WI-B*	*WI-K*	*BD*	*CD*	*UA*	*EI*
1. Pay or Report Crime	Y	Y	Y	Y	Y	Y
2. Pay or Face Lawsuit	N	N	N	N	N	N
3. Sober Work or Expose Drinking	N	N	N	N	Y	N
4. Pay or Reveal Recipe	Y	Y	N	Y	Y	Y
5. Pay or Publish Book	N	N	N	Y	Y	Y
6. Pay or Expose Cheating	Y	Y	Y	N	Y	Y
7. Withdraw or Expose Cheating	N	N	Y	N	Y	Y
8. Cut Tree or Publish Photos	Y	Y	Y	N	Y	N
9. Pay or Report Smoking	Y	Y	N	N	Y	N
10. Pay or Report Crime	Y	N	Y	N	Y	Y
11. Pay Penalty or Foreclose	Y	Y	N	N	N	N

Key: *WI-B and WI-K* – Wrongful Intention Theory of Berman and Katz, respectively
BD – Breach of Duty Theory of Feinberg
CD – Continuing Domination Theory of Fletcher
UA – Usurping Authority Theory of Lindgren
EI – Efficient Information Allocation Theory of Isenbergh
Y = this theory would impose liability in this scenario
N = this theory would not impose liability in this scenario

which of the theories best reflects participants' views. Below is an explanation of why each of the theories gives the pattern of criminalization set out in the table.

a. Wrongful Intention. Mitchell Berman and Leo Katz both offer theories of blackmail as the wrongful exploitation of the recipient of the threat by the maker of the threat. Under Berman's view, the threat itself provides evidence of the blackmailer's wrongful motivations or beliefs. Had the blackmailer been interested in disclosing the information (or engaging in whatever other conduct he threatens), he would simply have done so. The willingness to exchange silence (or other nonaction) for personal gain indicates that if the blackmailer's demand is not satisfied and he carries out the threat, he will be doing so in retaliation for not getting what he sought rather than out of a good faith desire to inform the party receiving the information. Katz similarly thinks that a retaliatory motivation can make an otherwise innocuous disclosure, or other threatened act, wrongful.[69]

Both Berman and Katz would find five of the scenarios to describe blackmail based on this retaliatory dimension: Scenario 1 ("Pay or Report Crime [$1,000]"), Scenario 4 ("Pay or Reveal Recipe"), Scenario 6 ("Pay or Expose Cheating"), Scenario 8 ("Cut Tree or Publish Photos"), and Scenario 9 ("Pay or Report Smoking"). In each case, Brian will accept money—or, in Scenario 8, the cutting down of the tree—in exchange for keeping secret whatever information he has, indicating that if he later discloses what he knows, he will not be doing so for the right reasons, but only because the recipient of the threat did not satisfy his desire to get paid.

Scenario 10 ("Pay or Report Crime [$1]") involves a similar threat, but presents the one case where Berman and Katz would disagree about the outcome. For Berman, if the willingness to keep one's silence about a known crime indicates a wrongful motivation, the magnitude of the demand does not change the wrongfulness of the threat.[70] For Katz, on the other hand, even a wrongfully motivated threat ceases to be blackmail if the demand is too trivial, and a demand for $1 does not rise to the level of substantiality Katz would require.[71]

Scenario 11 ("Pay Penalty or Foreclose") counts as blackmail for both Berman and Katz. Here Brian has the authority to make Victor pay the bank a penalty (and to foreclose if Victor does not), but he is exercising that authority for wrongful reasons, seeking to cause harm to Victor rather than make his decision on more neutral and fair grounds.

---

[69] *See* Katz, *supra* note 814 (discussing a position on retaliation as wrongful motivation making threatened conduct "immoral").

[70] *Cf.* E-mail from Mitchell Berman to Paul Robinson, June 5, 2009 (agreeing that Berman's theory "does not have an exclusion for trivial demands").

[71] *See, e.g.,* E-mail from Leo Katz to Paul Robinson, June 9, 2009 (claiming that in this scenario, the threat is "too insignificant to count as immoral"); [Katz memo sent 11/21/08] ("At some point the threatened misconduct is just too trivial. There is some line to be drawn .... Where is that line? We probably have discretion about where to draw it. The only thing we are compelled to do by logical consistency is to have such a line.").

The remaining four cases are not blackmail under this theory, as they involve situations where the threat is not driven by any wrongful purpose, but by a good faith desire to achieve a fair outcome for all concerned.

b. Breach of Duty. Under Feinberg's theory, it is acceptable to prohibit a threat as blackmail if it would also be justifiable for the law to prohibit, or mandate, the threatened act. Where the law imposes a duty, a person may not threaten to violate that duty (as occurs where the threatened act is prohibited), nor may he offer to violate the duty in exchange for compensation (as occurs where the threatened act is mandated). Further, even if the law does not currently recognize a given duty, where the duty is one the law *should* recognize, Feinberg argues for both adopting that duty and treating threats (or offers) to violate it as blackmail. For example, Feinberg maintains that revelation of some truthful but damaging information should be treated as defamation, and threats to reveal such information should be treated as blackmail.[72] The test, then, can be stated as follows: if it would be proper for the law to impose a duty to act in a certain way, then it would also be proper for the law to treat a threat or offer to violate that duty as blackmail.

Four of the scenarios are blackmail under Feinberg's theory because they involve *offers* to violate a duty: situations where the blackmailer's *failure* to do what he proposes to do would be improper. Feinberg explicitly discusses cases such as Scenario 1 ("Pay or Report Crime [$1,000]") and Scenario 10 ("Pay or Report Crime [$1]"), involving offers to breach one's duty to report criminal activity.[73] As to Scenario 10, Feinberg even points out that in his view, even a modest demand still counts as blackmail if it involves a violation of one's obligations, or civic duty to community,[74] such as nondisclosure of crime). Scenario 6 ("Pay or Expose Cheating") and Scenario 7 ("Withdraw or Expose Cheating") both contain a promise on the part of would-be police officers, such as Brian, to expose cheating by other applicants, and Brian's offer to Victor would violate that promise in both cases.

One other case would also constitute blackmail under Feinberg's theory. Under the theory, threats to violate a legal duty are blackmail whether the source of a legal duty is civil or criminal. For example, if someone would be entitled to bring a private lawsuit against another for disclosing secret information in violation of his privacy, then the threat to disclose that information can be treated as blackmail.[75] Scenario 8 ("Cut Tree or Publish Photos"), where Brian uses a special device to take compromising photographs of Victor in his own home and threatens to make them public, presents just such a situation, as Victor would almost certainly have a tort claim against Brian for invasion of privacy.

Feinberg's breach-of-duty theory finds that a threat is not blackmail if there is no duty in either direction, but the maker of the threat should be legally free either

---

[72] *See* FEINBERG, *supra* note 824, at 254–56.

[73] *See id.* at 241–45.

[74] *See id.* at 262.

[75] *See id.* at 250–51.

to engage in the threatened conduct or not. Three of the cases involve situations where the person making the threat is in possession of certain secret information and neither has, nor plausibly should have, any legal obligation either to disclose or to conceal such information. In Scenario 3 ("Sober Work or Expose Addiction"), Brian might arguably have a moral responsibility to tell his employer of Victor's addiction, but it seems dubious to claim that his failure to do so should subject him to legal liability, either criminally or civilly. In the other cases—Scenario 4 ("Pay or Reveal Recipe"), Scenario 5 ("Pay or Publish Book"), and Scenario 9 ("Pay or Report Smoking")—Brian is clearly free to decide whether or not he should reveal what he knows, as Victor's secret behavior is neither illegal nor dangerous.

The other two cases, Scenario 2 ("Pay or Face Lawsuit") and Scenario 11 ("Pay Penalty or Foreclose"), involve situations where the maker of the demand is legally entitled to what he is demanding and therefore clearly violates no duty in making the request for it.[76]

c. Continuing Domination. The criteria for establishing blackmail under George Fletcher's theory is whether the threat involves a demand that is both significant and capable of repetition, thus having the potential to create an ongoing relationship of dominance and subordination between the blackmailer and the victim. Three of the scenarios count as blackmail under this theory. All three involve situations where the blackmailer makes a demand for money that could easily be replicated even if the recipient of the threat pays the money, because the blackmailer will retain access to the information that grounds the threat: Scenario 1 ("Pay or Report Crime [$1,000]"), Scenario 4 ("Pay or Reveal Recipe"), and Scenario 5 ("Pay or Publish Book").

A fourth case, Scenario 10 ("Pay or Report Crime [$1]"), also involves such a threat, but would not count as blackmail for Fletcher because the demand is not "substantial." A "minimal" demand, such as the request for $1 in this case, is insufficient to create the degree of subordination Fletcher considers to be the gravamen of blackmail.[77] The other scenarios involve threats that cannot be repeated, so that no continuing pattern of domination can be established.

d. Usurping Authority. Under James Lindgren's theory, "blackmail is a way that one person requests something in return for suppressing the actual or potential interests of others. To get what he wants, the blackmailer uses leverage that is less his than someone else's."[78] Often this involves making a threat "to release damaging information" that some other party might want to know.[79] In Scenario 1 ("Pay or Report Crime [$1,000]"), Scenario 6 ("Pay or Expose Cheating"), and Scenario 10 ("Pay or Report Crime [$1]"), Brian seeks personal gain by using information in which law enforcement authorities (and the public at large) would have an interest. In Scenario

---

[76] *See id.* at 264–66 (noting that demands made under a legal claim of right are justifiable and not blackmail).

[77] *See* Fletcher, *supra* note 818, at 1627.

[78] Lindgren, *supra* note 841, at 672.

[79] *Id.* at 672.

4 ("Pay or Reveal Recipe"), Brian seeks money to withhold information that would interest the bakery's customers. In Scenario 9 ("Pay or Report Smoking"), Brian seeks money in return for keeping from Teresa information that she would want to know.

Similar, though perhaps less intuitive, results obtain under Lindgren's theory for Scenario 5 ("Pay or Publish Book")[80] and Scenario 8 ("Cut Tree or Publish Photos"). Here also, Lindgren's theory finds the threat to be blackmail, on the basis that Brian is somehow selling out the public's interest in obtaining secret, even salacious information about a private citizen.[81]

Finally, Scenario 3 ("Sober Work or Expose Addiction") and Scenario 7 ("Withdraw or Expose Cheating") are also blackmail under Lindgren's theory. In both cases, though Brian does not seem to seek anything for his own benefit, what he asks of Victor departs from what the relevant third party would demand in Brian's stead (and Brian is aware of this). Scenario 3 makes clear that if the employer knew about Victor's substance abuse problem, it would fire Victor under the "zero tolerance" policy. Brian is additionally demanding things (such as the donation to charity) that the employer would not be in a position to demand. Accordingly, though Brian might not be advancing his own interests over the employer's, he is pursuing a remedy at odds with what the entitled, but ignorant, third party would pursue. Scenario 7 is similar; indeed it presents an even stronger case for blackmail under Lindgren's theory, because here not only is Brian making a demand that might be incongruent with what the police force would do, but Brian is also violating his own promise to turn in cheaters to the proper authorities. Accordingly, Brian knows himself to be substituting his own judgment for that of another authorized decision maker.

For two cases, there is no third party whose interests are infringed by Brian's demand to Victor. In Scenario 2 ("Pay or Face Lawsuit"), Brian is not advancing the rights or interests of a third party, but his own rights to payment for damage to his car.[82] In Scenario 11 ("Pay Penalty or Foreclose"), Brian's position as an agent of the bank entitles him to impose the penalty, and he is arguably protecting the interests of the bank by doing so. Even if his motivation is not to advance the interests of the bank alone, the bank's position has not been compromised in any way—indeed, the bank is the source of Brian's authority and has delegated to Brian exactly the power he is exercising in this situation.

e. Efficient Information Allocation. Four of the scenarios are clearly blackmail of Isenbergh's first variety: both Scenario 1 ("Pay or Report Crime") and Scenario 6 ("Pay or Expose Cheating") involve situations where the information could form

[80] Lindgren discusses this precise situation. *See id.* at 683 ("Consider also the biographer or memoirist who seeks money to refrain from publishing a book that will damage someone's reputation. Publishing would further the writer's lawful business, but seeking money to refrain from ruining someone's reputation or business is blackmail.").

[81] *See id.* at 672 ("[S]elling the right to inform others of embarrassing (but legal) behavior involves suppressing the interests of those other people.").

[82] *See id.* at 713–14 ("For example, assume a person believes he has been tortiously and criminally harmed by another person. All authorities agree that it is legitimate for the injured party or his lawyer to threaten to file a civil suit for damages.").

the basis for a criminal prosecution. Two other scenarios are just as clearly *not* blackmail for Isenbergh: in both Scenario 2 ("Pay or Face Lawsuit") and Scenario 11 ("Pay Penalty or Foreclose"), Brian is directly enforcing legal rights that he has the authority to enforce.

For the remaining cases, the issue under Isenbergh's test is whether there has been any "prior course of dealing" between Brian and Victor; if not, the disclosure threat would be blackmail. In Scenario 4 ("Pay or Reveal Recipe"), the case does not specify whether Brian obtained the information about Victor's cupcake recipe fortuitously or through deliberate effort, but there is no indication of any previous relationship, so Isenbergh would treat the case as blackmail. The same seems true for Scenario 5 ("Pay or Publish Book"), where it is clear Brian was deliberately researching the details of Victor's life for the sake of uncovering what information he could.

This case indicates that Isenbergh's account has a difficult time dealing with cases of journalism or other investigation, where the researcher is, in Isenbergh's terms, engaged in "systematic information-farming" though not "bent only on profit from suppressing what they have uncovered."[83] Are such cases blackmail, because non-prohibition would promote excessive fruitless investigations, or non-blackmail, because the researcher is as or more likely to find (and disclose) useful public information as damaging private secrets, and is not planning at the outset to "bargain" with the target to keep the information secret? Under Isenbergh's test, such cases are blackmail, though it is by no means clear whether such treatment is in keeping with Isenbergh's underlying goals. A basic concern of Isenbergh (as with other law-and-economics thinkers) is to ensure that information ends up where it is most highly valued, and it is not clear in these cases whether the threat recipient values secrecy more than the public would value the information—though often the researcher, with the option of selling the information to either party, might be in the best position to decide.

In the remaining three cases, Brian and Victor do have a preexisting relationship, so Isenbergh's test would not treat any of them as blackmail. In Scenario 9 ("Pay or Report Smoking") and Scenario 3 ("Sober Work or Expose Drinking"), the implication is that Brian obtained the information fortuitously, so the result is consistent with Isenbergh's underlying principle. In such situations it also seems likely that Victor would be the "lowest cost avoider of untoward disclosure, and there is no obvious reason to protect [Victor] from bearing the full cost of preserving his own secrets."[84] The result of non-blackmail in the final case, Scenario 8 ("Cut Tree or Publish Photos"), is somewhat curious, since Brian has engaged in deliberate snooping with a specific view to using its fruits as the basis of a threat. Here again, though, perhaps an individual should bear the burden of taking steps to prevent neighbors from spying. Further, it also seems likely that Victor values

---

[83] *See* Isenbergh, *supra* note 850, at 1929.

[84] *Id.* at 1931.

nondisclosure of the photos more than the public would value access to them: their main, and perhaps only, value lies in Victor's desire to keep them private.

3. STATUTORY LIABILITY PATTERNS

An aim of this study was also to test which statutory approach in current law best captures the participants' views. Building upon the analysis of current statutes in section B, which suggested the existence of three common statutory approaches, each scenario was analyzed using the legal criteria summarized in Table 83 below.

Using these criteria, the three statutory approaches would generate criminalization for the 11 scenarios in the patterns set out in Table 84 below.

The MPC (broad-broad) jurisdictions would find liability for Brian in Scenarios 1, 4, 5, 6, 8, 9, and 10. However, Brian would get the exception offered by the MPC in Scenarios 2 and 7, as his purpose in those situations was to make Victor act in a way reasonably related to the circumstances surrounding Brian's threat. In Scenario 3, Brian will get the exception, but does not satisfy the MPC's offense requirements in any case, because he does not have purpose to restrict Victor's freedom of action "to his detriment."[85]

TABLE 83. } Legal Criminalization Criteria

e. **Model Penal Code (broad-broad)**[1] (Broad offense definitions, broad exceptions).
Did Brian, with purpose unlawfully to restrict Victor's freedom of action to his detriment, threaten to commit a criminal offense, accuse anyone of a criminal offense, or expose a secret ending to subject any person to hatred, contempt, or ridicule?
Brian is not liable if he believed the secret to be true and his action was limited to compelling Victor to behave in a way reasonably related to the circumstances which were the subject of the accusation, or exposure. Examples of permissible behaviors for Brian to compel include making Victor desist from further misbehavior, making Victor fix a previous wrong, or making Victor refrain from taking any action or responsibility for which Brian believes that Victor is not qualified.

f. **Narrow-narrow jurisdictions**[2] (Narrow offense definitions, narrow exceptions).
Did Brian threaten to expose a secret, accuse anyone of a crime, or threaten injury to Victor's property or reputation with intent to obtain Victor's property?
Brian is not liable if he was owed the property as compensation for property or services, or as restitution for harm done to Brian.

g. **Broad-narrow jurisdictions**[3] (Broad offense definitions, narrow exceptions).
Did Brian threaten to expose a secret, accuse anyone of a crime, or threaten injury to Victor's property or reputation with intent to coerce Victor into taking or refraining from action, or with intent to obtain Victor's property?
Brian is not liable if he was owed the property as compensation for property or services, or as restitution for harm done to Brian.

[1] AK, CT, HI, KY, NJ, NY, ND, PA, WA. Note that these do not necessarily share the MPC language but have the same effect.
[2] AL, AZ, DE, GA, ID, LA, ME, MS, NE, NH, SD, UT, (CA, NC, OH, OR). Note that the final four states listed are narrow-broad; in practice this formulation has identical results to narrow-narrow.
[3] AR, CO, DC, FL, IL, IN, IA, MD, MA, MI, MN, MO, MT, NM, RI, TN, VT, WI.

[85] Model Penal Code §212.5(1)(d).

TABLE 84. } Legal Liability Analysis

Scenario	MPC	N-N	B-N
1. Pay or Report Crime	Y	Y	Y
2. Pay or Face Lawsuit	N	N	N
3. Sober Work or Expose Drinking	N	N	Y
4. Pay or Reveal Recipe	Y	Y	Y
5. Pay or Publish Book	N	N	N
6. Pay or Expose Cheating	Y	Y	Y
7. Withdraw or Expose Cheating	N	N	Y
8. Cut Tree or Publish Photos	Y	N	Y
9. Pay or Report Smoking	Y	Y	Y
10. Pay or Report Crime	Y	Y	Y
11. Pay Penalty or Foreclose	N	N	N

Key: MPC – MPC (broad-broad) jurisdictions
N-N – narrow-narrow jurisdictions
B-N – broad-narrow jurisdictions)
Y – this statutory group typically would impose liability in this case
N – this statutory group typically would not impose liability in this case

It is difficult to formulate a "model" broad-narrow statute because of their different drafting styles, but under this type of statute liability would be expected for Brian in every scenario.[86] The critical difference between this category and the broad-broad category relates to the nature of the exception: in every scenario in which the MPC would give an exception, the narrow-narrow statutes would not. Brian does not have a right to any of the property demanded in Scenarios 1, 5, 6, 9, and 10, thus he will not get an exception. If he did have a right to the money, however, he could get an exception per a broad-narrow statute.

For the narrow-narrow statutes, it is, again, difficult to formulate a "model," but these statutes will find liability for Brian in Scenarios 1, 5, 6, 9, and 10. Predictably, the only differences between the broad-broad statutes and these are seen in the situations where Brian demands action from Victor, rather than compensation; a narrow-narrow statute will not criminalize the actor who makes this type of demand. If a situation arose in which the actor demanded only compensation that was owed him, these statutes would find no liability.

Of the jurisdictions in the "other" category, the four "broad prohibition" statutes would impose liability for Brian in all scenarios, and the five "narrow prohibition" statutes would impose liability in Scenarios 1, 5, 6, 9, and 10, tracking the narrow-narrow jurisdictions' results.

[86] Scenario 2 presents a problem for some of the statutes in this group. Twelve of the statutes in this category would definitely find Brian guilty in that scenario, five would probably find him guilty (if Brian's threat was malicious, he would be guilty of the blackmail offense; if it was not, he would not be), and one would probably not find him guilty (IL requires that Brian threaten to act without lawful authority; he clearly has the legal right to print a news story).

4. RESULTS AND DISCUSSION

a. Manipulation-Check Results. The results of the manipulation-check questionnaire are set out in Table 85, which can be compared to the desired subject perceptions described in Table 81. Average responses greater than zero are a "yes" response; those below zero are a "no" response.

Although the concepts being manipulated here are quite complex and abstract, a comparison to Table 81 suggests that these results are quite good. The one response of the 66 that is not the desired perception described in Table 85 is set out in bold. The four responses that indicate indifference—those that do not statistically significantly differ from zero, meaning a neutral response—are in italics. (Later in our analysis we introduce specific analyses that attempt to compensate for these subject misperceptions.[87])

The good manipulation-check results reported in this study are not the result of either good luck or a special talent in drafting scenarios, but rather the result of dozens of manipulation-check mini-field tests together with three formal manipulation-check pilot tests. After each test, adjustments were made to the scenarios' texts, which were then retested.

The larger point here is that criminal law theorists who undertake such studies can benefit significantly from partnering with a well-trained social psychologist and

TABLE 85. } Manipulation-Check Results

#	Scenario Q:	WI	BD	CD	UA	SD
1	Pay or Report Crime	1.1	2.2	2.2	2.3	2.6
2	Pay or Face Lawsuit	-2.4	-0.7	-1.2	-0.6	2.7
3	Sober Work or Expose Drinking	-2.2	*0.3*	-0.4	0.5	2.9
4	Pay or Reveal Recipe	2.3	-1.9	2.0	1.5	4.1
5	Pay or Publish Book	-0.4	-1.4	1.4	1.2	3.2
6	Pay or Expose Cheating	1.3	0.8	**0.6**	2.1	3.0
7	Withdraw or Expose Cheating	-1.5	1.0	-0.5	*0.4*	3.3
8	Cut Tree or Publish Photos	2.7	2.5	-0.5	1.5	2.8
9	Pay or Report Smoking	2.2	-1.7	-0.7	2.0	3.0
10	Pay or Report Crime	0.9	2.2	2.1	2.2	1.0
11	Pay Penalty or Foreclose	1.5	-0.6	*-0.1*	*-0.1*	3.1

Key: *WI* – Wrongful Intention Theory of Berman and Katz

BD – Breach of Duty Theory of Feinberg

CD – Continuing Domination Theory of Fletcher

UA – Usurping Authority Theory of Lindgren

SD – substantial demand (2 or less suggests subject thought Brian's demand was not substantial)

+ = 'yes' response – = 'no' response

---

[87] *See infra* text following Table 87 (showing correlation between predictions and subjects' liability responses, conditioned on subjects' manipulation-check responses).

from having a good deal of patience for the unexpected trials that reliable experimental work inevitably brings.

b. Liability Results. The subjects' criminalization judgments are set out in Table 86. The theory predictions from Table 82 and the statutory liability patterns from Table 84 are reproduced for comparison purposes. The points at which a theory or a statutory approach disagrees with the subjects' views, on average, are marked in bold.

All of the liability averages are statistically significantly different from zero, except for that for Scenario 5, set in italics. That scenario was the one in which the author of a biography gave the subject of the biography an opportunity to compensate him for his work to date in return for not publishing damaging information that he had found during his research work. The problem was not one of different subjects perceiving the scenario differently and, therefore, coming to different liability conclusions. As is apparent from Table 85 above, the Scenario 5 manipulations for all four types of theories tested worked. The subjects simply disagreed with one another about whether there should be criminal liability in such a case. The resulting average of 0.2 was not statistically significantly different from zero, which meant "unsure." Because of this, the below analysis mainly excludes consideration of Scenario 5.

At least one of the six theories disagreed with the subjects on every scenario (except the two screening scenarios, Scenarios 1 and 2, of course). This is as planned. The scenarios were constructed to test the differences between the theories. The more theories the subjects' responses for a given scenario contradicted, the more support those responses would tend to provide for the theory or theories supporting the result. The maximum support for any given theory would be a scenario where only that theory, and no others, predicted a given result and the subjects' responses generated that result. On the other hand, the clearest evidence of disagreement with a given theory would be if only that theory predicted a given result and the subjects chose the opposite result.

Two scenarios generated liability results that disagreed with the predictions of three theories: Scenario 7 (BD, UA, EI) and Scenario 9 (BD, CD, EI). Another three scenarios had results that disagreed with two theories: Scenario 8 (CD, EI), Scenario 10, and Scenario 11 (both versions of WI). Three scenarios gave results that conflicted with the prediction of only one theory: Scenario 3 gave a result that conflicted with one theory (UA), Scenario 4 (BD), and Scenario 6 (CD). As discussed earlier, the results of Scenario 5 were inconclusive.

A simple way to test the relative descriptive adequacy of the various positions is to simply count to see how many of their predictions bear out when looking at the mean liability judgments for the 10 scenarios with significant liability results presented in Table 86. Here's the scorecard:

10: MPC Broad-Broad
9: Wrongful Intention (Berman); Narrow-Narrow
8: Wrongful Intention (Katz); Usurping Authority (Lindgren); Broad-Narrow
7: Breach of Duty (Feinberg); Efficient Allocation (Isenbergh)
6: Continuing Domination (Fletcher)

TABLE 86. } Criminalization Results (and Comparisons)

Scenario	Mean	Y/N	*WI-B*	*WI-K*	*BD*	*CD*	*UA*	*EI*	*MPC*	*N-N*	*B-N*
1. Pay or Report Crime	2.5	Y	Y	Y	Y	Y	Y	Y	Y	Y	Y
2. Pay or Face Lawsuit	-2.5	N	N	N	N	N	N	N	N	N	N
3. Sober Work or Expose Drinking	-1.6	N	N	N	N	N	**Y**	N	N	N	**Y**
4. Pay or Reveal Recipe	1.3	Y	Y	Y	**N**	Y	Y	Y	Y	Y	Y
5. Pay or Publish Book	*0.2*	–	*N*	*N*	*N*	*Y*	*Y*	*Y*	*N*	*N*	*N*
6. Pay or Expose Cheating	1.6	Y	Y	Y	Y	**N**	Y	Y	Y	Y	Y
7. Withdraw or Expose Cheating	-1.1	N	N	N	**Y**	N	**Y**	**Y**	N	N	**Y**
8. Cut Tree or Publish Photos	2.3	Y	Y	Y	Y	**N**	Y	**N**	Y	**N**	Y
9. Pay or Report Smoking	0.7	Y	Y	Y	**N**	**N**	Y	**N**	Y	Y	Y
10. Pay or Report Crime	1.5	Y	Y	**N**	Y	**N**	Y	Y	Y	Y	Y
11. Pay Penalty or Foreclose	-0.5	N	**Y**	**Y**	N	N	N	N	N	N	N

Key: *WI-B and WI-K* – Wrongful Intention Theory of Berman and Katz, respectively
BD – Breach of Duty Theory of Feinberg
CD – Continuing Domination Theory of Fletcher
UA – Usurping Authority Theory of Lindgren
EI – Efficient Information Allocation Theory of Isenbergh
MPC – MPC (broad-broad) jurisdictions
N-N – narrow-narrow jurisdictions
B-N – broad-narrow jurisdictions)
Y = this theory would impose liability in this scenario
N = this theory would not impose liability in this scenario

c. The Theories. As is apparent from Table 86, no liability theory exactly matches the subjects' liability judgments, although the Wrongful Intention Theory, especially the Berman version, comes quite close. Apart from Scenario 5 (the scenario on which the subjects themselves substantially disagreed about the proper result), the only scenario the theory got wrong was Scenario 11, in which Brian, a bank official, does what the bank has authorized him to do but with a wrongful intention. The subjects, on average, said no liability, while the Wrongful Intention Theory would impose liability. All four of the other theories got this liability prediction correct. On the other hand, this was the scenario on which there was the most disagreement among the subjects (apart from Scenario 5): a majority of 51.2 percent versus a minority of 39.5 percent (with 9.3 percent undecided). Thus, the Wrongful Intention Theory does accurately capture the views of a substantial minority of the subjects.

Each other theory had more points of disagreement with the subjects. The Katz version of the Wrongful Intention Theory had the same disagreements with subjects as did the Berman version but, in addition, turned out wrong about the one aspect on which the Katz and the Berman versions disagreed: Scenario 10. The subjects were happy to impose criminal liability even though the demand itself was not substantial (only for $1), while Katz would have taken the trivial demand as barring liability.

Lindgren's Usurping Authority Theory did slightly less well, with two points of disagreement: Scenarios 3 and 7. In both cases, Lindgren's theory would impose liability, but the subjects did not, even though they recognized that Lindgren's relevant factor was present, that is, the manipulation checks were positive (though modestly so). More generally, Lindgren's theory was only weakly predictive where it indicated liability, but was the second most strongly predictive theory (after Berman's) where it predicted *no* liability, including an accurate prediction of no liability for Scenario 11, the only one Berman's theory predicted incorrectly.

Feinberg's Breach-of-Duty Theory had three points of disagreement with subjects (beyond the Scenario 5): Scenarios 4, 7, and 9—and the disagreements were in both directions. The disagreement on Scenarios 4 ("Pay or Reveal Recipe") and 9 ("Pay or Report Smoking") is hardly surprising, as both bear some similarity to the classic adultery-disclosure blackmail scenario that Feinberg's theory excludes from liability. In both situations, the person making the threat has access to potentially reputation-harming information that he has no obligation to share with anyone, and offers to reveal that information unless paid. Subjects would treat such situations as blackmail, though Feinberg would not. Yet Feinberg would impose liability in Scenario 7 ("Withdraw or Expose Cheating"), though subjects would not.

As with Feinberg's theory, Isenbergh's Efficient Information Allocation Theory had three points of disagreement with subjects: Scenarios 7, 8, and 9. And, again, the disagreements were in both directions: for Scenario 7, Isenbergh would favor liability, but the subjects rejected it, whereas for Scenario 8, Isenbergh would oppose liability but the subjects favored it (quite strongly). In Scenario 9, subjects were willing to impose liability though Brian clearly obtained the information fortuitously rather than by "information farming." It seems unlikely that subject's intuitions were driven by the considerations Isenbergh finds relevant—which is not a direct critique of Isenbergh, of course, as his account of blackmail made no claim to reflect public moral sentiment.

The Continuing Domination Theory of Fletcher had four points of disagreement with subjects: Scenarios 6, 8, 9, and 10. Like Katz, Fletcher takes the position that threats should only constitute blackmail if the blackmailer's demand is above some threshold level of significance. As with Katz, the subjects' willingness to impose liability in Scenario 10, involving a demand of $1, indicates this aspect of Fletcher's theory does not accord with popular intuitions. The other three scenarios for which Fletcher's predictions depart from actual responses also err in the same direction: subjects imposing liability where Fletcher's theory would not. Scenario 6, however, does not truly count against Fletcher, for the subjects' manipulation-check response for that Scenario was positive for Fletcher's theory, indicating they believed its criterion was satisfied; so their willingness to impose liability for that scenario actually aligns with what Fletcher would predict given the subjects' own understanding of the case. For Scenarios 8 and 9, however, the manipulation-check test for Fletcher's theory is negative, yet the subjects' liability response is positive, indicating they are not following Fletcher's ongoing-subordination account of blackmail. Both cases are constructed so that Brian could not repeat his demand of Victor, and the subjects perceived this feature of both scenarios, but were willing to impose liability nonetheless.

Finally, it is worth noting the lack of support for the abolitionist position. Subjects supported liability in 6 of the 11 scenarios tested. Only one subject who completed the survey imposed no liability for any of the 11 scenarios. Moreover, this person responded in a manner consistent with predictions for the manipulation checks for only 17 of the possible 55 theory items, raising doubts about how seriously the subject took the survey. The empirical data suggests that the abolitionist position is inconsistent with community views.

d. The Statutory Schemes. It turns out that the statutory schemes did better overall than the theorists in predicting the subjects' liability views. Indeed, setting aside Scenario 5, the Model Penal Code's broad-broad approach matched the subjects' views exactly, the only one to do so! The consonance between the statutory approach and the subjects' intuitions is all the more remarkable given the Model Penal Code's overtly utilitarian focus and disavowal of any effort to track public moral sentiment—though it is possible the Code's drafters were more influenced by considerations of moral blameworthiness than they let on.[88]

The other two statutory options seemed to fall short insofar as they departed from the Model Penal Code's approach. The broad-narrow approach, which defines the offense expansively (like the Model Code) but recognizes fewer exceptions, erred in the direction of imposing liability in two cases where the subjects would not: Scenarios 3 and 7. On the other hand, the narrow-narrow approach, which defines the offense itself less broadly, failed to impose liability in one scenario where the subjects would, Scenario 8—which was also the scenario which had the second-strongest pro-liability result, nearly as strong as the result for Scenario 1, the archetypal blackmail case. It seems, then, that so far as community sentiment is concerned, the "narrow offense" approach is too exclusive, and the "narrow exception" approach too inclusive, in determining which threats count as blackmail.

---

[88] *See, e.g.*, Chapter 6; Paul H. Robinson, *Why Does the Criminal Law Care What the Lay Person Thinks is Just? Coercive vs. Normative Crime Control*, 86 VA. L. REV. 1839 (2000).

e. Effect of Seriousness of Threat and Wrongfulness of Victim's Undisclosed Conduct. Set out in Table 87 below are the results of the last three questions in the manipulation-check questionnaire (*e*, *f*, and *g*). Recall that these three questions asked subjects for a quantitative assessment of the extent of the seriousness of the demand, the threat, and the victim's secret, rather than just the binary choice of agree-disagree or yes-no asked in the manipulation-check and the criminalization questions, respectively.

A correlation was computed for each subject between the liability judgments she supplied for each of the 11 scenarios with the 11 ratings she gave across the scenarios for demand, for disclosure, and for secret. The median correlations observed between liability and each of these factors were .01, .41, and .06, respectively. Of these, only Disclosure was significantly different from zero (by signed rank test, $W = 3760, p < .001$). In other words, the more harmful a subject viewed Brian's threat of disclosure to be, the more likely she was to assess criminal liability for the action, but the relationship between the other factors and liability was not significant.

The absence of correlation between the magnitude of the demand and the subjects' liability judgments across the battery of 11 scenarios suggests that Katz and Fletcher's adherence to a "trivial demand exception" for blackmail does not accord with lay intuitions. The correlation between subjects' liability judgments and their estimates of the harmfulness of disclosure offers some indirect support for the perspective (shared by Berman, Katz, and Fletcher) that the recipient of the threat is the true victim of the blackmail offense. As the potential harm to the recipient increases, so does the subjects' support for liability. Finally, the absence of correlation between subjects' liability judgments and their moral assessment of the victim's behavior offers some reassurance that their views about blackmail are not driven purely by their sympathy (or lack of sympathy) for the victim.

TABLE 87. } Subject Evaluations of Extent of Demand, Disclosure & Secret

Scenario	*e. Demand*	*f. Disclosure*	*g. Secret*
1. Pay or Report Crime	2.6	4.7	4.78
2. Pay or Face Lawsuit	2.7	2.3	3.2
3. Sober Work or Expose Drinking	2.9	3.8	2.8
4. Pay or Reveal Recipe	4.1	3.9	1.5
5. Pay or Publish Book	3.2	3.7	2.6
6. Pay or Expose Cheating	3	4.1	4.1
7. Withdraw or Expose Cheating	3.3	3.9	4.1
8. Cut Tree or Publish Photos	2.8	4.1	0.3
9. Pay or Report Smoking	3.0	3.7	1.3
10. Pay or Report Crime	1.0	4.8	4.8
11. Pay Penalty or Foreclose	3.1	4.5	2.5
Correlation with subject liability judgment	0.01	0.41	0.06

Key: *e* – How substantial was the demand?

f – How harmful would disclosure have been?

g – How wrongful was the victim's conduct to be revealed?

D. Conclusion

This chapter presents a study that reveals that the Model Penal Code's legal formulation and Mitchell Berman's theoretical account are better than their existing rivals at capturing shared intuitions regarding blackmail. One important shared trait of these two versions of blackmail is that both see blackmail as a form of extortion—a category traditionally limited to conditional threats to engage in *criminal* acts, such as a threat to injure someone unless paid. The Model Penal Code's coverage of blackmail falls within its broader extortion offense (entitled "Criminal Coercion"[89]), and Berman's theory seeks to justify the criminalization of blackmail on the ground that it constitutes a variety of extortion. The study indicates that lay understandings of blackmail share the position that its gravamen involves harm to the recipient of the threat, rather than some third party or generalized social interest. (Further, and significantly, the study indicates that some other factors that might be considered relevant to the blackmail inquiry are *not* seen that way: general lay intuitions regarding blackmail do not seem to attach any significance to the magnitude of the blackmailer's demand, or to the nature of the information the blackmailer threatens to disclose.)

More specifically, as Berman's theory claims, lay intuitions seem to accord with the position that blackmail amounts to extortion because of the blackmailer's bad faith or improper motivations. The blackmailer's central interest is to benefit himself, and his means of pursuing that interest displays his willingness to wrong the other person, either by forcing that person to sacrifice money (or something else) or by subjecting that person to the harm the blackmailer knows the threatened act will cause.

At the same time, however, and unlike Berman's theory, lay intuitions seem to view some demands as objectively legitimate even if their subjective motivation in a given case is improper. Thus a person whose demand seeks to vindicate a valid legal or societal interest, as in Scenario 11, is not seen as engaging in blackmail even if his underlying motivation is to harm the recipient rather than to advance the legitimate interest. This sentiment accords with the Model Penal Code's exception where the putative blackmail threat is made for the sake of "compelling the other to behave in a way reasonably related to the circumstances which were the subject of the [threat], as by desisting from further misbehavior [or] making good a wrong done. . . ."[90]

Taken together, the theoretical basis Berman excavates for blackmail and the more practical objective constraints the Model Penal Code imposes might suggest a formulation of "criminal coercion" that embraces, but also limits, the scope of blackmail, perhaps along the lines of the following:

---

[89] Model Penal Code §212.5(1). Section (1)(a) is traditional extortion; sections (1)(b)&(c) are common situations of blackmail.

[90] *Id.*

Criminal Coercion

(1) A person commits criminal coercion if he demands money or other valuable consideration as a condition of refraining from any act he intends or knows would cause harm to another person.

(2) For purposes of subsection (1), "harm" may include physical injury, financial deprivation, or substantial psychological stress.

(3) Exception. It is not an offense under subsection (1) if the actor believed his demand to be justified as a means of advancing a legitimate legal or societal interest.[91]

Such a formulation illuminates and makes explicit the general normative intuitions that seem to underlie popular sentiment while also drawing lines that prevent blackmail from being a purely subjective offense concerned only with culpability and not with objectively unjustified harm.

The study also suggests some more general conclusions about criminal law and theory. First, whether discussing blackmail, or other offenses, or more general normative issues of punishment, nearly all theorists rely on what they take to be popular moral intuitions—but they can't all be right. Further, which (if any) of them are right is a testable proposition. Accordingly, empirical work regarding lay intuitions can provide meaningful critique or illumination of theory. The study put the blackmail tests to the test, and the results provide strong support for one theory and much weaker support for others.

Finally, though some may not find the contention novel or surprising, this study may lend further credence to the claim that some aspects of criminal law are, if anything, over-theorized. The intellectual "paradox" of blackmail has given rise to a host of explanatory theories, most rooted in an effort to reflect and justify shared moral intuitions, yet many of those theories miss their mark rather widely, and none accords with popular intuitions as well as the Model Penal Code, a document purporting to advance a purely pragmatic agenda rather than to embody any deep or wide moral commitments. Many of the theorists who have gone to great lengths to advance and defend a principled justification of the blackmail offense might have done better by simply asking people what they think.

---

[91] The exact text of the statutory provision depends in part on the other provisions in the code of which the provision would be part, especially its General Part provisions, as well as the style of its Special Part provisions, such as the extent to which it prefers objective example lists over general criterion definitions. See, for example, the specific prohibited threat descriptions in Model Penal Code §212.5(1)(a)–(d).

20 }

Testing Competing Theories: Justification Defenses

This chapter offers a second example of how empirical research can inform theoretical analysis, in this instance, to help resolve a dispute between two opposing theories over the best way to characterize the nature of justification defenses. Justification defenses, such as self-defense and law enforcement authority, are common in every jurisdiction. They exculpate a person whose conduct otherwise would constitute a criminal offense but for the presence of special justifying circumstances that make the conduct accepted or even encouraged.[1] (In contrast, excuse defenses are given, even if what the person did was wrongful and should not have been done, because some characteristic of the person or her situation leaves her blameless for the offense.) While justification defenses are recognized in every jurisdiction, there is much debate about their underlying theory, and thus, their proper formulation. At the core of the debate is the following question: are justification defenses given because the actor's deed avoids a greater harm, or because she acted for the right reason?

The *deeds theory* of justification justifies conduct that avoids a greater harm, and thus, it is conduct that would be happily tolerated under similar circumstances in the future. Justified conduct under this theory is conduct where the actor has done the right deed. The *reasons theory* looks not to the deed but to the reason for the deed. The reasons theory gives a defense when a person acts for the right reason, generally *trying* to avoid a greater harm. The dispute between the two theories concerns the focus of justification: Is it the *objectively* justified nature of the deed or the actor's *belief*, mistaken or not, that she was justified in acting?

Each side buttresses its philosophical arguments with claims that its theory better tracks people's intuitions of justice.[2] This chapter uses the social science research methods similar to those in part III to examine people's intuitions on the subject. Section A gives a fuller examination of the deeds and reasons theories, and how

---

[1] *See generally* PAUL H. ROBINSON & MICHAEL T. CAHILL, CRIMINAL LAW ch. 8 (2nd ed. 2012).

[2] *See*, e.g., authorities cited at Paul H. Robinson, *Competing Theories of Justification: Deeds v. Reasons*, *in* HARM AND CULPABILITY 45, 47–49 (A. P. Simester & A.T.H. Smith eds., Oxford 1996); GEORGE P. FLETCHER, RETHINKING CRIMINAL LAW 556–57 (1978).

they would decide differently the outcome of cases. Section B predicts how the community would view various cases were they to follow one theory or the other, while section C reports the study results and its implications for the two theories. The chapter is drawn primarily from my article with John Darley, *Testing Competing Theories of Justifications*.[3]

A. Competing Theories of Justification

In many cases, an actor's conduct will be both objectively and subjectively justified. The actor believes her conduct avoids a greater harm and she acts to avoid that greater harm, thereby satisfying the reasons theory, and her conduct does in fact avoid a greater harm, thereby satisfying the deeds theory. But in many other cases, the deeds and reasons theories clash and give different results, and it is these cases of conflict that are the focus of this study.

When the reasons theory of justification is adopted (often called the "subjective" theory), the standard justification formulation provides that "an actor is justified if he *believes* that the conduct is necessary" to defend against unlawful aggression, to make an arrest, to maintain order on the vehicle, and so on.[4] Under this reasons theory, a person will get a justification defense as long as she believes that the justifying circumstances exist. Whether they actually exist or not is irrelevant.

Under a deeds theory (often termed an "objective" theory), the rationale for justification is whether or not the conduct is something society wants the actor to perform due to the justifying circumstances and to have others perform under similar circumstances in the future. The test for justification is whether on balance the conduct in fact avoids a net societal harm (in the broadest sense of harm). An actor's reasons may be relevant to liability under other criminal law doctrines: A mistaken reasonable belief that the conduct is justified may exculpate under an excuse defense. Conversely, a mistaken belief that the conduct is not justified may inculpate as an impossible attempt offense. But an actor's reasons are not relevant under the deeds theory in determining whether a justification defense is available.

This is the point of dispute in the theory of justification: Is the objectively justified nature of the *deed* central, as the deeds theory would have it, or irrelevant, as the reasons theory suggests?

Many, if not most, writers have signed on in support of the reasons theory and in opposition to the deeds theory,[5] some suggesting that the latter is

---

[3] Paul H. Robinson & John M. Darley, *Testing Competing Theories of Justifications*, 76 N.C. L. Rev. 1095, 1098–1108, 1124–35 (1998).

[4] *See, e.g.*, Model Penal Code Article 3 (describing justification formulations).

[5] *See, e.g.*, Michael Corrado, *Notes on the Structure of a Theory of Excuses*, 82 J. Crim. Law & Criminology 465, 489 (1991); Kent Greenawalt, *The Perplexing Borders of Justification and Excuse*, 84 Colum. L. Rev. 144 (1984); Austin W. Scott, Substantive Criminal Law 685 (St. Paul, Minnesota 1986); John Cyril Smith and Brian Hogan, Criminal Law 37 (6th ed., Butterworth-Heinemann1988).

"absurd,"[6] unfair,[7] or unduly burdensome.[8] (It is worth noting that the first two of these objections are based on the moral intuitions of the writers, coupled with their certainty that others share their moral intuitions.) The minority argues that a deeds theory of justification is better for a variety of reasons, including that it generates liability results that are more just and that better match collective intuitions of what is just.[9]

Most, but not all, state criminal law appears to follow the reasons theory,[10] although there is often some ambiguity as to which theory of justification they actually adopt despite the apparent clarity of first appearances.[11] The Model Penal Code formulation is quoted above: an actor is justified if she *believes* that her conduct is necessary for defense.[12]

The contrasts between the two theories are illuminated when one considers how the deeds theory and the reasons theory suggest different results at each of their two conflict points: (1) where the actor mistakenly believes her conduct is not justified (the unknowingly justified actor), and (2) where the actor mistakenly believes her conduct is justified (mistake as to a justification).

1. UNKNOWINGLY JUSTIFIED ACTOR

Assume a person's conduct is objectively justified but he does not realize this; he mistakenly believes it is unjustified. For example, the person mugs a jogger, only to find out that the victim was a club-wielding attacker. Whether the beating of the attacker-thought-to-be-a-jogger is justified depends on whether it is the quality of the *deed* or the actor's *reason* for it that provides the rationale for justification defenses.

Under the deeds theory, where the person's conduct in fact avoids a greater societal harm but the person is unaware of this, the conduct is justified despite the actor's ignorance. However, the person's belief that the conduct is not justified will give rise to attempt liability (assuming the jurisdiction punishes legally impossible attempts, as most do[13]). Thus, the use of force against the attacker-thought-to-be-a-jogger is justified, and the actor will have a defense to the substantive offense for assault, but the actor will be liable for an attempted assault. Attempt is an offense that exists to

---

[6] Brian Hogan, *The Dadson Principle*, 1989 CRIM. L. REV. 679, 680 (1989).

[7] Arnold Loewy, *Culpability, Dangerousness, and Harm: Balancing the Factors on which Our Criminal Law is Predicated*, 66 N.C. L. REV. 283, 289 (1988).

[8] Kevin McMunigal, *Disclosure and Accuracy in the Guilty Plea Process*, 40 HASTINGS L.J. 957, 979 (1989).

[9] Paul H. Robinson, *Competing Theories of Justification: Deeds vs. Reasons, in* HARM AND CULPABILITY 45, 61–67 (A.T.H. Smith & A. Simester, eds., Oxford University Press 1996).

[10] *See* authorities cited at 2 PAUL H. ROBINSON, CRIMINAL LAW DEFENSES §184(b) (1984).

[11] *See* Robinson, *Competing Theories supra* note 908, at 51–54.

[12] *See, e.g.*, Model Penal Code, §§3.02(1), 3.03(3)(a), 3.04(1), 3.05(1)(b), 3.06(1), and 3.07(1) (emphasis added).

[13] *See* authorities collected at 1 PAUL H. ROBINSON, CRIMINAL LAW DEFENSES §85(c) n.28.

punish just such manifested intention to commit an offense, where the harm or evil of the offense does not in fact occur, a situation analogous to that of the unknowingly justified actor who has manifested an intention to act unjustifiably but in fact no net societal harm has occurred.

Under the reasons theory, if the justifying circumstances exist but the actor is unaware of them and acts for a different purpose, the reasons theory denies a justification defense. If the reason behind the deed rather than the deed itself, then the force used against the attacker-thought-to-be-a-jogger is not justified. While it might have been the right deed, necessary for self-defense, it was for the wrong reason.

2. MISTAKE AS TO A JUSTIFICATION

More common is the reverse case: a person's conduct is objectively unjustified, but the person subjectively and mistakenly believes that it is justified. In such cases of mistaken justification, the actor believes that her conduct avoids a greater harm when in fact it does not. The club-wielding attacker, when successfully overcome and dragged to the street light, turns out to be a jogger carrying a flashlight whose bulb is out. Whether beating the jogger-mistaken-for-an-attacker is justified depends again on whether the justification defense is given (1) because the conduct in fact is justified, or (2) because the person acts for a justified reason.

Under a reasons theory, the force used against the jogger-mistaken-for-an-attacker is justified because it is used for the purpose of self-defense. The actor's reason is right even if the conduct is wrong. Under the deeds theory, a person who mistakenly believes that the conduct is justified is not justified, although the person may gain an excuse defense if the mistake is reasonable or perhaps mitigation even if it is not.[14]

Note that in this case the end result under the two theories seems to be the same. The difference is primarily a labeling matter: The person who reasonably but mistakenly believes that her conduct is justified is "justified" under the reasons theory but only "excused" under the deeds theory. This difference may have practical implications for third parties. For example, a jurisdiction might criminalize resistance to justified force, like a lawful arrest, yet allow resistance to excused force, like that of the psychotic aggressor.[15] This common approach creates problems for use of the reasons theory. Presumably one wants the victim to be able to lawfully resist the actor who is mistaken as to a justification. The jogger mistaken for a mugger ought to be able lawfully to resist the misguided attack. However, if the attacker mistakenly believes she is justified and, as the reasons theory would have it, that makes her "justified," then the criminal code must do some fancy dancing to reach the proper

---

[14] *See, e.g.,* Model Penal Code §3.09(2).

[15] *See, e.g.,* Model Penal Code §3.11(1) (defining "unlawful force," which triggers a right of justified defensive force, is including the attack of the psychotic aggressor but excluding privileged (objectively justified) force, such as that used to make a lawful arrest).

result. It must create a special rule that allows defenders to defend against these special kinds of justified attacks but not other kinds of justified attacks.

But putting aside this third party complication for the reasons theory, the result of the two theories is the same for the actor at hand. Both the deeds theory's excuse defense and the reasons theory's justification defense exculpate the actor who mistakenly believes she is justified. Yet, the different views of justification may show themselves in another aspect of defense formulations that has been the subject of much disagreement: the proper treatment of mistake as to a justification. All agree that a reasonable mistake as to a justification ought to fully exculpate. What is the proper treatment of an unreasonable mistake as to a justification?

A majority of jurisdictions permit a mistake as to a justification defense only if the actor's mistake is reasonable. An unreasonable mistake, reckless or negligent, gives no defense and generates full liability for the substantive offense.[16] A minority of jurisdictions gives a complete defense for reasonable mistake but also allow mitigation for an honest but unreasonable mistake.[17] The level of liability, that is, the extent of the mitigation given, typically is tied to the level of culpability of the mistake: A negligent mistake, being less culpable than a reckless mistake, gives a greater mitigation than does a reckless mistake.[18]

The few jurisdictions that take the deeds approach in formulating their justification defenses objectively (e.g., North Dakota, the Proposed Federal Criminal Code) all give mitigations for unreasonable mistakes as to justification.[19] In contrast, a majority of the jurisdictions that take a reasons approach and formulate their justification defenses subjectively take the all-or-nothing approach, giving no mitigation or defense for unreasonable mistakes as to a justification.[20] This pattern suggests a connection between the deeds-reasons dispute and the dispute over the proper treatment of unreasonable mistakes as to a justification. But the fact is there is no logical reason why the reasons theory should demand an all-or-nothing approach.

One could speculate about the source of the apparent correlation between the reasons theory and the all-or-nothing approach. If one views mistaken justification as a justification, it would be easy to conclude that an all-or-nothing approach is needed. After all, all or nothing is the way objective justification does operate. Either the actor's conduct avoids a greater harm and is to be encouraged or at least tolerated in the future, or it does not avoid a greater harm and is to be discouraged in the future. When the subjective reasons theory of justification combines objective justification and mistaken subjective justification under the same label of "justified," it should be no surprise that such creates the tendency to treat a mistaken justification as if it were a true objective justification. It should also be no

---

16 *See* authorities at 2 Paul H. Robinson, *supra* note 909, at §184(a) n.1, 395–98.

17 *Id.*

18 *See, e.g.,* Model Penal Code §3.09(2).

19 *See* N. D. Cent. Code §12.1-05-01 et seq. For a list of jurisdictions that have at least one objective justification statute, *see* 2 Paul H. Robinson, *supra* note 909, §122 n.19.

20 *See* authorities at 2 Paul H. Robinson, *supra* note 909, at §184(a) n.1, 395–98.

surprise to see mistake as to a justification treated, like all other justifications, as an all-or-nothing issue.

This same possibility for confusion does not exist under the deeds approach to formulating justifications. The deeds theory distinguishes true objective justifications from mistakes as to a justification, and treats the latter as excuses. Objective justifications are properly all-or-nothing matters. Mistake as to a justification, like other excuses, just as clearly are not all-or-nothing matters. Excuses function as part of law's adjudication of an actor's blameworthiness for a violation. Blameworthiness exists on a continuum, as is evident by the doctrines that contribute to this function.

Previous writings on the different functions of criminal law, have pointed out that objective justifications serve the ex ante rule articulation function, telling people the rules for future conduct, while the excuses, including mistaken justification, performs an ex post adjudication function, assessing the degree of liability and punishment for a violation of the rules of conduct.[21]

In performing the adjudication function, doctrines commonly express degrees of liability and punishment. For example, criminal codes typically recognize levels of culpability: purpose, knowledge, recklessness, and negligence. The law also recognizes mitigations for partial excuses in both its definition of offenses—for example, the extreme mental or emotional disturbance mitigation in homicide[22]—and its sentencing rules—for example, the federal sentencing guideline authorization for sentence reduction below the guidelines for offenders influenced by coercion, duress, or diminished capacity.[23] Under the deeds theory, mistakes as to a justification are seen as excuses, and like other doctrines for the adjudication of an actor's blameworthiness, the resulting liability may reflect a continuum of liability. Reasonable mistakes may excuse entirely, while the culpability inherent in unreasonable mistakes may suggest something less: mitigation rather than a defense.

B. Liability Predictions

A belief that the community's views are more accurately reflected in doctrine based upon a deeds theory of justification is a minority view. But it is predicted here that, it matters to lay persons whether a net societal harm actually occurs or not, just as it matters to them whether a prohibited result, such as a resulting death, occurs or not. In particular, the community will see the unknowingly justified actor as deserving the reduced liability of attempt rather than the full liability that would come from denying a justification defense.

---

[21] *See* Paul H. Robinson, *A Functional Analysis of Criminal Law*, 88 Nw. U. L. Rev. 857, 889–96 (1994); *Rules of Conduct and Principles of Adjudication*, 57 U. Chi. L. Rev. 729–71 (1990).

[22] *See, e.g.*, Model Penal Code §210.3(1)(b).

[23] *See, e.g.*, United States Sentencing Commission Guidelines Manual §§5K2.12, 5K2.13 (Nov. 1, 1995).

As to the reverse case of mistake as to a justification, it is predicted that the community will see unreasonable mistakes as a justification as deserving of mitigation, in contrast to the majority rule in the United States. Below is described exactly how these general claims translate into specific predictions with regard to the liability results of the scenarios used in the study.

1. CONTRAST CASES

Scenarios 1 through 6 are cases to serve as points of contrast to the justification test cases:

a. Intentional (Unjustified) Burning. Scenario 1 is a case included for comparison purposes. It presents the prototype case of a burning that is intentional and for which no claim of justification exists, similar to that which forms the basis for the other scenarios.

> Jake is angry with his neighbor over a dispute about use of water from a creek that the two share. When he knows that his neighbor is away, he sets fire to the neighbor's three acres of corn. Because the field is bounded on all sides by dirt roads, and there is no wind, it is clear that the burning will create no danger beyond that of destroying the corn. The fire destroys the entire crop.

The liability here is expected to be somewhere midscale because the offense is against only property. As discussed in chapter 13, it is not likely to inspire the heavy penalties at the higher end of the scale. Its purpose is to give a liability rating against which one can compare the liabilities assigned to other scenarios.

b. Attempted (Unjustified) Burning. Scenario 2 is another contrast case similar to Scenario 1 except that the harm intended does not actually come about. "... Just as Jake sets the fire, the neighbor unexpectedly returns and puts it out before it does any harm."

A crime like this typically is treated as an "attempt," as compared to that in Scenario 1, which is referred to as the "substantive offense." As discussed in chapter 12, the expected liability here will be substantially less than that imposed in Scenario 1, even though the actor's conduct and intention are identical in the two cases. The fact is that the vast majority of lay persons share a strong intuition that whether or not the planned harm does or does not occur makes a difference; the occurrence of harm does increase the punishment deserved. No claim of justification is at issue in Scenario 2.

c. Created Risk of (Unjustified) Burning, Realized—Reckless Commission. Scenario 3, yet another contrast case, differs from Scenario 2 in that the actor only risks the burning, rather than intending it. But as in Scenario 1, here the harm actually comes about.

> Like all of the local farmers, Jake routinely piles dry cornhusks near where they are cut and eventually burns them. Jake has one such pile near his neighbor's fields. Jake wants to get the pile burned quickly; the previous year he

> waited and the pile got soaked by rain. He is aware that high winds are forecast for today; winds that create a real risk that his fire will jump the gap between his trash pile and his neighbor's corn fields. Despite this danger, Jake burns his trash pile, hoping the fire will not jump to his neighbor's crop. The winds come and the fire jumps to his neighbor's crop. The fire destroys the entire crop.

The expected liability here, as in Scenario 2, is less than that in Scenario 1. Such an offense typically is termed a "crime of recklessness."

d. Created Risk of (Unjustified) Burning, Unrealized—Endangerment. Scenario 4, another contrast case, is similar to Scenario 3, but here, the harm luckily does not come about.

"...Despite this danger, Jake burns his trash pile, hoping the fire will not jump to his neighbor's crop. The winds come but, Jake is lucky, the fire does not jump to his neighbor's crop."

The expected liability here is less than in Scenario 3. Liability also will be less than in Scenario 2 because here the actor does not intend the harm but only risks it. This is an application of the principle noted in chapter 12, section D that greater punishment is due for greater culpable state of mind; intending to burn is more culpable than intending to create a risk of burning, all other things being equal. Offenses like this commonly are termed "endangerment" offenses. No claim of justification is at issue in the scenario.

These four cases present variations of the culpability and harm variables, as is evident from Table 88.

e. Attempted Risk Creation—Attempted Endangerment. Scenario 5 is a contrast case in which the actor thinks he is creating a criminal risk, but in fact no such risk is created. In other words, it is a case of attempted endangerment rather than the actual endangerment of Scenario 4. "...Despite this danger, Jake burns his trash pile, hoping the fire will not jump to his neighbor's crop. It turns out that the weather forecast was in error about the wind. Jake's burning never creates any danger to his neighbor's field."

It is expected that even less liability will be given than Scenario 4. In Scenario 4, a risk of the harm was in fact created, while here no such risk is created; the actor only mistakenly believes that it is created. Scenario 5 (risk intended but no risk occurs) bears the same relation to Scenario 4 (risk intended and risk occurs)

TABLE 88. } Interrelation of Contrast Cases 1 through 4

	Harm	No Harm
Intentional	Scenario 1 Substantive Offense	Scenario 2 Attempt
Reckless	Scenario 3 Reckless Offense	Scenario 4 Endangerment

Scenario 5. Attempted Risk Creation—Attempted Endangerment

that Scenario 2 (burning intended but does not occur) bears to Scenario 1 (burning intended and occurs). No claim of justification is at issue in the scenario.

f. Intentional Justified Burning. Scenario 6 is the final contrast case, one in which the burning occurs but is clearly justified, under both a reasons and a deeds theory. Not only did the objective circumstances that make the burning the right thing to do actually exist, but the actor knows of the justifying circumstances and acts because of them.

> Jake hears over his Citizen's Band radio that lightning has started a fire upwind from his and his neighbor's fields and the local town and that the fire is burning toward the town and endangering the people who live there. He can see the smoke from the approaching fire and calculates that if he burns his neighbor's corn crop he can create a firebreak that will stop the fire. (Remember that Jake's own field is not located where it could serve as a firebreak.) Jake knows that his neighbor is not available to ask for permission, and he burns the fields. The fire destroys the entire crop. Because of his quick work the town and its inhabitants are saved.

It is expected that Jack will get a complete defense in this scenario.

Together these six contrast cases give the full range of possible liability, as well as a variety of intermediate points. They give results of considerable intrinsic interest in their own right, but more importantly for the present purposes, they allow for interpretation of the liability results of the remaining six scenarios. By using them as a point of comparison, the contrast scenario can be used for each test scenario most relevant from the point of view of the competing theories, from a case of an intentional unjustified burning to a completely justified burning, or any one of the many possibilities between those two extremes on the continuum of liability. Taken together, these six cases represent all of the obvious variations of a non-justification case to which the subjects' responses might be compared.

2. TEST CASES

Scenarios 7 through 11 are justification test cases:

a. Unknowingly Justified Burning. Turn now to the scenarios that discriminate between the two competing theories. Scenario 7 is the case of the unknowingly justified actor.

> Jake is angry with his neighbor over a dispute about use of water from a creek that the two share. When he knows that his neighbor is away, he sets fire to the neighbor's three acres of corn. Because the field is bounded on all sides by dirt roads, it is clear that the burning will create no danger beyond that of destroying the neighbor's corn. The fire destroys the entire crop. *Unbeknownst to Jake*, lightning has started a fire upwind from his and his neighbor's fields and the local town and the fire is burning toward the town and endangering the

> people who live there. His burning the field creates a firebreak: the town and its inhabitants are saved.

Recall that the deeds theory, which is suggested to better represents community views, predicts this liability to be similar to that of Scenario 2, the attempt case. The actor's liability is based entirely upon his intention to burn without justification, the classic rationale for punishing an attempt. The reasons theory predicts that the actor will have no defense and therefore will be liable for the full offense, the same as liability as seen in Scenario 1.

b. Knowingly Justified Burning but with Bad Motive. Scenario 8 is a case where the justifying circumstances exist and the actor knows about them, but he acts for a bad motive, rather than for a justificatory purpose.

> Jake hears over his Citizen's Band radio that lightning has started a fire upwind from his and his neighbor's fields and the local town and that the fire is burning toward the town and endangering the people who live there. He can see the smoke from the approaching fire and calculates that if he burns his neighbor's corn crop he can create a firebreak that will stop the fire. (Remember that Jake's own field is not located where it could serve as a firebreak.) Jake has no interest in saving the town; the townspeople have always been unfriendly to him. Further, Jake is angry with his neighbor over a dispute about use of water from a creek that the two share. He decides to use the fire as an excuse to burn his neighbor's corn crop. Without asking his neighbor for permission, he burns the fields. The fire destroys the entire crop. Because of his quick work the town and its inhabitants are saved.

This is an interesting case because, as stated in section A, most jurisdictions implement the reasons theory by defense formulations that require only that the actor "believe" that the justifying circumstances exist. They do not require that the actor act for the justifying "purpose," even though "purpose" is a standard culpability level commonly required by other criminal law doctrines. Contrary to the legal rules, which give the same complete defense for either a justificatory purpose or just knowledge of the justifying circumstances, the community may find a difference between the two cases.

The prediction is that, while the person who acts for the justificatory purpose, as in Scenario 6, will receive a complete defense, no liability, the person who acts only knowing of the justifying circumstances but with a purpose other than to avoid the greater harm, will have some level of liability imposed.

A strict reasons theory might give no defense here. While the actor knew of the justifying circumstances, they were not his reason for acting. But the reasons theory as adopted in current law treats this actor as fully justified, thus imposing no liability.

The deeds theory would give this actor a significant discount from full liability, at least as great as that given the unknowingly justified actor, because while his motive may be bad, his conduct is objectively justified. On the other hand, the actor in Scenario 8 at least does not think that he is causing a net harm, and therefore it is expected that he will have less liability than the unknowingly justified actor of Scenario 7, who does think so.

c. Mistake as to Justification, Reasonable. These first two test scenarios present variations on the unknowingly justified actor. The next three scenarios consider the reverse case of the actor who mistakenly believes he is justified. The person setting the fire thinks that he has a justification for doing so, but his reasons for thinking this become increasingly poorly grounded.

Scenario 9 presents the case of a reasonable mistake as to a justification.

> Jake hears over his Citizen's Band radio that lightning has started a fire upwind from his and his neighbor's fields and the local town and that the fire is burning toward the town and endangering the people who live there. In the past, Citizen's Band radio reports have often been true, but also often false. Jake stops two cars that are racing into town, and both confirm that "there is a big, out of control fire, heading this way." (Any reasonable person would think there was a destructive fire coming.) Jake can see the smoke from the approaching fire and calculates that if he burns his neighbor's corn crop he can create a firebreak that will stop the fire. (Remember that Jake's own field is not located where it could serve as a firebreak.) Jake knows that his neighbor is not available to ask for permission, and he burns the fields. The fire destroys the entire crop. It turns out that the radio report was in error. The smoke was from a controlled burn being done by a crew of local foresters and presented no danger to the town or any of the surrounding area.

Both deeds and reasons theories would give a complete defense. Only the labeling would be different. The deeds theory would consider the actor excused; the reasons theory would consider the actor justified. All jurisdictions agree that a full defense is appropriate in this case; no issue of mitigation arises. Both the deeds theory and the reasons theory predict no liability.

d. Mistake as to Justification, Negligent. Scenario 10 is a case of a negligent mistake as to a justification.

> In the past, Citizen's Band radio reports have often been true, but also often false. Jake doesn't think of this, and although a reasonable person would do so, Jake doesn't think to check on the truth of the report, but there is no doubt in his mind that it is a dangerous fire. Jake can see the smoke from the approaching fire and calculates that if he burns his neighbor's corn crop he can create a firebreak that will stop the fire.

Those jurisdictions that require a reasonable mistake for a defense, a majority of reasons theory jurisdictions, would deny any defense here and would impose full liability, as in Scenario 1. The jurisdictions that do recognize mitigation for an unreasonable mistake as to a justification, which includes the few deeds jurisdictions, will impose more liability than the complete defense in Scenario 6, but notably less than the full liability of Scenario 1 that the majority view predicts.

e. Mistake as to Justification, Reckless. Scenario 11 is a case of a reckless mistake as to a justification, where there is greater culpable state of mind than in Scenario 10, but the actor still honestly and sincerely believes that he is acting justifiably.

> In the past, Citizen's Band radio reports have often been true, but also often false. Jake remembers this fact, and realizes there might not be a dangerous fire, but doesn't check on the truth of the report. He can see the smoke from the approaching fire and calculates that if he burns his neighbor's corn crop he can create a firebreak that will stop the fire.

The majority all-or-nothing approach again would give no defense and would impose full liability, as in Scenario 1. The mitigation approach again would give a mitigation from full liability, although not as much as the mitigation given in Scenario 10. Thus, it is predicted that the liability here will be greater than that in Scenario 10, but markedly less than that in Scenario 1.

The predictions and those consistent with current law are summarized in Table 89. Generally, it is expected that the subjects will agree with the predictions of the deeds theory and with mitigations for unreasonable mistakes as to a justification.

TABLE 89. } Summary of Liability Predictions

Contrast Cases	
Scenario	**Expectation**
1. Intentional commission of substantive offense	Baseline
2. Attempt	<1
3. Reckless commission	<1
4. Endangerment	<2 and 3
5. Attempted endangerment	<4
6. Justified commission	No liability

Test Cases		
Scenario	**Our Predictions (Deeds Theory)**	**Predictions Consistent with Current Law (Reasons Theory)**
7. Unknowingly justified burning	= 2 (attempted burning)	= 1 (no defense; full liability)
8. Justifying knowledge without justificatory purpose	> 6, but < 7	= 6 (complete justification)
9. Reasonable mistake as to justification (MJ)	= 6 (complete excuse)	(complete justification)
10. Negligent MJ	> 6, but < 1	= 1 (no defense; full liability)
11. Reckless MJ	> 6 and 10, but < 1	= 1 (no defense; full liability)

C. Liability Results

The mean liability for each of the scenarios is set out in Table 90.

1. CONTRAST CASES

First, consider the results for the cases that were designed to provide comparative information for the test cases. The Scenario 1 contrast case of intentional burning with no claim of justification has a liability mean of 4.65 (equivalent to about 10 months imprisonment). This result is what one might expect given the nature of the offense, a property offense in which no risk to persons is created.

The Scenario 2 contrast, the attempt case, has a liability of 3.52 (just over four months). This result is consistent with the expectation of substantially reduced punishment based solely on the fortuitous absence of the intended harm. Indeed, the ratio of penalties between Scenarios 1 and 2 is consistent with those jurisdictions that set the grade of an attempt as one grade less than or at half the penalty of the substantive offense.[24] Recall that on the exponential penalty scale, one unit is equivalent to one offense grade in a typical modern American criminal code, and that each higher grade typically doubles the penalty of the previous grade.

Scenario 3, in which the actor creates a risk of burning that is realized, is given a liability of 2.69 (6.2 weeks). As predicted, it is less than the liability in Scenario 1; here the actor does not intend the harm but only risks it. The importance of this

TABLE 90. } Liability Means

Scenario	Liability Mean	Imprisonment Equivalent
CONTRAST CASES		
1. Intentional (unjustified) burning	4.65	~ 10 months
2. Attempted (unjustified) burning	3.52	~ 4 months
3. Created risk of (unjustified) burning, realized	2.69	~ 6 weeks
4. Created risk of (unjustified) burning, unrealized	0.48	essentially no punishment
5. Attempted risk creation	0.42	essentially no punishment
6. Intentional justified burning	0.57	essentially no punishment
TEST CASES		
7. Unknowingly justified burning	3.63	~ 4 months
8. Knowingly justified burning but with bad motive	2.10	~ 2 weeks
9. Mistake as to justification, reasonable	1.10	~ 2 days
10. Mistake as to justification, negligent	2.02	~ 2 weeks
11. Mistake as to justification, reckless	2.33	~ 4 weeks

[24] *See* the statutes listed at Paul H. Robinson, Fundamentals of Criminal Law 297 (2nd ed. 1995).

difference in culpability level often is reflected by corresponding differences in penalties. For example, in homicide cases, this same culpability difference results in an intentional killing being punished as murder with life or long-term imprisonment or death, while a reckless killing is punished as manslaughter with a maximum penalty more in the range of 10 years.[25]

Scenario 4, a case of risk creation where the harm risked goes unrealized, receives a liability of 0.48, which is essentially no punishment (a liability mean of 1.0 is equivalent to one day imprisonment). No liability was assigned by 36.5 percent of subjects. Another 42.3 percent gave liability but no punishment. The remaining 21.2 percent gave punishment ranging from one day to six months. The deeds theory predicted low liability, from the concurrence of both the discount for no resulting harm, seen in Scenario 2, and the discount for lower culpability level, seen in Scenario 3. This additive nature of different discounts from the full intentional substantive offense was discussed in chapter 18, section C. The liability result here seems a neat accumulation of the 1.1 discount from the full offense seen in Scenario 2 and the 2.0 discount seen in Scenario 3. Thus, a perfectly additive discount would be 3.1. The liability result here shows a 3.2 discount. It seems unlikely, however, that this additive discounting always will be quite so neat. This substantial reduction is consistent with current law's treatment of such matters. In homicide, for example, creating a risk of death that is unrealized is punished as endangerment, which typically carries a maximum of only one year,[26] as compared to life imprisonment or death for murder.

Scenario 5 presents the case of attempted endangerment. As expected, the liability mean is low, 0.42. The result is only slightly less than the result in Scenario 4 (endangerment), and that small difference is not statistically significant. A difference between the two was predicted, with Scenario 5 less than Scenario 4, to reflect the absence in Scenario 5 of the risk that in fact is created in Scenario 4. The assumption is that the difference does not appear because the Scenario 4 liability is already so low no further reduction is possible. In Scenario 4, 78.8 percent of the subjects impose no punishment. That leaves little room to distinguish Scenario 5 as a case of even less blameworthiness. (In Scenario 5, 86.5 percent imposed no punishment.) If scenarios with a more serious base offense are used, such as homicide, the distinction that was expected might appear here.

Scenario 6, the final contrast case, is an intentional justified burning. As expected, it received essentially no punishment. Its liability mean was 0.57. No liability was assigned by 38.5 percent of the subjects. Another 40.4 percent gave liability but no punishment. The remaining 21.2 percent gave punishment ranging from one day to one year. This baseline is not as low as expected but still reflects the predicted

---

25 *See, e.g.,* Model Penal Code §§210.3(2) (making manslaughter a second degree felony), 6.06 (setting the maximum term of imprisonment for second degree felonies at 10 years).

26 *See, e.g., id.* §§211.2 (making reckless endangerment a misdemeanor), 6.06 (setting the maximum term of imprisonment for misdemeanors at one year).

judgment that the vast majority of subjects see this as a case of little or no blameworthiness, despite the fact that an intentional harm is caused.

To summarize the contrast case results, the results came out as predicted. Those predictions, it will be remembered, were based on two principles: a liability discount given when the harm risked did not actually occur; and a liability discount given as the harm risked altered from intentional, to reckless, to justified.

2. CASES FOR WHICH THE THEORIES OF JUSTIFICATION HAVE DIFFERENT PREDICTIONS

The first two test cases examine the community's views on cases critical to the deeds-reason debate. In Scenario 7, presenting the unknowingly justified actor, the two theories predict starkly different results, and the deeds theory predictions are confirmed. The perpetrator in Scenario 7 received a liability mean of 3.63 (just over 4 months). This result is not statistically different from the attempt contrast case in Scenario 2, as the deeds theory predicts. Such liability is dramatically less than the 4.65 liability (about 10 months) for the substantive offense that the reasons theory predicts. The deeds theory is clearly more consistent with community views on this matter.

Scenario 8 presents the case of the actor who knows of the justifying circumstances but who acts for other, non-justificatory motives. Recall that current law would give a complete defense in such a case, although logic would seem to suggest that a strict reasons theory would give no defense. The liability mean is 2.10 (2.6 weeks), not the complete defense that current law would provide—only 7.8 percent of the subjects assigned a verdict of no liability—and not the full liability that the reasons theory logically would seem to suggest. It is consistent, however, with the deeds theory prediction of liability somewhat less than that of the unknowingly justified actor. The actor is entitled to at least the discount given the unknowingly justified actor because his act is objectively justified; a greater harm is in fact avoided. Unlike the unknowingly justified actor, however, this actor's liability for attempt is less clear. His knowledge of the justifying circumstances may suggest to him that his conduct is not in fact criminal, thus he does not have the clear intention to violate the law that the unknowingly justified actor has. He might be viewed less as breaking the law than as taking advantage of it. In any case, the results again are consistent with the deeds view and inconsistent with the reasons view.

Turn next to the three scenarios in which the perpetrator, mistakenly believing that the town was in danger of a fire, set his neighbor's fields on fire to provide a firebreak. The reasonableness of the mistake varied across these three scenarios. Scenario 9 presents the case of a reasonable mistake as to a justification. Both reasons and deeds theories would give a complete defense. The subjects give liability of 1.10 (2.3 days), which is higher than expected. Further, only 17.3 percent gave the complete defense verdict of "not guilty." On the other hand, 42.3 percent gave liability but no punishment. Perhaps these subjects are concerned about the implications of giving a complete defense in a case where the conduct in fact is not justified in an objective sense. There is reason to think that they should be concerned, as discussed below in section D.3 which presents a proposal to revise acquittal verdicts.

Scenarios 10 and 11 are cases of unreasonable mistakes as to a justification. In Scenario 10, the actor honestly believes his conduct is justified but is mistaken and his mistake is negligent rather than reasonable. That is, a reasonable person in the actor's situation would have been aware of a risk that the contemplated conduct was not justified. In Scenario 11, the actor similarly honestly believes his conduct is justified and is similarly wrong. But here his mistake is more culpable; he is reckless. That is, he is aware of a risk that his conduct might not be justified, although on balance, he concludes that it is justified. He disregards the risk (that the conduct might not be justified) and proceeds with the conduct. In other words, he makes a reckless mistake as to a justification.

As expected, the subjects impose greater liability in these two cases than in the case of the reasonable mistake. Further, liability is greater in the case of greater culpability in making the mistake: 2.02 (two weeks) for the negligent mistake, 2.33 (about four weeks) for the reckless mistake. But this range of liability is considerably less than that imposed by current law's majority rule, which denies any defense or mitigation and imposes full substantive liability. In the context of this burning offense, current law's assignment of no defense would give the perpetrator ten months imprisonment, as imposed in Scenario 1, not the two weeks and four weeks that Scenarios 10 and 11, respectively, actually received. In conclusion, the subjects would very much support recognition of mitigations for unreasonable mistakes as to a justification. These results suggest that the Model Penal Code's mitigations of this sort should have not been so regularly rejected by state criminal code drafters.

D. Implications for Criminal Law Reform

With the results current in the reader's mind, this section examines the question of how criminal codes might be modified if one were to base a reformulation on the community intuitions reported here.

The results reported in the previous section confirm that much is right in current criminal law formulation. However, the results also frequently challenge criminal code formulations and suggest a variety of criminal law reforms. These alterations would involve the reformulation of offense definitions, altered formulations of what count as defenses, and an altered system of trial verdicts.

1. FORMULATION AND GRADING OFFENSES

While the study was designed to examine defenses related to justification, the results, specifically those in the contrast cases, say something about how the law ought to define offenses. In many respects, the results support the general approach of current law.

A comparison of Scenarios 1 and 2 illustrates that, although the actor's conduct and culpable state of mind are the same in the two cases, the existence of a resulting harm matters greatly in assessing liability and punishment. This outcome confirms findings in chapter 12, section B. It provides grounds to criticize that minority of state criminal codes that follow the Model Penal Code in grading attempts the same as the substantive offense.[27] The Code would have graded the offenses in Scenarios 1 and 2 the same, but the subjects gave the attempt less than half the punishment of the completed offense.

A comparison of the results in Scenarios 1 and 3, as well as in Scenarios 2 and 4, confirms current law's view that the actor's culpability level ought to have a large effect on degree of liability. Intentionally causing or trying to cause harm is dramatically more blameworthy than being reckless as to causing the same harm. This norm supports current law's grading of offenses according to culpability level, as in homicide, where intentional killing (murder) is graded more seriously than reckless killing (manslaughter).

But given the near universality of this rule, across a wide range of contexts, it also may be appropriate to criticize current law for limiting the use of culpability levels in grading to a few serious offenses. The results suggest that an actor's culpability level is significant in offenses far less serious than homicide. Even in the pure property offenses tested here, the effect of culpability level was dramatic. The intentional burning (Scenario 1) received more than seven times the punishment of the reckless burning (Scenario 3). Each point on the liability scale is equivalent to approximately one grade in a modern American criminal code. Thus, if the results here were followed, reckless burning would be graded two grades less than intentional burning. Current law, in contrast, typically grades intentional and reckless (and negligent) burning the same.[28]

2. FORMULATION OF DEFENSES

The results in the contrast cases also say something about defenses. A comparison of the results in Scenarios 1 and 6 shows clearly that a "lesser evils defense," as it is called, has strong intuitive support among the subjects. A plain language version of the defense might read like this: "You may act in a way that would otherwise be a crime if your conduct is necessary to avoid a more serious harm or evil than that caused by your conduct."[29] About half of American jurisdictions do not recognize such a defense,[30] and many of those that have recognized the defense in one case

---

[27] *See, e.g.,* Model Penal Code §5.05(1); CONN. GEN STAT. ANN. §53A-51; N.J. STAT. ANN. §2C:5-4(a); PA. CONS. STAT. ANN. tit. 18, §905(a).

[28] *See, e.g.,* Model Penal Code §220.3(1)(a).

[29] Paul H. Robinson, Peter D. Greene, and Natasha R. Goldstein, *Making Criminal Codes Functional: A Code of Conduct and a Code of Adjudication*, 86 J. CRIM. LAW AND CRIMINOLOGY 304, 344 (1996) (Appendix A, section 67).

[30] *See* authorities listed in 2 PAUL H. ROBINSON, *supra* note 909, §124 n.1 (1984).

or another have declined to codify it, leaving its availability and formulation in doubt.[31] The strength of intuitive support for the defense suggests that it ought to be formally recognized through codification everywhere.

The five test cases offer the most important new information with implications for criminal law reform. As noted in the previous section, the results in Scenario 7, as compared to Scenarios 1 and 2, suggest that the unknowingly justified actor ought to be treated as an attempter, not as a perpetrator of a full substantive offense. He has in fact avoided a greater harm; there is no net harm. An objective formulation of justification defenses, like the one quoted in the paragraph above, would achieve this result, for it would give a justification defense to the unknowingly justified actor, who would then be liable only for attempt under a provision like the Model Penal Code's: "A person is guilty of an attempt to commit a crime if, acting with the kind of culpability otherwise required for commission of the crime, he purposely engages in conduct which would constitute the crime if the attendant circumstances were as he believes them to be;..."[32] Under the circumstances as the unknowingly justified actor believes them to be, he is committing the crime; hence he is liable for an attempt to commit the crime.

In addition to justification defenses objectively defined, the law must provide a defense provision governing mistake as to a justification that would give a defense to the actor who mistakenly believes her conduct is justified. The results of Scenario 8, as compared to Scenario 6, suggest that such a provision should be formulated to give a complete defense only if the actor acts for the justificatory purpose; it ought not be enough that she simply knows of the justifying circumstances, if these were not her reason for acting. As noted above, only 7.8 percent of the subjects gave a defense to an actor who knew of the justifying circumstances but acted out for a different, malevolent motive. This result suggests that a complete defense ought to be given not where an actor "*believes* her conduct is necessary to avoid a threatened greater harm," but only where she engages in the offense conduct "*in order to* avoid a threatened greater harm."

One may wonder, however, whether such an increased defense requirement has practical utility. It is not impossible, but certainly difficult, for a court to know whether an actor acts for the proper purpose. An actor who knows of the justifying circumstances generally would have little difficulty persuading a court that the proper purpose is the source of her motivation. Further, the case where the justificatory purpose is not present, as in Scenario 8, will be rare. All things considered, it may not be worth the trouble to have the defense formulation distinguish between purpose and simple belief.

The real dispute in formulating the mistake as to a justification defense is whether to allow mitigation for an unreasonable mistake. As noted above, the results in Scenarios 10 and 11 show that the subjects give a significant mitigation in such cases

---

[31] *See id.*

[32] Model Penal Code §5.01(1)(a).

from the full liability given in Scenario 1. The current law's majority rule, then, is badly out of step with the subjects' views. In the case of a reckless mistake, the subjects would give one tenth the liability given for the full offense. For a negligent mistake, the subjects would give one twentieth of that for the full offense. These are substantial mitigations, in cases in which current law commonly gives none.

How might code drafters formulate mistake as to a justification defenses to incorporate this mitigation approach? The basic defense might read something like the following: "An actor is excused for her conduct constituting an offense if her conduct would be justified had the attendant circumstances been as she believed them to be." The effect of this provision would be to provide a mistake as to a justification excuse to a person who honestly believed her conduct to be justified. Another provision would then impose liability upon those actors whose mistakes were culpable, varying the level of liability with the level of culpability of the mistake.[33] Such a provision might provide: "When an actor is reckless or negligent in assessing the circumstances that justify her conduct, the mistake as to a justification excuse [quoted above] is not available for an offense for which recklessness or negligence, as the case may be, is sufficient to establish liability."[34] Thus, a person who intentionally kills another believing that such killing is justified but who is reckless in having such a belief, would be liable for only reckless homicide (manslaughter), not intentional homicide (murder). A person who is negligent in so believing would be liable for only negligent homicide.

3. REFORM OF ACQUITTAL VERDICT FORMS

Recall the peculiar results in Scenario 9, in which the actor makes an entirely reasonable mistake, is blameless, and few subjects impose any significant punishment, yet only 17.3 percent give the actor a defense. If the subjects thought that no punishment is appropriate, why would they impose liability? The puzzle here presents a nice illustration of the general point made above, and helps to illustrate the usefulness of the acquittal verdict reform first suggested there.

One argument made in support of the deeds theory is that it helps make a distinction that is important to effective operation of criminal justice: the distinction between (1) conduct not punished because it is the right thing to do—it avoids a greater harm and one would want it to be performed under similar circumstances in the future; and (2) conduct not punished because, while it is wrong—it does not avoid a greater harm, one would not want it performed in similar circumstances in the future, but the actor in fact is blameless for performing the wrongful conduct. Recall from the introduction to this chapter that this is the classic distinction between a justification and an excuse. The deeds theory allows this distinction to be

[33] This is the structural approach of the Model Penal Code. *See* Model Penal Code §3.09(2).

[34] This language is modeled after Model Penal Code §3.09(2). It suffers from a number of technical problems that are beyond the scope of this book. *See* Paul H. Robinson, Criminal Law 463–64 (1997).

made manifest by distinguishing cases of mistake as to a justification from cases of objective justification, labeling the former excuses and only the latter justifications.

Under this approach, an actor acquitted under a justification defense provides an example to others of conduct that they are free to repeat in similar circumstances in the future. An actor excused under a mistake as to a justification excuse, in contrast, provides an example to others of conduct that they ought not perform in similar circumstances in the future. The actor is being acquitted *despite* her wrongful conduct. The reasons theory, by combining truly justified conduct with mistake as to a justification by terming both "justified," makes it impossible to make this distinction.

This tension between judging the *actor* and judging the *act* may well have influenced the subjects in Scenario 9, in which 71.2 percent gave the actor essentially no punishment—either no liability, liability but no punishment, or one day imprisonment, which might have been seen as a symbolic gesture. If no punishment is the strong majority view of the group, why did only 17.3 percent give a defense, no liability? They may well have been concerned about the precedential effect of such outright acquittals, the message that it would send to others. Would it be taken to weaken the prohibition against such burnings generally?

That is, certainly a danger in a system like the current one, which does not distinguish between justified conduct, which the law is happy to have repeated by others in similar circumstances, and excused conduct, which the law does not want repeated. Both cases are acquitted under current practice with the same verdict of "not guilty." If the only choice available is "not guilty," with no justification or excuse distinction, jurors are likely to feel uncomfortable acquitting in cases of excuse, for fear of the ease with which the verdict can be misunderstood. On the other hand, they also would feel uncomfortable exposing to substantial punishment with a "guilty" verdict a person they thought blameless.[35]

The subjects were offered a way out of this dilemma and they embraced it. They are offered a choice of "liability but no punishment," which gives them the opportunity to avoid punishing a blameless actor but also to condemn the conduct as something that ought not be repeated.

While this approach is a useful research device and has revealed interesting information, it is not a solution to the practical problem in real life, for juries have little role in the sentencing process. Once they give a verdict of "liability" of any sort, it is for the court to sentence. The offense for which the jury convicts sets a statutory maximum above which the sentencing judge cannot go, but, unless they give a defense, they cannot otherwise assure that the actor will get no punishment or only symbolic punishment, as the study allows its subjects. Further, the "liability but no punishment" option has the disadvantage of imposing liability on a blameless defendant. In the real world, where criminal conviction can bring moral condemnation and stigmatization, as well as other collateral disadvantages in jobs, licensing,

---

[35] *See* Paul H. Robinson, Structure and Function in Criminal Law 146–48 (Oxford 1997).

and the like, such liability is unfair. Thus, even if jurors had sentencing power, this solution to the problem—liability with no punishment—has the effect of imposing the condemnation and stigma of criminal conviction on a blameless offender who does not deserve it. Jurors are forced between the two bad choices of doing injustice or undermining the prohibition against such conduct in the future.

The better resolution is to formally recognize distinct acquittal verdicts of "justified" and "excused," in which the former approves of the actor's conduct and the latter disapproves of it. An objectively justified actor receives a verdict of "justified," thereby approving of the conduct, while the actor who mistakenly believes she is justified is "excused," thereby disapproving of the conduct.[36]

E. Conclusions

The results reported here illustrate the potential usefulness of social science research for resolving disputes in criminal law theory. Properly constructed studies can resolve competing claims among criminal law theorists over which theory or rule better accords with people's intuitions of justice. Here the deeds theory of justification better accords with community views than the reasons theory.

Further, such studies also generate specific reform proposals that would make the criminal justice system more just in its operation. The results in this study suggest both a reformulation of many aspects of offense definitions, as well as reforms to justification defenses and defenses and mitigations for mistake as to a justification, and suggest a reform of jury acquittal verdicts. Upon the researchers examination and hopefully upon the reader's examination, these suggestions for reform appear coherent, and are ones that adequately balance the competing considerations that govern judgments about these difficult cases in which the reason for and the outcome of the perpetrator's acts are in conflict. They are, in other words, reasonable candidates for code adoption. Reforms of this sort, that bring criminal law's principles of justice closer to those of the community, increase the law's moral credibility, which in turn increases its long-term effectiveness in crime control.

---

[36] Details for such a verdict system can be found in other works. *See id.* at 204–07.

21 }

Guiding Judicial Discretion: Extralegal Punishment Factors

The criminal law's formal criteria for assessing punishment are typically contained in criminal codes, the rules of which fix an offender's liability and the grade of the offense. Those rules commonly look to an offender's blameworthiness, taking account of both the seriousness of the harm or evil of the offense as well as an offender's culpability and mental capacity. Courts generally examine these desert-based factors as they exist at the time of the offense. Modern crime-control theory sometimes prompts code drafters to look also at certain circumstances beyond the offense itself—such as at prior criminal record—on the grounds that such factors relate to the crime-control goals of deterrence and incapacitation.[1]

A look at how the punishment decision-making process actually works in practice, however, suggests that courts and other decision makers frequently go beyond the factors that the criminal law formally recognizes. It is these extralegal punishment factors (XPFs) that are the subject of this chapter. XPFs include matters as diverse as an offender's apology, remorse, history of good or bad deeds, public acknowledgment of guilt, special talents, old age, extralegal suffering from the offense, as well as forgiveness or outrage by the victim, and special hardship of the punishment for the offender or his family. Such XPFs can make a difference at any point in the criminal justice process at which decision makers exercise discretion, such as when prosecutors decide which charge to press; when judges decide which sentence to impose; when parole boards decide when to release a prisoner; and when executive officials decide whether to grant clemency; as well as in less-visible exercises of discretion, such as in decisions by police officers and trial jurors.

What effect, if any, are these XPFs having in the exercise of discretion by criminal justice decision makers? What effect should they have? If such XPFs should be taken into account, how should this be done? These are the questions addressed here.

Section A sketches the variety of XPFs that are being given effect and illustrates decision makers' reliance on them. For each XPF examined here, some claim

---

[1] *See generally* Paul H. Robinson, Distributive Principles of Criminal Law: Who Should Be Punished How Much? (2008) (addressing the various considerations commonly utilized in apportioning punishment).

has been made, through explicit argument or open practice, that reliance on the factor in determining punishment is appropriate. The support for some XPFs has blossomed into official approval in appellate court opinions or in sentencing guidelines, usually signaling decision makers that the factor may be relied on, but rarely requiring it.

There are good reasons to want to know how people feel about XPFs as a basis for adjusting punishment, as detailed in part II. Section B reports the results of an empirical study, showing which factors have intuitive support among lay persons and to what extent. Section C examines the implications of these findings for criminal justice reform. This chapter is drawn primarily from portions of my article with Sean Jackowitz and Dan Bartels, *Extralegal Punishment Factors: A Study of Forgiveness, Hardship, Good-Deeds, Apology, Remorse, and Other Such Discretionary Factors in Assessing Criminal Punishment*.[2]

A. Extralegal Punishment Factors

Extralegal punishment factors (XPFs), as defined here, include any factor that may influence the determination of what punishment an offender should receive other than (1) factors relating to the harm or evil of the offense, (2) factors relating to the blameworthiness of the offender in committing the offense, or (3) factors relating to the classic coercive crime-control principles of deterrence or incapacitation. Many, if not most, factors considered at sentencing, even discretionary factors, are not XPFs. The mental capacity of the offender may influence a judge's determination of the appropriate sentence, yet it is a factor that relates to the offender's blameworthiness, hence not an XPF as defined here. The notion of "mercy" may be an XPF as defined here, but in fact is sometimes used to refer to the consideration of factors such as an offender's youth, prior record, or rotten social background,[3] which relate directly to notions of blameworthiness and deserved punishment. A more narrow meaning of mercy, which refers to foregoing punishment that is in fact deserved, might well include reference to XPFs—such as forgiveness by the victim or hardship to the offender's family.

Legislatures or sentencing commissions have recognized some XPFs as permissible grounds for aggravation or mitigation, but they rarely gives rise to a requirement that a sentencing judge do so.[4] Rather, XPFs come into play when judges exercise their sentencing discretion, "taking into consideration various factors relating both to

---

[2] Paul H. Robinson, Sean Jackowitz, & Daniel M. Bartels, *Extralegal Punishment Factors: A Study of Forgiveness, Hardship, Good-Deeds, Apology, Remorse, and Other Such Discretionary Factors in Assessing Criminal Punishment* (UNIV. PA. L. SCH., Pub. Law Research Paper No. 11-12, 2011).

[3] *See, e.g.*, Richard Delgado, *"Rotten Social Background": Should the Criminal Law Recognize a Defense of Severe Environmental Deprivation?* 3 LAW & INEQ. 9, 10 (1985) (suggesting that socioeconomic deprivation may mitigate criminal responsibility and warrant recognition as a criminal defense).

[4] In the Model Penal Code formulation, for instance, the presence of some XPF in a death penalty case may give rise to a mandatory mitigation. *See* MODEL PENAL CODE §210.6 (2001) (withdrawn 2009).

offense and offender."[5] In the federal context, for example, Congress clamped down on judicial discretion by creating the U.S. Sentencing Commission and empowering it to enact mandatory Sentencing Guidelines. This discretion reemerged in the wake of the Supreme Court's decision in *United States v. Booker*,[6] which "stripped the Guidelines of the force of law" and "enhanced the position of the judge" to make discretionary sentencing decisions.[7] Thus, the decision of whether to mitigate or aggravate punishment in light of some XPF begins and often ends with the sentencing judge; and consistency in the application of XPFs to specific cases is lacking, even though an XPF can have a real effect on the amount of punishment an offender receives.[8]

Rather than examine every plausible XPF, the only ones examined were those for which there is some defensible argument that has been made, or could be made, for seriously taking them into account. For example, while some decision makers might in fact be influenced by an offender's race or physical attractiveness,[9] no one seriously argues that such practices *should* be followed. The goal here is in providing guidance to reformers, so only those XPFs that have at least some colorable claim to legitimacy were considered. The 18 factors discussed below fit these criteria. None directly relates to offense harm, offender blameworthiness, or coercive crime-control principles, and each either has at least some apparent use in current practice or support by punishment theorists.

The 18 XPFs are divided into four general categories: XPFs that relate to (1) the offender's reaction to his own offense, (2) the victim's or public's reaction to the offense, (3) the offender's status or character, and (4) the collateral hardship that normal punishment may cause the offender or third parties.

1. OFFENDER REACTION TO THE OFFENSE: REMORSE, APOLOGY, AND ACKNOWLEDGMENT OF GUILT

An offender's conduct *after* an offense typically has no effect on his blameworthiness *for* the offense. All of the information necessary to assess blameworthiness generally exists as soon as the offense has been committed. Nonetheless, what

[5] Apprendi v. New Jersey, 530 U.S. 466, 481 (2000).

[6] *See* 543 U.S. 220, 245 (2005) (Breyer, J., remedial opinion) (finding "the provision of the federal sentencing statute that makes the Guidelines mandatory . . . incompatible with today's constitutional holding." (internal citations omitted)).

[7] Nancy Gertner, *A Short History of American Sentencing: Too Little Law, Too Much Law, or Just Right*, 100 NW U. L. REV. 691, 706 (2010).

[8] In federal court, inconsistency in guideline departures was apparent even before *Booker*. *See* Michael S. Gelacek et al., *Departures under the Federal Sentencing Guidelines: An Empirical and Jurisprudential Analysis*, 81 MINN. L. REV. 299, 363–65 (1996).

[9] *See* David A. Abwender & Keyatta Hough, *Interactive Effects of Characteristics of Defendant and Mock Juror on U.S. Participants' Judgement and Sentencing Recommendations*, 141 J. SOC. PSYCHOL. 603 (2001) (demonstrating through empirical study that the physical attractiveness of an offender may be influential in punishment determinations by juries); Paul Skolnick & Jerry I. Shaw, *The O.J. Simpson Criminal Trial Verdict: Racism or Status Shield?*, 53 J. SOCIAL ISSUES 503 (1997) (finding that considerations of race may place a role in punishment determinations).

an offender does after committing an offense may have an effect on the proper level of punishment, at least insofar as lay people intuit. This section examines the extralegal punishment factors that most commonly take into account post-offense conduct.

a. Acknowledgment of Guilt. Perhaps the most widely recognized XPF is a defendant's acknowledgment of guilt. In federal court, the discount is formalized: The U.S. Sentencing Guidelines Manual calls for a two-step decrease in offense level if "the defendant clearly demonstrates acceptance of responsibility for his offense."[10] The Guidelines Commentary lists seven factors for judges to take into account in determining whether a defendant qualifies, including "truthfully admitting the conduct comprising the offense[]" and "the timeliness of the defendant's conduct in manifesting the acceptance of responsibility."[11] The Commission has also noted that additional mitigation "may be warranted" when "the defendant voluntarily discloses to authorities the existence of, and accepts responsibility for, the offense prior to the discovery of such offense, and if such offense was unlikely to have been discovered otherwise."[12] But a defendant who acknowledges his guilt only after he is convicted cannot expect much leniency. The guidelines make clear that "this adjustment is not intended to apply to a defendant who puts the government to its burden of proof"; only in "rare situations" may an offender demonstrate acceptance of responsibility *and* go through the ritual of a trial.[13]

Acknowledgment of guilt is also a powerful mitigator in many state courts. A few states parallel the federal guidelines with statutes providing that judges should consider a defendant's acknowledgment of guilt at sentencing.[14] It is more common, however, for states to require more from defendants than merely an acknowledgment of their wrongdoing. New Jersey, for example, allows judges to consider "the willingness of the offender to cooperate with law enforcement authorities" as a mitigating factor.[15] In fact, New Jersey judges are prohibited from considering a guilty plea without more,[16] though in this regard New Jersey is an outlier. Other states allow a mitigation when offenders provide assistance to authorities but do not explicitly bar judges from considering an acknowledgment of guilt in and of

---

[10] U.S. SENTENCING GUIDELINES MANUAL §3E1.1 (2010).

[11] *Id.* §3E1.1 cmt. n.1.

[12] *Id.* §5K2.16.

[13] U.S. SENTENCING GUIDELINES MANUAL §3E1.1 cmt. n.2 (2010).

[14] *See* GA. CODE ANN. §17-10-2(a) (allowing a judge to consider a "plea[] of guilty" as a mitigating factor); N.C. GEN. STAT. §15A-1340.16(e)(11) (listing as a mitigating factor when "[p]rior to arrest or at an early stage of the criminal process, the defendant voluntarily acknowledged wrongdoing in connection with the offense to a law enforcement officer."); CAL. CT. R. 4.423(b)(3) (recognizing mitigating factors in cases where "[t]he defendant voluntarily acknowledged wrongdoing before arrest or at an early stage of the criminal process").

[15] N.J. STAT. ANN. §2C:44-1(b)(12).

[16] *Id.*§2C:44-1(c)(1) ("A plea of guilty by a defendant or failure to so plead shall not be considered in withholding or imposing a sentence of imprisonment.").

itself.[17] Some theorists have advocated a reduction in punishment where an offender has admitted guilt, irrespective of his motivation.[18]

b. True Remorse. "True remorse" involves a sincere expression of contrition for the commission of the offense. Such remorse might be expressed independently of, or in conjunction with, an acknowledgment of guilt. Several writers have advocated the use of true remorse as a mitigator of punishment. Jeffrie Murphy writes that "[t]he repentant person has a better character than the unrepentant person, and thus the repentant person—on this theory—simply deserves less punishment than the unrepentant person."[19] In the same vein, Austin Sarat has argued that "remorse blunts the edge of retribution; it engenders forgiveness.... [a]nd, if not forgiveness, remorse at least seems to call for mitigation of punishment."[20]

Several jurisdictions treat true remorse as a discretionary consideration. The United States Sentencing Guidelines suggest that "a downward departure...*might* be considered where a defendant, motivated by remorse, discloses an offense that otherwise would have remained undiscovered."[21] Many states similarly permit the use of remorse as a mitigating factor.[22] The Supreme Court of Florida, for example, has held that "any convincing evidence of remorse may properly be considered in mitigation of the sentence."[23] As recently as 2002, an Indiana Supreme Court overturned a sentence due in part to a failure to consider testimony pertaining to the offender's expressions of remorse for her crime.[24] Some state statutes also allow evidence of a *lack* of remorse to be used as an aggravator for criminal sentencing.[25] State courts in some instances have sanctioned aggravation for lack of remorse through case law.[26] Analyses have shown that sentencing judges commonly give lighter punishment to remorseful offenders.[27]

c. Apology. A simple expression of apology from the offender to the victim of a crime is often thought to be worthy of consideration as a mitigation. The sentencing

---

17 *See* Robinson, Jackowitz, & Bartels, *Extralegal Punishment Factors*, *supra* note 937, at n. 20.

18 *See, e.g.,* Frank H. Easterbrook, *Plea Bargaining as Compromise*, 101 YALE L. J. 1969 (1992); Robert E. Scott & William J. Stuntz, *Plea Bargaining as Contract*, 101 YALE L.J. 1909 (1992).

19 JEFFRIE MURPHY, REPENTANCE, PUNISHMENT, AND MERCY, IN ETZIONI & CARNEY, REPENTANCE: A COMPARATIVE PERSPECTIVE 143, 157 (1997).

20 AUSTIN SARAT, REMORSE, RESPONSIBILITY, AND CRIMINAL PUNISHMENT: AN ANALYSIS OF POPULAR CULTURE, IN THE PASSIONS OF LAW 169 (Susan Bandes ed., 1999).

21 U.S. SENTENCING GUIDELINES MANUAL §5K2.16 (2004) (emphasis added).

22 State v. Trostle, 951 P.2d 869, 887 (Ariz. 1997); Jackson v. State, 684 So. 2d 1213, 1238 (Miss. 1996); State v. Allen, 994 P.2d 728, 764 (N.M. 2000).

23 Pope v. State, 441 So.2d 1073, 1078 (Fla. 1983). Florida also recognizes remorse as a mitigating factor by statute. FLA. STAT. §921.0026(2)(j) (recognizing as a mitigating factor when "[t]he offense was committed in an unsophisticated manner and was an isolated incident for which the defendant has shown remorse.").

24 *See* Crawford v. State, 770 N.E.2d 775 (Ind. 2002).

25 *See* OHIO REV. CODE ANN. §2929.12(D)(5).

26 *See, e.g.,* McAbee v. State, 770 N.E.2d 802, 806 (Ind. 2002); People v. Griswold, 747 N.Y.S.2d 872, 873 (N.Y. App. Div. 2002); State v. Mollicone, 746 A.2d 135, 138 (R.I. 2000); State v. Clegg, 635 N.W.2d 578, 580 (S.D. 2001).

27 *See, e.g.,* STANTON WHEELER ET AL., SITTING IN JUDGMENT: THE SENTENCING OF WHITE-COLLAR CRIMINALS 115–18 (1992).

courts of most states draw a significant distinction, however, between apology and remorse, generally refusing to recognize the former as a legitimate reason to mitigate, at least not without some other indication that it signals the latter. "Courts often view [simple statements of apology] as per se inadequate and take offense to the notion that saying "sorry" is enough."[28] Often, courts will closely parse the language of an offender's statement of apology in order to determine whether true remorse is present. Examples of such refusals to mitigate based on a close examination of an offender's apology abound: an Indiana court concluded that an offender's statement that he was "very sorry about what happened," was "'equivocal at best' and 'well short of a full acceptance of responsibility.'"[29] The Rhode Island Supreme Court similarly upheld a trial court's denial of apology-based mitigation on the grounds that "[t]he trial justice apparently detected no salt in [offender's] tears; nor do we."[30] The Pennsylvania Superior Court affirmed a trial court's unmitigated sentence due to a lack of credible remorse, holding favorably that "in reply [to offender's apologies and excuses] the sentencing court noted '[w]e heard your talk... but talk is cheap. You are judged on your actions.'"[31]

One area in which a bare apology (without any indication of remorse) seems to be acceptable for consideration in state courts is in capital sentencing, during which sentencing juries may "not be precluded from considering, as a mitigating factor, any aspect of a defendant's character or record and any of the circumstances of the offense that the defendant proffers as a basis for a sentence less than death."[32] The sentencing jury is, of course, not required to give weight to all mitigating factors advanced by the offender, but states cannot prohibit consideration of an apology in capital sentencing.[33]

2. VICTIM OR PUBLIC REACTION TO THE OFFENSE (UNRELATED TO DESERT): VICTIM FORGIVENESS; DEMAND FOR MORE PUNISHMENT, OR FOR LESS; PUBLIC OUTRAGE

Parties other than offenders in criminal cases may exert influence on the amount of punishment imposed. Extralegal punishment factors involving such parties include opinions and representations to the court made by victims or third parties, many of whom have no relation to the events that led to the prosecution, but who are nonetheless interested in the punishment imposed on the offender.

a. Forgiveness by Victim. In the unusual case in which a victim forgives an offender prior to sentencing, an argument might be made that the victim's feelings—even absent requests for leniency—should play a role in determining the appropriate

---

[28] Bryan H. Ward, *Sentencing without Remorse*, 38 LOY U. CHI. L.J. 131, 143 (2006)

[29] *Id.* at 144 (quoting Price v. State, 765 N.E.2d 1245 (Ind. 2002)).

[30] *Id.* at 144–45 (quoting State v. Thornton, 800 A.2d 1016 (R.I. 2002)).

[31] Commonwealth v. Tirado, 870 A.2d 362 (Pa. Super. Ct. 2005).

[32] Lockett v. Ohio, 438 U.S. 586, 604–05 (1978) (emphasis omitted).

[33] *Id.*

punishment. Stephanos Bibas has argued that "the state should take the victim's interests into account by giving weight to the victim's forgiveness."[34] According to Bibas, doing so will promote emotional healing on the part of the victim, humble the offender, place the victim above the offender in the societal power continuum, and satisfy victims' psychological needs.[35]

Courts routinely hear victim opinions through victim impact statements. Indeed, 48 states protect the rights of victims to participate in allocution in sentencing, and in the remaining 2 states judges have discretion to allow victim participation.[36] Some victims will choose to use their statement as an opportunity to express forgiveness for the offender.

b. Victim Punishment Demand. As opposed to the simple fact of victims' emotional expressions, this punishment factor concerns actual demands by a victim or some other party, either for greater or lesser punishment. Such punishment demands may arise apart from any forgiveness on the part of the victim. The life sentence imposed on Aaron McKinney, one of two teenagers convicted for the brutal murder of Matthew Shepard, is illustrative.[37] Although Shepard's parents never forgave McKinney for his crime, they insisted that prosecutors refrain from seeking the death penalty.[38] Instead, McKinney was given a plea agreement of life in prison without parole.[39]

Some have argued in favor of permitting victims to express their views of the appropriate punishment level of punishment.[40] While it is common practice to allow victims to offer general impact statements, only a few states give crime victims a right to offer sentence recommendations.[41] In some states, victim impact statements are expressly forbidden from including sentencing requests. In Texas, for example, victims are generally precluded from offering such opinions.[42] The Court of Appeals of Texas has held that "[o]n the question of punishment [the opinions of non-expert witnesses] have little value, because the witnesses are in no better position to form an opinion than the jury itself, and the allowance of such opinions in evidence would constitute merely an appeal to sympathy or prejudice."[43]

---

[34] Stephanos Bibas, *Forgiveness in Criminal Procedure*, 4 Ohio St. J. Crim. L. 329, 338 (2007).

[35] *Id.*

[36] Paul G. Cassell, *In Defense of Victim Impact Statements*, 6 Oh. St. J. Crim. L. 611 (2009).

[37] Susan Bandes, *When Victims Seek Closure: Forgiveness, Vengeance, and the Role of Government*, 27 Fordham Urb. L.J. 1599, 1600 (2000) (examining a case study of a victim's family who influenced the sentencing decision of the court).

[38] *Id.*

[39] *Id.*

[40] Cassell has argued that such victim-impact statements "promote justice without interfering with any legitimate interests of criminal defendants.... [They] help convey valuable information to sentencing judges and have other beneficial effects." Cassell, *supra* note 971, at 611.

[41] *See, e.g.,* Ohio Rev. Code Ann. 2930.13 (C)(4) (providing that victims can include in their statements a "recommendation for an appropriate sanction or disposition for the defendant"); Randell v. State, 846 P.2d 278 (Nev. 1993) (construing Nev. Rev. Stat. Ann. §176.015 to allow victims to give testimony as to the proper sentence for an offender).

[42] Gross v. State, 730 S.W.2d 104 (Tex. Crim. App. 1987).

[43] *Id.*

When victims express an opinion, they commonly request harsh punishment for the offender,[44] as in one Nevada case where a victim stated, "I wish that [the offenders] would spend the rest of their lives in jail and that they would die there. And have every torment possible that a jail can give them."[45] Paul Cassell has argued that "even if victim impact statements lead to harsher penalties in general or to a longer sentence in a particular case, that would hardly provide a convincing reason for banning them."[46] Cassell bases this argument on the premise that "some emotion is inherently desirable in a criminal process." He suggests that victim impact statements illustrate the emotional impact of the crime, which might not be properly understood if the victim were presented as a "shadowy abstraction."[47]

Less commonly, victims may request a lower sentence than is normally imposed. There are few examples in state courts of such victim requests for leniency. In 2009, the Court of Appeals of Michigan affirmed imposition of a sentence lower than the maximum permissible, observing that "[t]he trial court considered the victims' request for leniency and imposed a shorter sentence than it would have without the request."[48] Similarly, another Michigan court affirmed a downward departure based on a victim's letter asking for leniency, explaining that "the request of the victim [and one other factor] 'keenly' and 'irresistibly' grab our attention and are of 'considerable worth' in deciding the length of the sentence."[49]

A Florida appeals court came to the opposite conclusion when faced with a similar question: while "[t]he trial court also found that a downward departure sentence was justified based on the victim's request for a non-incarcerative sentence," the appeals court concluded that because "[g]enerally, mitigating circumstances supporting a downward departure ameliorate the level of the defendant's culpability," the victim's request was not an acceptable ground for a downward departure.[50] Nonetheless, this does not seem to be a categorical rule in Florida—while other cases have overturned downward departures based on victim requests,[51] some Florida courts have approved of such departures.[52]

c. Public Punishment Demand. Public opinion is not generally considered an acceptable factor for a judge to consider in criminal sentencing. It may commonly play an important role, but not one that is openly acknowledged. Presumably, a state's legislature has already considered community views on appropriate levels of punishment

---

[44] *See* Wayne A. Logan, *Opining on Death: Witness Sentence Recommendations in Capital Trials*, 41 B.C. L. Rev. 517, 529 n.73 (2000) (collecting sources).

[45] *Randell*, 846 P.2d at 279.

[46] Cassell, *supra* note 971, at 636.

[47] *Id.*

[48] People v. Smith, 2009 WL 2136903.

[49] People v. Washington, 2004 WL 243369.

[50] State v. Knox, 990 So.2d 665 (Fla. App. 2008).

[51] *See, e.g.,* State v. Ussery, 543 So.2d 457 (Fla. App. 1989).

[52] *See, e.g.,* State v. Bernard, 744 So.2d 1134, 1136 (Fla. App. 1999); State v. Powell, 696 So.2d 789, 791 (Fla. App. 1997).

when they graded offenses and set sentencing ranges or guidelines. Appellate courts generally regard any sentence modifications made by judges for this XPF to be in error. The Vermont Supreme Court, for example, overturned an aggravated sentence imposed after a trial judge allowed into evidence 22 petitions calling for a sentence increase. The court held that "[t]he trial judge appears to have been influenced by these petitions and the close public scrutiny at the sentence review hearing. By admitting the petitions into evidence he unwittingly injected bias, prejudice and public clamor into the case. [We thus] must remand the case... and require that the hearing be held before a different judge."[53]

The Supreme Court of New Jersey has come to the same conclusion under different facts, holding that "[p]remising a sentencing decision on public outcry against a particular defendant is no mere technical error. It is nothing less than the surrender of our criminal justice system to public pressure."[54] Finally, the United States Supreme Court has also disapproved of the use of public opinion in sentencing, holding that "[t]here can be no doubt that [the constitutional safeguards attaching to criminal procedure] embrace the fundamental conception of a fair trial, and that they exclude influence or domination by either a hostile or friendly mob. There is no room at any stage of judicial proceedings for such intervention; mob law is the very antithesis of due process."[55]

Despite this bar on the consideration of public opinion, sentencing judges are still confronted with such evidence. During the sentencing phase of the trial of Lewis "Scooter" Libby, the presiding judge received over 200 letters expressing an opinion as to the appropriate punishment for Libby.[56] While the judge in that case explicitly denied considering these letters,[57] the possibility remains that other judges in similar situations might succumb to public pressure and consider public sentiment, regardless of whether such consideration is acknowledged.

3. OFFENDER STATUS OR CHARACTERISTICS (UNRELATED TO COMMISSION OF THE OFFENSE): PAST GOOD, OR BAD, CHARACTER OR DEEDS; REHABILITATION; SPECIAL TALENTS

Many of an offender's characteristics, though unrelated to his or her blameworthiness for the offense, nonetheless may influence the amount of punishment imposed. In assigning punishment, a decision maker may take into account, for example, the offender's status within a community, the offender's past actions or character, or the offender's present characteristics unrelated to the offense. Some have argued that

---

[53] State v. Rice, 483 A.2d 248 (Vt. 1984).

[54] State v. Humphreys, 444 A.2d 569 (N.J. 1982).

[55] Cox v. Louisiana, 379 U.S. 559 (1965).

[56] *See* Scott Sundby, *The Libby Letters: Reflections on Sentencing and Mercy in a Post-Booker World* (Washington & Lee Pub. Legal Studies Research Paper Series, Accepted Paper 2009-2, 2009), *available at* http://papers.ssrn.com/sol3/papers.cfm?abstract_id=1354254.

[57] *Id.*

many such characteristics ought to be considered in setting punishment for criminal offenses, despite the fact that they do not relate to the law's traditional desert or crime-control criteria for liability and punishment.

a. Offender's Good Deeds or Character. The previous good works of an offender can render him more sympathetic in the eyes of the community and in some cases those of the court. Peter Henning has argued that, at least in the context of white collar crimes, "consideration of prior good works [is] an appropriate issue in deciding sentences for defendants."[58] Other authors agree; Douglas Berman has written that "every sentencing system (guideline or otherwise) provides for sentence enhancements (often huge enhancements) based on such a record of prior bad deeds. Doesn't it make some logical sense for a sentencing system to similarly provide for sentence reductions based on a notable record of prior good deeds such as military service?"[59]

During the sentencing phase of most trials, prior convictions typically act as an aggravating factor.[60] However, "[f]ew jurisdictions explicitly recognize prior good acts as a mitigating sentencing factor. Trial judges have occasionally reduced an offender's sentence on the basis of prior good actions that are unrelated to the conviction, such as military service or charitable work."[61] Decisions recognizing good character as a mitigating factor have been overturned by higher courts or frowned upon by the U.S. Sentencing Commission.[62] Unlike the federal courts, North Carolina explicitly addresses prior deeds and character in its sentencing provisions: the state's felony sentencing statute allows for mitigation in the case of a previous honorable discharge from the military,[63] or if the person "has been a person of good character or has had a good reputation in the community."[64] Tennessee courts have recognized military service as a mitigating factor at sentencing,[65] and several other states refer to "character" as a possible consideration in sentencing.[66]

Although there is disagreement over the general issue, the picture is clearer in the context of capital sentencing. The Supreme Court held in *Lockett v. Ohio* that

---

[58] Peter J. Henning, *Prior Good Works in the Age of Reasonableness*, 20 FED. SENT'G REP. 187, 187 (2008).

[59] Douglas A. Berman, *Sentencing Law and Policy: Should Prior Military Service Reduce a Sentence? Available at* http://sentencing.typepad.com/sentencing_law_and_policy/2006/04/should_prior_mi.html (Apr. 14, 2006, 09:12).

[60] *See, e.g.,* U.S. SENTENCING GUIDELINES MANUAL §4A1.1 (2010) (instructing sentencing judges to take an offender's criminal history into account when setting his sentence).

[61] Carissa Byrne Hessick, *Why Are Only Bad Acts Good Sentencing Factors?*, 88 B.U. L. REV. 1109, 1111 (2008).

[62] *Id.*

[63] N.C. GEN. STAT. §15A-1340.16(e)(14)

[64] *Id.* §15A-1340.16(e)(12).

[65] *See, e.g.,* State v. Overton, No. 02C019510-CC00303, 1997 WL 287665, at *3 (Tenn. Crim. App. June 2, 1997) ("With respect to the appellant's military service, honorable military service may always be considered as a mitigating factor consistent with the purposes of the 1989 Sentencing Act.").

[66] For a summary of these states, see Robinson, Jackowitz, & Bartels, *Extralegal Punishment Factors*, *supra* note 937, at n. 70.

"the Eighth and Fourteenth Amendments require that the sentencer, in all but the rarest kind of capital case, not be precluded from considering, as a mitigating factor, any aspect of a defendant's character or record and any of the circumstances of the offense that the defendant proffers as a basis for a sentence less than death."[67] Thus, the admissibility of evidence of good deeds or character is constitutionally guaranteed and may be introduced as a possible mitigating factor in the sentencing phase of all death penalty cases.[68]

On the federal level, the U.S. Sentencing Guidelines do allow for mitigation in rare instances outside of capital cases. As the guidelines themselves state, "Military, civic, charitable, or public service; employment-related contributions; and similar prior good works are not *ordinarily* relevant in determining whether a departure is warranted."[69] The use of such evidence, under extraordinary circumstances, has been upheld in several circuits.[70]

b. Offender's Bad Deeds or Character. The consideration of an offender's bad character—distinct from his criminal history, which is often formally included in punishment criteria because of its usefulness in identifying dangerous offenders[71]—is often advanced as a factor appropriate for consideration in punishment.[72] For example, in his dissenting opinion in *Dawson v. Delaware*, Justice Thomas argued that evidence that a criminal offender was racist was relevant at sentencing.[73] There, Thomas argued that the offender's racist character was itself evidence of other culpable conduct, and therefore appropriate to consider as a rebuttal to mitigating character evidence as well as an indication of future dangerousness.[74] Similarly, Garvey has argued that evidence of character, good or bad, can be appropriately considered for punishment purposes, albeit in the limited context of determining whether to grant or withhold mercy in capital sentencing.[75]

State courts commonly consider offenders' character and prior acts in sentencing, even when offenders' prior actions or characteristics are unrelated to the crime at issue. For example, the Indiana Supreme Court upheld a sentence based on a trial court's finding that the offender "was 'incorrigible' and had been away from home without permission" and "had given birth to two children by the age of

---

67 438 U.S. 586 (1978).

68 Hessick, *supra* note 996, at 1119.

69 U.S. Sentencing Guidelines Manual §5H1.11 (2004) (emphasis added).

70 *See, e.g.*, United States v. Rioux, 97 F.3d 648 (2d Cir. 1996).

71 *See* U.S. Sentencing Guidelines Manual ch. 4, pt. A, introductory cmt. (2010) ("A defendant with a record of prior criminal behavior is more culpable than a first offender and thus deserving of greater punishment.").

72 Rachael A. Hill, Comment, *Character, Choice, and "Aberrant Behavior": Aligning Criminal Sentencing with Concepts of Moral Blame*, 65 U. Chi. L. Rev. 975 (1998) (citing Duff, 12 L & Phil at 363 (cited in note 30) "[An offender] is convicted if and because his action warranted an inference to an undesirable character-trait; it is that character-trait which the law condemns and punishes.").

73 503 U.S. 159, 171 (1992) (Thomas, J. dissenting).

74 *Id.* at 173–74.

75 Stephen P. Garvey, *"As the Gentle Rain From Heaven": Mercy in Capital Sentencing*, 81 Cornell L. Rev. 989 (1996).

eighteen."[76] On review, the court found these factors (among others) to be reasonable sentence aggravations. Arizona courts have similarly held that sentencing judges "should consider not only the circumstances of the offense charged but also the moral character and past conduct of the defendant himself" in assigning punishment.[77]

c. Rehabilitation. Rehabilitation has had a tortuous history in American punishment law and practice. Previously forming the foundation of penal policy at both the federal and state level,[78] rehabilitation has been roundly criticized as a vague, hard-to-apply concept in practice.[79] Nevertheless, rehabilitation continues to play a role in some sentencing courts, particularly in states that still have indeterminate sentencing.[80]

Rehabilitation of an offender as a factor in determining punishment amount is most commonly considered at parole hearings, where the parole board might consider rehabilitation in its decision whether to grant early release. While in some cases rehabilitation may take place before sentencing, judges are more likely to consider an offender's potential for rehabilitation and impose less punishment in cases where rehabilitation seems likely. Some, such as Mae Quinn, argue that "good defense lawyers have long collected mitigating evidence from the inception of the case and presented proof of rehabilitation, when appropriate, in plea negotiations and in seeking leniency at sentencing."[81] Particularly in the context of juvenile justice, defendants often argue that the potential for rehabilitation is a worthy consideration in sentencing.[82]

The U.S. Sentencing Guidelines provide that one of the factors to be considered by the administrating court is "post-offense rehabilitative efforts (e.g. counseling or drug treatment)."[83] In applying this mitigation, the Eastern District of New York held that "rehabilitation 'cannot be served if a defendant can look forward to nothing beyond imprisonment'.... It is doubtful whether [the normally imposed sentence] provides such hope."[84] The Second Circuit has concluded that, while it is inappropriate to provide harsher sentences to promote rehabilitation, it can be

---

[76] Davidson v. State, 558 N.E.2d 1077 (Ind. 1990).

[77] State v. Castano, 360 P.2d 479, 480 (Ariz. 1961).

[78] *See* Marvin E. Frankel, Criminal Sentences: Law without Order (1973).

[79] *See id.*

[80] *See* Jeremy Travis & Sarah Lawrence, The Urban Inst., Beyond the Prison Gates: The State of Parole in America 4–7 (2002), *available at* http://www.urban.org/UploadedPDF/310583_Beyond_prison_gates.pdf (noting the continued prevalence of parole boards and indeterminate sentencing in America).

[81] Mae C. Quinn, *An RSVP to Professor Wexler's Warm Therapeutic Jurisprudence Invitation to the Criminal Defense Bar: Unable to Join You, Already (Somewhat Similarly) Engaged*, 48 B.C. L. Rev 539, 574 n.181 (2007).

[82] *See, e.g.*, Connie de la Vega & Michelle Leighton, *Sentencing our Children to Die in Prison: Global Law and Practice*, 42 U.S.F. L. Rev. 983, 1008 (2008) ("The harsh sentences dispensed in adult courts do not take into account...their potential for rehabilitation and reintegration into society.").

[83] U.S. Sentencing Guidelines Manual §3E1.1 (2004).

[84] Simon v. United States, 361 F. Supp. 2d 35 (E.D.N.Y. 2005).

appropriate to consider for downward sentencing departures—giving reduced sentences to offenders who appear especially likely to be rehabilitated.[85]

The Supreme Court recently endorsed rehabilitation as a punishment factor. In *Pepper v. United States*,[86] the petitioner, who had been convicted of a drug offense, litigated his sentence for over five years.[87] During that time, petitioner not only completed a prison-based drug rehabilitation program, he also enrolled in a local community college, attained a supervisory role at a part-time job, and started a family. According to the Court, this evidence of rehabilitation "support[ed] a downward variance from the advisory [Sentencing] Guidelines range."[88] The change in conduct since his initial sentence "provided the most up-to-date picture of Pepper's 'history and characteristics.'"[89]

In the states, courts have often held that potential for rehabilitation can be a mitigating factor.[90] Interestingly, some states *require* consideration of the potential for rehabilitation in certain situations. In South Dakota, for example, "a life sentence should only be imposed where the facts and previous convictions make rehabilitation so unlikely that the interests of society are best served by lifetime incarceration."[91] Illinois has a broader requirement that rehabilitation be considered in sentencing: "There are dual considerations in sentencing. The seriousness of the offense *and* rehabilitation of the offender both are to be given weight."[92]

In most state and federal courts, the consideration of an offender's rehabilitative potential is purely discretionary. Even where a court must consider rehabilitation, as in South Dakota or Illinois, considerable discretion still remains as to the amount of mitigation, if any, with which to credit the offender.

d. Unique Talents or Special Value of Contributions to Society. The special talents of an offender may be relevant to punishment decisions where the decision maker recognizes that punishment may deprive society of those talents. William Berry has argued: "A potential example of when such mitigation would be appropriate is one in which an essential contributor to an underprivileged community commits a minor offense, and the harm to the state of giving him a custodial sentence, because of the consequences of his corresponding absence, outweighs the small diminishment in achieving retributive or utilitarian punishment goals that results from mitigation."[93] For example, a small town doctor accused of theft might be given a reduced or non-incarcerative sentence so as to keep his medical services

---

[85] United States v. Maier, 975 F.2d 944 (2d Cir. 1992).

[86] Pepper v. United States, No. 09-6822, 2011 WL 709543 (U.S. Mar. 2, 2011).

[87] *Id.* at *7–8.

[88] *Id.* at *10.

[89] *Id.* (quoting 28 U.S.C. §3553(a)(1)).

[90] Hitchcock v. Dugger, 481 U.S. 393, 398 (1986); State v. Godsey, 60 S.W.3d 759, 786 (Tenn. 2001).

[91] State v. Bult, 529 N.W.2d 197, 200 (S.D. 1995).

[92] People v. Young, 529 N.E.2d 497, 501 (Ill. 1988).

[93] William W. Berry III, *Extraordinary and Compelling: A Re-Examination of the Justifications for Compassionate Release*, 68 MD. L. REV. 850, 883 (2009).

available to the town's citizens. Similarly, a great artist or novelist might be given a reduced sentence so that society will not be deprived of her artistic contributions.

Some scholars have argued in the context of punishment in military courts that an offender's "special talents" should be taken into account in sentencing.[94] The value of the offender to his organization may be a mitigating factor worthy of consideration; a long sentence deprives the service of the offender's talents, and that deprivation must be balanced against the harm the offender has caused.[95]

An illustration of the consideration of unique talents can be seen in the dramatic story of Frank Abagnale, Jr.[96] During a criminal career spanning several continents and ultimately costing the victims of his various scams over $2.5 million, Abagnale gained extensive knowledge and skill in the methods employed by counterfeiters and other fraudsters.[97] Upon his ultimate capture, he was sentenced to serve 12 years in federal prison.[98] Despite his sentence, Abagnale was released after serving fewer than 5 years on the condition that he use his knowledge and experience to assist the Federal Bureau of Investigation—essentially that he use what he had learned as a criminal to capture others.[99] The use of his talents in apprehending criminals and preventing further crime had no bearing on his blameworthiness for his past offenses, but it may be argued that society as a whole benefitted more from their use than from his incarceration.[100]

4. SUFFERING APART FROM OFFICIAL PUNISHMENT: SPECIAL HARDSHIP FROM OFFENSE OR FROM PUNISHMENT, FOR OFFENDER OR FAMILY OR OTHERS; PAYMENT OF CIVIL COMPENSATION

Finally, the appropriate punishment to be imposed on an offender may be affected by special hardship that the punishment would impose on the offender himself or on third parties that depend on or care for him. Old age may be a specific example of this kind of special vulnerability to punishment's effect, but it also invokes sympathy for other reasons. Situations where an offender has already paid substantial civil compensation to the offender are also part of this aspect of the calculus of proper punishment.

---

[94] Russell W.G. Grove, *Sentencing Reform: Toward a More Uniform, Less Uninformed System of Court-Martial Sentencing*, 1988 Army Law. 26, 32 (suggesting that special talents, among other factors, be included in presentence reports).

[95] *Id.*

[96] *See* Stan Redding & Frank W. Abagnale, Jr., Catch Me If You Can: The True Story of a Real Fake (2000).

[97] *Id.* at 885.

[98] *Id.*

[99] *Id.* Abagnale has since made a career of teaching others, both in and out of law enforcement, about issues of fraud prevention. *Abagnale & Associates*, http://www.abagnale.com.

[100] It is notable that in the decades since his release, Abagnale has made full restitution to nearly all of his victims. Peter Ross, *Man On The Run; The Racy Life of the World's Most Notorious Con Man Has Been Immortalised by Leonardo DiCaprio in Catch Me If You Can. But the Real Frank Abagnale is a Reformed Character Who's Now Chasing the Bad Guys For a Living,* The Sunday Herald at 3 (Jan. 26, 2003).

a. Special Offender Hardship Resulting from the Offense. Many offenders suffer as a result of their actions irrespective of any criminal punishment levied. Should this self-caused suffering be taken into account in assessing punishment amount? Consider, for example, a drunk driver who accidentally kills his daughter in an auto accident. That the intoxicated driver is guilty of a crime is clear. However, unlike many others convicted of the same offense, such an offender must also endure the loss of a loved one. Should the emotional pain perhaps justify a reduction in punishment?

In many jurisdictions, an offender who has suffered as a result of her offense can introduce this suffering to argue for a reduced sentence. However, without an additional showing of exceptional circumstances, such suffering is generally not enough to justify a discounted sentence. In Michigan, for example, the state supreme court overturned a trial court's downward departure from state sentencing guidelines where the offender "had already paid a significant price for his crimes, namely the loss of his family and employment," on the grounds that "neither loss grabs our attention as being exceptional."[101] It seems likely that an "exceptional" amount of suffering could trigger a valid downward departure, however it is unclear what might constitute such suffering.

Similarly, in 2009 the Supreme Court of Washington approved use of such an XPF when it overturned an accomplice-to-DUI conviction.[102] There, the defendant was the only survivor of a group of seven intoxicated persons involved in a single-car crash.[103] Though the trial court found the defendant guilty, the supreme court reversed, writing that

> While we would not hesitate to condemn Hedlund's conduct as reprehensible and indeed criminal, neither do we find it absurd to say that she has been punished enough. Her lack of judgment permitted the loss of the lives of her fiancé as well as several friends, and she spent months rehabilitating from her own severe injuries; further legal penalties would be dwarfed by the suffering she has already endured.[104]

The federal courts have also approved some downward departures based on offenders' prior suffering. In sentencing an offender convicted of filing a false tax return, a trial court disregarded the U.S. Sentencing Guidelines' 10- to 16-month recommended sentence and instead imposed only a term of probation and a fine, noting in part that the offender had already suffered substantially and "had been treated for depression due to the stress of the instant investigation.'"[105] The D.C. Circuit affirmed the sentence, holding that the "District Court's conclusion rests on precisely the kind of defendant-specific determinations that are within the special competence of sentencing courts."[106]

---

[101] People v. Dean, No. 266438, 2006 WL 3077520, at *2 (Mich. App. Oct. 31, 2006).

[102] City of Auburn v. Hedlund, 201 P.3d 315 (Wash. 2009).

[103] *Id.*

[104] *Id.*

[105] United States v. Gardellini, 545 F.3d 1089 (2008) (quoting district court decision).

[106] *Id.*

b. Special Hardship from Punishment. Offender suffering from his official punishment is rarely a grounds for mitigation—for good reason: punishment, at least in its retributivist justification, is for the purpose of causing offender suffering. However, in some cases, unusual hardship can result from the imposition of a traditional sentence. Hardship beyond that typically inherent in and intended by a sentence may be used as a mitigating factor, especially when the hardship is born by a dependent of the offender or another innocent third party.[107] For example, a single parent who commits a crime for which he would normally be sentenced to a long prison term might receive a mitigated sentence because his child would be left with no guardian if the full sentence were imposed.

Others argue that in some situations, the likelihood that punishment will cause atypical and severe harm to the offender could justify mitigating a punishment.[108] William Berry has argued that "the early release of an inmate because of a terminal illness will not unduly compromise the utilitarian goals of incapacitation, deterrence, and rehabilitation. The terminal illness will substantially reduce the risk of dangerousness, the need for rehabilitation, and will not impede any deterrent effect of the sentence."[109] In short, the value inherent in compassion can outweigh the interests sacrificed by exercising it. Others agree with Berry's argument but advocate different means to account for excessive hardships. For example, Kobil and others advocate the use of the clemency power in situations of old age or illness. If, for example, a 10-year sentence is given to an offender with a life expectancy of 5 years, these scholars argue that the punishment amounts to a life sentence and may be cruel or disproportionate.[110] The recent compassionate release of Abdelbaset Ali Mohmed Al Megrani, convicted of involvement in the bombing of Pan Am Flight 103 in the late 1980s, is illustrative of this sort of argument.[111] The Scottish Government allowed Al Megrani, suffering from terminal prostate cancer and expected to live no more than three months, to return to his native Libya to die.[112]

The Federal Sentencing Guidelines provide for a reduction in sentence where the offender suffers from "an extraordinary physical impairment...; e.g., in the case of a seriously infirm defendant, home detention may be as efficient as, and less costly than, imprisonment."[113] This provision has been applied to make departures from the guidelines where, for example, a white collar offender in extremely poor health was sentenced to probation and home detention in lieu of incarceration because imprisoning the offender might cause his death.[114]

---

[107] *See, e.g.*, 730 ILCS 5/5-5-3.1(a)(12).

[108] Berry, *supra* note 1028.

[109] *Id.*

[110] Daniel T. Kobil, *The Quality of Mercy Strained: Wresting the Pardoning Power from the King*, 69 Tex. L. Rev. 569 (1991).

[111] *Lockerbie Bomber Freed From Jail*, BBC News, Aug. 20, 2009, http://news.bbc.co.uk/2/hi/uk_news/scotland/south_of_scotland/8197370.stm.

[112] *Id.*

[113] U.S. Sentencing Guidelines Manual §5H1.4 (2004).

[114] U.S. v. Coughlin, 2008 WL 313099 (W.D.Ark. 2008).

Notably, there is another federal hardship provision, albeit one not often used: in the event of "extraordinary and compelling" terminal illness, debilitating physical condition, or death or incapacitation of the only family member who is able to care for a minor child, a prisoner may be released upon a motion by the director of the Bureau of Prisons.[115] In practice, the Bureau of Prisons has used this "compassionate release" extremely rarely, and then only for terminally ill inmates.[116]

c. Hardship for Offender's Family or Other Third Parties. Compassionate release maybe thought warranted when incarceration of a parent may cause hardship to dependents: "[I]n some situations, allowing an offender to care for his or her child could supplement the rehabilitative process by providing the inmate with an important responsibility. The impact on deterrence will be negligible and, as a result, will not forbid mitigation in this context."[117]

Both federal and state courts permit consideration of hardships inflicted upon third parties. The U.S. Sentencing Guidelines address this concern, stating that "family ties and responsibilities are not ordinarily relevant in determining whether a departure may be warranted." The guideline's commentary explains that in order to make a departure based on such factors, a court should look to a non-exhaustive list of factors including danger to members of offender's family as a result of the offense. Additionally, there are explicit requirements for a departure based on loss of caretaking or financial support.[118] As noted above, both federal and state death penalty cases have much looser evidentiary standards at sentencing; as such, in many cases, familial hardship is introduced as a mitigating factor.[119]

The states generally allow for mitigation based on potential harm to third parties caused by extended incarceration of an offender. Indiana's Penal Code, for example, permits a sentence mitigation if "[i]mprisonment of the person will result in undue hardship to the person or the dependents of the person."[120] Note, however, that the Indiana Supreme Court has held that a mitigation is not *required* in these circumstances. "Many persons convicted of serious crimes have one or more children and, absent special circumstances, trial courts are not required to find that imprisonment will result in an undue hardship."[121] The use of third party hardship as a mitigating factor (and its accompanying interpretation) is mirrored in many other states,[122] though some states restrict the mitigation to extraordinary circumstances.

---

[115] 18 U.S.C. §3582(c)(2) (2006).

[116] *See* Berry, *supra* note 1028, at 866.

[117] *Id.*, at 887.

[118] U.S. SENTENCING GUIDELINES MANUAL §5H1.6 (2004).

[119] *See, e.g.*, People v. Ochoa, 966 P.2d 442, 506 (Cal. 1998) ("Sympathy for a defendant's family is not a matter that a capital jury can consider in mitigation, but that family members may offer testimony of the impact of an execution on them if by so doing they illuminate some positive quality of the defendant's background or character.").

[120] IC 35-38-1-7.1(b)(10).

[121] Dowdell v. State, 720 N.E.2d 1146 (Ind. 1999)

[122] See, *e.g.*, 730 ILCS 5/5-5-3.1(a)(11); N.C. Gen. Stat. §15A-1340.16(e)(17); N.D. Cent. Code §12.1-32-04(11).

New Jersey, for example, only allows a mitigation based on hardship when "having regard to the character and condition of the defendant, [the court] is of the opinion that his imprisonment would be a serious injustice which overrides the need to deter such conduct by others."[123] This "serious injustice" standard may be "met only in 'truly extraordinary and unanticipated circumstances.'"

There is some evidence that this XPF surreptitiously plays a role in sentencing. In one 2007 study, trial judges in Pennsylvania were presented with factorial surveys comprised of short vignettes designed to test the judges' sentencing decisions for offenders in various familial roles (and whose punishments, it follows, would have varying impacts on others).[124] It was observed that judges were most likely to give significant decreases in the likelihood of incarceration for offenders in the role of caregiver (both "caregiver only" and "caregiver and financial provider").[125] This effect was observed for offenders of either sex for nearly all familial roles—the only familial role that did not significantly reduce the likelihood of incarceration was economic provider.[126]

d. Old Age. Youth is often taken as a consideration in criminal sentencing, as mandated by juvenile offender provisions and other considerations specific to young offenders. Immaturity may prevent an appreciation the wrongfulness of one's conduct and thereby undermine an offender's blameworthiness. Elderly offenders have no such claim to make, yet there is some support for an old age mitigation. Andrew Ashworth, for example, has argued that age is a relevant consideration in setting appropriate levels of punishment, since it may take the prime years away from young offenders and may be unduly burdensome on older offenders.[127]

In practice, many states seem to have allowed the use of age as a factor in punishment[128]. The Michigan Supreme Court has held that "a 'term of years' must be an indeterminate sentence less than life. It must be something that is reasonably possible for a defendant actually to serve."[129] Importantly, however, this holding does not require that a court make a factual determination as to how long an offender is expected to live; it is only a general requirement for courts to consider.[130] One study found that Pennsylvania judges were less likely to incarcerate older offenders, and that older offenders received shorter sentences than their younger counterparts; however,

---

[123] State v. Roth, 471 A.2d 370 (N.J. 1984).

[124] Tina L. Freiburger, Familial Paternalism in the Courtroom: A Comprehensive Examination of Male and Female Criminal Sentences (Aug. 2007) (unpublished Ph.D. dissertation, Indiana University of Pennsylvania), *available at* http://proquest.umi.com/pqdlink?did=1320951021&Fmt=7&clientId=79356&RQT=309&VName=PQD.

[125] *Id.*

[126] *Id.*

[127] Andrew Ashworth, Sentencing and Penal Policy 276–77 (1983) (arguing that equality of impact means that both older and younger offenders should receive a sentencing discount because of the special hardship prison would entail)

[128] *See, e.g.,* N.D. Cent. Code §12.1-32-04(12).

[129] People v. Moore, 439 N.W.2d 684 (Mich. 1989).

[130] *Id.*

the study offered little insight as to the causes of this discrepancy.[131] Other studies have reached "conflicting conclusions" about the impact of old age on punishment.[132]

The United States Sentencing Guidelines state that "age may be a reason to depart downward in a case in which the defendant is elderly and infirm and where a form of punishment such as home confinement might be equally efficient as and less costly than incarceration."[133] At least two circuits have narrowly interpreted this provision, both of which require all four elements (age, infirmity, efficiency, and cost effectiveness) in order to allow a reduced sentence.[134] Even within other, less strict circuits, the provision is rather rarely used.[135]

While several jurisdictions allow the use of age as a mitigating factor on a discretionary basis, at least one state explicitly forbids its consideration unless it has a direct implication for an offender's blameworthiness. Arizona courts have held that "extreme youth or old age only becomes a mitigating factor when, because of immaturity or senility, the defendant lacks substantial judgment in committing the crime."[136] The Tennessee Supreme Court has come to a similar conclusion based on a sentencing guideline much like Arizona's.[137] That court's pronouncement only allows the consideration of old age as a punishment factor where age might implicate the offender's ability to "appreciate the nature of his conduct" and requires that age be viewed in context, considering "education, maturity, experience, mental capacity or development."[138]

e. Payment of Substantial Civil Compensation to the Victim. Judges often adjust punishment in light of civil payments when the punishment is a fine or restitution. Indeed, when courts impose restitution orders, it is settled practice that they should offset against the amount to impose with "payments actually made by the defendant to the victim,"[139] though the fact that a civil proceeding is pending is insufficient to reduce punishment.[140] State courts often are statutorily authorized to mitigate sentences in light of substantial civil compensation.[141]

---

[131] William E. Adams, Jr., *The Intersection of Elder Law and Criminal Law: More Traffic Than One Might Assume*, 30 Stetson L. Rev. 1331, 1346 (2001) (Darrell Steffensmeier & Mark Motivans, *Sentencing the Older Offender: Is There an "Age Bias"?*, in ELDERS, CRIME, AND THE CRIMINAL JUSTICE SYSTEM: MYTH, PERCEPTIONS, AND REALITY IN THE 21ST CENTURY 185, 185 (Max B. Rothman et al. eds., 2000). Similar results were observed in the federal courts, despite the stricter guidelines applicable there.

[132] *Id.* at 1347 (citing William E. Adams, Jr., *The Incarceration of Older Criminals: Balancing Safety, Cost, and Humanitarian Concerns*, 19 NOVA L. REV. 465, 467 (1994)).

[133] U.S. SENTENCING GUIDELINES MANUAL §5H1.1 (2004).

[134] Thomas A. Long, Note, *The Federal Sentencing Guidelines and Elderly Offenders: Walking a Tightrope Between Uniformity and Discretion (and Slipping)*, 2 ELDER L.J. 69 (1994)

[135] *Id.*

[136] State v. de la Garza, 675 P.2d 295, 296 (App.1983), *disapproved of on other grounds by* State v. Thurlow, 712 P.2d 929, 932 (1986)

[137] State v. Adams, 864 S.W.2d 31 (Tenn. 1993).

[138] *Id.*

[139] CATHARINE M. GOODWIN ET AL., FEDERAL CRIMINAL RESTITUTION §14:7 (2010).

[140] *See id.* at §14.8 ("Even where a pending civil judgment or settlement is for the same harm as the restitution, courts generally disregard it in imposing restitution, because such a judgment might be subsequently changed, appealed, or amended.").

[141] *See* Alaska Stat. §12.55.155; Ca. St. Cr Cases R. 4.423(b)(5); N.C. Gen. Stat. §15A-1340.16(e)(5); N.D. Cent. Code §12.1-32.04(16); Tenn Code Ann. §40-35-113(5).

When pecuniary punishments are not solely at issue, federal courts under the U.S. Sentencing Guidelines have been hostile to the argument that restitution should reduce punishment. Allowing restitution to influence the sentencing decision, courts fear, may allow socioeconomic considerations to seep into the sentencing process.[142] As the Sixth Circuit has noted, courts "may not sentence a poor convict more harshly than a rich convict simply because the rich convict is better able to make restitution."[143]

Still, federal courts have acknowledged payment of civil compensation as a mitigating factor under §3E1.1(a) of the Sentencing Guidelines on the theory that such payments demonstrate "acceptance of responsibility for [the defendant's] offense."[144] On this theory, compensation is not a sign of hardship but rather an acknowledgment of guilt, and courts accordingly require the defendant's restitution to be accompanied by genuine expressions of sincerity. For instance, in *United States v. Szarwark*, the government succeeded in challenging the District Court's two-level reduction under §3E1.1(a) when the defendant, who was convicted of mail fraud, failed to collect money owed to him by the victim after the victim discovered the fraud.[145] The Seventh Circuit noted that the defendant's asserted restitution was "clearly not what the framers of the Sentencing Guidelines meant by voluntary payment."[146] By contrast, in *United States v. Oligmueller*, the Eighth Circuit upheld a downward departure when the defendant there voluntarily began paying back a fraudulent loan more than a year before he was indicted and worked 16-hour days, turned over his life insurance deposit, took an outside job, and gave up his home all in order to redeem the debt.[147]

B. A Study of Lay Intuitions of Extralegal Punishment Factors

What follows is a study of lay people's intuitions regarding extralegal punishment factors. It investigates whether and to what extent such factors influence lay judgments about how much punishment offenders should receive. The study was designed to elicit a basic understanding of the way in which people intuit extralegal punishment factors as well as to build a foundation for additional research.

---

[142] *Cf.* United States v. Chastain, 84 F.3d 321, 325 (9th Cir. 1996) ("Allowing a sentencing judge to reduce a defendant's sentence to preserve a defendant's job and facilitate restitution would introduce precisely the type of socio-economic disparity into sentencing that the Guidelines were designed to eliminate.").

[143] United States v. DeMonte, 25 F.3d 343, 347 (6th Cir. 1994).

[144] U.S. Sentencing Guidelines §3E1.1(a); *see also id.* cmt. n.1(c) ("In determining whether a defendant qualifies under subsection (a), appropriate considerations include... voluntary payment of restitution prior to adjudication of guilt....").

[145] 168 F.3d 993, 997 (7th Cir. 1999).

[146] *Id.*

[147] United States v. Oligmueller, 198 F.3d 669, 670 (8th Cir. 1999).

1. METHODOLOGY

Four hundred twenty-three subjects, representing a broad range of demographics,[148] were presented with five different "baseline scenarios," each describing the circumstances of a hypothetical criminal offense. Baseline scenarios were used to showcase different kinds of offenses: each of the five scenarios consisted of a simple paragraph-long narrative that focused on the offense while avoiding offender characteristics such as gender, ethnicity, or personality. These narratives, which the subjects read verbatim during the course of the survey, are set out in Table 91 below.

During the survey, subjects worked with one scenario at a time. For each scenario, they were first instructed to read the scenario narrative and then asked to report their intuitive judgments about how much punishment offender deserved for her crimes. Subjects answered using the scale set out in Figure 92.

After marking their judgments on this scale, subjects were given additional facts and asked whether those facts should have any effect on the amount of punishment imposed.

TABLE 91. } Baseline Scenarios

Scenario	Summary
Scenario A: Property Theft with Trespass	John does not have all the tools he needs for his workshop but knows of a family two streets over who sometimes leaves unlocked the door to the detached garage next to their house. When he next sees his chance, he enters the detached garage through the unlocked door and takes a medium-size electric drill, intending to keep it forever.
Scenario B: Personal Injury	Angry after overhearing another parent's remarks during a soccer match in which Alex's son is playing, Alex approaches the man after the game, grabs his coffee mug, knocks him down, then kicks him several times while he is on the ground, knocking him out for several minutes and causing cuts that require five stitches.
Scenario C: Governmental Corruption	David is the mayor of a moderately sized city, and has the responsibility of deciding between competing bids for the management of a youth detention facility. Company A has submitted the lowest bid, and is a reputable company that provides services to numerous other cities in the state. However, Company B's CEO recently visited David and offered him $5,000 in exchange for awarding the contract to his company, which has a long record of improper treatment of juveniles and has submitted a much higher bid. David takes the cash and gives the job to Company B. David is convicted of governmental corruption.
Scenario D: Death by Risk- Taking	Two vicious pit bulls that Brian keeps for illegal dog fighting have just learned to escape and have attacked a person who came to Brian's house. The police tell Brian he must destroy the dogs. Brian tells the police that he will, but does not actually intend to do so. The next day, the dogs escape again and maul to death a man delivering a package.
Scenario E: Intentional Death with Abduction	A woman at work reveals Mark's misdeeds to his employer, thereby getting him fired. Mark devises a plan to get even with her. The next week he forces the woman into his car at knife point and drives her to a secluded area where he shoots her to death.

[148] For more details on the nature of the sample, see Robinson, Jackowitz & Bartels, *supra* note 937, at 27–32.

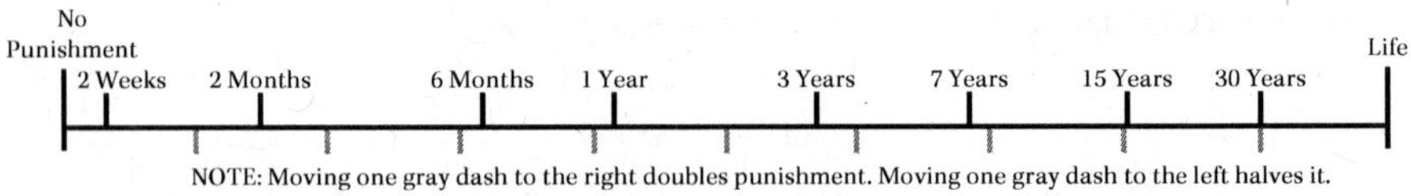

FIGURE 92. Scale Used by Subjects to Assign Punishment to Hypothetical Offenders

Subjects were shown one fact at a time, each fact corresponding to an XPF. When subjects answered "yes," they accessed the scale in Figure 92 and were instructed to indicate new punishment assignments. Baseline assignments were marked for reference.

Time markings on the scale are exponential, not linear. The hash marks below the line indicate the regular intervals of the scale, with each hash mark indicating a doubling or halving of punishment relative to the hash mark before or after it. Subjects did not have to figure out this exponential scale; they could look at the time scale marked above the line. Above-the-line marks correspond to grading levels typical to American criminal codes.[149]

The subjects' assignments of absolute liability were of little interest in this study;[150] rather, the focus here was on the willingness of the respondents to adjust their original punishment assignments in light of each separate XPF. The distance between any two hash marks (or, in fact, any two equivalent distances on the scale) is always equal in relative terms, corresponding to an increase or decrease in punishment. That is, no matter where one is on the scale, one additional hash mark is equal to a doubling of punishment. Hence, inter-subject comparison by *change in punishment*, expressed as distance traveled on the scale, is meaningful.

The results are reported throughout as changes in respondents' exponential scale numbers (ESNs). For example, an ESN change of +1 reflects a doubling of punishment from that originally given in the baseline scenario, and a change of –1 constitutes a halving of punishment, while a change of +2 by contract, represents a quadrupling of punishment. Table 93 illustrates these values.[151]

TABLE 93. } ESN Scale

ESN Value	–1	–0.8	–0.6	–0.5	–0.4	–0.2	0	0.2	0.4	0.5	0.6	0.8	1
% Change in	50%	57%	66%	71%	76%	87%	100%	115%	132%	141%	152%	174%	200%

ESN Value	–3	–2.5	–2	–1.5	–1	–0.5	0	0.5	1	1.5	2	2.5	3
% Change in	13%	18%	25%	35%	50%	71%	100%	141%	200%	283%	400%	566%	800%

[149] PAUL H. ROBINSON & JOHN M. DARLEY, JUSTICE, LIABILITY, AND BLAME: COMMUNITY VIEWS AND THE CRIMINAL LAW (1995).

[150] While perhaps agreeing on the relative blameworthiness rankings of at least "core crimes," subjects do not necessarily agree on absolute punishment levels.

[151] The values were derived as follows: The relationship between years of punishment and pixel position (p) is equal to: 86.562*ln(p) + 275.587. Using this equation, the percentage difference in punishment indicated by a distance of d pixels is equal to: e^(d/86.562).

The next part of the study concerns a series of facts that depicted the 18 XPFs discussed in section A. Each fact could plausibly prompt a respondent to depart from her baseline assignment of punishment. These facts are set out in Table 94.

Once subjects declined to change their initial punishment assignments or had the chance to revise the assignments, a new XPF fact was given. The instructions made clear that each of these alternative variations on the baseline scenario were to be considered independently of each other. The order in which the variations were presented was randomized. Moreover, respondents did not encounter every XPF in the study. About half of the respondents were randomly assigned to a survey

TABLE 94. } Extralegal Punishment Factor Variations

XPF	SCENARIO TEXT
A. Offender Reaction to the Offense	
1. Public Acknowledgment of Guilt	During a court hearing, the offender publicly acknowledges that he committed the offense, and enters a plea of guilty.
2. Public Acknowledgment of Guilt plus Apology	At a hearing in court, the offender publicly acknowledges that he committed the offense, enters a plea of guilty, and, on advice of counsel, publicly apologizes to his victims, who are present in court.
3. Truly Remorseful with Public Acknowledgment of Guilt and Apology	Sincerely remorseful about what he has done, the offender publicly acknowledges during a court hearing that he committed the offense, and pleads guilty. He publicly apologizes to his victims, who are present in court.
4. True Remorse, Public Acknowledgment of Guilt and Apology Immediately After Offense	Soon after the offense, the offender feels sincerely remorseful. While he is unable to undo his actions, he goes to his victims and apologizes. He turns himself into police, even though it is unlikely they would have caught him otherwise.
B. Victim or Public Reaction to the Offense	
5. Forgiveness by Victim	The victims, who are very religious people, have forgiven the offender for his offense.
6. Victim Wants Less or No Punishment	The victims, who are very religious people, want the offender's sentence for his offense to be substantially reduced.
7. Victim Wants More Punishment	The victims have expressed outrage over the offender's crime. They believe a lenient sentence will trivialize the offender's crime and the suffering he has caused and insist that he receive more severe punishment.
8. Public Outrage over Offense	After the offense, there is a good deal of news coverage about the offender's actions and their effects. The public expresses outrage over the offender's offense and demands that he receive harsher punishment.
C. Offender Status or Characteristics Unrelated to Commission of the Offense	
9. Rehabilitated	Through his participation in a rehabilitation program, the offender has come to appreciate the extent of the harm he caused, has changed his view about victimizing others, and is unlikely to commit a similar offense in the future.
10. Good Deeds Before Offense	For a year prior to his offense, the offender volunteered nearly every weekend to work at a homeless shelter and a charity soup kitchen.

(*Continued*)

XPF	SCENARIO TEXT
11. Good Deeds After Offense	For the year between the offender's offense and his conviction, the offender volunteers nearly every weekend at a homeless shelter and a charity soup kitchen.
12. Bad Deeds and Character	The offender is an avowed racist who has openly preached his views of racial supremacy and advocated policies that promote racial purity and segregation, including the prohibition of mixed-race marriages. His racism played no role in his offense.
13. Special Talents	The offender is a world-famous and extremely talented actor who has won many awards for his work, which is known particularly for touching and changing people's lives. His work has not only inspired many people, but also advanced the cause of art generally. Critics have marked the offender as likely to have a long and stellar career.
D. Suffering Apart from Official Punishment	
14. Already Suffering as a Result of the Offense	After the offense, the offender falls during his escape. As a result of his neck injuries, the offender will be paralyzed from the neck down for the rest of his life.
15. Has Already Paid Substantial Civil Compensation to the Victim	After the offender's conviction, but before his sentencing, the offender is found liable for his offense in a civil lawsuit, and pays his victims compensatory damages as well as special damages totaling three times compensatory.
16. Hardship for Offender's Family or Others	The offender's child has a serious disease that requires daily care and attention. Because the offender's wife is dead and he has no other living family, either The offender must provide the care or the child will be put in state custody. The extent of his punishment will affect how much care and support he can give to his child.
17. Hardship for Offender Himself	Several weeks after the offense, the offender is in an automobile accident. As a result of neck injuries, he will be paralyzed from the neck down for the rest of his life.
18. Old Age	At the time of the offense, the offender is 80 years old and in poor health. A person in his condition may not have long to live.

that tested only the XPFs listed in groups A and D; the other half were randomly assigned to a survey that tested the XPFs listed in groups B and C. Thus, every respondent considered nine punishment factors per baseline scenario. They also repeated the process for all five scenarios, for a total of 45 variations.

In order to thwart concern about a "demand effect," the instructions made it clear that "no change" was an entirely acceptable response. In fact, 71.8 percent of all responses were for "no change."[152] Moreover, 23.3 percent of the time respondents did not record a change for *any* XPF in a given scenario.[153] With these trends in mind, there seems little reason for concern about a demand effect.[154]

Once data collection was completed, two values were computed. The first, referred to as "XPF popularity," is the percentage of respondents who indicated

[152] Out of 16,749 recorded responses, 12,018 were "no change" (71.8 percent).

[153] Counting each scenario separately, respondents ran through a set of XPF questions 1861 times. Respondents did not record any change to their initial punishment assignment 434 times (23.3 percent).

[154] More details on the methodology of the study can be found at Robinson, Jackowitz & Bartels, *supra* note 937, at 27–32.

that they would change their initial punishment assignment in light of the XPF in question. The second, referred to as "XPF magnitude," is the amount by which respondents on average altered their initial punishment assignment. XPF magnitude was calculated based on the exponential scale numbers (ESNs) reported in the survey, with a response of "no change" averaged into the value as zero. Whenever an XPF magnitude value is reported, a negative ESN connotes a mitigation in punishment and a positive ESN connotes an aggravation of punishment.[155]

2. METHODOLOGICAL NOTE: A SHIFT FROM IMPLICIT TO EXPLICIT RANKING

Recall the discussion in chapter 2 regarding the high level of agreement of people's intuitions of justice across demographics for matters relating to the core of wrongdoing. It was relative blameworthiness upon which people agree, not the absolute amount of punishment. Some people punish more severely generally, setting a high endpoint for the continuum of punishment. Others punishment less severely, setting a lower endpoint. Thus, even though people may agree on relative blameworthiness, the absolute amounts of punishment they impose may be different.

The standard methodology used in part III and described in chapter 12, section A, deals with this situation by comparing the average liability for the different scenarios within a study. The differences in the liability averages among the different scenarios show the subjects' judgments of relative blameworthiness. Each scenario average may reflect an underlying distribution of liability amounts, rather than a single agreed upon amount but, because each subject assigns liability to each scenario, the different perspectives on liability severity generally "wash out" when the liability scores are averaged.

A potential weakness of this approach is that it assumes that a subject's view on general punishment severity influences all of the subject's liability judgments in the same way. While it seems likely that this is an acceptable assumption, at least for pioneering work that seeks a first rough survey of the punishment assignment landscape, more sophisticated research methods can do better. With a better understanding of the importance of the difference between judgments about relative blameworthiness and about punishment continuum endpoint, a better methodology might be to have subjects explicitly rank scenarios first, then add their absolute liability amounts in a second step. This would allow the data to be analyzed for ranking comparisons directly, without having to make any assumption about the effects of a subject's general sentencing severity.

Under this approach, a subject is given a set of scenarios, as usual, but is asked first to rank them in order of deserved punishment. This can be done by having each scenario on a card, for example, and having the subjects order the cards on a

[155] Note that three of the 18 XPFs were designed to be aggravators: XPF 7 ("Victim Wants More Punishment"), XPF 8 ("Public Outrage over Offense"), and XPF 12 ("Bad Deeds/Character").

table. This approach, and an internet version of it, was used in the studies reported in chapters 2 and 4. The subject is then asked to record the letter, number, or title identifier of each scenario in its determined order on a sheet, next to a liability scale, such as that below. The subject then draws a line from each scenario identifier to the point on the liability scale that shows the absolute amount of punishment the subject would impose in the case. This method allows the researcher to collect both pure ranking data as well as data on absolute liability amount. The latter are useful because they show the groupings of scenarios and the relative spacing of the scenarios along the punishment continuum.

3. SUPPORT FOR ADJUSTING PUNISHMENT IN LIGHT OF EXTRALEGAL PUNISHMENT FACTORS

Table 95 gives the average punishment assigned for each baseline scenario (that is, without consideration of any XPF), with an ESN-scale value translated into a term of imprisonment as it appeared on the survey's punishment scale. Table 96 shows the popularity and weight given to various XPFs when complementing the baseline scenario.

The histogram in Figure 97 shows the distribution of ESN values from all recorded responses. An overwhelming 71.8 percent of responses indicated "no change" and were recorded as 0. The remaining 27.9 percent of responses were between +10 and -10, with the responses having a negatively skewed unimodal distribution centered on 0. Since only a few XPFs aggravated punishment,[156] most ESN values recorded were negative.[157]

In broadest outline, the data suggests that there is indeed support among lay people for punishment factors that have traditionally been excluded from the criminal law's liability and punishment rules. Every XPF tested had some support, even in relation to scenario E ("Intentional Killing and Abduction"), the most serious offense. A number of XPFs enjoyed the support of a majority of study participants (those italicized in Table 96), with support reaching as high as 77 percent for one XPF.

It is equally true, however, that most XPFs do not have majority support, even in scenario A, which sets out the least serious offense in the survey. In scenario A,

TABLE 95. } Average Punishment for Each Baseline Scenario

Scenarios:	A. Theft with Trespass	B. Personal Injury	C. Governmental Corruption	D. Causing Death by Risk-Taking	E. Intentional Killing and Abduction	Average for All Baseline Scenarios
Prison Term in Years	1	1.3	6.1	14.2	49.7	14.5

[156] XPFs 7, 8 and 12 were designed to be aggravators, and XPF 13 ("Special Talents") turned out to be one.

[157] Individual histograms for each offense and XPF variation are on file with author.

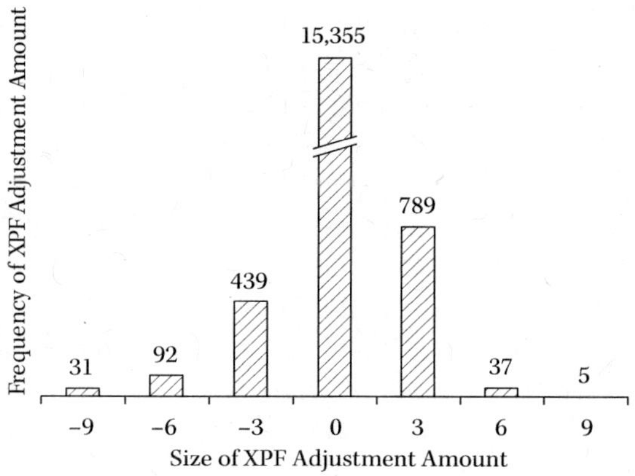

FIGURE 97 Frequency of XPF Adjustment Amounts

half of the XPFs had the support of less than a third of the participants. While, if the margin of error is taken into account, as many as eight XPFs may have enjoyed majority support, only two unquestionably did. Scenario A, in fact, was unlike other scenarios in this regard: only in two other instances did an XPF command clear majority support. For scenario E, the most serious offense, only one XPF received the support of even a third of study participants.

4. EFFECT OF BASELINE OFFENSE ON XPF ADJUSTMENTS TO PUNISHMENTS

The results suggest that XPF popularity and XPF magnitude depend on the underlying offense at issue. The differences between columns, including the column averages at the far right of Table 96, show that both XPF popularity and magnitude decrease substantially as the seriousness of the offense increases. In most instances, the drop in popularity moves in a consistently downward procession across the five baseline offenses as seriousness increases.

But this "offense effect" is not consistent for all XPFs. Popularity for some of the least popular XPFs remains at the same low level across all offenses.[158] Some XPFs show a drop-off in popularity of only a third,[159] while two relatively popular XPFs exhibit a decline in popularity of only a fifth.[160] This inconsistency in the way

---

[158] This is true for XPF 7 ("Victim Wants More Punishment), XPF 8 ("Public Outrage over Offense"), and XPF 12 ("Bad Deeds/Character"). *See supra* Table 96.

[159] This occurs with the unpopular XPF 13 ("Special Talents") as well as the moderately popular XPF 2 ("Public Acknowledgment of Guilt and Apology without Remorse"), XPF 4 ("True Remorse, Acknowledge Guilt, and Apology Immediately After Offense"), XPF 11 ("Good Deeds after Offense"), XPF 17 ("Hardship for Offender Himself"), and XPF 18 ("Old Age"). *See id.*

[160] This occurs in two relatively popular XPFs: XPF 15 ("Has Already Paid Civil Compensation") and XPF 16 ("Hardship for Offender's Family or Others"). *See id.*

TABLE 96. } XPF Popularity and Magnitude, Ordered by Overall Popularity

SCENARIOS: XPFs:	A. Theft with Trespass		B. Personal Injury		C. Governmental Corruption		D. Causing Death by Risk-Taking		E. Intentional Killing and Abduction		Row Averages	
4. True Remorse, Acknowledge Guilt, and Apology Immediately After Offense	***76.9%***	−0.94	***65.6%***	−0.66	***70.8%***	−1.15	*48.7%*	−0.51	40.1%	−0.33	*60.5%*	−0.72
9. Rehabilitated	*52.5%*	−0.32	*51.4%*	−0.26	41.8%	−0.29	42.9%	−0.32	30.9%	−0.26	44.0%	−0.29
15. Has Already Paid Substantial Civil Compensation to the Victim	***64.6%***	−0.88	*53.3%*	−0.62	*44.3%*	−0.68	28.4%	−0.24	14.1%	−0.04	41.0%	−0.49
3. Truly Remorseful with Public Acknowledgment of Guilt and Apology	*52.3%*	−0.42	*47.7%*	−0.36	37.9%	−0.37	28.4%	−0.21	20.8%	−0.11	37.5%	−0.29
16. Hardship for Offender's Family or Others	*50.3%*	−0.68	*51.3%*	−0.63	40.5%	−0.77	28.9%	−0.53	8.3%	−0.09	35.9%	−0.54
14. Has Been Punished Enough – Already Suffering from his Offense	*46.2%*	−0.76	37.4%	−0.37	28.2%	−0.49	39.6%	−0.81	14.1%	−0.36	33.2%	−0.56
2. Public Acknowledgment of Guilt Plus Apology	*44.6%*	−0.39	42.1%	−0.29	29.7%	−0.24	20.3%	−0.14	14.6%	−0.04	30.3%	−0.22
17. Hardship for Offender Himself	*45.1%*	−0.67	31.3%	−0.48	26.7%	−0.76	23.9%	−0.53	13.0%	−0.37	28.0%	−0.56
6. Victim Wants Less or No Punishment	39.7%	−0.28	32.4%	−0.21	16.4%	−0.20	24.9%	−0.27	18.9%	−0.15	26.5%	−0.22

1. Public Acknowledgment of Guilt	32.3%	−0.20	35.2%	−0.19	25.6%	−0.20	21.8%	−0.15	15.6%	−0.05	26.2%	−0.16
18. Old Age	32.8%	−0.33	26.2%	−0.34	21.5%	−0.35	20.8%	−0.41	9.9%	−0.12	22.3%	−0.31
7. Victim Wants More Punishment	19.6%	+0.09	19.0%	+0.11	24.9%	+0.05	23.2%	+0.07	15.4%	+0.00	20.4%	+0.06
11. Good Deeds After Offense	25.7%	−0.16	29.1%	−0.14	16.4%	−0.12	16.9%	−0.09	9.7%	−0.05	19.6%	−0.11
5. Forgiveness by Victim	31.3%	−0.25	22.5%	−0.29	13.0%	−0.07	16.4%	−0.19	12.0%	−0.10	19.1%	−0.18
12. Bad Deeds/Character	14.0%	+0.04	20.7%	+0.15	19.8%	+0.01	15.8%	+0.04	14.9%	+0.01	17.0%	+0.05
8. Public Outrage Over Offense	16.2%	+0.09	17.3%	+0.06	16.9%	+0.00	14.7%	+0.16	12.6%	−0.03	15.6%	+0.05
10. Good Deeds Before Offense	20.1%	−0.08	20.1%	−0.11	15.2%	−0.18	11.9%	−0.05	7.4%	−0.04	15.0%	−0.07
13. Special Talent	14.0%	+0.12	12.3%	+0.03	10.7%	−0.02	10.2%	+0.02	5.7%	−0.03	10.6%	+0.02
Column Averages	37.7%	−0.33	34.2%	−0.26	27.8%	−0.32	24.3%	−0.23	15.4%	−0.12	27.9%	−0.25

N.B.: XPF popularity values significantly greater than 50% (i.e., above the margin of error) are bolded. Popularity values within the margin of error are italicized.

in which popularity declines as offense seriousness increases suggests that the interaction between XPF and the underlying offense is quite complex and more than just a reflection of a punishment factor's initial popularity.

In addition to XPF popularity, XPF magnitude is similarly affected by switching among baseline scenarios. In Table 98 below, XPF magnitude is listed by scenario (taken from the lower half of each cell in Table 96), but this time include additional information about whether the figures in any row are significantly different from one another—that is, whether the magnitude of an XPF for a given offense differs significantly from the magnitude of the same XPF for a different offense.

Table 98 shows that there is a complex interactive effect between a punishment factor and the underlying offense. For example, the magnitude of XPF 15 ("Has Already Paid Substantial Civil Compensation to the Victim") displayed in scenarios A, B, and C diminished considerably in scenarios D and E. XPF 9 ("Rehabilitation") displayed a different tendency: the factor's magnitude remained consistent across all scenarios. Interestingly, XPF magnitude does not always depend on the seriousness of the underlying offense. For example, XPF 4 ("True Remorse, Acknowledge Guilt, and Apology Immediately After Offense") displayed greater magnitude when applied to scenario C than when applied to scenario B, even though scenario C was considered the more serious offense.[161]

5. RELATIVE RELATION AMONG XPFS BY POPULARITY

Table 99 below presents in each column the relative popularity of each XPF. XPFs are ranked according to their popularity, that is, the percentage of subjects who indicated that the factor should affect the baseline punishment assignment. XPFs are ordered according to their overall support, as provided in Table 95 above.

The relative popularity of an XPF varies depending on the baseline offense. This is itself no surprise. Subsection 3 has shown that there is some interactive effect between XPF popularity and offense. More surprising is that there is some general consistency in XPF ranking across the different kinds of offenses. XPFs that have a low relative rank for one scenario commonly have a similarly low rank for other scenarios; XPFs that have a high relative rank for one kind of offense tend to maintain that approximate ranking for other offenses. Such consistency is found in XPFs at all ranges of popularity. For example, XPF 13 ("Special Talents") ranks as the XPF with the least popularity for all five scenarios.[162] Likewise, XPF 2 ("Public Acknowledgment of Guilt Plus Apology") varies only slightly in rank, from 6th to 12th among the baseline scenarios.[163]

Some XPFs, however, change noticeably in their relative popularity, especially for the homicide offenses in scenarios D and E. The second most popular XPF—XPF 15

---

[161] *See supra* Table 96.

[162] *See supra* Table 99 (ranking XPF 13 as 18 – 18 – 18 – 18 – 18).

[163] *See id.* (ranking XPF 2 as 8 – 6 – 6 – 12 – 8).

TABLE 98. } Effects of Baseline Crime Scenario on XPF Magnitude

SCENARIOS: XPFs:	A. Theft with Trespass	B. Personal Injury	C. Governmental Corruption	D. Causing Death by Risk-Taking	E. Intentional Killing and Abduction
4. True Remorse, Acknowledge Guilt, and Apology Immediately After Offense	**−0.94** $_{ab}$	**−0.66** $_{bc}$	**−1.15** $_{a}$	**−0.51** $_{cd}$	**−0.33** $_{d}$
9. Rehabilitated	−0.32	−0.26	−0.29	−0.32	-0.26
15. Has Already Paid Substantial Civil Compensation to the Victim	**−0.88** $_{a}$	**−0.62** $_{a}$	**−0.68** $_{a}$	**−0.24** $_{b}$	**−0.04** $_{b}$
3. Truly Remorseful with Public Acknowledgment of Guilt and Apology	**−0.42** $_{a}$	**−0.36** $_{a}$	**−0.37** $_{a}$	**−0.21** $_{ab}$	**−0.11** $_{b}$
16. Hardship for Offender's Family or Others	**−0.68** $_{a}$	**−0.63** $_{a}$	**−0.77** $_{a}$	**−0.53** $_{a}$	**−0.09** $_{b}$
14. Has Been Punished Enough – Already Suffering from his Offense	**−0.76**	**−0.37**	**−0.49**	**−0.81**	**−0.36**
2. Public Acknowledgment of Guilt Plus Apology	**−0.39** $_{a}$	**−0.29** $_{ab}$	**−0.24** $_{abc}$	**−0.14** $_{bc}$	**−0.04** $_{c}$
17. Hardship for Offender Himself	−0.67	−0.48	−0.76	−0.53	−0.37
6. Victim Wants Less or No Punishment	−0.28	−0.21	−0.2	−0.27	−0.15
1. Public Acknowledgment of Guilt	−0.2	−0.19	−0.2	−0.15	−0.05
18. Old Age	**−0.33**	**−0.34**	**−0.35**	**−0.4**	**−0.12**
7. Victim Wants More Punishment	+0.09	0.11	+0.05	0.07	0
11. Good Deeds After Offense	−0.16	−0.14	−0.12	-0.09	−0.05
5. Forgiveness by Victim	**−0.25**	**−0.29**	**−0.07**	**−0.19**	**−0.1**
12. Bad Deeds/Character	0.04	0.15	0.01	0.04	+0.01
8. Public Outrage Over Offense	+0.09	0.06	0	0.16	−0.03
10. Good Deeds Before Offense	−0.08	−0.11	−0.18	−0.05	−0.04
13. Special Talent	**0.12**	**0.03**	**−0.02**	**0.02**	**−0.03**
Column Averages	**−0.33** $_{a}$	**−0.26** $_{bc}$	**−0.32** $_{ab}$	**−0.23** $_{c}$	**−0.12** $_{d}$

N.B.: Rows are bolded when the null hypothesis of no difference among scenarios may be rejected at the $p<0.05$ level.

TABLE 99. } Rank by Popularity of XPFs for Each Scenario

SCENARIOS: XPFs:	A. Theft with Trespass	B. Personal Injury	C. Governmental Corruption	D. Causing Death by Risk-Taking	E. Intentional Killing and Abduction	Overall Rank
4. Remorse, Public Acknowledgment of Guilt, Apology—Immediately after Offense	1	1 (66%)	1 (71%)	1 (49%)	1 (40%)	1 (61%)
9. Rehabilitated	3	3 (51%)	3 (42%)	2 (43%)	2 (31%)	2 (44%)
15. Already Paid Civil Compensation	2 (65%)	2 (53%)	2 (44%)	6 (28%)	10 (14%)	3 (41%)
3. Remorse, Public Acknowledgment, Apology	4 (53%)	5 (48%)	5 (38%)	5 (28%)	3 (21%)	4 (38%)
16. Hardship for Offender's Family	5 (50%)	4 (51%)	4 (41%)	4 (29%)	16 (8%)	5 (36%)
14. Already Suffering from his Offense	6 (46%)	7 (37%)	7 (28%)	3 (40%)	9 (14%)	6 (33%)
2. Public Acknowledgment of Guilt, Apology	8 (45%)	6 (42%)	6 (30%)	12 (20%)	8 (15%)	7 (30%)
17. Special Hardship for Offender	7 (45%)	10 (31%)	8 (27%)	8 (24%)	11 (13%)	8 (28%)
6. Victim Wants Less Punishment	9 (40%)	9 (32%)	14 (16%)	7 (25%)	4 (19%)	9 (27%)
1. Public Acknowledgment of Guilt	11 (32%)	8 (35%)	9 (26%)	10 (22%)	5 (16%)	10 (26%)
18. Old Age	10 (33%)	12 (26%)	11 (22%)	11 (21%)	14 (10%)	11 (22%)
7. Victim Wants More Punishment	15 (20%)	16 (19%)	10 (25%)	9 (23%)	6 (15%)	12 (20%)
11. Good Deeds After Offense	13 (26%)	11 (29%)	15 (16%)	13 (17%)	15 (10%)	13 (20%)
5. Forgiveness by Victim	12 (31%)	13 (23%)	17 (13%)	14 (16%)	13 (12%)	14 (19%)
12. Bad Deeds/ Character	17 (14%)	14 (21%)	12 (20%)	15 (16%)	7 (15%)	15 (17%)
8. Public Outrage Over Offense	16 (16%)	17 (17%)	13 (17%)	16 (15%)	12 (13%)	16 (16%)
10. Good Deeds Before Offense	14 (20%)	15 (20%)	16 (15%)	17 (12%)	17 (7%)	17 (15%)
13. Special Talent	18 (14%)	18 (12%)	18 (11%)	18 (10%)	18 (6%)	18 (11%)

("Has Already Paid Substantial Civil Compensation to the Victim")—drops to 6th for the reckless-killing scenario and 10th for the murder scenario. In other words, it is not simply that XPF popularity falls as the seriousness of the offense increases, but that XPF popularity in relation to other XPFs also falls as the underlying offense becomes more serious.

For some XPFs, the drop-off in relative popularity occurs just for the murder case. For example, XPF 16 ("Hardship for Offender's Family or Others") holds steady at either 4th or 5th place for most offenses but drops dramatically to16th for murder.[164] Similarly, XPF 14 ("Already Suffering From Offense") ranks between 3rd and 7th in scenarios A through D, but drops to 9th place in scenario E.[165]

In contrast, some XPFs become relatively more popular as the underlying offense becomes more serious. For example, XPF 8 ("Public Outrage over Offense") moves from 16th in scenario A to 12th in scenario E. Another aggravator of relatively weak popularity—XPF 12 ("Bad Deeds and Character")—similarly increases its popularity relative to other XPFs, at least for the most serious offense, murder.[166] But this raises an interesting interpretive issue. It may be that XPFs like these two increase in rank not because the logic of the mitigation is more compelling as applied to serious offenses but rather because other mitigations are less persuasive and the rankings of these XPFs increase primarily because they hold their popularity while others lose theirs.

One final interesting pattern of this sort is found in the pair of XPFs relating to victim desire for more or for less punishment. The relative popularity of XPF 6 ("Victim Wants Less or No Punishment") increases its rank from midrange for non-homicide offenses to 4th for murder. At the same time, XPF 7 ("Victim Wants More Punishment") moves from 15th place in scenario A to 6th place in scenario E. Thus, victim views on punishment appear to be taken into account more as offense seriousness rises.

6. DEMOGRAPHIC DIFFERENCES

In conducting the study, data was collected on the respondents' race, marital status, gender, income, age, and education level. Race, marital status, and gender were each coded as categorical variables (i.e., variables with two or more categories with no intrinsic ordering to the categories), while income, age, and education level were recorded as continuous variables (i.e., the relative values are ordered and magnitudes are straightforwardly interpretable).[167]

a. Demographic Differences and Popularity. The study took note of differences in XPF popularity by race, marital status, and gender. Values were derived based on this popularity throughout different demographics. Positive values indicate that

---

[164] *See id.* (ranking XPF 16 as 5 – 4 – 4 – 4 – 16).

[165] *See id.* (ranking XPF 17 as 7 – 10 – 8 – 8 – 11).

[166] *See id.* (ranking XPF 12 as 17 – 14 – 12 – 15 – 7).

[167] For a more in-depth presentation of the findings discussed here, see Robinson, Jackowitz & Bartels, *supra* note 937, at 34–56.

white, unmarried, or male subjects changed punishment more often than did nonwhite, married, or female subjects; negative values indicate that nonwhite, married or female subjects changed punishment more often. For instance, the value -23.6 percent, as reported for XPF 15 in scenario A, indicates that XPF popularity among nonwhite respondents exceeded XPF popularity among white respondents by 23.6 percent.

Race. Race seems to have the greatest demographic effect on popularity of XPFs. In the 15 mitigation XPFs,[168] XPF popularity among whites was significantly greater than among nonwhites in 17 of the 65 variations. XPF popularity was significantly greater among nonwhites in only 1 variation. But it was not that whites were generally more sympathetic to all offenders. In the three aggravation XPFs, XPF popularity among white subjects was significantly different from XPF popularity among nonwhites in ten of the fifteen variations, while in none of these variations was XPF popularity greater among nonwhites. Generalizing across all XPFs shows that whites adjusted punishment significantly more than nonwhites in three scenarios, while generalizing across all scenarios shows that whites adjusted punishment significantly more than nonwhites for 13 of the 18 XPFs. XPF popularity among whites exceeded XPF popularity among nonwhites by a statistically significant 5.7 percent.

Gender. Gender has less of an effect on XPF popularity than does ethnicity. XPF popularity among males was often greater than among females. In the 15 mitigation XPFs, males adjusted punishment significantly more often than did females in 7 of 75 variations. Females adjusted punishment significantly more than males in only 2 variations. In none of the 3 aggravation XPF variations did gender produce a statistically significant difference between genders, though XPF 12 ("Bad Deeds/Character") did show an overall significance. Column averages show that, generalizing across all XPFs, males were more likely to make a punishment adjustment than females in 3 of the 5 scenarios. Across all scenarios XPF popularity among males was significantly greater than among females for 6 of the 18 XPFs. Overall XPF popularity among males exceeded XPF popularity among females by a statistically significant 3.4 percent.

Marital Status. Marital status seems to have the least effect of the demographic factors. In the 15 mitigation XPFs, XPF popularity among unmarried respondents was significantly more than among married respondents in 2 of the 75 variations, and in both cases XPF popularity was greater among unmarried respondents. In the 3 aggravation XPFs, XPF popularity among unmarried respondents was greater than among married respondents in 2 of the 15 variations; in one instance XPF popularity among unmarried respondents was greater and in the other instance XPF popularity among married respondents was greater. Column averages show that, generalizing across all XPFs, unmarried subjects adjusted punishment significantly more often than did married respondents in only 2 of the 5 scenarios. Generalizing

---

[168] Three of the XPFs invited aggravations of punishment, as noted in *supra* Table 96.

across scenarios XPF popularity among unmarried respondents was significantly greater than among married respondents for 2 of the 18 XPFs. Overall XPF popularity among unmarried respondents exceeded XPF popularity among married respondents by a slight though statistically significant 1.7 percent.

In overview, XPF popularity among white, male, or unmarried respondents was greater than among nonwhite, female, or married respondents, though the actual difference was slight: only 5.7 percent, 3.4 percent, and 1.7 percent, respectively. This pattern held true in scenarios B and D, where across all XPFs white, male, or unmarried subjects tended to record more adjustments than did their nonwhite, female, or married counterparts, but again with single-digit differences. For XPFs across scenarios, all but the three most popular XPFs showed significant differences in XPF popularity among at least one demographic group, but again the extent of the differences rarely reached above single digits.

Income. Income seems to have a weak effect on XPF popularity. Income significantly correlates with XPF popularity in only two XPF variations: XPF 4 under scenario D and XPF 11 under scenario D. Generalizing across scenarios, income only has a significant effect on XPF 4, suggesting that at least for XPF 4 ("True Remorse, Acknowledge Guilt, and Apology Immediately After Offense"), as income increases so too does the XPF's intuitive appeal. XPF 4 seems to be an isolated example, however. Generalizing across XPFs, income has no significant effect on XPF popularity. Similarly, generally across all responses there was no significant correlation between income and XPF popularity.

Age. In some variations, age seems to play a significant role in determining whether to apply an extralegal punishment factor. Significance was found in 18 of the variations tested, though the size of the correlation was minimal in all. Notably, with a few exceptions, where correlation with age was significant, as age increased the likelihood that a respondent changed his punishment decreased. Indeed, generalizing across scenarios, this sort of relationship was found in XPFs 3, 4, 7, 8, 9, and 15 and generally across all responses there was a slight negative correlation between XPF popularity and age (-0.02).

Education. Education also seemed to play a significant role in some variations. Significance was found in 11 of the variations tested. Generalizing across XPFs, there was a slight though significant correlation found between education and XPF popularity in responses to scenarios A ("Theft") and B ("Assault"). Generalizing across scenarios, 7 XPFs showed some correlation with education, all but 1 of them negative.[169] That significance was found generally for XPFs 14 through 18, which constitute Group D ("Suffering apart from Official Punishment"), suggests that as education level increases Group D's rationale is less persuasive. Still, the correlation is slight. Across all responses, a slight negative correlation was found to be significant.

[169] XPFs 5, 14, 15, 16, 17, and 18 demonstrated a negative correlation with education. XPF 4 demonstrated a positive correlation.

To summarize, in the vast majority of XPF and base scenario variations, there are no demographic differences.[170] However, some variations did show some differences. Being white, male, unmarried, older, richer, or more educated, generally predicted a greater willingness to give the XPF mitigations tested here, though there are exceptions. We do not know, on these analyses, if there is an interactive effect among these demographic variables.

7. SUMMARY OF STUDY CONCLUSIONS

There is support among lay people for punishment factors that have traditionally been excluded from the criminal law's liability and punishment rules. Every XPF tested had some support, even in relation to scenario E ("Intentional Killing and Abduction"), the most serious offense. A number of XPFs enjoyed support of a majority of study participants, with support reaching as high as 77 percent for the most popular XPF. On the other hand, most XPFs did not gain the support of a majority of study participants. Even for a relatively minor offense like that in scenario A ("Theft with Trespass"), factors that are quite common in practice or are advocated for by criminal law theorists failed to persuade many study participants.

Nevertheless, lay intuitions about extralegal punishment factors are actually quite nuanced and sophisticated. The seriousness of the underlying offense almost always influenced decisions about whether, in light of some punishment factor, to grant a punishment reduction. The seriousness of the offense also affected decisions about the size of the change in punishment, if any were to be made. Moreover, some punishment factors seem better suited for certain types of crimes than others. Few punishment factors have appeal no matter what the underlying offense. For example, while XPFs like paying substantial civil compensation were popular mitigating factors when the underlying offense was not serious, once a human death was involved XPFs like victim forgiveness overtook them in popularity.

For the most part, lay judgments across demographics proved remarkably consistent. Differences attributable to age, income, or education level were few and slight. Likewise, while there were differences between whites and nonwhites, males and females, and married and unmarried respondents, neither XPF popularity nor XPF magnitude tended to differ in most cases among these demographic groups. Of the demographic variables tested, race seemed to have the biggest effect: whites were more likely to adjust punishment in response to XPFs than nonwhites especially in response to mitigation XPFs, although whites were not more sympathetic to offenders overall and the overall effect of was race was relatively small.

---

[170] For an analysis of the effect of demographic on the magnitude of change in XPF effect, *see* Robinson, Jackowitz & Bartels, *supra* note 937, at 43–50.

C. Implications for Criminal Justice Rules and Practices

For many, if not most, of the XPFs noted in section A there are ongoing discussions about the propriety of their use in assessing punishment. And many are part of larger debates, such as those regarding plea bargaining, restorative justice, the role of public outrage in sentencing, and the victims' rights debate on victim participation in sentencing. These discussions commonly focus on a variety of utilitarian and desert concerns, but all of them are affected by the findings reported in section C.

Two findings of section C have broad implications for criminal justice reform. First, the high level of disagreement regarding some XPFs highlights the problem of disparity in application. Second, the high level of agreement in supporting the use of some XPFs and in rejecting the use of others suggests that adjudication practices that conflict with these views are likely to undercut the system's moral credibility with the community it governs and, thereby, its ability to harness the powerful forces of normative and social influence.

1. DISAGREEMENTS ABOUT XPFS AND THE PROBLEM OF DISPARITY IN APPLICATION

As section A notes, there exist a myriad of points in the criminal justice process at which a decision maker may choose to take account of, or to ignore, the existence of an XPF. A prosecutor may consider, or ignore, extralegal punishment factors when deciding to prosecute an offender or when negotiating a plea bargain. A judge may consider, or ignore, an XPF at sentencing, occasionally upon legal authority, but more typically in the exercise of her sentencing discretion. In some trials, XPFs may come out during trial testimony and may be taken into account by jurors in determining a trial verdict, or not. And in some sentencing regimes,[171] juries also participate in the sentencing process and may consider, or ignore, an XPF in that context. Finally, parole boards and corrections officials may consider XPFs, or not, in deciding when to release an offender.

There seems general agreement that a central feature of fairness and justice is consistency in the application of punishment. Similar offenders committing similar offenses ought to receive similar punishment. One's punishment ought to depend upon one's offense, culpability, and capacities, not upon the luck, good or bad, of the decision maker one happens to draw.[172]

---

[171] *See* Nancy J. King & Susan R. Klein, *Essential Elements*, 54 VAND. L. REV. 1467, 1510 (2001) (noting that by the mid-20th century, 13 states continue to allow sentencing by juries).

[172] *See* S. Rep. No. 98–225, at 45–46 (1983) ("Sentencing disparities that are not justified by differences among offenses or offenders are unfair both to offenders and to the public."), *reprinted in* 1984 U.S.C.C.A.N. 3182, 3182–3562; Michael M. O'Hear, *National Uniformity/Local Uniformity: Reconsidering the Use of Departures To Reduce Federal-State Sentencing Disparities*, 87 IOWA L. REV. 721, 729 (2002). In *U.S. v. Booker*, Justice Breyer announced that Congress's basic goal in passing the Sentencing Act was increased uniformity in punishment. 543 U.S. 220, 253 (2005). The concept of uniformity can be described simply as encapsulating the "twin goals of (i) similar treatment of similarly situated offenders and (2) different treatment of differently situated offenders." *Id.*

Yet, as section A makes clear, there are many XPFs on which there is enormous disagreement as to the propriety of their application, even when people are considering the exact same XPF for the exact same offense and offender, as occurs in the study. In more than twenty percent of the cells in Table 96 (19 of 90), the subjects were almost evenly split, 40 to 60 percent or closer. In more than a quarter of the cells (25 of 90), there is a dissent of more than a third of the subjects. In almost half of the cells (43 of 90), a quarter or more of the subjects are dissenting.

There is little reason to think that these high levels of disagreement on some applications of some XPFs disappear among the police, prosecutors, judges, jurors, parole boards, and other criminal justice system decision makers.[173] Yet, clearly it would be unacceptable if the chances that one's punishment depended on the luck of the draw on a decision maker were at these levels.

Indeed, even more egregious are situations where an offender falls under a decision maker holding an idiosyncratic view. Imagine an offender being judged by a decision maker who falls into a small group of dissenters. More than half the cells (48 of 90) in Table 96 show a minority view of 25 percent of less. Some of the XPFs had a dissenting group as small as 6 percent. A lack of guidance in the application of XPFs invites the problem explicitly noted by the Senate: offenders receiving "more favorable or less favorable treatment because he happens to be sentenced by a particular judge."[174]

The potential for disparity in application is exacerbated by the demographic differences in assessing XPFs. While there is much agreement across demographics, there also is some disagreement. An offender's punishment ought not depend upon the particular demographic characteristics of the decision maker, be it sentencing judge, sentencing jury, or prosecuting attorney exercising discretion in striking a plea and sentence agreement.

Thus, if XPFs are to be relied upon in assessing punishment, there are good reasons to provide an articulation of rules governing their use or at least some informal guidance, both to better avoid abuse and to improve the uniformity in their application among different decision makers. For all offenders, punishment ought to depend upon the same set of factors relevant to the case, not upon the personal preferences and idiosyncrasies of the individual decision maker.

The strong trend in American criminal justice is to attempt to guide the exercise of discretion as much as possible, in large part out of a commitment to equality of treatment among similarly situated offenders. Toward that end, some parts of

---

[173] As a general matter, there is disagreement between the population at large and sentencing officials on how strict the criminal justice system should be. *See* Stephanos Bibas, *Transparency and Participation in Criminal Procedure*, 81 N.Y.U. L. Rev. 911, 928 (2006) (reviewing studies). As to what factors to take into account at sentencing, there is good reason to think that the judgment of criminal justice officials will often depart from that of non-specialists. *See* Michael Tonry, *The Functions of Sentencing and Sentencing Reform*, 58 Stan. L. Rev. 37, 43–45 (2005) (detailing the ways in which different people view the purposes of sentencing).

[174] S. Rep. No. 98–225, at 79 (1983), *reprinted in* 1984 U.S.C.C.A.N. 3182, 3262.

the system have experimented with using guidelines—some American jurisdictions have developed sentencing guidelines, parole release guidelines, or charging guidelines. As we better understand the effect that people give to XPFs, we will be better able to construct guidelines that articulate principles to guide reliance upon XPFs, wherever they may be used.

2. STRONG SUPPORT FOR, OR OPPOSITION TO, AN XPF AND THE PROBLEM OF UNDERMINING THE LAW'S MORAL CREDIBILITY

As argued in part II, there is reason to believe that there is good utility in a criminal justice system that distributes liability and punishment in accordance with citizens' shared intuitions of justice. If the criminal law is to build moral credibility with the community it governs, it should regularly take account of XPFs that have strong support in that community, a practice not now done, at least in any consistent fashion. For example, true remorse demonstrated by acknowledgment of guilt and apology before being a suspect (XPF 4) had strong support among lay persons in the study and dramatically reduced punishment. Indeed, it was supported by a majority of participants for all offense scenarios except for the two homicide cases. A criminal justice system that ignores such an XPF risks being seen as deaf to the community's views of proper punishment.

At the same time, maintaining the criminal law's moral credibility with the community also means avoiding reliance upon XPFs that the community rejects as irrelevant to punishment. Seven of the XPFs had average support across all scenarios of 20 percent or less (XPFs 7, 11, 5, 12, 8, 10, and 13, in decreasing order of support).[175] Allowing decision makers to rely upon these XPFs risks undermining the criminal law's moral credibility, thereby potentially undermining the law's ability to harness the powerful forces of normative and social influence.

Of course, these conclusions are not without caveats. While the improper consideration (or lack thereof) of an XPF might have detrimental effects on the law's moral credibility, this can only occur if the treatment of the XPF is publicized.[176] This is heavily dependent on accurate, detailed reporting by the media. If, for example, a court ignores an XPF in sentencing a defendant despite that factor's importance to the public, the law's moral credibility may only be harmed if the public learns that the XPF was ignored. Conversely, a court applying XPFs in accordance with the public's wishes might nonetheless be seen as unjust where the media fails to provide details of sentencing decisions. When a sentence is reported in isolation, which is the traditional news coverage approach, it may seem inappropriate, yet an examination of a fuller collection of cases may suggest that it is indeed just the sentence this offender deserves, given his relative blameworthiness.

---

[175] *See supra* table 96.

[176] *See* chapter 8, sections B and D; Paul H. Robinson & John M. Darley, *Intuitions of Justice: Implications for Criminal Law and Justice Policy*, 81 S. CAL. L. REV. 1, 18–31 (2007).

D. Conclusion

Section A documents a wide variety of factors that can influence punishment in current practice but that are generally not recognized by existing criminal law. These XPFs can influence the judgment of decision makers throughout the criminal justice process, such as when prosecutors decide what charge to press, when judges decide which sentence to impose, when parole boards decide when to release a prisoner, and when executive officials decide whether to grant clemency, as well as in less-visible exercises of discretion, such as in decisions by police officers and trial jurors. Many XPFs are part of larger debates, such as those regarding plea bargaining, restorative justice, the role of public outrage sentencing, and the debate over victims' right to participate in sentencing.

As the empirical findings reported in part B make clear, there is broad support for use of some XPFs in determining punishment (and all XPFs had some support). On the other hand, most XPFs have only minority support: half had the support of less than a third of the study participants. The extent of an XPF's support, and the extent of the effect it had in adjusting punishment, was commonly dependent upon the nature of the underlying offense. Interestingly, the relative popularity among the XPFs also was dependent upon the nature of the underlying offense. Some XPFs were popular or unpopular throughout, but for others' popularity changed, as with losing relative popularity as the offense is more serious. Both the level of support and the effect of some XPFs depended upon the demographic characteristics of a subject. For example, being white, male, unmarried, older, richer, or more educated, commonly predicted a greater willingness to give the XPF mitigations tested here, though there are exceptions. Finally, there were differences in the treatment of some XPFs, for some kinds of offenses, between the local and national sample.

The study findings suggest a variety of implications for criminal law and justice policy and practice. If the criminal justice system is to maintain its moral credibility with the community it governs, and thereby harness the powerful forces of social and normative influence, it cannot be seen as giving deference to an XPF that the community rejects nor as ignoring an XPF that the community broadly supports, yet this does indeed happen in current practice.

Where do all of these studies get us? Some piecing together of the conclusions with a synthesis of the ideas would be something I would like to see as a reader. What are the questions to be asked in the future on these topics? What are the things that should be done? All of these questions have been asked before, but they have not really been answered in a full and straightforward manner. At each step in the reading the reader is less equipped than at this final stage to fully tackle the range of ideas presented. A conclusion that did that would be powerful and help to bring the book's message home.

22 }

Intuitions of Justice & the Utility of Desert

Criminal law scholars have commonly accepted that people did not agree and would not ever agree on what punishment is deserved in a specific case, possibly due to the very subjective, complex, and value-dependent nature of judgments of blameworthiness. Yet the empirical studies reported here show the common wisdom to be false, for there are many points of agreement across all demographics (chs. 1 and 2). It is not agreement on the absolute amount of punishment but rather agreement on the relative blameworthiness among different cases. This consensus necessarily produces a specific amount of punishment when the high number of noticeably different cases is rank ordered on the continuum of available punishment, which has a limited number of meaningfully different punishment points.

This agreement does not touch all offenses and all factors but only what one might call the "core" of wrongdoing, which is limited primarily to offenses of violence and nonconsensual takings. As one moves out from this core of agreement by adding other factors or offenses, the extent of agreement breaks down (ch. 4). The larger point here is that, rather than a sea of disagreement on everything, as was thought, there is a continuum from a core of issues on which there is almost near unanimity, to increasing disagreement out at the culturally dependent periphery.

How can it be that there is high agreement across demographics on relative blameworthiness for any set of cases, a judgment so seemingly subjective and complex? One theory is that such judgments are the product of a specialized learning system shared by all humans. There is much evidence to support this view, but the accumulating evidence is not yet conclusive (ch. 3). Humans might also learn to gauge justice in the same general way they learn other things, and the high level of agreement comes from the fact that everyone's learning is overwhelmingly influenced by some universal condition, such as living within a group.

For law and policy makers, it may not matter which explanatory theory is ultimately proven correct. Both lead to the same conclusion on the point most relevant to criminal law: whatever the source of people's shared intuitions of justice, those intuitions are something to which system designers and social reformers would be wise to give special attention. Reformers ought not to assume they can simply educate people out of a core intuition of justice the way they would persuade people to change their views on a purely reasoned matter.

The presence of high levels of agreement across demographics suggests that the source of the sense of justice on core issues is deeply embedded and not easily influenced. Different demographic factors—income, education, race, political orientation, marital status, religion, gender—can have enormous effect in shaping people's views. To find high agreement across demographics means that the judgment at issue is immune to all of these powerful influences. If it is immune to these powerful influences, it will not be so easily changed by reformers, at least not with the kind of intrusions on personal autonomy that a liberal democracy would be likely to permit (ch. 5).

This reduced malleability has important implications for where reformers concentrate their efforts. For example, they ought not to waste resources trying to persuade people to not want to punish serious wrongdoing, as some reformers would do (ch. 11). They could find it unfeasible to persuade the community that serious resulting harm, such as causing death, ought to be insignificant in assessing punishment—that only an actor's intention should be relevant, as some scholars would argue.[1] At the same time, understanding the nature of people's judgments about justice can help reformers tailor their programs for greater effectiveness (ch. 5).

It is not only the nonmalleable nature of some lay judgments about justice that are important to criminal law but also the content of those judgments. Part III reviews community views on a wide range of liability and punishment issues, touching nearly every kind of issue a criminal code or sentencing guideline drafter might have to address. Lawmakers and reformers ought to pay close attention to such studies of the content of lay judgments of justice, and move beyond the past half century of criminal law formulations, which reflect little restraint in adopting rules that conflict with community views (ch. 7).

As observed throughout this book, studies now show that deviations from "empirical desert" are not cost free. Lay people have sophisticated and nuanced judgments of justice (ch. 1, part III), and liability and punishment rules that intentionally conflict with those judgments will undermine the criminal law's moral credibility with the community, which in turn will undermine the community's willingness to defer to the criminal law, to assist and support it, and to internalize its expressed norms (chs. 8 and 9). Specifically, gaining a reputation for regularly and intentionally relying upon rules incompatible with community views can promote subversion of and resistance to the criminal justice system, can undermine the effective yet cheap normative influence of stigmatization, can reduce people's willingness to defer to the criminal law in cases of normative ambiguity, and can subvert the criminal law's ability to shape community norms and to induce people to internalize the norms expressed in the law.

In part because of their own limitations, and in part because of their conflict with community views, the traditional "coercive crime-control" mechanisms of

---

[1] *See, e.g.*, Stephen J. Schulhofer, *Harm and Punishment*, 122 U. PA. L. REV. 1497, 1498–1503 (1974); LARRY ALEXANDER, KIMBERLY KESSLER FERZAN, AND STEPHEN MORSE, CRIME AND CULPABILITY (2009); Model Penal Code §5.05(1).

general deterrence and incapacitation ought to be replaced with the "normative crime-control" principle that has criminal law track community views as reflected in empirical studies of "empirical desert." The community of reference in any given situation is the one that will be bound or affected by the rule or practice being formulated, be it a federal criminal code, a state sentencing guideline, or a city sentencing practice.

The crime-control power of tracking community views, and the crime-control cost of law's conflicting with them, no doubt explain why even the Model Penal Code drafters of the 1950s, enthusiastic advocates of the then newly energized "coercive crime-control" strategy, nonetheless compromised their deterrence and incapacitation programs when the logic of those programs would take the criminal law too far from community judgments of justice (ch. 6).

The claim here is not that criminal law should never deviate from a community's judgments of justice. Those judgments might be unjust, or the law might have to delineate aspirational goals for community values (ch. 10). But reformers should appreciate the potential cost of such deviation and persuade themselves beforehand that the potential benefits outweigh those costs.

What is needed to inform policy makers and criminal law and sentencing guideline drafters (and even sentencing judges, ch. 21) is a comprehensive research effort to map lay judgments of justice. The studies reported in part III are only a rough sketch of the contours of the landscape when we actually need a high-resolution photograph. That research also should be used to test the claims in scholarly debates. As part IV illustrates, many scholarly theories are rooted in claims about how people assess blameworthiness and thus can be empirically tested.

The presentations here offer a new perspective on the age-old retributivist-utilitarian debate. In the classic view, the two are in inevitable and unavoidable tension. The criminal justice system must either devote itself to most effectively fighting crime and to most faithfully doing justice, or it must compromise one to advance the other. The studies show that a criminal law based upon empirical desert can strengthen crime control. Empirical desert is not true deontological desert, of course, but it may be the best close approximation of it that one can hope to construct in the real world. Thus, it may well be that the best way to fight crime is to do justice.

TABLE OF CASES

Adams; State v., 864 S.W.2d 31 (Tenn. 1993), 511*n*137–38
Adkins; People v., No. 257845, 2006 WL 142120 (Mich. Ct. App. 2006), 118
Alexander; United States v., 471 F.2d 923 (D.C. Cir. 1973), 229–30
Allen; State v., 994 P.2d 728 (N.M. 2000), 497*n*22
Anders; State v., 277 N.E.2d 554 (Ohio 1972), 117*n*35
Apprendi v. New Jersey, 530 U.S. 466 (2000), 495*n*5
Archbold v. State, 397 N.E.2d 1071 (Ind. App. 1979), 416*n*4
Auburn, City of v. Hedlund, 201 P.3d 315 (Wash. 2009), 507*n*102–4

Bernard; State v., 744 So.2d 1134 (Fla. App. 1999), 500*n*52
Bethea v. United States, 365 A.2d 64 (D.C. 1976), 117*n*35
Billingslea v. Texas, 780 S.W.2d 271 (Tex. Crim. App. 1989), 204*n*23
Booker; United States v., 543 U.S. 220 (2005), 495*n*6, 529*n*172
Brawner; United States v., 471 F.2d 969 (D.C. Cir. 1972), 228–29
Bult; State v., 529 N.W.2d 197 (S.D. 1995), 505*n*92

Castano; State v., 360 P.2d 479 (Ariz. 1961), 504*n*77
Chastain; United States v., 84 F.3d 321 (9th Cir. 1996), 512*n*142
City of. *See name of city*
Clark v. Arizona, 548 U.S. 735 (2006), 115–16, 123, 127
Clayton; State v., 656 S.W.2d 344 (Tenn. 1983), 117*n*34
Clegg; State v., 635 N.W.2d 578 (S.D. 2001), 497*n*26
Commonwealth v. *See name of opposing party*
Coughlin; United States v., 2008 WL 313099 (W.D. Ark. 2008), 508*n*114
Cox v. Louisiana, 379 U.S. 559 (1965), 501*n*55
Crawford v. State, 770 N.E.2d 775 (Ind. 2002), 497*n*24

Davidson v. State, 558 N.E.2d 1077 (Ind. 1990), 504*n*76
Dawson v. Delaware, 503 U.S. 159 (1992), 503
de la Garza; State v., 675 P.2d 295 (App.1983), 511*n*136
Dean; People v., No. 266438, 2006 WL 3077520 (Mich. App. Oct. 31, 2006), 507*n*101
DeMonte; United States v., 25 F.3d 343 (6th Cir. 1994), 512*n*143
Dowdell v. State, 720 N.E.2d 1146 (Ind. 1999), 509*n*121
Drew; People v., 583 P.2d 1318 (Cal. 1978), 117*n*34

Eggers; State v., No. 2 CA-CR 05–0320, 2005 WL 5829847 (Ariz. Ct. App. 2005), 115
Etzweiler v. State, 125 N.H. 57, 480 A.2d 870 (N.H. 1984), 311–12, 316, 317

Gardellini; United States v., 545 F.3d 1089 (2008), 507*n*105–6
Garnett v. Maryland, 632 A.2d 797 (Md. 1993), 118–19, 123, 127
Godley v. Commonwealth, 343 S.E.2d 368 (Va. Ct. App. 1986), 117*n*35
Godsey; State v., 60 S.W.3d 759 (Tenn. 2001), 505*n*91
Goldstein; United States v., 883 F.2d 1362 (7th Cir. 1989), 120*n*57
Grauerholz; State v., 654 P.2d 395 (Kan. 1982), 117*n*34
Griswold; People v., 747 N.Y.S.2d 872 (N.Y. App. Div. 2002), 497*n*26
Gross v. State, 730 S.W.2d 104 (Tex. Crim. App. 1987), 499*n*42–43

Haas; State v., No. A-05-804, 2006 WL 996535 (Neb. Ct. App. 2006), 118, 123, 127
Hailey v. Fenner & Beane, 246 S.W. 412 (Tex. Civ. App. 1922), 452*n*67
Harmelin v. Michigan, 501 U.S. 957 (1991), 113–14, 123, 127
Herron v. State, 287 So. 2d 759 (Miss. 1974), 117*n*34
Hitchcock v. Dugger, 481 U.S. 393 (1986), 505*n*90
Humphreys; State v., 444 A.2d 569 (N.J. 1982), 501*n*54

Jackson v. State, 286 Md. 430, 408 A.2d 711 (1979), 378*n*23
Jackson v. State, 684 So. 2d 1213 (Miss. 1996), 497*n*22
Jaffe; People v., 185 N.Y. 497, 78 N.E. 169 (1906), 417*n*6
Janis; United States v., 428 U.S. 433 (1976), 205*n*35
Johnson; State v., 399 A.2d 469 (R.I. 1979), 117*n*35

Keeler v. Superior Court, 470 P.2d 617 (Cal. 1970), 204*n*23
Knox; State v., 990 So.2d 665 (Fla. App. 2008), 500*n*50
Kost; State v., 290 N.W.2d 482 (S.D. 1980), 117*n*34

Leocal v. Ashcroft, 543 U.S. 1 (2004), 119*n*40
Lockett v. Ohio, 438 U.S. 586 (1978), 498*n*32–33, 502
Lockhart; State v., 490 S.E.2d 298 (W. Va. 1997), 117*n*35
Louisiana v. Moore, No. 2006-KA-1979, ; 2007 WL 914637 (La. App. 1 Cir. Mar. 28, 2007), 119, 123, 127

Maier; United States v., 975 F.2d 944 (2d Cir. 1992), 505*n*85
McAbee v. State, 770 N.E.2d 802 (Ind. 2002), 497*n*26
McHoul; Commonwealth v., 226 N.E.2d 556 (Mass. 1967), 117*n*35
Mollicone; State v., 746 A.2d 135 (R.I. 2000), 497*n*26
Moore; People v., 439 N.W.2d 684 (Mich. 1989), 510*n*129–30
Morissette v. U.S., 342 U.S. 246 (1952), 119*n*41
Mott; State v., 931 P.2d 1046 (Ariz. 1997), 116
Munn v. State, 658 P.2d 482 (Okla. 1983), 117*n*34

Ntshona; United States v., 156 F.3d 318 (2d Cir. 1998), 120*n*57

Ochoa; People v., 966 P.2d 442 (Cal. 1998), 509*n*119
Oligmueller; United States v., 198 F.3d 669 (8th Cir. 1999), 512*n*147
Overton; State v., No. 02C019510-CC00303, 1997 WL 287665 (Tenn. Crim. App. June 2, 1997), 502*n*65

Parsons v. State, 2 So. 854 (Ala. 1887), 106*n*39
Parsons v. State, 81 Alaska 577 (D. Alaska 1887), 338*n*9

Peaslee; Commonwealth v., 177 Mass. 267, 59 NE 55 (1901), 417*n*8
People v. *See name of opposing party*
Pepper v. United States, No. 09-6822, 2011 WL 709543 (U.S. Mar. 2, 2011), 505*n*86–89
Plummer; State v., 374 A.2d 431 (N.H. 1977), 117*n*34
Poole v. State, 625 P.2d 1163 (Nev. 1981), 117*n*34
Pope v. State, 441 So.2d 1073 (Fla. 1983), 497*n*23
Powell; State v., 696 So.2d 789 (Fla. App. 1997), 500*n*52
Price v. State, 765 N.E.2d 1245 (Ind. 2002), 498*n*29
Prince; United States v., 110 F.3d 921 (2d Cir. 1997), 114

Randell v. State, 846 P.2d 278 (1993), 500*n*45
Regina v. Cogan & Leak, [1976] 1 QB 217 (CA, Crim Div), 416*n*3
Regina v. Richards, [1974] 1 QB 776 (CA, Crim Div), 416*n*2
Rice; State v., 483 A.2d 248 (Vt. 1984), 501*n*53
Rioux; United States v., 97 F.3d 648 (2d Cir. 1996), 503*n*70
Rivera; State v., 27 A.3d 676 (N.H. 2011), 311*n*10
Roadenbaugh; State v., 673 P.2d 1166 (Kan. 1982), 117*n*34
Roth; State v., 471 A.2d 370 (N.J. 1984), 510*n*123
Ruffin v. State, 270 S.W.3d 586 (Tex. Crim. App. 2008), 116*n*32
Rummel v. Estelle, 445 U.S. 263 (1980), 112, 123, 127, 152
Rummel v. Estelle, 587 F.2d 651 (5th Cir. 1978), 112, 123, 127

Schwimmer; People v., 66 A.D.2d 91, 411 N.Y.S.2d 922 (1978), *aff'd,* 47 N.Y.2d 1004, 420 N.Y.S.2d 218, 394 N.E.2d 288 (1979), 416*n*5
Simon v. United States, 361 F. Supp. 2d 35 (E.D.N.Y. 2005), 504*n*84
Smith; People v., No. 284828, 2009 WL 2136903 (Mich. Ct. App. July 16, 2009), 500*n*48
State v. *See name of opposing party*
Szarwark; United States v., 198 F.3d 669 (8th Cir. 1999), 512

Thornton; State v., 800 A.2d 1016 (R.I. 2002), 498*n*30
Thurlow; State v., 712 P.2d 929 (1986), 511*n*136
Tirado; Commonwealth v., 870 A.2d 362 (Pa. Super. Ct. 2005), 498*n*31
Trostle; State v., 951 P.2d 869 (Ariz. 1997), 497*n*22

United States v. *See name of opposing party*
Ussery; State v., 543 So.2d 457 (Fla. App. 1989), 500*n*51

Vickers; State v., 291 S.E.2d 599 (N.C. 1982), 117*n*34

Washington; People v., No. 235241, 2004 WL 243369 (Mich. Ct. App. Feb. 10, 2004), 500*n*49
White; State v., 456 P.2d 797 (Idaho 1969), 117*n*35

Yates v. State, 171 S.W.3d 215 (2005), 116–17, 123, 127
Young; People v., 529 N.E.2d 497 (Ill. 1988), 505*n*93

TABLE OF MPC

1.02(2), 10*n*20
1.02(2)(a), 10
1.02(2)(a)(i), 10
1.02(2)(a)(ii), 10*n*20
1.13(9), 302*n*4
1.13(16), 105*n*28, 107*n*51
2.01(1), 269*n*18
2.02(1), 303*n*5
2.02(2), 301*n*1
2.02(2)(a)(ii), 106*n*40
2.02(2)(b)(ii), 106*n*41
2.02(2)(c), 105*n*29, 105*n*30
2.02(2)(d), 105*n*29, 105*n*30, 107*n*52, 329*n*15
2.02(3), 105*n*27, 302*n*2, 303*n*5, 304*n*7
2.02(comment 4), 330*n*16
2.03(1)(a), 385*n*26, 386*n*28
2.03(2)(b), 104*n*18, 386*n*27
2.03(3)(b), 104*n*18
2.04(1), 303*n*6
2.04(3)(b), 105*n*36
2.05(1)(a), 119*n*44
2.06(1), 418*n*12
2.06(2), 418*n*12
2.06(3)(a), 311*n*9
2.06(3)(a)(ii), 261*n*15, 377*n*20, 418*n*12, 419*n*13
2.06(4), 312*n*11, 377*n*20
2.06(6)(c)(ii), 106*n*37
2.06(7), 416*n*3
2.08(2), 106*n*43
2.08(4), 227*n*51, 347*n*14
2.08(5)(b), 319
2.09, 353*n*15
2.09(1), 99*n*5, 105*n*35, 107*n*44, 228*n*52
2.12(1), 105*n*32
2.12(2), 104*n*19
2.12(3), 105*n*33
2.13(1)(a), 354*n*16
2.13(1)(b), 107*n*45, 354*n*16
3.02(1), 474*n*12

3.02(1)(a), 105*n*34
3.03(3)(a), 474*n*12
3.04(1), 106*n*42, 107*n*49, 474*n*12
3.04(2)(b)(i), 279*n*7
3.05(1)(b), 474*n*12
3.06(1), 474*n*12
3.06(5), 289*n*11
3.07(1), 294*n*14, 474*n*12
3.07(2)(b), 294*n*15, 296*n*17
3.09(1)(b), 279*n*6
3.09(2), 279*n*5, 475*n*14, 476*n*18, 490*n*33, 490*n*34
3.09(3), 294*n*16
3.11(1), 475*n*15
4.01(1), 106*n*38, 338*n*8, 338*n*10
4.10, 347*n*13
5.01(1)(a), 417*n*7, 489*n*32
5.01(1)(c), 105*n*31, 242*n*5, 249, 417*n*9
5.01(4), 254*n*13
5.03(1)(a), 416*n*5
5.03(1)(b), 416*n*5
5.03(comments 398-402), 416*n*5
5.05(1), 102*n*12, 404*n*2, 418, 488*n*27
6.06, 485*n*25, 485*n*26
6.08, 291*n*12
7.03(1), 100*n*6
7.07(3), 100*n*6
210.2, 104*n*25
210.2(1)(a), 377*n*19
210.2(1)(b), 378*n*34
210.3(1)(a), 377*n*19
210.3(1)(b), 105*n*26, 477*n*22
210.3(2), 485*n*25
210.4(1), 377*n*19
210.6, 494*n*4
210.6(1)(d), 100*n*6
211.1, 291*n*12
211.1(2)(a), 104*n*25
211.2, 485*n*26
212.5(1), 470*n*89
212.5(1)(a), 470*n*89
212.5(1)(a)-(d), 417*n*91
212.5(1)(b), 470*n*89
212.5(1)(c), 470*n*89
212.5(1)(d), 450*n*55, 462*n*85
213.1(1), 102*n*13, 369*n*12, 369*n*14, 369*n*15
213.1(1)(a), 370*n*16

213.1(1)(d), 374*n*17
213.1(2), 369*n*14, 369*n*15
213.1(2)(b), 370*n*16
213.3(1), 369*n*15
213.3(1)(a), 370*n*16
213.4(2), 370*n*16
213.4(8), 370*n*16
213.6(1), 119*n*45
213.6(2), 369*n*13
213.6(4), 370*n*16
220.1(1), 102*n*14
220.1(3), 104*n*20
220.2(3), 104*n*22
220.3(1)(a), 488*n*28
221.2(3)(c), 107*n*50
223.1(3)(c), 107*n*47, 107*n*48
223.2, 102*n*15
223.3(1), 107*n*46, 107*n*50
223.3(3), 107*n*46, 107*n*50
223.5, 104*n*21
242, 330*n*16
250.2(1)(b), 104*n*23
250.10, 104*n*24
Article 3, 473*n*4

INDEX

abolitionist movement, 89, 210. *See also* restorative justice movement
abolition of punishment, 209–15
- blackmail as noncrime, 449, 468
- concept, 209–10
- core of wrongdoing, 22, 34
- insanity defense (*See* insanity defense)
- punishment replacement, abolitionists view, 210
- restorative justice movement, 210–15

abortion, radicalization of protesters, 80–81
accident/mistake defenses, culpability, 303–5
accomplices
- attempt liability, objective requirements of complicity, 261–68
- binary *vs.* category judgments, 407
- complicity liability, 261
- contributions to offense, 407
- effects of success or failure of killing on liability for the accomplice, 266
- felony murder, culpability, 377, 381
- gradations in liability, 268
- grading, 268, 377, 381, 390
- liability
  - culpability as to resulting death, 315
  - effects of success or failure of killing, 266
  - gradations in liability, 268
  - as related to object requirements of complicity, 263
- liability as related to object requirements of complicity, 263
- liability assigned to the accomplices as a function of involvement, 266
- masterminding, 265–67
- minimum required contribution, 261
- nuanced judgments, liability, 16
- objective requirements of complicity, 261–68
- results of study, 267–68
- sentencing, accomplice discount, 390
- study, 262–67
- U.S. Sentencing Commission Guidelines, 261

accumulated social learning, 58–62
- absence of variation among groups, differences in situation and culture, 59–60
- children's views, inconsistency with developmental data, 60
- developmental data, inconsistency with, 60
- intuitional knowledge and learned knowledge, characteristics distinguished, 60–61
- language and social learning, 61–62
- moral dumbfounding, 61
- teaching inarticulate lessons, difficulties, 61–62
- trolley problem, 61

acquittal verdict forms, reform of, 490–92
adjudication principles
- culpability (*See* culpability)
- excuse doctrines (*See* excuse defenses)
- grading (*See* grading)

adjudication procedures, promoting legitimacy, 202–7
- double jeopardy, 204
- exclusionary rule, 203
- fairness and justice, 203–7
- *mala in se* crimes, 206
- moral credibility *vs.* legitimacy, 205–7
- points of tension, 203–5
- resolving the conflict, 205–7

age, extralegal punishment factors (XPFs), 527
Alexander; U.S. v., 229–30, 235, 236
ALI test (Model Penal Code), 338–39, 347
Anglo American criminal law
- attempt liability, objective requirements test, 247–48
- omission liability (*See* omission liability)

animal studies evidence, evolutionary origins of justice, 41–44, 55
- cooperation, 42–44
- human morality, development, 44
- negative reciprocity, 43
- primates, 41–44
- punishment patterns, 41–44
- reciprocity, 43
- retribution, 44
- revenge system, 43
- sense of fair treatment, 42

attempt liability, 256–57
- accomplices, 261–68
- Anglo American criminal law, 247–48
- attempt scenarios, 244
- community views and the law, disagreement, 403–4
- dangerous proximity test, 248, 252–53, 256

attempt liability (*Cont.*)
desistance, 244, 249–50, 253–54, 257
determination tests, 248–49
inchoate liability, 248, 254
intent to commit offense, 252
Model Code Provisions, attempts graded same as completed offense, 248
nuanced judgments, 14–15
objective requirements, 247–53
older common law legal tests, 248
remorse factor, 256–57
renunciation, 253–55, 257
state laws, 248
substantial step test, 249, 275
theft offense, liability for degrees of conduct, 251
completed theft offense, 250–51
no liability, or liability but no punishment, 251
undoing the offense, 244, 250, 253–54, 256, 405, 515

Bazelon, David L., 228–30
behavioral economics studies, 20–21
Benthamite deterrence theory, 72, 145
binary *vs.* category judgments, 406–8
BKH criticism, response to, 82–94
abolitionist movement, 89
aspects of offenses included, 83–84
C&C agreement study, 83–87
construction of scenarios, 84
"core," 82–87
core of agreement issues, 87–91
criminal liability and punishment rules in conflict with people's judgment, 91–92
cultural dependence, 84
definition of core, 83
level of agreement as to what is criminal, 85–87
malleability of people's judgments about justice, 88–91
meaningless core of agreement, 87–88
possible points of disagreement, 87–93
property rights and cultural diversity, 86–87
"Punishment Realism," 92–94
reform realism, 92–93
sexual offenses, 85
social reformers, 92–93
blackmail, 439–71
act and threat of blackmail are wrongful, 441
breach of duty theory, 443–46, 458–59
categories and examples, statutory approach, 450–52
coercion, 443
competing theories of blackmail, 440–49
continuing domination, 442–43, 459
crime against the threat recipient, 441–43
crime against third parties, 443–47
criminalization, 448, 456, 462, 466
demand disclosure and secrets, extent of, 469
design and methodology, 453–55
efficient information allocation, 460–62
extent of demand disclosure and secrets, 469
liability analysis, statutory, 463
liability results, 465–66
liberalization position, 449
manipulation-check, 453
correct answers, 456
liability results, 465–66
questions for criteria of theories, 455
results, 464–66
seriousness of threat, wrongfulness of victims undisclosed conduct, 469
theories, 466–68
meta-blackmail, 449
noncrime, abolitionist position, 449, 468
public officials, exception, 448
reflective equilibrium, 441, 443
results, 464–70
statutory schemes, 468
seriousness of threat, wrongfulness of victim's undisclosed conduct, 469
societal harm, 447–49
statutory approach, 450–52, 462–63
statutory schemes, 468
subject evaluation, extent of demand disclosure and secrets, 469
testing community views, 453–69
theories, 441–47, 466–68
theory predictions, 455–62
third parties, crime against, 443–47
usurping authority, 446–47, 459–60
wrongful intentions, 457–58
blamelessness, exercising mercy, 222–26
disagreements about XPFs, application disparity, 224–26
nature and virtue of mercy, 222–23
sentencing disparities, 224–26
U.S. Sentencing Commission, creation, 225
XPF popularity and magnitude, 226, 520–21
XPFs and lay intuitions, 223–24
blameworthiness assessments, 402
brain imaging studies, 76
brain science evidence, evolutionary origins of justice, 44–48, 55
anatomical and functional specialization, 45
case of Phineas Gage, 45
functional MRIs, 46
morality intuitions, 46–48

brainwashing. *See* coercive indoctrination (brainwashing)
Brawner; U.S. v., 228–29
breach of agreement or deception in exchanges, 75–76
breach of duty theory, blackmail, 443–46, 458–59
Breyer, Stephen, 11–12

Cabraga, Alex, 231–34
C&C agreement study, 83–87
changing people's judgments of justice, 70–94, 533–34
  abolitionist movement, 89
  abortion, radicalization of protesters, 80–81
  Benthamite deterrence theory, 72, 145
  BKH criticisms, responses to, 82–94
  brain imaging studies, 76
  brainwashing (*See* coercive indoctrination (brainwashing))
  breach of agreement or deception in exchanges, 75–76
  childhood period, 79–80
  cigarette smoking, public education campaigns, 71, 77–78
  coercive indoctrination (*See* coercive indoctrination (brainwashing))
  core intuitions, 75
  core of agreement issues, 82–91
    aspects of offenses included, 83–84
    BKH criticisms, responses to, 82–94
    C&C agreement study, 83–87
    construction of scenarios, 84
    cultural dependence, 84
    definition, 83
    level of agreement as to what is criminal, 85–87
    manipulating analogy to core wrong, public education campaigns, 77–79
    meaningless core of agreement, 87–88
    sexual offenses, 85
  costly of infliction of punishment, 76
  crimes against property, 76
  criminal liability and punishment rules in conflict with people's judgment, 91–92
  demographics and culture, 75
  difficulties in changing intuitions, 71–74
  drunk driving, public education campaign, 71, 77
  gaming studies, 76
  group induced conclusions, 80
  immoralizing and de-moralizing behaviors, 81
  insider trading, efforts to change judgments concerning, 78–79
  internalization of group beliefs, 79–82
  intuitions of justice that can and cannot be changed, 74–76
  intuitive nature as a determining factor, 74–75
  male "affinity groups" and "rape myth beliefs," 81
  malleability of people's judgments about justice, 88–91
  malum in se offenses, 75
  manipulating analogy to core wrong, public education campaigns, 77–79
  meaningless core of agreement, 87–88
  moral judgments, 80–82
  Mother's Against Drunk Driving (MADD), 71, 77
  POWs, coercive indoctrination (brainwashing), 72–73, 230–31, 234, 235
  Prohibition (Volstead Act), 74
  property rights and cultural diversity, 86–87
  prototypes of wrongdoing actions, research on, 76
  public education campaigns, 77–79
  "Punishment Realism," 92–94
  reasoning system, 72
  reform programs, 71, 77–79
  reform realism, 92–93
  same-sex marriage, 71
  social reformers, 71, 77–79, 92–93
  Stockholm Syndrome, 73–74
  tagged action, 79
  wrongdoing and blameworthiness, change proposals, 70–71
child development evidence, evolutionary origins of justice, 48–54, 55
  blameworthiness, factors beyond offense seriousness, 52–53
  cross-cultural developmental studies, 53–54
  estimation of seriousness of wrongful conduct, 51–52
  intentional *vs.* unintentional actions, 52
  moral, conventional and prudential rules, distinguished, 49–51
  moral rules, universally applicable, 53–54
  moral wrongs distinguished from violations of convention, 50–51
  older children, moral and prudential rule distinction, 50–51
  predictable stages of development, 48–49
  relative ranking of wrongful acts, 54
  social conventions, differing perceptions of specific wrongful conduct, 54
  sophistication of children underestimated in early research, 49
  subtle and complex judgments at early age, 49–53
  Western world, 52–54

childhood period, internalization of group beliefs, 79–80
children
involuntary intoxication, immaturity and, 346–53
juveniles, adult prosecution of, 114–15
origins of justice (*See* child development evidence, evolutionary origins of justice)
social learning origins of justice, 60
why children obey the law, 153
cigarette smoking, public education campaigns, 71, 77–78
citizens' arrest. *See* citizens' law enforcement authority
citizens' law enforcement authority, 293–99
deadly and non-deadly force scenarios, 294–97, 299
liability, 295
limitations, 294
Model Penal Code, 296
perceptions, 298
coercion
blackmail, 443
crime control factors, 101
duress and entrapment defenses, degree of coercion, 356–57
entrapment, nuanced judgments, 16
person of reasonable firmness
coercive indoctrination (brainwashing), 227–28
jury speculation rules, 107
lay judgments of justice, 99, 105, 107
coercive crime-control doctrines
conflict with desert, 111–20
"crime-control" scenarios, 123
"milestone" and "crime-control" scenarios, 121–23
sentencing disparity identified, 124–28
TESS (Time Sharing Experiments in the Social Sciences), 123–24
testing the perceived justice of, 120–28
coercive crime-control principles
difficulty of detection, 100
failing to take account of factors relevant to, 100–101
grading factors, 100–101
incapacitation and rehabilitation strategies, 100
likelihood of capture, 100
limitations, 142–52
U.S. Sentencing Commission guidelines, 101
coercive indoctrination (brainwashing), 72–74, 226–36
Bazelon, David L.; judgments, 228–30
"but for" cause, inadequacy, 227–30
Cabarga, Alex, 231–34
coercion and reasonable firmness, 227–28
definition, 227
Durham argument, 228–29
empirical desert, 234–36
Hearst, Patty, 73, 230, 231
indoctrination effect, 234
POWs, 72–73
Tenneson, Richard, 230–31, 234, 235
rotten social background excuse, 231–36
skepticism about excuse, 235
Tenneson, Richard, 230–31, 234, 235
traditional excuse theory, 227–28
U.S. v. Alexander, 229–30, 235, 236
U.S. v. Brawner, 228–29
cognitive and control dysfunction (insanity defense), 340, 342, 345, 347–49, 360, 402
community views
law and, 401–14
agreement, 402
binary *vs.* category judgments, 406–8
criminal liability without punishment, 408–10
disagreement, 402–6
jury as resolver of law-community conflicts, 410–12
omission liability, duty to rescue, 408–9
social reformers decision to deviate from, 196–202
complicity
accomplices (*See* accomplices)
culpability requirements, 310–18
elevation view, 313, 317
continuing domination theory, 442–43, 459
contrast cases, 478–80, 484–86
attempted risk creation, 478–80
created risk, 478–79
intentional, 478, 480
interrelation of contact cases 1 through 4, 479
liability results, 484–86
cooperation
animal studies, 42–44
evolutionary origins of justice, 36–37
moral credibility, cooperation with criminal justice system, 177, 179, 180–83, 186–88
obedience, cooperation with criminal justice system, 156, 158–59
selective cooperation, 37
core intuitions, changing people's judgments of justice, 75
core of wrongdoing
abolition of punishment, 22, 34
agreement issues, 82–91
agreements on, 18–34
aspects of offenses included, 83–84
behavioral economics studies, 20–21

BKH criticisms, responses to, 82–94
C&C agreement study, 83–87
construction of scenarios, 84
costs to inflict punishment, 20–21, 39, 76
cross-cultural studies, 21–22
cultural dependence, 84
domestic studies, seriousness of wrongdoing, 23–26, 31
exceptions, 22–23
face pain scale, ranking, 31
face-to-face interviews, 25
Ghandi, Mahatma, 22
Human Universal, intuition to punish wrongdoing, 22–23
in-person testing, limits of agreement study, 29–32
Internet testing, limits of agreement study, 28, 32–34
intuitions on the relative seriousness of wrongdoing, studies, 23–28
intuition that serious wrongdoing should be punished, 19–23
Jesus Christ, 22
magnitude estimation, face-to-face interviews, 25
questionnaire studies, 19–22
relative blameworthiness, 23–28
studies, 29–34
TESS program (Time-Sharing Experiments for the Social Sciences), 33
testing the limits of agreement, 28–34
Ultimatum Game, 20–21
understating extent of agreement, 25–26
U.S. Sentencing Commission, sentencing guidelines, 18–19

creating criminal risk, 257–60
contrast cases, 478–80, 484–86
culpable state of mind, 258
grading, 259
justification defenses, testing competing theories, 478–80
liability as function of risk and injury, 260
liability for creation of risk, 258–59
minimum standards, 257
probability and harm variables, 259

crime control utilitarians, 97

criminal-civil system distinction, 218–22
advantages of separate systems, 218–19
blurring system distinction, detrimental effect, 219–22
criminalization, 219–20
criminal label, 218, 221
criminal system conveys messages, 219
duplication costs, 219
human desire to make moral judgments, 218
moral condemnation, 220–21
moral credibility, 220–21
regulatory offenses, criminalization, 220, 221
severe sanctions, access to, 221
stigmatization and conduct of potential offenders, 221–22
strict and vicarious liability, 220
tort liability, 220

criminality, common law to modern law codes, 415–38
attempts, minimum requirements, 420
bilateral and unilateral agreement requirements, 416
discounts, 430–33
doctrinal shift in views, 416–19
estimate of discount size, 432
grading, discounting model, 431
implications, 429–33
inchoate liability, 417, 419
murder cases, discounting models, 433
objectivist *vs.* subjectivist, 418, 419–21
offense conduct, 417
pattern of criminalization difference, theories, 416–21
prototype deviations, 430
substantial step, 417
testable empirical issues, 421
traditionalist *vs.* modernist views, 418, 419–21
white collar business crimes and special organized crime offenses, 416

criminalization doctrines, 237, 239–76
accomplices, objective requirements of complicity, 261–68
Anglo American criminal law
attempt liability, objective requirements test, 247–48
omission liability (*See* omission liability)
attempt liability, 256–57
attempt scenarios, 244
dangerous proximity test, 248, 252–53, 256
desistance, 244, 249–50, 253–54, 257
objective requirements test, 247–53
blackmail, 448, 456, 462, 466
creating a criminal risk, 257–60
malum prohibitum offenses, 239
objective requirements
attempt liability, 247–53
complicity of accomplices, 261–68
omission liability (*See* omission liability)
research methodology, testing lay judgments of justice, 240–47
secondary prohibitions, general explanation, 240, 275–76
victimless crimes, 239

criminal law reforms, 215–16
acquittal distinction, 216
burden of proof, shifting burden to defendant, 215
implications for, 487–92
formulation and grading offenses, 487–88
formulation of defenses, 488–90
grading offenses, 487–88
reform of acquittal verdict forms, 490–92
procedural and institutional reforms, 216
social reformers (*See* social reformers)
statute of limitation reforms due to scientific advances, 215
criminal risk. *See* creating criminal risk
cross-cultural development studies
accumulated social learning, absence of variation among groups, 59–60
agreements on core of wrongdoing, 21–22
BKH criticisms, responses to, 84, 86–87
changing people's judgments of justice, 75
child development evidence, evolutionary origins of justice, 53–54
cultural dependence and "core," responses to BKH criticisms, 84
evolutionary origins of justice, 53–54
prison sentences, disagreements about intuitions of justice, 65
property rights and cultural diversity, responses to BKH criticisms, 86–87
culpability, 301–35
accomplices
felony murder, culpability, 377, 381
liability, culpability as to resulting death, 315
binary *vs.* category judgments, 407
community views and the law, disagreement, 403
complicity, requirements, 310–18
creating criminal risk, culpable state of mind, 258
felony murder, grading doctrines, culpability, 377–85
grading
felony murder, 377–85
mistake/accident defenses, 303–5
negligence
individualization of objective standard of, 327–34
social reformers, 197
offense requirements, 302–10
proof of, 301–2
recklessness, 311–18, 329
social reformers, recklessness and negligence, 197
voluntary intoxication, 318–27
cultural dependence, 84
cultural diversity
property rights, response to BKH criticism, 86–87
culture, 75. *See also* cross-cultural development studies

death penalty, religious variables, 64–65
deeds theory, 472–77, 480–83, 485–86, 490, 492
defense of property, use of force, 287–93
community views and the law, disagreement, 405–6
deadly force, 292, 293
liability for the use of force, 288
necessity of force, assessment, 290–92
non-deadly force, 287, 290–91
study and results, 288–93
subjects' perceptions of the use of force, 289
democratic process, production of liability rules communities *see* as unjust, 128–39
designer laws, 137
factors, 128–29
government as media information source, 131–34
headline crimes, 134–36
longer sentences and public fear, 136–37
media
coverage of general crime issues, 131–34
government as information source, 131–34
headline crimes, 134–36
legislators and media, 132–34
news packages, 132
omission of facts vital to understanding sentences, 130–31
as primary motivator of public opinion, 133–34
role in shaping public perception, 132
skewed perception of sentences, 130–31
overbroadening of category, 135
politicians, 129, 139–40
legislators and media, 132–34
next-election vulnerability, 138–39
polling studies, 129–30
public choice perspective, 138
soft on crime, 139
polling studies, 129–30
prototype of crime, 134–36
public fear, 136–38
voter views, 129
demographics
culture and demographics, 75
extralegal punishment factors (XPFs), 525–28
race and demographics, 64–65
deontological desert, 97
concepts explained, 164–65
empirical desert and, 163–67

lay judgments of justice, current law's deference to, 97
designer laws, 137
deterrence, 143, 144–49
aggregated-effect studies, 147–48
amount of punishment, 145
Benthamite deterrence theory, 72, 145
complications, 145–46
costs and benefits of crime
difficulty establishing, 147
discounting future benefits and costs, 145–46
discounting future benefits and costs, 145–46
duration neglect, 146
dynamic of deterrence, 146
exaggeration of likelihood of rare events, 145
exaggeration of one's own abilities, 145
human nature, 146
increasing deterrence, 148
intuitively assessing punishment, 169–71
learning the pain, 146
prerequisites, 144
probability of punishment, 145
strengths & weaknesses, 149
subjective well-being studies, 146
timing and delay of punishment, 146–47
deviations from empirical desert, 189–207
adjudication procedures, promoting legitimacy, 202–7
double jeopardy, 204
exclusionary rule, 203
fairness and justice, 203–7
mala in se crimes, 206
moral credibility *vs.* legitimacy, 205–7
points of tension, 203–5
resolving the conflict, 205–7
advancement of interests other than crime control, 194, 196
community views, social reformers decision to deviate from, 196–202
cost and benefit determination, 195
crime control, 193, 194–95
extralegal punishment factors (*See* extralegal punishment factors (XPFs))
general deterrence, 195
incapacitation of dangerous persons, 194–95
inconspicuous deviations, 193
inevitable deviations, 190–91
justifying deviations, 193–96
moral credibility, 194
moral divisions within the community, 190–91
primary principle of empirical desert, 193
Prohibition example, 190–91
reforms to existing deviations from empirical desert, 215–17
rehabilitation, 194
right-spirited deviations, promoting justice, 191–93
sentencing judges, 196
social reformers, advice for altering empirical desert, 196–202
societal interests, 196
special deterrence, 194
disagreements about intuitions of justice, 63–69, 533
abstraction and politicization process, 64
apparent disagreements, 63–65
cross-culture variables, prison sentences, 65
demographics and race, 64–65
gender variables, 65
Internet-based rankings, study, 65–68
misleading sources, 63–64
paper-based rankings, study, 65–67
poor testing methods, 63–64
religious variables, death penalty, 64–65
responses to BKH criticisms, 85–87
sources of disagreement, 64–65
stereotyping, 64
true disagreement studies, ranking scenarios, 65–68
distributive principles, 142–52
deterrence (*See* deterrence)
empirical desert (*See* empirical desert as a distributive principle, criticisms)
excuse defenses, 143–44
rehabilitation, 148–49
doing justice as central concern, 208–9
double jeopardy, 204
drug offense penalties, 113–14
drunk driving, public education campaign, 71, 77
duplication costs, criminal-civil system distinction, 219
duress and entrapment defenses, 353–60
degree of coercion, 356–57
liability and subjects' perceptions as related to duress and entrapment, 356
objective formulation of entrapment, 354, 358–59, 360
predisposition of individual, 358, 359
subjective formulation of entrapment, 354, 359, 360
types of defenses, 353–55
duress defense, 99
***Durham* argument,** 228–29
dysfunction. *See* excuse defenses

education, extralegal punishment factors (XPFs), 527–28
empirical desert
deviations (*See* deviations from empirical desert)
distributive principle (*See* empirical desert as a distributive principle, criticisms)

empirical desert as a distributive principle, criticisms, 167–74
deterrence or incapacitation, intuitively assessing punishment, 169–71
disagreements, 168–69
media coverage, 171–72
political views, 171–72
potential immorality, 172–74
reflective equilibrium, 173
shared intuitions, problematic tendency to rely upon, 173
unfounded claims, 174
utilitarian theories, competition from, 173–74
vagueness, 167–68
entrapment. *See* duress and entrapment defenses
entrapment and coercion, nuanced judgments, 16
entrapment and duress and entrapment defenses, 353–60
ESN scale, 514
***Etzweiler* case,** 311–12, 316, 317
evolutionary origins of justice, 36–41
ability of group to be able to punish, shared intuitions contribute to, 39
advantageous intuitions, relative consistency, 40–41
animal studies evidence, 41–44, 55
brain science evidence, 44–48, 55
child development evidence, 48–54, 55
cooperation, evolution of, 36–37
costs and benefits, 37–41
costs associated with having diverging intuitions, 40–41
costs of inflicting punishment, 39
deserved and undeserved punishment, distinction, 39
empirical support, 41–56
human sociality and predisposition, 36–38
imposition of costs against wrongdoer, 39
infliction of punishment as generating benefits for individuals, 38–41
reciprocity, 37
selective cooperation, 37
social exchange principles, 37, 38–40
third party interactions, why humans care about, 38
Western world, punishment in hands of criminal justice system, 39
exclusionary rule, 203
excuse defenses, 143–44
brainwashing (*See* coercive indoctrination (brainwashing))
coercive indoctrination (*See* coercive indoctrination (brainwashing))
cognitive and control dysfunction (insanity defense), 340, 342, 345, 347–49, 360, 402
community views and the law, agreement, 402
deterrence, 144–49
distributive principles, 142–52
duress and entrapment (*See* duress and entrapment defenses)
duress defense, 99
entrapment (*See* duress and entrapment defenses)
immaturity and intoxication, 346–53
incapacitation and rehabilitation strategies, 99–100
insanity defense (*See* insanity defense)
involuntary intoxication, 346–53
lay judgments of justice, recognizing excuse defenses, 98–100
nature of excusing dysfunction, 98
recognizing excuse defenses, 98–100
special deterrence arguments, 99
extralegal punishment factors (XPFs), 493–532, 535
acknowledgment of guilt, 496–97
age, 527
apology, 497–98
demographic differences, 525–28
differences and popularity, 525–26
disagreements about XPFs and the problem of disparity in application, 529–31
education, 527–28
ESN scale, 514
extralegal punishment factor variations, 515–16
gender, 526
implications for criminal justice rules and practices, 529–31
income, 527
lay intuitions XPFs, 512–29
marital status, 526–27
methodology, 513–17
offender reaction to the offense, 495–98
offender status or characteristics, 503–4
popularity and magnitude, XPF ordered by overall popularity, 520–21
race, 526
rehabilitation, 504–5
relative relation among XPFs by popularity, 522–25
scale used by subjects to assign punishment to hypothetical offenders, 514
strong support for, or opposition to, an XPF and the problem of undermining the law's moral credibility, 531
suffering apart from official punishment, special hardship, 506–12
support for adjusting punishment in light of extralegal punishment factors, 518–19

true remorse, 497
unique talents or special value of contributions to society, 505–6
victim or public reaction to the offense (unrelated to desert), 498–501

face pain scale, ranking, 31
felony manslaughter, 404
felony murder, 119
accomplice, 377, 381
community views and the law, disagreement, 404
felony murder rule, 377–78, 384
grading, culpability, 377–85
lay judgments of justice, conflicts with current law, 119
liability, 379–80
liability as function of role and state of mind as to killing, 381
sentencing, 381–83

Gage, Phineas, 45
gender variables
disagreements about intuitions of justice, 65
extralegal punishment factors (XPFs), 526
severity of sentences, 24–25
Ghandi, Mahatma, 22
Goetz, Bernhard, 410
government as media information source, 131–34
grading, 362–400
accomplice discount, 390
accomplices, 268, 377, 381, 390
aggregable and non-aggregable offenses, 394–95, 398
Baltimore survey, seriousness ratings, 363–66
causation requirements, 385–93
causation study, 386–88, 392
coercive crime-control principles, 100–101
community views and the law, disagreement, 405
comparative grading, 366–67
consecutive and concurrent sentencing, 393
creating criminal risk, 259
criminality, common law to modern law codes, 431
criminalization doctrine, 367
criminal law reform, implications for formulation and grading offenses, 487–88
culpability, felony murder, 380, 381
felony murder, culpability, 377–85
grading distinctions, 362–69, 399–400
inchoate offenses, 102, 103, 108
justification defenses, testing competing theories, 487–88
legal cause requirement, 386, 388
liability, 386–93
lookout, liability, 388–90
multiple offense discount, 393–94
multiple offenses, punishment, 393–99
necessary *vs.* sufficient cause, 387–88, 392
objectivist *vs.* subjectivist criminality, 423–25, 428
operating principles used to grade, 368–69
perpetrator liability, 388–92
result elements included in offense definitions, Model Penal Code, 103
seriousness, 363–68
sexual offenses, 369–77
total liability, 396–97
U.S. Sentencing Commission Guidelines, 393, 394, 396
group interests preferred over individual interests, 57

habitual offender statutes, 112–13
headline crimes, 134–36
Hearst, Patty, 73, 230, 231
homosexual couples. *See also* same-sex marriage
sexual offenses, 369, 373, 376
human cognitive skills, limitations, 57–58
human desire to make moral judgments, 218
human sociality and predisposition, 36–38
Human Universal, intuition to punish wrongdoing, 22–23

immaturity
children (*See* headings under *children*)
involuntary intoxication and, 346–53
individual scenarios, 349–50
liability, 348
low cognitive impairment, 351
McNaughten test, 347
Model Penal Code ALI test, 347
subjects' perceptions of immaturity and involuntary intoxication cases, 349
immoralizing and de-moralizing behaviors, 81
incapacitation and rehabilitation strategies, 99–100
incapacitation of dangerous persons, 149–52
cloaking preventative detention as criminal justice, 149–52
justifying deviations, 194–95
strengths & weaknesses, 149
incapacitation or deterrence, intuitively assessing punishment, 169–71
inchoate liability, 248, 254, 417, 419
inchoate offenses, grading, 102, 103, 108
income, extralegal punishment factors (XPFs), 527
indoctrination
brainwashing (*See* coercive indoctrination (brainwashing))

insanity defense, 98, 143, 336–46
abolition or narrowing of, 115–17
cognitive and control dysfunction, 340, 342, 345, 347–49, 360, 402
controversy over defense, 346
criminal liability judgment comparisons, 341–43
judging standards and distinctions of ordinary persons, 338
lay judgments of justice, 98, 106, 115–17
lay understandings of legal definitions, 337
McNaughten test, 338–39, 344, 347
Model Penal Code ALI test, 338–39
questions, 344, 345
recognizing excuse defenses, 98
surveys and experiments, 336–37
vague standards, 106
insider trading, efforts to change judgments concerning, 78–79
internalization of group beliefs, 79–82
Internet-based rankings
disagreements about intuitions of justice, study, 65–68
Internet-based studies
core of wrongdoing, limits of agreement, 28, 32–34
disagreements about intuitions of justice, ranking scenarios, 65–68
Internet testing, core of wrongdoing
discussion, 34
face-to-face contact, motivation, 33
flipping scenarios, 33
limits of agreement study, 28, 32–34
TESS program (Time-Sharing Experiments for the Social Sciences), 33
intoxication
immaturity, involuntary intoxication, 346–53
involuntary intoxication, immaturity and, 346–53
McNaughten test, 347
Model Penal Code ALI test, 347
Mother's Against Drunk Driving (MADD), 71, 77
negligence as to becoming, 402
voluntary intoxication, culpability, 318–27
intuitional judgments, 5–8
degrees of badness, 7
heuristics and biases research, 6
moral dumbfounding, 7–8
perception of reasoning, 6–7
primary claim, 5–6
process and content, two cognitive systems, 6–7
statistical reasoning, 6
trolley problem, 7–8
intuitions of justice, disagreements. *See* disagreements about intuitions of justice
involuntary intoxication. *See also* intoxication
immaturity and involuntary intoxication, 346–53
individual scenarios, 349–50
liability, 348
low cognitive impairment, 351
McNaughten test, 347
Model Penal Code ALI test, 347
subjects' perceptions of immaturity and involuntary intoxication cases, 349

judgments about justice, 1–94
blameworthiness, 1–3
changing people's judgments of justice, 70–94, 533–34
core of wrongdoing, 1–3
disagreements about intuitions of justice, 63–69, 533
as human universal, agreements on a core of wrongdoing, 18–34
as intuitional, 5–8
as nuanced, 12–16
shared intuitions of justice, origins, 35–62, 533
jury as resolver of law-community conflicts, 410–12
jury speculation rules, 106–8
justification defenses, testing competing theories, 402, 472–92
acquittal verdict forms, reform of, 490–92
actor, unknowingly justified, 474–75
burning
knowingly justified burning, bad motive, 481–82
unknowingly justified burning, 480–81
competing theories of justification, 473–77
contrast cases, 478–80, 484–86
deeds theory, 472–77, 480–83, 485–86, 490, 492
formulation of defenses, 488–90
grading offenses, 487–88
implications for criminal law reform, 487–92
liability predictions, 477–83
liability results, 484–87
mistake as to justification, 475–77
negligent, 482–83
reasonable, 482
recklessness, 483
reasons theory, 472–76, 481–82, 486, 491–92
justification doctrines, 277–300
citizens' law enforcement authority, 293–99
defense of property, use of force, 287–93
research methodology, testing lay judgments of justice, 240–47
self-defense, use of deadly force, 278–87
juveniles, adult prosecution of, 114–15

knowing *vs.* reckless assistance
culpability, complicity, requirements, 316

lay judgments of justice
conflicts with current law, 110–40, 534
current law's deference to, 97–109, 535
explanations for deference, 108–9
law's liability assessment for complicity *vs.*, 111
standards, 103–8
legal code *vs.* individual moral intuitions, 200–202
legislators and media, 132–34
longer sentences and public fear, 136–37
lookout, liability, 388–90

***mala in se* crimes,** 206
male "affinity groups" and "rape myth beliefs," 81
***malum in se* offenses,** 75
***malum prohibitum* offenses,** 239
marital status, extralegal punishment factors (XPFs), 526–27
McNaughten test, 338–39, 344, 347
media
coverage of general crime issues, 131–34
government as information source, 131–34
headline crimes, 134–36
legislators and media, 132–34
news packages, 132
omission of facts vital to understanding sentences, 130–31
as primary motivator of public opinion, 133–34
role in shaping public perception, 132
skewed perception of sentences, 130–31
media coverage, 171–72
mentally handicapped people, sexual offenses, 373–74
mercy. *See* blamelessness, exercising mercy
meta-blackmail, 449
mistake/accident defenses, culpability, 303–5
mistake as to justification, 482–83
Model Penal Code
rules, 98–103
Section 1.02(2)(a), text of, 10n20
standards, 103–8
Model Penal Code ALI test, 338–39, 347
moral condemnation, criminal-civil system distinction, 220–21
moral credibility
compliance, affect of morality on, 184–88
cooperation with criminal justice system, 177, 179, 180–83, 186–88
criminal-civil system distinction, 220–21
disutuility of justice studies, 176–88, 534
justifying deviations, 194
perceptions of moral legitimacy, affect on compliance, 185–87
previous studies, 184–88
recent empirical studies, 177–84
social reformers, 197–99
tax law, compliance, 187–88
unjust prime, 186
why people obey the law, 157–58, 163
XPFs and the problem of undermining the law's moral credibility, 531
moral credibility *vs.* legitimacy, 205–7
moral divisions within the community, 190–91
moral dumbfounding, 7–8, 61
moral judgments, 80–82
Mother's Against Drunk Driving (MADD), 71, 77
multiple offenses, punishment, 393–99

negligence
culpability, individualization of objective standard of negligence, 327–34
characteristics to individualize reasonable person standard, 329–31, 333
criminal negligence, 328
improper risk taking judgments, 328
liability and culpability in core cases, 331
negligence standard, factors, 332
reasonable person standard, 327–31, 333
recklessness, 329
culpability, social reformers, recklessness and negligence, 197
mistake as to justification, 482–83
next-election vulnerability, politicians, 138–39
nuanced judgments, 12–16
accomplice liability, 16
attempt liability, objective requirements, 14
characteristics of particular offender, 16
coercion and entrapment, 16
complicity liability, objective requirements, 15
different causal chains, 15
effect of mistakes in various contexts, 14–15
liability and punishment scenarios, 13–16
magnitude estimation, 13
objective requirements, 14–15
omission to act that results in death, 15
small factual differences among cases, liability differences, 13–16
use of deadly force in self-defense, 14

obedience. *See* why people obey the law
objective requirements
attempt liability, 247–53
complicity of accomplices, 261–68
nuanced judgments, 14–15

objectivist *vs.* subjectivist criminality, 418, 419–21
existing criminal law, implications, 435–38
grading, 423–25, 428
identification, 421–22
liability results, 423
offense grading issues, 423–25, 428
offense minimum requirements, 425–28, 430
pure objectivists, 429
traditionalist *vs.* modernist views, 418, 419–21
offense requirements, culpability, 302–10
circumstance element, 302
conduct element, 302–3
core *vs.* collateral element, 310
liability as a function of culpability level, 306
minimum liability requirements, 309–10
Model Penal code, 306–8, 310
objective elements, 303
offense definitions, 302–3
omission liability, 268–75
Anglo American law, 269, 275–76
community views and the law, 408–9
duty to rescue, 264–74, 408–9
liability as a function of the degree of sacrifice necessary to rescue, 273
liability for commission and omission, 271
nuanced judgments, omission to act that results in death, 15
respondents' perceptions of commission and omission cases, 272
restrictive views, criticisms, 269–70
why people obey the law, 158
open-ended code provisions, vague standards, 105–6
open-ended justice, 107
overbroadening of category, 135
overcriminalization, 159–60

paper-based rankings study, disagreements about intuitions of justice, 65–67
persuasion *vs.* contempt, social reformers, 200–202
political views, 171–72
politicians, 129, 139–40
legislators and media, 132–34
next-election vulnerability, 138–39
polling studies, 129–30
public choice perspective, 138
soft on crime, 139
polling studies, 129–30
POWs, coercive indoctrination (brainwashing), 72–73
Tenneson, Richard, 230–31, 234, 235
preventative detention, avoidance, 217
Prohibition (Volstead Act), 74, 190–91
property. *See also* defense of property, use of force
crimes against property, changing people's judgments of justice, 76
rights and cultural diversity, 86–87
property defense. *See* defense of property, use of force
prototype deviations, criminality, 430
prototype of crime, 134–36
prototype perception and resistance to particular law, 161
prototypes of wrongdoing actions, 76
public choice perspective, politicians, 138
public education campaigns, 77–79
public fear, 136–38
public officials, blackmail, 448
punishment. *See also* sentencing
abolitionist movement, 89, 210
abolition of punishment, 209–15
costly of infliction of punishment, 20–21, 39, 76
deserved and undeserved punishment, distinction, 39
extralegal punishment factors (*See* extralegal punishment factors (XPFs))
infliction of punishment as generating benefits for individuals, 38–41
"Punishment Realism," 92–94

questionnaire studies, core of wrongdoing, 19–22

race
demographics and race, 64–65
extralegal punishment factors (XPFs), 526
rape
cohabiting people, 372–73, 375–76
consensual intercourse with underage partner, statutory rape, 369–70, 373–74, 376
male "affinity groups" and "rape myth beliefs," 81
statutory rape, 369–70, 373–74, 376
stranger rape, 370–71, 372
rape reformers, 197–99, 200
reasonable person standard, 327–31, 333
reasoning system, changing people's judgments of justice, 72
reasons theory, 472–76, 481–82, 486, 491–92
reciprocity, evolutionary origins of justice, 37, 43
recklessness
created criminal risk, reckless commission, 478–79
culpability, 311–18, 329
knowing *vs.* reckless assistance, culpability, 316
mistake as to justification, 483
negligence, 105, 197
reflective equilibrium, 173, 441, 443
reform programs. *See* social reformers

reform realism, 92–93
reforms. *See* criminal law reforms
reforms to existing deviations from empirical desert, 215–17
regulatory offenses and violations, criminalization, 119–21
rehabilitation, 148–49
extralegal punishment factors (XPFs), offender status or characteristics, 504–5
justifying deviations, 194
rehabilitation and incapacitation strategies, 99–100
relative blameworthiness, 23–28
religious variables, death penalty, 64–65
research methodology, 240–47
attempt scenarios, 244
designing scenarios, 243–46
level of detail provided in scenario, 245–46
manipulation checks, 245–47
randomization, 244
scenario research, explained, 240–43
within-subjects design, 243
restorative justice movement, 210–15
acceptance of purely restorative justice practices in American society, study, 213–14
concept explained, 210–11
human nature, 212
multiple justice aims, 214–15
punishing serious wrongdoing, making people not care about, 212–13
realistic concept, questioning, 211–12
retribution urges seen as unhealthy, 210, 211
retributive practices, support for banning, 214
result elements included in offense definitions, 101–3
coercion crime control factors, 101
false impression resulting harm is significant, 101–3
Model Penal Code, grading, 103
unsuccessful or attempted crimes, 102
retribution
animal studies evidence, evolutionary origins of justice, 44
restorative justice movement, 210, 211, 214
retributivists, 97
risk creation. *See* creating criminal risk
rotten social background excuse, 231–36
rules common in modern criminal code, 97–103
rules of conduct
doctrines of criminalization (*See* criminalization doctrines)
doctrines of justification (*See* justification doctrines)
same-sex marriage, 71. *See also* homosexual couples
secondary prohibitions, general explanation, 240, 275–76
selective cooperation, 37
self-defense
community views and the law, disagreement, 405–6
self-defense, use of deadly force, 278–87, 405–6
boundaries of liability, 279
code-subject discrepancy, 282–83
conditions, 278–79
defensive and nondefensive killing scenarios, 280–81
degree of perceived threat, 282
jury as resolver of law-community conflicts, 410, 411
liability, 280–81
maximum force allowed, 283
nuanced judgments, 14
pattern distinctions, 286
retreat rule, 283–84
sentencing. *See also* extralegal punishment factors (XPFs); U.S. Sentencing Commission guidelines
accomplice discount, 390
blamelessness, sentencing disparities, 224–26
consecutive and concurrent sentencing, 393
cross-cultural development studies, 65
disparity identified, 124–28
felony murder, 381–83
Justice Breyer opposition to basing sentencing guidelines on desert, 11–12
justifying deviations, sentencing judges, 196
longer sentences and public fear, 136–37
media, omission of facts vital to understanding sentences, 130–31
media, skewed perception of sentences, 130–31
multiple offenses, punishment, 393–99
sexual offenses
BKH criticism, response to, 85
changing people's judgments of justice, 85
community views and the law, disagreement, 402–3
consensual intercourse, 369–70, 373–74, 376
consensual intercourse with underage partner, statutory rape, 369–70, 373–74, 376
core of agreement issues, 85
forcible intercourse, 369, 372–73, 375
grading, 369
grading doctrines, seriousness, 369–77
homosexual couples, 369, 373, 376
liability, 370
mentally handicapped people, 373–74
offense distinctions, 370–72

sexual offenses (*Cont.*)
rape, cohabiting people, 372–73, 375–76
same-sex marriage, 71
stranger rape, 370–71, 372
subjects' perception, 371
shared intuitions, origins of, 35–62
shared intuitions of justice, origins, 35–62, 533
Simon, Herb, 58
social exchange principles, 37, 38–40
social learning, origins of justice, 56–62
accumulated social learning, 58–62
spontaneous social learning, 56–58
social reformers
advice for altering empirical desert, 196–202
BKH criticism, response to, 92–93
changing people's judgments of justice, 71, 77–79
community views, decision to deviate, 197
legal code *vs.* individual moral intuitions, 200–202
limitations and techniques, changing norms, 199–200
managing benefits *vs.* risks of reform programs, 200–202
moral credibility, 197–99
persuasion *vs.* contempt, 200–202
rape reformers, 197–99, 200
recklessness and negligence, problem with culpability requirements, 197
reform programs, 71, 77–79
social sanctions, reasons why people obey the law, 152–53
societal harm, blackmail, 447–49
societal interests
justifying deviations, 196
soft on crime, politicians, 139
special deterrence, 143
justifying deviations, 194
spontaneous social learning, 56–58
standards, lay judgments of justice, 103–8
coercion, person of reasonable firmness, 107
explicit reliance upon lay judgments of justice, 104
insanity defense, 106
jury speculation rules, 106–8
negligence, definition, 107
open-ended code provisions, 105–6
open-ended justice, 107
precision and specificity, 103
reasonable reliance on official statement of law, 105–6
recklessness and negligence, 105, 197
vague standards, 103–6
stereotyping
disagreements about intuitions of justice, 64
stigmatization, 154–55, 221–22
Stockholm Syndrome, 73–74
strict and vicarious liability, criminal-civil system distinction, 220
strict liability, 117–19

tax law, compliance, 187–88
Tenneson, Richard, 230–31, 234, 235
TESS (Time Sharing Experiments in the Social Sciences), 33, 123–24, 128
three strikes law, 112–13
tort liability
criminal-civil system distinction, 220
traditional excuse theory, 227–28
trolley problem, 7–8, 61

Ultimatum Game, 20–21
U.S. Sentencing Commission guidelines
agreements on core of wrongdoing, 18–19
drug offense penalties, 114
Justice Breyer opposition to basing sentencing guidelines on desert, 11–12
vagueness of desert, 11–12
usurping authority theory, 446–47, 459–60

vagueness of desert, 8–12
concept of desert, 9
empirical desert as a distributive principle, criticisms of, 167–68
Justice Breyer opposition to basing sentencing guidelines on desert, 11–12
Model Penal Code Section 1.02(2)(a), text of, 10n20
punishment continuum, 11
U.S. Sentencing Commission, 11–12
vague standards, 103–6
insanity defense, 106
open-ended code provisions, 105–6
reasonable reliance on official statement of law, 105–6
recklessness and negligence, 105, 197
vicarious and strict liability, 220
victimless crimes, 239
vigilantism, avoiding, 155–56
voluntary intoxication, culpability, 318–27. *See also* intoxication
faultless killing scenarios, 324
liability, 321
pre-intoxication culpability as to killing, 319–21, 323, 326
voter views, 129

Western world, evolutionary origins of justice, 39, 52–54
why people obey the law, 152–63

barriers to deviant behavior, 152–53
borderline cases, gaining compliance, 162–63
children, 153
cooperation with criminal justice system, 156, 158–59
deviation from community views of justice, 156–57
internal moral sanctions, 152–53
legal codes and moral codes, 158–61
moral credibility, 157–58, 163
omission liability study, 158
overcriminalization, 159–60
persuasive power of the law, shaping societal norms, 161–62
prototype perception and resistance to particular law, 161
social sanctions, 152–53
societal norms, persuasive power of the law, 161–62
stigmatization, 154–55
vigilantism, avoiding, 155–56

wrongdoing and blameworthiness, change proposals, 70–71

wrongful intention theory, blackmail, 441–42

XPFs. *See* extralegal punishment factors (XPFs)